Intelligent Applications for Heterogeneous System Modeling and Design

Kandarpa Kumar Sarma
Gauhati University, India

Manash Pratim Sarma
Gauhati University, India

Mousmita Sarma
SpeecHWareNet (I) Pvt. Ltd, India

A volume in the Advances in Systems Analysis,
Software Engineering, and High Performance
Computing (ASASEHPC) Book Series

Information Science
REFERENCE
An Imprint of IGI Global

Managing Director:	Lindsay Johnston
Managing Editor:	Austin DeMarco
Director of Intellectual Property & Contracts:	Jan Travers
Acquisitions Editor:	Kayla Wolfe
Production Editor:	Christina Henning
Development Editor:	Brandon Carbaugh
Cover Design:	Jason Mull

Published in the United States of America by
Information Science Reference (an imprint of IGI Global)
701 E. Chocolate Avenue
Hershey PA, USA 17033
Tel: 717-533-8845
Fax: 717-533-8661
E-mail: cust@igi-global.com
Web site: http://www.igi-global.com

Library of Congress Cataloging-in-Publication Data

Intelligent applications for heterogeneous system modeling and design / Kandarpa Kumar Sarma, Manash Pratim Sarma, and Mousmita Sarma, editors.
     pages cm
 Includes bibliographical references and index.
  ISBN 978-1-4666-8493-5 (hardcover) -- ISBN 978-1-4666-8494-2 (ebook) 1. Expert systems (Computer science) 2. Automatic control. 3. Heterogeneous computing. I. Sarma, Kandarpa Kumar, editor. II. Sarma, Manash Pratim, 1984- editor. III. Sarma, Mousmita, editor.
  QA76.76.E95I53477 2015
  006.3'3--dc23
                                        2015010288

This book is published in the IGI Global book series Advances in Systems Analysis, Software Engineering, and High Performance Computing (ASASEHPC) (ISSN: 2327-3453; eISSN: 2327-3461)

British Cataloguing in Publication Data
A Cataloguing in Publication record for this book is available from the British Library.

For electronic access to this publication, please contact: eresources@igi-global.com.

Advances in Systems Analysis, Software Engineering, and High Performance Computing (ASASEHPC) Book Series

Vijayan Sugumaran
Oakland University, USA

ISSN: 2327-3453
EISSN: 2327-3461

Mission

The theory and practice of computing applications and distributed systems has emerged as one of the key areas of research driving innovations in business, engineering, and science. The fields of software engineering, systems analysis, and high performance computing offer a wide range of applications and solutions in solving computational problems for any modern organization.

The **Advances in Systems Analysis, Software Engineering, and High Performance Computing (ASASEHPC) Book Series** brings together research in the areas of distributed computing, systems and software engineering, high performance computing, and service science. This collection of publications is useful for academics, researchers, and practitioners seeking the latest practices and knowledge in this field.

Coverage

- Enterprise Information Systems
- Parallel Architectures
- Engineering Environments
- Performance Modelling
- Computer System Analysis
- Computer Networking
- Computer Graphics
- Virtual Data Systems
- Distributed Cloud Computing
- Software engineering

IGI Global is currently accepting manuscripts for publication within this series. To submit a proposal for a volume in this series, please contact our Acquisition Editors at Acquisitions@igi-global.com or visit: http://www.igi-global.com/publish/.

Titles in this Series

For a list of additional titles in this series, please visit: www.igi-global.com

Delivery and Adoption of Cloud Computing Services in Contemporary Organizations
Victor Chang (Computing, Creative Technologies and Engineering, Leeds Beckett University, UK) Robert John Walters (Electronics and Computer Science, University of Southampton, UK) and Gary Wills (Electronics and Computer Science, University of Southampton, UK)
Information Science Reference • copyright 2015 • 519pp • H/C (ISBN: 9781466682108) • US $225.00 (our price)

Emerging Research in Cloud Distributed Computing Systems
Susmit Bagchi (Gyeongsang National University, South Korea)
Information Science Reference • copyright 2015 • 447pp • H/C (ISBN: 9781466682139) • US $200.00 (our price)

Resource Management of Mobile Cloud Computing Networks and Environments
George Mastorakis (Technological Educational Institute of Crete, Greece) Constandinos X. Mavromoustakis (University of Nicosia, Cyprus) and Evangelos Pallis (Technological Educational Institute of Crete, Greece)
Information Science Reference • copyright 2015 • 432pp • H/C (ISBN: 9781466682252) • US $215.00 (our price)

Research and Applications in Global Supercomputing
Richard S. Segall (Arkansas State University, USA) Jeffrey S. Cook (Independent Researcher, USA) and Qingyu Zhang (Shenzhen University, China)
Information Science Reference • copyright 2015 • 672pp • H/C (ISBN: 9781466674615) • US $265.00 (our price)

Challenges, Opportunities, and Dimensions of Cyber-Physical Systems
P. Venkata Krishna (VIT University, India) V. Saritha (VIT University, India) and H. P. Sultana (VIT University, India)
Information Science Reference • copyright 2015 • 328pp • H/C (ISBN: 9781466673120) • US $200.00 (our price)

Human Factors in Software Development and Design
Saqib Saeed (University of Dammam, Saudi Arabia) Imran Sarwar Bajwa (The Islamia University of Bahawalpur, Pakistan) and Zaigham Mahmood (University of Derby, UK & North West University, South Africa)
Information Science Reference • copyright 2015 • 354pp • H/C (ISBN: 9781466664852) • US $195.00 (our price)

Handbook of Research on Innovations in Systems and Software Engineering
Vicente García Díaz (University of Oviedo, Spain) Juan Manuel Cueva Lovelle (University of Oviedo, Spain) and B. Cristina Pelayo García-Bustelo (University of Oviedo, Spain)
Information Science Reference • copyright 2015 • 745pp • H/C (ISBN: 9781466663596) • US $515.00 (our price)

DISSEMINATOR OF KNOWLEDGE

www.igi-global.com

701 E. Chocolate Ave., Hershey, PA 17033
Order online at www.igi-global.com or call 717-533-8845 x100
To place a standing order for titles released in this series, contact: cust@igi-global.com
Mon-Fri 8:00 am - 5:00 pm (est) or fax 24 hours a day 717-533-8661

Table of Contents

Section 3
Communication

Detailed Table of Contents

Section 1
HCI and Intelligent System Design

This section includes six contributions related to review and experimental work on the area of Human Computer Interaction (HCI) and Intelligent System Design.

Chapter 1
Jens Alfredson, Saab Aeronautics, Sweden
Ulrika Ohlander, Saab Aeronautics, Sweden

This chapter highlights important aspects of an intelligent fighter pilot support for distributed unmanned and manned decision making. First the background is described including current trends within the domain, and characteristics of a decision support system are discussed. After that a scenario and example situations are presented. The chapter also includes reflections of an intelligent fighter pilot support for distributed unmanned and manned decision making from the joint cognitive systems view, regarding human interoperability, and function allocation.

Chapter 2
Razib Hayat Khan, Norwegian University of Science & Technology (NTNU), Norway

To meet the challenge of conducting quantitative analysis at the early stage of the system development process, this chapter introduces an extensive framework for performance modeling of a distributed system. The goal of the performance modeling framework is the assessment of the non-functional properties of the distributed system at an early stage based on the system's functional description and deployment mapping of service components over an execution environment. System's functional description with deployment mapping has been specified using UML. To analyze the correctness of the UML specification style, we have used temporal logic, specifically cTLA, to formalize the UML model. We have shown in detail how UML models are formalized by a set of cTLA processes and production rules. To conduct the performance evaluation of a distributed system, the UML model is transformed into analytic model SRN. We have specified an automated model transformation process to generate SRN model from UML, which is performed in an efficient and scalable way by the use of model transformation rules.

Chapter 3

Pushpanjalee Konwar, Assam Don Bosco University, India

Hemashree Bordoloi, Assam Don Bosco University, India

Elecrooculogram (EOG) signal extraction is critical in the working of any electrooculography aided system based upon the tracking of the ocular movement of the eye dipole. In this chapter the signals captured using sensors (electrodes), are first amplified, then the noise is removed and then digitized, before being transferred to controller for movement of the wheelchair. Finally, from the muscle sensor, the output is directly being given to the controller to reach the target and complete the control of the movement of the wheelchair. Initially, a potentiometer is used instead of the Ag-Agcl electrodes to test the strength of signal obtained due to the movement of the eyes. Using this wheelchair is quite an advantage because this chair helps a physically handicapped person to move freely without being dependent on anyone else. The research provides a new method for human-machine interface system.

Chapter 4

Saurav Goswami, Assam Don Bosco University, India

Semina Mehjabin, Assam Don Bosco University, India

Parismita A. Kashyap, Assam Don Bosco University, India

This chapter discusses about a prototype of Driverless Train Operation (DTO) mode. In DTO, driving is controlled and monitored automatically, without human assistance. A train attendant can intervene in emergencies. The automatic driving system takes care of the departure, the movement between two stations, and the automatic and precision stopping of the train and opening of the doors. If required, the door is automatically opened again. When passenger volume is high, additional trains are automatically sent into operation straight from the depot at the push of a button. The driverless metro train in our work is basically an embedded system based framework, which is designed to provide solutions for smooth a human machine interface while controlling high speed metro train using automated actuation and regulation mechanisms. In this work, the modeling of the metro train is done in a more precise way using an AVR microcontroller.

Chapter 5

Bhaswati Mandal, Gauhati University, India

Manash Pratim Sarma, Gauhati University, India

Kandarpa Kumar Sarma, Gauhati University, India

This chapter presents a method for generating binary and multiclass Support Vector Machine (SVM) classifier with multiplierless kernel function. This design provides reduced power, area and reduced cost due to the use of multiplierless kernel operation. Binary SVM classifier classifies two groups of linearly or nonlinearly separable data while the multiclass classification provides classification of three nonlinearly separable data. Here, at first SVM classifier is trained for different classification problems and then the extracted training parameters are used in the testing phase of the same. The dataflow from all the processing elements (PEs) are parallely supported by systolic array. This systolic array architecture provides faster processing of the whole system design.

Chapter 6

Puspalata Sah, Centre of Plasma Physics, Institute for Plasma Research, India
Kandarpa Kumar Sarma, Gauhati University, India

Detection of diabetes using bloodless technique is an important research issue in the area of machine learning and artificial intelligence (AI). Here we present the working of a system designed to detect the abnormality of the eye with pain and blood free method. The typical features for diabetic retinopathy (DR) are used along with certain soft computing techniques to design such a system. The essential components of DR are blood vessels, red lesions visible as microaneurysms, hemorrhages and whitish lesions i.e., lipid exudates and cotton wool spots. The chapter reports the use of a unique feature set derived from the retinal image of the eye. The feature set is applied to a Support Vector Machine (SVM) which provides the decision regarding the state of infection of the eye. The classification ability of the proposed system for blood vessel and exudate is 91.67% and for optic disc and microaneurysm is 83.33%.

Section 2
Signal Processing

This section is consisted of six contributions related to review and experimental work on the area of biomedical signal processing, speech signal processing and image processing.

Chapter 7

S. R. Nirmala, Gauhati University, India
Pratiksha Sarma, Girijananda Chowdhury Institute of Management and Technology, India

Biological signals can be classified according to its various characteristics like waveform shape, statistical structure and temporal properties. Among various bioelectric signals, one of the most familiar signal is the ECG. It is a signal derived from the electrical activity of the heart. The heart is an important organ which supplies body with oxygen. ECG is widely used in monitoring the health condition of the human. Cardiac arrhythmias can affect electrical system of the heart muscles and cause abnormal heart rhythms that can lead to insufficient pumping of blood and death risks. An important step towards identifying an arrhythmia is the classification of heartbeats. Modern analysis of electrical activity of the heart uses simple as well as sophisticated algorithms of digital signal processing. With the advent of technology, automatic classification of electrocardiogram signals through human-computer interactive systems has received great attention. This chapter discusses some computer assisted classification techniques based on statistical features extracted from ECG signal.

Chapter 8

Devkant Swargiary, Don Bosco College of Engineering & Technology, India
Joydeep Paul, Don Bosco College of Engineering & Technology, India
Ruhul Amin, Don Bosco College of Engineering & Technology, India
Hemashree Bordoloi, Don Bosco College of Engineering & Technology, India

Eye ball detection can be used for controlling certain applications. In this chapter, we describe the formulation of an eye ball detection system for design of an obstacle detection and avoidance technique. The obstacle detector is used with a vehicle and works by determining the location of an obstacle in the vicinity of a test object. The obstacle's distance is gauged from the test object in terms of corresponding voltages. The system uses image processing to detect the eye of the driver. If the eye of the driver is closed for a longer period than the threshold period then the image processing block sends a signal to the sensor which automatically takes control of the test vehicle.

Chapter 9

Prolonged Diabetes causes massive destruction to the retina, known as Diabetic Retinopathy (DR) leading to blindness. The blindness due to DR may consequence from several factors such as Blood vessel (BV) leakage, new BV formation on retina. The effects become more threatening when abnormalities involves the macular region. Here automatic analysis of fundus images becomes important. This system checks for any abnormality and help ophthalmologists in decision making and to analyze more number of cases. The main objective of this chapter is to explore image processing tools for automatic detection and grading macular edema in fundus images.

Chapter 10

Diabetes maculopathy has become one of the rapidly increasing health threats worldwide. The complication of diabetes associated to retina of the eye is diabetic retinopathy. A patient with the disease has to undergo periodic screening of eye. The ophthalmologists use colour retinal images of a patient acquired from digital fundus camera for disease diagnosis. Limited number of ophthalmology specialists in most of the countries motivates the need for computer based analysis of retinal images using image processing techniques. The results of this process may be used in applications such as, to classify the retinal images into normal and diseased. This could reduce the workload of ophthalmologists, also aid in diagnosis, to make measurements and to look for a change in progression of disease. Some computer based retinal image analysis methods used for the application are briefed in this chapter.

Chapter 11

In the present scenario, vision based hand gesture recognition has become a highly emerging research area for the purpose of human computer interaction. Such recognition systems are deployed to serve as a replacement for the commonly used human-machine interactive devices such as keyboard, mouse, joystick etc. in real world situations. The major challenges faced by a vision based hand gesture recognition system include recognition in complex background, in dynamic background, in presence of multiple gestures in the background, under variable lighting condition, under different viewpoints etc. In the context of sign language recognition, which is a highly demanding application of hand gesture recognition system, coarticulation detection is a challenging task. The main objective of this chapter is to provide a general overview of vision based hand gesture recognition system as well as to bring into light some of the research works that have been done in this field.

Chapter 12

Mousmita Sarma, Gauhati University, India
Kandarpa Kumar Sarma, Gauhati University, India

Acoustic modeling of the sound unit is a crucial component of Automatic Speech Recognition (ASR) system. This is the process of establishing statistical representations for the feature vector sequences for a particular sound unit so that a classifier for the entire sound unit used in the ASR system can be designed. Current ASR systems use Hidden Markov Model (HMM) to deal with temporal variability and Gaussian Mixture Model (GMM) for acoustic modeling. Recently machine learning paradigms have been explored for application in speech recognition domain. In this regard, Multi Layer Perception (MLP), Recurrent Neural Network (RNN) etc. are extensively used. Artificial Neural Network (ANN) s are trained by back propagating the error derivatives and therefore have the potential to learn much better models of nonlinear data. Recently, Deep Neural Network (DNN)s with many hidden layer have been up voted by the researchers and have been accepted to be suitable for speech signal modeling. In this chapter various techniques and works on the ANN based acoustic modeling are described.

Section 3
Communication

This section includes three contributions which represent recent advances in communication and related areas.

Chapter 13

Irfan Habib, Assam Don Bosco University, India
Atiqul Islam, Assam Don Bosco University, India
Suman Chetia, Assam Don Bosco University, India
Samar Jyoti Saikia, Assam Don Bosco University, India

A radio-controlled (RC) aircraft is controlled remotely by a hand-held transmitter and a receiver within the craft. The working mechanism of such an arrangement designed using an AT89S51 microcontroller is reported in this chapter. The primary focus of the chapter is to describe the design of the interfacing of transceiver module with AT89S51 microcontroller and control the movement of the aircraft according to the instruction given remotely. The microcontroller reads the input given by the user and transmits the data to the receiver at the aircraft. The receiver module receives the transmitted signal and demodulates it and gives the data as serial sequence of bits at the output. The serial data are then given to the decoder which transforms the data from serial to parallel. This set of data is used to control motors and any related device. A special coding technique is used to secure the transmitted data.

Chapter 14

Banty Tiru, Gauhati University, India

Power Line Communication (PLC) uses the available power line as a communication medium. The purpose of this chapter is to present the salient features, current trend and future scope of PLC with emphasis in the Indian context. Unlike other channels available, power lines are harsh media for data transfer and require efficient modeling and simulation techniques to propose and implement suitable mitigation schemes for achieving acceptable performance. Designed equipments have to adhere to strict mandates at the national and international levels to account for issues related to electromagnetic compatibility (EMC). In spite of this, PLC is expected to occupy an important place in the networking market in applications of smart grid and as a component of heterogeneous/hybrid communication system. The chapter is also backed by results from experiments carried on a typical power line in a test site with a presentation of noise, transfer characteristics, modeling and an estimate of the channel capacity.

Chapter 15

This chapter describes the use of certain interleavers for use in a wireless communication set for better accuracy and constancy of the transmitted data. Different interleaver techniques and methods are explored, including the variation of associated system parameters. The performance derived is discussed and the most suitable design is ascertained which is essential for better reliability of a wireless communication system. Bit Error Rate (BER), computational time, mutual information and correlation are the parameters analysed, in case of four types of interleavers viz. general block interleaver, matrix interleaver, random interleaver and convolutional interleaver, considering a fading environment. The hardware implementation using a block interleaver is reported here as a part of this work that shows encouraging results and maybe considered to be a part of a communication system with appropriate modifications.

Preface

Of late, intelligent system and related designs have become important instruments of innovative designs for automated control and interaction with computers and machines. Such systems depend upon methods and tools for solving complex learning and decision-making problems under uncertain and continuously varying conditions. A range of areas covering many disciplines of science, engineering and technology in a composite form, incorporating modifications with certain autonomy and decision making in methods and instruments constitute intelligent system design. Frameworks based on knowledge-aided systems, natural-language processing, machine learning, data mining, adaptive robotics, etc working in concert have driven research and innovation towards design of intelligence aided approaches of interaction between human and machine. These aspects currently have been receiving attention not only from the research community but have also influenced social dimensions. Such aspects need proper discussion, documentation and discrimination. The present book titled *Intelligent Applications for Heterogeneous System Modelling and Design* is a collection of selected submissions derived out of continuous research in the related areas. The book is intended to provide a compilation of contemporary research and include certain significant contributions representing critical developments in intelligent and emerging system design. Considerable work has been reported in this area and there is always a necessity to compile such works. This book is an attempt in this direction and is intended to include some of the recent works related to intelligent and emerging system design. The book attempts to cover the recent trends in intelligent and emerging system design using a range of tools including soft-computation. The book includes review, discussion and experimental work in the areas of communication, computation, vision sciences, device design, fabrication, upcoming materials and related process design etc. Its objective is to provide a glimpse about the ongoing and emerging areas of research in the areas of intelligent and emerging system design and related domains.

Several chapters are included in the book. Jens Alfredson et. al discusses intelligent support to fighter pilots operating with distributed unmanned and manned platforms and decision making. This chapter highlights important aspects of an intelligent fighter pilot support for distributed unmanned and manned decision making. First the background is described including current trends within the domain, and characteristics of a decision support system are discussed. After that a scenario and example situations are presented. The chapter also includes reflections of an intelligent fighter pilot support for distributed unmanned and manned decision making from the joint cognitive systems view, regarding human interoperability, and function allocation.

Razib Hayat Khan et. al discusses the quantitative analysis of a complex distributed system, at the early stage of the system development process is always an essential and intricate endeavour. To meet the challenge of conducting quantitative analysis at the early stage, this chapter introduces an extensive framework for performance modelling of a distributed system. The goal of the performance modelling framework is the assessment of the non-functional properties of the distributed system at an early stage based on the system's functional description and deployment mapping of service components over an execution environment. System's functional description with deployment mapping has been specified using UML. To analyse the correctness of the UML specification style, we have used temporal logic, specifically cTLA, to formalize the UML model. We have shown in detail how UML models are formalized by a set of cTLA processes and production rules. To conduct the performance evaluation of a distributed system, the UML model is transformed into analytic model SRN. We have specified an automated model transformation process to generate SRN model from UML, which is performed in an efficient and scalable way by the use of model transformation rules.

Detection of diabetes using bloodless technique is an issue which is in the limelight of research in the field of machine learning and artificial intelligence (AI). It primarily intends to contribute towards faster and efficient means of detection and subsequent diagnosis of diabetes. Here, in a chapter by Sah et. Al. working of a system designed to detect the abnormality of the eye with pain- and blood-free method is discussed. The typical features for diabetic retinopathy (DR) are used along with certain soft computing techniques to design such a system. The essential components of DR are blood vessels, microaneurysms, haemorrhages and exudates. This chapter formulate a framework for bloodless diagnosis of diabetes using a unique feature set derived from the retinal image of the eye. The feature set is applied to a soft computational tool Support Vector Machine (SVM) which provides us the decision regarding the state of infection of the eye. The classification ability of the proposed system for blood vessel and exudate is 91.67% and for optic disc and microaneurysm is 83.33%.

Medical issue are vital for human survival, hence have been a fertile area of application of knowledge –aided systems. Such an aspect has been covered by Medhi et. al. Prolonged Diabetes Mellitus causes massive destruction to the retina, known as Diabetic Retinopathy (DR) leading to blindness. DR has become the most prominent cause of the new cases of blindness occurred in individuals of aged 20-70 years among world population. The blindness due to DR may consequence from several factors such as (a) Blood vessel (BV) leakage and new BV formation on retina at severe stages lead to retinal detachment causing irreversible vision loss; (b) The peripheral vision loss occurs due to imbalance of Optic Disc (OD) to Cup ratio and its central depression Cup are the bright region of retina) resulting from Glaucoma; (c) The effects become more threatening when abnormalities involves the macular region. The macula—and its center fovea—of the retina are responsible for sharp vision. The accumulation of abnormalities over fovea leads to blindness. Patients diagnosed with diabetes are therefore must have to undergo regular eye examination at least once a year, to find out the presence of DR. A non-invasive, low cost method for obtaining retinal photographs is Fundus photography. Thus, now-a-day's ophthalmologists mostly use fundus photograph for the analysis of DR. The number of eye care professionals with the essential skills to diagnose DR is currently inadequate compared to the number of cases registered with DR. There are many unidentified cases because of the high cost involved in screening procedures. Under these circumstances, mass screening would not be possible. Here automatic screening comes into picture. Automatic screenings are performed on fundus images and algorithms are applied. An automatic report can be recorded by the system to check out any abnormality. This approach will help the ophthalmologists to analyze more number of cases. The main objective of this chapter is to analyze macular edema in fundus images and use image processing tools for its automatic detection and grading. After detection, the macular regions are to be marked for the identification of maculopathy stages. The Macular Edema (ME) severity stages are located based on the presence of abnormalities from neighborhood of macula towards its center. In this chapter, a study on analysis of macular edema is performed and an algorithm is introduced for the same.

Sharma et. al have covered another related area in a chapter. Biological signals can be classified according to its various characteristics like waveform shape, statistical structure and temporal properties. Among various bioelectric signals, one of the most familiar signal is the ECG. It is a signal derived from the electrical activity of the heart. The heart is an important organ which supplies body with oxygen. ECG is widely used in monitoring the health condition of the human. Cardiac arrhythmias can affect electrical system of the heart muscles and cause abnormal heart rhythms that can lead to insufficient pumping of blood and death risks. An important step towards identifying an arrhythmia is the classification of heartbeats. Modern analysis of electrical activity of the heart uses simple as well as sophisticated algorithms of digital signal processing. With the advent of technology, automatic classification of electrocardiogram signals through human-computer interactive systems has received great attention. This chapter discusses some computer assisted classification techniques based on statistical features extracted from ECG signal.

How biological signals and intelligent systems can be combined for assistance of persons with special requirements have been demonstrated in a chapter by Bordoloi et. al. This chapter describes a real-time control machinery of wheelchair system using Electrooculography (EOG) signals. The system was initially verified using a test signal which had been provided by a 10k potentiometer. The movement of the human eye signal is used as a control signal for the wheel chair movement, called human-machine interface (HMI) system. The goal is to design a sophisticated EOG based system which can prove to be a supportive mechanism for physically handicapped person.

Importance of intelligent control has been highlighted by Kashyap et. al. in a chapter related to locomotive engine control. This chapter discusses about a prototype of Driverless Train Operation (DTO) mode. In DTO, driving is controlled and monitored automatically, without human assistance. A train attendant can intervene in emergencies. The automatic driving system takes care of the departure, the movement between two stations, and the automatic and precision stopping of the train and opening of the doors. If required, the door is automatically opened again. When passenger volume is high, additional trains are automatically sent into operation straight from the depot at the push of a button. The driverless metro train in our work is basically an embedded system based framework, which is designed to provide solutions for smooth a human machine interface while controlling high speed metro train using automated actuation and regulation mechanisms. In this work, the modelling of the metro train is done in a more precise way using an AVR microcontroller.

Communication continues to improve the way people remain connected and build greater reach. Certain works in this area has been highlighted in the book. Das et. al. discuss design of interleavers and application in stochastic wireless channels. Wireless communication is an inevitable part of modern technology. It plays a significant role in almost every sphere such as education, communication, entertainment, etc. In wireless communication, accuracy and constancy of the transmitted data is always an issue, therefore continuous attempts are being carried out in order to accomplish ascertainable results over several wireless media. Different techniques and ideas are suggested and executed for this purpose. Still there remains certain limitations in the system which needs to be addressed. So in order to mitigate such limitations, a technique called interleaving is proposed here. The use of interleaver can enhance the performance of wireless communication up to a great extent. Here in this chapter, some system parameters are discussed and analysed, which are important to determine the performance of a wireless communication system. Bit Error Rate (BER), computational time, mutual information and correlation are the parameters analysed, using four types of interleavers viz. general block interleaver, matrix interleaver, random interleaver and convolutional interleaver, considering a fading environment. Efforts to design hardware architectures have yielded encouraging results, yet there are considerable amount of challenges which are to be met during implementation. The hardware implementation using a block interleaver is reported as performed as a part of this work that shows encouraging results and maybe considered to be a part of a communication system with appropriate modifications.

Wireless communication has grown largely in last decade and it is constantly expanding. It can also be used for data communication to control various remote devices such as airplanes, cars etc. Data security plays a vital role in these kinds of design issues. Different coding schemes can be used to encrypt the data. Such possibilities have been reported by Saikia et. al. in the chapter, the authors reported the implementation of a simple and unique coding scheme by generating a bit sequence to secure the data transmission along with already available coding schemes. A radio-controlled plane or aircraft, often called RC aircraft or RC plane, is controlled remotely by a hand-held transmitter and a receiver within the craft. The receiver controls the corresponding servos that move the control surfaces based on the position of joysticks on the transmitter, which in turn affect the orientation of the plane. Flying RC aircraft as a hobby has been growing worldwide with the advent of more efficient motors, lighter and more powerful batteries and less expensive radio systems. Scientific, government and military organizations are also utilizing RC aircraft for experiments, gathering weather readings, aerodynamic modeling and testing, and even using them as drones or spy planes.

Tiru et. al discuss about using the available power line as a communication media for various requirements. With the advance of digital signal processing techniques, power line carrier communication (PLCC) have come out as a strong competitor in the networking market. The power line network is heterogeneous in nature constituted of pieces of transmission line of different characteristics and loaded with variable loads offering a most unsuitable channel for signal transfer. The workable devices have to overcome the harsh channel conditions using complex mitigation schemes; adhering to strict mandates at the national and international levels. In spite of these, PLCC offers a market for investors and researchers alike due to its cost effectiveness and promising efficiencies in utilities leading to sustainable development. This chapter describes the salient features and the future prospect of this communication technique.

The book has a rich collection of works related to human machine interface. Mandal et. al. discuss about the design of power aware systolic processor design for certain computer vision applications. Real-time implementation is becoming necessary for a wide range of applications related to computer vision and image processing, security, bio-informatics, and several other areas. Efficient hardware implementations of machine-learning techniques yield a variety of advantages over software solutions which includes increased processing speed, reliability and battery life as well as reduced cost and complexity. Efforts to design hardware architectures have yielded encouraging results, yet there are considerable amount of challenges which are to be met during implementation. This chapter presents a method for generating binary and multiclass Support Vector Machine (SVM) classifier with multiplierless kernel function. This design provides reduced power, area and reduced cost due to the use of multiplierless kernel operation. Binary SVM classifier classifies two groups of linearly or nonlinearly separable data while the multiclass classification provides classification of three nonlinearly separable data. Here, at first SVM classifier is trained for different classification problems and then the extracted training parameters are used in the testing phase of the same. The dataflow from all the processing elements (PEs) are parallely supported by systolic array. This systolic array architecture provides faster processing of the whole system design.

A review of important vision based gesture recognition is presented by Choudhury et. al. In the present scenario, vision based hand gesture recognition has become a highly emerging research area for the purpose of human computer interaction. Such recognition systems are deployed to serve as a replacement for the commonly used human-machine interactive devices such as keyboard, mouse, joystick etc. in real world situations. The major challenges faced by a vision based hand gesture recognition system include recognition in complex background, in dynamic background, in presence of multiple gestures in the background, under variable lighting condition, under different viewpoints etc. In the context of sign language recognition, which is a highly demanding application of hand gesture recognition system, co articulation detection is a challenging task. The main objective of this chapter is to provide a general overview of vision based hand gesture recognition system as well as to bring into light some of the research works that have been done in this field.

Authentication, verification etc are integral issues of intelligent system design. Such issues are highlighted by Kashyap et. al. Authentication and identification is a fundamental issue to critical part in many security protocols. The Three Phase Security System is an especially designed system to provide best possible security for places where only authorized persons are allowed. The system comes with the combination of three technologies i.e. RFID (Radio Frequency Identification), Password and, Fingerprint Impression. Passwords or smart cards have been the most widely used authentication methods due to easy implementation and replacement. However, one can easily steal the RFID tag or hack the password. fingerprint scanner which is now a day's quite popular for its demand and efficiency holds an important place in security system. But alone a fingerprint scanner also cannot guaranty a protected system, because of various new and advanced fingerprint manipulation technology. This leads to the development of 3 phase security system: using RFID, password and fingerprint which is likely to overcome certain limitations. Moreover, the system is designed such that a random number or alphanumeric code of fixed length is automatically generated by the system and is sent to the mobile number of the user with the help of Global System for Mobile Communication (GSM) modem via short messaging service (SMS) connected for login verification. . The system also creates a log containing check-in of each user along with basic information of user. This ensures the reliability of the system and makes it difficult to breach.

Sarma et. al highlights some of the issues related to a soft-computing framework related to speech processing. Acoustic modelling of the sound unit is a crucial component of Automatic Speech Recognition (ASR) system. This is the process of establishing statistical representations for the feature vector sequences for a particular sound unit so that a classifier for the entire sound unit used in the ASR system can be designed. Current ASR systems use Hidden Markov Model (HMM) to deal with temporal variability and Gaussian Mixture Model (GMM) for acoustic modelling. Recently machine learning paradigms have been explored for application in speech recognition domain. In this regard, Multi Layer Perception (MLP), Recurrent Neural Network (RNN)etc. are extensively used. Artificial Neural Network (ANN) s are trained by back propagating the error derivatives and therefore have the potential to learn much better models of nonlinear data. Recently, Deep Neural Network (DNN)s with many hidden layer have been up voted by the researchers and have been accepted to be suitable for speech signal modelling. In this chapter various techniques and works on the ANN based acoustic modelling are described.

These are expected to constitute a ready reference for subsequent researches. The document is intended for a wide audience constituted by students, researchers, academicians, professionals, practitioners etc. Readers related to intelligent and emerging system design through mathematical and computational modeling and experimental designs shall find the book to be a new addition to the already existing repository. The book is specifically intended for a wide audience who are broadly involved in the domains of electronics and communication engineering, electrical engineering, cognitive system design, mathematics, computer science, other applied informatics domains and related areas.

There had been a thorough scrutiny of the submissions. The first stage was chapter proposal submission. Each of the proposals submitted have been thoroughly reviewed. Next, complete chapters were requested to the approved proposals. After the chapters were submitted, another round of review was conducted and detailed comments were passed on to the authors to make necessary revisions. The modified, revised and updated manuscripts were again subjected to another round of review and the decisions regarding inclusion taken. In this process, inputs from the editorial advisory board members were helpful. The editors are thankful to the reviewers who despite their busy schedules have shared their time to provide the feedbacks by carefully going through the submissions. The entire process was tedious and the final outcome had been due to the dedication of the team involved including the staff members of IGI Global. It has been a pleasant experience. If the contents in the book motivate researchers to take up work in this area, the efforts of the editorial team shall be considered to have been rewarded.

Kandarpa Kumar Sarma
Gauhati University, India

Manash Pratim Sarma
Gauhati University, India

Mousmita Sarma
SpeecHWareNet (I) Pvt. Ltd, India

Acknowledgment

The editors acknowledge the contributions by the authors, reviewers and the students, researchers and faculty members who have contributed in the respective ways in making the compilation of the volume possible.

Section 1
HCI and Intelligent System Design

This section includes six contributions related to review and experimental work on the area of Human Computer Interaction (HCI) and Intelligent System Design.

Chapter 1
Intelligent Fighter Pilot Support for Distributed Unmanned and Manned Decision Making

Jens Alfredson
Saab Aeronautics, Sweden

Ulrika Ohlander
Saab Aeronautics, Sweden

ABSTRACT

This chapter highlights important aspects of an intelligent fighter pilot support for distributed unmanned and manned decision making. First the background is described including current trends within the domain, and characteristics of a decision support system are discussed. After that a scenario and example situations are presented. The chapter also includes reflections of an intelligent fighter pilot support for distributed unmanned and manned decision making from the joint cognitive systems view, regarding human interoperability, and function allocation.

INTRODUCTION

This chapter aims at, identifying and systematically describe, system characteristics and contextual constraints of an intelligent fighter pilot support system for distributed unmanned and manned decision making. Specifically an analysis based on a literature review of state-of-the-art is presented as well as domain specific lessons learned from systems design within this field. Also, the chapter contributes more generally to guide and motivate students and researchers to perform similar contributions in adjacent domains of intelligent applications for heterogeneous system modelling and design.

In the technology-intensive domain of fighter aircraft it is important to design for human factors by regarding what is special about that specific context (Alfredson & Andersson, 2013), and to successfully apply cognitive design principles (Alfredson, Holmberg, Andersson, & Wikforss, 2011). For instance, human-centred automation guidelines could be applied to the fighter aircraft domain (Helldin, Falkman, Alfredson, & Holmberg, 2011). Also, design principles for adaptive automation and aiding have been

DOI: 10.4018/978-1-4666-8493-5.ch001

provided by Steinhauser, Pavlas and Hancock (2009). Already today and more so in future contexts, a fighter pilot has to interact with intelligent applications for heterogeneous systems where transparency is important (Helldin, 2014).

BACKGROUND

In the early days of aviation keeping the aircraft in the air was hard enough. The aviators were fully occupied by piloting. However, after some years of progress within the domain the aircraft could be better controlled in the air and there was also time to regard other activities. The pilots found time not only to aviate but also to navigate. In the military domain pilots could communicate what they had observed on the ground after they had landed, which could provide important reconnaissance information. Later, the history of military aviation is full of various types of aircraft performing very different missions in numerous scenarios. Fighter pilots of today make use of a flight control system or an "autopilot" or other functions to aid the piloting of the aircraft. Also, modern fighters are equipped with advanced sensor suits, high tech weapon systems, electronic warfare systems and many other subsystems that a modern fighter pilot has to manage. If you were ever given the opportunity to look at the instrumentation of a modern fighter aircraft performing a tactical mission you would probably see that instrumentation and displays to a great deal is used for tactical considerations and not only for flight instrumentation. The role of a fighter pilot has been transformed over time; from pilot to tactical decision maker.

This long term trend has led to current situations where a fighter pilot has to manage several tactical subsystems simultaneously and, at the same time, assess on going parallel tactical situations on the ground and/or in the air and make fast and important decisions to provide influence of the situations. Many situations are very applicable to naturalistic decision making as it were characterised by Klein, Orasanu, Calderwood, and Zsambok (1993). Situations are often complex, uncertain and dynamic characterised by high stakes, potentially risking both own and others life under extreme time pressure, calling for naturalistic decision making. Also, demanding situations may appear suddenly when performing almost any military mission, either it is an air-to-air mission, an air-to-surface mission or a reconnaissance mission. Also civil aviation can at times also be very demanding and dynamic at times, even though the military component of foes influencing the situation adds an extra need for specific decision making and corresponding decision support.

Today, and even more so in future aircraft systems, the pilot has to regard and interact with more and more information, if this trend will keep developing in the same direction and pace. This trend increases the need to support decision making. At the same time, there is a trend towards increasing abilities to support decision making. For instance, the computational power of modern avionics has increased substantially and the human-machine interaction technology has been improved, providing fighter aircraft engineers with new means of supporting fighter pilot interaction during demanding situations. There has been a long term trend towards increasing communication abilities between pilots not only including oral communication but also various means of data communication, allowing new means of communication between pilots as well as with command and control functions and more. Also, the cognitive ability for technical agents that the fighter pilot is in contact with, either direct by own manipulation and control, or indirect through another human, is increasing. Examples of technical agents that could influence the situation for a fighter pilot is a decision support system in the own aircraft as well as equivalent systems on other platforms, autonomous or highly automated unmanned aircraft or command and control decision support systems, as well as intelligent support systems for planning and evaluating the own mission. Also, some technical agents possess ability to support each other with data, including situation assessments, status of own system capabilities etcetera.

The further this trend is going the greater the abilities become to distribute decision making. One cognitive agent, human or technical, could very well pre-process information that another agent is making a decision based on, that yet another agent is executing etcetera. There are also tactical needs to distribute abilities between various cognitive agents. For instance, it might be more acceptable to expose unmanned systems to high risk settings at the same time as a human agent is assigned to judge the situation supported be decision support technology, all being distributed in the total system by location and/or in time. At the same time a parallel trend is emerging towards more and more competent unmanned aircraft, as the technology for unmanned systems is matured, possessing a wide spectrum of abilities. Hence, new opportunities to generate intelligent fighter pilot support for distributed unmanned and manned decision making emerge.

Within various civil sectors different trends that emphasize user subjective impression such as Kansaei Engineering (Nagamachi, 1989; 2011; Schütte, 2005) or user experience from the user-centred design tradition (Norman, Miller & Henderson, 1995; Hassenzahl & Tractinsky, 2006) have influenced design. Even though there have been variations in the actual design for military systems there has, for a long time, been an emphasis on performance as the utter importance for military systems. Even though concepts as mental workload and situation awareness has been used a lot to guide the design of military systems, their link to performance has been central and has been scrutinized for the fighter aircraft domain (Castor 2009; Svensson, Angelborg-Thanderz, & Sjöberg, 1993; Svensson, Angelborg-Thanderz, Sjöberg, & Olsson, 1997; Svensson & Wilson, 2002).

Also, it is of special importance that the performance of the total system is high rather than only the performance of individual subsystems, not to risk sub optimization. This is one of the reasons for why the joint cognitive system perspective (Hollnagel & Woods, 1983; 2005; Woods & Hollnagel, 2006) is a powerful base for analysis. However, for pragmatic reasons the system boundaries set for the analysis have to map the system level of the design process it is intended to support. Even though it is very important for a future user of a system that it supports the work that will be conducted in the applied context, not all these conditions are known when the design is performed and not all conditions could be influenced by the design decisions. Not knowing all design conditions and their relevance when conducting the design is a problem that has to be handled during the design and is sometimes referred to as the envisioned world problem (Dekker, 1996; Dekker & Woods, 1999). The fact that conditions other than the ones considered in the design process affect end users, can be regarded in the design process by assumptions and analysis, but cannot be controlled by system design alone. Conditions concerning the human, the methods used in the applied context, organizational factors and technology developed by other design organizations are all examples of factors of importance for the performance but with little or no influence from the system design process. To regard this broader scope, however, the design could be put in a wider context, such as the NATO human view presented by Handley and Smillie (2008).

Apart from striving to optimize the system design for users of the system currently being designed, the developing organisation may also have long term technology development goals. There has, for instance, been a long term trend towards highly automated systems and autonomy where the design organisation may have ambitions and visions. One way to handle this is to develop a strategy that aims towards that all products and product versions should be usable as well as to cope with the long term trend towards partial or fully autonomous systems. The strategy could include an automation strategy that could also assist in designing which functions to automate and which not to automate. To optimize the system design for users of the system the strategy could regard which activities humans are better at, which activities technical systems performs better, and which activities are best performed together by humans and technical systems, by thoughtful function allocation. Also, this function allocation does not have to be static, but designed to be dynamic. If the automation strategy involves guidance on how the dynamics of the function allocation should be designed it is more likely that the system design is more useful in aiding the user achieving high performance.

THE DECISION SUPPORT SYSTEM

Modern fighter aircraft are equipped with a range of sensors in order to give the pilot a view of the tactical environment and to support the launching of weapons. The information from the sensors is collected by the decision support system (DSS) which identifies and assesses the potential targets and threats and provides the analysed information to the pilot. The DSS controls the sensors and decides in what direction they should search and for what kinds of objects. The DSS helps the pilot to make decisions about actions, for example to dispense countermeasures and provide recommendations for delivery of weapons. The collected picture of the current situation the pilot receives from compiled information is often referred to as situation awareness (SA). It is crucial that the pilot can establish and maintain a high degree of SA in stressful dynamic situations with short time to take decisions.

SA and mental workload are widely used concepts among developers and system designers of human-machine interaction (HMI). Endsley (1988) defines SA as "The perception of the elements in the environment within a volume of time and space, the comprehension of their meaning, and the projection of their status in the near future". This construct is commonly used to explain why things went wrong and lack of SA is concluded as the cause of many accidents. Dekker and Hollnagel (2004) raise concerns about this use and label the constructs as "Folk Models". They argue that the concept is intuitively understood but not defined in a way that can be scientifically proven. Rather, one label is substituted for another, instead of trying to decompose into measurable parts. They propose that operator performance should be used as measure to validate design instead. Parasuraman, Sheridan and Wickens (2008) respond that these constructs do indeed have a scientific base and argue that the SA construct is useful in cognitive engineering. They argue that SA represents a continuous diagnosis of the state of a dynamic world. There is a "truth" and the user´s SA tells something about how much of this truth that is known to him, which has also been argued by Alfredson (2007). The term SA is widely used when formulating requirements for the development of interfaces and to describe the desirable performance of systems, such as DSS. In the case of fighter aircraft and DSS, SA could be regarded from two perspectives. The first is the picture of the situation the pilot gets from the sensors through the DSS, assuming that the DSS collects all the information that needs to be collected. In this case the pilot´s SA is depending on how good the DSS is to convey the information and this largely depends on the display interface. But it is not certain that the sensors have picked up everything there is to know. An object can be present but hidden and suddenly appear and surprise the pilot, by for example stealth technology. In this case it is rather the technical system which have faulted, not the pilot. Can the pilot be blamed for missing something the sensor system did not pick up?

The DSS is aiding the pilot in the tactical tasks of the mission; it is not connected to the actual flying of the aircraft. The complete SA should therefore be considered to include both awareness of the status of the aircraft (fuel etc.), the navigation and flying of the aircraft, knowing where the team members are and what they are doing and knowledge of the potential targets and threats in the environment. DSS supports the pilot in a part of his complete task. The discussed system is a hypothetical DSS in a fighter aircraft; it is simplified, and modelled for the purpose of this study.

The sensors on the aircraft are typically radar, electronic warfare, and infrared based systems that either actively (by sending out and receiving signals) or passively (by picking up signals) detect objects in the environment. This is performed at a distance greater than the human eye can see; therefore this kind of scenario is labelled beyond visual range (BVR). Here we will not get into the sensor technology, only presume that information about objects is obtained from the sensors and that the sensors need to be controlled and optimized in order to deliver the best possible measurements. Also, measurements made by other aircraft in the same tactical unit and the command and control (C2) will enter the DSS via data link.

The information that enters the DSS from the sensors typically consists of measurements of distances and bearings to various objects. The DSS fuses the information from the different sources to establish a fused object to make further analysis on. Then the DSS makes an estimate of what kind of aircraft it is most likely to be. Objects can for instance be classified as fighter, attack or other (transport, surveillance aircraft). The DSS also tries to establish the identity of the aircraft such as for example friendly, neutral, unknown or hostile.

The information is typically displayed to the pilot as a symbol on a digital moving map. The graphics on the map should optimally contain all the information the pilot needs.

In Figure 1 the flow of data and commands between the pilot and the sensors via the DSS is pictured. The top functionalities for this system would be:

- Fuse data from different sensor sources
- Classify objects, (fighter, attack or other)
- Identify objects, (friendly, hostile, unknown)
- Assess situation, prioritize from most hostile object
- Control sensors for further measurements

Figure 1. Overview of the analysed system

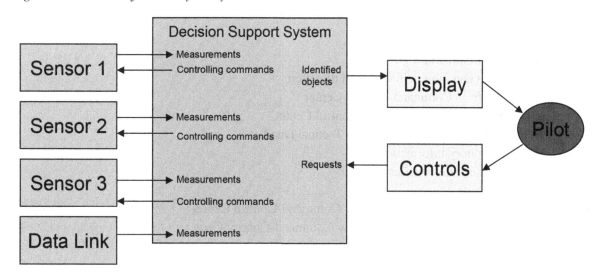

It can be noted here that both the pilot and the DSS make assessments of the situation and both the pilot and the DSS can select objects for closer monitoring. But, as a rule, the pilot should always have the last word and the system adapt to his requests. Also, it should be noted that the term DSS usually refers to a system which helps in sorting out alternative ways of acting and aid the user in decision making. The DSS in this context should do a little more than that. It optimizes the use of the sensors and controls them according to pilot command in detail in order to extract as much information from the environment as possible. Aiming at high level interaction between the DSS and the pilot, a higher level of automation could influence the pilot to think more higher-level thoughts that has been shown in a commercial aviation context by Casner and Schooler (2014).

SCENARIO AND EXAMPLE SITUATIONS

Ollero and Maza (2007) listed the following civil application areas for unmanned aerial vehicles (UAV): "Aerial photography and cinematography", "Aerial mapping", "Meteorology", Environmental monitoring", "Agriculture and forestry", "Inspection", "Law enforcement and security applications", Disasters and crisis management", "Fire fighting", "Traffic surveillance", "Communications", and "Civil engineering", but also concluded that currently the main UAV applications are within the defence domain. Also in the future there will be defence related applications for unmanned aircraft. Even though the future scenarios are not known in detail, they will probably be related to the scenarios of today, for manned and unmanned aircraft.

There are a lot of possible scenarios were an intelligent fighter pilot support for distributed unmanned and manned decision making could be used. Below we are presenting an example scenario and discussing how it could be modified to represent one possible scenario for such an intelligent fighter pilot support. An example scenario could be an air-to-air scenario with beyond visual range conditions. "Beyond Visual Range (BVR) means a scenario where the enemy is engaged before they can be seen visually. This is possible due to the performance of the sensors available to the formation, either their own sensors (primarily the aircraft radars), and the sensors and information available to the fighter controller" (Castor, 2009, p. 21). Helander and Skinnars (2000a) used cognitive walkthrough for evaluation of cockpit design. The following breakdown of subtasks for an air-to-air combat beyond visual range has been identified and presented by Helander & Skinnars (2000b):

1. Waiting in aircraft ready to take off
    1.1 Sitting in aircraft waiting
    1.2 Start within one minute in specified direction
2. Receive order from Command-Control Center
3. Identify connection with Command-Control Center
    3.1 Receive uuencoded information on Tactical Display
    3.2 Receive auditory information
    3.3 Group Commander verifies mission
4. Take off from base
5. Follow directional commands given by Command-Control Center
6. Follow geographical command given by Command-Control Center
7. Determine target

       7.1 Commander coordinates mission

       7.2 Commander communicates mission

       7.3 Prioritize goals for own delivery of weapons

8.   Achieve advantageous position

       8.1 Determine advantageous position

       8.2 Navigate to advantageous position

       8.3 Verify advantageous position

9.   Prepare missile for target

       9.1 Verify target position

       9.2 Use radar information from outside source

       9.3 Use own radar to measure naval targets

10.   Deliver missile

       10.1 Select advantageous time for delivery

       10.2 Deliver missiles

11.   Supervise situation

       11.1 Verify results from weapons delivery

12.   Finish mission

       Modify plans for return

13.   Navigate to base assigned by Command-Control Center

       13.1 Check navigation points (position, radar or visual)

       13.2 Communicate with Traffic Control

       13.3 Select approach mode for landing

       13.4 Land aircraft

       13.5 Report mission

14.   Select strategy to avoid attack against own aircraft

       14.1 Divert maneuver and drop weapons

       14.2 Let the aircraft drop and swing towards the ground

       14.3 Escape

       14.4 Disturb through

       14.5 Close range Air-to-Air, see section below

       14.6 Attack bomber aircraft using IR missiles, see Air-to-Surface below (pp. 16-17)

A complementary view containing some relevant technical and tactical parameters of air combat is suggested by Johansson (1999):

Jamming, electronic countermeasures and radar warning receiver

- Range of own jamming versus enemy radar
- Radar warning receiver range and accuracy

Radar

- Radar modes (e.g. Track While Scan, Continuous Wave)
- Aircraft radar range and angle of coverage

Weapon characteristics

- Mean speed
- Maximum range

- ○ Missile seeker opening distance

Aircraft behaviour and tactics

- ○ Absolute and relative altitude of aircraft in engagement
- ○ Absolute and relative speed of aircraft in engagement
- ○ Thrust
- ○ Geometry, i.e. the relative position and ranges of the aircraft within the twoship or fourship to the enemy, and to other friendly aircraft, e.g. attack aircraft that are being escorted
- ○ Aggressive or defensive stance and risk taking
- ○ Intentions and Rules of Engagement for both sides
- ○ Active versus passive use of radar

Numerical superiority

- ○ Number of own aircraft
- ○ Number of enemy aircraft

Command and Control

- ○ Radar coverage for air surveillance radars (i.e. other friendly radars on the ground or in the air)
- ○ Fighter controllers' threats classification capabilities

Loadout on aircraft

- ○ Fuel
- ○ Weapons loadout (quoted from Castor, 2009, p. 24).

There are various ways of performing BVR-combat, using various tactics and strategies and various systems and subsystems. However, as expressed by Castor (2009): "Regardless of engagement scenario the pure tactical goal would be to shoot down as many as possible of the enemy aircraft, while not getting shot down yourself" (p. 21). When new systems and subsystems are developed, often also new tactics are evolved in parallel. The use of manned and unmanned aircraft together is one example of that. Ollero and Maza (2007) has described challenges with multiple heterogeneous unmanned aerial vehicles, and more specifically Alfredson, Lundqvist, Molander, and Nordlund (2010) has described challenges related to the collaboration between a manned fighter aircraft and an unmanned aerial reconnaissance vehicle. Future fighter pilots have to interact, direct or indirect, with manned as well as unmanned fellow air vehicles in various scenarios and situations. How BVR-combat will then be performed is highly dependent on the capabilities of the future system and one speculation is that the potentials of distributed decisions will be explored further and that several users and technical systems will act together. The following situations, illustrated in Figure 2 and Figure 3, are examples that can be considered for analysis. They represent situations that are both tactically important and could also help illustrate the performance of the total system. The first case includes a team where one or several members are not using their radar in order not to emit energy and reveal themselves. One team member is relaying on the information he receives from the rest of the team via data link. It is crucial in this situation that the other team members are aware of this fact and realize that they are contributing with important information for this team member, for the situation depicted in Figure 2.

Another example is when a team is performing reconnaissance, see Figure 3. The total area of interest for the team is marked on the map and it should also be noted that it is a volume in space not just a flat area. How does each team member know what area to search next and how can the team best keep track of where the others recently have been searching?

Figure 2. Example situation. Team measurement (intersecting).

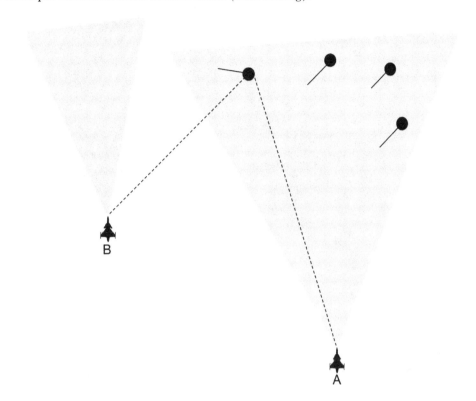

THE JOINT COGNITIVE SYSTEMS VIEW

One way to describe users and technical systems is to regard them as a joint cognitive system – JCS (Hollnagel & Woods, 1983; 2005; Woods & Hollnagel, 2006). Agents in such a JCS could very well be interdependent to fulfil the tasks of the JCS that could act as one unit, although distributed in space. This chapter explores how the JCS perspective could be applied to an intelligent fighter pilot support for distributed unmanned and manned decision making. Later, what to automate is discussed. Such an analysis will benefit from distinguishing between various types of automation suited for specific tasks with known user cognitive demands (Taylor, Reinerman-Jones, Szalma, Mouloua, & Hancock, 2013). Similar to a study from the automotive domain on context adaptable driver information (Davidsson & Alm, 2014), this chapter will describe what do whom need and want when.

Often researchers that are applying the JCS approach argue that traditionally the focus in the field of Human Factors engineering has been to the interface between the user and the machine/computer (HMI) and therefore the purpose of the total system is at risk to be lost. Too much energy is spent on designing the interface instead of trying to optimize the output from the system. The JCS approach shifts the attention towards the functionality and performance. The JCS is not defined by what it is but rather by what it does.

A JCS can be defined in different ways depending on the analysis but at least it consists of a human user (who is regarded as a cognitive system) and an artefact. A cognitive system is defined by Hollna-

Figure 3. Example situation. Team reconnaissance.

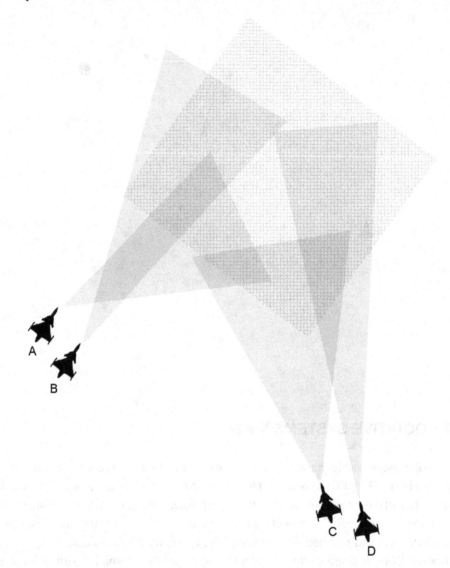

gel and Woods (2005) as "a system that can modify its behaviour on the basis of experience so as to achieve specific anti-entropic ends" (p.22). The term anti-entropic here refers to the systems ability to resist the increase in entropy, i.e. the amount of disorder. An artefact is defined as something made for a specific purpose.

What parts of the system that should be included in the JCS analysis can be different depending on the context but typically the things that can be controlled should be included. An example is when analysing traffic the driver and the car are obviously included. But the roads can also be embraced since they are possible to control and change. The weather in the other hand is excluded. Even though the weather does influence traffic it can not be controlled and changed. The JCS in this case consists of the pilot, the aircraft and the DSS together. In this view the DSS is an artefact that mediates the relationship between the sensors and the pilot. The interaction is considered to be with the world through the artefact rather than with the artefact itself. The borders of the JCS can also be expanded to include several cooperating aircraft depending on the scope of the analysis. For example, the analysis can be done for a team of aircraft some of which can be unmanned and the JCS in this case would consist of several agents.

The artefact can be categorized depending on how transparent it appears to the user and how the user perceives it. In the transparency dimension there are two extremes, hermeneutic or transparent. In the case the artefact is transparent it is experienced by the user as a part of him rather than as a part of the application. It is easy for the user to build and maintain a mental model. The artefact can either serve as an extension of the user´s body and mind and therefore the relationship is considered to be embodied. In this case the artefact is transparent and it is experienced by the user as a part of him rather than as a part of the application. The other dimension the artefact can be analysed in is as an interpreter and in this role it does all the communication between the user and the process. The artefact is opaque or non-transparent and is experienced more as being part of the process rather than the operator. In the case with the DSS the pilot cannot have any experience of what is going on than through the artefact since the scenario is taking place at a distance out of his sight and a lot of data fusion and identification is done by the system. This is considered to be an extreme case when the operator is dependent of the artefact, and the relation is labelled hermeneutic and means that the operator must go through the artefact to get to the world (Hollnagel and Woods, 2005). Another dimension of viewing the artefact is as either a tool or prosthesis. A tool is an artefact that amplifies the user´s cognitive functions while prosthesis rather takes over functions from the user. The DSS is a complex system and it will substitute the pilot in the control of the sensors and alleviate in the fusion of data, therefore it will be regarded as prosthesis. The transparency-exchangeability relation as proposed by Hollnagel and Woods (2005) distinguishes between two dimensions:

- Transparency: Hermeneutic vs. Embodiment
- Exchangeability: Tool vs. Prosthesis

The DSS is situated towards hermeneutic and prosthesis, that could be described as low transparency and high exchangeability. The combination of hermeneutic and prosthesis relation makes it challenging to develop a system that the user will understand and perform well with. It is probably advisable to try to design and construct the system in order for it to be perceived by the user as more of a tool with more transparency even if it is "actually" a hermeneutic prosthesis as in the case with the DSS. Our goal of the design would be to try to move towards tool and embodiment, striving for high transparency and low exchangeability.

The hermeneutic relation implies that is not possible for the pilot to have any experience of what is going on besides than through the DSS. However, one way for pilots to go "beside" the DSS would be to look at raw sensor data and try to make the assessments by themselves. This means that they would want to have access to the direct measurements from each sensor as well as the fused objects. The designers will then have to consider if this shall be provided. The risk being that the system gets even more complicated with many low level functions.

HUMAN INTEROPERABILITY

To regard the contribution from the design process in a wider context other aspects than technical has to be included in the analysis. Often new technology that is to be developed has very high expectations to meet increasing operational needs of the future that could not always be met. From studies of the command and control domain Persson (2014) has shown that several expected advantages of future technologies have not been met. However, relating technology to a wider context including human aspects when developing the technology may both adjust the expectations of the technology to more realistic levels as well as increasing the actual benefits from the technology by develop it considering for instance human operability, A network model for human interoperability proposed by Handley (2014) including the human view (Handley & Smillie, 2008) is applying the eight aspects: *Concept, Constraints, Functions, Roles, Human network, Training, Metrics,* and *Human dynamics.* The human view "…provides an integrated set of products that can be used to inform and influence system design, especially for network-enabled systems" (Handley, 2014, p. 351). One of the main benefits for this kind of analysis is that it potentially aids human interoperability into systems design and support collaboration. Below, these aspects are discussed in the light of intelligent fighter support for distributed unmanned and manned decision making.

The human view product *Concept* is about the human in relation to operational demands and system components. This is a very high-level representation, and for an intelligent fighter support for distributed unmanned and manned decision making it is essential to have an idea of human contributions to decisions in this context. Figure 4, below, provides a depicted overview of cognitive agents, amongst some are supposed to be human. Cognitive agents in this context could for instance be an unmanned aircraft or any human interacting with that aircraft or a decision support system either on a manned aircraft, on the ground or distributed between several aircraft etcetera. Operational demands in this kind of setting are very much determined by the concept of operation in applied scenarios. As discussed above there are a variety of potential scenarios to regard for this kind of systems, amongst a BVR-combat is only one. However, it is assumed that the role of the human is important for total system performance and that several humans have to cooperate together with unmanned systems and intelligent subsystems for mission success. The abilities of system components are highly dependent on the technologies used in this systems and subsystems. However, some general abilities could be defined such as the ability for a technical system to be used as means of communication between human agents, or the ability for a technical system to aid a distributed decision process together with other technical systems and/or humans, or to autonomous execute tasks etcetera. Later in this chapter the ability and potential benefit of distributing tasks through function allocation will be further discussed.

The human view product *Constraints* is about the capabilities and limitations of the human in the system. Sub views presented by Handley and Smillie (2008) are: Manpower Projections, Career Progression, Establishment Inventory, Health Hazards, Human Characteristics, and Personnel Policy. Several of these categories contain aspects that could not at all, or only indirectly, be controlled by design decisions in a technical design process. However, it is important to regard these aspects also in the design process by making assumptions and analysis of potential future constraints of relevance for the technical systems under development. The human characteristics including physical characteristics of a pilot performing a mission is very relevant, if not crucial to regard in the design process. In fighter aircraft of today mental workload demands are occasionally very high and information overload could affect the performance negatively. A context where more information is available and decisions are designed to be distributed between several cognitive agents could very well add to mental demands if this is not

Figure 4. The figure depicts an overview of cognitive agents in a joint cognitive system that supplies an intelligent pilot support for distributed unmanned and manned decision making.

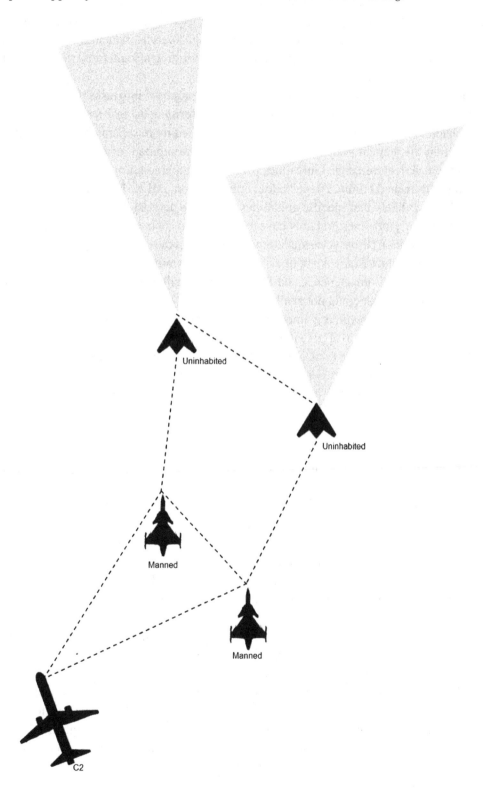

supported by technology, training and organisational measures. Aspects to regard to design for human factors in development of fighter aircraft has been addressed by Alfredson and Andersson (2013) and what is special about a fighter pilot compared to many other users is that the pilot community is in some sense homogeneous, due to for instance selection and training. Apart from mental demands fighter pilots also have to cope with high G-loads, visually demanding environments and more, which also limits the potential design of a fighter aircraft.

The human view product *Functions* is about functions decomposed into tasks that have been allocated to the human, including a justification for why a human is performing the task and not a technical system. Later in this chapter function allocation is going to be discussed more separately. Apart from the actual function allocation this human view product includes the development of interface design guidelines dependent on the task requirements. Guidelines for human-centered automation have been studied for the fighter aircraft domain (Helldin, 2014; Helldin & Erlandsson, 2012; Helldin, Falkman, Alfredson, & Holmberg, 2011). It is likely that specific guidelines have to be defined or current guidelines have to be modified. For instance, guidelines probably have to be adjusted concerning principles of interaction for dynamic function allocation between various cognitive agents, as the competences of these agents evolve.

The human view product *Roles* is about a job function defining specific behaviour, and includes: Responsibility, Authority, Competencies, and Multiplicity (Handley & Smillie, 2008). Several of these categories contain aspects that could not at all, or only indirectly, be controlled by design decisions in a technical design process. However, it is important to regard these aspects also in the design process by making assumptions and analysis of potential future constraints of relevance for the technical systems under development. It is important to map the roles to the function allocation, and also to decide if roles are to be regarded as static or if they could change over time.

The human view product *Human Network* is about the human-to-human communication patterns, including team aspects, but also technology for distributed cognition, shared awareness etcetera. The human view product human network also includes type of interaction, such as coordination, supervision etcetera. Although much of the human-to-human communication only use technology for communication purposes there might also be indirect influence from technology to human-to-human communication. For instance reported Lyons and Stokes (2012) indications of that human-human reliance could become biased towards lower behavioural reliance on human aids when confronted to conflicting information from automation. For intelligent fighter support for distributed unmanned and manned decision making it is likely that humans will have to collaborate to achieve mission objectives. Also, there will be someone formally in command. However, apart from the formal structure there might be informal structures of a human network influencing the mission outcome and even formal and/or informal networks between human and non-human cognitive agents, possible expanding the scope of this human view product, if not handled in another human view product.

The human view product *Training* is about how aspects concerning training will affect the human. Most training aspects are partly or only indirectly controlled by design decisions in a technical design process. It is important to regard these aspects in the design process by making assumptions and analysis of potential future constraints of relevance for the technical systems under development. For instance, functionality for embedded training has a clear link between the design during the development process and the use of the future product in its operational use. Especially for intelligent fighter pilot support for distributed unmanned and manned decision making the implications to train for missions with mixed manned and unmanned components has to be regarded.

The human view product *Metrics* is about human factors metrics and human related performance criteria, target values etcetera. Involving human factors assessment, this product is broad and assessments may be effected by concerns in any of the other human view products. Recently, Berggren, Nählinder, and Svensson (2014) described important aspects of assessing command and control effectiveness. Regarding intelligent pilot support for distributed unmanned and manned decision making it is important not only to regard human factors assessment at the level of human system interaction for all humans involved, but also include assessment of behaviour and performance of the total system, including a joint cognitive system approach.

Last, but not least, the human view product *Human Dynamics* is about change over time and may concern any of the other products. Handley and Smillie (2008) provides the following examples of elements that the human view product Human Dynamics may include: states and state changes, conditions, time units, and performance measures. Scenarios belong to this human view product and for intelligent fighter pilot support for distributed unmanned and manned decision making it is important to regard not only the operational scenarios, such as the BVR-combat case described above, but also various use cases and examples of how a flexible system may perform in different ways in given operational scenarios.

FUNCTION ALLOCATION

Function allocation design challenges has to be regarded for an intelligent fighter pilot support for distributed unmanned and manned decision making, to achieve a high performing total system. There is a long research tradition in using knowledge of what humans are good at and machines are good at for achieving better design. For instance Fitts (1951) suggested principles to allocate functions between man and machine. Even though substitution-based function allocation methods have been criticised (Hollnagel, 1999; Dekker & Woods, 2002) it is still contributing to design in various domains. Also, dynamic function allocation described as levels of automation (Sheridan & Verplank, 1978; Taylor, 1997) is still contributing to design in various domains. However, Defense Science Board (2012), suggests to "abandon the debate over definitions of levels of autonomy and embrace a three-facet (cognitive echelon, mission timelines, human-machine system trade spaces) autonomous systems framework…" (p. 2).

Five key requirements for effective function allocation proposed by Feigh and Pritchett (2014), in a model of human-automation function allocation (Pritchett, Kim, & Feigh, 2014) are described below, that is: 1) *"Each agent must be allocated functions that it is capable of performing"*, 2) *"Each agent must be capable of performing its collective set of functions"*, 3) *"The function allocation must be realizable with reasonable teamwork"*, 4) *"The function allocation must support the dynamics of the work"*, and 5) *"The function allocation should be the result of deliberate design decisions"*. Each of these aspects could be applied to the context of an intelligent fighter pilot support for distributed unmanned and manned decision making. By such an approach all cognitive agents, human and technical systems are analysed together which could be perceived as unsophisticated for any human that perceives human abilities and behaviour to be very different from those of technical systems. The analysis will for instance risk describing human characteristics in technical terms and thereby reduce humans into information processing agents. Also the opposite critique could be expressed, risking anthropomorphism when a technical system and its behaviour is analysed together with human agents. However, first, this analysis and the requirements below is not intended to mirror every aspect of a system in use, but is used to guide design decisions. Secondly, the reason for applying the requirements is that there are differences between the agents and if there are significant differences it is more challenging to develop methods and requirements that could be applied to all these various agents. However, it is due to the fact that there are significant differences between the agents that methods and requirements are needed to support the design process.

The first requirement proposed by Feigh and Pritchett (2014); *Each agent must be allocated functions that it is capable of performing*, is about each particular function relative to the capabilities of the agent that has been allocated the function. In the tradition of Fitts (1951) lists has described what men are better at and what machines are better at, in general. Specifically for an intelligent fighter pilot support for distributed unmanned and manned decision making an estimation of abilities of agents in that context has to be performed. In this context it is not only of interest which agent is better at performing a task, but also the risk/cost of performing a task has to be regarded since many missions may include substantial risks. For instance, if the performance of a task is associated to an increased risk of being shot down, there would be an incentive to allocate such a task to an unmanned rather than a manned aircraft as far as possible. Also, from either an economical or military strategically point of view it might be that some assets, either a flying platform itself or its subsystems or carried loads, may be very valuable and thereby the risk level of that entity should be minimized in comparison to other entities.

The second requirement; *Each agent must be capable of performing its collective set of functions*, is about understanding the agents limited resources. Even though one agent might be the best agent to perform the task according to its characteristics (e.g. according to a list of what men are better at and what machines are better at) it might not be prioritised or might not even be possible for that agent to perform the task due to the collective set of functions. For instance, workload might constrain the performance of a task, either the task might risk being performed badly or not performed at all due to high workload. For a technical system it might be limitations in processing capability or lack of memory or any other technical constraint, whilst for a human agent it might be an overload of some mental capability. Specifically for the fighter domain the visual demands of a fighter pilot has been very high at times. Team spatial working memory has been shown to affect team performance in networked supervisory control of unmanned air vehicles (McKendrick, Shaw, de Visser, Saqer, Kidwell, & Parasuraman, 2014). Specifically for an intelligent fighter pilot support for distributed unmanned and manned decision making it is also important to regard the spatial positioning of the aircraft relative each other before allocating the tasks, since some tasks may be better performed at one position rather than another. Also, in some military missions each agent's ability to perform a collective set of functions might vary a lot, due to for instance radar jamming or decreased functionality due to enemy fire etcetera.

The third requirement; *The function allocation must be realizable with reasonable teamwork*, is about teamwork functions that coordinates the work across the agents. In this sense human agents as well as technical systems are team members that have to communicate, interact and coordinate their actions. Some tasks need teamwork to be performed, whilst other tasks may be better performed by teamwork although they might have been possible to perform to some degree by a single agent. Specifically for an intelligent fighter pilot support for distributed unmanned and manned decision making it is important to consider the spatial positioning of the aircraft also for teamwork considerations. For instance, the distance between two aircraft that both use a passive sensor, such as an infra-red-search-and-track (IRST) sensor, is very important for determining the position of an object of interest. Also, the relative positioning of aircraft might be of importance for tactical reasons such as establishing potential threats at an enemy over a longer period of time etcetera.

The fourth requirement; *The function allocation must support the dynamics of the work*, is about the on going response to the work environment for each agent as well as for the total system. When functions are interdependent this could be more or less obvious and sometimes it is not obvious at all, but the function allocation should support the agents to cope with the dynamics of the situation. An alternative approach that could complement the striving of allocating functions to when they are needed is to gain resilience by increasing a team's ability to perform during unexpected conditions. Specifically for an intelligent fighter pilot support for distributed unmanned and manned decision making it is important to regard fast and drastic changes in the work setting, to cope with events such as aircraft that has been shut down or the sudden appearance of stealth aircraft on the battle scene etcetera. Also, the rules of engagement (ROE) that defines what to do during various circumstances has to be regarded at the same time as the function allocation supports the dynamics of the work.

The fifth and last of the requirements proposed by Feigh and Pritchett (2014); *The function allocation should be the result of deliberate design decisions*, is about integrating function allocation into the design process. In general it is important to make deliberate design decisions concerning function allocation early in the design as these decisions often influence the choice of technology to be used and very much influence criteria for human-machine interaction. Specifically for an intelligent fighter pilot support for distributed unmanned and manned decision making it is important to consider the very long life time of aircraft as well as the long cycles for development of new products compared to many other domains. Also, it is important not only to make deliberate design decisions on the function allocation of a specific aircraft, manned or unmanned, but also on the total system level of several cognitive agents collaborating using several manned and unmanned aircraft.

DISCUSSION

The purpose of the analysed DSS is to perform tasks for the pilot such as object search and identification. Both system complexity and time constraints would make it very difficult if not impossible for the pilot to both manually control the sensors and conclude from the data what kind of object is being measured. It would be very difficult for the pilot to go into the details and set up the sensors in the most optimal way. Not long ago the radar was to a large extent controlled by the pilot on a fairly low level and the raw data was plotted on a screen. In this setting the pilot probably felt that he was in control of the process and understood what the system was doing. When he had trouble locating and identifying an object he tried a different mode or perhaps changed some parameters. With the DSS the aim is to achieve a more capable system working at a faster pace with several channels of information. The challenge is to keep the pilot feeling in control and knowing what is going on in the system and still achieve powerful and fast automated functions by the DSS.

The division of decisions between the DSS and the pilot could include a strategy such as that the DSS handles for instance rule based decisions or suggestions, which can be predicted and programmed in the system (automated). The pilot could take the more difficult decisions, such as if to launch a weapon. He is able to adapt to the changing environment which is difficult for the DSS to manage. The type of decisions can serve as a guide to what functions should belong to the pilot and the DSS respectively.

The main purpose of the DSS is to measure objects with such good quality that weapons can be launched at hostile objects. Identification and classification of the objects is a key capability of the JCS. The performance of the DSS in the identification and classification of the objects is crucial. If the pilot experiences that the performance is bad there is a risk that he will lose trust in the DSS and perhaps try to make the assessment himself without the aid of the DSS. It is probably not possible to have total transparency in how the DSS controls and takes the decisions. Sometimes sophisticated algorithms are used and they can for example rely on Bayesian probability which is perhaps not totally intuitive. But in the case of uncertainty a measure to indicate this to the pilot could be provided.

CSE and the JCS view stress the need to design systems starting from the functionality and the purpose of the JCS. In this view it becomes clear why the system is being built and the requirements on the total system including the user can be identified. However, at some point during the development the need to make an interface between the artefact and the user still arises. Guidelines for what to automate and design style guides helps in the development.

CONCLUSION

To conclude, some long term trends have been identified for the domain. The role of a modern fighter pilot has transformed from pilot to tactical decision maker. Already today, and even more so tomorrow, the fighter pilot has an increasing need to be provided with decision support, and fortunately there are also an on-going parallel trend supporting this by technical progress. There are also increasing opportunities for distributing decision making, even between manned and unmanned aircraft.

Just like many other military applications it is important for an intelligent fighter pilot support for distributed unmanned and manned decision making to prioritize performance, and not only the performance of an individual aircraft and its subsystems but also the total system engaged in a mission, that could involve manned as well as unmanned aircraft in a JCS. It is important to have an automation strategy to achieve this at the same time as long term technology development goals for the design organization could be reached. The domain is characterized by long life cycles and long development times for aircraft compared to many other domains.

The automation strategy could specifically strive to help the DSS to be perceived as highly transparent and not very exchangeable, as a design goal. It is likely that specific guidelines has to be developed concerning principles of interaction for dynamic function allocation and it is important to map roles to the function allocation, regardless if the they are constant over time or not, taking into account both formal and informal structures among active cognitive agents. Concerning a DSS it is a challenge to keep the pilot feeling in control and knowing what is going on in the system and it is probably not possible to possess total transparency in how the DSS functions, but in the case of uncertainty a measure to indicate this to the pilot could be provided. As a part of an automation strategy guidelines could be provided to aid the development. For instance, the human pilot's ability to adapt to the changing environment could very well be explored further together with a DSS.

Specifically for intelligent fighter pilot support for distributed unmanned and manned decision making, concerning function allocation, it is important to not only regard which agent is best at performing a task but also to regard the risk/cost of performing a task in this kind of potentially hazardous context. Also, the risk of decreased functionality such as jammed radar or a shot down aircraft has to be regarded, as well as other drastic changes and dynamics of a mission. Another important factor to specially regard is the spatial positioning of aircraft which impact both the performance of an individual aircraft as well as team work between aircraft for certain tasks during a mission.

ACKNOWLEDGMENT

This research has been supported by the Swedish Governmental Agency for Innovation Systems (Vinnova) through the National Aviation Engineering Research Program.

REFERENCES

Alfredson, J. (2007). *Differences in situational awareness and how to manage them in development of complex systems* [Doctoral dissertation No. 1132]. Linköping, Sweden: Linköping University.

Alfredson, J., & Andersson, R. (2013). Designing for Human Factors in the Technology-Intensive Domain of Fighter Aircraft. *International Journal of Aviation Technology, Engineering and Management, 1*(2), 1–16. doi:10.4018/ijatem.2013070101

Alfredson, J., Holmberg, J., Andersson, R., & Wikforss, M. (2011). Applied cognitive ergonomics design principles for fighter aircraft. In D. Harris (Ed.), *Proceedings of the 9th International Conference on Engineering Psychology and Cognitive Ergonomics (EPCE 2011)* (pp. 473–483). Springer-Verlag. doi:10.1007/978-3-642-21741-8_50

Alfredson, J., Lundqvist, A., Molander, S., & Nordlund, P.-J. (2010). Decision support for the Gripen aircraft and beyond. *Proceedings of the 27th International Congress of the Aeronautical Sciences ICAS 2010.*

Berggren, P., Nählinder, S., & Svensson (2014). *Assessing command and control effectiveness: Dealing with a changing world.* Farnham, England: Ashgate.

Casner, S. M., & Schooler, J. W. (2014). Thoughts in flight: Automation use and pilots' task-related and task-unrelated thought. *Human Factors, 56*(3), 433–442. doi:10.1177/0018720813501550 PMID:24930166

Castor, M. (2009). *The use of structural equation modeling to describe the effect of operator functional state on air-to-air engagement outcomes* [Doctoral dissertation No. 1251]. Linköping, Sweden: Linköping University

Davidsson, S., & Alm, H. (2014). *Context adaptable driver information – Or, what do whom need and want when?* Applied Cognitive Ergonomics.

The role of autonomy in DoD systems. (2012). Defense Science Board Washington DC: Undersecretary of Defense.

Dekker, S. W. A. (1996). Cognitive complexity in management by exception: Deriving early human factors requirements for an envisioned air traffic management world. In D. Harris (Ed.), Engineering psychology and cognitive ergonomics, Volume I: Transportation systems (pp. 201-210). Aldershot, England: Ashgate.

Dekker, S. W. A., & Woods, D. D. (1999). Extracting data from the future: Assessment and certification of envisioned systems. In S. Dekker & E. Hollnagel (Eds.), *Coping with computers in the cockpit* (pp. 131–143). Aldershot, England: Ashgate.

Dekker, S. W. A., & Woods, D. D. (2002). MABA-MABA or Abracadabra: Progress on human automation cooperation. *Cognition Technology and Work, 4*(4), 240–244. doi:10.1007/s101110200022

Endsley, M. R. (1988). Situation Awareness global assessment technique (SAGAT). *Proceedings of the IEEE National Aerospace and Electronics Conference* (pp. 789-795). New York: IEEE.

Feigh, K. M., & Pritchett, A. R. (2014). Requirements for effective function allocation: A critical review. *Journal of Cognitive Engineering and Decision Making, 8*(1), 23–32. doi:10.1177/1555343413490945

Fitts, P. M. (1951). Human engineering for an effective air navigation and traffic control system. Ohio State University Research Foundation Report.

Handley, H., & Smillie, R. (2008). Architecture framework human view: The NATO approach. *Systems Engineering, 11*(2), 156–164. doi:10.1002/sys.20093

Handley, H. A. H. (2014). A network model for human interoperability. *Human Factors, 56*(2), 349–360. doi:10.1177/0018720813493640 PMID:24689253

Hassenzahl, M., & Tractinsky, N. (2006). User experience – a research agenda. *Behaviour & Information Technology, 25*(2), 91–97. doi:10.1080/01449290500330331

Helander, M., & Skinnars, Ö. (2000a). Use of cognitive walkthrough for evaluation of cockpit design. *In Proceedings of the 44th Annual Meeting of the Human Factors and Ergonomics Society* (pp.616-619). Santa Monica, CA: Human Factors and Ergonomics Society. doi:10.1177/154193120004400619

Helander, M., & Skinnars, Ö. (2000b). *Use of cognitive walkthrough for evaluation of cockpit design (HFA Paper No.2000-01)*. Linköping, Sweden: Swedish Centre for Human Factors in Aviation.

Helldin, T. (2014). *Transparency for Future Semi-Automated Systems* [Doctoral dissertation]. Örebro, Sweden: Örebro University.

Helldin, T., Falkman, G., Alfredson, J., & Holmberg, J. (2011). The Applicability of Human-Centred Automation Guidelines in the Fighter Aircraft Domain. *Proceedings of the 29th Annual European Conference on Cognitive Ergonomics* (pp.67-74).Universitätsdruckerei Rostock, Germany doi:10.1145/2074712.2074727

Hollnagel, E. (1999). From function allocation to function congruence. In S. Dekker & E. Hollnagel (Eds.), *Coping with computers in the cockpit* (pp. 29–53). Aldershot, England: Ashgate.

Hollnagel, E., & Woods, D. D. (1983). Cognitive systems engineering: New wine in new bottles. *International Journal of Man-Machine Studies, 18*(6), 583–600. doi:10.1016/S0020-7373(83)80034-0

Hollnagel, E., & Woods, D. D. (2005). *Joint cognitive systems: Foundations of cognitive systems engineering*. Boca Raton, FL: Taylor & Francis. doi:10.1201/9781420038194

Johansson, C. (1999). Modellering av luftstridsavdömningar [Air Combat Resolution Modeling]. Linköping, Sweden: Linköping Institute of Technology.

Klein, G., Orasanu, J., Calderwood, R., & Zsambok, C. (Eds.). (1993). *Decision making in action: Models and methods*. Norwood, NJ: Ablex.

Lyons, J. B., & Stokes, C. K. (2012). Human-human Reliance in the context of automation. *Human Factors, 54*(1), 112–121. doi:10.1177/0018720811427034 PMID:22409106

McKendrick, R., Shaw, T., de Visser, E., Saqer, H., Kidwell, B., & Parasuraman, R. (2014). Team performance in networked supervisory control of unmanned air vehicles: Effects of automation, working memory, and communication content. *Human Factors, 56*(3), 463–475. doi:10.1177/0018720813496269 PMID:24930169

Nagamachi, M. (1989). *Kansei Engineering*. Tokyo: Kaibundo.

Nagamachi, M. (2011). *Kansei/Affective Engineering*. Boca Raton, FL: CRC Press.

Norman, D., Miller, J., & Henderson, A. (1995). *What you see, some of what's in the future, and how we go about doing it: HI at Apple Computer. Proceedings of CHI* (p. 155). New York: ACM Press.

Ollero, A., & Maza, I. (2007). *Multiple hetrogenous unmanned aerial vehicles. Springer Tracts on Advanced Robotics*. NY: Springer. doi:10.1007/978-3-540-73958-6

Parasuraman, R., Sheridan, T., & Wickens, C. (2008). Situation Awareness, Mental Workload and Trust in Automation: Viable, Empirically Supported Cognitive Engineering Constructs. *Journal of Cognitive Engineering and Decision Making, 2*(2), 140–160. doi:10.1518/155534308X284417

Persson, M. (2014). *Future technology support of command and control: Assessing the impact of assumed future technologies on cooperative command and control* [Doctoral dissertation]. Uppsala, Sweden: Uppsala University.

Pritchett, A. R., Kim, S. Y., & Feigh, K. M. (2014). Modeling human-automation function allocation. *Journal of Cognititve Engineering and Decision Making, 8*(1), 33–51. doi:10.1177/1555343413490944

Schütte, S. (2005). *Engineering emotional values in product design – Kansei engineering in development* [Doktoral dissertation No. 951]. Linköping, Sweden: Linköping University.

Sheridan, T. B., & Verplank, W. (1978). Human and Computer Control of Undersea Teleoperators. Cambridge, MA: Man-Machine Systems Laboratory, Department of Mechanical Engineering, MIT.

Steinhauser, N. B., Pavlas, D., & Hancock, P. A. (2009). Design principles for adaptive automation and aiding. *Ergonomics in Design, 17*(2), 6–10. doi:10.1518/106480409X435943

Svensson, E., Angelborg-Thanderz, M., & Sjöberg, L. (1993). Mission challenge, mental workload and performance in military aviation. *Aviation, Space, and Environmental Medicine, 64*(11), 985–991. PMID:8280046

Svensson, E., Angelborg-Thanderz, M., Sjöberg, L., & Olsson, S. (1997). Information complexity: Mental workload and performance in combat aircraft. *Ergonomics, 40*(3), 362–380. doi:10.1080/001401397188206 PMID:11536799

Svensson, E., & Wilson, G. F. (2002). Psychological and psychophysiological models of pilot performance for systems development and mission evaluation. *The International Journal of Aviation Psychology, 12*(1), 95–110. doi:10.1207/S15327108IJAP1201_8

Taylor, G. S., Reinerman-Jones, L. E., Szalma, J. L., Mouloua, M., & Hancock, P. A. (2013). What to automate: Addressing the multidimensionality of cognitive resources through systems design. *Journal of Cognitive Engineering and Decision Making, 7*(4), 311–329. doi:10.1177/1555343413495396

Taylor, R. M. (1997). Human-Electronic Crew Teamwork: Cognitive Requirements for Compatibility and Control with Dynamic Function Allocation. In M. J. Smith, G. Salvendy, & R. J. Koubek (Eds.), *Design of Computing Systems, 21B* (pp. 247–250). Amsterdam: Elselvier.

Woods, D. D., & Hollnagel, E. (2006). *Joint cognitive systems: Patterns in cognitive systems engineering*. Boca Raton, FL: Taylor & Francis. doi:10.1201/9781420005684

Chapter 2
Utilizing UML, cTLA, and SRN:
An Application to Distributed System Performance Modeling

Razib Hayat Khan
Norwegian University of Science & Technology (NTNU), Norway

ABSTRACT

To meet the challenge of conducting quantitative analysis at the early stage of the system development process, this chapter introduces an extensive framework for performance modeling of a distributed system. The goal of the performance modeling framework is the assessment of the non-functional properties of the distributed system at an early stage based on the system's functional description and deployment mapping of service components over an execution environment. System's functional description with deployment mapping has been specified using UML. To analyze the correctness of the UML specification style, we have used temporal logic, specifically cTLA, to formalize the UML model. We have shown in detail how UML models are formalized by a set of cTLA processes and production rules. To conduct the performance evaluation of a distributed system, the UML model is transformed into analytic model SRN. We have specified an automated model transformation process to generate SRN model from UML, which is performed in an efficient and scalable way by the use of model transformation rules.

INTRODUCTION

Distributed software system typically deploys in a resource-limited environment that is mainly constrained by rigorous performance requirements. In a distributed system, system functional behavior is normally distributed among several objects. The overall behavior of the system is composed of the partial behavior of the distributed objects of the system. It is essential to capture the behavior of the distributed objects for appropriate analysis to evaluate the performance related factors of the system at the early design stage. Distributed software systems offer functionalities to the end users by utilizing the distributed components behavior that leads to complex specification as each distributed component provides the partial functionalities of the whole system. Hence, modeling plays an important role in the whole design process of the distributed system to capture partial component behavior efficiently for qualitative

DOI: 10.4018/978-1-4666-8493-5.ch002

and quantitative analysis. As functionality is basically a service spanning over several components, we thus need a specifications describing the collaboration of various distributed components. We therefore introduce a specification style in which a self contained specification block models all functional aspects and collaboration of distributed objects in encapsulated ways that can be reused. We apply UML (Unified Modeling Language) collaborations to express static properties and UML activities to model collaborative detailed behavior as reusable specification of building blocks which in turn provide the facility to build service and adjust the system functions rapidly rather than start the development process from scratch (OMG, 2009a). Reusability makes the developer task easy and faster as system of a specific domain can be built by applying the reoccurring building blocks that are selected from existing libraries. Another advantage of reusable building block utilizing collaboration oriented modeling is that it supports the convergence of Information and Communication Technology (ICT) modeling concept. In particular, we can encapsulate the specific properties of component of certain domain in reusable building block. Thus developers familiar with the concept of different domain of ICT should have less trouble to create sound distributed system using the building block of existing domain (Kraemer & Herrmann, 2006). Besides, considering collaboration diagram helps to compose the system from the subtask of the participants which are relevant for drawing the system's overall functional behavior. Above all, collaboration oriented approach provides a way to group chunks of interaction behavior contributed by the most pertinent actors of the system.

Furthermore, we consider system execution architecture to realize the deployment of the service components. Abstract view of the system architecture is captured by the UML deployment diagram which defines the execution architecture of the system by identifying the system components and the assignment of software artifacts to those identified system components (OMG, 2009a). Considering the system architecture to generate the performability model resolves the bottleneck of system performance by finding a better allocation of service components to the physical nodes. This needs for an efficient approach to deploy the service components on the available hosts of distributed environment to achieve preferably high performance and low cost levels. The most basic example in this regard is to choose better deployment architectures by considering only the latency of the service. The easiest way to satisfy the latency requirements is to identify and deploy the service components that require the highest volume of interaction onto the same physical resource or to choose resources that are connected by links with sufficiently high capacity (Csorba, Heegaard, & Hermann, 2008).

In order to guarantee the precise understanding and correctness of the model, the approach requires formal reasoning on the semantics of the language used and to maintain the consistency of the building blocks and their composition. Temporal logic is a suitable option for that. In particular, the properties of super position supported by compositional Temporal Logic of Action (cTLA) make it possible to describe systems from different view points by individual processes that are superimposed (Hermann, 1997; Hermann & Krumm, 2000). Here, we focus on the definition of cTLA/c, a style of cTLA that allows us to formalize the collaboration service specifications given by UML activities and also to define the formal semantics of deployment diagram. By expressing collaborations as cTLA processes, we can ensure that a composed service maintains the properties of the individual collaborations it is composed from. Moreover, the semantic definition of collaboration, activity and deployment in form of temporal logic is implemented as a transformation tool which produces TLA$^+$ modules (Slåtten, 2007). These modules may then be used as input for the model checker TLC (Yu, Manolios, & Lamport, 1999). The tool also generates a number of theorems, so that collaborations may be analyzed for more advanced properties than simple syntactic checks.

Standalone UML diagram is not capable of incorporating performance related parameters. So it is indispensable to extend the UML model to incorporate the performance related Quality of Service (QoS) information to allow evaluating the properties of a system with respect to performance related behavior. Hence, the UML models are annotated according to the *UML profile for MARTE: Modeling & Analysis of Real-Time Embedded Systems* (OMG, 2009b). This profile helps to maintain consistency between system design and implementation with respect to requirement specification. It provides facilities to annotate models with information required to perform specific analysis. Especially, MARTE focuses on performance and schedulability analysis. It fosters the construction of models that may be used to make quantitative predictions regarding real-time and embedded features of systems taking into account system components characteristics.

In order to allow the quantitative evaluation, the resulting UML software model is transformed into Stochastic Reward Net (SRN) model (Ciardo, Muppala, & Trivedi, 1992). The model transformation process is guided by the model transformation rules that have been utilized to provide a scalable model transformation approach for large and multifaceted distributed systems. The model transformation rules are designed in such a generalized way so that software model of different application domains can be transformed in a faster and automated fashion. We will focus on the SRN model as performance model generated by our framework due to having some prominent and interesting properties such as priorities assignment in transitions, presence of guard functions for enabling transitions that can use entire state of the net rather than a particular state, marking dependent arc multiplicity that can change the structure of the net, marking-dependent firing rates, and reward rates defined at the net level.

A number of approaches have been pursued to construct the performance model from system design specification. Lopez-Grao *et al.* proposed a conversion method where annotated UML activity diagram is formalized using generalized stochastic petrinet model (Lopez-Grao, Merseguer, & Campos, 2004). In Cooper, Dai, and Deng (2003), the authors presented an overview of their aspect-oriented Formal Design Analysis Framework (FDAF) and how it can be used to design and analyze performance properties. In Moura, Borges, and Mota (2012), the author experienced annotating UML class diagrams with fragments of the Object-Z specification language. Another approach is proposed by IBM where the Object Constraint Language (OCL) is used as a standard formal specification language to formalize UML diagrams (Warmer & Kleppe, 1999). In Theelen, Putten, and Voeten (2004), the author proposed Software/Hardware Engineering (SHE) method that enables constructing formal executable models based on the expressive modeling Parallel Object-Oriented Specification Language (POOSL). The related works mentioned above still lack of a complete formal semantics and capabilities to prove the properties and refinements as well as fails to provide the formal representation of concurrent activities. Some other efforts have been taken to outline formal definition of UML model and mostly the works are based on UML statechart diagram and sequence diagram (Yongfeng, Liu, Li, Zhang, & Wu, 2010; Shuhao, Wei, & Zhichang, 2004; Merayo, Nu'n~ez, & Rodrı'Guez, 2008; Andolfi, Aquilani, Balsamo, & Inverardi, 2000; Cardoso, & Blanc, 2001). UML activity diagram is not thoroughly investigated while generating performance model for software performance analysis except some of the works presented in (Cooper et al., 2003; Eshuis, and Wieringa, 2001; Petriu, and Shen, 2002).

The objective of the chapter is to provide an extensive performance modeling framework that provides a transformation process to generate SRN performance model from UML specification style. The semantics of the input UML model for the framework such as collaborations, activities and deployment model have been realized formally by the cTLA/c technique to understand the formalism of reusable collaborative building block. The output model is a SRN performance model through which we attain a precise and formal way of representing and evaluating the large and complex distributed system efficiently considering inter-node communication and the occurring of other events. The mapping process to demonstrate the correspondence between formalized UML diagram and SRN model has been illustrated in details. The main focus of this chapter is on the framework, mostly without the model validation and performance evaluation steps. The chapter is mainly based on the continuation of our previous works presented in (Khan and Heegaard 2011; Khan and Heegaard 2010a, 2010b).

DESCRIPTION OF THE PERFORMANCE MODELING FRAMEWORK

The detail description of our performance modeling framework is outlined in this section. This section addresses the service specification with deployment and annotation phase as well as describes the automated model transformation process.

Service Specification

The performance modeling framework utilizes collaboration as main specification units for service specification. The specifications for collaborations are given as coherent, self-contained reusable building blocks. The structure of the building block is described by UML 2.2 collaboration. The building block declares the participants (as collaboration roles) and connection between them. The internal behavior of building block is described by UML activity. It is declared as the classifier behavior of the collaboration and has one activity partition for each collaboration role in the structural description. For each collaboration use, the activity declares a corresponding call behavior action referring to the activities of the employed building blocks. For example, the general structure of the building block t where it only declares the participants A and B as collaboration roles and the connection between them is defined as collaboration use t. The internal behavior of the same building block. The activity $transfer_{ij}$ (where $ij = AB$) describes the behavior of the corresponding collaboration. It has one activity partition for each collaboration role: A and B. Activities base their semantics on token flow (OMG, 2009a). The activity starts by placing a token when there is a response (indicated by the streaming pin res_A or res_B) to transfer by either participant A or B. After completion of the processing by the collaboration role A, the token passes through the fork node f where the flow is divided into two branches. One branch is directly forwarded to the streaming pin req_B as a request sent to the collaboration role B. Another flow is directed to the join node j. After completion of the processing by the collaboration role B, the token passes through the decision node δ where only one branch either x or y will be activated. If flow marked with x activates it will then pass through the join node j. If both the incoming flow of the join node j arrive the join node j will be activated. If flow marked with y activates it will then pass through the merge node m. The outgoing flow of the merge node will be activated when either of the incoming flow arrives.

In order to generate the performance model, the structural information about how the collaborations are composed is not sufficient. It is necessary to specify the detailed behavior of how the different events of collaborative building blocks are coupled. For delineating the detail behavior, UML collaborations and activities are used complementary to each other; UML collaborations focus on the role binding and structural aspect, while UML activities complement this by covering also the behavioral aspect (Kraemer & Herrmann, 2006). For this purpose, call behavior actions are used. Collaboration is represented by call behavior action referring to the respective activity of building blocks. Each call behavior action represents an instance of a building block. For each activity parameter node of the referred activity, a call behavior action declares a corresponding pin. Pins have the same symbol as activity parameter nodes to represent them on the frame of a call behavior action. Arbitrary logic between pins may be used to synchronize the building block events and transfer data between them. By connecting the individual input and output pins of the call behavior actions, the events occurring in collaboration can be coupled with each other. The initial node () indicates the starting of the activity. The activity is started at the same time from each participant A and B. After being activated, each participant starts its processing of the request which is mentioned by call behavior action Pi (Processingi, where i = A, B). Completions of the processing by the participants are mentioned by the call behavior action di (Processing_donei, i = A, B). After completion of the processing, the responses are delivered to the corresponding participants indicated by the streaming pin res. The response of the collaboration role A will be forwarded to B and vice versa, which is mentioned by then collaboration t: transferij (where ij = AB).

UML Deployment Diagram

Deployment diagram shows a system's physical layout, specifying which pieces of software run on what pieces of hardware (OMG, 2009a). The main items on the deployment diagrams are physical nodes connected by communication paths. A physical node can host software artifacts. Listing an artifact within in a physical node indicates that the artifact is deployed to that node in the running system.

Stating deployment mapping of service components: We model the system as collection of N interconnected physical nodes. Our objective is to find a deployment mapping for this execution environment for a set of service components available for deployment that comprises the service. Deployment mapping **M** is defined as: $\mathbf{M}=(C \rightarrow N)$, where C is a number of service components instances and physical nodes N. We consider three types of requirements in the deployment problem where the term cost is introduced to capture several non-functional requirements those are later on utilized to conduct performance evaluation of the systems:

(1) Service components have execution costs
(2) Collaborations have communication costs and costs for running of background process to conduct the communication known as overhead cost
(3) Some of the service components can be restricted in the deployment mapping to specific physical nodes which are called bound components.

Furthermore, we observe the processing cost that physical nodes impose while host the service components and also the target balancing of cost among the physical nodes available in the network. Communication costs are considered if collaboration between two service components happens remotely, i.e. it happens between two physical nodes (Csorba, Heegaard, & Hermann, 2008). In other words, if two service components are placed onto the same physical node the communication cost between them will be ignored. This holds for the case study that is conducted in this paper. This is not generally true, and it is not a limiting factor of our framework. The cost for executing the background process for conducting the communication between the collaboration roles is always considerable no matter whether the collaboration roles deploy on the same or different physical nodes. Using the above specified input, the deployment logic provides an optimal deployment architecture taking into account the QoS requirements for the service components providing the specified services. We then define the objective of the deployment logic as obtaining an efficient (low-cost, if possible optimum) mapping of service components onto the physical nodes that satisfies the requirements in reasonable time. The deployment mapping providing optimal deployment architecture is mentioned by the cost function F(**M**), that is a function that expresses the utility of deployment mapping of service components on the physical resources with their constraints and capabilities by satisfying non-functional properties of the system. The cost function is designed to reflect the goal of balancing the execution cost and minimizing the communication cost. This is in turn utilized to achieve reduced task turnaround time by maximizing the utilization of system resources while minimizing any communication between processing node. Hence, it will offer a high system throughput, taking into account the expected execution and inter-node communication requirements of the service components on the given hardware architecture (Khan & Heegaard, 2011). Cost function F(M) derivation is described in Khan (2014), which is beyond the scope of this chapter.

Annotation of UML Model

In order to annotate the UML diagram we use several stereotypes and tagged values according to the *UML profile for MARTE* (OMG, 2009b). The stereotypes are the following:

- *SaStep* defines a step that begins and ends when decisions about the allocation of system resources are made.
- *ComputingResource* represents either virtual or physical processing devices capable of storing and executing program code. Hence, its fundamental function is to compute.
- *Scheduler* is a stereotype that brings access to a resource following a certain scheduling policy mentioned by tagged value *schedPolicy*.
- *GaExecHost* can be any device which executes behavior, including storage and peripheral devices.
- *SaSharedResource* is dynamically allocated to schedulable resources by means of an access policy.

The tagged values are the following:

- *execTime*: The duration of the execution time is mentioned by the tagged value *execTime* which is the average time in our case. The execution cost of service component is expressed by this tagged value in the annotated UML model.
- *deadline* defines the maximum time bound on the completion of the particular execution segment that must be met. The overhead cost and communication cost between the service components are specified by this tagged value in the annotated UML model.
- *resmult* Indicates the multiplicity of a resource. It may specify the maximum number of instances of the resource considered as available. By default only one instance is available.
- *capacity* defines the number of permissible concurrent users.

The flow between P_A and d_A are annotated using stereotype *SaStep* and tagged value *execTime* which defines that after being deployed in execution environment the collaboration role A needs t_1 seconds and collaboration role B needs t_2 seconds to complete their processing by the physical node. After completion of the processing, communication between A and B is achieved in t_3 seconds while the overhead time to conduct this communication is t_4 seconds which is annotated using stereotype *saStep* and two instances of *deadline* – *deadline$_1$* defines the communication time and *deadline$_2$* is for overhead time.

Formalizing UML Diagrams

So far we introduce the UML diagram in a descriptive and informal way. In order to understand the precise formalism of the UML model and for the correct way of model transformation we need to present the UML model with the help of formal semantics. The formal semantics of UML model thus helps us to implement the model very efficiently for providing the tool based support of our modeling framework. Before introducing the formalization of the UML model at first we illustrate the temporal logic more specifically cTLA that has been applied to formalize the UML model (Hermann, 1997; Hermann & Krumm, 2000).

Temporal Logic and cTLA

Temporal logic is well suited to formally define the behavior of the distributed system (Manna & Pnueli, 1992). The temporal logic can be distinguished in two categories: linear time logics (LTL), which express behaviors by set of infinite sequences of states and computational tree logic (CTL), which is branching time logic modeling the state orders by tree structure (Kraemer & Hermann, 2007a).

A well-known LTL is Leslie Lamport's Temporal Logic of Actions (TLA) which is logic for specifying and reasoning about concurrent systems (Lamport, 2002). Systems and their properties are represented in the same logic, so the assertion that a system meets its specification and the assertion that one system implements another are both expressed by logical implication. System's behavior is described by special state transition method as well as fairness properties by TLA. The TLA coupling method by means of states is common to several element specifications (Martin & Leslie, 1995). However, this specification style makes it difficult to create constraint-oriented models in which properties reflecting partial system behavior spanning over several components are specified (Vissers, Scollo, Sinderen, & Brinksma, 1991). As our collaboration oriented models support exactly this specification style, we use the cTLA (Hermann, 1997; Hermann & Krumm, 2000). This is a variant of TLA which provides couplings based on jointly executed transitions enabling to glue interacting constraints nicely. Moreover, cTLA makes the description of state transition systems in a process-like style.

A cTLA processes are used to model resources or constraints of a system (Kraemer & Hermann, 2007a). A simple cTLA process which specifies the activity of component A already visualized in UML activity diagram. In the process header, the process name and a list of process parameters are mentioned. The parameters enable to model several shapes of process instances by a single process type (Kraemer & Hermann, 2007a). For example, the process parameter TT describes the signature of the tokens modeled by a particular UML activity so that we can use the process A for various token formats. As said, a cTLA process models a state transition system, the state of which is described by variables. In the example process, we use the variables x distinguishing if the component A is P_A or d_A and tv storing the data of an activity token passing it. The set of initial states which hold in the beginning of executing a process are defined by the predicate INIT. Here, the variable x is initially P_A while tv contains any data set from TT. The transitions are specified by actions (e.g., **start**) which are predicates on a pair of a current and a next state. Variable identifiers in simple form (e.g., x) refer to the current state while variables describing the successor state occur in the primed form (e.g., x'). The conjuncts of an action referring only to variables in the current state specify the enabling condition while those with primed variable identifiers express the state change. Thus, the action start is enabled if variable x is "P_A" while its execution leads to a new process state change in which x carries the new value "d_A". Actions may have parameters modeling transfer between processes. For instance, *start* has the parameter *it* of type *TT* describing the data set of a token arriving at the component *A* which is stored in the variable *tv*. Actions can be distinguished into two classes. External actions denoted by the keyword ACTIONS may be coupled with actions of other processes. In contrast, internal actions defined in a compartment headed with INTERNAL ACTIONS must not be joined with actions of the process environment so that they express purely local process behavior (Kraemer & Hermann, 2007a). Formally, a cTLA process can be expressed as a TLA-formula, the so-called canonical formula C:

$$C \triangleq INIT \land \square[\exists it, ot \in TT : start(it) \lor expire(ot) \lor expireAndRestart(it, ot)]_{\langle i, tv \rangle}$$

The conjunct at the left side of the formula states that the predicate INIT holds in the first state of every state sequence modeled by *C*. The conjunct on the right side starts with the temporal operator □ ("always") specifying that the expression right to it has to hold in all states of all state sequences. The TLA expression $[pp]_{\langle i, tv \rangle}$ defines that either the pair predicate *pp* holds or that a stuttering step takes place in which the annexed variable identifiers do not change their state (i.e., $x' = x \land tv' = tv$ holds). We listed the disjunction of the process actions as pair predicate *pp* in which the process parameters are existentially quantified. This models a state change in the process that always corresponds to the execution of one of its actions using any action parameters of the set TT. Thus, the cTLA processes specifies that the first process state fulfills INIT and that all state changes follow the process actions or are stuttering steps (Kraemer & Hermann, 2007a).

Formalizing UML collaboration: The concept of UML collaborations as introduced here is rather structural and describes a structure of collaborating elements (UML, 2009a). Although UML enables collaborations, being so-called behavioral classifiers, refer to behaviors in form of interactions, state machines or activities, the specification of these behaviors is not elaborated formally. It demands for a precise formal semantics describing the structure and behavior of collaborations. This does by far not exclude UML; on the contrary, such a well-defined formal basis enables us using different UML diagrams, utilizing their specific advantages where appropriate. For this reason, we define the cTLA style cTLA/c used to model collaborations in a way that several diagram types can be formalized (Kraemer & Hermann, 2007a).

To illustrate cTLA/c, a structure of the collaboration as well as collaboration from an abstract, external viewpoint. It is a process realized between the collaboration roles' c_1 and c_2. While most of the behavior may be executed internally to the collaboration, we need some mechanisms to couple the collaborations with others during composition if necessary (Kraemer & Hermann, 2007a). For example, the end of one collaboration could trigger the start of another one, or collaborations may exchange data. For this, two principle solutions exist: communication by variables and synchronously executed actions. Only relying on the first one (i.e., allowing only producer/consumer synchronization) implies buffering, so that it would always take two execution steps for collaboration to influence another one. In some cases, however, following the idea of constraint-oriented modeling, we may want to describe that events happen at the same time in several collaborations. Thus, both interaction principles can be useful, and cTLA/c is laid out to support both of them. For synchronous couplings, we simply conjoin the cTLA actions of different collaborations, while for buffered communication; we assume that the collaborations are linked to a special collaboration modeling the buffered communication (Kraemer & Hermann, 2007a).

The externally visible cTLA actions a_1, a_2, and a_3 can be used to couple *Cl* with other collaborations. A cTLA process for the structure of the collaboration can be seen as following tuple:

$$Cl = (Clrl)$$

where collaboration role associated with the *Cl* is defined by the set $Clrl = \{ c_1, \ldots, c_n \}$.

A cTLA process of behavior of collaboration can be seen as a tuple:

$$Cl_{bhv} = (Clrl, Act_{int}, Act_{ext}, p_{act}, c_{dmp})$$

Clrl have the same meaning as in *Cl*. In addition, the actions modeling interaction with the environment of the collaboration are described by the set Act_{ext}, while Act_{int} models behavior that is not visible from the outside. Each action is attached to a collaboration role via function $[p_{act} = (Act \rightarrow Clrl)]$.

Formalizing Activities for representing the behavior of collaboration: We use UML activities to express the behavior of collaborations in our performance modeling framework. UML collaboration is complemented by an activity which uses one separate activity partition for each collaboration role. In the terms of cTLA/c, an activity partition corresponds to a collaboration role.

The semantics of UML activities is based on Petri nets (UML, 2009a). Thus, an activity basically describes a state transition system, with the token movements as the transitions and the placement of tokens within the graph as the states. In consequence, the variables of a cTLA/c specification model the actual token placement on the activity while its actions specify the flow of tokens between states. Flows may cross partition borders. According to the cTLA/c definition and due to the fact that the partitions are implemented by distributed components, flows moving between partitions are modeled by means of communication buffers while states assigned to activity nodes are represented in cTLA/c by local variables.

Certain variables of cTLA/c collaboration may be triggers. For activities, triggers are represented by initial activity elements starting a flow in the beginning and flows crossing a partition border in which a token in the corresponding communication buffer is triggered to forward to the receiving partition. Moreover, a token may be triggered from the activity environment which is expressed by flow passing pins at the border of call behavior actions. This leads to flows which — from a local view of a single activity — are non-triggered. Of course, in order to achieve lively flows, non-triggered partial flows have to be connected with other flows in a way that in the system description all flows start at a triggering activity element (Kraemer & Hermann, 2007a). In the following, an activity is given by the tuple:

$$Act = (activity \ elements, \ flows, \ type, \ part, \ location)$$

with the set of activity elements, [flows $\subseteq$ (activity elements $\times$ activity elements)] describes the set of flows between activity elements, [type $\in$ (activity elements $\rightarrow$ Type)] assigns to each activity element a type which is an part of the set *Type* = {*initial, fork, join, merge, decision, waiting, timer, receive, send, input, output, operation, callBehavior, input-Pin, output-Pin*}, *part* models the set of partitions, [location = (activity elements $\cup$ flows $\rightarrow$ SUBSET part \ { })] assigns each element and flow a non-empty set of partitions. Here, all activity elements except for call behavior actions must only be mapped to exactly one partition while flows may belong to several partitions as they can arbitrarily cross partition borders. In addition to the tuple Act, we define function outgoing and incoming as [(outgoing, incoming) = (activity element $\rightarrow$ SUBSET flows)] that gives us the set of incoming and outgoing flows of an activity element.

In particular, only decision and fork elements have more than one outgoing flow, and only merge and join elements have more than one incoming flow (Kraemer & Hermann, 2007a).

To define the semantics of activities using cTLA/c, we opted for an approach that makes direct use of the mechanisms of cTLA (Kraemer & Hermann 2007a). We describe for some activity element types as separate cTLA processes which are introduced in the Appendix A. This already helps to understand the semantics of the activity elements. We introduce only the cTLA processes for initial elements, call operations, and transfer flows which are necessary to understand the example sketched in this chapter. A complete documentation comprising the cTLA processes for all activity elements is provided in (Kraemer & Hermann, 2007a). We introduce some generic data types to discuss cTLA process used as process parameters. Here, we assume that a list of variables is expressed by a single record element. *VT* describes the types of all variables in a partition. The signature set of the tokens is represented by the type *TT*, while *ET* is an enumeration providing each flow a unique identifier in an activity (Kraemer & Hermann, 2007a).

Production Rules for cTLA/c Actions for UML activities: We decide to present the method producing the system actions from the local process actions as a set of rules, so that each activity element can be discussed separately. There are two types of rules (Kraemer & Hermann, 2007a):

- Rules that create a new action. These rules treat triggering nodes like incoming transfer flows as well as flows starting at an input or output pin of a call behavior action. They simply start the construction of a new action.
- Rules that replace an existing action. These rules model the continuation of a flow. They start at a flow that is not triggering, take the already produced action *act* for the upstream graph, and add a conjunct *c* to the existing action, so that a new action $act^*=act \wedge c$ is created. This new action replaces the existing one.

Each production rule presented below is divided into two parts. The first part refers to the structure of an activity and defines the activity flows resp. activity elements for which the rule can be used. Moreover, the cTLA action to be replaced is listed. We also need to remember when traversing activities which of its flows still have to be visited. In a production rule, we therefore use the function [*toVisit* ∈ (Act → subset *ET*) storing for a particular cTLA action of which the flows still to be passed. The second part shows the effect of the rule. It gives instructions whether a new action should be created or an existing one should be replaced, and how the emerging action is constructed. It also declares any changes to the function *toVisit* by updating the set of flows still to be visited for an action. The actions under construction have the signature (Kraemer & Hermann, 2007a):

act (it: TT; ot: [ET→TT]; iv: VT; ov: [ET→VT]; is, os: SUBSET TT; last: SUBSET ET)

The parameter *it* specifies the value of the token when the flow starts. While the function *ot* describes the token signature after leaving a particular flow. Similarly, parameters *iv* and *ov* describe the values of the local variables after the flow starts and after traversing a particular flow. Signals sent within an action are described with parameter *os*, and signals received are specified by *is*. Parameter *last* keeps track of the flows in an action after those the flow stops. This is needed to support the storage of the auxiliary variables. In the following, we will show the rules for initial nodes, operations, and transfer flows. The remaining rules are listed in Kraemer and Herrmann (2007b).

Initial Elements: As an INITIAL element is a trigger, it is the starting point for the production of an action. The rule is enabled for an initial element x with an outgoing flow e. It creates action *act*, which is coupled with action *start* to the process instance corresponding to the initial element, p_x. As the flow is not yet finished, *last* is empty. The element neither produces any output signals ($os = \{\}$) and does not change the value of the variables or token, so that *ov* and *ot* remember their respective initial values for this flow. As we continue the production of the action with whatever comes after flow e, we store it as still to be visited.

Transfer Flows: Flows crossing partition borders are handled by two rules, TRANSFERLEAVE modeling the leaving of the current partition, and TRANSFERENTER for flows entering a partition. TRANSFERLEAVE is a rule that adds a conjunct invoking *send* on process p_t modeling the buffered communication. As the flow ends where it leaves the partition, the flow is removed from the flows that must be visited but entered to the set *last* describing final flows. The rule for receiving (not shown) is similar to an INITIAL element. It creates a new action referring to the triggered action for receiving of the transfer process.

Call Operation Actions: As described above, operations are modeled as functions that assign new values to the token passing through it as well as the variables, modeled by the cTLA process OPERATION with its action *execute*. This action is coupled with the original one, and the production continues with the outgoing flow of the operation. The values *ot* and *ov* for the outgoing flow j reflect the changes carried out by the operation which are described by the action parameters new_v and new_t.

The produced action conforms to the constraints in cTLA/c (Kraemer & Hermann, 2007a).

- The production of an action always stays within the partition where the production started. Flows leaving a partition terminate the production of an action by a corresponding send action of a transfer process. Consequently, all produced actions can be assigned to exactly one participant of the cTLA/c process under construction.

Box 1.

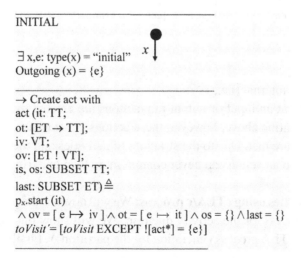

Box 2.

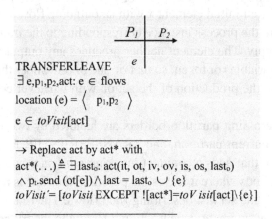

Box 3.

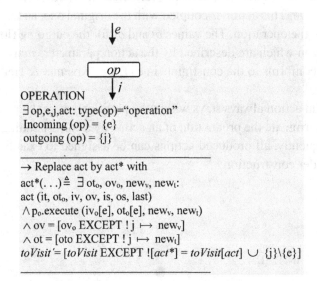

- Actions are by default internal (i.e., $\in Act_{int}$).
- Just for flows starting at an input or output pin, actions are created that do not contain a trigger. According to the definition above, however, these actions are external and the cTLA/c claims for non-triggered actions are met. Due to the structure of activities and the layout of the rules, a sub-graph corresponding to an action can never contain more than one trigger.

Example of UML activities using cTLA/c process: We will now use the production rules to generate the parts of the cTLA/c process for the activity diagram. We will show the stepwise generation of the actions for the partition A. cTLA process generation for the partition A. Firstly, we instantiate processes x, e_1, o_1, e_2, o_2, and e_3 for the corresponding activity elements.

Step 1: We start with the initial element x and apply rule INITIAL to flow e_1, which leads to the construction of action act_1. As no signal has been sent yet, os is empty. There is no final flow, as the flow continues. The variables did not change with the initial element, such that ov contains the same value as iv for flow e_1. The same applied for the value of the token managed by ot.

act_1 (it: TT; ot: [ET → TT]; iv: VT; ov: [ET ! VT]; is, os: SUBSET TT; last: SUBSET ET)$\triangleq$

x.start (it)

$\wedge$ov = ["e_1" → iv]$\wedge$ ot = ["e_1" → it]

$\wedge$os = { }$\wedge$last = { }

Step 2: We continue with the flow by applying rule OPERATION to the call operation action o_1 and the already created action act_1. It is replaced by act_2 which is an extension of act_1. The operation is a function $o1nav$ that computes new values for all the variables in the partition, and an $o1nto$ that computes the value of a new token.

act_2 (.......)$\triangleq$

x.start (it)

$\wedge$ov = ["e_1" → iv, "e_2" → o1nav [iv, it]]

$\wedge$ot = ["e_1" → iv, "e_2" → o1nto [iv, it]]

$\wedge$os = { }$\wedge$last = { }

$\wedge$op.execute (iv, it, o1nav [iv, it], o1nto [iv, it])

Step 3: To handle the second call operation action o_2 we apply the rule OPERATION same as step 2. The new action will be act_3 which will be the extension of act_2.

act_3 (.......)$\triangleq$

x.start (it)

$\wedge$ov = ["e_1" → iv, "e_2" → o1nav [iv, it], "e_3" → o1nav [iv, it]]

$\wedge$ot = ["e_1" → iv, "e_2" → o1nto [iv, it], "e_3" → o1nto [iv, it]]

$\wedge$os = { }$\wedge$last = { }

$\wedge$op.execute (iv, it, o1nav [iv, it], o1nto [iv, it])

Step 4: When we continue with action act_3 and flow e_3, we apply rule TRANSFERLEAVE and replace it by action act_4 that simply adds a conjunction sending the token. As the set of flows to visit is empty for this flow, this is an action presents in the final process.

$act_4(\ldots\ldots) \triangleq$

x.start (it)

$\land ov = [\text{``}e_1\text{''} \rightarrow iv, \text{``}e_2\text{''} \rightarrow o1nav \ [iv, it], \text{``}e_3\text{''} \rightarrow o1nav \ [iv, it]]$

$\land ot = [\text{``}e_1\text{''} \rightarrow iv, \text{``}e_2\text{''} \rightarrow o1nto \ [iv, it], \text{``}e_3\text{''} \rightarrow o1nto \ [iv, it]]$

$\land os = \{ \ \} \land last = \{e_3\}$

$\land op.execute \ (iv, it, o1nav \ [iv, it], o1nto \ [iv, it])$

$\land e_3.send \ (o1nto \ [iv, it]);$

In a similar way, we can produce the cTLA actions for modeling flows of partition *B* and also other activities. All-in-all, the production rules give a powerful means to formalize UML activities as they are used in our modeling framework. If necessary, the generation process can be automated as done in Slåtten (2007) for checking activities with the model checker TLC (Yu, Manolios, & Lamport, 1999).

Formalizing UML deployment diagram: The concept of UML deployment diagram is pretty structural and describes a structure of the execution environment by identifying a system's physical layout, specifying which pieces of software run on what pieces of physical nodes and how nodes are connected by communication paths. For deployment modeling, we use the following tuple as additional invariant which is also a part of the style cTLA/c:

$$D = (N_L, L, L_A, SA, D_{mp})$$

We define the physical nodes in our execution environment by the set $N_L = \{n_1 \ldots n_n\}$. As well the list of the communication links in the execution environment is illustrated by the set $L = \{l_1 \ldots l_n\}$. Function $L_A = [L \rightarrow N_L]$ defines the association of a link with physical nodes where each link can be associated with exactly two physical nodes. $SA = \{s_1 \ldots s_n\}$ is a set that defines the software artifacts exist in the execution environment. Function $D_{mp} = \{SA \rightarrow N_L\}$ defines the deployment mapping of software artifact to a physical node where each software can be mapped to only one physical node.

Model Transformation Phase

We define model transformation rules that will transform the input annotated UML model into SRN model. The process of model transformations. Since annotated UML models will be translated into SRN, we will give a brief introduction about SRN model and the motivation behind choosing this model. SRN is based on the Generalized Stochastic Petri net (GSPN) (Trivedi, 2001) and extends them further by introducing prominent extensions such as guard functions, reward functions, and marking dependent firing rates (Ciardo, Muppala, & Trivedi, 1992). A guard function is assigned to a transition. It specifies the condition to enable or disable the transition and can use the entire state of the net rather than just the number of tokens in places. Reward function defines the reward rate for each tangible marking of Petri Net based on which various quantitative measures can be done in the Net level. Marking dependent firing rate allows using the number of token in a chosen place multiplying the basic rate of the transition. SRN model has the following elements: Finite set of the places (drawn as circles), Finite set of the transition defined as either timed transition (drawn as thick transparent bar) or immediate transition (drawn as thin black bar), set of arcs connecting places and transitions, multiplicity associated with the arcs, and marking that denotes the number of token in each place. SRN model is mentioned formally by the 6-tuple $\{\mathbf{\Phi}, \mathbf{T}, \mathbf{A}, \mathbf{K}, \mathbf{N}, \mathbf{m_0}\}$ in the following way (Trivedi, 2001):

$\mathbf{\Phi}$ = Finite set of the places

$\mathbf{T}$ = Finite set of the transition

$A \subseteq \{\Phi \times T\} \cup \{T \times \Phi\}$ is a set of arcs connecting Φ and T

$\mathbf{K}$: T $\rightarrow$ {Timed (time>0), Immediate (time = 0)} specifies the type of the each transition

$\mathbf{N}$: A$\rightarrow$ {1, 2, 3...} is the multiplicity associated with the arcs in A

m: $\Phi \rightarrow \{0, 1, 2...\}$ is the marking that denotes the number of tokens for each place in Φ. The initial marking is denoted as m_0.

In order to keep the service specification model and analytical model consistent with each other, the process of model transformation is driven by the model transformation rules, which provide an efficient, scalable, and automated approach to conducting model transformation for large, complex, and multifaceted distributed systems. By considering the semantic definition of the SRN models, we provide the model transformation rules to generate performance model. Rules for generating performance SRN model can be divided into two categories:

Rule 1: Deployment mapping of a collaboration role
Rule 2: Deployment mapping of collaboration

Rule 1: Deployment mapping of a collaboration role: Rule 1 addresses the generation of an SRN model of a collaboration role with deployment mapping, (where Pi = Processing of ith collaboration role and di = Processing performed of the ith collaboration role). Mainly, rule 1 has been utilized to model the load of a physical node. For each physical node, there must be an upper bound of the execution of the process in parallel with that node. The execution of the process is only possible when the node has the capacity to do so. When the collaboration role of a building block deploys onto a physical node, the equivalent SRN model. Initially, place PPn contains q (where integer q > 0) tokens, which define the upper bound of the execution of the processes in parallel with a physical node n, and the timed transition do will fire (which symbolizes the execution of the process i) only when there is a token available in both the place Pi and PPn. The place PPn will again receive its token back after firing of the timed transition do, indicating that the node is ready to execute other processes deployed on that node.

When the collaboration role of a building block deploys onto a physical node the equivalent SRN model is represented by 6-tuple in following way:

$\Phi = \{Pi, di, PPn\}$

$T = \{do, exit\}$

$A = \{\{(Pi \times do) \cup (do \times di)\}, \{(PPn \times do) \cup (do \times PPn)\}, \{(di \times exit) \cup (exit \times Pi)\}\}$

$K = (do \rightarrow Timed, exit \rightarrow Immediate)$

$N = \{(Pi \times do) \rightarrow 1, (do \times di) \rightarrow 1, (PPn \times do) \rightarrow 1, (do \times PPn) \rightarrow 1, (di \times exit) \rightarrow 1, (exit \times Pi) \rightarrow 1\}$

$m_0 = \{(Pi \rightarrow 1\}, (di \rightarrow 0), (PPn \rightarrow q)\}$

Rule 2: Deployment mapping of collaboration: Rule 2 addresses the generation of an SRN model of collaboration. The collaboration connects only two collaboration roles in bidirectional manner, where roles are deployed on the same or different physical nodes. When collaboration roles i and j are deployed on the same physical node n, the timed transition tij in the SRN model is only realized by the overhead cost, as in this case, communication cost = 0. When collaboration roles i and j are deployed on the different physical nodes n and m, the timed transition tij in the SRN model is realized by both the overhead cost and communication cost.

The SRN model of a collaboration where collaboration connects only two collaboration roles those deploy on the same physical node can be represented by the 6-tuple in the following way:

$\Phi = \{Pi, di, Pj, dj, PPn\}$

$T = \{doi, doj, tij\}$

$A = \{(Pi \times doi) \cup (doi \times di), (PPn \times doi) \cup (doi \times PPn), (di \times tij) \cup (tij \times Pi), (Pj \times doj) \cup (doj \times dj), (PPn \times doj) \cup (doj \times PPn), (dj \times tij) \cup (tij \times Pj)\}$

$K = \{(doi, doj, tij) \rightarrow Timed\}$

$N = \{((Pi \times doi), (doi \times di), (PPn \times doi), (doi \times PPn), (di \times tij), (tij \times Pi), (Pj \times doj), (doj \times dj), (PPn \times doj), (doj \times PPn), (dj \times tij), (tij \times Pj)) \rightarrow 1\}$

$m_0 = \{(Pi \rightarrow 1), (di \rightarrow 0), (Pj \rightarrow 1) (dj \rightarrow 0), (PPn \rightarrow q)\}$

Similar to the above, the SRN model of collaboration can be represented by the 6-tuple, where collaboration connects only two collaboration roles in bidirectional way and the roles are deployed on different physical nodes.

Model transformation for components presented in Activity diagram: In this following section, we will describe the model transformation process of the some of the elements of the activity diagram that might be presented in the reusable building block:

The decision node in UML activity diagram activates one of the outgoing flows which are realized by the immediate or timed transitions in the SRN model according to the performance annotation requirement. The activation of outgoing flow in UML activity diagram is achieved based on a condition or a criterion that means the decision is not random. So we attach guard functions with immediate or timed transition in the equivalent SRN model of the decision node during the model transformation so that the decision is not made randomly. Guard function is associated with a condition based on which the activation of the transition will be permitted. For example, immediate transition tyes is associated with a guard function [gr] which will capture the same condition to be activated as outgoing flow yes in the activity diagram. If the condition of the guard function [gr] is fulfilled the associated transition will be activated. In the same way, it is also possible to associate a guard function with immediate transition tno instead of transition tyes and can conduct the same process for the activation of outgoing flow.

In case of merge node, the outgoing flow is activated when either of the incoming flow arrives. This event is captured by using the immediate or timed transitions in the SRN model according to the performance annotation requirement to activate the outgoing flow in the SRN model.

The timer node in UML activity diagram is represented by the timed transition in the corresponding SRN model.

In case of join node, after all incoming flows arrive; the outgoing flow starts which is realized by the immediate or timed transition in the SRN model according to the performance annotation requirement.

The fork node is realized by the split of incoming flow into several outgoing flows which is represented by the immediate or timed transition in the SRN model according to the performance annotation requirement.

Correspondence between UML and SRN Model Using Mapping Rules

The mapping process to demonstrate the correspondence between UML diagram and SRN model has been mentioned in the below. The mapping process is driven by the by the mapping rules listed below:

1. Activity element *operation* will be mapped into a *place* in SRN model
2. Activity element *flow* will be converted into a *timed transition* except the flows that start from *initial* element
3. Activity element *initial* will be converted into a *token* that will be reflected in the initial marking of the corresponding *place* in SRN model
4. If more than one flow cross the same partition border in UML activity diagram where direction of flows opposite to each other, the flows will be joined by single *timed transition* in the SRN model
5. *Flow* that does not cross the partition border in UML activity diagram will be realized by the *execution cost* in the corresponding timed transition of the SRN model where cost will be derived from the annotated UML model of the corresponding collaboration role. (Here cost ↔ time)
6. *Flow* that crosses the partition border in UML activity diagram will be realized by the *overhead cost* in the corresponding *timed transition* of the SRN model if the two partitions are associated with same physical node in the deployment mapping shown in UML deployment diagram where cost

will be derived from the annotated UML model of the corresponding collaboration, otherwise rate of the timed transition that crosses the partition border will be realized by both the *communication* and *overhead cost*. (Here, cost ↔ time)

7. For each physical node in the system execution environment, there exists a corresponding *place* in the SRN model which contains q (where q> =1) token which defines the upper bound of the execution of the processes in parallel by that physical node. This also ensures the execution of the process only when the physical node has that capacity to execute. So the *timed transition* in the SRN model which is realized by the *execution cost* will get one incoming arc from the corresponding *place* in the SRN model for the physical node. One outgoing arc also generates from that *timed transition* which connects to the corresponding *place* for the physical node.

8. Activity element *decision node* will be represented through *immediate* or *timed transitions* in SRN model according to the performance annotation requirement to active its outgoing flows where the one of the *immediate transitions* are associated with the guard function to activate

9. Activity element *merge node* will be represented through *immediate* or *timed transitions* in SRN model to activate its outgoing flow according to the performance annotation requirement where the outgoing flow is activated when either of the incoming flows arrive

10. Activity element *timer* will be mapped into *timed transition* in SRN model

11. Activity element *join* node will mapped into *immediate* or *timed transition* in the SRN model according to the performance annotation requirement

12. Activity element *fork* node will mapped into *immediate* or *timed transition* in the SRN model according to the performance annotation requirement

Focusing on the mapping rules, the correspondence between UML model and SRN model is illustrated below with respect to model transformation rule 2. The formal representation of the UML models that has been utilized as input for the model transformation process. According to the model transformation rule 2, the formal representation of the collaboration is represented as:

- $t_{ij} = \{i, j\}$; where collaboration role associated with the collaboration t_{ij} is defined by set $\{i, j\}$.

According to the model transformation rule 2, the formal representation of the activity diagram is mentioned as:

- Set of activity elements: $\{x, e_1, o_1, e_2, o_2, e_3, y, e_4, o_3, e_5, o_4, e_6\}$
- Set of flows between activity elements: $\{e_1 \subseteq (x \times o_1), e_2 \subseteq (o_1 \times o_2), e_3 \subseteq (o_2 \times y), e_4 \subseteq (y \times o_3), e_5 \subseteq (o_3 \times o_4), e_6 \subseteq (o_4 \times x)\}$; where $e_1 \subseteq (x \times o_1)$ means that edge e_1 connects the activity elements x and o_1
- type assigns each activity element a type; where x, y are *initial* elements, o_1, o_2, o_3, o_4 are known as *operation* elements, and $e_1, e_2, e_3, e_4, e_5, e_6$ are flow elements
- Set of partition in the activity diagram is represented as $\{i, j\}$; which means there is only two activity partition i and j
- Set of location: $\{\{x, o_1, o_2\} \to i, \{y, o_3, o_4\} \to j, \{e_1, e_2\} \to i, \{e_4, e_5\} \to j, \{e_3, e_6\} \to \{i, j\}\}$; where $\{x, o_1, o_2\} \to i$ means that elements x, o_1, and o_2 are located in the partition i

Furthermore, formal representation of the deployment mapping is mentioned as:

- $D_{mp} = (\{i, j\} \rightarrow n$; which means that software components i and j deploys in physical node n
- $D_{mp} = (\{i \rightarrow n\}, \{j \rightarrow m\})$; which means that software component i deploys onto physical node n and component j deploys onto physical node m

Applying the mapping rules to show the correspondence between UML model and SRN model for model transformation rule 2 (activity diagram) and SRN model is mentioned in Table 1. According to the mapping rule 1, activity element operations o_1, o_2, o_3, and o_4 will be mapped to place P_i, d_i, P_j, and d_j. According to the mapping rule 7, for physical nodes n and m, the corresponding places will be PP_n and PP_m. Considering mapping rule 2, activity element flows e_2 and e_5 are represented by the timed transition do_i $(P_i \times d_i)$ and $do_j(P_j \times d_j)$ in the SRN model where do_i connects the places P_i and d_i, and do_j connects the places P_j and d_j. Activity element flows e_3, e_6 are represented by the single timed transition $t_{ij}((d_i \times P_j) (d_j \times P_i))$ according to the mapping rule 4 where the incoming places for this transition are d_i and d_j and outgoing places for this transition are P_j and P_i. Following the mapping rules 3, because of initial elements x and y of activity diagram places P_i and P_j get one taken each in the SRN model. According to rule 7, places PP_n and PP_m each will be assigned q (q > = 1) token in the SRN model for defining the upper bound of the execution of the processes in parallel by physical nodes n and m. When collaboration roles i and j deploy on the same physical node n timed transitions do_i and do_j will be connected by incoming arcs from the place PP_n and out going arcs will be connected to place PP_n from timed transitions do_i and do_j following the mapping rule 7. When collaboration roles i and j deploy on the different physical nodes n and m timed transitions do_i and do_j will be connected by incoming arcs from the places PP_n and PP_m and out going arcs will be connected to place PP_n and PP_m from timed transitions do_i and do_j following the mapping rule 7. According to rule 6, timed transition t_{ij} in the SRN model will be realized by the overhead time when collaboration roles i and j deploy on the same physical node n and timed transition in the SRN model will be realized by the overhead time and communication time when collaboration roles i and j deploy on the different physical nodes n and m. According to rule 5, timed transitions do_i and do_j in the SRN model will be realized by the execution time whether collaboration roles i and j deploy on the same physical node n or different physical nodes n and m.

The SRN model as output of the model transformation process for model transformation rules. We have designed the model transformation algorithms utilizing the above model transformation rules to generate the corresponding SRN model from the annotated UML model. These algorithms are given in Appendix B.

CONCLUSION

We present a novel approach for model based performance modeling of distributed system which spans from capturing the system dynamics through UML diagram as reusable building block to efficient deployment of service components in a distributed manner by specifying the QoS requirements. System dynamics is captured through UML collaboration and activity oriented approach. The behavior of the collaboration and the composition of collaboration to highlight the overall system behavior are demonstrated by utilizing UML activity. Furthermore, quantitative analysis of the system is achieved by automatically generating SRN performance model from the UML specification style. The transformation

Table 1. Correspondence among collaboration diagram, activity diagram, deployment diagram, and SRN model

Element of Activity Diagram	Element of SRN Model	Element of Deployment Diagram
Operation	Place	Physical node
O_1, O_2, O_3, O_4	P_i, d_i, P_j, d_j	n, m
	PP_n, PP_m	
flow	timed transition (associated places)	
e_2, e_5	$do_i(P_i \times d_i), do_j(P_j \times d_j)$	
e_3, e_6 (cross partition border)	$t_{ij}((d_i \times P_j)(d_j \times P_i))$	
Initial element	Initial marking	Physical node
x, y	$P_i \rightarrow 1, P_j \rightarrow 1$	n, m
	$PP_n \rightarrow q, PP_m \rightarrow q$	
Collaboration role	**Timed transition (associated places) for utilizing physical node capacity**	**Deployment mapping**
i, j	$do_i(PP_n \times PP_n), do_j(PP_n \times PP_n)$	$\{i, j\} \rightarrow n$
	$do_i(PP_n \times PP_n), do_j(PP_m \times PP_m)$	$(i \rightarrow n, j \rightarrow m)$
Collaboration role	**Timed transition (associated time) that crosses partition border**	**Deployment mapping**
i, j	t_{ij} (overhead time)	$\{i, j\} \rightarrow n$
	t_{ij} (overhead time + communication time)	$(i \rightarrow n, j \rightarrow m)$
Collaboration role	**Timed transition (associated cost) does not cross partition border**	**Deployment mapping**
i, j	(do_i, do_j) (execution time)	$\{i, j\} \rightarrow n$ or $(i \rightarrow n, j \rightarrow m)$

from UML diagram to corresponding SRN elements like states, different pseudostates, and transitions is proposed. While performing the transformation, the UML diagrams such as collaboration, activities, and deployment are formalized using cTLA that captures the behavior of the collaborative system specification. We apply cTLA as a foremost background technique to understand the formalism of collaborative specifications expressed in other languages, such as UML. In our approach, we use UML collaborations in combination with activities, and have therefore presented how they can be transformed to cTLA/c specifications and in this way provide them with a non-ambiguous formal semantics. The provision of a formal semantics does not end in itself but, is a central ingredient for the automated development of high-quality software. It is the basis for meaningful semantic checks as, for instance, to be done with the model checking approach introduced in Slåtten (2007). Performance related QoS information is taken into account and included in the SRN model with equivalent timing and probabilistic assumption for enabling the performance modeling of the system at the early stage of the system development process. Future work includes providing the automated model checking of cTLA formalisms of UML using TLC (Yu, Manolios, & Lamport, 1999).

REFERENCES

Andolfi, F., Aquilani, F., Balsamo, S., & Inverardi, P. (2000). Deriving performance models of software architecture for message sequence charts. *Proceedings of the Workshop On the Softaware and Performance* (pp. 45-57). New York, NY: ACM. doi:10.1145/350391.350404

Cardoso, J., & Blanc, C. (2001). Ordering actions in sequence diagram of UML. *Proceedings of the International conference on Information Technology Interfaces* (pp. 3-14). Croatia: IEEE.

Ciardo, G., Muppala, J., & Trivedi, K. S. (1992). Analyzing concurrent and fault-tolerant software using stochastic reward nets. *Journal of Parallel and Distributed Computing, 15*(1), 255–269. doi:10.1016/0743-7315(92)90007-A

Cooper, K., Dai, L., & Deng, Y. (2003). Modeling performance as an aspect: a UML based approach. *Proceedings of the 4th workshop on AOSD modeling with UML*. San Francisco, CA.

Csorba, M., Heegaard, P., & Hermann, P. (2008). Cost-Efficient deployment of collaborating components. Proceedings of the 8th IFIP WG 6.1 *International conference on Distributed applications and interoperable systems* (pp. 253-268). Oslo, Norway. Springer. doi:10.1007/978-3-540-68642-2_20

Eshuis, R., & Wieringa, R. (2001). A comparison of Petri net & activity diagram variants. *In Proceedings of the International collaboration on Petri Net technologies for modeling communication based systems* (pp. 93-104). Berlin, Germany. Springer.

Herrmann, P. (1997). Problemnaher korrektheitssichernder entwurf von hochleistungsprotokollen. [Dissertation]. Universitat Dortmund.

Herrmann, P., & Krumm, H. (2000). A framework for modeling transfer protocols. *Computer Networks, 34*(2), 317–337. doi:10.1016/S1389-1286(00)00089-X

Khan, R. H. (2011). Performance and performability modeling framework considering management of service components deployment [Dissertation]. Norwegian University of Science and Technology.

Khan, R. H., & Heegaard, P. (2010). From UML to SRN: A performance modeling framework for managing behavior of multiple collaborative session and instances. *Proceedings of the International Conference on Computer Design and Application* (pp. 72-80). Qinhuangdao, China. IEEE.

Khan, R. H., & Heegaard, P. (2010). A performance modeling framework incorporating cost efficient deployment of collaborating components. *Proceedings of the International Conference of the Software Technology and Engineering* (pp. 340-349). San Juan, PR. IEEE. doi:10.1109/ICSTE.2010.5608859

Khan, R. H., & Heegaard, P. (2011). A Performance modeling framework incorporating cost efficient deployment of multiple collaborating components. *proceedings of the International Conference Software Engineering and Computer Systems* (pp. 31-45). Pahang, Malaysia. Springer. doi:10.1007/978-3-642-22170-5_3

Kraemer, F. A., & Hermann, P. (2007a). Formalizing collaboration-oriented service specifications using temporal logic. *Proceedings of the International conference on networking and electronic commerce research conference (pp.* 194-220). Italy.

Kraemer, F. A., & Herrmann, P. (2006). Service specification by composition of collaborations-an example. *Proceedings of the WI-IAT workshops* (pp. 129-133). Hong Kong. doi:10.1109/WI-IATW.2006.121

Kraemer, F. A., & Herrmann, P. (2007b). Semantics of UML 2.0 Activities and Collaborations in cTLA [Avantel Technical Report 3]. Norwegian University of Science and Technology.

Lamport, L. (2002). *Specifying Systems*. New York: Addison-Wesley.

Lopez-Grao, J. P., Merseguer, J., & Campos, J. (2004). From UML activity diagrams to SPN: application to software performance engineering. *Proceedings of the 4th International conference on software and performance* (pp.25-36). New York, NY. ACM.

Manna, Z., & Pnueli, A. (1992). *The Temporal Logic of Reactive and Concurrent Systems*. Berling: Springer-Verlag. doi:10.1007/978-1-4612-0931-7

Martin, A., & Leslie, L. (1995). Conjoining Specifications. *ACM Transactions on Programming Languages and Systems, 17*(3), 507–535. doi:10.1145/203095.201069

Merayo, M. G., Núñez, M., & Rodríguez, I. (2008). Formal testing from timed finite state machines. *Computer Networks, 52*(2), 432–460. doi:10.1016/j.comnet.2007.10.002

Moura, P., Borges, R., & Mota, A. (2012). Experimenting formal methods through UML. Retrieved November 19 2012, from http:// www.imamu.edu.sa/ DContent/ IT_Topics/ Experimenting Formal Methods through UML.pdf

OMG. (2009a). OMG Unified Modeling Language (OMG UML) Superstructure. Version 2.2. *Object management group*. Retrieved from http://www.omg.org/spec/UML/22/Superstructure/PDF/

OMG. (2009b). UML Profile for MARTE: Modeling and analysis of real-time embedded systems. Version 1.0. *Object management group*. Retrieved from http://www.omg.org/omgmarte/Documents/Specifications/08-06-09.pdf

Petriu, D., & Shen, H. (2002). Applying the UMl Performance Profile: Graph grammar based derivation of LQN models from UML specifications. *Proceedings of the TOOLS* (pp. 159-177). Springer-Verlag. doi:10.1007/3-540-46029-2_10

Shuhao, L., Ji, W., Wei, D., & Zhichang, Q. (2004). A framework of property-oriented testing of reactive systems. *Chinese Journal of Electronics, 32*(12A), 222–225.

Slåtten, V. (2007). Model checking collaborative service specifications in TLA with TLC [Dissertation]. Norwegian University of Science and Technology.

Theelen, B., Putten, P., & Voeten, J. (2004). Using the SHE method for UML-based performance modeling. *Proceedings of the System specification and design languages* (pp. 143-160).

Trivedi, K. S. (2001). *Probability and statistics with reliability, queuing and computer science application*. New York: Wiley- Interscience.

Vissers, C. A., Scollo, G., Sinderen, M. V., & Brinksma, H. (1991). Specification Styles in Distributed System Design and Verification. *Theoretical Computer Science, 89*(3), 179–206. doi:10.1016/0304-3975(90)90111-T

Warmer, J., & Kleppe, A. (1999). *The object constraint language: Precise modeling with UML*. Edinburgh: Addison-Wesley.

Yongfeng, Y., Liu, B., Li, Z., Zhang, C., & Wu, N. (2010). The Integrated Application Based on Real-time Extended UML and Improved Formal Method in Real-time Embedded Software Testing. *Journal of networks*, 5(12), 1410-1416.

Yu, Y., Manolios, P., & Lamport, L. (1999). Model checking TLA+ specifications. In L. Pierre, & T. Kropf, (Eds), Proceedings of CHARME '99. 10th IFIP WG 10.5 Advanced research working conference on correct hardware design and verification methods. Springer, Verlag.

KEY TERMS AND DEFINITIONS

Collaborative Building Block: UML collaboration is the main specification unit of the collaborative building block which captures the interaction between the software components. The behavioral aspect of the collaborative building is defined by the UML activity.

Distributed System: A distributed system consists of multiple autonomous computers that communicate through a computer network. The computers interact with each other in order to achieve a common goal.

Model Transformation: To transform the UML model into analytical model (e.g, markov, SPN, SRN) is defined as model transformation.

Reusable Building Block: Collaborative building block is called as reusable building block as it is archived in a library for later reuse.

Self-Contained Encapsulated Building Block: Collaborative building block is also defined as self-contained encapsulated building block as each building block captures the local behavior and interaction between the software components in it. Each building block is self described and independent to each other.

Service: A software system to achieve some goals in a computing environment.

Software Component: A software component is a module that encapsulates a set of related functions.

System: A system is a set of interacting or interdependent components forming an integrated whole.

System Physical Component: System physical component is the device or node where the software components deploy.

UML Profile: Profile in UML is defined using stereotypes, tag definitions, and constraints that are applied to specific model elements, such as Classes, Attributes, Operations, and Activities. A Profile is a collection of such extensions that collectively customize UML for a particular domain or platform.

APPENDIX A

cTLA Process of Activity Elements

Initial Nodes: The variable x is the flag describing the place at an initial node. The place is only filled in the initial system state (value "idle") while it will remain empty when the activity is running (value "active"). The leaving of the token from the initial node is modeled by the action *start* which must only be executed if the token is in its place (i.e., $x =$ *"idle"*) and removes the token ($x =$ *"processing"*). The action parameter t specifies the signature of the token. Since that is not defined explicitly, it may contain any correct value of set *TT*. *start* is a trigger action modeling the start of a new token flow.

PROCESS Initial (TT: Any)

VARIABLES x: {"idle", "processing"};

INIT ≜ x = "idle";

ACTIONS

start(t: TT) ≜ x = "idle" ∧ t ∈ TT ∧ x´ = "processing" ;

END

Transfer Flows: The queue modeling the transfer of a token from one partition to another one is modeled by the variable q. It stores for every received token the corresponding signature and delivers this information in FIFO order. The arrival of a token with the signature *it* at the partition border is specified by the action *send* while *receive* models the consumption of a token with signature *ot*. According to this definition, the action *send* is assigned to the partition from which the flow leads to the partition border while *receive* is part of the one consuming the token. *receive* is a trigger action.

PROCESS Transfer (TT: Any)

VARIABLES q: Queue (TT);

INIT ≜ q = EMPTY;

ACTIONS

Send (it: TT) ≜ q´ = append (q, it);

Receive (ot: TT) ≜ q ≠ EMPTY ∧ ot = first (q) ∧ q´ = tail (q);

END

Call Operation Actions: An operation may change the values of local auxiliary variables of the partition, in which it is defined, as well as the signature of the token flowing through it. We describe operations by the stateless cTLA process *Operation*, which takes two functions as parameters *nv* and *nt*. These parameters reflect that a call operation action may change both the signature of the tokens and the auxiliary variables. Consequently, *nv* is a function that describes the operation's effect on the values of the auxiliary variables. Similarly, *nt* describes the deriving of new token values. The method *execute* models the computation of new values according to these functions. As action parameters it uses *iv* expressing the auxiliary variable setting and specifying the token signature before executing the operation. The new value of the auxiliary variables and the new token signature are described by the action parameters *ov* and *ot*.

PROCESS Operation(nv: $[VT \times TT \rightarrow VT]$; nt: $[VT \times TT \rightarrow TT]$)

ACTIONS

execute (iv: VT; it: TT; ov: VT; ot: TT) $\triangleq$ ov = nv [iv, it] $\wedge$ ot = no [iv, it];

END

APPENDIX B

Model Transformation Algorithm

Input of transformation algorithm is defined as follows:

- *Nodes:* A non-empty list of physical nodes
- *CollaborationRoles:* A non-empty list of collaboration roles
- *Mappings:* A non-empty list of mappings from *CollaborationRoles* to *Nodes* as pairs
- *ExecCost:* A non-empty list of collaboration roles and their associated execution costs as tuple
- *CommCost:* A non-empty list of collaboration roles that participate in the communication and associated communication and overhead cost as tuple

Output of transformation algorithm is defined as follows:

- A file named "Output.txt" that contains the SRN model of the system

The algorithms are presented in the follwoing:

Algorithm 1: generateRates (ExecCost, Mappings, CollaborationRoles)

1   Open file *"Output.txt"* in append mode
2   **for** each tuple *(C_i ExecCost$_i$)* in the *ExecCost* list **do**
3   *rate* ← 1/ *ExecCost$_i$*
4   Write to file *"func rate"* + *i* + *"()"* + *rate*
5   **for** each tuple *(C_m, N_n)* in the **Mappings** list do
6   **if** $C_i = C_m$ **then**
7   *node* ← N_n
8   **end if**
9   **end for**
10   **for** each tuple (C_p, N_q) in the *Mappings* list **do**
11   **if** *node* = N_q **then**
12   *roleIndex* ← index of C_p in the *CollaborationRoles* list
13   **if** *firstItem* **then**
14   Write to file *"#(p"* + *roleIndex* + *")"*
15   **else**
16   Write to file *"+ #(p"* + *roleIndex* + *")"*
17   **end if**
18   **end if**
19   **end for**
20   Write to file *")"* + *newline*
20   **end for**
21   **return**

Algorithm 2: generatePlaces (Nodes, CollaborationRoles)

1   Open file *"Output.txt"* in append mode
2   **for** each element (C_i) in the *CollaborationRoles* list **do**
3   Write to file *"P$_i$ 1"*
4   Write to file *"D$_i$ 0"*
5   **end for**
6   **for** each element (N_i) in the *Nodes* list **do**
7   Write to file *"PΩ$_i$ 10"*
8   **end for**
9   **return**

Algorithm 3: generateTimedTransition (CollaborationRoles, CommCost, Mappings)

1   Open file "Output.txt" in append mode
2   **for** each element (C_i) in the *CollaborationRoles* list **do**
3   Write to file "*t*" + *i* + "*gendep rate*" + *i* + "()"
4   **end for**
5   **for** each tuple (K_i, C_m, C_n, *CommCost*$_p$, *OverheadCost*$_q$) in the *CommCost* list **do**
6   *roleIndex$_1$* ← index of C_m in *Mappings* list
7   *roleIndex$_2$* ← index of C_n in *Mappings* list
8   *node$_1$* ← corresponding node at *roleIndex$_1$* in *Mappings* list
9   *node$_2$* ← corresponding node at *roleIndex$_2$* in *Mappings* list
10   **if** node$_1$ ≠ node$_2$ **then**
11   *cost* ← *CommCost$_p$* + *OverheadCost$_q$*
12   **else**
13   *cost* ← *OverheadCost$_q$*
14   **end if**
15   **cost** ← 1/*cost*
16   Write to file "K_i" + "*ind*" + cost
17   **end for**
18   **return**

Algorithm 4: generateInputArcs (Nodes, CollaborationRoles, Mappings, CommCost)

1   Open file "Output.txt" in append mode
2   **for** each element (C_i) in the *CollaborationRoles* list **do**
3   Write to file "*Pi ti 1*"
4   **end for**
5   **for** each tuple (C_i, N_j) in the *Mappings* list **do**
6   *roleIndex* ← index of C_i in *CollaborationRoles* list
7   *nodeIndex* ← index of N_j in *Nodes* list
8   Write to file "p_Ω" + *nodeIndex* + "*t*" + *roleIndex* + "*1*"
9   **end for**
10   **for** each tuple (*Ki, Cm, Cn, CommCostp, OverheadCostq*) in the *CommCost* list **do**
11   *roleIndex$_1$* ← index of C_m in *CollaborationRoles* list
12   *roleIndex$_2$* ← index of C_n in *CollaborationRoles* list
13   Write to file "*d*" + *roleIndex$_1$* + " "+ K_i + "*1*"
14   Write to file "d" + roleIndex$_2$ + " " + K_i + "*1*"
15   **end for**
16   **return**

Algorithm 5: generateOutputArcs (Nodes, CollaborationRoles, Mappings, CommCost)

1   Open file "Output.txt" in append mode
2   **for** each element (C_i) in the *CollaborationRoles* list **do**
3   Write to file "$t_i\, d_i\, 1$"
4   **end for**
5   **for** each tuple (C_i, N_j) in the *Mappings* list **do**
6   *roleIndex* ← index of C_i in *CollaborationRoles* list
7   *nodeIndex* ← index of N_j in *Nodes* list
8   Write to file "*t*"+ *roleIndex* + "*pp*" + *nodeIndex* + "*1*"
9   **end for**
10   **for** each tuple $(K_i, C_m, C_n, CommCost_p, OverheadCost_q)$ in the *CommCost* list **do**
11   *roleIndex$_1$* ← index of C_m in *CollaborationRoles* list
12   *roleIndex$_2$* ← index of C_n in *CollaborationRoles* list
13   Write to file "K_i" + "*p*" + *roleIndex$_1$* + "*1*"
14   Write to file "K_i" + "*p*" + *roleIndex$_2$* + "*1*"
15   **end for**
16   **return**

Chapter 3
An EOG Signal based Framework to Control a Wheel Chair

Pushpanjalee Konwar
Assam Don Bosco University, India

Hemashree Bordoloi
Assam Don Bosco University, India

ABSTRACT

Elecrooculogram (EOG) signal extraction is critical in the working of any electrooculography aided system based upon the tracking of the ocular movement of the eye dipole. In this chapter the signals captured using sensors (electrodes), are first amplified, then the noise is removed and then digitized, before being transferred to controller for movement of the wheelchair. Finally, from the muscle sensor, the output is directly being given to the controller to reach the target and complete the control of the movement of the wheelchair. Initially, a potentiometer is used instead of the Ag-Agcl electrodes to test the strength of signal obtained due to the movement of the eyes. Using this wheelchair is quite an advantage because this chair helps a physically handicapped person to move freely without being dependent on anyone else. The research provides a new method for human-machine interface system.

INTRODUCTION

Recently, various bio-signals are used to control the physical devices such as mouse, joysticks, key-board etc. In medical science, numerous assistive technologies are providing to help the handicapped persons. Bio-signals are generally detected from the excitable tissues of the human body that is, nerve and muscle cells. Electrooculography (EOG), electromyography (EMG), etc. are the examples of such signals. In this work the EOG signal has been used to control a wheelchair (Wissel & Palaniappan, 2011).

However, the first step of acquiring signals starts with positioning of electrodes followed by filtering and amplifying units respectively. The actual placement of electrode is required to determine electrical activity caused by eye movements. The placement of Ag/AgCl electrodes is important for acquiring a good signal from the eyes. The overall placement of the electrodes can be represented as shown in Figure 1.

DOI: 10.4018/978-1-4666-8493-5.ch003

Figure 1. Electrodes placement for EOG signal

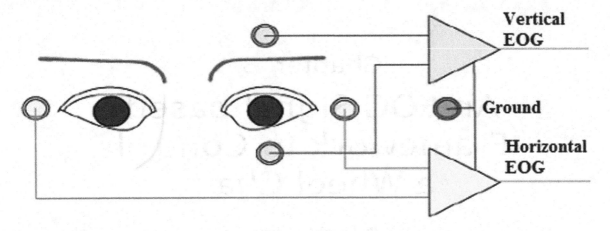

The generation of the electro-occulogram (EOG) signal is due to the hyperpolarization and depolarization of retinal cells. The measurement of horizontal eye movements is done by the placement of a pair of electrodes at the outside of the left and right eye. Horizontal EOG is measured as a voltage by means of electrodes strategically placed as close as possible to the canthus of each eye. Similarly, vertical EOG is measured as a voltage by means of electrodes placed just above the eye (Choudhury, Venkataramanan, Nemade & Sahambi, 2005). The entire idea of the approach is to design a system for the paralysed persons and the use of wheelchair proves to be a very important factor for mobility among disabled as well as the quadriplegic, which may cause by road accident, falling from the high position or severe diseases. The initial purpose of the wheelchair is actually aimed to give more freedom for these people to do basic things on their own, such as carrying items from one place to another and manoeuvre (Rokonuzzaman. et al., 2012). The mobility of the wheelchair users can be aided according to the level of injuries of a user has, or depending on the capability of the user to handle the wheelchair. It is very crucial in translating the eye movement into a correct motion input. Any wrong judgment of eye movement input classification will lead to a fault motion instruction of the wheelchair (Borea, Boquete, Maza, Lopez & Lledo, 2013).

OBJECTIVE OF THE WORK

A system consists of a DC motor with wheel and coupled with a servo motor. The speed reversal and the left-right direction control is the main scope this work. By the resulting signal of the potential difference caused by eye movements a voltage difference is measured between the cornea and the retina. The resting potential ranges from 0.4mV to 1mV and a pair of electrodes are commonly used to detect this signal, but the voltage difference when there's an eye movement can be as small as just some micro volts. Depending on the eye's position, an electrode is more positive or negative with respect to the ground electrode. Therefore, the recorded signal is either negative or positive as per the movement of eyes (Pradeep, Govada & Swamy, 2013). A manual switch operation, the servo mechanism and the DC motor speed reversal can be done respectively.

BACKGROUND

There are many literatures describing the technical background of the EOG signals. Some of the important terms in the EOG detection process are as given below:

1. **BIOELECTRICAL SIGNALS:** Bioelectrical signals are very low amplitude and low frequency electrical signals that can be measured from biological beings, using electrodes. Examples- ECG, EEG, EMG, EOG etc. (Merino, Rivera, Gomez, Molina & Dorronzoroa, 2010).
2. **BIOELECTRIC POTENTIAL:** A voltage produced by a tissue of the body, particularly muscle tissue during a contraction. Bioelectric phenomenon is of immense importance to biomedical engineers because these potentials are routine recorded in modern clinical practice. There are two types of bioelectric potentials which are as follows:
3. **RESTING POTENTIAL:** The excitable membrane resting potential is one that brings the membrane into a steady state. It is that value at which the total membrane current is zero (otherwise, we have a changing potential and the membrane is not at rest). Before intracellular electrodes, it was supposed that all permeable ions were individually in equilibrium (i.e., in which case there would be a total absence of transmembrane ion flow). Bioelectric potentials are a result of electrochemical activity of excitable cells (in neurons, muscular or glandular system). The resting potential of a cell is steady difference in electric potentials between internal and external environment of the cell. Typical values of resting potentials are in range of 50 mV to 100 mV (reference point out of the cell). The resting potential is the result of an unequal distribution of ions across the membrane. The resting potential is sensitive to ions in proportion to their ability to permeate the membrane (Borea, Boquete, Maza, Lopez & Lledo, 2013).
4. **ACTION POTENTIAL:** Changes in Ion Permeability allows inward Na flux and triggers an increased outward K flux through voltage gated ion channels. As result a transient change in Membrane Potential occurs. The change in ion permeability is triggered by transient depolarization of the membrane
5. **ARDEN RATIO:** The arden ratio can be calculated by the given formula:

6. $$\text{Arden Ratio} = \frac{\text{The maximal height of the potential in the light}\left(\text{light peak}\right)}{\text{The maximal height of the potential in the dark}\left(\text{dark peak}\right)} \times 100\%$$

BRIEF INTRODUCTION ON THE WHEELCHAIR MECHANISM SYSTEM

Over the years, the neurophysiology and biomechanics of muscle systems have been investigated quite extensively based on the research of surface EMG signal. As the measurement of given muscle activity, surface Electromyography (EMG) signals represent the electrical activity of a muscle during contraction. More elaborate research had been attempted by the researchers around the world to abstract the features of EMG in motion and to classify the movement patterns (Pradeep, Govada & Swamy, 2013). The surface EMG signals are complex, non stationary time sequence that can be considered as direct reflection of the muscle activity. In this work EMG signals collected from the muscles responsible for the movement of human eyes are used as the controlling signal for the wheelchair movement.

The chapter presents a solution for those kinds of disabled people who are unable to spend a lot of money to buy a fancy or sophisticated wheelchair which does not need any on board computer or any other expensive instruments. A simple structure and user friendly control system is used to control the wheelchair navigation using only the movement of eyes. Generally this type of design would suit most to the people who are totally disabled, that means completely unable to move their hand, leg or head.

PRIMARY MECHANISMS USED TO FIXATE ON OBJECTS

One of the most important functions your eyes can perform is to "fix" or "lock" on specific objects. When you "fix" on an object, you position your eyes so that the image of the object is projected onto your retina at the area of greatest acuity, the fovea. Muscular control of your eyes works to keep the image on your fovea, regardless of whether the object is stationary or moving.

There are two primary mechanisms used to fixate on objects in visual field:

1. **VOLUNTARY FIXATION MECHANISM:** Voluntary fixation allows directing visual attention and locking onto the selected object.
2. **INVOLUNTARY FIXATION MECHANISM:** In voluntary fixation allows you to keep a selected object in your visual field once it has been found. In voluntary types of eye movements, you can fixate on another person from across a crowded room. Voluntary fixation involves a conscious effort to move the eyes. This mechanism is used to initially select objects in your visual field, and once selected, your brain "hands off" the task to involuntary fixation. Even when you fixate on a stationary object, your eyes are not still but exhibit tiny, involuntary movements. There are three types of involuntary movements: tremors, slow drifts, and flicking:
    ◦ **Tremors:** a series of small tremors of the eyes at about 30-80 Hz (cycles/sec).
    ◦ **Slow drifts:** involuntary movements that result in drifting movements of the eyes. This drift means that even if an object is stationary, the image drifts across the fovea.
    ◦ **Flicking movements:** As the image drifts to the edge of the fovea, the third involuntary mechanism causes a reflex flicking of the eyeball so that the image is once again projected onto the fovea. The drifting movements and flicking movements will be in opposite directions. If the drifting movement is to the left, the flicking movement will be to the right, although it may not be 180 opposite of the drifting movement. Another set of motions is used when you read or when objects are streaming past you, e.g., when you watch the world go by while riding in a train. Rather than a smooth tracking motion, reading usually involves voluntary, larger movements, known as saccades, or fixating on a series of points in rapid succession. Typically, the eye will spend about 10% of the time moving from fixation point to fixation point, with the other 90% of the time fixating on words, although there is much variation.

Eye movement can be recorded as an electrooculogram (Khan, Memon, Jat & Khan, A., 2012), a recording of changes in voltage that occur with eye position. Electric potentials are generated across the Cornea and Retina of the eyes as a result of the movement of eyeballs within the conductive environment of the skull. This is referred to as the Cornea-Retinal Potential (CRP) and is the source of the electrooculogram (EOG) signal. Electrically, the eye is a spherical "battery," with the positive terminal in front at the cornea, and the negative terminal behind at the retina of the eyeball. The potential between the front and back of the eyeball is about 0.4-1.0 mV. By placing electrodes on either side of the eye, you can measure eye movement up to $\pm 70^0$, where 0^0 is in front and $\pm 90^0$ is directly lateral or vertical to the eyes. The electrodes measure the changes in potential as the cornea moves nearer or further from the recording electrodes. When the eye is looking straight ahead, it is about the same distance from either electrode, so the signal is essentially zero. When the front of the eyeball, the cornea, is closer to the positive electrode, that electrode records a positive difference in voltage (Noor & Ahmad, 2013).

ANATOMY BEHIND THE MOVEMENT OF HUMAN EYE

Movement of human eye is governed by the extra ocular muscles. A unique and exclusive combination of muscle(s) is responsible for a particular movement of the eye ball. For this reason EOG signals have been chosen as the control parameter of the system. Figure 2 shows the six different extra ocular muscles of the human eye.

As seen from Figure 2, there are three pairs of muscles which control the movement of human eye. From Figure 3, it can be found that which muscle(s) are responsible for a particular direction of gaze.

MECHANISM OF ELECTROOCULOGRAM SIGNALS

The eye is a seat of a steady electric potential field that is quite unrelated to light stimulation (Desai, 2013). Figure 4 shows the eye and its major components. In fact, this field may be detected with the eye in total darkness or with the eyes closed. It can be described as a fixed dipole with positive pole at the cornea and negative pole at the retina. The magnitude of this corneoretinal potential is in the range 0.4-1.0 mV (Wu, Liao, Lu, Jiang, Chen & Lin, 2013). It is not generated by excitable tissue but, rather, is attributed to the higher metabolic rate in the retina. The polarity of this potential difference in the eyes of invertebrates is opposite to that of vertebrates. This potential difference and the rotation of the

Figure 2. Six extra ocular muscle responsible for the movement of eye

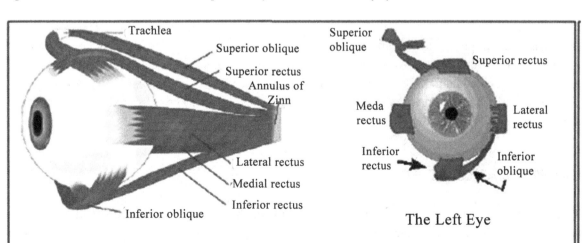

Figure 3. Pictorial representation of the muscle combination for a particular direction of gaze

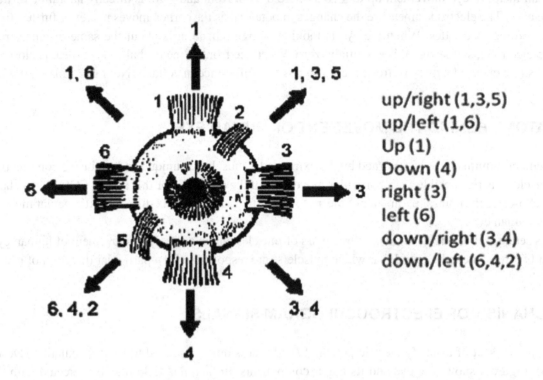

up/right (1,3,5)
up/left (1,6)
Up (1)
Down (4)
right (3)
left (6)
down/right (3,4)
down/left (6,4,2)

eye are the basis for a signal measured at a pair of periorbital surface electrodes. The signal is known as the electrooculogram, (EOG). It is useful in the study of eye movement. The retinal cellular structure is shown in Figure 5.

The measurement of horizontal eye movements can be done by the placement of a pair of electrodes at the outside of the left and right eye (outer canthi). With the eye at rest the electrodes are effectively at the same potential and no voltage is recorded. The rotation of the eye to the right results in a difference of potential, with the electrode in the direction of movement (i.e., the right canthus) becoming positive relative to the second electrode.

Ideally the difference in potential should be proportional to the sine of the angle. The opposite effect results from a rotation to the left, as illustrated. The calibration of the signal may be achieved by having the patient look consecutively at two different fixation points located a known angle apart and recording the concomitant EOGs. Typical achievable accuracy is $\pm 2°$, and maximum rotation is $\pm 70°$ however, linearity becomes progressively worse for angles beyond $30°$. Typical signal magnitudes range from 5-20 $\mu V/°$.

IMPLEMENTATION OF EOG

The generation of the Electrooculogram (EOG) signal is due to the hyper polarization and depolarization of retinal cells. However, the first step of acquiring signals starts with positioning of electrodes followed by filtering and amplifying units respectively (WEI & Huosheng, 2011). The actual placement

Figure 4. The eye and its major components

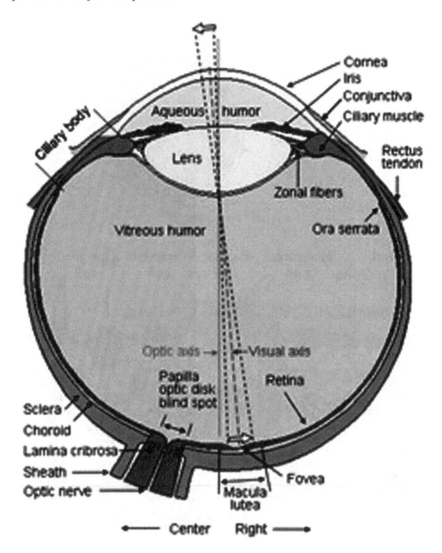

of electrode is required to determine electrical activity caused by eye movements. The placement of Ag/ AgCl electrodes is important for acquiring a good signal from the eyes. The overall placement of the electrodes can be represented as shown in Figure 6.

The measurement of horizontal eye movements is done by the placement of a pair of electrodes at the outside of the left and right eye (Ahsan, Ibrahimy & Khalifa, 2009). Horizontal EOG is measured as a voltage by means of electrodes strategically placed as close as possible to the canthus of each eye. Similarly, vertical EOG is measured as a voltage by means of electrodes placed just above the eye. With the eye at rest no voltage is recorded. The rotation of the eye to the right results in a difference of potential, with the electrode in the direction of movement (i.e., the right) becoming positive relative to the second electrode. Ideally the difference in potential should be proportional to the sine of the angle.

Figure 5. The retinal cellular structure

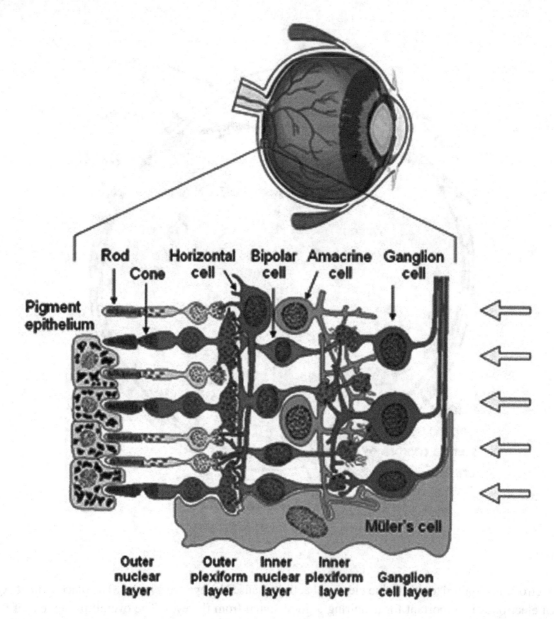

The entire idea of the approach is to design a system for the paralysed persons and the use of wheelchair proves to be a very important factor for mobility among disabled as well as the quadriplegic, which may cause by road accident, falling from the high position or severe diseases (Yathunanthan, Chandrasena, Umakanthan, Vasuki & Munasinghe, 2008). The initial purpose of the wheelchair is actually aimed to give more freedom for these people to do basic things on their own, such as carrying items from one place to another and maneuver. The mobility of the wheelchair users can be aided according to the level of injuries of a user has, or depending on the capability of the user to handle the wheelchair. It is very crucial in translating the eye movement into a correct motion input. Any wrong judgment of eye movement input classification will lead to a fault motion instruction of the wheelchair.

Figure 6. Electrodes placement for EOG signal

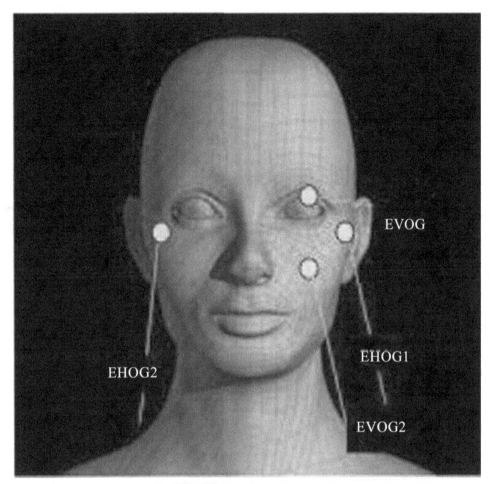

COMPLETE STRUCTURE OF THE SYSTEM

The complete structure of the system is described in Figure 7. After the extraction of the signal, the output is provided as the input signal for the filtration and amplifier block (Fatourechi, Bashashati, Ward, & Birch, 2007). This block plays a vital role as because the extracted signal obtained has very low

Figure 7. Tentative Block Diagram

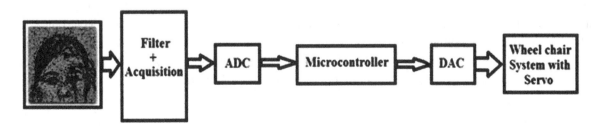

Figure 8. Complete structure of the system

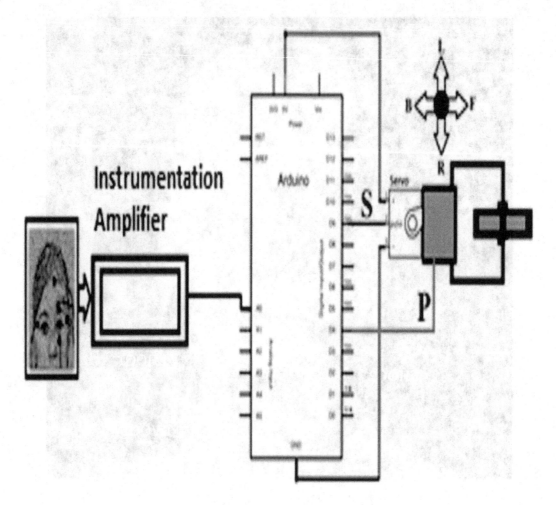

amplitude and noise. After completion of the amplification and filtration, the signal is being provided to the A_0 pin of the Arduino Microcontroller. The advantage of using Arduino is that it has inbuilt ADC and DAC. The final output is supplied to the wheelchair mechanism block. The complete structure of the system is depicted in Figure 8 (Yagi, 2010).

Since the strength of the voltage signal is very low and noise sensitive, an amplification circuit with proper filter has to be designed to acquire the signal for the process. Generally an instrumentation amplifier and a low pass filter or sometimes a band pass filter are used to amplify the signal and remove the noise from the signal respectively. But a muscle sensor has the feature to filter and rectify electrical activity of a muscle; outputting 0-Vs Volts depending on the amount of activity in the selected muscle, where Vs signifies the voltage of the power source. One of the best features of a muscle sensor is that it has improved adjustable gain. So instead of designing an amplification circuit with proper filtration circuit, a v3 technology muscle sensor is much preferred over an amplification circuit.

INITIAL EXPERIMENTAL SETUP

The initial experimental Set consisted of a 10 k potentiometer used as a test signal instead of Ag-AgCl electrodes which has to be actually used to extract EOG signal. Figure 9 shows a preliminary set up which consist of the pot connected to the A_0 pin of the microcontroller as an input signal.

CONTROL LOGIC STEPS FOR THE PRELIMINARY WORK USING A 10K POTENTIOMETER:

Step 1: Select Analog Pin (A_0) to read the test signal. A potentiometer is used to provide test signal.
Step 2: Design a control pulse for driving the servo motor which is used to move the wheel right to left or vice-versa.

#Loop start:

(a)   Read the value of the potentiometer, by smooth rotation of the potentiometer knob.
(b)   A scaling factor has been design to map the angular rotation 0^0 to 180^0
(c)   Sets the position of the servo according to the scaling factor designed to map the angular rotation 0^0 to 180^0
(d)   A small delay has been introduced to reach the servo at desired position.

Loop end.

Figure 9. Preliminary Set Up

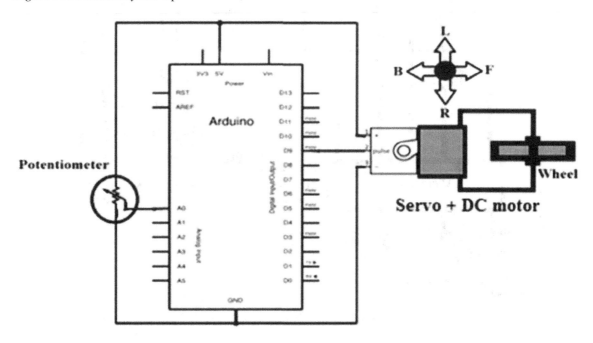

Step 3: Now, to change the position of the servo, manually rotate the potentiometer knob and verify it

To control the forward and backward movement of the wheel, a motor driver is used along with the servo motor. The left and right direction of the wheel is controlled by the servo motor. The experimental set up using the motor driver is shown in Figure 10.

CONTROL LOGIC STEPS FOR THE PRELIMINARY WORK USING SERVO AND DC MOTOR:

A motor driver is used to drive the dc motor in either forward or backward directions (Gao, Lei, Song, Yu & Ge, 2006). If the DIR pin state changes LOW to HIGH and vice-versa, the direction of the DC motor is also changed. The servo motor, attached with the microcontroller pin servo pin, is used to drive the complete dc motor in either left or right directions as per controlled PWM pulses. Instead of real EOG signal in the horizontal movement of the eye, the potentiometer is regulated to verify the left-right direction control. The manual switch is used to move the DC motor in either direction. In future, the movement of the eye in the vertical direction will be used as a speed control of DC motor. The control logic steps using servo and driver are shown in Figure 11.

Figure 10. Experimental Set up Using Motor Driver

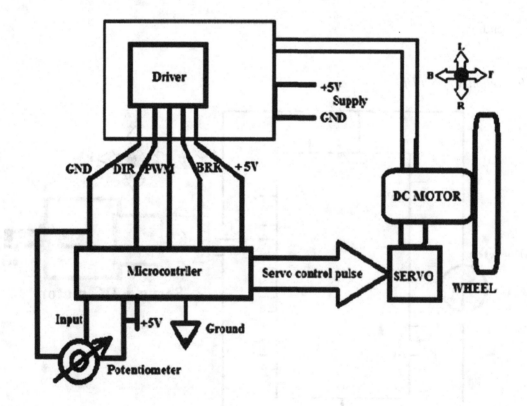

Figure 11. Control logic steps using servo and driver

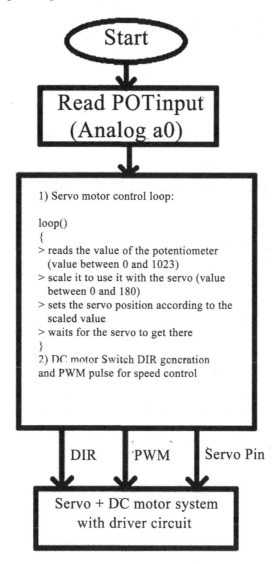

1. **MOTOR DRIVER:** It is a simple TTL/CMOS based interface that can connect directly to the I/O of an MCU. It has a breaking feature that can guarantee immediate halt on the shaft of motors in most high power applications and also includes protection circuitry to avoid any electrical fluctuations affecting the normal operation of an MCU.
2. **MICROCONTROLLER LOGIC:** There are 5 pins available in the motor driver to operate the dc motor which holds the wheel. The servo motor has 3 pins: ground (black), 5V (red) and control pulse (yellow). A digital logic has been implemented using microcontroller kit- Arduino UNO.

In this work, the 5 pins of motor driver are controlled using microcontroller I/Os. Pin 7 of the microcontroller is assigned to reverse the speed of the motor as a switch. Pin 7 is connected to the DIR pin of the driver to reverse the speed of the wheel. The PWM pin and the BRK (Break) pin is kept at active high and active low respectively (given in the datasheet). Ground (GND) must be connected for the protection of the circuits and electric closed path. Pin 11 (LRdir) is a PWM pulse for controlling the servo direction. A potentiometer is used to change the duty ratio of PWM pulse.

PIN ASSIGNMENT

The pin assignment of the microcontroller and system is given in Table 1.

EXPERIMENTAL SET UP USING Ag-AgCl ELECTRODES

The experimental set-up consists of a dc motor, a servo motor, a microcontroller and a muscle sensor. The initial set up consisted of a 10k pot as input which has been replaced by electrodes. The muscle sensor has inbuilt instrumentation amplifier and a filter as shown in Figure 12.

A v3 technology muscle sensor is much preferred over an amplification circuit. Various detailed study resulted in the usage of "advanced technologies v3 muscle sensor" instead of designing an amplification circuit with proper filtration circuit (Wadhwani & Yadav, 2011). A muscle sensor is used

Table 1. Pin assignment of the microcontroller

Microcontroller Pin	Driver circuit and Servo
Pin 7	DIR
Pin 11	ServoPin
5V Pin	PWM, BRK

Figure 12. Experimental set up using Ag- AgCl electrodes along with servo motor

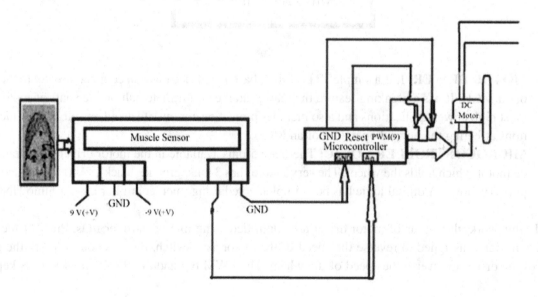

to give the signal extracted using electrodes to the microcontroller. The servo motor, attached with the microcontroller pin Servo Pin, is used to drive the complete dc motor in either left or right directions as per controlled PWM pulses. Figure13 illustrates the operation of the dc motor without a driver. It explains the movement of the wheel which is connected directly to the muscle sensor. Initially for servo motor the input is given through the microcontroller for the left right movement of the wheel but for the dc motor it is directly connected to the muscle sensor without any control logic to check the movement of the wheel. In future instead motor driver will be used for the backward and forward movement of the wheel to reach the objective as expected. The experimental set up using dc motor is shown in Figure 13.

For verification of the output, the signal is displayed using cathode ray oscilloscope. The connection is directly given from the muscle sensor which extracts the EOG signal sensing the potential difference to the CRO as depicted in Figure 14.

The specifications are given in Table 2.

Figure 13. Experimental set up using dc motor

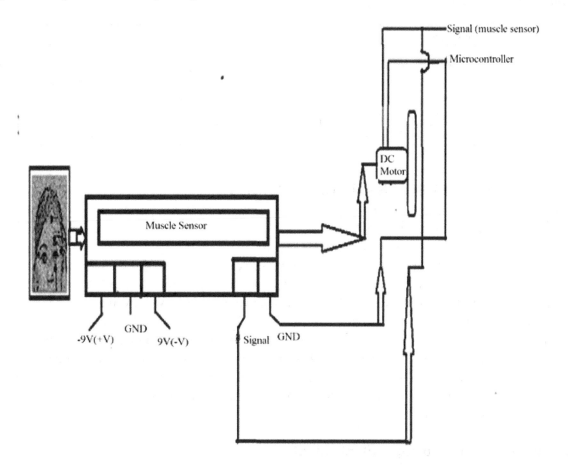

Figure 14. Experimental set up using cathode ray oscilloscope

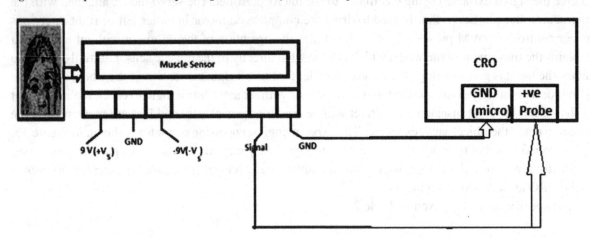

Table 2. Specifications

Name of the components	Quantity	Specifications
Microcontroller kit	1	Arduino Uno
DC motor with wheel	1 set	5V, 1.8W
Servo motor	1	Hitec, HS-55
Muscle Sensor	1	Advanced Technologies
Electrodes	3	Ag-AgCl

EXPERIMENTAL RESULTS AND DISCUSSIONS

1. Results (Using Test Signal)

Initially a 10k potentiometer was used to verify the movement of the servo and DC motor. Analog input voltage between 0 and 5V is converted into 10 bit digital values, i.e. integer values between 0 and 1023 as shown in Figure 15. Thus, by varying the input analog voltage from 0V to 5V, the servo angle can be varied from 0° to 180° as shown in Figure 16.

Initially, suppose the wheel is moving in the forward direction and PWM is fixed at a particular duty ratio as shown in Figure 17. Now if the switch is changed to the opposite direction, the outputs at the pin 10 and 9 are also changed the voltage level as shown in Figure 18. By changing the duty ratio of the PWM pulse using potentiometer, the direction is controlled using servo operation which is shown in Figure 19 and Figure 20.

2. Results (Using Ag-AgCl Electrodes)

For subject 1, as shown in Figure 21, signal is obtained using electrodes, depicting the potential difference created due to the left right movement of the eyes.

Figure 15. Analog to Digital Conversion

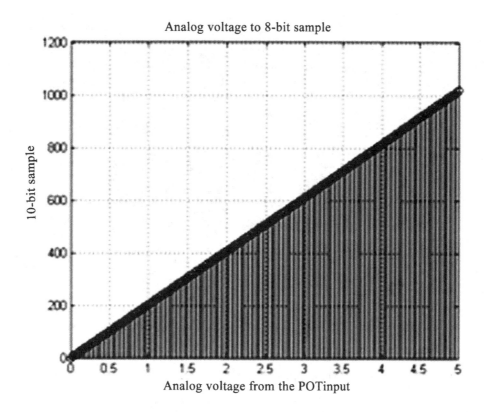

Figure 16. Analog voltage mapping for angular position

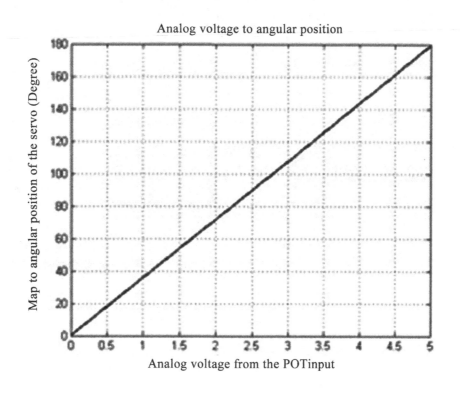

Figure 17. (1) PWM (2) Output A (3) Output B

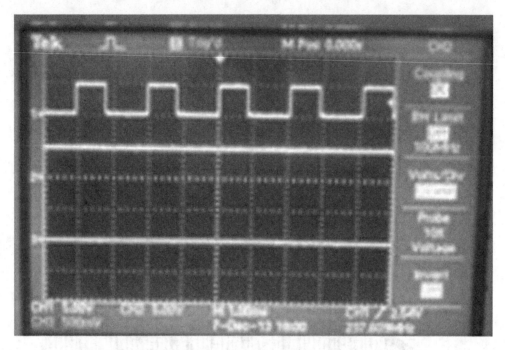

Figure 18. (1) PWM (2) Output A (3) Output B

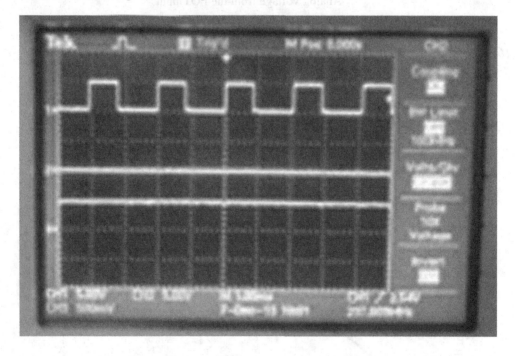

Figure 19. PWM duty change-a

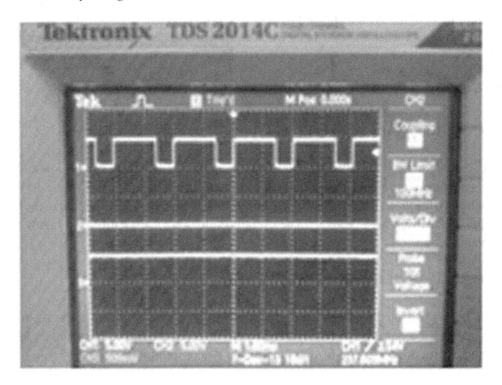

Figure 20. PWM duty change-b

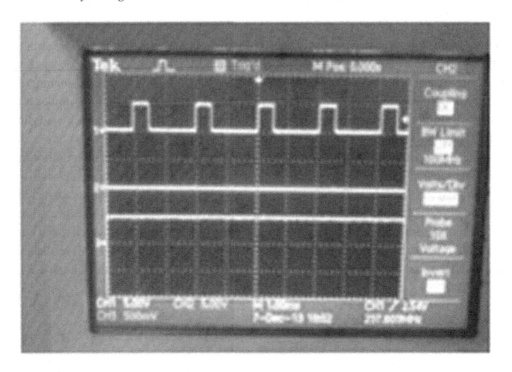

For subject 2, as shown in Figure 22, it has been observed that for a certain instant of time when there is no movement of the eyes, no potential difference is created and a steady waveform is obtained describing the movement when the eyes balls were steady without any left-right or forward-backward movement.

3. DISCUSSIONS

- **USING TEST SIGNAL:**

By changing the duty ratio of the PWM, the left-right direction of the wheel can be controlled. More than 50% of +5V moves the wheel in the right hand direction where less than 50% of the +5V changes the motor in the left direction. The switch enables the wheel in the forward direction and in the backward for active high and active low respectively. The overall results were satisfactory. The Figure 23 shows the experimental set up.

- **USING AG-AGCL ELECTRODES:**

Using the signals extracted from eyes, the system provides satisfactory results. The Ag-AgCl electrodes were placed for acquiring satisfactory signal from the eyes. As shown in Figure 24, the output obtained with an input of 18V is 11.4 V after amplification and filtration.

CONCLUSION

Using test signal, the system provides satisfactory results. Using various experimental results, the miniature version of the system has proved that it can provide satisfactory outcomes under all possible circumstances. Test signal was replaced by Ag-AgCl electrodes to extract the signals from eyes. The observations made from the outcome of the system were as per the expected results. Using various experimental results, the miniature version of the system has proved that it can provide satisfactory outcomes under all possible circumstances. In future a motor driver will be used to control the forward and backward direction of the dc motor using EOG signal to reach the objective as expected.

The chapter has proposed the design of the wheelchair along with its simple but effectual system design mechanism. The accuracy and performance of the system depends greatly on the signal acquisition. The test signal results were satisfactory. Test signal was replaced by Ag-AgCl electrodes to extract the signals from eyes. The observations made from the outcome of the system were as per the expected results. By means of various experimental results, the miniature version of the system has proved that it can provide satisfactory outcomes under all possible circumstances. In future a motor driver will be used to control the forward and backward direction of the dc motor using EOG signal to reach the objective as expected.

Figure 21. Subject 1 potential difference

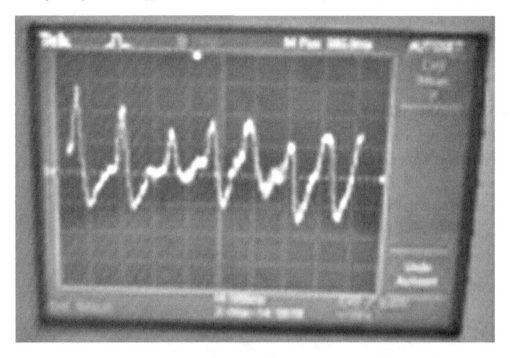

Figure 22. Subject 2 potential difference

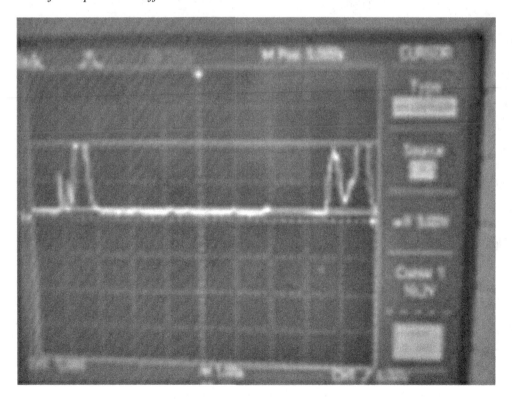

THE VITAL ROLE OF THE WORK

The change in the movement of eyes made a wheelchair- meant to carry a physically challenged person, move to places within the range of the patient. The mechanism designed used motors of very low power. We know,

Torque = weight / wheel radius

Circumference = radius x pi

Rpm = desired speed / circumference

So depending upon the weight of the person and chair required, as well the radius of the wheel, the motor can be selected for the specific torque.

Figure 23. Experimental Set up

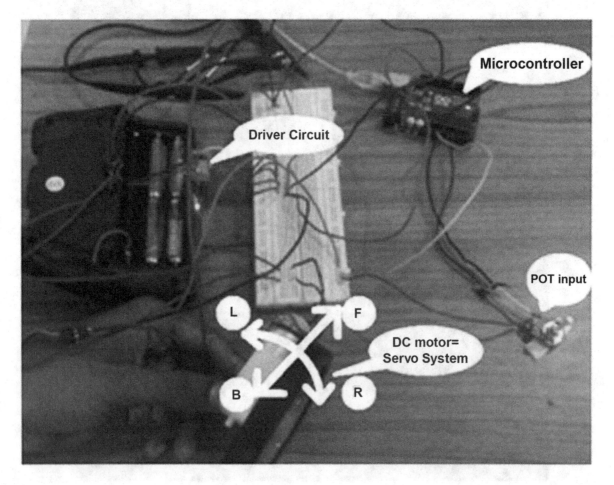

Figure 24. Output waveform

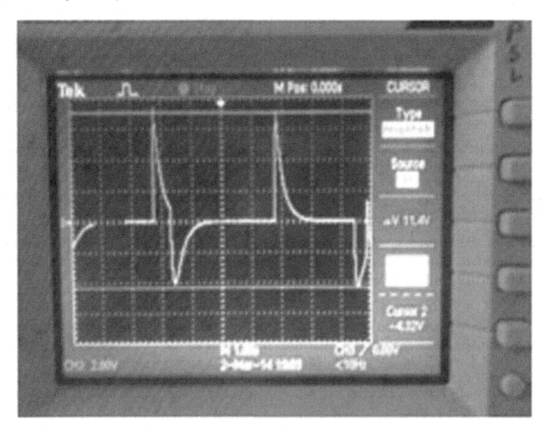

FUTURE PROSPECTS

The research done in the thesis prevailed over some of the awaiting processes. The designed mechanism does play a significant and vital role in the field of medical science. In future a motor driver will be used to control the forward and backward direction of the dc motor using EOG signal to reach the objective as expected. The PWM is used to control the speed of the DC motor. In this work, it is not included due to full fill the main objective of the work and kept it in active HIGH as given in the datasheet. In future, it will be using to control the speed of the DC motor.

ACKNOWLEDGMENT

The authors would like to thank Mriganka Gogoi, Assitant Professor, and Samar Jyoti Saikia, Assistant Professor, of Assam Don Bosco University for their immense help and support in preparing and doing the work.

REFERENCES

Ahsan, R., Ibrahimy, M., & Khalifa, O. O. (2009). EMG Signal Classification for Human Computer Interaction: A Review. *European Journal of Scientific Research, 33*, 480–501.

Borea, R., Boquete, L., Maza, M., Lopez, E., & Lledo, A. G. (2013). EOG Technique to Guide a Wheelchair. Retrieved from https://www.researchgate.net/publication/228965183_EOG_Technique_to_guide_a_wheelchair

Choudhury, S. R., Venkataramanan, S., Nemade, H. B., & Sahambi, J. S. (2005). Design & Development of a novel EOG Biopotential Amplifier. *IJBEM, 7*(1), 271–274.

Desai, Y. S. (2013). Natural Eye Movement & its Application for Paralyzed Patient. *International Journal of Engineering Trends and Technology, 4*(4), 679–686.

Fatourechi, M., Bashashati, A., Ward, R. K., & Birch, G. E. (2007). EMG and EOG artifacts in brain computer interface systems: A survey. *Clinical Neurophysiology, 118*(3), 480–494. doi:10.1016/j.clinph.2006.10.019 PMID:17169606

Gao, Z., Lei, J., Song, Q., Yu, Y., & Ge, Y. (2006). Research on the Surface EMG Signal for Human Body Motion Recognizing Based on Arm Wrestling Robot. *Proceedings of International Conference on Information Acquisition* (pp. 1269-1273). USA

Khan, A., Memon, A., Jat, Y., & Khan, A. (2012). Electrooculogram Based Interactive Robotic Arm Interface for Partially Paralytic Patients. *International Journal of Information Technology and Electrical Engineering, 1*(1), 1–4.

Merino, M., Rivera, O., Gomez, I., Molina, A., & Dorronzoroa, E. (2010). A Method of EOG Signal Processing to Detect the Direction of Eye Movement. *Sensor Device Technologies and Applications*, 100-105. DOI: .10.1109/SENSORDEVICES.2010.25

Noor, N. M., & Ahmad, S. (2013). Analysis of Different Level of EOG Signal from Eye Movement for Wheelchair Control. *International Journal of Biomedical Engineering and Technology, 11*(2), 175–196. doi:10.1504/IJBET.2013.055043

Pradeep, S. G., Govada, A., & Swamy, K. (2013). Eye Controller Human Machine Interface. *International Journal of Advanced Research in Computer and Communication Engineering, 2*(5), 2205–2209.

Rokonuzzaman, M., Ferdous, S. M., Tuhin. R. A., Arman, S. I., Manzar, T. & Hasan, N. (2012). Design of an Autonomous Mobile Wheel Chair for Disabled Using Electrooculogram (EOG) Signals. *Mechatronics: Recent Technological and Scientific Advances*, 41-53, DOI:10.1007/978-3-642-23244-2_6

Wei, L., & Huosheng, H. (2011). Towards Multimodal Human-Machine Interface for Hands-free Control: A survey [Technical Report: CES–510]. HU. University of Essex, United Kingdom.

Wadhwani, A. K., & Yadav, M. (2011). Filtration of ECG signal By Using Various Filter. *International Journal of Modern Engineering Research, 1*(2), 658–661.

Wissel, T., & Palaniappan, R. (2011). Considerations on Strategies to Improve EOG Signal Analysis. *International Journal of Artificial Life Research, 2*(3), 6–21. doi:10.4018/jalr.2011070102

Wu, S. L., Liao, L. D., Lu, S. W., Jiang, W. L., Chen, S. A., & Lin, C. T. (2013). Controlling a Human–Computer Interface System With a Novel Classification Method that Uses Electrooculography Signals. *IEEE Transactions on Bio-Medical Engineering, 60*(8), 2133–2141. doi:10.1109/TBME.2013.2248154 PMID:23446030

Yagi, T. (2010). Eye-gaze interfaces using electro-oculography. *Proceedings of International workshop on eye gaze in intelligent human machine interaction* (pp. 1-5). CA, USA.

Yathunanthan, Y., Chandrasena, L. U. R., Umakanthan, A., Vasuki, V., & Munasinghe, S. R. (2008). Controlling a Wheelchair by Use of EOG Signal. *Proceedings of 4th International Conference on Information and Automation for Sustainability (pp.* 283-288), Doi:10.1109/ICIAFS.2008.4783987

KEY TERMS AND DEFINITIONS

Cornea-Retinal Potential: The corneoretinal potential, the resting potential, which is defined as the difference in potential between the cornea and the posterior pole of the eye.

Electrooculography (EOG/E.O.G.): It is a technique for measuring the corneo-retinal standing potential that exists between the front and the back of the human eye. The resulting signal is called the electrooculogram. Primary applications are inophthalmological diagnosis and in recording eye movements. Unlike the electrorctinogram, the EOG does not measure response to individual visual stimuli.

EOG Signals: The eye is a seat of a steady electric potential field that is quite unrelated to light stimulation. In fact, this field may be detected with the eye in total darkness and/or with the eyes closed. It can be described as a fixed dipole with positive pole at the cornea and negative pole at the retina. The magnitude of this corneoretinal potential is in the range 0.4-1.0 mV. It is not generated by excitable tissue but, rather, is attributed to the higher metabolic rate in the retina. The polarity of this potential difference in the eyes of invertebrates is opposite to that of vertebrates. This potential difference and the rotation of the eye are the basis for a signal measured at a pair of periorbital surface electrodes. The signal is known as the electro-oculogram (EOG). It is useful in the study of eye movement. It is useful in the study of eye movement.

HMI System: Human–machine interface is the part of the machine that handles the human–machine interaction. Membrane switches, rubber keypads and touch screens are examples of that part of the Human Machine Interface which we can see and touch.

Physically Handicapped: A physical disability is a limitation on a person's physical functioning, mobility, dexterity or stamina. Other physical disabilities include impairments which limit other facets of daily living, such as respiratory disorders, blindness and epilepsy.

Posterior Pole of the Eye: The posterior pole is the back of the eye, usually referring to the retina between the optic disc and the macula.

Chapter 4
Driverless Metro Train with Automatic Crowd Control System

Saurav Goswami
Assam Don Bosco University, India

Semina Mehjabin
Assam Don Bosco University, India

Parismita A. Kashyap
Assam Don Bosco University, India

ABSTRACT

This chapter discusses about a prototype of Driverless Train Operation (DTO) mode. In DTO, driving is controlled and monitored automatically, without human assistance. A train attendant can intervene in emergencies. The automatic driving system takes care of the departure, the movement between two stations, and the automatic and precision stopping of the train and opening of the doors. If required, the door is automatically opened again. When passenger volume is high, additional trains are automatically sent into operation straight from the depot at the push of a button. The driverless metro train in our work is basically an embedded system based framework, which is designed to provide solutions for smooth a human machine interface while controlling high speed metro train using automated actuation and regulation mechanisms. In this work, the modeling of the metro train is done in a more precise way using an AVR microcontroller.

INTRODUCTION

In metro systems, automation refers to the process by which responsibility for operation management of the trains is transferred from the driver to the train control system (Punetha, Kumar, & Mehta, 2013). The various grades of automation range from driver-assisting functions for control of the brakes and automatic speed control of a train through automatic and precise stopping of a train in stations, opening and closing a train's doors to possible remote control and fully automatic metro operation without drivers. The Automated operation in a train generally consists of two components, the automatic train

DOI: 10.4018/978-1-4666-8493-5.ch004

control and the automatic train protection systems. Automatic train control reduces the involvement of human in the operation of trains. The automatic train protection system reduces the cause of the alarm in the train. It ensures the safe driving of trains at all times. Automatic Train Control (ATC) systems work within an overall signaling system with interlocking, automatic train supervision, track vacancy detection and communication functions, route setting and train regulation. The ATO and ATC systems work together to maintain a train within a defined tolerance of its time table. The combined system will marginally adjust operating parameters such as the ratio of power to coast when moving and station dwell time, in order to bring the train back to the timetable slot defined for it. There is no driver, and no staff assigned to accompany the train. Automatic Train Protection (ATP) is the system and all equipment responsible for basic safety. It avoids collisions, red signal overrunning and exceeding speed limits by applying brakes automatically. A train protection system continuously monitors its speed, however, (Siemens, 2013) controlling the heavy crowd during the rush in a metro station is indeed a difficult task for a train attendant than a programmed machine. Folks in a station can ignore a person but not a machine.

This paper discusses about a prototype of Driverless Train Operation (DTO) mode. In DTO, driving is controlled and monitored automatically, without human assistance. A train attendant can intervene in emergencies. The automatic driving system takes care of the departure, the movement between two stations, and the automatic and precision stopping of the train and opening of the doors. If required, the door is automatically opened again. When passenger volume is high, additional trains are automatically sent into operation straight from the depot at the push of a button. The Underground Railway for Kolkata solved the problems to some extent. Later on the metros in Delhi, Mumbai and Bangalore came into operation. Such big metropolitan cities suffer daily from over passenger as the number of passengers using a city metro has been increasing steadily per day (Davies, 2000).

The driverless metro train in our work is basically an embedded system based, which is designed to bring out solutions to such types of burning problem and to face new challenges in an innovative and proactive manner. In this work, the modeling of the metro train is done in a more precise way using an AVR microcontroller. We implemented a line follower robot which we considered as a prototype for the metro train. The railway track is shown in black and white lines. The white line signifies the railway line over which the train moves whereas the black ones depict the railway stations. As the train is obstructed by black lines in between it, it halts and after that a buzzer blows and the door of the train opens automatically. As the passengers get inside the train the sensor attached to the door detects the number of passengers entering or leaving the train and displays the exact number of vacancy or seat capacity available in it along with an announcement inside the train. In our model, the information for the passengers is made available using a simple graphical interface and an announcement system designed on Visual Basics (VB). Finally, at the limit of the passengers, the buzzer blows again and the door closes automatically. The train moves out of the station and continue moving till it reach the next station. Following the same procedure the train moves in the same manner across different stations. Programming is done well to operate different parts of the system.

RELATED WORK

In order to establish a safe, reliable railway system, it is important to achieve an integrated system that comprehensively controls individual subsystems throughout the entire process, including design, manufacturing, procurement, installation, testing and commissioning.

The paper speaks about a fully automatic system which is designed in a skillful and improved manner to understand the new technology used in modern metros across continents like Asia, Europe, North America, and more recently South America and the Middle East. The metro train equipped with a microcontroller which function according to some sensors and controls different operations in the train. However, with the same concept, many other Authors & Journals have tried to design models like Artificial Landmark using IR Coding (Wang, Ning, Cao, De Schutter, & Van den Boom, 2011), line follower Robot in Health Care Management Systems (Punetha, Kumar, & Mehta, 2013), Robot for Path Finding & Obstacle Evasion (Bajwa, Nigar, & Arshad, 2010), Double Line Follower Robot (Banuchandar, Kaliraj, Balasubramanian, Deepa, & Thamilarasi, 2012). The work of Voice IC and RF reader in automated place announcement system in metro train gives the idea of the new announcement system.

Some of the related works speaks about an Intelligent Decentralized ATC (ID-ATC) approach based on the Multi-Agent systems theory (Sridhar, 2012), current ATO system and new fuzzy control method (Sandidzadeh & Shamszadeh, 2012). Few works deals with the reduction of time and to provide safety to the road users by reducing the accidents (Khafri & Jahanian, 2012). A documentary study on ATP enlightens the safety of automatic trains over other trains (Nguyen, 2011).

THEORETICAL BACKGROUND

The heart of our system is the AVR microcontroller which can also be named as the main control station of the train. It controls the movement, announcement and different operations of the train. The most of the important components that has built the system are:

1. Microcontroller Atmega32
2. LM324 comparator
3. Motors
4. L293D driver
5. Max232
6. RS232

AVR Microcontroller

The ATmega32 is a low-power CMOS 8-bit microcontroller based on the AVR enhanced RISC architecture. By executing powerful instructions in a single clock cycle, the ATmega32 achieves throughputs approaching 1 MIPS per MHz allowing the system designed to optimize power consumption versus processing speed. The Atmel AVR core combines a rich instruction set with 32 general purpose working registers. All the 32 registers are directly connected to the Arithmetic Logic Unit (ALU), allowing two independent registers to be accessed in one single instruction executed in one clock cycle. The resulting architecture is more code efficient while achieving throughputs up to ten times faster than conventional CISC microcontrollers. The ATmega32 provides the following features like it has 32Kbytes of In-System Programmable Flash Program memory with Read-While-Write capabilities, 1024bytes EEPROM, 2Kbyte SRAM, 32 general purpose I/O lines, 32 general purpose working registers this is

Figure 1. Atmega32A

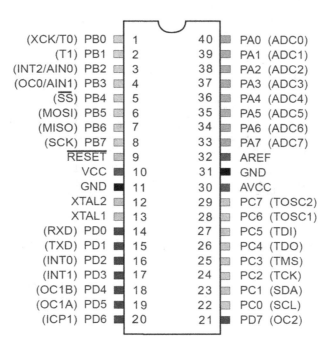

the reason why it is termed as Atmega32, On-chip Debugging support and programming, three flexible Timer/Counters with compare modes, Internal and External Interrupts, a serial programmable USART, a byte oriented Two-wire Serial Interface, an 8-channel, 10-bit ADC with optional differential input stage with programmable gain (TQFP package only), a programmable Watchdog Timer with Internal Oscillator, an SPI serial port, and six software selectable power saving modes. By combining an 8-bit RISC CPU with In-System Self-Programmable Flash on a monolithic chip, the Atmel ATmega32 is a powerful microcontroller that provides a highly-flexible and cost-effective solution to many embedded control applications, (Mazidi, Naimi, & Naimi, 2012). Fig. 1 shows the pin configuration of ATmega32.

LM324 Op-amp

The comparator compares the analogue inputs from sensors with a fixed reference voltage. If this voltage is greater than the reference voltage the comparator outputs a low voltage, and if it is smaller the comparator generates a high voltage that acts as input for the decision-making device (microcontroller). This reference voltage can be adjusted by changing the value of the 10-kilo-ohm preset. (Engineers Garage, n.d). Fig. 2 shows the pin configuration of LM327.

Motors

Gear motors are complete motive force systems consisting of an electric motor and a reduction gear train integrated into one easy-to-mount and configure package. This greatly reduces the complexity and cost of designing and constructing power tools, machines and appliances calling for high torque at relatively

Figure 2. LM324 (Engineers garage, n.d)

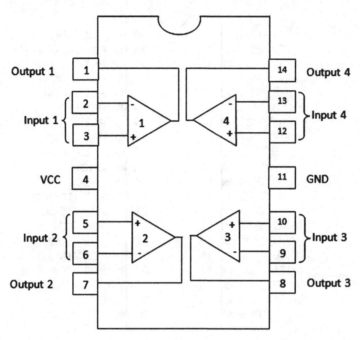

low shaft speed or RPM (here we have used 60 RPM). Gear motors allow the use of economical low-horsepower motors to provide great motive force at low speed such as in lifts, winches, medical tables, jacks and robotics. They can be large enough to lift a building or small enough to drive a tiny clock C.

L293D Driver

The L293D is designed to provide bidirectional drive currents of up to 600-mA at voltages from 4.5 V to 36 V and are quadruple high-current half-H drivers. This device is designed to drive inductive loads such as relays, solenoids, dc and bipolar stepping motors, as well as other high-current/high-voltage loads in positive-supply applications.. Drivers are enabled in pairs, with drivers 1 and 2 enabled by 1,2EN and drivers 3 and 4 enabled by 3,4EN.When a enable input is high, the associated drivers are enabled and their outputs are active and in phase with their inputs. When the enable input is low, those drivers are disabled and their outputs are off and in the high-impedance state. With the proper data inputs, each pair of drivers forms a full-H (or bridge) reversible drive suitable for solenoid or motor. (Punetha, Kumar, & Mehta, 2013). Fig. 3 shows the pin configuration of L293D.

MAX232

The MAX232 is a dual driver/receiver that includes a capacitive voltage generator to supply TIA/EIA-232-F voltage levels from a single 5-V supply. Each receiver converts TIA/EIA-232-F inputs to 5-V TTL/CMOS levels. These receivers have a typical threshold of 1.3 V, a typical hysteresis of 0.5 V, and can accept ±30-V inputs. Each driver converts TTL/CMOS input levels into TIA/EIA-232-F levels. (Society of Robots, n.d). Fig. 4 shows the pin configuration of max232.

Figure 3. Pin configuration of L293D (Mukhopadhyay, 2012)

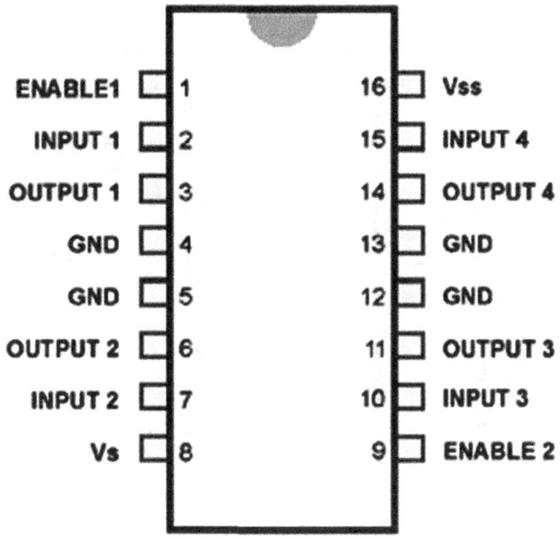

```
           ENABLE1 ☐ 1        16 ☐ Vss
           INPUT 1 ☐ 2        15 ☐ INPUT 4
          OUTPUT 1 ☐ 3        14 ☐ OUTPUT 4
               GND ☐ 4        13 ☐ GND
               GND ☐ 5        12 ☐ GND
          OUTPUT 2 ☐ 6        11 ☐ OUTPUT 3
           INPUT 2 ☐ 7        10 ☐ INPUT 3
                Vs ☐ 8         9 ☐ ENABLE 2
```

RS232

The USB_RS232 cables are a family of USB to RS232 levels serial UART converter cables incorporating FTDI's FT232RQ USB to serial UART interface IC device which handles all the USB signalling and protocols. The cables provide a fast, simple way to connect devices with a RS232 level serial UART interface to USB. The integrated electronics also include the RS232 level shifter plus Tx and Rx LEDs which give a visual indication of traffic on the cable (if transparent USB connector specified).

SYSTEM MODEL

1. Block Diagram:

The system block diagram is designed showing different blocks of components and their inputs and results. The total voltage supply is 5V with a current of 2Amp. The current requirement is high as require by the H-bridge IC to drive four motors with two of them connected in parallel.

Figure 5 shows the system block diagram which consists of various aspects and equipments. For easy understanding and flexibility the entire work is divided into the categories: the train, railway track and the internal system. The train consists of four wheels and a door. The train is simply designed as a line follower robot whose movements are controlled by the geared motors and direction by the IR sensors. The track is designed by drawing white lines in between black so that it will follow the white line and stop whenever it come across a CROSS Sign indicating its arrival at the next station. At this point a buzzer gets horned for a few seconds and train door opens immediately. The passengers will board or leave during that period of time, after which it gets closed and moves toward the next destination. Whenever the sensors detect any black line, the Microcontroller gets high and accordingly output signals are generated to run the motors. But the current supplied by the microcontroller to drive the motor is

Figure 4. Pin configuration of max232 (Society of Robots, n.d.)

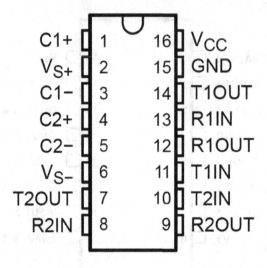

Figure 5. Block Diagram

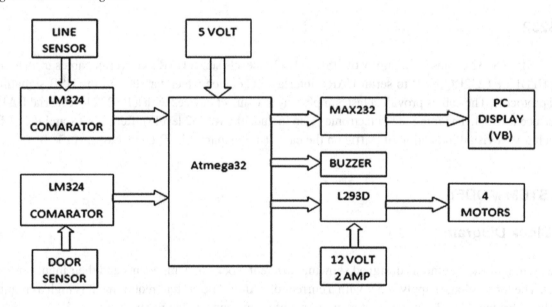

small. Therefore a motor-driver IC is used. It provides sufficient current to drive the motor. Normal DC gear-head motors require current greater than 250mA. ICs like 555 timers, ATmega16 Microcontroller, 74 series ICs cannot supply this amount of current. Directly connecting motors to the output of any of the above IC's, may cause serious damages. For controlling motor in both directions H Bridge (L293D) circuit is used. L293D gave us an output current of 600mA and peak output current of 1.2A per channel. Moreover for protection of circuit from back EMF output diode are included within the L293D. The output supply high is external supply has a wide range from 4.5V to 36V which has made L293D a best choice for DC motor driver. Motor power that is requiring is 12V with 200rpm. The rotation of the DC motor can be control by combinations of A and B in programming assembling. For the track sensing part special light sensors: IR transmitter-receiver along with an op-amp is used. When the sensor is above the white background the light falling on it from the source reflects to the sensor, and when the sensor is above the black background the light from the source doesn't reflect to it as shown in Fig. 6.

The sensor senses the reflected light to give an output, which is fed to the comparator. The comparator compares the analogue inputs from sensors with a fixed reference voltage. If this voltage is greater than the reference voltage the comparator outputs a low voltage, and if it is smaller the comparator generates a high voltage that acts as input for the decision-making device (microcontroller). This reference voltage can be adjusted by changing the value of the 10-kilo-ohm preset. (Goswami, Mehjabin, Basumatary, Goswami, & Kashyap, 2014).

The heart of our project is also the internal system that consists of a buzzer, signal led, PC interface (for voice& display) all of which are interfaced in the Microcontroller. In our model, the information for the passengers is made available using a simple graphical interface designed on Visual Basics (VB). For displaying purposes a PC is interfaced with the microcontroller using serial port communication that displays the maximum seat capacity; seat vacancy and number of passenger boarded and left the train. It also shows the status of current station as well as the next station the train will reach. Simultaneously voice announcements will be made announcing the seat capacity, and for alerting the current and next station. Along with all the above parts there is a small buzzer to indicate the arrival and departure of the train and few signal LEDs indicating the opening and closing of the door.

2. Circuit Description

Figure 7 shows the entire circuit diagram of the system. The strength of the entire circuit is the voltage source which is of 5V and current of 2 Amp. All the components are operated within the threshold of this voltage source. The port A of the microcontroller that is the ADC ports are used as system inputs. The LM324 compare out the sensor inputs to the port A and the L293D drives four motors accordingly which is connected through port C. Max232 establishes the connection between the system and the PC

Figure 6. IR reflecting surface

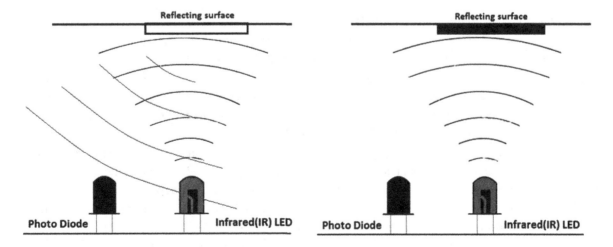

Figure 7. Circuit Diagram

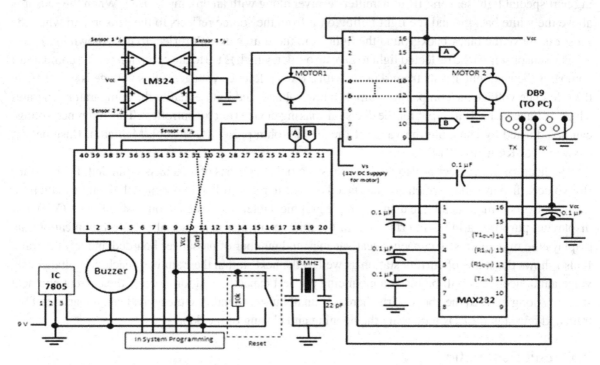

through RS-232 pins. Port B sends a signal out as soon as the train reaches at the station and the buzzer beep for few seconds. A second comparator signal is taken as input by the microcontroller which is the responses of the sensors placed near the door. The working of all the components takes place in fraction of seconds with smart synchronization between the PC and the system.

3. Sensor Description

The working of the model is directly dependent upon the response of the sensors that are used throughout the project. It can also be called as a sensor based model. From the rolling of the motors to the controlling of the crowd every bit of work is confide in sensor.

A **sensor** is a device that measures a physical and sensible quantity and converts it into a signal which can be read by an observer or by an electronic instrument. It is a device, which responds to an input quantity by generating a functionally related output usually in the form of an electrical or optical signal. A sensor's sensitivity indicates how much the sensor's output changes when the measured quantity changes. Ideal sensors are designed to be linear to some simple mathematical function of the measurement, typically logarithmic. The output of such a sensor is an analog signal and linearly proportional to the value or simple function of the measured property. The sensitivity is then defined as the ratio between output signal and measured property. For an analog sensor signal to be processed, or used in digital equipment, it needs to be converted to a digital signal, using an analog-to-digital converter.

Our eyes are detectors which are designed to detect visible light waves (or visible radiation). Infrared radiation is the portion of electromagnetic spectrum that is invisible to human eyes. Infrared radiation lies between the visible and microwave portions of the electromagnetic spectrum. Infrared waves have wavelengths longer than visible and shorter than microwaves, and have frequencies which are lower than visible and higher than microwaves. Infrared is broken into three categories: near, mid and far-infrared. Near-infrared refers to the part of the infrared spectrum that is closest to visible light and far-infrared refers to the part that is closer to the microwave region. Mid-infrared is the region between these two. The region roughly from 0.75μm to 1000 μm is the infrared region.

Figure 8. shows an IR transmission and reception system. An infrared sensor or IR sensor is an electronic device that emits and/or detects infrared radiation in order to sense some aspect of its surroundings. Infrared sensors can measure the heat of an object, as well as detect motion.

IR Sensors work by using a specific light sensor to detect a select light wavelength in the Infra-Red (IR) spectrum. Various types of detectors are used in IR sensors. Important specifications of detectors are Photosensitivity or Responsivity. Higher is the Responsivity the better is the output current. Here we have used a p-i-n photo detector to detect the output of an infrared source. The transmission medium is the atmosphere. Due to which the impact of sun rays during the day time highly affect the output response of the photo detector.

IR Sensor comprises of IR transmitter and IR receiver. Without an efficient IR receiver, an IR sensor is incomplete. IR transmitters are basically sources of light characterized by high amount of spontaneous emission of photons as current passes across the p-n junction diode. A sufficient amount of light generated from the IR transmitter falls on the detecting surface of the photo detector lead to the increase of electric field across the junction. (Roman Osorio, Romero, Mario Peña, & Juárez, 2006).

IR transmitter may be LED, colored LED, IR LED and IR receiver is a photo detector or a photo diode. Photo detectors are classified according to their responsivity and surface area of detection.

The circuit in Fig. 9 is a low cost and low range infrared object detection module that you can be made at home easily by using IR sensors. We have used a photodiode and IR LED to make this simple circuit.

The IR led keeps transmitting IR infrared rays up to some range. When some object comes in the IR infrared range, the IR waves hits the object and comes back at some angle, photo diode detects the IR rays and generates a corresponding voltage thereby working as a sensor.

The point is that it reflects all colors except black color objects. This is due to absorption of light by the black color. So, if the IR rays falls upon any black object, the rays won't gets reflected back thus absorption takes place by the black object and the photo detector will not be able to detect any obstacle in front of it.

Track Sensor

This activation is done via different Programming for different inputs. The four positions of the four IR sensor pairs are placed as shown in the Fig. 10.

As long as the front and the central sensors are detecting white lines, the robot will move in the forward direction. Similarly for a left turn, only the 1st and fourth sensor will be above the white lines while

Figure 8. IR transmission and reception

Figure 9. Sensor Circuit

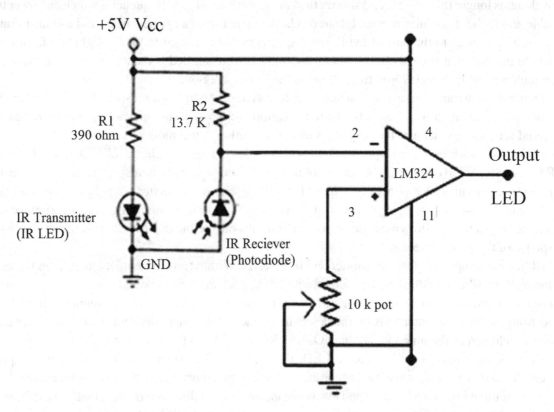

Figure 10. Line sensors beneath the train

the 2nd and third will receive white lines. For the right turn, 3rd and 4th will be pushed towards the white line and the 2nd and 1st towards black line. For the train to come to a halt, we have designed a junction of all 4 white lines such that each Sensor will be upon a white line. At this time the door sensors will start operating.

Door Sensor

Two sensors are placed near the door as well for counting the number of passengers boarding & leaving the train. Passengers leaving the train in a particular station are sensed by the inner sensors while those boarding the train are sensed by outer sensors. Here we used small thermocol papers to indicate the passengers which we handled manually to check the system operation. Every time a person enters the train, the 1st Sensor gets cut and microcontroller counts and adds one with the current value of the number of passengers that have entered inside the train. Similarly, when a person tries to leave from inside, it cuts the second sensor and a value is decrement, with the increase in seat capacity. In this way until it reaches up to the maximum limitation, the process continues to work properly. Thereafter a delay is provided right after which the door gets locked and no more entry/exit can be made. Fig. 11 shows the door sensors designed for this purpose.

4. Flow Chart

Figure 12 shows the flow chart of the entire system.

Figure 11. Door sensors of our robot

Figure 12. Flow Chart of the system

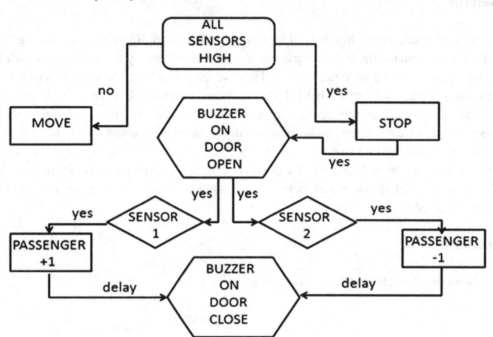

RESULTS AND DISCUSSIONS

This section describes the various experimental results obtained in the work. The results obtained can be classified into different sections for understanding the display part as well as the announcement part. The responses of the various sensors are also explained here.

The display section comprises of a Mini Laptop placed at the stack of the robot for easy portability and smooth momentum. The serial communication holds the connection between the robot and the PC which is done through RS232 serial interfacing with the help serial to USB cable connected to one of the USB port of the Laptop.

A Visual Basic form is being designed showing the image of three main functions of the system. These are following three functions are:

1. Counter working as a crowd control system
2. Information of the current station and the succeeding one.
3. Speech generation for regular announcements.

Counter Working as a Crowd Management System

A **counter** counts the number of times a particular event or process has occurred. Regarding our system, the event is the movement of the passengers through the train door. When the movement is sensed by the sensor immediately the counter goes high. This quick response of the sensor led to the increase of the values of number of passengers boarded or left the train by one. Meanwhile depending up the action of the passenger the seat vacancy also changes.

There is a particular limit to which passengers are allowed to board the train beyond its maximum capacity the counter stops. It depends entirely on the maximum seat capacity allotted during the process. This is done to avoid congestion inside the train and to provide a crowd free journey, so that the people are comfortable in their respective seats during the whole journey.

Information of the Current Station and the Succeeding One

Mostly the stations have the facility to provide information about the current location of the train and sometimes the next location as well. This whole concept is put inside the running train and is displayed before the passengers as soon as the train is about to reach a particular station. Moreover, there is also some voice announcements made simultaneously in case if a passenger is poor in vision.

The data regarding the station name and next location to be reached is programmed according to the sequence order of the stations. For a particular station, there are sequence numbers following which the name and its number is shown in the form. The data base for a particular city can be changed during coding if the locations are changed randomly.

Voice Generation for Regular Announcements

Speech and announcements are regularly observed in almost every big station in India. Broadcasting of new updates or new time schedule of trains is frequent over time. Here we are trying to help the people inside as well as outside the train to see and listen to the announcements. A person lack of good vision can depend upon this facility that we are trying to provide. These are same as the data displayed in the screen. Few extra speeches are added to make the announcement more interesting.

In the main VB form an object is created as SAPI which works as a train radio speaker and forces the Laptop system voice to speak out the text stated under the speaker. The text written are like station name, passenger boarded or left, seat vacancy, door opening or closing, and some other commercial speeches. Theoretically this text is converted into speech by SAPI and is spoken by the system. The system is trained to read only English language. The rate of the speech can be varied to give a clear recognizable sound.

In order to setup connection of the form with the system, initially some settings need to be done to function properly without any unauthorized error. There are few steps as explained below and shown in Fig. 13.

1. Open the exe file of the form in the main window of the desktop.
2. Before connecting close any other application running in the window screen to avoid lagging during the process.
3. Now, go to the serial communication group of the form. Check the port to which the serial to USB cable is connected.(This can be found by Right click-→My computer-→Manage→Device Management→Ports)
4. Another important option that allows choosing the Baud Rate (speed of the processor) is "Baud". Write the correct baud rate of the microcontroller you are using in the VB code.
5. After the baud rate is selected the settings are done. Now you can connect to your microcontroller directly. The connections will be established automatically.

Figure 13. Serial Communication establishment

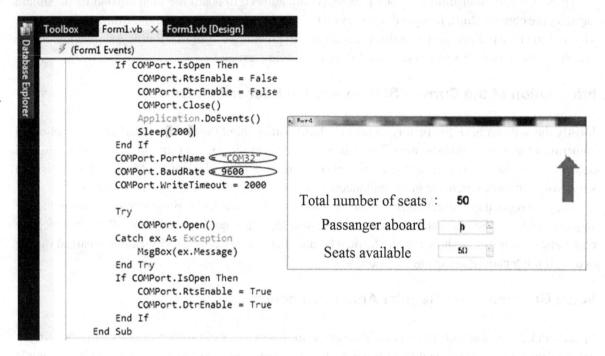

6. The connection is established between the PC and the system. The data can be transferred from any of the device.

7. After a successful data transmission/reception the serial port can be disconnected as soon as we stop debugging the VB program or closing down the application.

8. Disconnection can also be done during the ongoing transportation of data in case of emergency only but it there may be some error due to continuous ongoing data transmission between PC and the system.

Figure 14 shows the main graphical display when the train moves in the forward direction. The green arrow shown at the right corner of the display keeps on changing its pointer as the train moves in different directions. The arrow points toward right indicating right movement and left for left movement of the train. Thus, if the train turns, it is known to the passengers inside it by these symbols.

The graphical display also indicates the number of passengers boarded or left a particular station, the current station, and the seat vacancy. Fig.15 and 16 clearly indicates these. The values changes as a person enter or leave the train at each station. The values are positive integers that vary with the instant response of the microcontroller except for the "maximum capacity" which is fixed throughout the process. In the prototype discussed, the maximum seat capacity is assumed to be fifty.

The display of momentary action of the train door is programmed to a text label. The text is labeled as "Door open" or "Door close" according to the present action of the door as shown in Fig. 17 and 18.

Station name and its station number is arranged and presented in the form in a sequencing order. Altogether there are 10 stations naming important places and towns across the city. As the train moves to the next station the name and number changes giving the passengers inside the train the information

Figure 14. Direction of movement

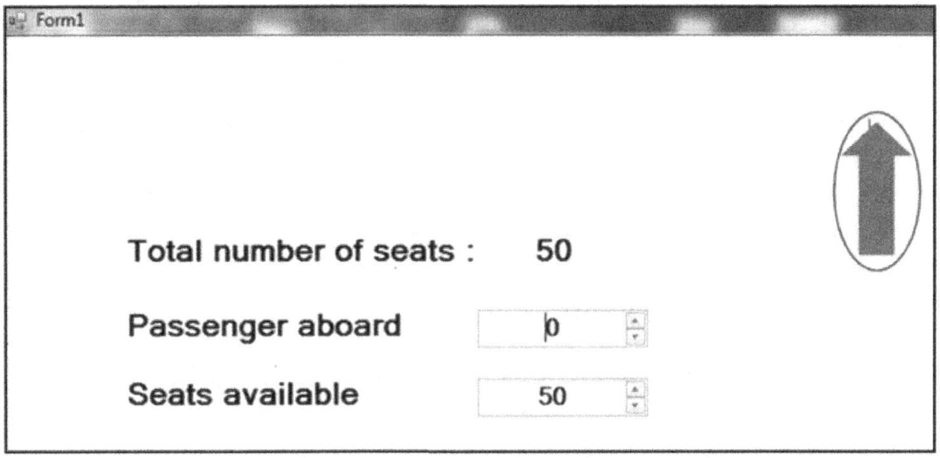

Figure 15. Numeric-up-down buttons

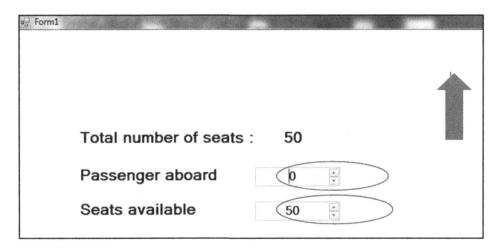

Figure 16. Home Menu Contents

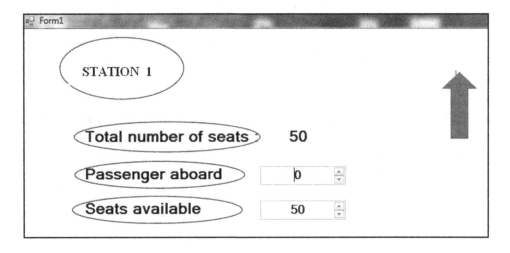

Figure 17. Door opens

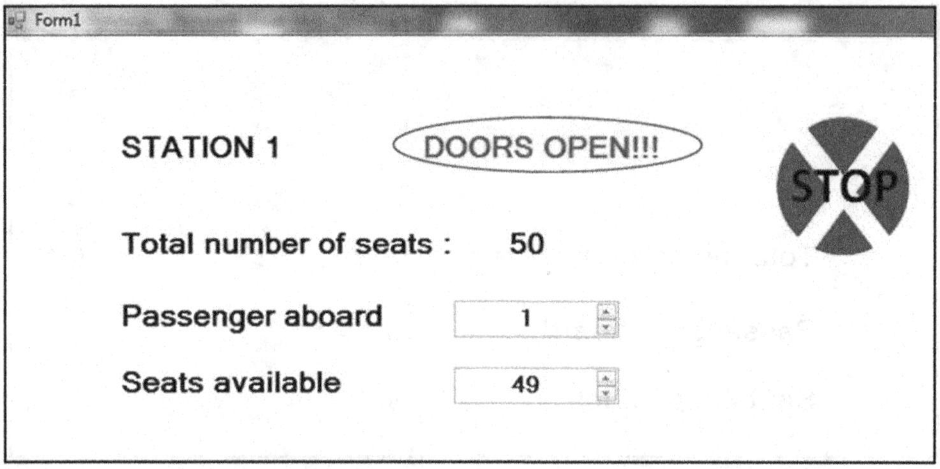

Figure 18. Door closes

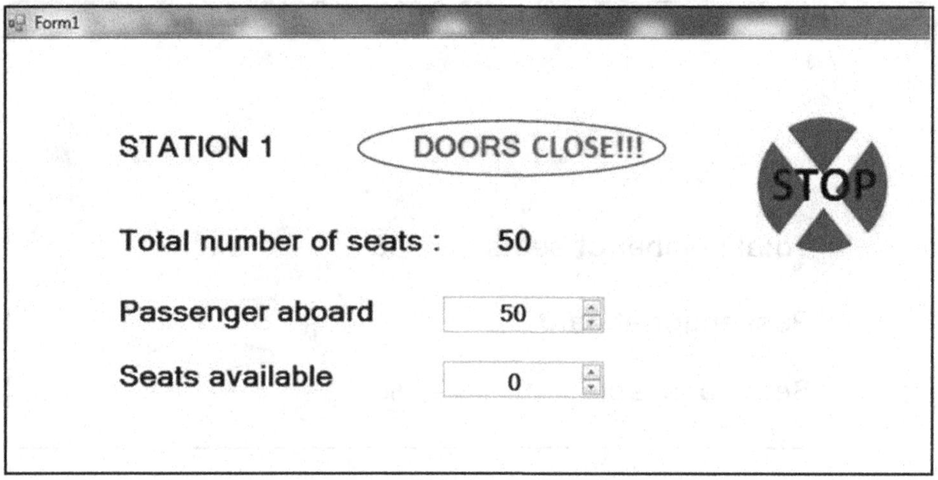

of the present station and the next station as well. Before the change occurs the pre-programmed voice speaks out the same information displayed at the screen.

In a real time system the graphical display is assumed to be present both inside and outside the train.

Sensor Responses

The door sensor operations are affected by a number of factors depending upon which a variety of sensor working ranges are calculated. Table 1. describes the length of detection and different values of 10k potentiometer for maximum and minimum range, experimented during different intervals of time.

From Table 1. It can be seen that the potentiometer values are same for both passengers leaving and boarding the train, but the distances of detection vary slightly.

Table 1. Sensitivity of door sensors

Range	Passenger Boarding (Pot value)	Distance of detection	Passenger leaving(pot value)	Distance of detection	Duration
Maximum	4k	2.5cm	4k	2.5	Day
Maximum	4.4k	6cm	4.4k	4.9cm	Night
Minimum	4.6k	1.8cm	4.5k	1.6cm	Night

The system deploys minimum manpower from automatic opening of doors to automatic voice announcements. It is fascinated with lower expenditure for staff (staff swallows a significant part of the costs of running a transport system). However, service and security personnel are common in automated systems. Thus, it is with very limited human intervention. It is a cost efficient product running with low power of 5v and 2amp current. Despite of other psychological concerns, driverless metros are safer than traditional ones.

FUTURE WORK

The prototype is just a small concept from a vast chapter of thousands of research works on mass rapid transport systems. Discovering flaws and errors over the mass system, led us put up steps to experiment with our system in a more aggressive manner .Some of the future scopes which can be enhanced for real time operation are:

i.   An obstacle detector which can be implemented by some more modifications to avoid collisions or sudden accidents.
ii.   For parallel movements of incoming and outgoing passengers, RFID tags will be used.
iii. To overcome simultaneous entry or exit through the door during heavy rush at the station faster responsive sensors can be used.
iv.   Emergency braking system can be implemented for urgent situations.

CONCLUSION

The concept of "**Driverless Metro Train with Automatic Crowd Management System**" is a model that has been tested to work efficiently to limit the crowd inside a metro train. The work will try to maintain high levels of availability and punctuality above the target levels, offering reliable and safe service to its users, and winning high praise and trust from the client. The expectation of introduction of door sensors and voice announcements will at least reduce the rush inside the station which will greatly contribute the modern technologies in each relevant field and the technological development of the railway industry by providing trains with feasibility to win higher service quality and faster speed. The results obtained are in tune to the expected outcomes which establishes the effectiveness of the entire system.

REFERENCES

Bajwa, I. S., Nigar, N., & Arshad, M. J. (2010). An Autonomous Robot Framework for Path Finding and Obstacle Evasion. *International Journal of Computer Science and Telecommunications*, *1*(1), 1–6.

Banuchandar, J., Kaliraj, V., Balasubramanian, P., Deepa, S., & Thamilarasi, N. (2012). Automated Unmanned Railway Level Crossing System. *International Journal of Modern Engineering Research*, *2*(1), 458–463.

Dewangan, A. K., Gupta, M., & Patel, P. (2012). Automation of Railway Gate Control Using Microcontroller. *International Journal of Engineering Research & Technology*, *1*(3), 1–8.

Davies, D. (2000). Automatic Train Protection for the Railway Network in Britain.

Engineers Garage. (n. d). Retrieved from http://www.engineersgarage.com/electronic-components/lm324n-datasheet

Goswami, S., Mehjabin, S., Basumatary, R., Goswami, S. R., & Kashyap, P. A. (2014). Fully Automatic Crowd Control System in Metro Train. *Proceedings of National Conference on Emerging Global Trends in Engineering & Technology*. Guwahati: Assam. Don Bosco University.

Khafri, Y. Z., & Jahanian, A. (2012). Improved Line Tracking System for Autonomous Navigation of High-Speed Vehicle. *International Journal of Robotics and Automation*, *1*(3), 163–174.

Mazidi, M. A., Naimi, S., & Naimi, S. (2012). *AVR Microcontroller and embedded system: Using C and Assembly Language*. USA: Pearson Custom Electronics Technology.

Mahdi, A. S., Al-Zuhairi. (2013). Automatic Railway Gate and Crossing Control based Sensors & Microcontroller. *International Journal of Computer Trends and Technology*, *4*(7), 2135–2140.

Mukhopadhyay, A. (2012). *Control a DC Motor using Arduino and l293d chip*. Retrieved from http://obliblog.wordpress.com/2012/05/30/control-motor-arduino-l293d-chip

Nguyen, H. N. (2011). *Automatic Train Control* [PDF document]. Retrieved from [REMOVED HYPERLINK FIELD]http://www.cs.swan.ac.uk/~csmarkus/.../Slides/Railway_Seminar_Talk6.pdf

Punetha, D., Kumar, N., & Mehta, V. (2013). Development and Applications of Line Following Robot Based Health Care Management System. *International Journal of Advanced Research in Computer Engineering & Technology*, *2*(8), 2446–2450.

ATMEGA32A-PU Atmel 8 Bit 32K AVR Microcontroller. (n. d.). *Protostack.com*. Retrieved from http://www.protostack.com/microcontrollers/atmega32a-pu-atmel-8-bit-32k-avr-microcontroller

Román Osorio, C., Romero, J. A., Mario Peña, C., & Juárez, I. L. (2006). Intelligent Line Follower Mini-Robot System. *International Journal of Computers, Communications & Control*, *1*(2), 73–83.

Sandidzadeh, M. A., & Shamszadeh, B. (2012). Improvement of Automatic Train Operation Using Enhanced Predictive Fuzzy Control Method. INTECH Open Access Publisher.

Rail Automation in Mass Transit Systems. (2013). Seimens. Munich: Media relations.

Siahvashi, A., & Moaveni, B. (2010). Automatic Train Control based on the Multi-Agent Control of Cooperative Systems. TJMCS, 1(4), 247-257.

Society of Robots. (n. d). Retrieved from http://www.societyofrobots.com/electronics_negative_voltages.shtml

Sridhar, V. (2012). Automated System Design For Metro Train. *International Journal on Computer Science and Engineering*, *1*(1), 30–41.

Wang, Y., Ning, B., Cao, F., De Schutter, B., & Van den Boom, T. J. J. (2011). A Survey on Optimal Trajectory Planning for Train Operations. *Proceedings of International Conference on Service Operations, Logistics, and Informatics (SOLI)*. Beijing. IEEE. doi:10.1109/SOLI.2011.5986629

Chapter 5

Design of a Power Aware Systolic Array based Support Vector Machine Classifier

Bhaswati Mandal
Gauhati University, India

Manash Pratim Sarma
Gauhati University, India

Kandarpa Kumar Sarma
Gauhati University, India

ABSTRACT

This chapter presents a method for generating binary and multiclass Support Vector Machine (SVM) classifier with multiplierless kernel function. This design provides reduced power, area and reduced cost due to the use of multiplierless kernel operation. Binary SVM classifier classifies two groups of linearly or nonlinearly separable data while the multiclass classification provides classification of three non-linearly separable data. Here, at first SVM classifier is trained for different classification problems and then the extracted training parameters are used in the testing phase of the same. The dataflow from all the processing elements (PEs) are parallely supported by systolic array. This systolic array architecture provides faster processing of the whole system design.

INTRODUCTION

Methods for efficiently classifying two or more groups of data are the area of interest for many researchers and scholars. Till date various solutions to classification problem have been proposed to classify two or more groups of data, each method carrying their own efficiency and deficiency. One of the significant methods was introduced in 1936 by R.A. Fisher which is a simple method to classify two or more groups of data known as Linear Discriminant Analysis (LDA). The main reason to choose LDA could be its Analytical and computational simplicity and low error rates. But there is a lack of a variety of

DOI: 10.4018/978-1-4666-8493-5.ch005

measurable continuous variables for relatively large data samples. This reduces the popularity of LDA. Another most significant method for classification was introduced in 1943 by Warren McCulloch and Walter Pitts was Artificial Neural Network (ANN). Because of its nature that a user can easily train the network with any dynamic and nonlinear examples and can classify any sets of data even without personal knowledge about the behavior of solved problem, it was quite popular during the period 1940-1990 before SVM was introduced. The newest classification method proposed is SVM which was introduced by Cortes and Vapnik in 1992. It is based on the concept of decision planes (Li, Zhu & Ogihara, 2006). This plane provides decision boundaries that help to discriminate classes with higher accuracies than the other known statistical classifier (Li, Zhu & Ogihara, 2006), (Preman & Suwapura, 1991). Though most SVM implementation based on software provides acceptable margins of accuracy, real time performance of such classifiers has always been an area of concern. Yet SVM classifiers have been preferred. This is because of the fact that unlike ANN, SVMs do not suffer from multiple local minima problems. Further, SVMs provide solutions to classification problems which are global and unique. Also, SVMs provide simple geometric implementation to class discriminations and provide sparse solution (Li, Zhu & Ogihara, 2006), (Preman & Suwapura, 1991). Moreover, unlike ANNs, SVMs have a computational complexity that doesn't depend upon the curse of dimensionality. ANNs are based on empirical risk minimization, while SVMs depend on structural risk minimization (Preman & Suwapura, 1991). As reported by open literature, existing general-purpose SVM architectures do not scale well in terms of required hardware resources, complexity, data transfer (wiring) and memory management. This is primarily because of two important constraints. First, the number of support vectors (SVs) and next, their dimensionality. An SVM with a small number of SVs, requires only a few computational modules. But several applications require a large number of high dimensional SVs.

The key consideration involved is related to reduction of the power requirement of the processor. Power reduction has become a crucial factor now days. Because as the power decreases, battery life as well as the life of whole hardware design increases. The vector product for the kernel module SVM consumes most of the time. This work presents a method for generating binary and multiclass SVM classifier with multiplierless kernel function. This design provides reduced power, area and reduced cost due to the use of multiplierless kernel operation. Binary SVM classifier classifies two groups of linearly or nonlinearly separable data while the multiclass classification provides classification of three linearly or nonlinearly separable data. Here, at first SVM classifier is trained for different classification problems and then the extracted training parameters are used in the testing phase of the same. The dataflow from all the processing elements (PEs) is parallely supported by systolic array. This systolic array architecture provides faster processing of the whole system design.

BACKGROUND

In the field of image processing, computer vision, bio-informatics, classification of data is an area of study for many researchers and scholars from the beginning. SVMs are dynamic and powerful learning methods which provide excellent generalization performance for a wide range of regression and classification problem. Previous software implementations of SVM have reported high classification accuracy. But software designs can't meet the real time requirements because these designs can't take the advantage of parallelism inherent in the SVM algorithm. Thus, the hardware implementation of SVM can increase total simulation time and synthesis time.

During the period of global warming, saving of power is the prime concern of the human society. From the low level system to the high level complex hardware design power reduction has become a major factor. Power consumption is directly related to the cost of design. As power consumption is more, heat production is also more which also raises the cooling requirement. Again as heat increased, the density of hardware design must be reduced, which raises the space requirement along with its associate cost. Reducing power can enhance the performance of a design and life period of a battery. Though power related costs may not be a major issue, but the power itself is a limited source. So, managing power requirement have become the need of today. In the field of classification efficient utilization of power is one of the major concerns. So, in this work we mainly concern about decreasing hardware complexity and reduction of power.

Literature Review

Designing different classifiers on systolic array came into practice since last 1980. Some of these implementations are discussed here:

The authors address the problem of finding efficient systolic arrays for vector and matrix multiplications in (Urquahart & Wood, 1984). Here, at first the authors discussed about the existing systolic arrays, both at the word and bit levels, then described some efficient arrays in the context of signal processing. Finally, three applications are outlined, namely, a convolver, an IIR filter and a linear classifier. Lastly, the authors came to a conclusion that the most convenient way of improving efficiency is to return to the idea of keeping coefficients static on the array. In (Canny, Whirter & Wood, 1984), a bit level systolic array for computing the convolution operation is described. The circuit proposed here is highly regular and ideally suited to VLSI chip design. It is also optimized in the sense that all the cells contribute to the computation on each clock cycle. This makes the array almost four times more efficient than the one which were previously described. The authors in (Arnaud, 1986) discuss how the architecture of bit level systolic array circuits which includes a single-bit coefficient correlator and a multi bit convolver can be modified to incorporate unidirectional data flow. This feature that is unidirectional data flow has some important advantages in terms of chip cascadability, fault tolerance and possible wafer-scale integration. In (Wang, Wci & Cheii, 1986), a word-level systolic array with 100% efficiency is described for the linear discriminant function classifier. When compared with two previous word-level linear classifier arrays, it not only saves the number of weighted vectors used in the inner product step cells, but also simplifies the chip's I/O design. In (Klass, 1991), a unidirectional flow systolic array with 100% efficiency is described for the linear discriminant classifier. The authors applied a two-stage transformation method to the previous reported contra flow array. In the first stage, the contra flow design is transformed into an equivalent design with unidirectional flow. In the second stage, a retiming of input data sequences is performed which is combined with further refinements in the clocking scheme which significantly increases the computation efficiency of the systolic array. The authors in (Shen and Oruc, 1990) present systolic mapping techniques that exploit the parallelism inherent in discrete Fourier transforms. It is established that, for an M dimensional signal, parallel executions of such transforms are closely related to mappings of an $(M+1)$ dimensional finite vector space into itself. Three examples of such parallel schemes are then described for the discrete Fourier transform of a two-dimensional finite extent sequence of size $N1 \times N2$. The first is a linear array of $N1 + N2 - 1$ processors and takes $O(N1N2)$ steps. The second is an $N1 \times N2$ rectangular array of processors and takes $O(N1 + N2)$ steps, and the third is a hexagonal array which uses $N1N2 + (N2-1)(N1+N2-1)$ processors and takes $O(N1+N2)$ steps. Each of these achieves asymptotically optimal speed up over a single processor implementation, even though the linear array takes $O(N2)$ time with $O(N)$ processors, and the other two take $O(N)$ time with $O(N2)$ processors. It should be noted that these time complexities can be reduced. This requires a butterfly network which is very costly to lay out in most circuit technologies including VLSI. The systolic implementations of multidimensional DFT described in this paper provides a good compromise between speed and cost. Here, systolic architectures for the implementation of ANN algorithms in custom VLSI and FPGA platforms is described in (Meher, 2010). The key techniques used for the design of basic systolic building blocks of ANN algorithms are discussed in detail. Moreover, the mapping of fully-connected unconstrained ANN, as well as, multilayer ANN algorithm into fully-pipelined systolic architecture is described with generalized dependence graph formulation. A mesh systolic array using GCN (giga connection), for a fast simulation of ANNs is presented in (Hiraiwa, Fujita & Arisawa, 1990). The PE of the GCN is composed of the RISC processor which have a large scale local memory, and high bandwidth first-in first-out devices. The mapping algorithm of the ANN onto the GCN is discussed and the multilayer feed forward network and Kohenen feature map are mapped onto the GCN by using this algorithm. Another parallelism that can be used for a stochastic ANN like the Boltzmann machine is also discussed. In (Khan & Nam, 1991), a novel design of neural networks using 2-dimensional systolic array is proposed. Two new techniques are discussed in the design, namely, 2-dimensional pipelining and multi rate processing (2 level clocking). This scheme of passing weights also saves area significantly since local storage area for the weights can be reduced. During the last few years, hardware designing of SVM has received lots of interest. Many designs have been developed in this field. Yet there are lot more refinement to be done. A one-layer recurrent neural network for SVM learning in pattern classification and regression is presented in (Cortes & Vapnik, 1995). The SVM learning problem is first converted into an equivalent formulation, and then a one-layer recurrent neural network for SVM learning is proposed. The proposed neural network is guaranteed to obtain the optimal solution of support vector classification and regression. Compared with the existing two-layer neural network for the SVM classification, the proposed neural network has allowed complexity for implementation. In (Reyna, Esteve, Houzet & Albenge, 2000), the authors utilize the uniformity behavior of the SVM decision function in the integrated vision system. The main module used in this system is SVM classifier. The authors proposed a parallel implementation on an FPGA programmed with VHDL for the reduction of the computation time. The authors in (Anguita, Boni & Ridella, 2003) proposed an SVM learning algorithm and elaborate its implementation on a field programmable gate array (FPGA). In (Genov & Cauwenberghs, 2003), the authors present a system for SVM in silicon which they named Kerneltron. This Kerneltron offers a 100- 10000 improvement in computation efficiency over the previous reported designs on digital signal processors. This high level of efficiency is obtained from the very large scale integration (VLSI). Architecture with massively parallel kernel computation. They used a two dimensional (2D) analog array of cells and input output vector components crossing in perpendicular directions altering from one stage to the next. In (Khan, Amold & Pottenger, 2005), the authors used Logarithmic Number System (LNS) system in digital SVM classifier which saves a considerable amount of hardware utilization with no significant loss of hardware utilization with no significant loss of accuracy in classification process. The author uses the LNS method because this utilizes the property of logarithmic compression for numerical operation. SVM kernels are basically vector multiplication and exponential operations which significantly improve the performance of kernel operations. A parallel architecture for

SVM to be implemented on Xilinx FPGA is presented in (Biasi, Boni & Zorat, 2005). Here, they used thousands of complex classification patterns from the high energy physics to obtain the results and also compared the performance of the architecture with the simpler sequential architecture. In (Cadambi, Durdanovic, Jakkula, Sankardass, Casatto, Chakradhar & Graf, 2009), the authors present a massively parallel FPGA based coprocessor. To take the advantage of large amount of parallelism in data of this application, both SVM training and classification is implemented in this coprocessor. In (Kyrkou & Theocharides, 2010), the authors introduce a design called Systolic Chain of Processing Elements (SCOPE) which was the first attempt of realization of generic systolic array in SVM for object detection and describes its embedded audio and video application. This design provides efficient memory management, reduced complexity and efficient data transfer mechanisms. As the size of the chain and kernel module can be changed in plug, the proposed architecture is generic and scalable and any changes can be done without affecting the overall architecture. The authors investigate three popular object detection algorithms in (Kyrkou, 2010). Neural Networks, Support Vector Machines, and the Viola-Jones detection frame- work. Two architectures are proposed, one for the Viola-Jones detection framework and one for Support Vector Machines, both based on systolic array designs. Moreover, an attempt is made to compare the three classification algorithms in order to provide directives and indications on which case each should be used. A successful design for a high performance, low- resource-consuming hardware for Support Vector Classification and Support Vector Regression is presented in (Llata, Guamizo & Calvino, 2010). The system has been implemented on a low cost FPGA device and exploits the advantages of parallel processing to compute the feed forward phase in support vector machines. In this paper we show that the same hardware can be used for classification problems and regression problems, and we show satisfactory results on an image recognition problem by SV multiclass classification and on a function estimation problem by SV regression. In (Kim, Lee & Cho, 2012), the authors designed a high performance circuit which supports both linear and nonlinear classification. Concerning the efficiency of classification a 48×96 or 64×64 sliding window with window strides is used. The circuit size is minimized here by sharing most of their sources used for linear and nonlinear classification. In (Patil, Sahula & Mandal, 2012), a power aware hardware implementation of multiclass SVM on FPGA using systolic array architecture is presented. Here, the authors used reconfiguration method for power reduction and compared it to the same design before reconfiguration..

Contribution

From the literature survey we can interpret that the above mentioned SVM techniques using systolic array did not focus on the power factor. These techniques used kernel module for classification which involves sequence of multiplication between test samples and SVs, consumes a high amount of power. As now a days power saving is one of the crucial factor, in this chapter we are introducing a power conscious design for SVM classification. We are able to reduce power of binary linear, nonlinear and multiclass SVM and also able to reduce power in classification applications like character recognition.

Organization of the Chapter

Section 1 provides a brief introduction and background about the topic and a brief overview of related works of implementation of SVM in hardware. A brief explanation about the classification tool used here that is SVM and its hardware systolic architecture are included in section 2. The description of the proposed approach and the system model are included in Section 3. Results are shown in Section 4. Conclusion and future work are included in Section 5.

THEORITICAL CONSIDERATIONS

SVM technique is mainly used for classification problem in various domains because it is efficient than other classification techniques like ANN, LDA. Again the hardware architecture of SVM is designed in systolic array. We are using the systolic array because of its parallel processing architecture which reduces the time consumption of a design.

Support Vector Machine

SVMs classify a group of elements according to some risk function called score value. This function is neither linear nor parametric. The score values enable to formulate SVM margin which is shown in Figure 1. Here, we briefly discuss about how SVM works. Let there be a new company j which is to be classified into class 1 or 0 as per SVM scores. Let the financial ratio's be defined as $x_j = (x_{j1}, x_{j2}, ..., x_{jd})$ where, x_j is a vector with is a vector with d financial ratios. The x_{jk} is the value of the financial ratio number k for company j, with $k - 1, 2, ..., d$. Next, let z_j be the related financial score of the company j which can be expressed as:

Figure 1. Geometrical representation of the SVM margin

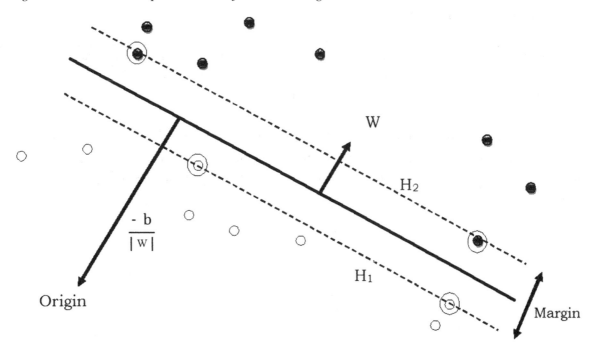

$$z = w_1 x_{j1} + w_2 x_{j2} + \dots + w_d x_{jd} + b \tag{1}$$

where b is constant. In a compact form:

$$z = x_j^T + b \tag{2}$$

Where w s are weights forming a vector. The score z is compared with a threshold which decides whether the company falls in class 1 or 0 according to certain related financial criteria.

In the case of a non-linear SVM, the score of a company is computed by substituting the scalar product of the financial ratios with a kernel function.

$$z_j = \sum y_i a_i < x_j.x_j > +b \rightarrow z_i = \sum a_i y_i k(x_j.x_j) + b \tag{3}$$

Kernels are symmetric, semi-positive definite functions satisfying the Mercer theorem. If this theorem is satisfied, this ensures that there exists a (possibly) non-linear φ map from the input space into some feature space, such that its inner product equals the kernel. The non-linear transformation φ is only implicitly defined through the use of a kernel, since it only appears as an inner product.

$$k(x_i, x_j) = < \varphi(x_i, x_j) > \tag{4}$$

Here we are going to discuss two cases of SVM, one is separable and another is non separable SVM, both of these cases are also implemented in our design.

The Separable Case of SVM

For separable case suppose we have taken two groups of samples: positive samples and negative samples which are linearly separable. The trained data x_i, where $i = 1, 2, \dots, l$ is labeled with $y_i \in \{-1, 1\}$. The samples which satisfy the condition $wx + b = 0$ are the samples lying on the hyperplane, where w is normal to the hyperplane, $\|b\| / \|w\|$ is the perpendicular distance from the hyperplane to the origin and $\|w\|$ is the Euclidian distance. Let $d+$ be the shortest distance of the hyperplane from the positive side and $d-$ from the negative side respectively. Then the margin of the separating hyperplane is $d+ + d-$. For this linear case the largest margin is calculated. Let all the training samples satisfy the following conditions:

$$x_i w + b \geq +1 \text{ for } y_i = +1 \tag{5}$$

$$x_i.w + b < +1 \text{ for } y_i = -1 \tag{6}$$

These two equations can be combined as following:

$$y_i(x_i.w + b) - 1 \geq 0, \forall i \tag{7}$$

Now consider the samples which satisfy the equation (5). These points lie on the hyperplane $H1$: $x_i w + b = +1$ with normal w and perpendicular distance from the origin $\|1 - b\| / \|w\|$ and the samples which satisfy equation (6) lie on the hyperplane $H2$: $x_i w + b = -1$ with normal w and perpendicular distance from the origin $\|-1 - b\| / \|w\|$. Therefore $d+ = d- = 1 / \|w\|$ then the value of margin becomes $2 / \|w\|$. No training data lies within hyperplane H1 and H2 which are two parallaly separated lines. Thus minimizing $\|w\|^2$ w. r. to constraint (7) we can achieve maximum margin hyperplane.

From the above calculations we can get Fig 5. The vectors nearest to the hyperplane H1 and H2 are called Support Vectors.

Now Lagrangian formulation is applied here. This is because of the following two reasons. The first is that the Lagrangian multiplier will replace the constraint (7) which is easier to handle and secondly, we will only get the vector product of training data and this would generalize this formulation to nonlinear case.

The hyperplane that minimizes equation (8) is the resultant hyperplane that optimally separates the group of samples.

$$\phi(\omega) = 1 / 2 \|w\|^2 \tag{8}$$

As equation (7) is satisfied, it is independent of b, Any change in b will move it in the normal direction to itself.

Under constrains of equation (7), the solution to the optimizing problem of equation (8) is given by the saddle point of Lagrange functional.

$$\phi(\omega, b, \alpha) = 1 / 2 \|w\|^2 - \sum_{i=1}^{l} \alpha_i (y^i [< \omega, x^i > + b] - 1) \tag{9}$$

Where α are the Lagrange multipliers. The Lagrangian is now should be maximized with respect to $\alpha \geq 0$ and should be minimized with respect to ω and b. Equation (9) is now converted to dual problem, which is much easier to solve. The dual problem is then given by equation (10),

$$\max W(\alpha) = \max(\min \phi(\omega, b, \alpha)) \tag{10}$$

The with respect to ω and b of the Lagrangian Φ would be as equation (11),

$$\partial \phi / \partial b = 0 => \sum_{i=0}^{l} \alpha_i y_i = 0$$

$$\partial \phi / \partial \omega = 0 => \omega = \sum_{i=0}^{l} \alpha_i y_i x_i \tag{11}$$

Hence from Equations (9), (10)and (11), the dual problem is,

$$\max W(\alpha) = \max -1/2 \sum_{i=1}^{l} \sum_{j=1}^{l} \alpha_i \alpha_j y_i y_j <x_i x_j> + \sum_{k=1}^{l} \alpha_k \tag{12}$$

Therefore, the solution to the problem is given by with equation (13) with constraints $\alpha \geq 0, i = 1, 2, ..., l$ and equation (14).

$$\alpha^* = \arg \min 1/2 \sum_{i=1}^{l} \sum_{j=1}^{l} \alpha_i \alpha_j y_i y_j <x_i x_j> - \sum_{k=1}^{l} \alpha_k \tag{13}$$

$$\sum_{j=1}^{l} \alpha_i y_i = 0 = 0 \tag{14}$$

The Lagrange multipliers are determined by solving equation (13) with constraint equation (14) and the optimal separating hyperplane is given by equation (15),

$$\omega^* = \sum_{i=1}^{l} \alpha_i y_i x_i$$

$$b^* = -1/2 <\omega^*, x_r + x_s> \tag{15}$$

Where, x_r and x_s are support vectors from each class which satisfies in equation (16)

$$\alpha_r, \alpha_s > 0, y_r = -1, y_s = 1 \tag{16}$$

Then, the classifier is given by equation (17).

$$f(x) = \mathrm{sgn}(<\omega^*, x> + b) \tag{17}$$

From kernel equation given by equation (18) we can come to a conclusion that the only points that satisfies equation (19) will have non-zero Lagrange multipliers and these sample points are entitled as SV.

$$\alpha_i (y^i [<\omega, x^i> + b] - 1) = 0, i = 1, 2, ..., l \tag{18}$$

$$y^i [<\omega, x^i> + b] = 1 \tag{19}$$

The Non-Separable Case of SVM

The main problem to classify non linear data is concerned with storage and manipulation of the high dimensional data. To solve this problem consider an example of second order products of two data samples i.e. $\chi = (x_1, x_2)$ and $\phi(x) = (x_1^2, \sqrt{2}x_1x_2, x_2^2)$.

The scalar product of two feature space vector of this type can be effortlessly evolved in terms of kernel function k.

$$(\phi(x)^T \phi(z)) = (x_1^2, \sqrt{2}x_1x_2, x_2^2)(z_1^2, \sqrt{2}z_1z_2, z_2^2)$$

$$= ((x_1, x_2)(z_1, z_2)^T)^2$$

$$= (x^T z)^2$$

$$= k(x, z)$$

It can be generalized as shown in equation (20) $x, z \in R^n$ and $d \in N$.

$$k(x, z) = (x^T z)^d \tag{20}$$

Thus the kernel function computes scalar product of x and z in dimension d .

Kernels are the one which enables the data to operate in higher dimensional feature space without computing their coordinates in higher dimensional space but using only inner product between the images of all pairs of data in the feature space. kernel should satisfy Mercer theorem and if this is satisfied then mapping can be done from input feature space to higher dimensional feature space. The Mercer's Theorem, which we will reproduce in the following, states that if the kernel function k gives rise to a positive integral operator, the evaluation of $k(x, z)$ can be expressed as a finite or infinite, absolute and uniformly convergent series, almost everywhere. This series then defines in another way a feature space and an associated mapping connected to the kernel k (Vanschoenwinkel, & Manderick, 2004).

SVM is generally a binary classifier but we can use non linear kernels for SVM so that it can classify non linear set of data. The simplest form of SVM is the binary SVM classifier and we can combine several such binary classifiers to form a multiclass classifier. This is possible by creating a binary classifier for each possible pair of classes.

In case of choosing a kernel we can choose any of the four kernels according to the ease of our design. As for the binary case, the data which are linearly separable, linear kernel is more efficient. For nonlinear case both the polynomial and radial basis functions are suitable. All the kernels satisfy the same goal of separating two classes of data but with different mathematical analysis. The most innovative kernel designs which are widely used because of their efficiency in mapping data to higher dimensional space are listed below (Preman, Suapura, 1991):

1) Linear: $K(\vec{x}, \vec{z}) = (\vec{x}.\vec{z})$

2) Polynomial: $K(\vec{x}, \vec{z}) = (1 + (\vec{x}.\vec{z}))^d$

3) Sigmoid: $K(\vec{x}, \vec{z}) = \tan((\vec{x}.\vec{z}) + \theta)$

4) Radial Basis: $K(\vec{x}, \vec{z}) = \exp((x - z)^2 / 2\sigma^2)$

Thus the kernels can side-step the problem that data are nonlinearly separable by implicitly mapping them into a feature space, in which the linear threshold can be used. Using a kernel is equivalent to solving a linear SVM in some new higher dimensional feature space. The non-linear SVM score is thus a linear combination, but with new variables, which are derived through a kernel transformation of the prior financial ratios. Linear kernel is one special case of Radial Basis Kernel and it is mainly used for binary data classification. It can efficiently classify two different groups of data samples which are binary linearly separable (Vanschoenwinkel & Manderick, 2004).

If we choose polynomial kernel, we have to set the degree of polynomial kernel which is here denoted by d to specify the degree for SVM classification. By default the minimum value of d is 1 which represents a binary classifier that is basically a straight line between two different classes. The degree 1 only works when there are two different classes which are linearly and distinctly separable. The maximum value of the degree that is d is infinite. As this parameter d increases the boundary between two classes of data becomes more accurate. The polynomial kernel function used in SVM represents the likeness of training samples in a feature space over polynomials of the original variables which permit learning of non-linear models (Goldberg & Elhadad, 2008). In machine learning, Radial Basis function (RBF) is quite popular kernel function of SVM. RBF network is used to find a set of weights for a curve fitting problem. The weights are in higher dimensional space (Schoelkopf, Sung, Burges, Girosi, Niyogi, Poggio & Vapnik, 1996). In RBF kernel $(x - z)^2$ may be recognized as the squared Euclidean distance between the two feature vectors and ¾ is a free parameter. Gaussian Radial Basis function kernel with a default scaling factor ¾ of 1. It can be varied according to the classification accuracy requirements of test samples. In Sigmoid kernel μ is a shifting parameter that controls the threshold of mapping and $\mu < 0$, is more suitable for the sigmoid kernel (Vanschoenwinkel & Manderick, 2004). Sigmoid Basis function is less popular than polynomial and radial basis function. In some cases polynomial shows better result while in some other cases radial shows the better performance. Polynomial kernel is quite popular in natural language processing (NLP). In (Chavhan, Dhore & Yesaware, 2010) the author experiments different kernels for speech recognition process and found that with $d = 1$ linear and polynomial kernel function shows same performance whatever the datasheet used. For $d = 10$ polynomial kernel shows the highest efficiency compared to all these latest machine learning algorithms. Thus, in our design also we are using this polynomial kernel function for binary nonlinear and multiclass classification. The main decision function of SVM classification is given by:

$$z_j = sign(\sum_{i=1}^{n} a_i y_i k(x_i, s_i) + b) \tag{21}$$

Binary SVM classifier is modified to get a multiclass SVM classifier. Here following approaches have been used for doing so:

1) Binary classifier: In this a binary classifier, all the patterns from class p are trained as positive samples and the other patterns from class q are trained as negative samples for the classifier pq.

When a new test sample is classified a vote is casted by the decision function in favor of one of the two classes. The class with maximum votes is the class of the new test sample.

2) Multiclass classifier: For the multiclass classifier, all the patterns of class p are trained with positive samples and the patterns from all other classes are trained as negative samples for the classifier p. The new test input belongs to the class which has the highest output value.

Systolic Array

Systolic architecture represents a network of processing elements (PE) that rhythmically compute and pass data through the system. These PEs regularly pump data in and out such that a regular flow of data is maintained. As a result, systolic system feature modularity and regularity, which are important properties for VLSI design. It is invented by Kung and Leiserson (1978). Ever since Kung proposed the systolic model its elegant solutions to demanding problems and its potential performance have attracted great attention. In physiology, the term systolic describes the contraction (systole) of the heart, which regularly sends blood to all cells of the body through the arteries, veins, and capillaries. Analogously, Systolic computer processes perform operations in a rhythmic, incremental, cellular and repetitive manner. Typically all PEs in systolic array are uniform and fully pipelined. i.e., all communicating edges among the PEs contain delay elements, and the whole system usually contains only local interconnections. However, some relaxations have been introduced to increase the utility of systolic arrays. These relaxations include use of not only local but also neighbor interconnections, use of data broadcast operations, and use of different PEs in the system especially at the boundaries (Parhi. 2012).

The major demands related to architectural issues in designing special purpose system are:

- Simple and regular design with low cost has always been a chief concern.
- Concurrency, communication and faster design.
- Balancing computation with I/O.

Systolic architectures is a solution to above challenges. It is an architectural concept originally proposed for VLSI implementation of some matrix operations. A systolic system consists of a set of interconnected cells, each capable of performing some simple operations. Because simple, regular communication and control structures have substantial advantages over complicate ones in design and implementation, cells in a systolic system are typically interconnected to form a systolic array or a systolic tree. Information in a systolic system flows between cells in a pipelined fashion and communication with the outside world occurs only at the boundary cells. Thus, in a systolic array, only those cells on the array boundaries may work as I/O ports for the system. Computational tasks can be conceptually classified into two families: compute bound computations and I/O-bound computations. In a computation, if the total number of operations is larger than the total number of input and output elements, then the computation is compute-bound, otherwise it is I/O-bound. For example, the ordinary matrix-matrix multiplication algorithm represents a compute-bound task, since every entry in a matrix is multiplied by all entries in some row or column of the other matrix. Adding two matrices, on the other hand, is I/O-bound, since the total number of adds is not larger than the total number of entries in the two matrices. It should be clear that any attempt to speed up an I/O bound computation must rely on an increase in memory bandwidth. Memory bandwidth can be increased by the use of either fast components (which could be expensive) or interleaved memories (which could create complicated memory management problems).

Speeding up a compute- bound computation, however, may often be accomplished in a relatively simple and inexpensive manner, that is, by the systolic approach. By replacing a single processing element with an array of PEs, or cells in the terminology of this article, a higher computation throughput can be achieved without increasing memory bandwidth. The function of this type of is analogous to that of the heart; it pulses data (instead of blood) through the array of cells. The crux of this approach is to ensure that once a data item is brought out from the memory it can be used effectively at each cell it passes while being pumped from cell to cell along the array. This is possible for a wide class of compute-bound computations where multiple operations are performed on each data item in a repetitive manner. Being able to use each input data item a number of times (and thus achieving high computation throughput with only modest memory bandwidth) is just one of the many advantages of the systolic approach. Other advantages, such as modular expansibility, simple and regular data and control flows, use of simple and uniform cells, elimination of global broadcasting, and fan-in and (possibly) fast response time, will be illustrated in various systolic designs in the next section (Kung). The systolic architecture can be used as special purpose processor for the following reasons-

- For its simple and regular design.
- systolic array are faster because of their concurrency in communication.
- They are modular to different goals.
- They have relatively low bandwidth of current I/O devices, which provides faster communication rate.

There are different types of systolic array. In the beginning, only one dimensional and two dimensional arrays are introduced. The newest systolic array implemented is planar array where we can feed the data through the boundary. Till date 4 different types of systolic array architecture are introduced:

- Linear array with 1D I/O: This array architecture is suitable for single I/O. It is a one dimensional (1D) systolic array. This array takes the inputs from the leftmost cell and gives the output through the rightmost cell (Milovanovic, Milovanovic, Randjelovic & Jovanovic, 2003). Using this type of systolic arrays have many advantages over the other types of arrays. This simple interconnection scheme requires minimum number of inputs/ outputs (I/O) in the sense that only two end cells communicate with the outside world. Thus, for each I/O operation, n-cell linear array can perform O(n) computations because of which I/O bandwidth can be minimized to a high extent for achieving high performance. This array has another important advantage that it can be safely synchronized by a single, global clock. The Figure of this array is shown in Figure 2.

Figure 2. 1D Linear systolic array

- Linear array with 2D I/O: This architecture allows additional control over the linear array. These types of systolic arrays have all properties similar to the linear I/O systolic array with one additional control over the whole array, all flowing in one direction (Milovanovic, Milovanovic, Randjelovic & Jovanovic, 2003). As these arrays have all the data and control flow in one direction, an efficient fault- tolerant techniques can be used to identify and reconstruction of the cells in the systolic array. It is shown in Figure 3.
- Planar array: This type of architecture allows I/O only through the boundary. It is 2D systolic array which are widely used in signal processing and image processing (Milentijevic, Milovanovic, Milovanovic & M.K. Stojcev, 1997). This architecture provides massive parallelism of data as we can feed the data from two directions. Figure of the same is shown in Figure 4.

Figure 3. 2D I/O Linear systolic array

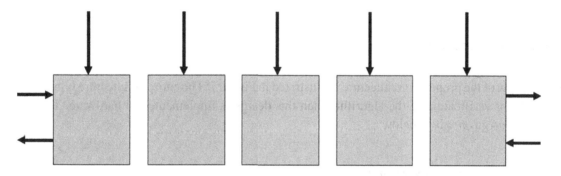

Figure 4. Planar systolic array

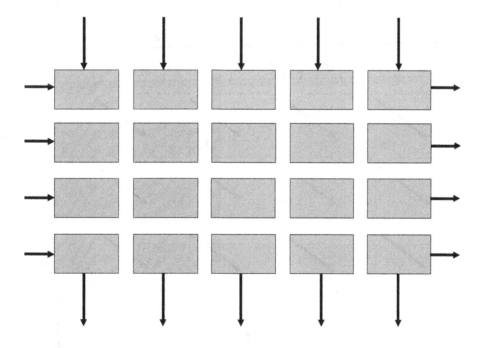

- Focal plane array: This array architecture has 3D I/O. This configuration allows I/O to each cell of the systolic array. The main disadvantage of the planar array is the speed limitation and the speed becomes considerably low while doing complex computation. So to compensate these limitations focal plane systolic arrays are designed. The focal array has many advantages over the planar array. These include higher speed, better extensibility, better partition ability, better fault tolerance capabilities, ease of cascading, ease of pipelining etc. Additionally, PE for these type of systolic array are simpler than that of the planar array (Chai, Wills & Jokerst, 1997). It is given in Figure 5.

Systolic Array can be used for many applications like Matrix Inversion and Decomposition, Polynomial Evaluation, Convolution, matrix multiplication, Image Processing, Systolic lattice filters used for speech and seismic signal processing. For parallel data transfer operation we have used systolic array. Here in each PE the data generated from the Matlab is stored and the input data feed to the PE in the manner as show in Figure 6.

PROPOSED APPROACH

The dataflow of the proposed architecture is illustrated in Figure 7. The entire architecture is implemented in Matlab for verification of the algorithm then this design is implemented in hardware. The steps of the whole design are given below:

Figure 5. Focal plane systolic array

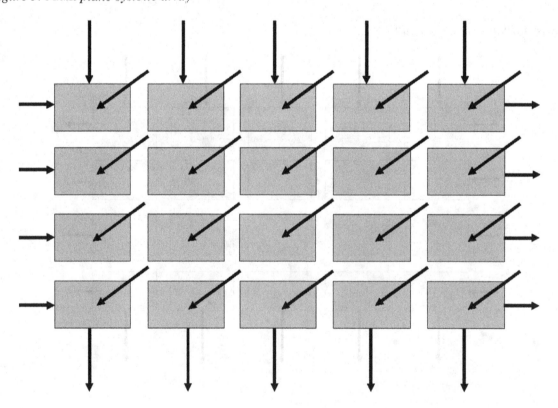

Figure 6. The systolic architecture

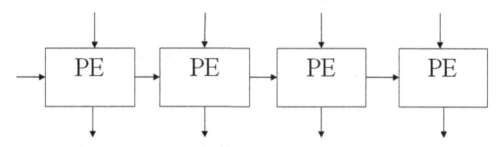

Figure 7. The Proposed architecture for binary linear SVM

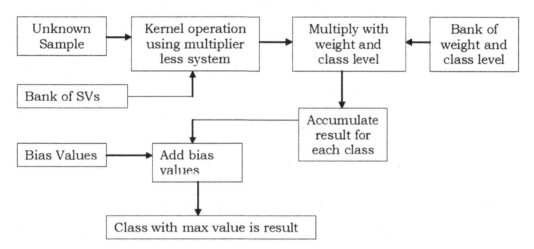

- The input to the PE is the test samples.
- Then the multiplierless kernel operation is performed which yield a scalar output.
- The scalar output value is then multiplied with alpha values and class levels. Class level is either +1 or -1.
- Each PE performs all these operations in a pipelined manner. Simultaneously, the input vector elements are passed to next PE.
- All the PEs give different scalar values which are stored in register and then these values are added classwise along with the bias value.
- The class which gives the maximum value is the class of the unknown input sample

In our proposed methodology, we have replaced the kernel vector product block with a multiplierless block. This block is introduced mainly for reduction of power utilization along with reduction of cost and hardware complexity. For this purpose in the proposed block we are using CSD, CSE algorithm. To gain massive parallelism are using systolic array. This increases the speed of the whole system.

Power Reduction Methodology

As power reduction is the major concern of this hour in the field of hardware designing of the classifiers. So, we have designed a power aware system. This power reduction is achieved by multiplierless block. Here, the vector product kernel module is replaced by shift and add operations, as the adders consumes less power and area as compared to the multipliers. Here we have used CSD block to reduce the number of ones contained in the test vector because CSD is a representation by which we can represent a floating point number with minimum number of ones. Again we have reduced the number of ones because reduction of number of ones means reduction of number of adders which indicates efficient utilization of area as well as reduction in power level. To simplify the hardware design model more we have used CSE method. This reduces the number of ones further. Thus, using these methodologies we have obtained a power conscious system for the binary linear, non linear and multiclass SVM.

The complexity of multiple constant multiplication (MCM) problem is dominated by the number of additions or subtractions used for MCM coefficient multiplications. To reduce the complexity of the coefficients, it can be expressed in the canonic signed digit (CSD) form. The CSD codes minimize the number of adders or subtracters required in each coefficient multiplications. The common subexpression elimination (CSE) methods have been proposed to make the multiplier block as simple as possible. These two algorithms are described in the following subsections.

Canonic Signed Digit (CSD) Representation

CSD is a number system by which we can represent a floating point number in two's complement form. The representation uses -1, 0, +1 (or -, 0, +) symbols only. With each position denoting the addition and subtraction of power of 2 (Coleman & Yurdakul, 2001). These encoding techniques contains 33 percentage fewer non-zero elements than 2's complement form which leads to efficient implementations of add/subtract networks in hardwired digital signal processing (DSP). The properties of a CSD number are listed below:

- No two consecutive bits in a CSD number are non-zero.
- CSD representation of a particular number is always unique.
- A CSD representation contains minimum possible number of ones.

Constants are generally expressed in 2's complement representation as $\sum a_i 2_i$ where, $-1, 0, a_i \in 0, 1, i = 0, K, n-2$ and n is the word length. If -1 is introduced into the value set of bit representation, it makes, $a_i \in \{1, 0, -1\}, i = 0, K, n-1$ and $a_j . a_{j+1} = 0, j = 0, K, n-2$. The constant a_i is said to be in CSD representation. For convenience, it is often written as N. For example, an integer 115 can be denoted as (01110011) in 2's complement representation and be denoted as (+00-0+0-) in CSD representation (Coleman & Yurdakul, 2001), (Parhi, 2012). Every constant in n-bit 2's complement representation can be uniquely expressed in n-bit CSD format. According to the definition of CSD representation, the number of nonzero bits of a constant in n-bits CSD representation is no more than $(n+1)/2$ where x denotes the largest integer no more than x. In CSD representation, the multiplication $x = 0.10100\overline{1}0010\overline{1}00\overline{1}$ can be computed as shown in Figure 8, where partial products are accumulated in a linear arrangement.

Figure 8. Linear arrangement for CSD representation

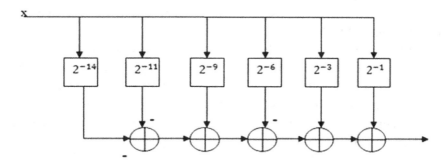

Common Subexpression Elimination (CSE)

CSE is an optimization algorithm that searches for identical expression and substitute a variable which holds the computed value in place of the expression. The main tasks of CSE algorithm are:

- Identification of different patterns present in the input.
- Choose one pattern for elimination.
- Elimination of all occurrences of the selected pattern.

Close observation on the multiplicators in CSD representation shows that some of the bit patterns occur more than once. For example, in a multiplicator (+0-00+0-) CSD, the bit pattern (+0-) CSD appears twice, so it can be extracted as a common subexpression and be reused. It is possible to make full use of this characteristic to reduce the computational complexity in the multiplierless implementation of MCM problem (Wu & Sun, 2003), (Takahashi & Yokoyama, 2005).

In our case we are using horizontal CSE method for reduction of adders. In the horizontal CSE method, we must be examined all combinations of non-zero bit patterns in a coefficient. Since a bit pattern can only be eliminated once, we must also detect the occurrence of the same patterns within each other. For example, the valid non-zero bit patterns of coefficient $010n010n$ are summarized in Table 1. In this case, patterns $10n$ and $100n$ are identified as most frequent for the coefficients. If two patterns have the same frequency (>1), the smallest pattern is chosen. Because, adder/subtracter structures with a bigger

Table 1. Non-zero bit patterns of coefficient "010n010n"

Bit pattern	Frequency
10n	2
10001	1
100000n	1
n01	1
n00n	1

wordlength cause a larger implementation area. Most common horizontal subexpressions resulting from the proposed method (i.e. $10n$ and $100n$) are extracted from the coefficient table represented in canonic signed digit (CSD) shown in Figure 9.

These two algorithms are then applied to support vectors. Then the shifting, add and subtraction operation is done here. As all the above algorithms are till now applied in case of FIR filters only, the algorithms are modified to work suitably for the SVM support vector coefficient. Complement representation can be uniquely expressed in n-bit CSD format. According to the definition of CSD representation, the number of nonzero bits of a constant in n-bits CSD representation is no more than $(n+1)/2$, where x denotes the largest integer no more than x.

RESULTS AND DISCUSSION

Binary Classification

In case of Binary classification this design is implemented for both binary linear and binary nonlinear classification operation. Here two groups of Fisheriris data setosa and nonsetosa for the training phase of linearly separable data and versilcolor and virginica for non-linearly separable data is taken. The data are trained in Matlab. Training phase of linear and nonlinear classification is shown in Figure 10 and Figure 11. This training phase generates support vectors (SV) s and alpha values. Then these values are

Figure 9. Horizontal CSE method

	-1	-2	-3	-4	-5	-6	-7	-8
h(0)	0	0	0	0	0	0	1	0
h(1)	0	0	0	1	0	1	0	n
h(2)	0	0	0	0	1	0	0	0
h(3)	0	0	0	0	0	1	0	n
h(4)	0	0	0	0	0	0	1	0
h(5)	0	0	0	0	1	0	0	0
h(6)	0	0	0	1	0	n	0	n
h(7)	0	0	0	0	1	0	0	1
h(8)	0	0	0	0	0	0	0	0
h(9)	0	0	0	1	0	0	n	0
h(10)	0	0	1	0	0	0	0	n
h(11)	0	1	0	n	0	0	0	n
h(12)	0	1	0	0	n	0	0	0

Figure 10. Trained Support Vectors for linear SVM

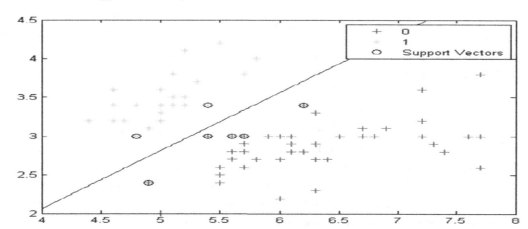

Figure 11. Trained Support Vectors for nonlinear SVM

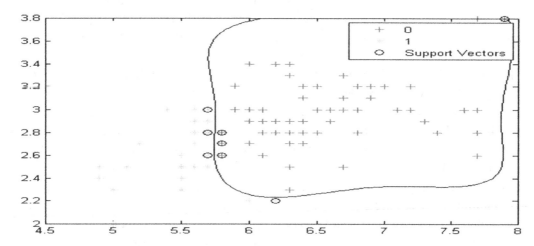

stored in the virtually generated processing elements in Matlab. Simultaneously, input sample vector is feed to each PE. The PE performs the multiplierless kernel operation and the decision function operation which decides the class label of the unknown input samples.

Here we use a multiplierless kernel operation. Thus instead of vector multiplication of the support vectors and test samples, we use shift add operation. The above procedure is done for each class. The dimension of different matrices of linear and nonlinear classification problem is shown in Table 2 and Table 3 respectively. For linear classification we use the linear kernel and for nonlinear we use the polynomial kernel. Here we have taken d=4.

Table 2. Dimension for different matrices for linear classification

Class	Test Vector	Support Vector	Kernel	Decision fn
Setosa	1×2	2×3	1×3	1×1
Non setosa	1×2	2×5	1×5	1×1

Table 3. Dimension for different matrices for nonlinear classification

Class	Test Vector	Support Vector	Kernel	Decision fn
Setosa	1×2	2×12	1×12	1×1
Non setosa	1×2	2×12	1×12	1×1

For linear case we get 8 SVs and non linear case we get 24 SVs. Hence we need a total of 8 and 24 multiplierless Kernel operations respectively in each PE which yields a scalar value; this is multiplied by the corresponding alpha and class levels. Simultaneously, Input vector elements are passed to next PE. Then the scalar values are classwise added together with the bias value. The class which gives maximum value is the class of unknown input vector. The parameters generated from the training phase are shown in Table 4. These values of the support vectors are their distance from the maximum marginal hyperplane. These SVs are the vectors residing nearest to the hyperplane. This Table also listed the corresponding alpha values of the support vectors. The alpha values are always positive. Here negative alpha value indicates the alpha values of the SVs which belongs to class 0 while positive alpha values indicate the alpha values of the SVs which belongs to class 1. Table V gives the output of applying CSD and CSE algorithm on some random values. For CSE in our design we have taken 101=6, 10-1=7, -101=-7, -10-1=-6, 1001=8, 100-1=9, -1001=-9, -100-1=-8.

The output of each PE for the input test vector [6 4] is summarized in Table 5. Here we can see that PE1, PE2, PE3, PE8 voted for class 1 and PE4, PE5, PE6 and PE7 voted for class 0. The output of the decision function for the classification is given in Table 6. Here we can see that this design can efficiently classify the data which establishes the strength of the system. The details of the number of multiplicators required for the kernel function using dot product and multiplierless kernel function is shown in Table 7. The profile summary i.e. the run time of all the functions used in our program is shown in Table 8. The output of nonlinear binary classification is shown in Table 9. Here also we can see that the multiplierless design efficiently classifying all the test vectors. Table 10 shows a comparison of number of multiplicators for binary classification. Here we can see that for binary linear classification the number of multiplicators reduces from 18 to 0 while for binary nonlinear classification the number of multiplicators reduces from 651 to 515.

Table 4. Support Vectors and corresponding Alpha Values

Support Vector	Support Vector	Alpha values
-1.2680	-0.2045	-0.9102
-0.5670	0.7251	-1.5000
-1.2680	-0.2045	-0.6834
-1.1512	-1.5990	0.4140
-0.3334	-0.2045	0.7500
-0.5670	-0.2045	0.7500
-0.2165	-0.2045	0.4296
0.3676	0.7251	0.7500

Table 5. Values after applying CSD and CSE Algorithms

Test Vector	Binary	CSD digit	CSE
4.2	100.0011001100	0+00.0+0-0+0-0+0-	0100070007000700
4.5	100.1	0+00.+00000000000	0800000000000000
5	101	0+0+.000000000000	0600000000000000
5.5	101.1	+0-0.-00000000000	7000-10000000000
6	0110	+0-0.000000000000	7000000000000000
3	0011	0+0-.000000000000	0700000000000000

Table 6. Output from the PEs

PE1	7.6693
PE2	0.7524
PE3	5.7583
PE4	-5.5075
PE5	-1.9263
PE6	-3.1650
PE7	-0.9095
PE8	3.8295

Table 7. Values of Linear Classification

Test Vector	Class
[4.2 2.1]	1
[4.2 2.5]	-1
[4.5 2.1]	1
[4.5 2.5]	-1
[4.5 4]	-1
[5 2.3]	1
[5 2.7]	-1
[5.5 2.5]	1
[5.5 2.9]	1
[5.5 3.2]	-1
[5.5 4]	-1
[6 2.5]	1
[6 3]	1
[6 4]	-1

Table 8. Profile Summary of Binary Linear Classification

Function Name	Calls	Total Time	Self Time
Input program	1	10.524 s	0.064 s
Decision	14	10.441 s	0.043 s
Multiplierless mul	244	9.709 s	0.760 s
PE1	14	1.937 s	0.070 s
PE2	14	1.239 s	0.006 s
PE3	14	1.217 s	0.008 s
PE4	14	1.216 s	0.011 s
PE5	14	1210 s	0.006 s
PE6	14	1.200 s	0.007 s
PE7	14	1.194 s	0.008 s
PE8	14	1.184 s	0.011 s
Csdigit	224	0.548 s	0.251 s
Cse_extract	224	0.256 s	0.119 s
Bi2de	11048	2.018 s	2.018 s
De2bi	7688	2.006 s	1.854 s

Table 9. Values of nonlinear classification

Test Vector	Class
[7 3.2]	1
[6 3.2]	1
[5.5 2.3]	-1
[6.5 2.8]	1
[5.7 2.8]	-1
[4.9 2.4]	-1
[6.6 2.9]	1
[5.2 2.7]	-1
[5.9 3]	1
[6 2.2]	-1
[6 2.9]	1
[5.6 2.9]	-1
[6.7 3.1]	1
[6 4]	-1

Table 10. Number of Multiplicators for Binary Classification

Classification	Dot product kernel function	Multiplierless kernel function
Linear	18	0
Nonlinear	651	515

Character recognition: An application specific design

We have applied our proposed approach for character recognition operation. For this purpose we have trained the SVM with sets of images of character "A" and "1" which generates SVs, alpha values and bias values. The parameters generated from the training phase are listed in Table 11. After training, it is efficiently classified in Matlab. Then we have implemented the classification process in hardware and have compared the resource utilization and power measurement using vector product kernel and using multiplierless kernel. The character "A" is taken here as class 0 and "1" is taken as class 1.

Internal Architecture of PE

We have efficiently classified the binary data in MATLAB. Again we have implemented the binary linear classification design in VIRTEX7 xc7vx485t and binary nonlinear classification design in VIRTEX VIRTEX7 xc7vx485t. The trained data is taken from Matlab simulation only. Then in each PE we store one support vector and its corresponding alpha and class label values. Each support vector has two elements. Internal architecture of PE is shown in Figure 12. In each PE vector operation of SV and input vector is performed, generating a scalar value which is stored in registers. This value is then multiplied with alpha and class label simultaneously input vector elements are passed to next PE.

Hardware Implementation Results of Binary Linear Classification

The output of CSD conversion block is shown in Table 12. The CSD output is of 13 bits where 5 bits are taken for decimal value and 8 bits are taken for floating. This number of bits we have taken here as per requirement of our design. The CSD digit is binary encoded into a sign bit xis and a magnitude bit xim. Under the sign=magnitude encoding $0 = 00; 1 = 01; -1 = 11$. In our design we have 8 PEs for binary linear classification and 24 PEs for binary nonlinear classification. The PE gives output of 37 bits where 5 bits are for decimal and 32 bits are for floating. The classification result is same as we have in MATLAB.

The primitive and black box uses of LUTs, DSP4s and clocks of binary linear classifier using vector product kernel module and using multiplierless kernel is given in Table 12 and Table 13. The design utilization summary of the vector product kernel module and using multiplierless kernel is given in Table

Table 11. Dimension for different matrices for character recognition of "A" and "1"

Class	Test Vector	Support Vector	Kernel	Decision fn
"A"	1×64	2×64	1×2	1×1
"1"	1×64	2×64	1×2	1×1

Figure 12. Internal architecture of PE

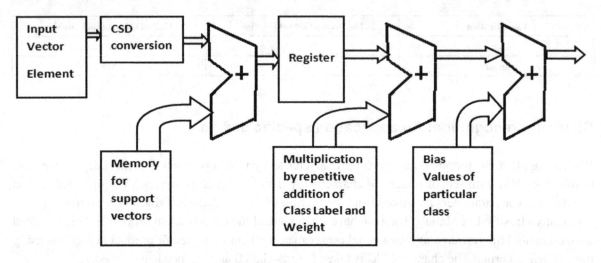

Table 12. Primitive and Black Box usage for vector product kernel of binary linear SVM

GND	1	MUXCY	978
INV	578	MUXF7	3
LUT1	69	VCC	1
LUT2	284	XORCY	1023
LUT3	323	IBUF	26
LUT4	43	OBUF	37
LUT5	249	IO buffers	63
LUT6	137	DSP48E1	18

Table 13. Primitive and Black Box usage for multiplierless kernel of binary linear SVM

GND	1	MUXCY	789
INV	372	MUXF7	6
LUT1	26	VCC	1
LUT2	187	XORCY	457
LUT3	294	IBUF	26
LUT4	217	OBUF	37
LUT5	232	IO buffers	63
LUT6	682	DSP48E1	0

14 and Table 15. This is obtained from the synthesis report of each design in XILINX. The power is measured using XILINX POWER ESTIMATOR (XPE) 14.1. This version is used for power measurement of 7 series FPGA. The on chip power summary report of both the vector product kernel module and multiplierless kernel for the binary linear classification is given in Table 16. The summary of power

Table 14. Device utilization summary for vector product kernel of binary linear SVM

Device: XILINX xc7vx485t-2ffg1157	Utilized	Available	Percentage Utilization
Number of Slice LUTs:	1683	303600	0.6%
Number used as Logic:	1683	303600	0.6%
Number with an unused Flip Flop:	1683	1683	100%
Number with an unused LUT:	0	1683	0%
Number of bonded IOBs:	63	600	10%
Number of DSP48E1	18	2800	0.6%

Table 15. Device utilization summary for multiplierless kernel of binary linear SVM

Device: XILINX xc7vx485t-2ffg1157	Utilized	Available	Percentage Utilization
Number of Slice LUTs:	2010	303600	0.7%
Number used as Logic:	2010	303600	0.7%
Number with an unused Flip Flop:	2010	2010	100%
Number with an unused LUT:	0	2010	0%
Number of bonded IOBs:	63	600	10%
Number of DSP48E1	0	2800	0%

consumption of the vector product kernel module and multiplierless kernel for the binary linear classification is given in Table 17. From Table 14 and Table 15, we can interpret that the LUT usage in vector product kernel model is 0.6% while the LUT usage in multiplierless kernel is 0.7% but the dsp usage is minimized from 0.6% in vector product kernel to 0% in the multiplierless kernel. We can justify this increment in number of LUTs. As we are using CSD algorithm and add and shift operation in multiplierless binary SVM instead of vector multiplication the logic increases in multiplierless binary SVM. But this has no effect on the power factor which is demonstrated in Table 16. Here as the resource utilization (LUT) is higher in multiplierless kernel so the logic consumes higher power in multiplierless kernel than the vector product kernel. All the other power consumption factors like clock, PLL, I/O, device statistics and others consume almost same power for multiplierless kernel and the vector product kernel, only we can find a difference in power consumption in case of the dsp. As dsp consumes more power in vector product kernel, the total power consumption decreases from 1.493 to 1.479 using multiplierless kernel. So, we have achieved around 1% reduction in power in binary linear SVM.

Results of Hardware Implementation of Character Recognition

The primitive and black box uses of LUTs, DSP4s and clocks of character recognition SVM system using vector product kernel module and using multiplierless kernel is given in Table 18 and Table 19. The design utilization summary of the vector product kernel module and using multiplierless kernel is given in Table 20 and Table 21. This is obtained from the synthesis report of each design in XILINX.

Table 16. On- Chip Power Summary for binary linear SVM

On- chip	vector product kernel (W)	Multiplierless kernel (W)
Clock	0.005	0.002
Logic	0.012	0.014
PLL	0.114	0.114
Others	0.332	0.332
BRAM	0.000	0.000
I/Os	0.766	0.766
DSPs	0.012	0
Device Statistics	0.251	0.251

Table 17. Power consumption for binary linear SVM

Power (W)	Total(W)
Vector product Kernel	1.493
Multiplierless kernel	1.479

Table 18. Primitive and Black Box usage for vector product kernel of binary character recognition

GND	1	MUXCY	2787
INV	112	MUXF7	0
LUT1	118	VCC	1
LUT2	162	XORCY	3567
LUT3	1972	IBUF	68
LUT4	2159	OBUF	1
LUT5	346	IO buffers	69
LUT6	570	DSP48E1	20

Table 19. Primitive and Black Box usage for multiplierless kernel of binary character recognition

GND	1	MUXCY	2931
INV	119	MUXF7	0
LUT1	18	VCC	1
LUT2	263	XORCY	3256
LUT3	267	IBUF	26
LUT4	2363	OBUF	37
LUT5	1857	IO buffers	63
LUT6	691	DSP48E1	0

Table 20. Device utilization summary for vector product kernel of binary character recognition

Device: XILINX xc7vx485t-2-ffg1157	Utilized	Available	Percentage Utilization
Number of Slice LUTs:	5439	303600	1.7%
Number used as Logic:	5439	303600	1.7%
Number with an unused Flip Flop:	5439	5439	100%
Number with an unused LUT:	0	5439	0%
Number of bonded IOBs:	63	600	12%
Number of DSP48E1	20	2800	0.7%

Table 21. Device utilization summary for multiplierless kernel of binary character recognition

Device: XILINX xc7vx485t-2-ffg1157	Utilized	Available	Percentage Utilization
Number of Slice LUTs:	5473	303600	1.8%
Number used as Logic:	5473	303600	1.8%
Number with an unused Flip Flop:	5473	5473	100%
Number with an unused LUT:	0	5473	0%
Number of bonded IOBs:	63	600	12%
Number of DSP48E1	0	2800	0%

As we are implementing the character recognition system in VIRTEX 7 series, the power is measured using XILINX POWER ESTIMATOR (XPE) 14.1 because this version is used for power measurement of 7 series FPGA products. The on chip power summary report of both the vector product kernel module and multiplierless kernel for the character recognition SVM system is given in Table 22. The summary power consumption of the vector product kernel module and multiplierless kernel for the character recognition SVM system is given in Table 23 is minimized from 0.6% in vector product kernel to 0% in the multiplierless kernel. This increment in number of LUTs can be justified, as here we are using CSD

Table 22. On- Chip Power Summary for binary character recognition

On- chip	vector product kernel (W)	Multiplierless kernel (W)
Clock	0.005	0.002
Logic	0.038	0.041
PLL	0.114	0.114
Others	0.332	0.332
BRAM	0.000	0.272
I/Os	0.766	0.000
DSPs	0.015	0
Device Statistics	0.251	0.251

Table 23. Power consumption for binary character recognition

Power (W)	Total(W)
Vector product Kernel	1.522
Multiplierless kernel	1.506

algorithm and add and shift operation in multiplierless binary SVM instead of vector multiplication the logic increases in multiplierless binary SVM. In Table 22, we can see that the power consumption due to LUT usage can not affect power of the whole system. Here as the resource utilization (LUT) is higher in multiplierless kernel so the logic consumes higher power in multiplierless kernel than the vector product kernel. All the other power consumption factors like clock, PLL, I/O, device statistics and others consumes almost same power in case of multiplierless kernel and the vector product kernel except the dsp. As dsp consumes more power in vector product kernel, the total power consumption decreases from 1.522 to 1.506 using multiplierless kernel. So, we have achieved around 1.6% reduction in power in binary character recognition.

Hardware Implementation of Binary Nonlinear Classification

The primitive and black box uses of LUTs, DSP4s and clocks for binary non linear classifier using vector product kernel module and using multiplierless kernel is given in Table 24 and Table 25. The design utilization summary of the vector product kernel module and using multiplierless kernel is given in Table 26 and Table 27. The synthesis report estimates the resources used for every design implemented in Xilinx. The power is measured using XILINX POWER ESTIMATOR (XPE) 14.1. This version is used specifically for the 7 series XPE. The on chip power summary report of both the vector product kernel module and multiplierless kernel for the binary non linear classification is given in Table 28. The summary of power consumption of the vector product kernel module and multiplierless kernel for the binary non linear classification is given in Table 29. From Table 26 and Table 27, we can see that just like the binary linear case here also the percentage utilization of LUT slice and logic increases. In this case the increment of the LUT usage in vector product kernel module to the multiplierless kernel is 4.2% to 7% but the dsp usage is minimized from 23% in vector product kernel to 18% in the multiplierless kernel. This is because of the use of CSD algorithm and other logics to make the kernel module

Table 24. Primitive and Black Box usage for vector product kernel of binary nonlinear SVM

GND	1	MUXCY	9754
INV	3085	MUXF7	1
LUT1	1806	VCC	1
LUT2	2932	XORCY	9838
LUT3	2586	IBUF	26
LUT4	1562	OBUF	1
LUT5	445	IO buffers	27
LUT6	196	DSP48E1	651

Table 25. Primitive and Black Box usage for multiplierless kernel of binary nonlinear SVM

GND	1	MUXCY	2225
INV	2087	MUXF7	3
LUT1	1760	VCC	1
LUT2	3534	XORCY	5436
LUT3	4030	IBUF	26
LUT4	6379	OBUF	1
LUT5	1177	IO buffers	27
LUT6	46	DSP48E1	515

Table 26. Device utilization summary for vector product kernel of binary nonlinear SVM

Device: XILINX xc7vx7vx485t	Utilized	Available	Percentage Utilization
Number of Slice LUTs:	12612	303600	4.2%
Number used as Logic:	12612	303600	4.2%
Number with an unused Flip Flop:	12612	12612	100%
Number with an unused LUT:	0	12612	0%
Number of bonded IOBs:	27	600	4%
Number of DSP48E1	651	2800	23%

Table 27. Device utilization summary for multiplierless kernel of binary nonlinear SVM

Device: XILINX xc7vx7vx485t	Utilized	Available	Percentage Utilization
Number of Slice LUTs:	19023	303600	7%
Number used as Logic:	19023	303600	7%
Number with an unused Flip Flop:	19023	19023	100%
Number with an unused LUT:	0	19023	0%
Number of bonded IOBs:	27	600	4%
Number of DSP48E1	515	2800	18%

multiplier less. Thus number of LUT increases and dsp utilization decreases. In the nonlinear case for multiplierless kernel also 515 numbers of dsps are used. This is because we are using polynomial kernel of order 4. DSPs are extracted for the exponent operation of polynomial kernel. On chip power summary for binary nonlinear SVM is demonstrated in Table 28. Here as the resource utilization (LUT) is higher in multiplierless kernel so the logic consumes higher power in multiplierless kernel than the vector product kernel. All the other power consumption factors like clock, PLL, I/O, device statistics and others consumes almost same power for multiplierless kernel and the vector product kernel except the dsp.

Table 28. On- Chip Power Summary for binary nonlinear SVM

On- chip	vector product kernel (W)	Multiplierless kernel (W)
Clock	0.016	0.014
Logic	0.089	0.134
PLL	0.114	0.114
Others	0.332	0.332
BRAM	0.000	0.000
I/Os	0.766	0.766
DSPs	0.478	0.378
Device Statistics	0.255	0.255

But as the power consumption due to dsp is more in vector product kernel, the total power consumption decreases from 2.051 to 1.994 due to the use of multiplierless kernel. So we are successful in around 2.7% reduction in power in case of binary non linear SVM.

Multiclass Classification

In case of multiclass classification for the training phase all the three groups of Fisher iris data are taken. This training phase generates 74 SVs, 74 alpha values and 74 class labels as well as bias values for their corresponding classes. The output of training phase is shown in Figure 13, Figure 14 and Figure 15.The produced data is given in Table 30. The test samples are given as input to the multiplierless system. In the multiplierless block, to reduce the complexity of the coefficients, all the coefficients are expressed in the canonic signed digit (CSD) form as CSD codes minimize the number of adders or subtracters required in each coefficient multiplications. The common subexpression elimination (CSE) method has been used to make the multiplierless block as simple as possible. This further reduces the number of adders or subtractors. Then the multiplierless kernel operation is performed which yields a scalar output. The scalar output value is then multiplied with alpha values and class levels. Each PE performs all these operations in a pipelined manner. Simultaneously, the input vector element are passed to next PE. All the PEs give different scalar values which are stored in registers and then these values are added classwise along with the bias value. The class which gives the maximum value is the class of the unknown input sample. The output of multiclass classification is given in Table 31 and comparison of number of multiplicators used in vector product kernel and multiplierless kernel is shown in Table 32.

Table 29. Power consumption for binary nonlinear SVM

Power (W)	Total(W)
Vector product Kernel	2.051
Multiplierless kernel	1.994

Figure 13. Trained Support Vectors for multiclass SVM (separating class 1 from class 2 and 3)

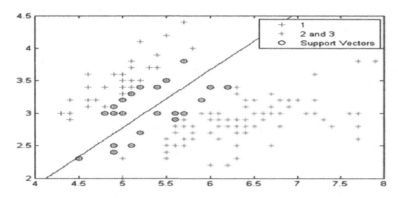

Figure 14. Trained Support Vectors for multiclass SVM (separating class 2 from class 1 and 3)

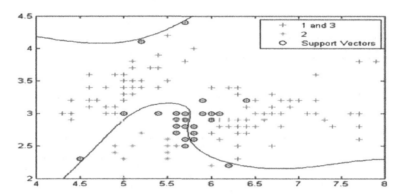

Figure 15. Trained Support Vectors for multiclass SVM (separating class 3 from class 1 and 2)

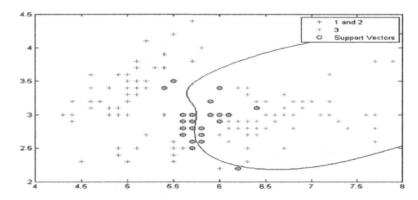

Multiclass Character recognition system: An application specific design

In our project, we will also check whether our proposed approach for multiclass SVM is efficient for any application specific design. For this purpose we are applying the multiplierless kernel in a 10 class problem of classifying numbers from 0 to 9. This recognition system can be used in many important

Table 30. Number of Support Vectors for each class

Sl No.	Group Names	No. of Training Samples	No. of Support Vectors	Bias Values
1	Class 1	50	12	1.0299
2	Class 2	50	30	-0.2240
3	Class 3	50	32	0.1719

Table 31. Values of Multiclass Classification

Test Vector	Class
[4.5 3]	1
[4.5 3.5]	1
[5 4]	1
[5.5 3.5]	1
[5 2.5]	2
[5.5 2.5]	2
[5.5 3]	2
[6 2.2]	2
[5.3 2.8]	2
[6.5 2.5]	3
7 2.9]	3
[6 2.9]	3
[7.5 2.5]	3
[7 2.3]	3

Table 32. Number of Multiplicators for Multiclass Classification

Dot product kernel function	Multiplierless kernel function
222	0

applications like number plate detection of vehicles etc. For this purpose, we have trained the SVM with sets of images of numbers 0 to 9. This phase will generate 48 SVs, alpha values and bias values. The parameters generated from the training phase are listed in Table 33. The output of the training phase is then used to classify the data. Here we also implemented the SVM design in hardware.

Hardware Implementation of Multiclass Classification

The primitive and black box uses of LUTs, DSP4s and clocks for multiclass classifier using vector product kernel module and using multiplierless kernel is given in Table 34 and Table 35. The design utilization summary of the vector product kernel module and using multiplierless kernel is given in Table 36 and

Table 33. Dimension for different matrices for number recognition of from "0" to "9"

Class	Test Vector	Support Vector	kernel	Decision fn
"0"	1×400	5×400	1×5	1×1
"1"	1×400	4×400	1×4	1×1
"2"	1×400	6×400	1×6	1×1
"3"	1×400	6×400	1×6	1×1
"4"	1×400	4×400	1×4	1×1
"5"	1×400	4×400	1×4	1×1
"6"	1×400	4×400	1×4	1×1
"7"	1×400	5×400	1×5	1×1
"8"	1×400	6×400	1×6	1×1
"9"	1×400	4×400	1×4	1×1

Table 37. The synthesis report estimates the resources used for every design implemented in Xilinx. The power is measured using XILINX POWER ESTIMATOR (XPE) 14.1. This version is used specifically for the 7 series XPE. The on chip power summary report of both the vector product kernel module and multiplierless kernel for multiclass classification is given in Table 38. The summary power consumption of the vector product kernel module and multiplierless kernel for the multiclass classification is given in Table 39. From Table 36 and Table 37, we can analyze that the percentage utilization of LUT and slice logic is very high in case of multiplierless kernel. This is because we have 74 PEs and in case of multiplierless kernel each PE carries all logics to perform multiplierless vector operation. Here in case of multiplierless kernel system, the LUT extraction is very high but as the dsp utilization ratio is 0% so the power is optimized. On chip power summary of multiclass SVM is demonstrated in Table 38. Here as the resource utilization (LUT) is higher in multiplierless kernel so the logic consumes higher power in multiplierless kernel than the vector product kernel. All the other power consumption factors like clock, PLL, I/O, device statistics and others consumes almost same power except dsp. As in case of vector product kernel the dsp power consumption is much higher due to use of large number of dsp units, the total power consumption decreases from 1.764 to 1.703 using multiplierless kernel. So we have reached to our goal that is around 3.5% reduction.

Table 34. Primitive and Black Box usage for vector product kernel of multiclass SVM

GND	1	MUXCY	12205
INV	6615	MUXF7	0
LUT1	493	VCC	1
LUT2	6005	XORCY	12552
LUT3	3139	IBUF	26
LUT4	540	OBUF	2
LUT5	12	IO buffers	28
LUT6	963	DSP48E1	222

Table 35. Primitive and Black Box usage for multiplierless kernel of multiclass SVM

GND	211	MUXCY	3352
INV	2695	MUXF7	0
LUT1	154	VCC	41
LUT2	4913	XORCY	3985
LUT3	7612	IBUF	26
LUT4	12874	OBUF	2
LUT5	712	IO buffers	28
LUT6	4400	DSP48E1	0

Table 36. Device utilization summary for vector product kernel of multiclass SVM

Device: VIRTEX7 xc7vx485t	Utilized	Available	Percentage Utilization
Number of Slice LUTs:	17767	303600	6%
Number used as Logic:	17767	303600	6%
Number with an unused Flip Flop:	17767	17767	100%
Number with an unused LUT:	0	23198	0%
Number of bonded IOBs:	28	600	4%
Number of DSP48E1	222	2800	8%

Table 37. Device utilization summary for multiplierless kernel of multiclass SVM

Device: VIRTEX7 xc7vx485t	Utilized	Available	Percentage Utilization
Number of Slice LUTs:	33360	303600	11%
Number used as Logic:	33360	303600	7%
Number with an unused Flip Flop:	33360	33360	100%
Number with an unused LUT:	0	33360	0%
Number of bonded IOBs:	28	600	4%
Number of DSP48E1	0	2800	0%

The output of the decision function for the multiclass classification is given in Table 3.10. Thus this design is also efficient for multiclass classification. Table 3.11 shows the number of multiplicators used in multiclass classification using vector product kernel function and multiplierless kernel function.

The computational complexity of matrix multiplication is $O(n^3)$. But as we have used here only adders and subtractors the computational complexity is $O(n)$.

Table 38. On- Chip Power Summary for multiclass SVM

On- chip	vector product kernel (W)	Multiplierless kernel (W)
Clock	0.010	0.002
Logic	0126	0.236
PLL	0.114	0.114
Others	0.332	0.332
BRAM	0.000	0.000
I/Os	0.766	0.766
DSPs	0.163	0.000
Device Statistics	0.253	0.253

Table 39. Power consumption for multiclass SVM

Power (W)	Total(W)
Vector product Kernel	1.764
Multiplierless kernel	1.703

Hardware Implementation Results of Multiclass Classification

The output of classification for input test vectors of image of numbers "0", "1", "2", "3", "4", "5", "6", "7", "8", "9" which are here taken as class "0001", "0010", "0011", "0100", "0101", "0110", "0111", "1000", "1001", "1010".

The primitive and black box uses of LUTs, DSP4s and clocks of multiclass character recognition SVM system using vector product kernel and multiplierless kernel is given in Table 40 and 41. The design utilization summary of the multiclass character recognition SVM using vector product kernel and multiplierless kernel is given in Table 42 and 43. This is obtained from the synthesis report of each design in XILINX. As we are implementing the character recognition system in VIRTEX 7 series, the power is measured using XILINX POWER ESTI MATOR (XPE) 14.1 because this version is used for power measurement of 7 series FPGA design. The on chip power summary report comparing vector

Table 40. Primitive and Black Box usage for vector product kernel of multiclass character recognition

GND	1	MUXCY	25293
INV	14748	MUXF7	1
LUT1	578	VCC	1
LUT2	1738	XORCY	24967
LUT3	7385	IBUF	204
LUT4	10349	OBUF	4
LUT5	31	IO buffers	208
LUT6	34	DSP48E1	576

Table 41. Primitive and Black Box usage for multiplierless kernel of multiclass character recognition

GND	1	MUXCY	30347
INV	17340	MUXF7	1
LUT1	945	VCC	1
LUT2	2360	XORCY	30111
LUT3	8552	IBUF	204
LUT4	10932	OBUF	4
LUT5	84	IO buffers	208
LUT6	91	DSP48E1	0

Table 42. Device utilization summary for vector product kernel of multiclass character recognition

Device: VIRTEX7vx485tffg1157	Utilized	Available	Percentage Utilization
Number of Slice LUTs:	34863	303600	11%
Number used as Logic:	34863	303600	11%
Number with an unused Flip Flop:	34863	34863	100%
Number with an unused LUT:	0	34863	0%
Number of bonded IOBs:	208	600	34%
Number of DSP48E1	576	2800	20%

Table 43. Device utilization summary for multiplierless kernel of multiclass character recognition

Device: VIRTEX7 xc7vx485t	Utilized	Available	Percentage Utilization
Number of Slice LUTs:	40304	303600	13%
Number used as Logic:	40304	303600	13%
Number with an unused Flip Flop:	40304	40304	100%
Number with an unused LUT:	0	40304	0%
Number of bonded IOBs:	63	600	34%
Number of DSP48E1	0	2800	0%

product kernel and multiplierless kernel based the character recognition SVM system is given in Table 44. The summary of power consumption of the vector product kernel module and multiplierless kernel for the character recognition is given in Table 45. From Table 42 and Table 43, we can interpret that the LUT usage in vector product kernel model is 11% while the LUT usage in multiplierless kernel is 13% but the dsp usage is minimized from 20% in vector product kernel to 0% in the multiplierless kernel. This increment in number of LUTs can be justified, as here we are using CSD algorithm and add and shift operation in multiplierless binary SVM instead of vector multiplication the logic increases in multiplierless binary SVM. In Table 44, we can see that the power consumption due to LUT usage can not affect power of the whole system. Here as the resource utilization (LUT) is higher in multiplierless

Table 44. On- Chip Power Summary for multiclass character recognition

On- chip	vector product kernel (W)	Multiplierless kernel (W)
Clock	0.015	0.002
Logic	0.246	0.285
PLL	0.114	0.114
Others	0.332	0.332
BRAM	0.000	0.000
I/Os	0.766	0.766
DSPs	0.423	0
Device Statistics	0.256	0.253

Table 45. Power consumption for multiclass character recognition

Power (W)	Total(W)
Vector product Kernel	2.153
Multiplierless kernel	1.752

kernel so the logic consumes higher power in multiplierless kernel than the vector product kernel. All the other power consumption factors like clock, PLL, I/O, device statistics and others consumes almost same power in case of multiplierless kernel and the vector product kernel except the dsp. As dsp consumes more power in vector product kernel, the total power consumption decreases from 2.153 to 1.752 using multiplierless kernel. So, here we have achieved 18% reduction in power in multiclass character recognition which is the maximum power reduction we obtained among all the system we tested using our proposed multiplierless kernel.

Summary

We have successfully implemented our design in three different classification problem systems. We are able to reduce significant amount of resource and power utilization. Comparison of number of multiplicators used for different classification problem is shown in Table 46. % reduction in power using

Table 46. Number of multiplicators for all the 4 classification problems

Classification	Dot product kernel fn	Multiplierless kernel fn
Binary linear	18	0
Binary non linear	20	0
Multiclass	651	515
Binary Character recognition	148	0
Multiclass Character recognition	576	0

proposed kernel for all the classification results is listed in Table 47. From this table we can see that the power decrement is high in case of binary nonlinear and multiclass kernel which are mainly used for real-time applications.

CONCLUSION

SVM is efficient in classification problems and has numerous applications in object detection, computer vision and image processing. It has been effectively implemented in software. But the hardware implementation of this continues to be challenging. Here, we have proposed the design of multiplierless kernel function which is suitable for binary and multiclass problems with both low and high dimension data. The proposed multiplierless kernel is used in case of binary linear, binary nonlinear and multiclass classification. All of these classification problems showing successful results in classifying the data. We have also implemented the above three different classification problems in hardware using multiplierless kernel module. Comparative analysis of these three classification problem is done using multiplierless kernel and the classification problem using conventional vector product kernel regarding resource utilization, shows better results. We are also able to lower the power requirement of the hardware design of all the three classification problem discussed here using the proposed multiplierless kernel compared to the vector product kernel. Hardware implementation of a binary and multiclass character recognition system using proposed kernel also shows successful results in terms of efficiency, power and hardware complexity. The multiplierless kernel design uses CSD and CSE based systolic array PEs which contribute toward lowering of processing cycles and also reduces power. These attributes make the system suitable for computer vision application involving high dimension data.

LIMITATION

The main limitation of the project is that this multiplierless kernel function operation is efficient for the linear and polynomial basis function not for the radial basis function. But from the comparative study of all the kernel function we come to know that linear kernel function is best for binary classification while for multiclass classification the polynomial basis function is considered to be best for most of the cases.

FUTURE DIRECTION

In future this idea can also be used in any detection problem using SVM. This approach can also be evaluated in image processing, bio-informatics and computer vision. To perform operations excluding

Table 47. Power reduction using multiplierless kernel compared to vector product kernel

Binary linear	Binary Character recognition	Binary non linear	Multiclass	Multiclass character recognition
1%	1.6%	2.7%	3.5%	18%

the kernel function, faster and efficient method could be explored in spite of the systolic array. This idea can also be translated to make a complete ASIC design for solving a real time classification problem which can also be helpful for proper analysis in terms of power, area, design complexity and speed.

REFERENCES

Anguita, D., Boni, A., & Ridella, S. (2003). A digital architecture for support vector machines: Theory, algorithm and FPGA implementation. *IEEE Transactions on Neural Networks*, *14*(5), 993–1009. doi:10.1109/TNN.2003.816033 PMID:18244555

Arnaud, J. (1986). Use of unidirectional data flow in bit level systolic array chips. *Electronics Letters*, *22*(10), 540–541. doi:10.1049/el:19860368

Biasi, I., Boni, A., & Zorat, A. (2005). A reconfigurable parallel architecture for SVM classification. *Proceedings of IEEE International Joint Conference on Neural Networks* (Vol. 5, pp. 2867 – 2872)

Burges, J. C. (1998). A Tutorial on Support Vector Machines for Pattern Recognition.

Buzbee, B., Wang, W. & Wang, A. A. (n. d.). Power Saving Approaches and Trade-off for Storage Systems. Florida State University.

Cadambi, S., Durdanovic, I., Jakkula, V., Sankaradass, M., Cosatto, E., Chakradhar, S., & Graf, H. (2009). A massively parallel FPGA-based coprocessor for support vector machines. *Proceedings of 17th IEEE Symposium on Field Programmable Custom Computing Machines* (pp. 115 -122). doi:10.1109/FCCM.2009.34

Canny, M., Whirter, M. J. G., & Wood, K. W. (1984). Optimized bit level systolic array for convolution. IEEE Proc. F, Commun, Radar and Signal Process, 6, 632-637.

Chai, S. M., Wills, D. S., & Jokerst, N. M. (1997). Systolic processing architectures using optoelectronic interconnects. *Proceedings of the Fourth International Conference on Massively Parallel Processing Using Optical Interconnections* (pp. 160-166). doi:10.1109/MPPOI.1997.609179

Chavhan, Y., Dhore, M. L., & Yesaware, P. (2010). Speech Emotion Recognition Using Support Vector Machine. *International Journal of Computers and Applications*, *1*(20), 6–9.

Coleman, J. O., & Yurdakul, A. (2001). Fractions in the canonical-signed-digit number system. *Proceedings of Conference on Information Sciences and Systems, the Johns Hopkins University*.

Cortes, C., & Vapnik, V. (1995). Support-vector networks, Machine Learning. *Journal Machine Learning*, *20*(3), 273–297. doi:10.1007/BF00994018

Genov, R., & Cauwenberghs, G. (2003). Kerneltron: Support Vector Machine in Silicon. [PubMed]. *IEEE Transactions on Neural Networks*, *14*(5), 1426–1434. doi:10.1109/TNN.2003.816345

Goldberg, Y., & Elhadad, M. (2008). splitSVM: Fast, space-efficient, non-heuristic, polynomial kernel computation for NLP applications. *Proceedings of the 46st Annual Meeting of the Association of Computational Linguistics*. doi:10.3115/1557690.1557758

Gunn, S. R. (1998). *Support Vector Machines for Classification and Regression*. University of Southampton.

Hiraiwa, A., Fujita, M., Kurosu, S., & Arisawa, S. (1990). Implementation of ANN on RISC processor array. *Proceedings of the International Conference on Application Specific Array Processors* (pp. 677 – 688). doi:10.1109/ASAP.1990.145502

Khan, E. R., & Nam, L. (1991) Two-dimensional multi rate systolic array design for artificial neural networks. *Proceedings on First Great Lakes Symposium on VLSI* (pp. 186 – 193). doi:10.1109/GLSV.1991.143964

Khan, F. M., Arnold, M. G., & Pottenger, W. M. (2005). Hardware-Based Support Vector Machine Classification in Logarithmic Number Systems. *Circuits and Systems, 2005. ISCAS 2005. Proceedings of IEEE International Symposium* (Vol. 5, pp. 5154 – 5157).

Kim, S., Lee, S. & Cho, K. (2012). Design of High-Performance Unified Circuit for Linear and Non-Linear SVM Classifications. *Journal of semiconductor technology and science*, 12(2), 162-167.

Klass, K. (1991). Efficient systolic array for linear discriminant classifier. *IEEE, Delft university of Technology*. (pp. 701-704).

Knuth, D. (1997). *The Art of Computer Programming* (3rd ed.). Addison Wesley.

Kung, H. T. Why Systolic Architectures? *Carnegie-Mellon University*.

Kyrkou, C. (2010). Embedded hardware architecture for object detection.

Kyrkou, C., & Theocharides, T. (2009). SCoPE: Towards a systolic array for SVM object detection. *Embedded Systems Letters, IEEE*, 1(2), 46–49. doi:10.1109/LES.2009.2034709

Li, T., Zhu, S., & Ogihara, M. (2006). Using discriminant analysis for multiclass classification: an experimental investigation (pp. 453-472). London: Springer, Verlag.

Llata, M. R., Guarnizo, G., & Calvino, M. Y. (2010). FPGA Implementation of a Support Vector Machine for Classification and Regression. Proceedings of *WCCI 2010 IEEE World Congress on Computational Intelligence* (pp. 2037-2041).

Madzarov, G., Gjorgjevikj, D., & Chorbev, I. (2009). A Multi-class SVM Classifier Utilizing Binary Decision Tree. *Informatica*, *33*, 233–241.

Mandal, B., Sarma, M. P., & Sarma, K. K. (2014). Design of Systolic array based Multiplierless SVM Classifier. Proceedings of *IEEE International Conference on Signal Processing and Integrated Networks* (pp. 35-39). Noida.

Meher, P. K. (2010). Systolic VLSI and FPGA Realization of Artificial Neural Networks. *Springer Berlin Heidelberg*, 7, 359–380.

Milentijevic, I. Z., Milovanovic, I. Z., Milovanovic, E. I., & Stojcev, M. K. (1997). The design of optimal planar systolic arrays for matrix multiplication. *Computers & Mathematics with Applications (Oxford, England)*, *33*(6), 17–35. doi:10.1016/S0898-1221(97)00028-X

Milovanovic, I. Z., Milovanovic, E. I., Randjelovic, B. M., & Jovanovic, I. C. (2003). Matrix multiplication on bidirectional systolic arrays. *FILOMAT*, *17*(17), 135–141. doi:10.2298/FIL0317135M

Parhi, K. K. (2012). VLSI digital signal processing system. New Delhi: Wiley India (P.) Ltd.

Patil, R. A., Gupta, G., Sahula, V., & Mandal, A. S. (2012). Power aware Hardware prototyping of multiclass SVM classifier through Reconfiguration. Proceedings of *25th International Conference on VLSI Design* (pp. 62-67). doi:10.1109/VLSID.2012.47

Preman, J. A., & Suapura, D. M. (1991). *Neural Networks: algorithms, application and programming techniques*. Addison-Wesly.

Reyna, R., Esteve, D., Houzet, D., & Albenge, M. F. (2000). Implementation of the SVM neural network generalization function for image processing. *Proceedings Fifth IEEE International Workshop on Computer Architectures for Machine Perception* (pp. 147 -151). doi:10.1109/CAMP.2000.875972

Schoelkopf, B., Sung, K., Burges, C., Girosi, F., Niyogin, P., Poggio, T., & Vapnik, V. (1996). *Comparing Support Vector Machines with Gaussian Kernels to Radial Basis Function Classifiers*. MA: Massachusetts Institute of Technology. Cambridge.

Shen, W., & Oruc, A. Y. (1990). Systolic array for multidimensional discrete transform. University of Maryland (Vol. 4, pp. 201-222).

Takahashi, Y., & Yokoyama, M. (2005). New Cost-effective VLSI Implementation of Multiplierless FIR Filter using Common Subexpression Elimination (pp. 1445-1448).

Urquahart, R. B. & Wood. (1984). Systolic matrix and vector multiplication methods for signal. *IEEE Proc. F, Commun., Radar and Signal processing,* 623-631.

Vanschoenwinkel, B., & Manderick, B. (2004). *Appropriate Kernel Functions for Support Vector Machine Learning with Sequences of Symbolic Data*. Vrije Universiteit, Brussel.

Wang, C., & Wci, C. & Cheii. (1986). Improved systolic array for linear discriminant function classifier. *Elecfron. Lr.*, *22*, 85–86.

Wu, Q., & Sun, Y. (2003). A Novel Algorithm for Common Subexpression Elimination in VLSI implementation of high speed multiplierless FIR Filters. Institute of Microelectronics, Tsinghua University, 1-7.

KEY TERMS AND DEFINITIONS

Kernel Methods: Kernel methods are the methods used for pattern analysis. They compute inner product between all pairs of data of images in the feature space to operate in higher dimension.

Multiple Constant Multiplications (MCM): The generation of a multiplier block from the set of constants is known as the multiple constant multiplication (MCM) problems.

Natural Language Processing: It is the study of artificial intelligence that concerned with the interaction between human and computer languages.

Processing Elements (PE): Systolic array is formed with many PEs arranged in matrix form. The PEs in a systolic array are similar and perform same arithmetic and logical operations.

Training Phase: It is one of the important phase of classification where the classifier is trained with data of known class so that it can classify unknown data.

Chapter 6
Bloodless Technique to Detect Diabetes using Soft Computational Tool

Puspalata Sah
Centre of Plasma Physics, Institute for Plasma Research, India

Kandarpa Kumar Sarma
Gauhati University, India

ABSTRACT

Detection of diabetes using bloodless technique is an important research issue in the area of machine learning and artificial intelligence (AI). Here we present the working of a system designed to detect the abnormality of the eye with pain and blood free method. The typical features for diabetic retinopathy (DR) are used along with certain soft computing techniques to design such a system. The essential components of DR are blood vessels, red lesions visible as microaneurysms, hemorrhages and whitish lesions i.e., lipid exudates and cotton wool spots. The chapter reports the use of a unique feature set derived from the retinal image of the eye. The feature set is applied to a Support Vector Machine (SVM) which provides the decision regarding the state of infection of the eye. The classification ability of the proposed system for blood vessel and exudate is 91.67% and for optic disc and microaneurysm is 83.33%.

INTRODUCTION

Diabetic retinopathy is the commonest cause of blindness and one of the commonest cause of vision defects in both developing and developed countries (Chaudhuri, Chatterjee, Katz, Nelson & Goldman, 1989). The World Health Organization (WHO) has estimated that, the number of adults with diabetes increasing alarmingly: from 135 million in 1995 to 300 million in 2025 (Premi, 2015). In India, this increases is expected to be greatest; 195 from 18 million in 1995 to 54 million in 2025. Studies done by the ICMR in the early 1970s had shown the prevalence of diabetes in India to be 2.5 and 1.5% in the rural

DOI: 10.4018/978-1-4666-8493-5.ch006

population. However recent reports have shown the prevalence to be in the range of 12% to 14% in the urban population. Of these patients with diabetes, over 20% are expected to be suffering from diabetic retinopathy. The prevalence of diabetes in the rural population is expected to be about 5%.

Diabetes is a disorder of metabolism. The energy required by the body is obtained from glucose which is produced as a result of food digestion (Chaudhuri, Chatterjee, Katz, Nelson & Goldman, 1989). Digested food enters the body stream with the aid of a hormone called insulin that is produced by the pancreas, an organ that lies near the stomach. During eating, the pancreas automatically produces the correct amount of insulin needed for allowing glucose absorption from the blood into the cells. In individuals with diabetes, the pancreas either produces too little or no insulin or the cells do not react properly to the insulin or the cells don't react properly to the insulin that is produced (Bevilacqua, Cambo, Cariello & Mastronardi, 2005). The buildup of glucose in the blood, overflows into the urine and then passes out of the body. Therefore, the body losses its main source of fuel even though the blood contains large amount of glucose. Basically there are three types of diabetes:

1) Diabetes caused as a result of auto immune problem. The immune system of the body destroys the insulin producing beta cells in the pancreas leading to no or less production of required insulin by the pancreas.
2) Diabetes due to malfunctioning of beta cell itself. This malfunction includes non production of insulin or situation known as insulin resistance (Wang, Hsu, Goh & Lee, 2000).
3) Third type is known as gestational diabetes. During this stage, the body resist the effect of insulin produced.

The effect of diabetes on the eye is called Diabetic Retinopathy (DR). It is known to damage the small blood vessel of the retina and this might lead to loss of vision. The disease is classified into three stages viz. Background Diabetic Retinopathy (BDR), Proliferate Diabetic Retinopathy (PDR) and Severe Diabetic Retinopathy (SDR). In BDR phase, the arteries in the retina become weakened and leak, forming small, dot like haemorrhages. These leaking vessels often lead to swelling or edema in the retina and decreased vision. In the PDR phase, circulation problems cause areas of the retina to become oxygen deprived or ischemic. New fragile, vessels develop as the circulatory system attempts to maintain adequate oxygen levels within the retina. This phenomenon is called neovascularisation. Blood may leak into the retina and vitreous, causing spots or floaters, along with decreased vision. In the SDR phase of the disease, there is continued abnormal vessel growth and scar tissue, which may cause serious problems such as retinal detachment and glaucoma and gradual loss of vision.

Diabetes is a major disease affecting a sizable portion of the humanity. Hence, detection of diabetes and its subsequent is a major challenge faced by the medical fraternity. Traditional methods of detection of diabetes involves pain and necessity of blood which has certain constraints including the possibility of contamination and related health hazards. Hence, there is a necessity to develop systems which are painless and also don't require blood samples. Detection of diabetes using bloodless technique is an issue which is in the limelight of research in the field of machine learning and artificial intelligence (AI). It primarily intends to contribute towards faster and efficient means of detection and subsequent diagnosis of diabetes. Here, we present the working of a system designed to detect the abnormality of the eye with pain- and blood-free method. The typical features for diabetic retinopathy (DR) are used along with certain soft computing techniques to design such a system. The essential components of DR are blood vessels, red lesions visible as microaneurysms, hemorrhages and whitish lesions i.e., lipid exudates and cotton wool spots. We formulate a framework for bloodless diagnosis of diabetes using a unique feature set derived from the retinal image of the eye. The feature set is applied to a soft computational tool Support Vector Machine (SVM) which provides us the decision regarding the state of infection of the eye. The classification ability of the proposed system for blood vessel and exudate is 91.67% and for optic disc and microaneurysm is 83.33%.

DIABETIC RETINOPATHY

Diabetic can affect the eye in a number of ways. It affects the retina, mainly the network of blood vessel lying within it. The name of this condition is diabetic retinopathy. There are four stages of diabetic retinopathy:

1) Mild nonproliferative retinopathy: At this early stage microaneurysms ocuurs. They are small areas of balloon like swelling in the retina's tiny blood vessels.
2) Moderate nonproliferative retinopathy: As the disease progress, some blood vessels that nourish the retina are blocked.
3) Severe nonproliferative retinopathy: Many more blood vessels are blocked, depriving several areas of the retina send signals to the body to grow new blood vessels for nourishment.
4) Proliferative retinopathy: At this advance stage, the signals sent by the retina for the nourishment trigger the growth of new blood vessels. This condition is called proliferative retinopathy. These new blood vessels are abnormal and fragile. These blood vessels have thin fragile walls. If they leak blood severe vision loss and even blindness can result.

There are two ways in which one's vision may be affected due to diabetic retinopathy.

1) Fragile, abnormal blood vessels can develope and leak blood into the centre of the eye, blurring vision. This is proliferative retinopathy and is the most advance stage of the disease.
2) Fluid can leak into the centre of the macula, part of the eye where sharp and straightahead vision occurs. The fluid makes the macula swell, blurring vision. This condition is called macular edema. It can occur in the any stage of diabetic retinopathy.

ABNORMALITIES ASSOCIATED WITH THE EYE

Abnormalities associated with the eye can be divided into two main classes, the first being disease of the eye, such as cataract, conjunctivitis, blepharitis and glaucoma. The second group is categorized as life style related disease such as life style related disease such as hypertension, arteriosclerosis and diabetes (Gardenr, Abcouwer, Barber & Jackson, 2011). When the retina is been affected as a result of diabetes, this type of disease is called Diabetic retinopathy (DR). DR occurrence have been generally categorise into three main form viz. BDR, PDR, SDR as discussed above. These three classes can occur in any of the form described below:

Microanurysms: These are the first clinical abnormality to be noticed in the eye. They may appear in isolation or in clusters as tiny, dark red spots or looking like tiny haemorrhages within the light sensitive retina. Their sizes ranges from 10-100 microns i.e. less than 1/12th the diameter of an average optics disc and are circular in shape (Sah & Sarma, 2013) at this stage, the disease is not eye threatening.

Haemorrhages: Occurs in the deeper layers of the retina and are often called plot haemorrhages because of their round shape.

Hard Exudates: These are one of the main characteristics of diabetic retinopathy and can vary in size from tiny specks to large patches with clear edges. As well as blood, fluid that is rich in fat and protein is containes in the eye and this is what leaks out to form the exudates. These can impair vision by preventing light from reaching the retina.

Soft Exudates: These are often called cotton wool spots and are more often seen in advance retinopathy.

Neuvascularisation: This can be described as abnormal growth of blood vessels in areas of the eye including the retina and is associated with vision loss. This occurs in response to ischemia, or diminished blood flow to ocular tissues. If these abnormal blood vessels grow around the pupil, glaucoma can result from the increasing pressure within the eye. These new blood vessels vessels weaker walls and may break and bleed, or cause scar tissue to grow that can pull the retina away from the back of the eye. When the retina is pulled away it is called a retinal detachment can cause severe vision loss, including blindness. Leaking blood can cloud the vitreous (the clear, jelly like substance that fills the eye) and block the light passing through the pupil to the retina, causing blurred and distorted images. In more advanced proliferate retinopathy, diabetic fiborous or scar tissue can form on retina (Lochan, Sah & Sarma, 2012).

The algorithm used in our case is classified in terms of five basic image processing and decision making categories. The associated primary subdivision are as follows:

- Preprocessing stages
    1. Correction of non-uniform illumination
    2. Color normalization
    3. Contrast enhancement
- Localization and Segmentation of Optic Disc
    1. Charecteristics of the optic Disc
    2. Optic Disc localization
    3. Optic disc segmentation
- Localization of Macula Fovea
    1. Characteristics of the macula and fovea
    2. Methods for localizing the macula and fovea
- Segmentation of retinal vasculature
    1. Charecteristics of the vaculature
    2. Method for segmenting the vasculature
- Localization and Segmentation of retinopathy
    1. Microaneurysms/ haemorrhages
    2. Exudates/ cotton wool spots

OVERVIEW OF THE DETECTION

The proposed system in a conceptualized form is depicted in Figure 1. It has several stages which are discussed in the subsequent sections.

Figure 1. System Model

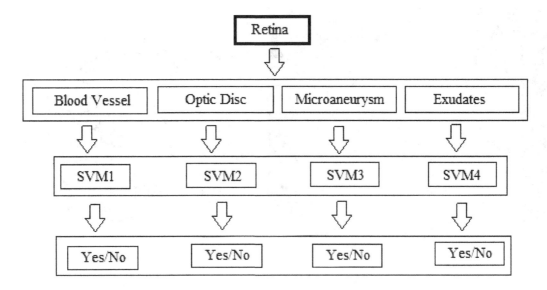

Detection of Blood Vessel

Information about retinal blood vessels is important for the diagnosis, treatment, evaluation, and clinical study of many diseases such as diabetes and hypertension (Ming, 2009). Changes in vessel morphology can indicate the current state and progression of a disease. For example, the diameter, shape, and colour of retinal arteries and veins can be used for grading the severity and progression of a number of diseases. Figure 2 shows the block diagram of the system adopted to detect the blood vessel (Vallabha, Dorairaj, Namuduri &Thompson, 2004).

Blood vessels are extracted in our work for the identification of diabetic retinopathy. The contrast of the fundus image tends to be bright in the centre and diminish at the side, hence pre-processing is essential to minimize this effect and have a more uniform image. After which, the green channel of the image is applied with morphological image processing to remove the optical disc. Image segmentation is then performed to adjust the contrast intensity and small pixels considered to be noise are removed. The obtained image would represent the blood vessel of the original image as indicated in Figure 3.

Figure 2. Block diagram to detect the blood vessel

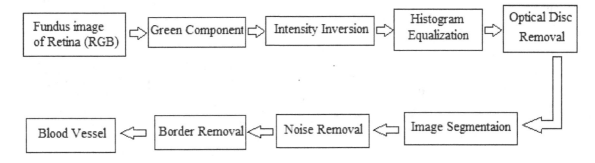

Figure 3. Input image with the extracted blood vessel

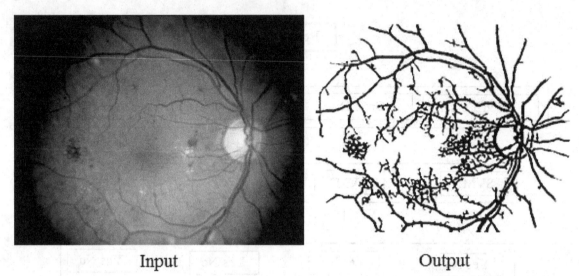

Input   Output

Detection of Microaneurysm

These are the first clinical abnormality to be noticed in the eye. They may appear in isolation or in clusters as tiny, dark red spots or looking like tiny haemorrhages within the light sensitive retina. Their sizes ranges from 10-100 microns i.e. less than $1/12^{th}$ the diameter of an average optics disc and are circular in shape (Ahmad, Mansoor, Mumtaz, Khan, & Mirza, 2014), at this stage, the disease is not eye threatening. Figure 4 shows the block diagram to detect the microaneurysm. The grayscale image is used to detect the circular border and optical disc mask. The green channel of the images first finds the edges using the Canny operator before removing the circular border to fill the enclosed small area. The image is contrast is stretched by applying adaptive histogram equalization before using edge detection to detect the outlines of the image. The larger area are then removed and applied with the AND logic to remove the exudates. The output is the microaneurysm Figure 5.

Figure 4. Block diagram to detect microaneurysm

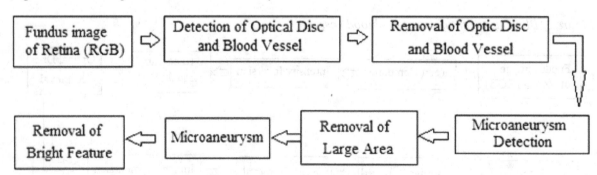

Figure 5. Input image with the detected microaneurysm

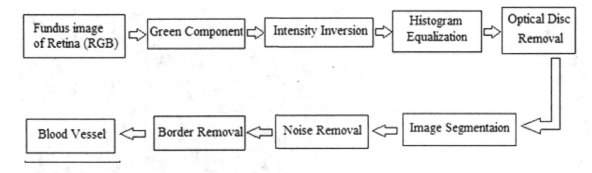

Detection of Optic disc

As the optical disc is made up of a group of bright spots, it is not suitable to use loops and locate the largest value. This would only point to one spot and most likely to be on the side of the optical disk. The mask required to cover the optical disk would be inefficient as it would be much larger and covers more details. Mask creation is used in the detection of blood vessels, exudates and microaneurysms. Gray scale image instead of the green channel is used as it is more efficient in the detection (Wang, Hsu, Goh & Lee, 2000).. The above lines would first and the maximum value for each of the 720 columns of the image before locating the largest value. The co-ordinates (row and column) of all brightness point (s) are than one point. After locating the optical disc, a mask needs to be created. The radius of the mask is given by:

$$R^2 = (x - h)^2 + (y - k)^2$$

where *h* and *k* are the coordinates (row and columns), *x* and *y* are the matrices. Figure 6 shows the block diagram for the detection of optic disc and Figure 7 shows extracted optic disc.

Figure 6. Block diagram to detect optic disc

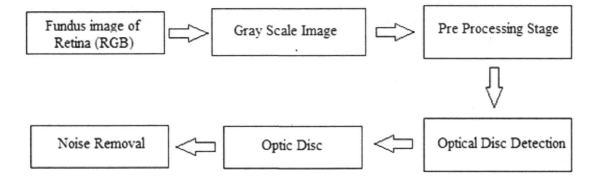

Figure 7. Input image with extracted optic disc

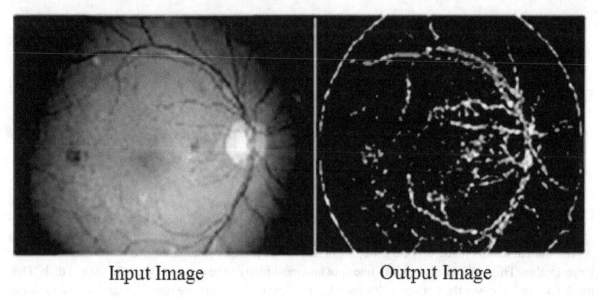

Input Image   Output Image

Detection of Exudates

Exudates appeared as bright yellow - white deposits on the retina due to the leakage blood from abnormal vessels. Their shape and size will vary with the different retinopathy stages. The grayscale image is first pre processed for uniformity before the morphological image processing is applied to remove the blood vessels and identify the exudates region (Vapnik, 1998). The exudates are detected after removing the border, optical disc and non exudates area. Figure 8 shows the block diagram to detect exudates. In Fig 9, we can see the extracted exudates from the input image.

PROPOSED SYSTEM

The proposed system is based on SVM which uses a feature set. The system provides us the decision regarding the state of infection of the eye for a range of samples considered for the purpose. In the recent years, SVM classifiers have demonstrated excellent performance as a soft computational tool in a variety of pattern recognition problem (Xu, Chan, 2003).

Figure 8. Block diagram to detect Exudates

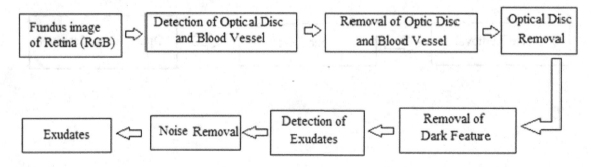

Figure 9. Input image with extracted exudates

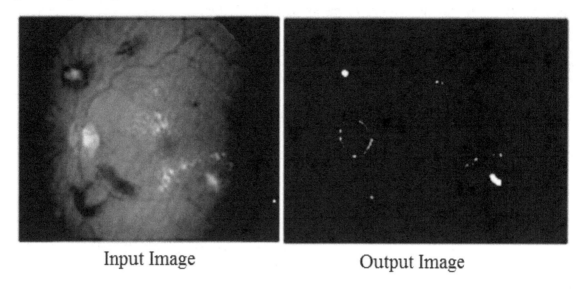

Input Image   Output Image

In a system based on SVM, the input space is mapped into a high dimensional feature space. Then, the hyper plane that maximizes the margin of separation between classes is constructed. The points that lie closest to the decision surface are called support vectors and directly affect its location (Gonzalez & Woods, 2002). When the classes are non-separable, the optimal hyperplane is the one that minimizes the probability of classification error as indicated in Figure 10.

Figure 10. Optimal hyperplane, margin and support vectors

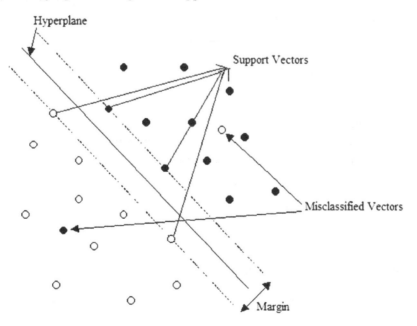

The general method of construction of the Optimal Hyperplane (HO) which separates from the data belonging to two different classes linearly separable is as follows:Let, $H : (w \cdot x) + b$ be the hyperplane, which satisfies the following condition:

$$y_i (w \cdot x_i + b) \geq 1 \ldots\ldots\ldots\ i = 1, \ldots\ldots, m$$

To find the optimal hyperplane amounts to maximizing the margin

$$M = \frac{2}{\|w\|}.$$

This is equivalent to minimize

$$\frac{\|w\|^2}{2}$$

under the constraint. This is a problem of minimization of a quadratic objective function with linear constraints

$$\min \frac{1}{2}\|w\|^2 \ \forall i, y_i(w.x_i + b) \geq 1$$

By applying the principle of Lagrange, one obtains the quadratic problem of programming of dimension m (a number of examples) according to

$$\max \sum_{i=1}^{m} \alpha_i - \frac{1}{2} \sum_{i,j} \alpha_i \alpha_j y_i y_j (x_i \cdot x_j) \forall i, \alpha_i \geq 0$$

where, α_i are the coefficients of Lagrange.

The solution for the optimum boundary w_0 is a linear combination of subset of the training data, $s \in \{1, \ldots\ldots\ldots , N\}$: the support vectors. These support vectors define the margin edges and satisfy the equality $y_i[(w_0 \cdot x_i) + b_0] = 1$, what is equivalent to:

$$VS = \{x_i | \alpha_i \rangle 0\} \ldots\ldots\ldots i = 1, \ldots..m$$

The function of classification *class(x)* is defined by:

$$class(x) = sign\big[(w_0 \cdot x) + b_0\big]$$

$$= sign\left[\sum_{x_i \in VS} \alpha_i y_i (x_i \cdot x) + b_0\right]$$

If *class (x)* is lower than *0, X* is in the class "-1" if not it is in the class 1.The typical kernel functions are listed below:

- Linear, $k(x, x') = x.x'$
- Polynomial, $k(x, x') = (x, x')^d \, ou(c + x.x')^d$
- Gaussian, $k(x, x') = e^{(-\|x - x'\|^2)/\sigma}$
- Sigmoid, $k(x, x') = \tanh(\alpha_0(x.x') + \beta_0)$

With the origin, the SVM were conceived primarily for the problems with 2 classes, however several approaches making it possible to extend this algorithm to the cases N classes were proposed. Generalization in the case multi-classes can be done in three different ways. In this paper, SVM is used as binary classifier.

EXPERIMENTAL DETAILS AND RESULTS

As discussed above, we take different fundus image of retina of both normal and diabetic effected. The different features (blood Vessel, microaneurysm, optic disc, exudates) extracted using the proposed algorithm (Ahmad et al., 2014) (Wang et al., 2000)and then these extracted features (Figures 3, 5, 7 and 9) are applied to the SVM classifier for classification. Next, we used 3 abnormal (abnormal1, abnormal2, abnormal3) samples and 3 normal (normal1, normal2, normal3) samples of retina. Thus, a total of nine combination of retina for training are obtained. Each sample is tested for twelve to fifteen times. The overall block diagram for our system is already shown in Figure 1. Tables 1, 3, 5 and 7 show testing data for features related to blood vessel, microaneurysm, optic disc and exudates respectively.

Table 1. Testing data for blood vessel

Test Sample	Correct Classification	Classification (%)
12	11	91.67
12	10	83.33
12	9	75
12	12	100
12	12	100
12	9	75
12	12	100
12	12	100
12	12	100

We tested our classifier system for different feature combination of normal and abnormal samples of retina (Table 9) and it shows that designed SVM classifier is able to classify from 87.49% to 91.67% (Tables 2, 4, 6 and 8) for different features and combination of different feature sets.

The outputs of the SVM classifier are shown in Tables 10, 11, 12 and 13 where, the blue arrow represents the weight vector and red is decision boundary. The experiment is performed for each Feature with threshold value: 0.735 and weight vectors (2.789 and -2.054) for blood vessel with threshold value: -0.691 and weight vectors (2.786 and -2.095) for optical disc, microaneurysm and exudates. The shadow around the decision boundary represent the minimum margin on the training data (the SVM algorithm finds the largest possible minimum margin). Circles and green lines indicate the support vectors of the classifier. The perpendicular distance of the decision boundary from the origin is $\left(-\theta / \|w\|\right)$, where θ the threshold is and w is the weight vector.

Table 2. Results of SVM classification for blood vessel

No.of training	No. Of Testing	No. Of Correctly Classified	Classification (%)
9	12	11	91.66

Table 3. Testing data for microaneurysm

Test Sample	Correct Classification	Classification (%)
12	10	83.33
12	8	83.33
12	12	100
12	11	91.67
12	9	75
12	9	75
12	10	83.33
12	10	83.33
12	11	91.67

Table 4. Results of SVM classification for microaneurysm

No.of training	No. Of Testing	No. Of Correctly Classified	Classification (%)
9	12	10	83.33

Table 5. Testing data for optic disc

Test Sample	Correct Classification	Classification (%)
12	12	100
12	8	66.67
12	10	83.33
12	9	75
12	11	91.67
12	11	91.67
12	10	83.33
12	9	75
12	10	83.33

Table 6. Results of SVM classification for optic disc

No.of training	No. Of Testing	No. Of Correctly Classified	Classification (%)
9	12	10	83.33

Table 7. Testing data for exudates

Test Sample	Correct Classification	Classification (%)
12	9	75
12	11	91.67
12	12	100
12	9	75
12	8	66.67
12	10	83.33
12	10	83.33
12	11	91.67
12	10	83.33

Table 8. Results of SVM classification for exudates

No.of training	No. Of Testing	No. Of Correctly Classified	Classification (%)
9	12	11	91.66

Table 9. Comparison of classification ability of SVM according to feature combination of Retina for DR

Combination of Features	Classification ability of SVM classifier (%)
Blood Vessel and Optic Disc	87.49
Blood Vessel and Microaneurysm	87.49
Blood Vessel and Exudates	91.66
Optic Disc and Microaneurysm	83.33
Optic Disc and Exudates	87.49
Microaneurysm and Exudates	87.49

Table 10. SVM output

Weight vectors: 2.789 and -2.054, Threshold value: 0.735	
Combination	**Output**
Normal1 +Abnormal1	
Normal1 +Abnormal2	
Normal1 +Abnormal3	
Normal2 +Abnormal1	
Normal2 +Abnormal2	
Normal2 +Abnormal3	
Normal3 +Abnormal1	
Normal3 +Abnormal2	
Normal3 +Abnormal3	

Table 11. Output of SVM for Microaneurysm

Weight vectors: 2.786 and -2.095, Threshold value: -.0691	
Combination	**Output**
Normal1 +Abnormal1	
Normal1 +Abnormal2	
Normal1 +Abnormal3	
Normal2 +Abnormal1	
Normal2 +Abnormal2	
Normal2 +Abnormal3	
Normal3 +Abnormal1	
Normal3 +Abnormal2	
Normal3 +Abnormal3	

Table 12. Output of SVM for Optic Disc

Weight vectors: 2.786 and -2.095, Threshold value: -.0691	
Combination	**Output**
Normal1 +Abnormal1	
Normal1 +Abnormal2	
Normal1 +Abnormal3	
Normal2 +Abnormal1	
Normal2 +Abnormal2	
Normal2 +Abnormal3	
Normal3 +Abnormal1	
Normal3 +Abnormal2	
Normal3 +Abnormal3	

Table 13. Output of SVM for Exudates

Weight vectors: 2.786 and -2.095, Threshold value: -.0691	
Combination	**Output**
Normal1 +Abnormal1	
Normal1 +Abnormal2	
Normal1 +Abnormal3	
Normal2 +Abnormal1	
Normal2 +Abnormal2	
Normal2 +Abnormal3	
Normal3 +Abnormal1	
Normal3 +Abnormal2	
Normal3 +Abnormal3	

Finally, the performance graph of the proposed system for different features of retina are shown in Figures 11, 12, 13 and 14 using bar diagram.

Our results show that the classifier is able to identify their class up to 91.67% for Blood vessel. For microaneurysm, optic disc and exudates percentage of classification ability of SVM classifier are 83.33%, 83.33% and 91.67% respectively. And for combined feature set classification ability of our system is from 87.49% to 91.67% (Table 9).

Figure 11. Performance graph of our system for Blood vessel (9 different trials)

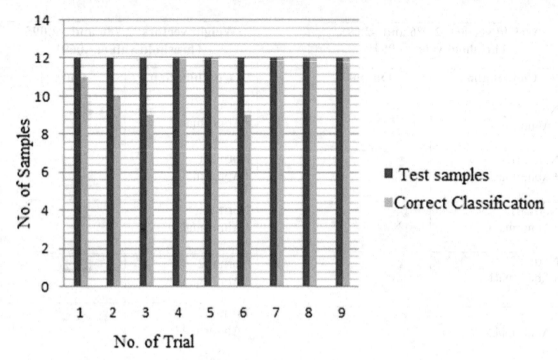

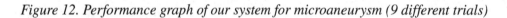

Figure 12. Performance graph of our system for microaneurysm (9 different trials)

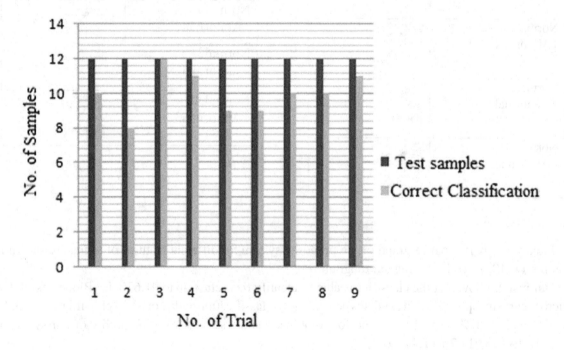

Figure 13. Performance graph of our system for Optic Disc (9 different trials)

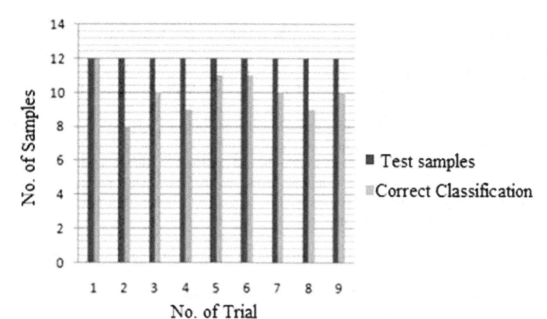

Figure 14. Performance graph of the proposed system for exudates (9 different trials)

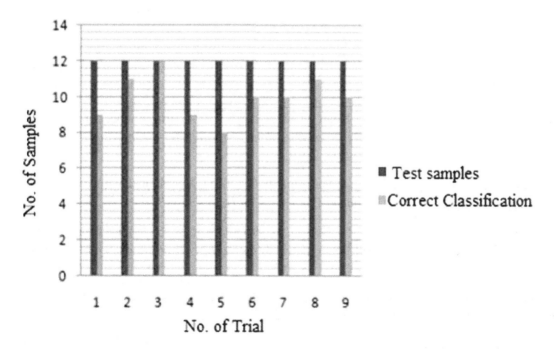

CONCLUSION

In this chapter, we presented a system to detect the abnormality (due to diabetes) of the eye with the focus to show the application of machine learning approaches for pain and blood-free method. Here, we designed a soft computational tool which can be trained with samples of the retina image and prior knowledge provided regarding the condition of diabetes as is indicated by the eye. The trained SVM classifier can be used repeatedly with samples of the retina image and decision regarding the state of diabetes can be generated. It has the capacity to deal with a decision making process regarding diabetes using retina image. The proposed system shows classification ability from 83.33% up to 91.66% for different features (blood vessel, microaneurysm, optic disc and exudates) and different feature combination set of retina. The advantage of such system shall be the speed of information processing, blood-less diagnosis, re-usabilty and help for subsequent advice/ suggestion for related treatment.

Some more advantages of our system are:

- Since we detect different features of diabetic effected retina, which help us to classify the diabetic effected and not effected retina. Which will also help us to know the different stages of diabetes
- Equalization of uneven illumination of the set of provided fundus image is one of the key success of this work. The quality of the images provided and used in the hospital is very low and very difficult for visual manual grading by the opthomologist. The quality of which is firstly improved by our method of illumination equalization.

In addition we can extend the work to crossover point classification which will help to classify more accurately.

REFERENCES

Ahmad, A., Mansoor, A., Mumtaz, R., Khan, M., & Mirza, S. (2014). Image processing and classification in diabetic retinopathy: A Review. *Proceedings of the 5th European workshop on visual information Processing* (EUVIP 2014) (pp 1-6). France. IEEE

Bevilacqua, V., Cambo, S., Cariello, L., & Mastronardi, G. (2005), A combined method to detect Retinal Fundus Features. *Proceedings of European Conference on Data Analysis.*

Chaudhuri, G. S., Chatterjee, S., Katz, N., Nelson, M., & Goldman, M. (1989). Detection of blood vessels in retinal images using two dimensional matched filters. *IEEE Transactions on Medical Imaging*, *8*(3), 263–269. doi:10.1109/42.34715 PMID:18230524

Gardenr, T. W., Abcouwer, S. F., Barber, A. J., & Jackson, G. R. (2011). An Integrated approach to diabetic retinopathy research. Arch. Ophthalmol., *129*(2), 230–235. PMID:21320973

Gonzalez, R. C., & Woods, R. E. (2002). *Digital Image Processing using MATLAB. 2nd edition.* New Delhi: Prentice Hall.

Lochan, K., Sah, P., & Sarma, K. K. (2012). Innovative Feature Set for Retinopathic Analysis of Diabetes and its Detection. *Proceeding of 2nd IEEE National Conference on Emerging Trends and Applications in Computer Science*, Shillong, India.

Ming, Y. F. (2009). Identification of diabetic retinopathy stages using digital fundus images using imaging [Master's thesis]. SIM University.

Premi, M.S. G. (2015). Novel approach for retinal blood vessels extraction and exudates segmentation. *Journal of Chemical and pharmaceutical Research*, 7(1), 792-797.

Sah, P., & Sarma, K. K. (2013). Detection of Blood Vessel and its application for Classifying Diabetic Retinopathy. *Journal of the Instrument Society of India*, 43, 72–74.

Vallabha, D. R. Dorairaj, Namuduri, K., Thompson, H. (2004). Automated Detection and Classiffication of Vascular Abnormalities in Diabetic Retinopathy. *Proceedings of 38th Asilomar Conference on Signals, Systems and Computers*.

Vapnik, V. (1998). *Statistical learning theory*. New York: Wiley.

Wang, H. H., Goh, W., K.G. & Lee, M. L. (2000). An effective approach to detect lesions in color retinal images. *Proceedings of IEEE Conference on engineering in medicine and biology Society*.

Wang, H., Hsu, W., Goh, K. G., & Lee, M. L. (2000). An effective approach to detect lesions in color retinal images. *Proceedings of IEEE Conference on Computer Vision and Pattern Recognition* (pp. 1-6).

Xu, P., & Chan, A. K. (2003). Support vector machine for multi-class signal classification with unbalanced samples. *Proceedings of the International Joint Conference on Neural Networks* (pp. 1116-1119). Portland, USA.

KEY TERMS AND DEFINITIONS

Canny Operator: Canny operator is an edge detector operator that uses a multi stage algorithm to detect a wide range od edges in images. It was developed by John F. Canny in 1986.

Diabetic Retinopathy: *Diabetic retinopathy* is a common complication of diabetes. It occurs when high blood sugar levels damage the cells at the back of the eye (known as the retina).

Hemorrhages: Hemorrhaging is the loss of blood escaping from the circulatory system.

Hyperplane: Hyperplane is the linear classifier with the maximum margin for a given finite set of learning patterns. A *Support Vector Machine* (*SVM*) performs classification by finding the *hyperplane.*

Kernel Function: In machine learning method, Kernel function is a class of algorithm for pattern analysis, whose best known member is the Support Vector Machine (SVM). The general task of pattern analysis is to find and study general types of relations (for example clesters, principle components, correlations, classifications) in datasets.

Machine Learning Method: Machine learning is a subfield of computer science that evolved from the study of pattern recognition and computational learning theory in artificial intelligence. Machine learning explores the construction and study of algorithms that can learn from and make predictions on data. Such algorithms operate by building a model from example inputs in order to make data driven predictions or decesionsdecisions.

Microaneurysms: Microaneurysm is a small swelling that forms on the side of tiny blood vessels. These small swellings may break and bleed into nearby tissue.

Optic Disc: Optic disc is a round area in the back of the eye where retinal nerve fibres collect to form the optic nerve.

Support Vector Machine: Support Vector Machine is a machine learning method for data classification. These type of machines are based on the concept of decision planes that define decision boundaries.

Section 2
Signal Processing

This section is consisted of six contributions related to review and experimental work on the area of biomedical signal processing, speech signal processing and image processing.

Chapter 7
A Computer Based System for ECG Arrhythmia Classification

S. R. Nirmala
Gauhati University, India

Pratiksha Sarma
Girijananda Chowdhury Institute of Management and Technology, India

ABSTRACT

Biological signals can be classified according to its various characteristics like waveform shape, statistical structure and temporal properties. Among various bioelectric signals, one of the most familiar signal is the ECG. It is a signal derived from the electrical activity of the heart. The heart is an important organ which supplies body with oxygen. ECG is widely used in monitoring the health condition of the human. Cardiac arrhythmias can affect electrical system of the heart muscles and cause abnormal heart rhythms that can lead to insufficient pumping of blood and death risks. An important step towards identifying an arrhythmia is the classification of heartbeats. Modern analysis of electrical activity of the heart uses simple as well as sophisticated algorithms of digital signal processing. With the advent of technology, automatic classification of electrocardiogram signals through human-computer interactive systems has received great attention. This chapter discusses some computer assisted classification techniques based on statistical features extracted from ECG signal.

INTRODUCTION

(This section gives a brief overview of the importance of biosignal ECG and its processing in medical field. It also discusses the motivation of processing the biosignal ECG with computer assisted methods followed by a brief literature review on such works performed by various researchers.)

The discovery of association of electricity with medical science dates back to 18th century which formed the basis of the study of the action of living tissues in terms of bioelectric potentials. Bioelectric phenomena are associated with the distribution of ions or charged molecules in a biologic structure and the changes in this distribution resulting from specific processes (Khandpur 2006). These signals give

DOI: 10.4018/978-1-4666-8493-5.ch007

pathological significance of a specific organ of human body. Biological Signals can be classified according to various characteristics of the signal including the waveform shape, statistical structure and temporal properties (Enderle et al. 2006).

Among various bioelectric signals, one of the most important signal under diagnosis is the electrocardiogram (ECG). ECG is a non-invasive clinical signal that records the electrical activity of the heart at the surface of the body. The heart is one of the most important organs in the body. It supplies the body with oxygen. The heart generates an electrochemical impulse, initiated by a group of nerve cells called the sinoatrial (SA) node. This result in a process called depolarization which propagates from cell to cell across the entire heart. The wave of depolarization causes the cells of the heart to contract and relax in a timely order and makes the heartbeat. As this action represents flow of electricity, it can be measured on the surface of the body by skin electrodes, placed at designated locations. The record of the propagation of this bio-signal is called as ECG (Enamet 2009).

The ECG was originally observed by Waller in 1899. W. Einthoven, in the year 1903, introduced the electrophysiology concept that includes the labels of the waves and it is still used today. ECG aims at extracting significant information of the cardiovascular system for diagnosing various condition of the heart such as conduction through the heart, disturbances in cardiac rhythm due to cardiac ischemia and infarction (Adams and Choi 2012).The diagnosis is possible as the pattern of electrical propagation of ECG is not random. It spreads over the structure of the heart in a coordinated pattern. Therefore, in order to better analyze the heart's activity, the morphology of ECG needs great attention. Any deviation in the ECG waveform, from the normal form, is an indication to abnormality or possible disease occurring in the heart. This is popularly known as arrhythmia. Cardiac arrhythmias are frequent reason of death around the world. Early detection of this cardiac arrhythmia would enable mankind to enhance better quality of life through effective treatments (Chazal et al. 2004).

An important step towards identifying an arrhythmia is the classification of heartbeats. The rhythm of the ECG signal can be determined by analyzing two consecutive heartbeats in the signal. However, the ECG signals being non-stationary in nature, it is very difficult to analyze them visually. Some heart disorders or arrhythmias might appear infrequently and such problems might require monitoring of ECG activity up to a week or so to successfully capture them. Many arrhythmias manifest as sequences of heartbeats with unusual timing or ECG morphology. The work of the cardiologist becomes tedious while tracking down such abnormalities. Also daily clinical practice generates large amount of signals during monitoring of patients and for diagnostics purpose. As a follow up to such possibilities, system for automatic classification of cardiac arrhythmias has become necessary and important for diagnosis of cardiac abnormalities. New computer assisted methods can simplify and speed up the processing of large volume of data. Among the available literature, some of the published works describing computer assisted methods are discussed below briefly.

Emanet et.al.(2009) presented an algorithm named Random Forest to classify five types of ECG beats using the ECG signals obtained from the MIT/BIH database were used to classify the five heartbeat classes (N, L,R, V, P). Feature extraction from the ECG signals for classification of ECG beats was performed by using discrete wavelet transform (DWT) with a classification accuracy of 99.8%. Wang et al. (2011) describes an effective electrocardiogram (ECG) arrhythmia classification scheme consisting of a feature reduction method combining principal component analysis (PCA) with linear discriminant analysis (LDA), and a probabilistic neural network (PNN) classifier to discriminate eight different types of arrhythmia from ECG beats. Their average classification accuracy was 99.71%. Hosseini et al. (2001)

describes a multi-stage network including two multilayer perceptron (MLP) and one self-organizing map (SOM) networks. The input of the network is a combination of independent features and compressed ECGdata. They classified six common ECG waveforms using ten ECG records of the MIT/BIH arrhythmia database. Their system achieved an average recognition rate of 0.883 within a short training and testing time. Gothwal et al. (2001) presented a method of ECG classification using Fast Fourier Transform (FFT) and Neural Network. They classified arrhythmias into Tachycardia, Bradycardia, Supraventricular Tachycardia, Incomplete BBB and Ventricular Tachycardia using MIT-BIH database with 98.48% accuracy.A method is proposed by Ghosh et al. (2005) to classify cardiac abnormalities like Cardiomyopathy, Myocardial infarction, Dysrhythmia, Myocardial hypertrophy and Valvular heart disease using Support Vector Machine (SVM). The classification is based on some patterns inherent in the features extracted by Continuous Wavelet Transform (CWT) of different ECG signals. The average classification accuracy of their system was 96%. Güler et al. (2005) used DWT features of the ECG signals for classifying beats into four types: normal beat, congestive heart failure beat, ventricular tachyarrhythmia beat, atrial fibrillation beat. The beats have been obtained from Physiobank database. Combined neural network (CNN) was used for classification and the classification accuracy of the system was 96.94%.Osowski et al. (2004) demonstrated the application of SVM for reliable heartbeat recognition. The authors used ECG data from the MIT-BIH arrhythmia database corresponding to the normal sinus rhythm and 12 types of arrhythmias. They applied two different preprocessing methods for generation of features. First method involved the higher order statistics (HOS) while the second method used Hermite characterization of QRS complex of the registered ECG waveform. The SVM classifier was fed with 12 inputs representing different arrhythmias. The classifier gives an output, indicating the category of the input signal. They applied the one-against-one strategy for multiclass recognition and their classification accuracy was 95.77% for Hermite preprocessing and 94.26% for HOS preprocessing. A different method is discussed by Ghosh et al. (2005) to classify cardiac abnormalities like Cardiomyopathy, Myocardial infarction, Dysrhythmia, Myocardial hypertrophy and Valvular heart disease. They used SVM for classification based on some patterns. The features extracted through Continuous Wavelet Transform (CWT) of different ECG signals are considered. The average classification accuracy obtained was 96%. Zhao and Zhang (2005) presented an approach to the feature extraction for reliable heart rhythm recognition. They employed two different methods for feature extraction. The first one is wavelet transform to extract the coefficients of the transform as the features of each ECG segment. The second method is the autoregressive (AR) modeling to obtain the temporal features of ECG waveforms. Then they used SVM with Gaussian kernel to classify different ECG heart rhythm. The overall classification accuracy for recognition of 6 heart rhythm types was 99.68%. A. Kampouraki et al. (2009) presented a classification method for heartbeat time series analysis using SVM. Statistical methods and signal analysis techniques were used to extract features from the signals. They investigated the classification rate for two real datasets, long-term ECG recordings of young and elderly healthy subjects; and long-term ECG recordings of normal subjects and subjects suffering from coronary artery disease. They results have been tested for various classifiers and found best results for SVM.

The rest of the chapter briefly describes the background of electrocardiogram, followed by some theoretical aspects considered for automatic classification of ECG. The theoretical basics of some feature extraction methods have also been presented.Along with that, two methods for ECG classification have been discussed in the later part of the chapter. The conclusion summarizes the contributions of the chapter and suggests some future work for such classification system that could be developed further.

BACKGROUND

Electrocardiography and Its Physiological Significance

The study of ECG can be basically divided into morphology and arrhythmology. Electrocardiographic morphology deals with interpretation of the shape (amplitude, width and contour) of the electrocardiographic signals whereas arrhythmology is devoted to the study of the rhythm (sequence and frequency) of the heart. The range for frequency of an ECG signal is 0.05Hz to 100 Hz and that of amplitude in volts is1mV to 10mV respectively (Iftikhar et al. 2012). In standard clinical electrocardiogram, signals are recorded with single lead or multiple lead configurations from the surface of human body. Each lead bears a good amount of clinically relevant diagnostic information. During normal sinus rhythm the sequence is always obtained as PQRST. Depending on heart rate and rhythm, the interval between waves of one cycle and another is varies. Figure 1 show an ECG signal marked with their amplitudes and time intervals. Each portion of the ECG waveform carries various types of information for the clinician

Figure 1. A typical ECG Waveform

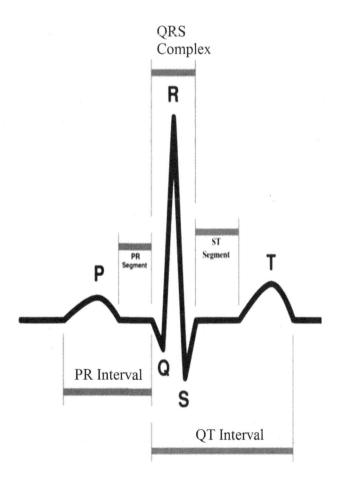

analyzing the patient's heart condition. Therefore the various morphologies, time durations, amplitudes are basic to characterizing the ECG waveform as normal or abnormal (Reddy 2006). The physiological significance of these local waves is presented below:

P-Wave

The electrical impulses initiated at sinoatrial node of right atrium starts atrial depolarization and produce the P wave on the electrocardiogram. P wave represents the composite electrical activation of right and left atria. The duration of P-wave is in the range of 80 to 100 ms. The maximum normal amplitude of P-wave is 0.25mV. Normal P-wave is never pointed or peaked. A P-wave with magnitude > 0.25mV signifies Right Atrial Enlargement (RLE) and a widened P wave indicates Left Atrial Enlargement (LAE). In case of hyperkalemia, P wave may be decreased in height.

Q Wave

First downward detection of the QRS complex is the Q-wave. Depolarization of the intra-ventricular septum is represented by the Q wave. A normal wave has duration less than 40ms and its amplitude is 25% of the amplitude of the R wave. Myocardial infarction shows a wide or deep Q wave.

PR Interval

The time interval between the atrial depolarization and the beginning of ventricular depolarization is the PR interval. The PR interval is measured from P wave to the Q wave or the R wave if the Q wave is absent. The normal PR interval is 120-200 ms. A short PR interval is observed in patients with Wolfe-Parkinson-White Syndrome. Prolonged PR interval is observed in ECG signals from patients with 1st degree atrioventricular (AV) block, 2nd degree AV block and rheumatic heart diseases.

R Wave

First upward detection of the QRS-complex is the R wave. A part of the ventricular depolarization cycle is represented by this wave. The presence of bundle branch block is indicated by a reverse or greatly disturbed R wave.

S Wave

The downward detection of QRS-complex is the S-wave. It represents the remaining part of the time period for ventricular depolarization. In the presence of bundle branch block, S-waves have irregular shapes.

QRS Complex

The QRS complex represents the depolarization of the myocardial cells of the ventricles. Its duration is normally 60ms to 100ms. Abnormal intraventricular conduction velocity is rejected as a change in the duration of QRS complex.

ST Segment

It represents the period from the end of systole to the beginning of repolarization of the ventricles. It has duration of 80ms to 120ms. It may appear as a flat line between the QRS complex and the T wave. The ST segment will become depressed with a long duration and large amplitude before it joins the T-wave during ischemia and it becomes elevated during Myocardial infarction.

T Wave

The ventricular repolarization is represented by the T-wave. Its duration is 100 ms to 250 ms and its amplitude is less than 0.5 mV.

QT Interval

The beginning of the QRS complex to the end of the T wave is represented by the QT-interval.Its duration varies between 350 ms to 450 ms. In higher heart rate the duration of the QT interval is reduced. The ventricular tachyarrhythmias leading to sudden cardiac death can be diagnosed from prolonged QT interval.

RR Interval

The RR interval is the heart rate which represents the duration of cardiac cycles.

ARRHYTHMIA

Arrhythmia (also known as cardiac dysrhythmia or irregular heartbeat) is a condition of the heart, in which the electrical activity of the heart is irregular or is faster or slower than normal. The heartbeat may be too fast (over 100 beats per minute) or too slow (less than 60 beats per minute), and may be regular or irregular. A heart beat that is too fast is called tachycardia and a heartbeat that is too slow is called bradycardia. Although many arrhythmias are harmless, but some can be serious or even life threatening. During an arrhythmia, the heart may not be able to pump enough blood to the body. Lack of blood flow can damage the brain, heart, and other organs.

Some of the reasons for irregular heart rhythm are cough, tobacco, cold medicines, and alcohol and diet pills. The people having rhythm disorders and severe symptoms of illness required to be treated to keep heartbeat normal. With rhythmic disorders the patient may feel that his heart is beating at a faster pace, can also experience pain in the chest, and may notice irregularities or missing heartbeat. The patient may also experience dizziness and breathlessness. Figure 2 shows five types of reference heartbeats. A few of the most general type of arrhythmias are discussed below.

Atrial Fibrillation

In atrial fibrillation, a common type of arrhythmia, electrical signals travel through the atria in a fast and disorganized way. This causes the atria to quiver instead of contract.

Premature Ventricular Contraction (PVC)

This is also known as ventricular premature beat (VPB) or extrasystole. Extrasystole is a form of abnormal heart beat in which ventricles contract prematurely. This is also taken as palpitations. The ventricle activates the depolarization of cardiac myocytes rather than sinoatrial node. Premature ventricle contractions impart heart rate anomalies. The properties of this turbulence are used to evaluate cardiac functions.

Left Bundle Branch Block (LBBB)

LBBB is a cardiac conduction abnormality seen on the electrocardiogram (ECG). In this condition, activation of the left ventricle is delayed, which results in the left ventricle contracting later than the right ventricle.

Right Bundle Branch Block (RBBB)

Right Bundle Branch Block (RBBB) is the imperfection of electric conduction system of heart. The right ventricle is not excited directly by electric impulses moving through the right bundle branch (RBB) in case of right bundle branch block, whereas the left bundle branch excites the left ventricle. The electric impulses move through left ventricle's myocardium to the right ventricle and activate the right ventricle.

Paced Beat (PB)

Paced beat is the pacemaker induced heartbeat in patients.

MIT-BIH DATABASE

A large number of databases are available at (physionet). MIT-BIH database is most widely used databases consisting of five arrhythmia classes. It contains 30 records of one lead as well as multi-lead. MIT-BIH arrhythmia database includes recordings of many common and life-threatening arrhythmias along with examples of normal sinus rhythm. It contains 48 recordings, each containing two 30-min ECG lead signals (denoted lead A and B). Table 1 shows the distribution of heartbeat types in MIT-BIH database. The signals in the database are sampled at 360Hz. Each record of the MIT-BIH database has its respective annotation file that gives various information of the signal such as the class of the heartbeat, fudicial points etc.

COMPUTER AIDED TECHNIQUES FOR ARRHYTHMIA CLASSIFICATION

The most significant technological advancement of the 20th century is the computer which plays an important role in cardiac investigations. Over the past few years, automatic classification of electrocardiogram signals through human-computer interactive systems has received great attention. Computerized

Figure 2. Reference waveform for the five heartbeat type

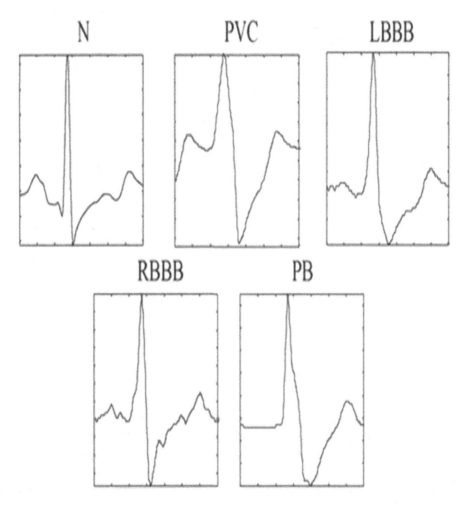

Table 1. Distribution of N, PB, LBBB, RBBB and PVC beats in MIT-BIH database

Heartbeat Type	ECG Recordings Containing the Respective Type
N	100-106, 108, 112-117, 119, 121-123, 200-203, 205, 208-210, 212, 213, 215, 217, 219-223, 228, 230, 231, 233, 234
PB	102, 104, 107, 217
LBBB	109, 111, 207, 214
RBBB	118, 124, 207, 212, 231, 232
PVC	100, 102, 104-109, 111, 114, 116, 118, 119, 121, 123, 124, 200-203, 205, 207-210, 213-215, 217, 219, 221, 223, 228, 230, 231, 233, 234

interpretation is made possible because of availability of digitized ECG signals. To this signals, various mathematical techniques of signal processing can be applied for analyzing the condition of the heart (Reddy 2006). A system that is capable of recognizing particular patterns may be divided into several stages. A generalized block diagram for classification of ECG signals is shown in Figure 3.

Figure 3. Block Diagram of an ECG Classification system

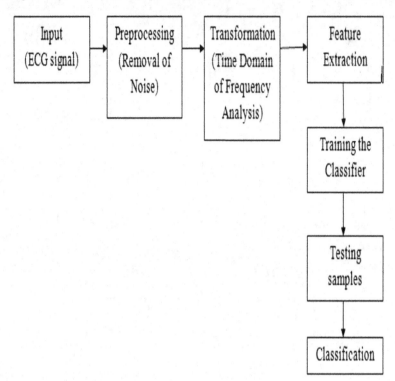

Modern analysis of electrical activity of the heart uses simple as well as sophisticated algorithms of digital signal processing. Successful classification of heartbeats is generally achieved by proper processing of ECG signals. The processing of single or multichannel ECG is preceded by an important preprocessing stage. In the pre-processing block, signal is amplitude and time normalized. Then the signal is processed based on time domain, frequency domain and time-frequency domain. The first two domains belong to classical methods. New algorithms are usually implemented in time-frequency domain which combines advantages of classical methods. Biomedical signal processing algorithm also requires appropriate classifiers in order to best categorize variety in bioelectric signals. Neural networks have been treated as powerful classifier to deal with ECG arrhythmia classification problems. Approaches of utilizing ANN have found their application in processing non-linear signals, classification and optimization.

Pre-Processing of ECG Signals

The input to an ECG classification system is the raw beat obtained from a patient. The raw ECG signal may contain a few undesired signals or other artifacts. Noise elimination is an important signal processing task. The most common types of noises and artifacts present in ECG signal are baseline wander; dc offset noise, electrode motion artifacts, powerline interference and EMG noise. Processing of ECG emphasizes the signal and at the same time it deemphasizes the undesired and unwanted part or parts of the signal hence improving the signal quality for more accurate analysis and measurement Baseline wander is a low-frequency artifact present in raw ECG signal whose spectral content is below 1 Hz. It appears due to perspiration, respiration, body movement and poor electrode contact. It can be filtered out by applying linear filtering methods (Enamet2009), butterworth digital filter (Palaniappan et al. 2008) or wavelet transform (Rabee et al.2012). Power line interference is caused by improper grounding of the ECG equipment and interference from nearby equipment. It can be done by linear or nonlinear filtering (Sharma 2012). Dc offset noise can be removed by FFT filtering (Sarma2013).

Processing of ECG Signals

The main purpose of classification of ECG signals is selection of components from complex one-dimensional non-periodic time series and searching for important features in it. In classification applications, selecting a proper subset of features is an important task. A feature is an important attribute or characteristics of a signal that differentiate it from others. Feature extraction is a critical and an essential part of ECG beat classification systems. It is the process of reducing the number of samples and retains the characteristic features, necessary for classification. Feature selection serves two main purposes. First, it makes training a classifier more efficient by decreasing the size of the effective features. Second, it increases classification accuracy by eliminating noisy features. A noisy feature is one that when added to the main feature set, increases the classification error (Kohli and Verma, 2011). Generally the analysis is carried out by transforming the signal data into specific domain: time-domain, frequency domain (Fourier Transform) or time-frequency domain (Wavelet transform). Fourier transform analysis provides the signal spectrum or range of frequency amplitudes within the signal. Wavelet can provide a time versus frequency representation of the signal and works well on non-stationary data (Rabee2012). Other algorithms use morphological features (Chazal2004), heart beat temporal or interval features and statistical features (Kicmerova2009). The Principal Component analysis (PCA) (Wang et al. 2011), Linear Prediction Coding (LPC), Independent Component Analysis (ICA) are a few of the statistical features used for feature extraction. Some of the feature set for analysis of ECG is discussed below:

Principal Component Analysis (PCA)

PCA is a well-established technique for feature extraction and dimensionality reduction. Itis a statistical method used to select features for classification application. This technique is appropriate when we have obtained measures on a number of observed variables and wish to develop a smaller number of artificial variables. It is based on the assumption that mostinformation about classes is contained in the directions along which the variations are the largest (Kohli and Verma, 2011). These directions or artificial variables are called principal components that will account for most of the variance in the observed variables. The principal components may then be used as predictor or criterion variables in subsequent analysis. The first component extracted in a principal component analysis accounts for a maximal amount of total variance in the observed variables. Under typical conditions, this means that the first component will be correlated with at least some of the observed variables. It may be correlated with many. The second component extracted will have two important characteristics. First, this component will account for a maximal amount of variance in the data set that was not accounted for by the first component. Again under typical conditions, this means that the second component will be correlated with some of the observed variables that did not display strong correlations with component 1. The second characteristic of the second component is that it will be uncorrelated with the first component. Literally, if we were to compute the correlation between components 1 and 2, that correlation would be zero. The remaining components that are extracted in the analysis display the same two characteristics: each component accounts for a maximal amount of variance in the observed variables that was not accounted for by the preceding components, and is uncorrelated with all of the preceding components. A PCA proceeds in this fashion, with each new component accounting for progressively smaller and smaller amounts of variance (this is why only the first few components are usually retained and interpreted). When the analysis is complete, the resulting components will display varying degrees of correlation with the observed variables, but are completely uncorrelated with one another (Barret2004).Considering a vector of n random variables x for which the covariance matrix is $\sum$ the principal components (PCs) can be defined by

$$z = Ax$$

where z is the vector of n PCs and A is the n by n orthogonal matrix with rows that are the eigenvectors of $\sum$. The eigen values of $\sum$ are proportional to the fraction of the total variance accounted for by the corresponding eigenvectors, so the PCs explaining most of the variance in the original variables can be identified (Wang et al. 2011).

Linear Predictive Coding (LPC)

Among various feature extraction methods, linear prediction is one of the powerful signal analysis techniques in the method of feature extraction. LPC is a technique of time series analysis that is used to predict future values of a signal as a linear function of previous samples. The basic solution of the LPC system to determine the forward coefficients of the signal is the difference equation, which expresses each sample of the signal as a linear combination of previous samples. Such an equation is also called a linear predictor, which is better known as Linear Predictive Coding. The estimate is done by minimizing the mean-square error between the predicted signal and the actual signal. The most common representation of the linear prediction model is

$$\hat{x}(n) = -\sum_{i=0}^{p} a_i x(n-i)$$

where $\hat{x}(n)$ is the predicted signal value, $x(n-i)$ is the previous observed values, a is the predictor coefficient and p is the order of the LPC. The order p decides the accuracy of prediction. The good prediction can be achieved with optimal determination of the filter coefficients. In order to design filter coefficients coder attempts to minimize mean square error. The error generated by the estimate is then the difference of the predicted value and the actual value:

$$e(n) = x(n) - \hat{x}(n)$$

where x(n) is the true signal value.

Wavelet Transform

Conventional data processing is done in either the time domain (moments, correlations, etc.) or in the frequency domain (power spectra, etc.). Wavelet processing combines the two, allowing the denition of local spectral properties and the ability to zoom in on local features of the signal. To simplify language, we use 'time-frequency', with implied reference to time series for the data, in this text; the use of the spatial-spectral alter-native for spatial data is straightforward. A wavelet is a basis function (an elementary building block to analyze and synthesize the signal) characterized by:

- Its shape and its amplitude, to be selected by the user
- Its scale (frequency) and location (time) relative to the signal, spanning a range of interest to study a given phenomenon.

Wavelet coefficients are the scalar products of the signal with all dilated and translated wavelets. The set of wavelet coefficients thus obtained is indexed by position and scale (always positive) in the wavelet half-plane. The CWT performs a multiresolution analysis by contraction and dilatation of the wavelet functions. The discrete wavelet transform (DWT) uses filter banks for the construction of the multiresolution time-frequency plane filter. Unfortunately, computation of features based on continuous wavelet transform (CWT) is somewhat time consuming and is not suitable for large sized data analysis especially, on-line condition monitoring of tool which is of interest here. The Discrete Wavelet Transform (DWT) is based on sub-band coding. The real benefit in the use of DWT is an obvious reduction in computation time. It is easy to implement and demands less resources.

Discrete Wavelet Transform

DWT can be applied to extract the wavelet coefficients of discrete time signals. The proposed procedure makes use of multirate signal processing techniques. The multiresolution feature of the DWT allows the decomposition of a signal into a number of time scale function which correlates the wavelets to the signal. Each scale of the DWT represents a particular coarseness of the signal under study. The DWT provides very general technique which can be applied to many tasks in signal processing. One very important application is the ability to compute and manipulate data in compressed parameters which are technically termed as features (Ubeyli2007).The dilation function of the discrete wavelet transform can be represented as a tree of low and high pass filters, with each step transforming the low pass filter as shown in Figure 4. The original signal is successively decomposed into components of lower resolution, while the high frequency components are not analyzed any further. The maximum number of dilations that can be performed in a data with 2N samples using DWT is N discrete levels. The wavelet coefficients are calculated for each wavelet segment, giving a time-scale function relating the wavelets correlation to the signal. Thus, the ECG signal, consisting of many data points, can be compressed into a few parameters, which characterize the behavior of the signal. This feature of using a smaller number of parameters to represent the ECG signal is particularly important for recognition and diagnostic purposes.

Classification of ECG Signals

Classification unit does the work for its diagnostic decision. In most cases, the classification method is usually based on a set of training patterns that has already been classified or labeled. This type of training is called supervised learning. Presently, Artificial Neural Networks (ANNs) are widely applied in the area of processing non-linear signals, classification and optimization. ANN is a conventional classifier used for various classification problems. In processing of ECG signals, multilayer layer perceptron (MLP)

Figure 4. Filter Bank representation of DWT dilation

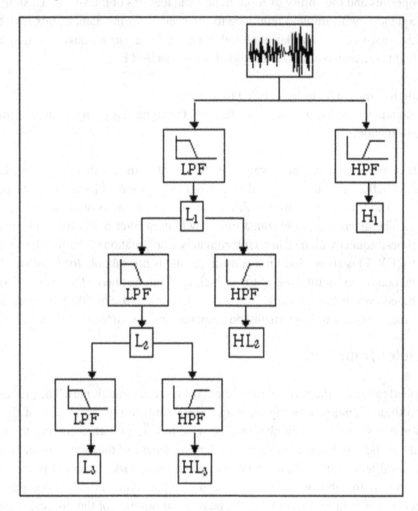

(Sarma2014), radial basis function (RBF) networks and learning vector quantization (LVQ) networks are widely used. Also support vector machine (SVM) have emerged as powerful classifiers for general purpose pattern recognition (Ghosh et al. 2005). It has been applied to problems with exceptionally good performance on a range of binary classification tasks. Types of ANN with unsupervised learning used in bio-signal processing include Hopfield network, self organizing map networks. Two of the important classifiers are discussed below:

Artificial Neural Network (ANN)

Inspired by the way biological nervous systems such as human brains process information; an ANN is an information processing system which contains a large number of highly interconnected processing neurons. These neurons work together in a distributed manner to learn from the input information, to coordinate internal processing, and to optimize its final output. The basic structure of a neuron can be theoretically modeled as shown in Figure 5, where X (X_i, i = 1, 2...n) represent the inputs to the neuron

Figure 5. An artificial Neuron

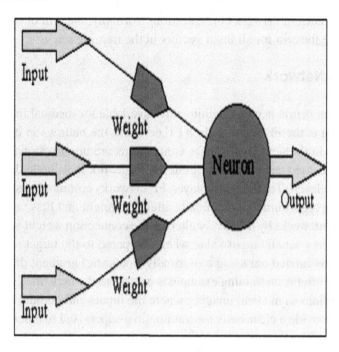

and Y represents the output. Each input is multiplied by its weight w_i, a bias b is associated with each neuron and their sum goes through a transfer function f(:). As a result, the relationship between input and output can be described as follows:

$$Y = f(X(w_i x_i + b))$$

$$Y = f(X(w_i x_i + b)) \quad \text{where i} = 1 \text{ to n}$$

What makes a great difference between ANN and traditional computer systems is the fact that computers are only able to follow a series of particular instructions and offer solutions that are already known. ANN process information in the same way as the human brain does. Therefore, ANN may be described as artificial intelligence (Kicmerova2009). There are a range of transfer functions available to process the weighted and biased inputs. Via selection of suitable transfer functions and connection of neurons, various ANNs can be constructed to be trained for producing the specified outputs. The learning system for ANNs in medical image processing generally includes supervised learning and unsupervised learning.

In supervised learning, a network is trained using a set of inputs and outputs (targets). For each training case there will be a set of input values and one or more associated output values, and the goal is minimize the networks overall output error for all training cases by iteratively adjusting the neuron connection weights and bias values using a specific training algorithm. In unsupervised learning, the training data set does not include any target information. Normally, a function is defined that measures the suitability or accuracy of the network. This function, often referred to as a cost function, is dependent on the networks application and normally uses both the input values and the networks output value(s) to produce a cost for the current network configuration. Normally, the aim of unsupervised learning is to minimize or maximize the cost for all input vectors in the training set.

Feed-Forward (FF) Network

There are several different neural network architectures available for medical imaging applications, but one of the most common is the FF network. In a FF network, the neurons in each layer are only connected with the neurons in the next layer. These connections are unidirectional, which means signals or information being processed can only pass through the network in a single direction, from the input layer, through the hidden layer(s) to the output layer. FF networks commonly use the Back-Propagation (BP) supervised learning algorithm to dynamically alter the weight and bias values for each neuron in the network. The algorithm works by iteratively altering the connection weight values for neurons based on the error in the networks actual output value when compared to the target output value. The actual modification of weights is carried out using a (normally stochastic) gradient descent algorithm, where the weights are modified after each training example is present to the network. FF networks are particularly suitable for applications in medical imaging where the inputs and outputs are numerical and pairs of input/output vectors provide a clear basis for training in a supervised manner.

Multilayer Perceptron (MLP) Neural Network

MLP is an important class of neural network. This type of neural network consists of a set of sensory units that constitute the input layer and one or more hidden layer of computation modes. The multilayer perceptrons are used with supervised learning and have led to the successful back-propagation algorithm. The disadvantage of the single layer perceptron is that it cannot be extended to multi-layered version. In MLP networks there exists a non-linear activation function. The widely used non-linear activation function is logistic sigmoid function. The MLP network also has various layers of hidden neurons. The hidden neurons make the MLP network active for highly complex tasks. The input layer of MLP generally consists of units equal to number of features in the training dataset. In the output layer, the number of units corresponds to the number of output classes. The quantity of hidden units contained in the middle generally varies between these two numbers. It is better to use smaller number of hidden units than the number of inputs as too many hidden units can lead to overtraining and hence give poor test results. If the number of hidden units is too low, then it might be problem for the network to learn the training data. If the network achieves good results in the training and at the same time, gives poor test results, the quantity of hidden units should be decreased. On the other hand, if the network produces insufficient results in the training process, the amount of hidden units should be increased. The MLP thus can be trained in such way to give high computational efficiency (Sivanandan2006).

Support Vector Machine (SVM)

SVM is a machine learning method that is widely used for data analyzing and pattern recognizing. The SVMs introduced by Vapnik, are a relatively new technique for classification and regression tasks. It is method for estimation of parameters of linear classifies by minimizing the structural risk. It is basically developed for binary classification task and the aim is to find an optimal separating hyperplane (OSH).

Classifying of data has been one of the major parts in machine learning. The idea of support vector machine is to create a hyperplane in between data sets to indicate which class it belongs to. The challenge is to train the machine to understand structure from data and mapping with the right class label. SVM finds this OSH by maximizing the margin, which lies in some space, between the classes. Given training examples labeled either `yes' or `no', the maximum margin hyperplane splits the two conditions. For the best result, the hyper plane is so splited that it has the largest distance to the nearest training data points of any class. SVM first transforms input data into a higher dimensional space by means of a kernel function and then constructs a linear OSH between the two classes in the transformed space. Those data vectors nearest to the constructed line in the transformed space are called the support vectors (SVs) (Sivanandan2006). Figure 6 shows a classification process of SVM through OSH.

As described before, SVMs are intrinsically binary classifiers, but, the classification of ECG signals often involves more than two classes. In order to face this issue, a number of multiclass classification strategies have been adopted. The most popular ones are, the one-against-all(OAA) and the one-against-one (OAO) strategies. The OAA method constructs n SVM models for n-class problem. The ith SVM is trained with all of the training examples in the ith class with positive labels and all other examples with

Figure 6. SVM Classification

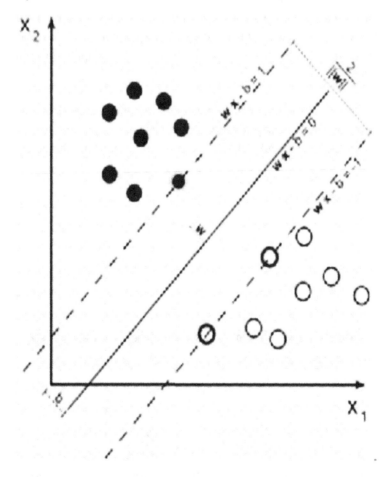

negative labels. The final output of the OAA method is the class that corresponds to the SVM with the highest output value. On the other hand, OAO for n class problem constructs n*(n-1)/2 decision functions for all the combinations of class pairs.

As discussed above, it is found that there are many methods available for ECG classification. Two of the techniques, considering a set of features and machine learning classifier, are discussed below:

Method 1: Implementation of MLP Classifier for ECG Classification Using LPC and PCA Based Features

LPC has been use dextensively in the analysis of vowel recognition in speech recognition systems because of its ability to detect poles. Even though the ECG signal is not a speech signal, it shows similar quasi-periodic properties to a phonetic segment of speech (Loong2010).LPC is used to compute the spectral coefficients of the ECG signal. PCA is another important method which has been widely used in statistical data analysis, feature extraction, feature reduction, and data compression. The goal of PCA is to transform one set of variables in *Rk* space into another set in *Rp* space containing the maximum amount of variance in the data where normally *p* is smaller than *k*. A method for ECG classification using LPC and PCA features is discussed here.

The raw ECG signal obtained from MIT-BIH database is pre-processed to remove dc offset. This is done by filtering the signal in the frequency domain. FFT is applied to the original signal and the lower frequency components are zeroed. This results in a low frequency offset removed signal with the baseline at zero reference line. On the resultant signal inverse FFT is applied to obtain a preprocessed signal as shown in Figure 7.

1. In the processing stages, a fraction of the signal centered on the R peak is extracted manually for each type of heartbeat. The R-peak points for all the heartbeat types are taken from the annotation text file available in the physiobank ATM. To ensure the important characteristic points of ECG

Figure 7. A pre-processed signal

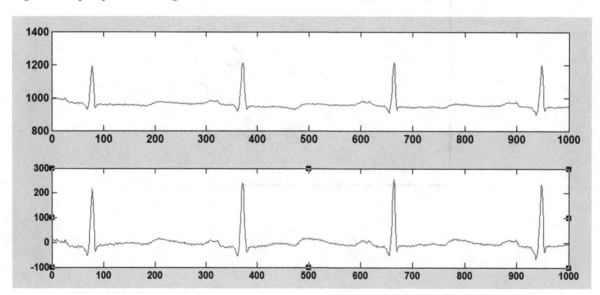

like P, Q, R, S and T, a total of 250 sampling points at a 360 Hz sampling rate, 100 sampling points before and 150 sampling points after the R-peak, are collected as one ECG beat sample for each type

2. It is found that beat-to-beat changes in ECG features such as QRS complex; T wave or P wave could be identified by LPC and PCA from multi-beat, single lead ECG recordings. The LPC gives future predictable coefficient of a particular heartbeat. LPCs of 20 heart beat samples are arranged as a matrix of 20x250, having LPC coefficients as the column elements. Then the mean vector of this matrix is calculated and considered as the feature vector. This process is repeated for other type of ECG beats also. Then the average of the LPCs for each type is taken as a feature vector and is fed to the classifier.

3. The PCA results in a change in the correlation between these features if there is a beat-to-beat change in ECG signal. For PCA, a matrix of each type is formed with 20x250 samples. Then the PCAs are found using that matrix. PCAs are then sorted in descending order and 80% of the values is taken as a feature vector to be fed to the classifier.

4. The combination of the above two features is also fed as a feature matrix to the classifier.

5. In the classification stage, a Feed-Forward Network with one input layer, two hidden layer and one output layer is proposed. The input layer consist of 250neurons with the transfer function of tan-sigmoid, the hidden layer consist of 150 and 50neurons in two-stages with the transfer function of log-sigmoid whereas the output layer consists of 5 neurons with the linear transfer function. MLP learns the behavior of theinput data using back propagation (BP) algorithm. The BP algorithm compares the result that is obtained in this step with the result that is expected. The MLP computes the error signal using the obtained output and desired output. The computed signal error is then fed back to the ANN and is used to adjust the weights such that with each iteration the error decreases and the neural model gets closer and closer to produce the desired output.

6. There are different training algorithms, while it is very difficult to know which training algorithm is suitable for a given problem. In order to determine the training algorithm, many parameters should be considered. For instance, the complexity of the problem, the number of data points in the training set, the number of weights, and biases in the network, and error goal to be evaluated. The results of the evaluated system is shown below:

The performance of the classifier is found to be better for PCA based features compared to LPC features as shown in Table 4 and 5. When the two features are combined, the classifier shows improved performance in classifying the first four types of heartbeats. For the case of PVC, the classifier performance is the average of LPC and PCA features. From the tables, it is found that overall. LPC feature

Table 2. Performance of the LPC feature used

Heartbeat Type	Total Beats Tested	Beats Tested Correctly	Classification Rate for LPC
N	40	35	87.5%
PB	40	36	90%
LBBB	40	34	85%
RBBB	40	34	85%
PVC	40	33	82.5%

Table 3. Performance of the PCA feature used

Heartbeat Type	Total Beats Tested	Beats Tested Correctly	Classification Rate for PCA
N	40	35	87.5%
PB	40	36	90%
LBBB	40	35	87.5%
RBBB	40	35	87.5%
PVC	40	35	87.5%

Table 4. Performance of the LPC+PCA feature used

Heartbeat Type	Total Beats Tested	Beats Tested Correctly	Classification Rate for LPC+PCA
N	40	37	92.5%
PB	40	36	90%
LBBB	40	37	92.5%
RBBB	40	35	87.5%
PVC	40	34	85%

set has an efficiency of 86%, PCA has 87.5% and combined feature set has 89.5%. As the beat selection is done manually, so the complete dataset was not taken. Signals in the dataset which had majority of a particular heartbeat type, were generally considered for the purpose. All these results are reported in Sarma et al. (2013).

Method 2: Implementation of MLP Classifier for ECG Classification Using DWT Based Features

ECG is bio-signal that is non-stationary in nature and wavelet transform is mainly devoted to the analysis of nonstationary signals. It is seen from the previous work that although PCA and LPC based feature set for ECG beat classification is found to be above average, but the problem faced while carrying out the work is the number of samples to be selected for the feature vector. As LPC and PCA generates feature samples equal to the number of samples used for training, it is difficult to decide the length of the feature vector to be fed to the classifier. Large number of samples can overtrain the system whereas less number of samples can undertrain the system. A trial and error analysis was carried for length of the feature vector to get the optimal results. In this consideration, an alternate feature analysis that has proved to be very efficient in signal analysis is wavelet transform.

The wavelet analysis block transforms the signal into different time-frequency scales. Wavelet analysis employs the expansion and contraction of basis function to detect simultaneously the characteristics of global and local of measured signal. Wavelets allow the decomposition of a signal into different levels of resolution called frequency octaves. The basis function (Mother Wavelet) is dilated at low frequencies and compressed at high frequencies, so that large windows are used to obtain the low frequency components of the signal, while small windows reflect discontinuities. The ability of wavelet to compute and manipulate data in compressed parameters is one of its very important applications.

Sub-band analysis is a form of transform coding that breaks a signal into a number of different frequency bands and analyse each one independently. A work in Sarma et al. (2014), undertaking sub-band analysis of wavelet coefficients have been discussed below:

ECG signals are first decomposed into 6 levels using biorthogonal wavelets with order N = 6.8 Each beat in each type of ECG signals consists of 250 data points. Then approximate and detailed coefficients were calculated based on 6 levels of decomposition of each beat. From the obtained approximate and detailed coefficients, subband energy (SE) and other parameters are calculated.

Subband Energy (SE): It is computed as the summation of square of the absolute values of the wavelet coefficients (C_n). It is mathematically defined as

$$SE_j = \sum_{n=1}^{N} |C_n|^2$$

where j is level of decomposition and N is the total number of coefficients in the subband.

Total Energy (TE): It is mathematically defined as the summation of all the subband energies obtained from wavelet decomposition.

$$TE = \sum SE_j$$

NormalisedSubband Energy (NSE): It is defined as subband energy divided by total energy.

$$NSE_j = \frac{SE_j}{TE}$$

Mean Subband Energy (MSE): It is the subband energy divided by the total number of coefficients in the subband.

$$MSE_j = \frac{SE_j}{N}$$

Relative Mean Subband Energy (RMSE): Mean subband energy divided by total MSE_j (TMSE).

$$RMSE_j = \frac{MSE_j}{TMSE}$$

The three parameters: NSE, MSE, RMSE are considered as feature set (FS) and fed to the MLP NN for classification purpose.

The MLP specification for this system is as follows: the input layer consist of six neurons with the transfer function of tan-sigmoid, the hidden layer consist of ten neurons with the transfer function of log-sigmoid whereas the output layer consist of five neurons with the log-sigmoid transfer function. The number of neurons in hidden layer is chosen in a trial and error basis and the results obtained are optimum for this case.

The inputs given to the input layer are MSE, NSE, RMSE, each trained and tested separately, whereas the outputs obtained are the class of ECG types: N, PB, PVC, LBBB, RBBB. The network is trained by resilient backpropagation algorithm and the mean squared error is taken as 0.001. The performance curves of training the MLP for NSE is shown in Figure 6 that of MSE is shown in Figure 7 and of RMSE is shown in Figure 8.

The classification rate obtained for the five classes using the three feature set is given in Table 5.

From Table 5, it is observed that for normal beat (N), the feature set RMSE and NSE show better results i.e. 91.6% and 100% respectively, compared to the other features. In case of paced beat (PB), RMSE gives 91.6%. The classification rate for left bundle branch block (LBBB) is 95.8% for NSE and RMSE. For right bundle branch block (RBBB), NSE gives 91.6% and RMSE gives 95.8%. In case pre-ventricular contraction (PVC) beat, NSE gives 95.8% and MSE gives 91.6%. Thus, considering all the above cases, it is seen that NSE, RSE has shown better results for most of the classes. Hence wavelet sub-band energy feature set discussed in this work can be considered as good feature set for ECG classification.

A comparative analysis of the classification accuracy of the above two methods with some other methods discussed in the literature is given in Table 6. While comparing, parameters taken into account are the number of heart beat types, the feature set and classifier used for classification.

From the classification table, it is seen that different feature set can provide different information for classification. The classification rate also depends on the type of classifier used. Some classifiers provide good classification rate for less number of classes. Multilayer perceptron neural network is a base class system widely used for any classification problem. Now-a- days SVMs are widely used for classification problems of larger number of classes.

Figure 8. Performance Curve of NSE

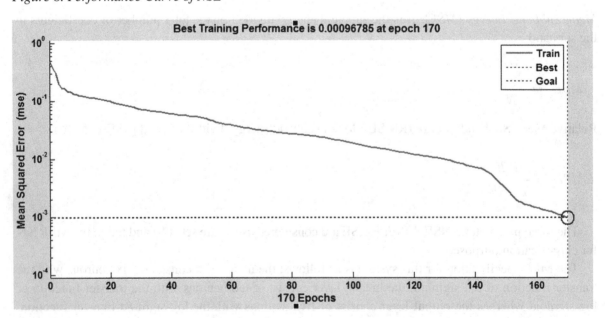

Figure 9. Performance Curve of MSE

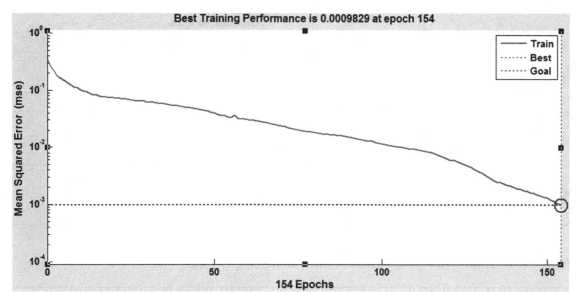

Figure 10. Performance Curve of RMS

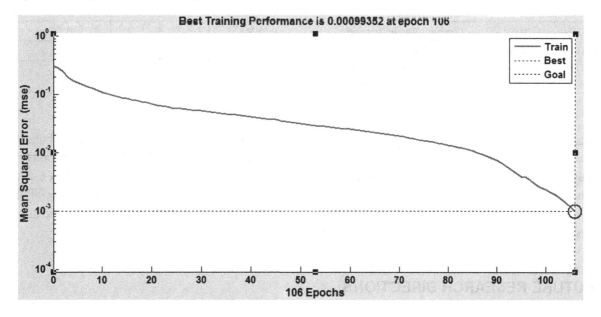

CONCLUSION

Biomedical signal processing methods have the potential to provide prior indication about the state of different organs in human body. A few of the efficient and simple framework for classification of ECG signal have been discussed in the chapter. In first method, a system for classification of ECG signals using LPC and PCA features was discussed. The feature vector is first applied individually and then in combination. Finally depending on the features vector applied for each type, ECG signals are classified

Table 5. Classification rate of FS used

Feature Set	Classification Types				
	N	PB	LBBB	RBBB	PVC
$NSE = \dfrac{SEj}{\sum SEj}$.	100%	83.3%	95.8%	91.6%	83.3%
$MSE = \dfrac{SEj}{N}$	79.1%	87.5%	79.1%	83.3%	91.6%
$RMSE = \dfrac{MSEj}{\sum MSEj}$	95.8%	91.6%	95.8%	95.8%	79.1%

Table 6. Comparison of discussed methods with some existing methods

Method Used	Feature Type	Classifier Used	No. of Classes	Classification Rate
Method 1	LPC and PCA	MLP	5	89.5%
Method 2	RMSE	MLP	5	91.6%
Ghosh et al (2005)	Continuos Wavelet Transform	SVM	5	93.2%
Güler et al. (2005)	Discrete Wavelet Transform	MLPNN	4	96.9%
Osowski et al. (2004)	Higher order statistics (IIOS) and Hermite coefficient (HER)	SVM	13	95.9%

into normal, paced beat, pre-ventricular contraction beat, left bundle branch block beat and right bundle branch block beat using multilayer perceptron neural network. This method is simple and gives good results for less number of classes. Secondly, another system for classification of ECG using wavelet energy based features has been discussed. In this system, DWT features have been used with SVM classifier to analyze and compare the classification accuracy with the first method. The developed classification system could aid the cardiologists in detecting the ECG arrhythmia in early stage.

FUTURE RESEARCH DIRECTIONS

As advances are made in technology, computer based methods are being widely used in bio-signal processing and biomedical instrumentation. Such techniques along with human interaction have shown to perform faster and better. It is also proved that they provide more accurate solution than conventional methods for signals that are highly complex and contain high level of noise. The classification technique can be further extended to discriminate other type of ECG arrhythmias such as atrial premature contraction, ventricular flutter wave, ventricular escape beat, Ventricular fibrillation, complete heart block etc. An automatic detection along with this classification system would help to make the diagnostic decision system more robust and complete.

REFERENCES

Adams, R., & Choi, A. (2012). Using Neural Networks to Predict Cardiac Arrhythmia. *Proceedings of Conference on Recent Advances in Robotics (pp. 1-6)*. Florida. doi:10.1109/ICSMC.2012.6377734

Barret, H. H. (2004). Foundation of Image Science (3rd ed.). Hoboken, New Jersey: John Wiley and Sons. U. K. Publications.

Chazal, P., Dwyer, M. O., & Reilly, R. B. (2004). Automatic Classification of Heartbeats Using ECG Morphology and Heartbeat Interval Features. *IEEE Transactions on Bio-Medical Engineering, 51*(7), 1196–1206. doi:10.1109/TBME.2004.827359 PMID:15248536

Emanet, N. (2009). ECG Beat Classification by using Discrete Wavelet Transform and Random Forest Algorithm. *Proceedings of International Conference on Soft Computing with Words and Perceptions in System Analysis Decision and Control* (pp. 1-4). Istanbul. doi:10.1109/ICSCCW.2009.5379457

Enderle, J. Blanchard, & S., Bronzino, J. (2006). Introduction to Biomedical Engineering (2nd eds). Elsevier.

Ghosh D., Midya, B. L., Koley, C., &Purkait, P. (2005). Wavelet Aided SVM Analysis of ECG Signals for Cardiac Abnormality Detection. *Proceedings of IEEE Indicon Conference* (pp. 9-13).

Gothwal, H., Kedawat, S., & Kumar, R. (2001). Cardiac Arrhythmia Detection in an ECG beat signal using Fast Fourier Transform and Artificial Neural Network. *Journal of Biomedical Science and Engineering* (pp. 289-296).

Guller, I., & Ubeyli, E. D. (2005). ECG beat classifier designed by Combined Neural Network Model. *Journal of Pattern Recognition, 38*(2), 199–208. doi:10.1016/S0031-3203(04)00276-6

Hosseini, H. G., Reynolds, K. J., & Powers, D. (2001). A Multi-Stage Neural Network Classifier for ECG Events. Proceedings of IEEE Engineering in Medicine and Biology Society. Istanbul, Turkey.

Iftikar, F., & Shams, A. (2012). A. Rhythm disorders - Heart Beat Classification of and Electrocardiogram Signal. *International Journal of Computers and Applications, 39*(11), 38–44. doi:10.5120/4867-7292

Kampouraki, A., Manis, G., & Nikou, C. (2009). Heartbeat Time Series Classification with Support Vector Machines. *IEEE Transactions on Information Technology in Biomedicine, 13*(4), 512–518. doi:10.1109/TITB.2008.2003323 PMID:19273030

Khandpur, R. S. (2006). *Handbook of Biomedical Instrumentation* (2nd ed.). Tata: McGraw Hill.

Kicmerova, I. D. (2009). Methods for Detection and Classification in ECG Analysis [Ph D. Thesis]. Brno University of Technology.

Kohli, N., & Verma, N. K. (2011). Arrhythmia Classification Using SVM with Selected Features. *IACSIT International Journal of Engineering and Technology, 3*(8), 122–131.

Lewalle, J., Farge, M., & Schneider, K. (n. d.). Wavelet Transforms (pp. 1378-1387). In C. Tropea, A. Yarin, & J. F. Foss (2007), *Springer Handbook of Experimental Fluid Mechanics, Vol. 1.*

Loong, J. L. C., Subari, K. S., & Abdullah, M. K. (2010). A New Approach to ECG Biometric System. *World Academy of Science. Engineering and Technology, 4*(8), 644–650.

Moody, G. B., & Mark, R. G. (2001, May-June). The impact of the MIT-BIH Arrhythmia Database. *IEEE Eng in Med and Biol,* 20(3), 45-50. Retrieved from http://www.physionet.org/physiobank/database/mitdb

Osowski, S., Hoai, L. T., & Markiewicz, T. (2004). Support Vector Machine-Based Expert System for Reliable Heartbeat Recognition. *IEEE Transactions on Bio-Medical Engineering, 51*(4), 582–589. doi:10.1109/TBME.2004.824138 PMID:15072212

Palaniappan, R., Gupta C. N. and Krishnan, S. M. (2008) Neural Network Classification of Premature Heartbeats. *Special Issue on Multimedia Data Processing and Classification* 3(3).

Rabee, A., & Barhumi, I. (2012). ECG Signal Classification using Support Vector Machine Based on Wavelet Multiresolution Analysis. *Proceedings of 11th International Conference on Information Sciences, Signal Processing and their Applications*: Special Sessions (pp. 1319-1323).

Reddy, D. C. (2006). *Biomedical Signal Processing- Principles and Techniques*. Tata: McGraw Hill.

Sarma, P., Nirmala, S. R., & Sarma, K. K. (2013). Classification of ECG using Some Novel Features. *Proceedings of IEEE International Conference on Emerging Trends and Computer Applications* (pp. 187-191). Shillong. doi:10.1109/ICETACS.2013.6691420

Sarma, P., Nirmala, S. R., & Sarma, K. K. (2014). ECG Classification using Wavelet Subband Energy based Features. *Proceedings of IEEE International Conference on Signal Processing and Integrated Networks (pp.* 785-790). Noida. doi:10.1109/SPIN.2014.6777061

Sharma, L. N. (2012). Multiscale Processing of Multichannel Electrocardiogram Signals [Ph D. Thesis]. Department of EEE, IIT Guwahati.

Sivanandam, S. N., Sumathi, S., & Deepa, S. N. (2006). *Introduction to Neural Networks using MATLAB 6.0. Computer Engineering Series*. Mc-Graw Hill.

Ubeyli, E. D. A. (2007). ECG Beat Classification Using Multiclass Support Vector Machines with Error Correcting Output Codes. *Digital Signal Processing, 17*(3), 675–684. doi:10.1016/j.dsp.2006.11.009

Wang, J. S., Chiang, W. C., & Ting, Y. C., Yang and Hsu, Y. L. (2011). An Effective ECG Arrythmia Classification Algorithm. *In proceedings of Bio-Inspired Computing and Applications.International Conference on Intelligent Computing* (pp. 545-550). China,

Zhao, Q., & Zhang, L. (2005) ECG Feature Extraction and Classification Using Wavelet Transform and Support Vector Machines. *Proceedings of International Conference on Neural Networks and Brain (ICNNB)* (Vol. 2, pp. 1089-1092).

ADDITIONAL READING

Jain, S., *Modeling & Simulation using Matlab-Simulink*. Wiley India

Sarma, K. K. *MATLAB Demystified-Basic Concepts and Application*. 1st Edition.Vikas Publishing House Pvt Ltd., New Delhi.

Stranneby, D. Walker, W. *Digital Signal Processing and Applications*. 2nd Edition.Elsevier.

Tan, L. *Digital Signal Processing-Fundamentals and Applications*.Elsevier.

Tompkins, W. J., *Biomedical Digital Signal Processing*. Prentice Hall of India Pvt Ltd.

KEY TERMS AND DEFINITIONS

Arrhythmia: An arrhythmia is a change in the regular beat of the heart.

Artificial Neural Network: Artificial Neural Networks are nonlinear information (signal) processing devices, which are built from interconnected elementary processing devices called neurons.

Classifier: In machine learning and statistics, classification is the problem of identifying to which of a set of categories, a new observation belongs, on the basis of a training set of data containing observations whose category membership is known. The system that performs this task is called classifier.

Feature: Feature is the important characteristic that helps the classifier to perform the classification.

Hyperplane: It is a subspace of one dimension less than its ambient space. A hyperplane of an n-dimensional space is a flat subset with dimension $n - 1$. By its nature, it separates the space into two half spaces.

Normal Beat: This is the beat of a normal human heart and its rate ranges from 60 to 100 bpm.

Perceptron: In machine learning, the perceptron is a classification algorithm that makes its predictions based on a linear predictor function combining a set of weights with the feature vector.

Chapter 8
Eye Ball Detection Using Labview and Application for Design of Obstacle Detector

Devkant Swargiary
Don Bosco College of Engineering & Technology, India

Ruhul Amin
Don Bosco College of Engineering & Technology, India

Joydeep Paul
Don Bosco College of Engineering & Technology, India

Hemashree Bordoloi
Don Bosco College of Engineering & Technology, India

ABSTRACT

Eye ball detection can be used for controlling certain applications. In this chapter, we describe the formulation of an eye ball detection system for design of an obstacle detection and avoidance technique. The obstacle detector is used with a vehicle and works by determining the location of an obstacle in the vicinity of a test object. The obstacle's distance is gauged from the test object in terms of corresponding voltages. The system uses image processing to detect the eye of the driver. If the eye of the driver is closed for a longer period than the threshold period then the image processing block sends a signal to the sensor which automatically takes control of the test vehicle.

INTRODUCTION

"*Eye Ball Detection Using LabVIEW & Obstacle Detector*" is all about taking control of the car when it senses that the driver is asleep. **"*Eye Ball Detection Using LabVIEW & Obstacle Detector*"** uses image processing to detect the eye of the driver. If the eye of the driver is closed for a longer period than the threshold period then the image processing block will send signal to the sensor which will automatically take control of the test vehicle.

It will detect obstacles such as other vehicle to avoid any kind of collision with them. Moreover it will detect the end of the road using edge avoider so that the car doesn't fall off into the valley or into a deep crater. Thereby it will find the shortest parking distance & it will park the car safely.

DOI: 10.4018/978-1-4666-8493-5.ch008

To monitor the condition of the driver we have used a camera. The camera will detect the movement of the eye ball of the driver. If the eye of the driver is closed for more than the threshold period of time then the obstacle sensor situated at the corners of the car will be activated. It will help the car to evade the other vehicles as obstacle (Reve & Choudhri, 2012).

For eye ball detection we are using LabVIEW software. With this software the camera can be made to track the eye ball of the driver. The threshold time is set regarding the blinking of the eyes of the driver and for inspecting in the vicinity in the interior of the car. Suppose this threshold time is around 5 seconds. If the eyes of the driver are closed for more than this threshold time of 5 seconds than a signal will be fed to the comparator which pass on the signal to the microcontroller. The microcontroller will eventually alert or activate the sensors. The sensors obstacle detector to be precise will sense the obstacles such as other vehicles so as to avert collisions (Kianpisheh, Mustaffa, Limtrairut & Keikhosrokiani, 2012).

The obstacle detector in this case is a circuit made with an IR sensor. In order to obtain a higher accuracy sonar sensor can be used in place of IR sensor. Figure 1 represents the block diagram of the proposed system.

We have designed a program entitled "Eye Detection using LabVIEW". Through this program we can control any system using the movement of the eye. The output of the program is accessed through the data acquisition card. When the eye of the user is open then we get a voltage of 5V and when the eye is closed then we get a voltage of 0V. By interfacing this program with a microcontroller we can control any kind of system

Image Processing Using LabVIEW

- The image processing block will capture the image of the driver in the 1ˢᵗ stage. The image will be fed to the buffer which will provide some temporary memory location for the continuous captured image acquired by the previous block, so that overlapping of the image doesn't takes place (LabVIEW, n.d.). Image processing block is shown in Figure 2.
- It is tougher to process a 3-D image (colour image or RGB) compared to a 2-D image (gray image). At 1ˢᵗ we will try to process a 2-D (gray) image.

Figure 1. Block Diagram of Intelligent Brake and Parking Assist System

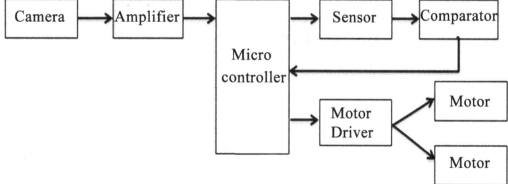

- In 4th block we will provide one reference image (template) with which every nascent captured image will be compared. If the template matches with the nascent images then the detector block will showcase the co-ordinates of the matching template pattern of the nascent image.
- After matching the template pattern the 5th block will give some particular signal (which will signify that template pattern is matched).

Basic Blocks Of LabVIEW And Their Details Used In Eyeball Detection

Vision Acquisition

The NI vision Acquisition wizard is launched by placing the express VI on the block diagram. Vision acquisition is shown in Figure 3. Select an acquisition source and configure an acquisition using NI-IMAQ, NI-IMAQdx, or simulate an acquisition by reading an AVI or image file from a folder. After an acquisition is configured, select control and indicators to be able to programmatically set in LabVIEW. Double-click the vision Acquisition Express VI to edit the acquisition (LabVIEW, n.d.).

Any image created by the express VI need to be disposed after use. Use the IMAQ Dispose.vi to clean-up the image output by the Express VI when they are no longer needed.

IMAQ Create VI

The IMAQ Create.vi as shown in Figure 4 is the VI which creates image buffers for use in LabVIEW vision applications. Ideally, the IMAQ Create.vi should be called at:

- There is an acquisition step, such as an IMAQ Snap or an IMAQ Grab, or
- There is a processing step that significantly changes the nature of the image, such as a threshold operation.

Whenever this VI is called, a unique name should be given to the Image Name input, as this will allocate a new image buffer. Occasionally, the same Image Name is passed to the IMAQ Create.vi. If this VI is called multiple times with the same Image Name, whatever data was present inside the image

Figure 2. Image Processing Block Using LabVIEW

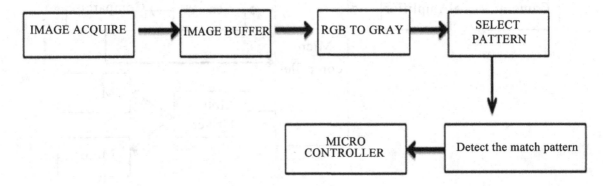

Figure 3. Vision Acquisition

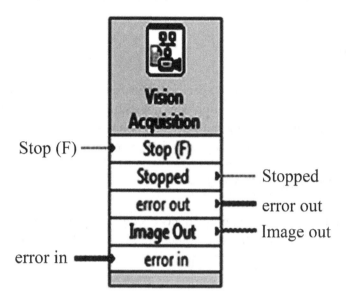

Figure 4. Image create VI

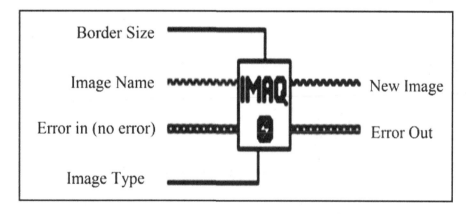

buffer is deleted and replaced by a 'NULL' image. This does not create a new space in memory, it simply overwrites the image. In general, always a unique name should be used.

Vision Assistant

When this Express VI is placed on the block diagram, NI vision Assistant is launched. Figure 5 shows the vision assistant wizard. We have created an algorithm using the vision Assistant processing functions. After an algorithm is created, the control and indicator is selected that the user wants to be programmatically set in LabVIEW. Double-click the vision Assistant Express VI to edit the algorithm (LabVIEW help, n.d.).

Unbundle By Name Function

It returns the cluster elements whose name is specified. The users do not have to keep track of the order of the elements within the cluster. This function does not require the number of elements to match the number in the cluster. After the user wires a cluster to this function, the user can select an individual element from the function. Cluster of name is shown in Figure 6.

IMAQ Extract Single Colour Plane VI

Single colour plane VI as shown in Figure 7 extracts a single plane from a colour image defines the colour plane to extract. Functions of different colour are shown in Table 1. The user can choose the colours as per the table:

BUILD ARRAY FUNCTION

It concatenates multiple arrays or appends elements to an n-dimensional array. The user also can use the Replace Array Subset function to modify an existing array. The connector pane displays the default data types for this polymorphic function (LabVIEW help, n.d.). Figure 8 represents array function.

Figure 5. Vision Assistant

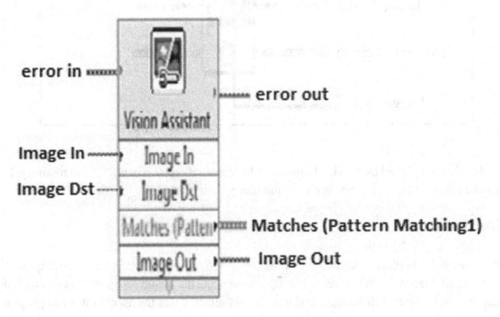

Figure 6. Cluster of Name

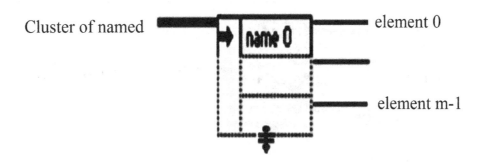

Figure 7. Single colour plane VI

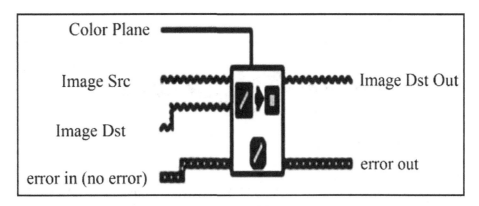

Table 1. Functions of different colours

Red(0)	(Default)Extracts the red colour plane
Green(1)	Extracts the green colour plane
Blue(2)	Extracts the blue colour plane
Hue(3)	Extracts the hue colour plane
Saturation(4)	Extracts the saturation colour plane
Luminance(5)	Extracts the luminance colour plane
Value(6)	Extracts the value colour plane
Intensity(7)	Extracts the intensity colour plane

Array to Cluster Function

Array to Cluster Function Conversion as shown in Figure 9 converts a 1D array to a cluster of elements of the same type as the array elements. Right click the function and select the Cluster Size from the shortcut menu to set the number of elements in the cluster. The default is nine. The maximum cluster

Figure 8. Array Function

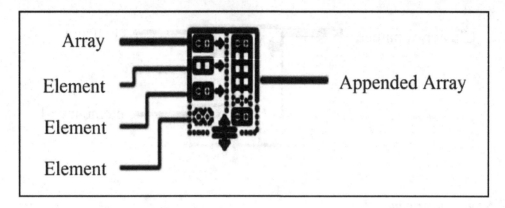

Figure 9. Array to Cluster Function Conversion

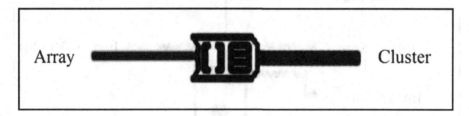

size for this function is 256. Use this function when you want to display elements of the same type in a front panel cluster indicator but want to manipulate the elements on the block diagram by their index values (LabVIEW help, n.d.).

Imaq Overlay Rectangle VI

It overlay a rectangle on an image. Overlays are non-destructive, which means that they do not overwrite the underlying pixel values (LabVIEW help, n.d.). Figure 10 represents Imaq Overlay Rectangle VI.

Figure 10. IMAQ Overlay Rectangle VI

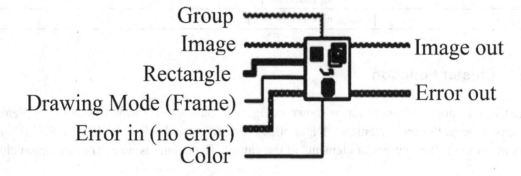

DESIRE OUTPUT OF EYE BALL DETECTION USING PATTERN MATCHING USING LABVIEW

The output of the eye ball detection using pattern matching as shown in Figure 11 is obtained.

SONAR

Sonar (originally an acronym for Sound Navigation and Ranging) is a technique that uses sound propagation (usually underwater, as in submarine navigation) to navigate, communicate with or detect objects on or under the surface of the water, such as other vessels.

Sonar sensors as shown in Figure 12 are useful ultrasonic rangefinders. They are capable of giving readings from 0 to 255 inches, with increments of 1 inch. A sonar sensor works by sending out a sonic pulse, which is then returned as an echo that is then returned to the sensor and analyzed (Chen, Hu & Chang, 2011).

Figure 11. Screenshot of Eye ball detection pattern

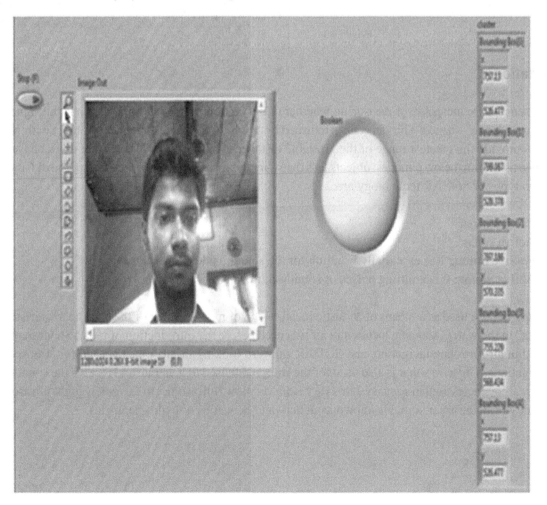

Figure 12. Sonar Sensor

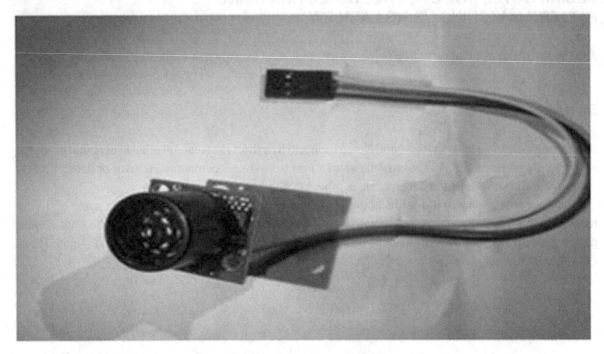

Limitations

Sonar sensors are incapable of measuring whether or not an object is small or large, since the signal the send out is "cone"-shaped. Thus an echo is returned by anything the pulse comes into contact with. Sonar sensors provide the greatest range of the available distance sensors (up to 21 feet), but do not have fine distance resolution below 6 inches; objects less than 6 inches away will have a recorded range of 6 inches.

Two types of SONAR technology are:

- Passive sonar
- Active sonar
  Passive Sonar: It is essentially listening for the sound made by system.
  Active Sonar: It is emitting pulses of sounds and listening for echoes.

Sonar may be used as a means of acoustic location and of measurement of the echo characteristics of "targets" in the water. Acoustic location in air was used before the introduction of radar. Sonar may also be used in air for robot navigation, and SODAR (upward looking in-air sonar) is used for atmospheric investigations. The term sonar is also used for the equipment used to generate and receive the sound. The acoustic frequencies used in sonar systems vary from very low (infrasonic) to extremely high (ultrasonic). The study of underwater sound is known as underwater acoustics or hydro-acoustics.

IR Sensor

Figure 13 represents IR transceivers that work by using a specific light sensor to detect a select light wavelength in the Infra-Red (IR) spectrum. When an object is close to the sensor, the light from the LED bounces off the object and into the light sensor. This results in a large jump in the intensity, which we already know can be detected using a threshold (Kong & Tan, 2008).

Detecting Brightness

Since the sensor works by looking for reflected light, it is possible to have a sensor that can return the value of the reflected light. This type of sensor can then be used to measure how "bright" the object is. This is useful for tasks like line tracking. Figure 14 represents operation of an IR sensor and Figure 15 represents mechanism of measuring brightness by an IR sensor. A brief comparison between a sonar sensor and IR sensor is given in Table 2.

Results and EXPERIMENTAL ANALYSIS

Eye Detection using LabVIEW

We have designed a program entitled "Eye Detection using LabVIEW". Through this program we can control any system using the movement of the eye. The output of the program is accessed through the data acquisition card. When the eye of the user is open then we get a voltage of 5V and when the eye is closed then we get a voltage of 0V. This is shown in Figure 16. By interfacing this program with a microcontroller we can control any kind of system.

The LED glows green when it detects the eye of the driver is open.

Figure 13. IR Transceiver

Figure 14. Depiction of the operation of an IR sensor

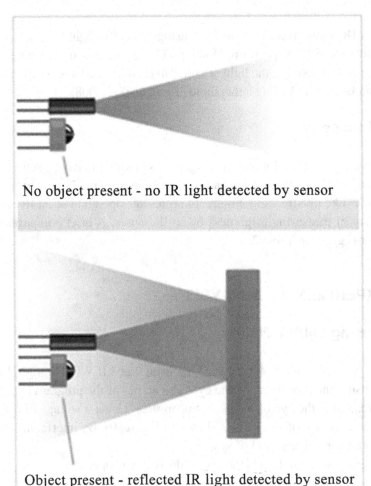

No object present - no IR light detected by sensor

Object present - reflected IR light detected by sensor

Obstacle Avoider with Sonar Sensor

We have designed an obstacle detector circuit with a sonar sensor. Bats use sonar mechanism as shown in Figure 17. A DC geared motor is connected with the obstacle detector circuit. The DC geared motor acts as the moving wheel of the car which will be stopped when the sonar sensor senses any obstacle in front of it. The obstacle detector circuit is being operated at 5 volts.

The microcontroller will activate the sonar. Then the sonar emits a mostly inaudible sound, time passes, then detects the return echo. It then immediately sends a voltage signal to the microcontroller, which by keeping track of the time that passes, can calculate the distance of the particular object detected.

The proximity of the vehicles will be calculated & the safe treading path will be estimated. The obstacle avoider will transmit the sonar beam which will strike back to the receiver after hitting the obstacles (other vehicles). The received signal will be in terms of voltage. The receiving voltages will be directly in terms of the distances. i.e., shorter the distance of the obstacles/ cars from the test vehicle the greater will be the output voltages of the sensor. Figure 18 shows interaction of robot with an obstacle. The microprocessor will compare the voltages & find the suitable path for parking (Mimbela & Klein, 2000).

Figure 15. Depiction of an IR sensor to measure brightness

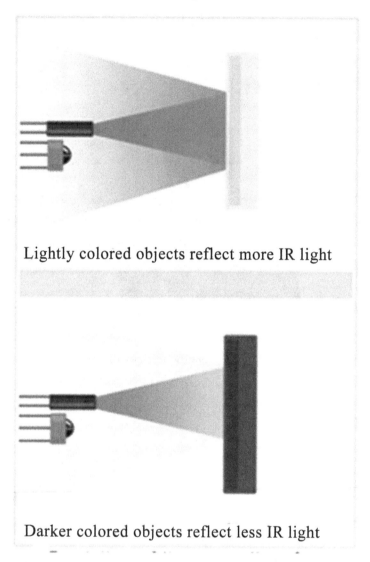

Table 2. Comparison between Sonar Sensor and Infrared Sensor

SONAR SENSORS	INFRARED SENSORS
1. Sonar sensors use sound instead of light for ranging, so ultrasonic sensors (some people call it sonar) can be used outside in bright sunlight.	1. Infrared sensors emit infrared light and therefore the sensors cannot work accurately outside or even inside, if there is direct or indirect sunlight.
2. Sonar sensor is expensive.	2. Infrared is cheap.
3. Sonar sensor more accurate, not good with absorbent objects like sponges), and wide beam.	3. Infrared has small beam, not good measuring distance to dark objects.

Figure 16. Screenshot of output of Eye ball detection

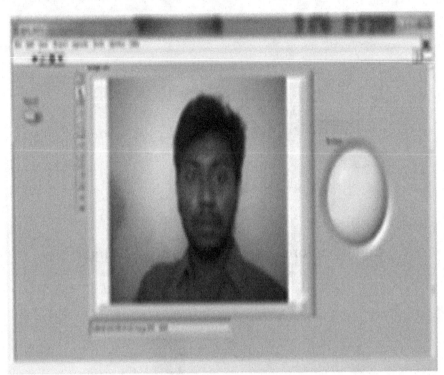

Figure 17. Sonar working in bats

Figure 18. Interaction of robot with an obstacle

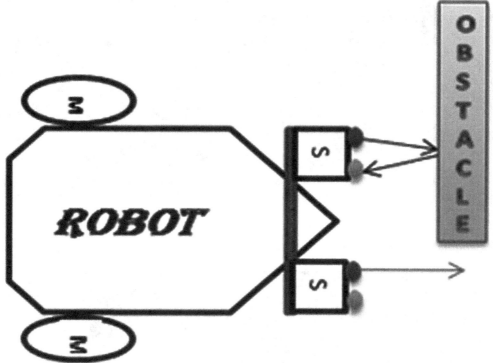

Working Principle

The sensor senses the light reflected from the surface and feeds the output to the comparator. If there is any obstacle in front then the light falling on it from the source reflects to the sensor, and if there is no obstacle in front then the source doesn't reflect to it. The sensor senses the reflected light to give an output, which is fed to the comparator. The comparator compares the analogue inputs from sensors with a fixed reference voltage. If this voltage is greater than the reference voltage, the comparator outputs a low voltage as shown in Figure 19, and if it is smaller, the comparator generates a high voltage, as shown in Figure 20, that acts as input for the decision-making device (microcontroller). This reference voltage can be adjusted by changing the value of the 10-kilo-ohm preset.

Interfacing Of Eye Detection Using LabVIEW With The Microcontroller

The eye detection program using LabVIEW is interfaced with the 8051 microcontroller kit and the prototype of the car. When the user eye is open the microcontroller gets a high signal and the prototype car keeps moving. When the eye of the user is closed the microcontroller get a low signal and the car stops moving. In this way the car can be controlled depending upon the eye movement of the user.

Figure 19. Output of Obstacle Detector without Obstacle [1.94 volts]

Figure 20. Output of Obstacle Detector with Obstacle [0.18 volts]

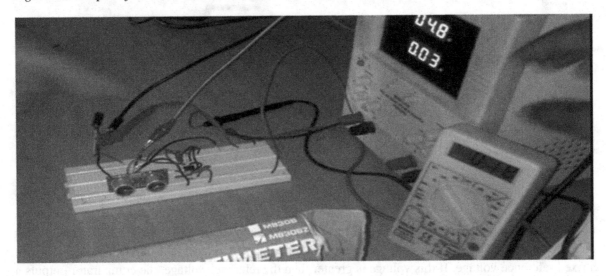

Experimental Analysis

Table 3 represents output of the sonar sensor with comparator and Table 4 represents the same without comparator.

CONCLUSION

Our system will override the manual control & will park the car in the shortest distance safely without waking up the driver. Use of the sonar sensors will be beneficial to drive the test vehicle both during day as well as night conditions.

Table 3. Output of Sonar Sensor with Comparator-LM324

INPUT VOLTAGE(volt))	DISTANCE(cm)	OUTPUT VOLTAGE(volt)
4.7	0	0.64
4.7	7.5	0.19
4.7	15	0.25
4.7	22.5	0.18
4.7	30	0.31
4.7	37.5	0.32
4.7	45	2.05
4.7	52.5	2.53
4.7	60	2.72
4.7	80	3.37

Table 4. Output of Sonar Sensor without Comparator-LM324

INPUT VOLTAGE(volt)	DISTANCE(cm)	OUTPUT VOLTAGE(volt)
4.7	0	0.12
4.7	7.5	0.14
4.7	15	0.16
4.7	22.5	0.14
4.7	30	0.22
4.7	37.5	0.18
4.7	45	1.38
4.7	50	1.47
4.7	60	1.5
4.7	90	1.85

The eye ball detection feature can be implemented in various systems ranging from security systems at homes to security systems at banks. Using the data acquisition card this feature can be accessed by the interfacing systems.

The implementation of brake and parking assist system is a boon for the mankind. At times when the braking is required at a flash in order to avoid the collisions or to minimize the effects of collisions, brake assist system proves to be beneficial. Moreover the users should bore the fact in minds that nothing can replace the response or action of the driver. So driver should remain alert while driving.

ACKNOWLEDGMENT

The authors would like to thank the Department of Electronics & Communication Engineering of Assam Don Bosco University for their support & assistance.

REFERENCES

Chen, M., Hu, C., & Chang, T. (2011). The Research on Optimal Parking Space Choice Model in Parking Lots. *Proceedings of International Conference on Computer Research and Development* (Vol. 2, pp. 93-97). Doi:10.1109/ICCRD.2011.5764091

Kianpisheh, A., Mustaffa, N., Limtrairut, P., & Keikhosrokiani, P. (2012). Smart Parking System (SPS) Architecture Using Ultrasonic Detector. *International Journal of Software Engineering and Its Applications*, 6(3), 51–58.

Kong, F., & Tan, J. (2008). A Collaboration-based Hybrid Vehicular Sensor Network Architecture. *Proceedings of International Conference on Information and Automation ICIA 2008* (pp. 584-589). Doi:10.1109/ICINFA.2008.4608067

LabVIEW help. (n. d). *General format*. Retrieved from http://www.ni.com/labview

LabVIEW. (n. d). In *Encyclopedia Wikipedia online*. Retrieved from http://en.wikipedia.org/wiki/LabVIEW

Mimbela, L. E. Y., & Klein, L. A. (2000). *A summary of vehicle detection and surveillance technologies used in intelligent transportation systems. Federal Highway Administration s (FHWA) Intelligent Transportation Systems Joint Program Office, the Vehicle Detector Clearinghouse*. NMSU.

Reve, S. V., & Choudhri, S. (2012). Management of car parking system using wireless sensor network. *International Journal of Emerging Technology and Advanced Engineering*, 2(7), 262–268.

KEY TERMS AND DEFINITIONS

ABS: Anti-lock braking system (ABS) is an automobile safety system that allows the wheels on a motor vehicle to maintain tractive contact with the road surface according to driver inputs while braking, preventing the wheels from locking up (ceasing rotation) and avoiding uncontrolled skidding. It is an automated system that uses the principles of threshold braking and cadence braking which were practiced by skillful drivers with previous generation braking systems. It does this at a much faster rate and with better control than a driver could manage.

DTMF: Dual-tone multi-frequency signaling (DTMF) is an in-band telecommunication signaling system using the voice-frequency band over telephone lines between telephone equipment and other communications devices and switching centers.

GSM: GSM (Global System for Mobile Communications, originally Groupe Spécial Mobile), is a standard developed by the European Telecommunications Standards Institute (ETSI) to describe protocols for second-generation (2G) digital cellular networks used by mobile phones.

IR: IR Sensors work by using a specific light sensor to detect a select light wavelength in the Infra-Red (IR) spectrum.

NI-IMAQ: Image acquisition drivers of LabVIEW.

Photosensitive Detectors: They are constructed to take advantage of the photoelectric effect, the emission of electrons from matter upon the absorption of electromagnetic radiation.

Pyroelectric Detectors: Pyroelectric detectors are infrared sensitive optoelectronic components which are specifically used for detecting electromagnetic radiation in a wavelength range from (2 to 14) μm.

SONAR: Sonar (originally an acronym for Sound Navigation and Ranging) is a technique that uses sound propagation (usually underwater, as in submarine navigation) to navigate, communicate with or detect objects on or under the surface of the water, such as other vessels.

USV: Unmanned surface vehicles (USV) or autonomous surface vehicles (ASV) are vehicles that operate on the surface of the water without a crew.

Chapter 9
An Approach for Automatic Detection and Grading of Macular Edema

Jyoti Prakash Medhi
Gauhati University, India

ABSTRACT

Prolonged Diabetes causes massive destruction to the retina, known as Diabetic Retinopathy (DR) leading to blindness. The blindness due to DR may consequence from several factors such as Blood vessel (BV) leakage, new BV formation on retina. The effects become more threatening when abnormalities involves the macular region. Here automatic analysis of fundus images becomes important. This system checks for any abnormality and help ophthalmologists in decision making and to analyze more number of cases. The main objective of this chapter is to explore image processing tools for automatic detection and grading macular edema in fundus images.

INTRODUCTION

The retina is a light sensitive tissue found at the back of the eye. It perceives light signal passed through the lens and accumulates at the center of retina called macula. The perceived signal is then send to the brain through optic nerve, where it is translated to the picture we see. The legitimate functioning of retina depends on constant supply of oxygen carried through blood vessel (BV)s (Diabetes Care, 2004; Diabetes Care, 2003;NHS Choices, 2014). Inadequate supply of oxygen gradually ceases the functionality of retina leading to vision complexities. There are various aspects causing impairment of the retina such as, hypertension, diabetes, old age, heart diseases etc. Various complexities of the retina is commonly known as 'Retinopathy'. Retinopathy begins with blockage of BV leading to blood leak over the retina. With gradual progression of the disease blood constituents like lipids and fatty materials also get deposited over retina. With deposition of such materials, the vision becomes blur. We may visualize it as being looking into an object through these depositions as shown Figure 1. As shown in second image of Figure 1 we observe the image as blur, because blood is not clear as water and the black region in the image represents the fatty material depositions over retina.

DOI: 10.4018/978-1-4666-8493-5.ch009

Figure 1. Normal vision vs. Vision with Retinopathy

The macula (Cataract and Laser Institute, 2012) of the retina consists of large number of cone cells located at the posterior pole of the eye, between the superior and inferior temporal arteries and is responsible for the central and sharp vision, for example, reading, watching television, writing, recognizing objects, colors etc. During progression of retinopathy, if depositions include macula or neighborhood of macula it is known as maculopathy. During maculopathy the vision severely gets effected and if not taken care at early stage, it may lead to vision loss. Various symptoms of maculopathy (Patient, 2014) includes, gradual loss of central vision causing obstruction or blurred patch as shown in Figure 2, distortion of image size and shape etc. As shown in the figure, the patient is able to see the clock but not the time.

Generally maculopathy occurs with age, (EyeSmart, 2013; ILMO, 2012) commonly known as Age related Macular Degeneration (AMD). Generally AMD starts after the age of 50. During AMD lipid structures leak from epithelial layer of eye and fall in neighborhood and/or over the macula. Maculopathy is also observed in younger age with patients having diabetes, known as Diabetic Macular Edema (DME). At initial stages of diabetes it is not much effective, but gradually with progression of disease the depositions will severely affect the vision and lead to blindness. Therefore one must go for regular eye examinations, at least once a year to avoid such complications. Ophthalmologists widely use fundus images for analysis of retinopathy. To investigate more features Optical Coherence Tomography (OCT) (EyeSmart, 2015) and Fluorescein angiography (MedlinePlus, 2015) are performed. The number of ophthalmologists compared to the retinopathy patients is very less with a ratio of 1:70,000. Thus, analysis of retinopathy with such huge extent is not easy. Many national screening programs have already started but will need time to meet the requirement. Automatic screening programs for analysis of retinopathy provides a helping hand in this regard. The automatic screening algorithms uses fundus images for analysis.

The chapter contains a direction towards automatic detection of maculopathy using fundus images. Few fundus image analysis methods for detection and grading of maculopathy have been presented

Figure 2. Effect of maculopathy in vision

along with the results and comparison statistics with existing methods. The organization of the chapter contains brief introduction of the fundus image and its imaging technique, discussion on various pathogens existence during maculopathy, literature review for the automatic detection approach, proposed methods and finally results.

FUNDUS PHOTOGRAPHY

Fundus means hollow, the eye is also a hollow organ and imaging of eye therefore called as Fundus Image / Photograph. Fundus imaging is the process whereby a 2D representation of the 3D semitransparent tissues projected onto imaging plane. The image intensities of the 2D image represent the amount of reflected light. Fundus camera as shown in Figure 3 is a low power microscope with an attached camera for fundus imaging or fundus photography, for imaging retina shown in Figure 4.

The fundus image shown in Figure 4 is authors own retinal image being taken at Biomedical Laboratory of Indian Institute of Technology, Guwahati. The fundus image shows the labelled retinal landmarks.

Figure 3. Fundus Camera
(Wikipedia, 2007).

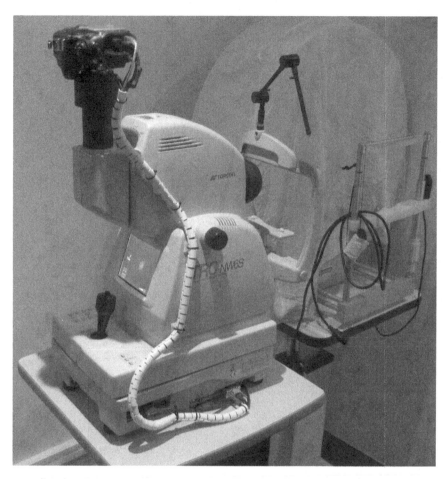

RETINOPATHY

Retinopathy is a sight threatening disease of the retina. Damage to the retina causes vision deficits and even blindness. The retina contains many blood vessels. Abnormalities in these vessels are a major cause of retinopathy. There are several types of retinopathy,

- **Retinopathy of Prematurity (ROP):** A child born too early doesn't have full grown retinal BVs. It will cause retinal disorders and may lead to retinal detachment.
- **Diabetic Retinopathy (DR):** During diabetes the retinal BVs were inadequate to provide proper oxygen supply to the retina causing DR.
- **Hypertensive Retinopathy:** High blood pressure causes alteration of the BVs leading to retinal dysfunctions.
- **Central Serous Retinopathy:** Accumulation of fluid behind the retinal layer causes blurred and poor night vision.

Figure 4. Fundus Image

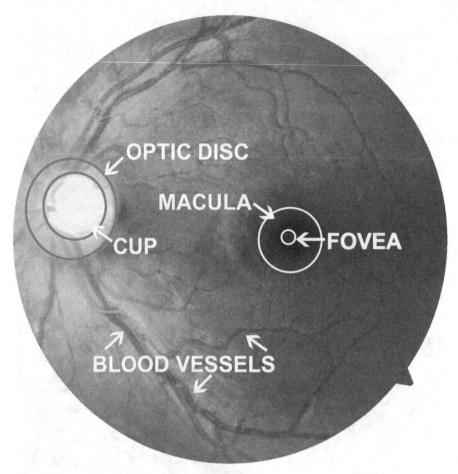

DIABETIC RETINOPATHY (DR)

DR (VRMNY, 2013; AOA, 2014; EyeSmart, 2013; RNIB, 2014) is one of the commonest causes of blindness in adults between 30 and 65 years of age in developed countries which happens because of diabetes mellitus. Retinal photocoagulation is an effective treatment, particularly if it is given at a relatively early stage when the patient is usually symptomless. Two types of changes are described in DR-background (Non-proliferative NPDR) and proliferative retinopathy. Background (NPDR) is the initial retinal capillary microangiopathy. The following changes are seen – basement membrane thickness, degeneration of pericytes and some loss of endothelial cells are found, capillary microaneurysms are found, waxy exudates accumulate in the vicinity of microaneurysms and lot hemorrhages in the deeper layer of retina are produced and soft cotton wool spots appear on the retina which are micro infarcts of nerve fiber layers of retina. After many years, retinopathy becomes proliferative. The following changes are seen in this case- Neovascularization at the OD, friability of newly formed blood vessels causes them to bleed easily and result in vitreous hemorrhages, proliferation of astrocytes and fibrous tissues around new blood vessels, fibro vascular and gliotic tissue contracts to cause retinal detachment and blindness.

Anomalies Due to DR

The clinical features of DR include- Microaneurysms, Hemorrhages, Exudates, Cotton wool spools, Intra-retinal micro vascular abnormalities and Neovascularization as shown in Figure 5.

- **Microaneurysms:** In most cases these are the earliest clinical abnormality detected. They appear as tiny, discrete, circular, dark red dots near to, but apparently different from, the retinal vessels. They look like tiny hemorrhages but they are in fact minute aneurysms arising mainly from the venous end of capillaries. They may give rise to retinal leakage of plasma constituents.
- **Hemorrhages:** These most characteristically occur in the deeper layers of the retina and hence are round and regular in shape and described as 'blot' hemorrhages. The smaller ones may be difficult to differentiate from microaneurysms and the two are often grouped together as 'dots and blots'. Superficial flame-shaped hemorrhages in the nerve fiber layer may also appear, especially if the patient is hypertensive.
- **Exudates:** These are characteristic of diabetic retinopathy. They vary in size from tiny specks to large confluent patches and tend to occur particularly in the peri macular area. They result from leakage of plasma from abnormal retinal capillaries and overlie areas of neuronal degeneration.
- **Cotton Wool Spots:** These are similar to retinal changes that occur in hypertension, and also occur particularly within five disc diameters of the OD. They represent arteriolar occlusions caus-

Figure 5. Anomalies due to DR
(Retinal Eye Care Associates, 2014)

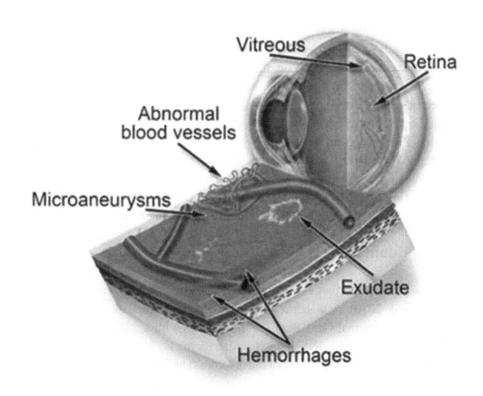

ing retinal ischaemia and, if it is numerous, may represent pre-proliferative diabetic retinopathy; they are most often seen in rapidly advancing retinopathy or in association with uncontrolled hypertension

- **Intra-Retinal Micro Vascular Abnormalities:** Intra-retinal micro vascular abnormalities (IRMA) are dilated, tortuous capillaries which develop in severe pre-proliferative retinopathy. They represent the remaining patent capillaries in an area of ischemic retina where most have been occluded.
- **Neovascularization:** New vessel formation may arise from the venous circulation either on the OD (NVD) or elsewhere in the retina (NVE), in response to widespread retinal ischemia. The earliest appearance is that of fine tufts of delicate vessels forming arcades on the surface of the retina. As they grow, they may extend forwards on to the posterior surface of the vitreous. They are fragile and leaky, and are liable to rupture during vitreous movement, causing a pre-retinal ('subhyaloid') or a vitreous hemorrhage. New vessels may be symptomless until hemorrhage appear, when there may be acute visual loss. Serous products leaking from these new vessels stimulate a connective tissue reaction, called gliosis and fibrosis. This first appears as a white, cloudy structure among the new vessels. As it extends, the new vessels may be obliterated and the surrounding retina is covered by a dense white sheet. By this stage, hemorrhage is less common but retinal detachment can occur through traction on adhesions formed between the vitreous and the retina, causing serious visual impairment.

MACULAR EDEMA

Although proliferative retinopathy is the most dramatic series of retinal lesions in diabetes, and may produce the most profound visual loss even to total blindness. The most common reason for visual impairment in diabetic individuals is macular edema. By definition macular edema is the result of an inflation of fluid in the retinal slab around the macula (Creteil, 2010). It causes vision loss by altering the functional cell relationship in the retina and promoting an inflammatory reparative response. Macular edema is a nonspecific sign of ocular disease. It may be viewed as a clinically relevant type of macular response to a retinal environment being altered. In most cases, it is associated with an alteration of the blood-retinal barrier (BRB). Macular edema may occur in a wide variety of ocular situations including uveitis, trauma, intraocular surgery, vascular retinopathies, vitreoretinal adhesions, hereditary dystrophies, diabetes, and age-related macular degeneration. The histopathological picture of this condition is an accumulation of fluid in the outer plexiform and inner nuclear and plexiform layers of the retina. The increase in water content of the retinal tissue characterizing macular edema.

Diabetic Macular Edema (DME)

Macular edema is the most important complication of diabetes mellitus leading to an impairment of visual sensitivity (Creteil, 2010). A diabetic macular edema is defined as a retinal thickening caused by the accumulation of intraretinal fluid and/or hard exudates within 2 disk diameters of the center of the macula, the fovea. The incidence of diabetic macular edema is closely associated with the degree of diabetic retinopathy and the duration and type of the disorder. The 25-year collective incidence in persons with type 1 diabetes mellitus is subjected to 29% for macular edema and 17% for clinically significant macular edema. There are two subtypes of diabetic macular edema, a focal and a diffuse form. Focal macular edema refers to localized areas of retinal thickening, caused by locus of vascular dysfunction, mainly microaneurysms, and less caused by intraretinal micro vascular abnormalities. Here fluid leakage occurs at a great extent, which is usually followed by hard exudates. The hard exudate pattern may be either focal or ring structured. Diffuse macular edema is caused by a general diffuse leakage from dilated retinal capillaries (and from microaneurysms and arterioles) throughout the posterior pole of the retina. It is usually observed in both eyes with the similar or extensively different degree of leakage. There are also classifications for ischemic and exudative macular edema. In most situations, a hybrid type can be observed.

A clinically significant macular edema (CSME) is the early DR study which includes features like thickening of the retina at or within 500 mm from fovea and presence of hard exudates obtained in the same region, if linked with thickening of the adjacent retina.

Age-Related Macular Degeneration (AMD)

Age-related macular degeneration (AMD) is the term applied to ageing changes without any obvious cause that occur in the macula in people with age 50 years and above. It begins with accumulation of lipid material as deposits beneath the retinal pigment epithelium (RPE). When focal collections of lipid material are present these are referred to as drusen and can be seen as pale yellow spots on fundus image. Generally drusen and RPE irregularities are not associated with disturbances of central vision. A proportion of people having these early alterations will progress to severe central vision loss when development of geographic atrophy and/or exudative disease occurs. AMD can be sub-classified into two major forms: the atrophic or dry form and the exudative or wet form. Atrophic macular degeneration without exudative changes does not generally lead to macular edema. The exudative form with choroidal neovascularization may cause a serous detachment of the overlying retina, resulting in CME. The presence of CME is more likely if the serous detachment of the macula has been present for 3-6 months or if the choroidal neovascular membrane has involved the sub foveal region.

LITERATURE SURVEY

A large numbers of articles have been published in the literature on retinal image analysis and segmentation of retinal features. For proper understanding they are classified as follows:

- Localization of Macula.
- Localization of Abnormalities.
- Analysis of maculopathy.

Localization of Macula

The macula is an oval-shaped highly pigmented yellow spot near the center of the retina (Siegel & Sapru, 2006). It is of diameter around 6 mm and is often defined as having two or more ganglion cells layers. Its center is called fovea, a small region that contains high concentration of cone cells in the eye. Fovea is responsible for central, high resolution vision.

The contrast of the macular region is often quite low and it may be wrapped by exudates or hemorrhages. As a result to obtain a global correlation often fails. The fovea is located approximately 2–2.5 disk diameters temporal to the optic disk (OD) and between superior and inferior temporal arteries. These positional constraints have been used by several authors to identify a small search area for the macula.

Siddalingaswamy, P. C. & Prabhu, (2010) have used the OD as the reference point and have used the positional constraint with respect to OD. The Macula is said to be situated 2 disc diameter (DD) temporal to OD and the mean angle between macula and the center of OD against the horizon is -2.3^0 to -8.9^0. In that area a rectangular search window has been created and the center of window having the lowest average intensity is taken as center of the macular region.

Mubbashar, M., Usman & Akram, (2011) also used OD the reference point and the maximum value is calculated in front of the OD. The mean of these maximum value is calculated and plotted on a thresholded image which gives the macula.

Sekher, Al-Nuaimy & Nandi, (2008) have searched for the vicinity of the OD. The candidate macula ROI is defined as the portion of a sector subtended at the center of the OD by 30^0 above and below the center of the OD and the image. The macula is identified by iteratively applying a threshold and then applying a morphological opening on the resulting blob.

Niemeijer, M., Abramoff & Bram, (2007) have used a different approach to locate macula. A cost function has been used combining local as well as global cues to detect anatomical structures in fundus images. The parametric model that has been used in this work can be given as $S_{result}=G(b,F,I,O)$, where G is the model ; b is a set of parameter, F is a cost function, I is the image and O the optimizing algorithm. So given a set of model parameters b, a certain configuration of the 16 points should be generated. Then, taking I and s as input the cost function F will generate a value for the current configuration indicating how well S fits to I. Optimization algorithm O will then attempt to find the b where F has the lowest value. When O has found the set of parameters where F is minimal, the corresponding point configuration is S_{result}.

Poshtyar,A., Ghassabi & Shanbehzadeh, (2011) used the spatial information of the optic cup to detect OD and macula. The fovea is assumed to have the row coordinate same as the row coordinate of middle pixel of the image (i.e. row/2) in ideal situation. But that isn't the usual case hence the row coordinate of fovea is assumed to be smaller or larger than the row coordinate of middle pixel of image, therefore is computed accordingly. The column coordinate of fovea is computed in each 1/8 of image which the OD is appeared. Macular area is an approximate ellipse with fovea coordinates in the center.

Singh, Joshi & Sivaswamy, (2008) have used the appearance of macula as a property to determine its location. Signal to Noise Ratio (SNR) boosting is performed to enhance the darker profile of macula. Green channel image is subtracted from complemented red channel image to retain the dark intensity information. The resultant image is later binarized to detect macula.

LOCALIZATION OF ABNORMALITIES

Microaneurysms, small outpunching of the capillary walls, are the first micro-vascular changes to appear and are sentinel markers for early diabetic retinopathy. With disease progression small intraretinal dot haemorrhages, often indistinguishable from Microaneurysms appear and later larger blot haemorrhages.

Excessive capillary permeability is manifest as retinal edema usually accompanied by lipid exudation. If the exudates are on the macula, it can be sight threatening (diabetic maculopathy). Figure 6 shows a fundus with abnormalities.

Detection of Microaneurysms

Quellec *et al.*, (Quellec et al., 2008) modelled the microaneurysms with 2-D rotation-symmetric generalized Gaussian function given by

$$f(r;\alpha;\gamma;\delta) = \gamma + \delta_{\exp}\left(\left(\frac{|r|}{\alpha}\right)^{\beta}\right)$$

where, $r = \sqrt{x^2 + y^2}$ and α are the parameters for modelling the lesion size, β is for modelling lesion sharpness, γ is for background intensity and δ is for modelling lesion height. Gaussian shape was found to be convenient for modelling wide range of shapes of MAs.

Figure 6. Fundus image with abnormalities
(IMAGERET, 2007)

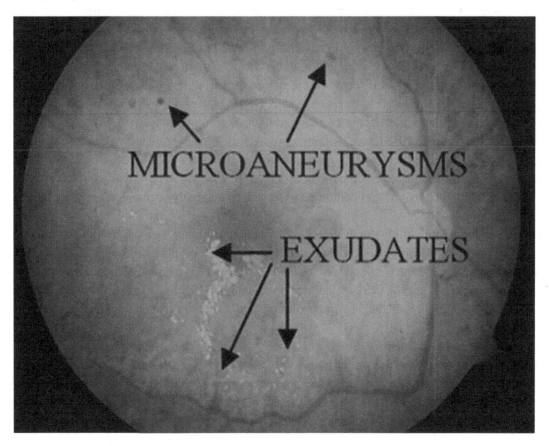

Hatanaka et al. 2008, (Hatanaka, Nakagawa, Hayashi, Hara & Fujita, 2008) proposes a new method for detection of haemorrhages. The author first performs brightness correction using hue-saturation-value (HSV) space. The brightness corrected value is given by:

$$B_C\left(i,j\right) = \sqrt{1-\left(V\left(i,j\right)-1\right)^2}$$

where, $V\left(i,j\right)$ = brightness value of HSV space. Then the $B_C\left(i,j\right)$ are processed by gamma correction. Gamma value was experimentally set at 1.5. First optic nerve head was extracted by thresholding method from green component of fundus image. Then haemorrhages were detected by density analysis. Two smooth images were made by using masks of 3×3 and 9×9. Then the difference of the pixel values of the two smoothed images was calculated and haemorrhages were detected. This method was not able to detect the haemorrhages connected to blood vessels.

Detection of Exudates

Drusens appear as yellowish, cloudy blobs in a retinal image. They exhibit no specific size or shape. The modification of size in individual drusens and their confluence seem to be an essential risk factor in developing macular degeneration. Exudates are characteristic of diabetic retinopathy. They vary in size from tiny specks to large confluent patches and tend to occur particularly in the perimacular area. They result as leakage of plasma from abnormal retinal capillaries and overlie areas of neuronal degeneration.

Walter et al. (2007) identified exudates from green channel using the gray-level variations. They have used the mathematical morphology for determining the contour of exudates after initial localization. This method has three parameters: local window (used for calculation of local pixel variation) and two threshold values. First threshold determines the minimum variation value within each local window. Exudates regions are found by first threshold value. Second threshold value represents the minimum value, by which candidate differs from its surrounding background pixels.

Harangi, B. & Hajdu, (2013) have extracted possible candidate exudate regions by applying morphological operations. These extracted regions are treated as initial mask for an active contour method. At the preprocessing level nine separate methods has been. Nine different boundaries are extracted for each of the exudates one by one and combined to fit best to manually segmented exudates in the training database.

Siddalingaswamy, P. C & Prabhu, (2010) have extracted candidate exudate by clustering technique, then the OD is removed from the clustered image to get rid of false positive. Later candidate region is segmented using morphological operations. The finely segmented candidate exudate region is overlaid on the green channel to get the marker image and the original green channel is used as the mask. Finally the exudate region are obtained by thresholding the difference between the original image and the reconstructed image.

Tariq, Akram, Shaukat & Khan, (2012) has initially extracted the candidate exudate. It is done in the following way- (1) blood vessels & dark lesions are removed by morphological closing (2) contrast of the exudates are improved by adaptive contrast enhancement (3) to further enhance the bright lesions Gabor kernel is convolved with the contrast enhanced image. The feature of this candidate regions is fed to a support vector machine (SVM) which determines whether it is an exudate or not.

Haniza, Hamzah & Hazlita, (2012) have used the strategy that involves the applications of fuzzy c-means (FCM) clustering, edge detection and OTSU thresholding to separate edge pixels of the exudates from the background. Then inverse surface thresholding is employed to extract the exudates. The FCM will segment the fundus images into the above five categories- the area outside of the eyeball, the blood vessel, the healthy background retina, the low intensity exudates (cotton wools) and the high intensity exudates (hard exudates). Since only the area containing exudates the ROI, only the last two groups is to be processed further. Once the region containing the soft and hard exudate is identified the rest of the area will be disregarded, then Prewitt operator is applied to identify the boundaries of the exudates. To avoid manually selecting a threshold value which can be effected by uneven illumination and contrast OTSU method is applied. The threshold splits the resulting image of the previous phase into the edge and non-edge pixels. Now OD is detected by applying variance intensity of the adjacent pixels. Now inverse surface is used to locate the OD and exudates. The intensity of the inverse surface is derived from the gradients of the original image and the negative image in four passes. The final inverse surface is the average of the four primary surfaces. The final step is to do surface thresholding so as to adjust the position of the inverse surface so that only the areas containing defects will intersect with the original image.

Welfer, D., Scharcanski & Marinho, (2010) have converted the RGB image to LUV color model then on L channel contrast enhancement has been done by applying Top Hat morphological operation on L channel followed by Bottom hat morphological operation on L channel. The top hat image is then added to, and bottom hat image is subtracted from the L channel which makes the bright area brighter and dark area darker. At this stage regional minima is obtained and a morphological reconstruction is done from the regional minima. The difference between the reconstructed image and the contrast enhanced image is obtained. The H- maxima transform is computed from the difference image. This image is further thresholded to give a coarsely segmented image which serves as the marker image for finer exudate detection. A morphological reconstruction of the marker is done. Again a difference image is obtained from the green channel and the reconstructed image. Again the image is thresholded which gives the final exudate lesion.

Analysis of Maculopathy

Maculopathy analysis depicts the accumulation of anomalies over and around neighborhood of macula. Depending on the region of presence of these anomalies maculopathy is classified into three stages namely mild, moderate and severe. The anomalies are classified as significant if they are within the range of macula neighborhood. Otherwise they are classified as non-significant macular edema. Automatic grading of maculopathy is performed by estimating the density and location of anomalies from the center of macula. The stages are classified as follows,

- **Mild:** If the anomalies lie far away from the macula neighborhood. At 2 OD diameter away from macula center.
- **Moderate:** If the anomalies lie in macula neighborhood. At 1 OD diameter away from macula center.
- **Severe:** If anomalies fall over the macula. The condition turns sight threatening when anomalies involves fovea. At $1/3^{rd}$ OD diameter from fovea center.

Very few papers have been published in the literature for maculopathy analysis, Deepak, K.S, & Sivaswamy, (2012) have performed global image analysis for determining exudates by analyzing motion pattern. Motion pattern formed on healthy fundus images were considered for generating test images. The test images were then compared with the motion pattern images containing exudates. The variation determines the amount of exudates present in the image. Same patterns were then generated for macular region to find out severity of maculopathy.

Siddalingaswamy, P.C, & Prabhu, (2010) have generated macular regions to identify maculopathy stages by determining the amount of exudates present over them. Here the author classifies the stages of maculopathy and performs the severity measurement.

Medhi, Nath & Dandapat, (2012) have detected macula using intensity property. BV removed green channel image and red channel image are processed to obtain the dark intensity region of fundus image and using an adaptive threshold macula region is identified. On the macular a mask is created to analyze severity of maculopathy. The exudates and microaneurysms are later detected using mathematical morphology. The amount of anomalies presence over macular mask determine the severity of the disease.

OPEN ISSUES AND MOTIVATION

Automatic detection and classification of maculopathy involves detection of anomalies presence over macular regions. In this direction we have to follow mainly three step analysis. The first stage involves identification of anomalies present in the image. Secondly gathering information of fovea location and lastly, to generate macular regions from fovea and to identify amount of anomalies present over them.

All the stages have various challenges and limitations of analysis. Various issues are mentioned as follows for each analysis step.

- *Detection of anomalies is a challenging task.* If the image is not illuminated properly, the intensity values of anomalies are near to those of the background. Classification applied on such images may lead to background classification along with abnormalities. Irregular shapes, varying structure and intensity of the unhealthy area also makes it difficult to classify them. The intensity of OD and exudates both appear bright in intensity. Therefore OD masking is essential before segmenting exudates. Improper masking of OD may result as misclassified unhealthy areas. The exudates may also be so near to OD that it might seem part of the OD. Microaneurysms are very close to the BV intensities. Thus classifying microaneurysms is also challenging.
- *The fovea is located at 2 OD diameter temporal to OD center.* Using this property the fovea location may be determined. The primary requirement of this method is to identify OD location. OD center is then to obtain from the detected OD. From the center using spatial relationship the region containing fovea is to be located. The main challenge in this analysis is to locate the exact position of OD center. If any exudate be misclassified as OD the whole process will fail. Another way of determining fovea is to locate the dark intensity region, as macula has dark profile. BV removal may be needed in this process as BVs also share the same intensity. The main limitation in this method is, if the macula region is not dark or not visible properly the algorithm fails. Also if hemorrhages lie with similar intensity they might get misclassified as fovea. Thus identifying fovea demands efficient algorithms.

- *Classification of maculopathy stages requires proper identification of fovea and OD diameter.* Using these properties different regions can be obtained and later presence of anomalies over them is identified and graded.

Considering all the pros and cons of automatic detection we present few methods to analyze macular edema.

METHODS FOR AUTOMATED ANALYSIS OF MACULAR EDEMA

The automatic detection of retinal landmarks is based combination of *inpainting, morphology and thresholding technique* applied to different color planes of fundus image. It is an approach for modification of RGB model by processing HSI and yCbCr color model. Before segmentation, the original fundus image has to undergo preprocessing for enhancement of the image quality. After segmentation of the anomalies grading is also performed to detect the severity of the disease (e.g. DR). The proposed algorithm is represented by the block diagram shown in Figure 7

PREPROCESSING

The diagnostic process of DR have been affected if the illumination of fundus image is not proper. Improper reflection of camera flash, retinal pigmentation etc. causes variation in illumination. Thus for reducing the image variability preprocessing step is very much significant for success of the algorithm.

The databases of fundus images which we worked have resolution and illumination variations. Thus we have to go through various illumination correction methods and generalize the images to a single resolution. Thus we have fixed all the images size to be 576×720. Depending on the properties of the images color normalization and contrast enhancement of the fundus photographs are needed. Various preprocessing tools were applied to the images depending on their intensity variations. Median filtering is performed in all the RGB planes to remove noise present in fundus. Contrast enhancement is applied on Hue plane and the enhanced image is converted back to RGB. For illumination equalization we consider all the RGB image planes and apply the algorithm. To apply CLAHE, RGB image is first converted to HSI color plane and enhancement is applied to intensity (I) plane. Then the $HSI_{modified}$ image is converted back to RGB color image which is contrast enhanced image. The Homomorphic filtering and White top transformations are applied on gray scale image. All these preprocessing techniques were described in (Harangi & Hajdu, 2013).

BLOOD VESSEL REMOVAL

The fundus image consists of numerous blood vessels (BV) having its boarders along different retinal land marks such as OD, macula causing difficulty for proper segmentation. Thus, BV network is removed using image inpainting method (Bertalmio, Sapiro, Caselles & Ballester, 2000). For BV to be inpainted the binary mask of BV is to be segmented. For segmentation of BV mathematical morphology is used.

Figure 7. Block diagram of proposed algorithm

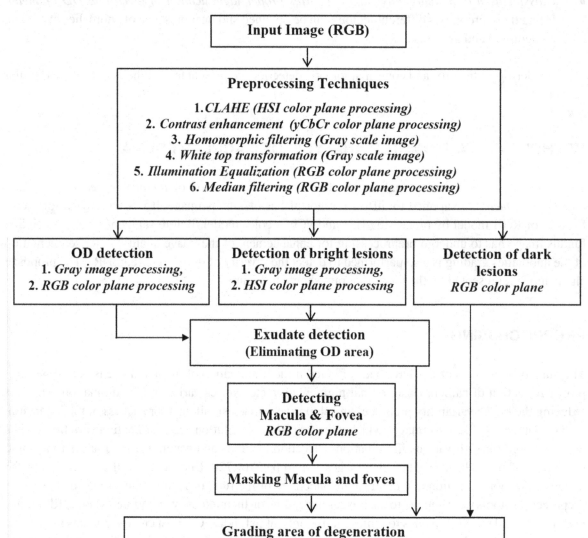

OD DETECTION AND MASKING

OD has maximum intensity pixels then other retinal landmarks. On the other hand exudates are also bright in nature having similar range of intensity values. Thus detection of exudates also finds OD. Therefore OD is to be located and masked before detecting exudates.

For detection of OD we have selected the intensity property and applied a threshold to detect the maximum intensity pixels. After correcting illumination on gray scale image we set a threshold of maximum 40 gray levels and detect the pixels having intensity within that range. After the pixels being detected we apply a mask of radius 70 from the center of detected region. This mask is then used to remove the OD in hue color plane as it will be used for detection of exudates.

Exudate Detection

For exudate detection we have performed three methods using different properties of image processing. To enhance exudate detection in all the cases we detect the outer boundary of the fundus image using morphological boundary tracing operations as preprocessing requirement. After the boundary being detected it is masked such that the boundary pixels don't interfere in exudate segmentation.

Method 1: The hue color plane of HSI color model contains the color information of all the pixels. The high valued pixel of hue plane corresponds to exudates. Using this property we have extracted out the exudates from color fundus image. First RGB image is converted to HSI color model and hue plane is extracted. In the hue plane a threshold of maximum 70 is applied and pixels above which are marked as exudates.

Method 2: Another method for exudate detection is applied on gray scale image. In this connection we have considered the BV and OD removed gray scale image and applied morphological closing to enhance the exudate area removing all the unwanted noisy pixels. Then a threshold is applied and pixels above which are marked as exudates.

Method 3: For feature extraction and pattern recognition, contour tracing is a handy preprocessing techniques performed on digital images. This is because of the contour pixels are small subset of the total number of pixels representing a pattern. As the contour of a given pattern is obtained, its different properties can be examined and used as features for pattern classification. The boundary tracing algorithm used in this connection is Moore-Neighbor tracing (Contour Tracing, 2000).

The BV removed image is used for this purpose. The boundary tracing algorithm is applied to all enhanced preprocessed image. The result of boundary extraction is then used to determine the area covered by the exudates. The image containing maximum area is considered to be the best result and it is chosen for further processing.

To display the exudates in the color image we have collected the coordinates of detected pixels and highlight those locations in original image by using a single color. This method have been taken from our previous work (Majumder & Medhi, 2014).

Microaneurysms (MA) Detection

The MAs are detected from the preprocessed images. Green channel of RGB color plane is used for the analysis. The mathematical morphology is used for MA detection. The outlines of the image is detected by canny edge detection method applied to the histogram equalized image. The circular boarder detected in preprocessing is removed. Subtracting the edge image gives the MAs. This image also contains the noisy pixels, like BVs and exudates. The image is then subtracted from the previous processed images containing exudates and BVs. Finally the MAs image is obtained. It is an enhancement of our previous method (Medhi, Nath & Dandapat, 2012).

Macula and Fovea Detection

For macular region detection we have performed two methods using different properties of image processing. The macula appears dark in intensity and the information is intact in RGB plane.

Method 1: It is the extension of the processed output obtained from the first exudate detection method. After the exudates are detected in hue plane the resultant HSI image is converted back to RGB image. In the RGB image green color plane contains the information of macula more than the other color planes. Thus a threshold is applied to obtain pixels with intensity value less than. The pixels detected are the macular region. On decreasing the threshold value the detected pixels represent fovea.

Method 2: This method have been taken from our previous work (Medhi, Nath & Dandapat, 2012). Blood vessel removed red channel and the green channel images of the preprocessed image are used for detection of macula. The green channel image is subtracted from complemented red channel image. A fixed global threshold is used and the macula is separated. On increasing the threshold value fovea is separated.

Grading Macular Edema

Maculopathy grading requires information of exudates detected in macular region (Severe stage), in neighborhood of macula (Moderate stage) and far away from macula (Mild stage). Thus for grading, regions of macula are to be determined earlier. The segmented pathogenic image is overlapped with all the macular masks. The area of overlapped region of abnormality and different macular masks are determined. The result shows the severity level of maculopathy, i.e. whether the patient is suffering from mild, moderate or severe case. After classification of the stages the amount of severity is determined by obtaining the ratio of overlapping pixels to the masks pixels.

MATERIALS/ DATABASE USED

For analysis three databases of fundus images were used which are available on the web, DRIVE (Digital Retinal Images for Vessel Extraction), DIRETDB1 and HRF (High-Resolution Fundus Image).

The DRIVE database (Image Sciences Institute, 2004) consists of 40 color image varying in quality with 584×565 pixels in TIFF format captured by Canon CR5 non-mydriatic 3CCD camera with a 45 degree field of view (FOV). It contains training set and test set having equal number of images out of which 7 images (15% of images) have signs of mild DR. The DIARETDB1 (IMAGERET, 2007) database consists of 89 color fundus images with 1500×1152 pixels and captured using 50 degree FOV digital fundus camera with varying imaging settings. Out of 89 images 5 images are normal and 84 images contain mild NPDR signs (94.39% of images). Among the mild NPDR sign images 47 retinal images (55.95% of images) contain hard exudates. HRF database (TECHNISCHE FAKULTAT, 2013) consists of 45 images with 3504×2336 pixels in JPG format captured by Canon CR-1 fundus camera with a 45° FOV. Out of 45 images 15 images (33.33% of images) have signs of DR and 15 images (33.33% of images) have signs of glaucoma.

RESULTS

The results obtained are divided into three methods. But image enhancement is the basic requirement of any one of the algorithm. Therefore we have performed six different image enhancement techniques to meet our requirements.

Preprocessing

Preprocessing of the input RGB image is performed initially before segmentation. After preprocessing the BV are removed using inpainting. Figure 8(a) shows original image and Figure 8(b)-(i) show the entire enhanced image obtained using the methods discussed in section 4.1. Figure 9(a)-(d) shows the blood vessel removed RGB, green plane, red plane and gray image.

Figure 8. (a) Original image RGB, (b) Median filtered image RGB, (c) Contrast enhanced image RGB, (d) CLAHE image RGB, (e) Illumination equalized image RGB, (f) Illumination equalized image Green Plane of RGB, (g) Original image Gray scale, (h) Homomorphic filtered image Gray scale and (i) White Top transformed image Gray scale.

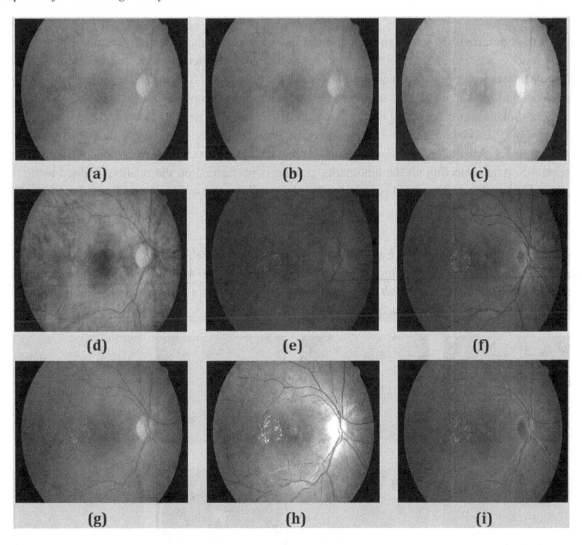

Figure 9. (a) BV removed image RGB, (b) BV removed image Green plane, (c) BV removed image Red plane and (d) BV removed image Gray scale.

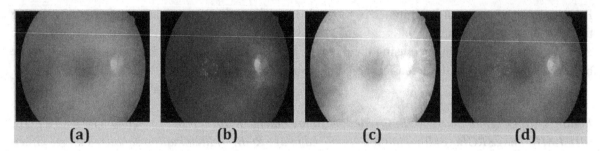

Method 1

This method describes the automatic detection of maculopathy using different color plane processing. In this process we first enhanced image by median filtering and then contrast enhancement for RGB image. Whereas for gray scale image we performed Homomorphic filtering. After enhancing, the OD is detected and masked using gray scale image and the co-ordinates of the mask are stored and applied to the color planes. In this method we don't require BV removal. After OD is masked the RGB$_{modified}$ is converted to HSI and the Hue plane is considered for determining the exudates, as described in method 1 of section 4.3. After exudates being determined the macula is detected, as mentioned in method 1 of section 4.5. After detecting all the landmarks grading is performed on the results obtained using the method described in section 4.6. Figure 10(a)-(h) shows all the steps of implementation for Method 1.

Figure 10. (a) Original image, (b) Enhanced image, (c) OD masked, (d) Exudates detected (green pixels), (e) Zoomed input image, (f) Exudates detected in zoomed image, (g) Macula detected and boundary of image formed, (h) Combined result showing all segmented image in different color. (Red=boundary, Green= fundus image, Black=exudates, Light brown=macula)

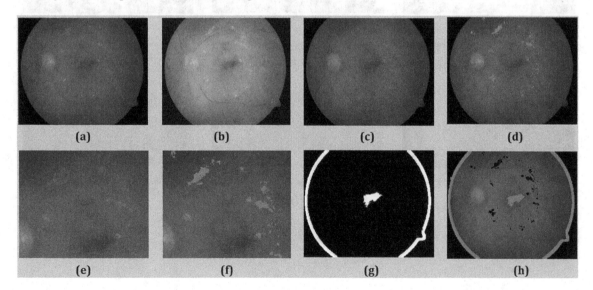

Here, image (a) is the original input image. Upon application of preprocessing the enhanced image is shown in image (b). Figure (c) represents the OD masked. Exudate detection is shown in image (d), and zoomed version in (f). Detected macula is depicted in image (g) and image (h) shows the combination of the detected sections together where fundus boundary in shown in red, exudates detected in black inside fundus and macula detected in light brown color.

Method 2

This method describes the automatic detection of maculopathy using intensity property of fundus as the macula appears dark in color and OD has maximum brightness. In this process we have used the BV removed green plane, red plane and gray scale image. The images are then enhanced using median filtering and CLAHE. As described in method 2 of section 4.5 we detect the macula and fovea. If we invert the original image OD appears as dark in intensity. Thus same method is implemented to detect the OD and removed for proper exudate detection. The microaneurysms and exudates are detected using gray scale image as shown in section 4.4 and 4.3 respectively. After detection of the land marks, grading is done as described in section 4.6. Figure 11 and 12 shows all the steps of implementation for Method 2.

Discussion: The proposed method detects macula and fovea on both normal and pathological images with 97.53% efficiency (158 out of 162). Out of 172 images of the databases 9 images have been eliminated from the analysis as the illumination of the images is very poor and/or macula regions doesn't have dark intensity profile. The method is also applied on images with anomalies. The selected images show severe level in 27 images with amount of overlapping region more than 25%. Moderate level is found in 22 images and 39 images show mild DR. The method is compared with the existing methods in the literature. The comparisons are given in Table I. The proposed method performs better.

Table 1. Performance comparison of Macula detection method

Method	Technique	Dataset	Accuracy
Li and Chutatape (Li & Chutatape, 2004)	ROI selection, Mathematical Morphology	Not Specified	100%
Niemeijer et al. (Niemeijer, Abramoff & Bram, 2007)	Point distribution and Cost Function	Local	94.40%
Sagar et al. (Sagar, Balasubramanian & Chandrasekaran, 2007)	ROI selection & morphology	DRIVE, STARE	96%
Singh et al. (Singh, Joshi & Sivaswamy, 2008)	Appearance Based	DRIVE, STARE	96.61%
Proposed Method	Morphology and thresholding Based	DRIVE, HRF,DIARETDB1	97.53%

Figure 11. (a) Original image RGB, (b) BV removed RGB and (c) Enhanced BV removed RGB (d) BV removed Red channel image of RGB, (e) BV removed Green channel image of RGB, (f) BV removed Gray scale image, (g) Enhanced BV removed Red channel image of RGB, (h) Enhanced BV removed Green channel image of RGB and (i) Enhanced BV removed Gray scale image

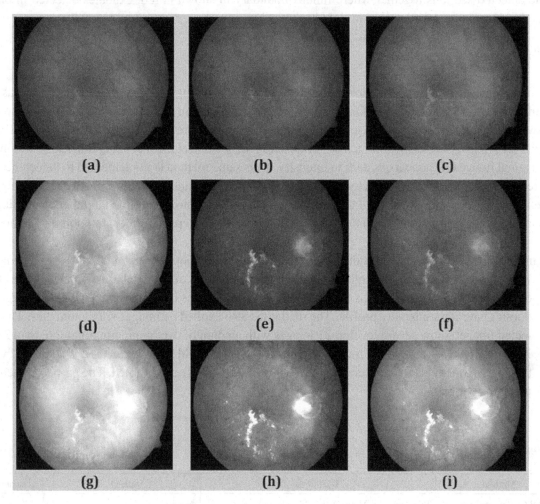

Method 3

In this method we propose a novel approach to detect exudates from multiple contours. Here we have considered the images enhanced by different methods as mentioned in section 4.1. And then determined the contours (method 3, section 4.3) of the anomalies. OD is priory removed from the images to avoid false detection. The areas of these boundaries are calculated and this descriptor is used to find the exudate present in the image if any. The boundary with the maximum area is declared to be the one with exudates as can be seen in results in Figure 13.

Discussion: The best method comprising maximum area is contrast enhancement output as obtained in the above implementation. Among the result obtained 10 images of DIARETDB1 results is shown in Table 2. Comparison of our work has been done based on Sensitivity analysis with manually segmented images shown in Table 3. The methodology is 100% sensitive to hard exudate. From

Figure 12. (a) Macula detected, (b) Fovea detected, (c) Anomalies detected, (d-f) Macula mask 1,2,3 (g-i) Overlapping of macular mask and anomalies for grading severe, moderate and mild stage respectively.

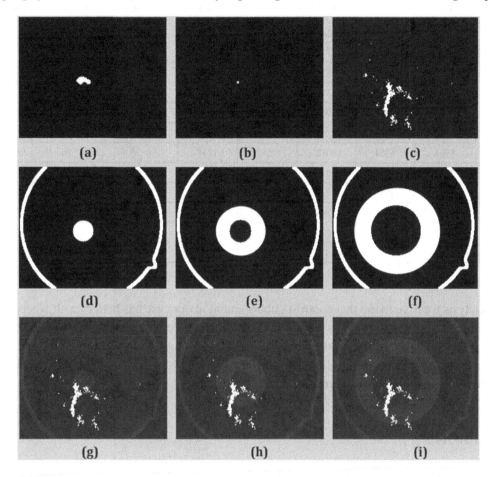

Figure 13. Preprocessed image after applying (a) Contrast Enhancement (b) CLAHE (c) Illumination equalization (d) White top transformation (e) Chromaticity normalization. (f)-(j) Boundary of the exudates detected respectively.

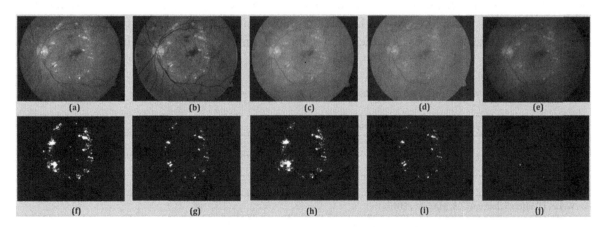

Table 2. Performance of proposed method for DIARETDB1

Images	Area using Method 1	Area using Method 2	Area using Method 3	Area using Method 4	Area using Method 5	Manual Segmentation	Sensitivity (%)	Best Method
Image 1	8856	5436	6578	3981	1100	9025	70	Method 1
Image 2	6753	1236	9876	4532	5686	7036	78	Method 1
Image 3	7854	3459	6375	2987	3475	8027	89	Method 1
Image 4	2865	3987	1065	1024	963	6692	85	Method 1
Image 5	9866	2562	1245	1136	784	11566	70	Method 1
Image 6	8963	6354	9012	2587	1245	9876	70	Method 3
Image 7	2834	7821	5632	4529	3254	5529	76	Method 1
Image 8	8919	3689	2371	6421	2351	9452	70	Method 1
Image 9	6789	1893	2346	5432	1853	7746	75	Method 1
Image 10	2965	2136	1978	3296	1241	3065	72	Method 1
Average	6666.4	3857.3	4647.8	3592.5	2195.2	7801.4	75.5	

the analysis we have found that contrast enhancement in our case has better result when compared with manual segmentation. Thus we can say that the preprocessing image of contrast enhancement has been more successful than the rest. The primary limitation of this method is for the images where the size of intensity of the exudates having nearby values as that of the background then the methodology did not produce promising result.

CONCLUSION

Automation for mass screening procedure has not been perfected. It has been found that the anatomy of each eye may vary from person to person. Hence automation is a challenging task. Here in this study we have aimed to determine an automated method for retinal image scanning and detection of macular degeneration. In this regard we have determined three methods for automatic analysis. It includes image properties such as intensity, chromaticity and appearance etc. Along with abnormality detection classification of severity is also determined. During the analysis it has been observed that due to improper illumination and reflections, images of the databases are not uniform in intensity. Thus these issues give

Table 3. Performance comparison of Exudate detection methods

Methods	Sensitivity (%)
Proposed Method	77.6
Harangi (Harangi & Hajdu, 2013)	76
T. Walter (Walter, 2007)	76
D. Welfer (Welfer, Scharcanski & Marinho, 2010)	19

rise to difference in anomalies intensity and if not properly equalized the exact amount of anomalies present could not been determined. Therefore in the third algorithm we have tried to identify the best preprocessing method. The advantage of our proposed algorithm for macular degeneration is that, it is independent of relative positions of macula from OD or BV. Although the algorithm detects macula but it will be more efficient if the preprocessing algorithms can be improved to have uniform intensities therefore it could be considered as future aspect.

REFERENCES

Bertalmio, M., Sapiro, G., Caselles, V., & Ballester, C. (2000). Image Inpainting. *Proceedings of the 27th Annual Conference on Computer Graphics and Interactive Techniques* (pp. 417–424), New York: ACMPress/Addison-Wesley.

Creteil, G. C. (2010). *Macular edema- a practical approach*. Paris: Karger.

Deepak, K. S., & Sivaswamy, J. (2012). Automatic assessment of macular edema from color retinal images. *IEEE Transactions on Medical Imaging*, *31*(3), 766–776. doi:10.1109/TMI.2011.2178856 PMID:22167598

Diabetic Retinopathy. (2012). *St. Luke's Cataract and Laser Institute*. Retrieved from http://www.st-lukeseye.com/conditions/DiabeticRetinopathy.html

Diabetic retinopathy. (2013). *NHS Choices*. Retrieved from http://www.nhs.uk/conditions/diabetic-retinopathy/Pages/Introduction.aspx

Diabetic Retinopathy [Image]. (2013). *Vitreous-Retina-Macula Consultants of New York*. Retrieved from http://www.vrmny.com/education-center/educational-topcs/diabetic-retinopathy.html

Diabetic Retinopathy. (2014). American Optometric Association. Retrieved from http://www.aoa.org/patients-and-public/eye-and-vision-problems/glossary-of-eye-and-vision-conditions/diabetic-retinopathy?sso=y

Diabetic Retinopathy [image]. (2014). Retinal Eye Care Associates. Retrieved from http://www.retinaleyecare.com/common/images/diabetic-retinopathy.jpg

DRIVE: Digital Retinal Images for Vessel Extraction. (2004). *Image Sciences Institute*. Retrieved from http://www.isi.uu.nl/Research/Databases/DRIVE

Flourescein angiography. (2012, September 17). *MedlinePlus*. Retrieved from http://www.nlm.nih.gov/medlineplus/ency/article/003846.htm

Fong, D., Aiello, L., Gardner, T.W., King, G.L., Blankenship, G., Cavallerano, J.D., Ferris III, F.L., & Klein, R. (2003). Retinopathy in Diabetes. *Diabetes Care*, 26(1), 226-229. Retrieved from http://care.diabetesjournals.org/content/26/1/226.full?sid=2012dd7a-64a7-4816-929d-46b3d4591a49

Fong, D., Aiello, L., Gardner, T.W., King, G.L., Blankenship, G., Cavallerano, J.D., Ferris III, F.L., & Klein, R. (2004). Retinopathy in Diabetes. *Diabetes Care*, 27(Supplement 1), s84-s87. Retrieved from http://care.diabetesjournals.org/content/27/suppl_1/s84.long

Ghuneim, A.G. (2000). *Moore-Neighbor tracing*. Retrieve from http://www.imageprocessingplace.com/downloads_V3/root_downloads/tutorials/contour_tracing_Abeer_George_Ghuneim/moore.html

Haniza, Y., Hamzah, A., & Hazlita, M. I. (2012). Exudates segmentation using inverse surface adaptive thresholding. *Journal of Measurement, Elsevier, 45*(6), 1599–1608. doi:10.1016/j.measurement.2012.02.016

Harangi, B. & Hajdu. (2013). Improving automatic exudate detection based on the fusion of the results of multiple active contours. *Proceedings of IEEE 10th International Symposium on Biomedical Imaging* (pp. 45-48). San Francisco, CA, USA. IEEE. doi:10.1109/ISBI.2013.6556408

Hatanaka, Y., Nakagawa, T., Hayashi, Y., Hara, T., & Fujita, H. (2008). Improvement of automated detection method of hemorrhages in fundus images. *Proceedings of IEEE 30th Annual International Conference on Engineering in Medicine and Biology Society* (pp.5429-5432). Vancouver, British Columbia, Canada. IEEE. doi:10.1109/IEMBS.2008.4650442

High-Resolution Fundus Image Database. (2007). *Department Informatik, Technische Fakultat*. Retrieved from http://www5.cs.fau.de/research/data/fundus-images/

Kauppi, T., Kalesnykiene, V., Kamarainen, J. K., et al. (2006). *DIARETDB1 database*. http://www2.it.lut.fi/project/imageret/diaretdb1/

Li, H., & Chutatape, O. (2004). Automated feature extraction in color retinal images by a model based approach. *IEEE Transactions on Bio-Medical Engineering, 51*(2), 246–254. doi:10.1109/TBME.2003.820400 PMID:14765697

Lowth, M. (2014). Macular disorders. *Patient*. Retrieved from http://www.patient.co.uk/doctor/macular-disorders

Maculopathy and macular degeneration. (2014). *ILMO.it*. Retrieved from http://www.ilmo.it/en/solutions/surgery-at-ilmo/vision-problems-and-eye-diseases /maculopathy-and-macular-degeneration/

Majumder, P., & Medhi, J. P. (2014). Automatic exudate detection based on amalgamation of results of multiple contours. *Proceedings of International Conference on Green Materials through Science, Technology and Management*. Assam, India.

Medhi, J. P., Nath, M. K., & Dandapat, S. (2012). Automatic grading of macular degeneration from color fundus images. *Proceedings of World Congress on Information and Communication Technologies* (pp. 511-514). IEEE. doi:10.1109/WICT.2012.6409131

Mubbashar, M., Usman, A., & Akram, M. U. (2011). Automated system for macula detection in digital retinal images. *Proceedings of Conference on Information and Communication Technologies* (pp. 1-5). Karachi. IEEE.

Niemeijer, M., Abramoff, M. D., & Bram, V. G. (2007). Segmentation of the Optic Disc, Macula and Vascular Arch in Fundus Photographs. *IEEE Transactions on Medical Imaging, 26*(1), 116–127. doi:10.1109/TMI.2006.885336 PMID:17243590

Poshtyar, A., Ghassabi, Z., & Shanbehzadeh, J. (2011) Detection of Optic Disc Center and Macula using Spatial Information of Optic Cup. In *Proceedings of 4th International Conference on Biomedical Engineering and Informatics* (pp.255-258). Shanghai: IEEE. doi:10.1109/BMEI.2011.6098351

Quellec, G., Lamard, M., Josselin, P. M., Cazuguel, G., Cochener, B., & Roux, C. (2008). Optimal wavelet transform for the detection of microaneurysms in retinal photographs. *IEEE Transactions on Medical Imaging, 27*(9), 1230–1241. doi:10.1109/TMI.2008.920619 PMID:18779064

Sagar, A. V., Balasubramanian, S., & Chandrasekaran, V. (2007). Automatic detection of anatomical structures in digital fundus retinal images. In *Proceedings of IAPR Conference on Machine Vision Applications* (pp. 483–486). Tokyo, Japan.

Sekher, S., Al-Nuaimy, W., & Nandi, A. K. (2008). Automated localisation of optic disc, and fovea in retinal fundus image. *Proceedings of 16th European Signal Processing Conference*. Lausanne, Switzerland. IEEE.

Siddalingaswamy, P. C., & Prabhu, K. G. (2010). Automatic grading of diabetic maculopathy severity levels. *Proceedings of International Conference on Systems in Medicine and Biology*. Kharagpur, India. doi:10.1109/ICSMB.2010.5735398

Siegel, A., & Sapru, H. N. (2006). B. Sun, (Ed.) Essential Neuroscience. Baltimore, Maryland: Lippincott Williams & Wilkins.

Singh, J., Joshi, G., & Sivaswamy, J. (2008). Appearance-based object detection in colour retinal images. *Proceedings of IEEE International Conference on Image Processing* (pp.1432-1435). IEEE. doi:10.1109/ICIP.2008.4712034

Tariq, A., Akram, M. U., Shaukat, A., & Khan, S. A. (2012). A computer aided system for grading of maculopathy. *Proceedings of Cairo International Biomedical Engineering Conference*. Cairo, Egypt. IEEE. doi:10.1109/CIBEC.2012.6473318

Understanding eye conditions related to diabetes. (2014). *RNIB*. Retrieved from http://www.rnib.org.uk/eye-health-eye-conditions-z-eye-conditions/understanding-eye-conditions-related-diabetes

Walter, T., Massin, P., Erginay, A., Ordonez, R., Jeulin, C., & Klein, J. C. (2007). Automatic detection of microaneurysms in colour fundus images. *Journal of Medical Image Analysis, 11*(6), 555–566. doi:10.1016/j.media.2007.05.001 PMID:17950655

Welfer, D., Scharcanski, J., & Marinho, D. R. (2010). A coarse-to-fine strategy for automatically detecting exudates in color eye fundus images. *Journal of Computerized Medical Imaging and Graphics, 34*(3), 228–235. doi:10.1016/j.compmedimag.2009.10.001 PMID:19954928

What is age-related Macular Degeneration? (2013). *Geteyesmart.org*. Retrieved from http://www.get-eyesmart.org/eyesmart/diseases/age-related-macular-degeneration/

What is Diabetic Retinopathy? (2013). *Geteyesmart.org*. Retrieved from http://www.geteyesmart.org/eyesmart/diseases/diabetic-retinopathy/

What is Optical Coherence Tomography? (2015). *Geteyesmart.org.*. Retrieved from http://www.geteye-smart.org/eyesmart/diseases/optical-coherence-tomography.cfm

Fundus camera picture. (2007). *Wikipedia*. Retrieved from http://en.wikipedia.org/wiki/File:Retinal_camera.jpg

ADDITIONAL READING

Baumann, W. B. (2007). *Developments in ophthalmology*. Karger.

Browning, D. J. (2010). *Diabetic retinopathy – evidence based management*. Springer. doi:10.1007/978-0-387-85900-2

Cheung, W., & Hamarneh, G. (2007). N-SIFT: N-dimensional scale invariant feature transform for matching medical images. *Proceedings of 4th IEEE International Symposium Biomedical Imaging*: From Nano to Macro. doi:10.1109/ISBI.2007.356953

Duh, E. (2008). *Diabetic retinopathy*. Humana Press. doi:10.1007/978-1-59745-563-3

Hammes, Porta (2010). Experimental approaches to Diabetic Retinopathy.

Kim, J. S., Ishikawa, H., Gabriele, M. L., Wollstein, G., Bilonick, R. A., & Kagemann, L. et al. (2010). Retinal nerve fiber layer thickness measurement comparability between time domain optical coherence tomography (OCT) and spectral domain OCT. *Investigative Ophthalmology & Visual Science*, *51*(2), 896–902. doi:10.1167/iovs.09-4110 PMID:19737886

Medhi, J. P., & Deka, D. (2014). Morphology based automatic classification of colour fundus image. In *Proceedings of International Conference on Green Materials Through Science, Technology and Management*. Assam, India.

Olk, R. J & Lee, C. M. (1993). Diabetic Retinopathy – Practical Management.

Saxena, S. (2012). *Diabetic retinopathy*. Jaypee.

Scanlon, Wilkinson, Aldington, & Matthews. (2009) *A Practical Manual of Diabetic Retinopathy Management.*

Strouthidis, N. G., Yang, H., Reynaud, J. F., Grimm, J. L., Gardiner, S. K., Fortune, B., & Burgoyne, C. F. (2009). Comparison of clinical and spectral domain optical coherence tomography optic disc margin anatomy. *Investigative Ophthalmology & Visual Science*, *50*(10), 4709–4718. doi:10.1167/iovs.09-3586 PMID:19443718

Wu, G. (2010). Diabetic retinopathy – the essentials.

KEY TERMS AND DEFINITIONS

Contrast Limited Adaptive Histogram Equalization (CLAHE): This is a type of adaptive histogram equalisation method used to enhance the contrast of an image. This method differs from ordinary adaptive histogram equalization in its contrast limiting. Unlike ordinary adaptive histogram equalization this method prevents the over amplification noise.

Cotton Wool Spots: These are fluffy white patches of the abnormal retinal image that occurs due to damage of nerve fibers.

Diabetic Macular Edema (DME): A retinal disease caused by complication of diabetes mellitus. DME affect the central vision the patient.

Diabetic Retinopathy (DR): A sight threatening retinal disease caused by complications of diabetes.

Exudates: Exudates are the lipid deposits in the retina which appear as bright yellow lesions.

Neovascularization: Growth of new blood vessels at the advance stage of diabetic retinopathy called as proliferative diabetic retinopathy.

Chapter 10

Computer Assisted Methods for Retinal Image Classification

S. R. Nirmala
Gauhati University, India

Purabi Sharma
Gauhati University, India

ABSTRACT

Diabetes maculopathy has become one of the rapidly increasing health threats worldwide. The complication of diabetes associated to retina of the eye is diabetic retinopathy. A patient with the disease has to undergo periodic screening of eye. The ophthalmologists use colour retinal images of a patient acquired from digital fundus camera for disease diagnosis. Limited number of ophthalmology specialists in most of the countries motivates the need for computer based analysis of retinal images using image processing techniques. The results of this process may be used in applications such as, to classify the retinal images into normal and diseased. This could reduce the workload of ophthalmologists, also aid in diagnosis, to make measurements and to look for a change in progression of disease. Some computer based retinal image analysis methods used for the application are briefed in this chapter.

INTRODUCTION

Modern medical imaging offers the potential for major advances in science and medicine as higher fidelity images are produced. It has developed into one of the most important fields within scientific imaging due to the rapid progress in computerized medical image visualization and advances in analysis methods (Dougherty 2011). Computer-aided diagnosis is a vital part of the early detection, diagnosis, and treatment of retinal pathologies. These accomplishments have allowed clinicians to make accurate and efficient diagnoses non-invasively. With medical imaging playing an increasingly prominent role in the diagnosis and treatment of diseases, the challenge is to effectively process and analyze the images in order to extract and interpret useful information about anatomical structures (Dougherty 2011). The number of people with eye diseases is increasing with an increase in the aged population worldwide. So, there is a relative decrease in ophthalmic services, especially in rural areas and developing countries.

DOI: 10.4018/978-1-4666-8493-5.ch010

Figure 1. Digital retinal image (a) Normal retinal image (b) diseased retinal image

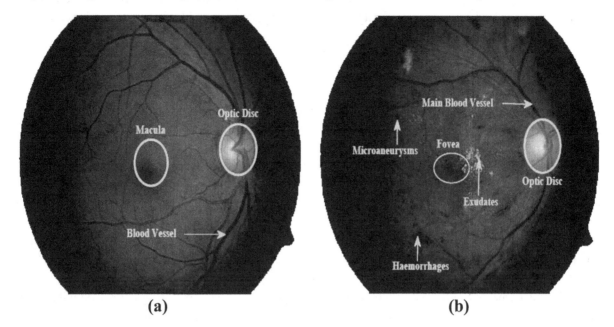

(a)   **(b)**

The World Health Organization (WHO) has launched "Vision 2020," a global initiative for the prevention of avoidable visual impairment by the year 2020 (Wild, Roglic, Green, Sicree & King, 2004). The main causes of global blindness are age-related macular degeneration (ARMD), glaucoma, cataract and diabetic retinopathy (DR). If these diseases are detected early and treated, then significant reduction in the progression of eyesight loss is possible.

Retina and Common Retinal Diseases

Retinal imaging and image processing play a crucial role in the care of patients with retinal diseases. Retina is the light sensitive layer at the back of the eye. Digital retinal images are captured by a special modality called fundus camera. Such an image obtained from a local eye hospital (Sri Sankaradeva Nethralaya) is shown in Figure 1. Typical features of normal retinal image include macula, optic disc (OD) and blood vessels as shown in Figure 1 (a). Macula is the dark, central retinal area. The centre of the macula is the fovea. It contains the highest concentration of photosensitive cells and is responsible for sharp central vision and reading vision. The OD is a bright yellowish region in the back of the eye where the optic nerve enters the eye. This also corresponds to the blind spot since there are no photosensitive cells in this location. The blood vessels radiating out from OD supply blood to nourish the inner retinal layers. The ophthalmologists examine the clinically important features in the retinal image for signs of various eye related diseases.

Some of the clinical symptoms of retinal disease are microaneurysms, haemorrhages and exudates as shown in Figure 1 (b). Microaneurysms are small saccular pouches caused by local distension of vessel walls and appear as small red dots. Haemorrhages are the abnormal bleeding of the blood vessels in the retina. Exudates are the fatty material deposited in the retina by leaky blood vessels which appear as bright yellow lesions. The distribution of these pathological signs helps the doctors to evaluate the health condition of the human eye. For example, the presence of exudates especially in relation to the fovea can be used to determine the severity of a disease called maculopathy. A brief description of the common retinal diseases is given below.

Diabetic Retinopathy (DR)

Diabetic retinopathy (DR) is the common complication of diabetes that affects the blood vessels in the retina. The blood vessels may be damaged by diabetes reducing the nourishment to the retina. In this condition, new fragile blood vessels develop on the surface of the retina. These abnormal blood vessels can break and bleed over the surface of the retina leading to microaneurysms (MAs) and haemorrhages.

Glaucoma

Glaucoma is a disease in which fluid pressure within the eye rises. Clear liquid flows in and out of the anterior chamber of the eye. This fluid nourishes the nearby tissues. If a patient has glaucoma, the fluid does not drain properly. This leads to fluid build-up and the pressure inside the eye rises. This increased pressure may damage the OD and result in the loss of vision. There is a small brighter region within the OD known as cup. The primary indication of glaucoma is the increased cup size. The ratio of the cup and optic disc diameter called cup-to-disc ratio (CDR), is an important structural indicator for assessing the presence and progression of glaucoma.

Diabetic Maculopathy (DM)

Diabetic maculopathy (DM) is a complication of retinopathy where exudates are present within the macular region. If maculopathy is not detected in the early stage then damage of the macula or visual field is irreversible and can lead to complete blindness. Severity of the maculopathy depends on the position of exudates from the center of macula. The condition where the locations of exudates are outside the macular region is considered as clinically non significant maculopathy. In this case the patient will not have any visible symptoms. In case of clinically significant maculopathy, exudates are present near the macula region. If the exudates are distributed around the center of the macula, the patient may experience a distorted vision. If the exudates are present on the macula center, then it affects the central vision of the eye.

Age-Related Macular Degeneration (ARMD)

Age-related macular degeneration (ARMD) is the leading cause of blindness in people over 50 years of age. It is caused by the damage to the macula. One of the symptoms of ARMD is the presence of fatty deposits called drusen on the retina. Because of ARMD, the property of the macula for seeing fine details and colour is lost.

Detection and Identifying Stages for DR and DM

Diabetic retinopathy is characterized by the presence of retinal lesions in a patient with diabetes. The earliest signs of DR are microaneurysms, small hemorrhages, cotton wool spots and exudates. Diabetic retinopathy is divided into various stages (Wilkinson et al. 2003; National Eye Institute, 1968) as follows:

1. **Nonproliferative Diabetic Retinopathy (NPDR):** It is the earliest stage of diabetic retinopathy. In this stage, damaged blood vessels in the retina begin to leak extra fluid and small amounts of blood into the eye. Depending on the presence and extent of these retinal lesions NPDR stage can be classified to mild, moderate or severe stages as follows:
    a. **Mild NPDR:** This is the earliest stage of retinopathy and usually does not affect the vision. However, deterioration of the blood vessels in the retina begins in this stage. Micro-aneurysms or flame-shaped haemorrhages start to develop in the retina in this stage but no other retinal lesion or abnormality associated with DM is present. Those with mild NPDR have a 5% risk of progression to PDR within 1 year and a 15% risk of progression to high-risk PDR within 5 years (Khan et al., 2005).
    b. **Moderate NPDR:** As the disease progresses, some blood vessels that nourish the retina are blocked. It is the intermediate stage of "mild" and "severe" stage. Micro-aneurysms or hemorrhages of greater severity occur in this stage. This results in cotton wool spots and exudates in the retina. The risk of progression to PDR within 1 year is 12% to 27%, and the risk of progression to high-risk PDR within 5 years is 33% (Khan et al., 2005).
    c. **Severe NPDR:** More blood vessels are blocked in this stage. This results in depriving several areas of the retina with their blood supply. These areas of retina send signals to the body to grow new vessels in order to compensate for the lack of nourishment.
2. **Proliferative Diabetic Retinopathy (PDR):** This is the advanced stage of DR where signals sent by the retina to the body for the lack of blood supply trigger the growth of new blood vessels. These new blood vessels are abnormal and fragile. They grow along the retina and along the surface of the clear jelly-like substance (vitreous gel) which fills the centre of the eye. Although they are fragile and abnormal, they do not cause vision loss. However, when their thin and weak walls leak blood, severe visual loss or even irreversible blindness occurs.

The new fragile, abnormal blood vessels can leak into the center of the retina called macula, the part of the eye where sharp, straight vision occurs. This fluid makes the macula swell. Accumulation of these fluids called exudates near the macula region leads to distortion of the central vision. This condition is called macular edema or Diabetic Maculopathy (DM) (National Eye Institute, 1968).

Hence, DM is a complication of retinopathy where exudates are present within the macular region. Usually DM does not show any symptoms in the early stages. Severity of the maculopathy depends on how close exudates are to the center of macula. If the exudates are present near the macula region then DM stages are classified as mild, moderate and sever stage (Wilkinson et al. 2003) as follows:

*   **Mild Stage:** This is the first stage of maculopathy with no visible symtoms. This stage marks the presence of some hard exudates in posterior pole but distant from the center of the macula. So, patient's vision may not be seriously affected in this stage.

- **Moderate Stage:** In this stage, exudate approaches the center of the macula but does not involve the center of macula called fovea.
- **Severe Stage:** In this stage, exudates involve the center of macula. This is the most sight threatening stage where there is a high risk of vision loss.

Screening is the simple procedure to detect retinal disorders (Dougherty 2011). A typical screening process involves the acquisition of retinal images from the patient followed by manual examination of individual image by medical experts in order to identify any signs of abnormalities. However manual data analysis for diagnosis in medical practice has become inadequate as number of patients is increasing. Hence a system for automatic classification of retinal images is required so that the medical experts can examine the diseased images more effectively.

This chapter gives an overview of computer assisted methods for retinal image analysis. The literature background describing various existing methods is explained in background section, different databases used for evaluating the methods are listed and two of the computer assisted methods are given in detail along with results and discussions.

BACKGROUND

It is important to monitor the retinal features for detection of various retinal diseases. Computer assisted methods can be very effective for this purpose. The detection of various clinical features is the first step in these methods. Many algorithms can be found in literature for detection of OD, macula, blood vessels and pathological signs such as microaneurysms, haemorrhages and exudates.

Detection of OD

OD detection can be useful for a number of applications. For example, the OD location can serve as a landmark for localizing and segmenting other anatomical structures such as the fovea (Youssif, Ghalwash & Ghoneim, 2008).

The method described in Sekher, Nuaimy and Nandi (2008) automatically localise both the OD and fovea. OD is localised by means of using the morphological operations and Hough transform. The fovea is localised by means of its spatial relationship with the optic disk, and from the spatial distribution of the macular structure. Morphological operation is used to analyse the shape of the OD. Then, magnitude gradient of the image is estimated. The boundary of OD and its centre are found by applying the Hough transform to the gradient image. After locating the optic disk, the macula region is determined by exploring the region in the vicinity of the image centre. The candidate macula ROI is defined as the portion of a sector subtended at the centre of the optic disk by an angle of 30° above and below the line between the image centre and the centre of the OD. The radius of the inner arc for this ROI is 1.5 times the OD diameter. The macula is identified within this ROI by iteratively applying a threshold, and then applying morphological opening on the resulting blob. Once the macula region is identified, the fovea is simply determined as the centroid of this blob.

The location can also be used for computing some important diagnostic indices for hypertensive retinopathy based upon vasculature (Li & Chutatape, 2004). Also, since the OD can be easily confounded with bright exudates, the detection of its location is important to remove it from a set of candidate exudates region (Sharma, Nirmala, & Sarma, 2013). The technique of projection of vertical edge pixels of the retinal image is used in Sharma et al. (2013) to detect the OD. The blood vessels that emerge from the OD are mainly in the vertical direction. So, the 1-D projection obtained has larger peaks near the OD region.

The concept of average brightness is used in Li and Chutatape (2004) to find the OD candidate regions for their model-based approach. Pixels with the highest 1% intensity levels were selected. The selected pixels were then clustered. Only large clusters were retained and small clusters were discarded. A model for OD was created by applying the principal component analysis (PCA) to a training set of 10 intensity normalized square subimages manually cropped around the OD. Then for each pixel in the candidate regions, the PCA transform was applied through a window with different scales. The OD was detected as the region with the smallest Euclidean distance to its projection onto the OD model.

OD can be detected by using various image processing techniques like Hough transform, active contour model (Osareh et al. 2002), gradient vector flow (GVF) (Thongnuch & Uyyanonvara, 2007).

Fuzzy C Means clustering (FCM) is used in Padmanaban and kannan (2013) to locate the OD in colour retinal image. Green plane of the colour image is used for detection of OD. Before locating the OD, median filter is applied to de-noise the image then region of interest (ROI) is extracted by selecting the maximum brightest points in the green plane. The approximate region of the optic disc is selected around these identified brightest points. The extracted ROI is used as input of FCM clustering technique. The cluster index of the maximum brightest point is selected as OD cluster and morphological operations are used to finalize the OD location.

A novel algorithm for OD localization is discussed in Godse and Bormane (2013). The green channel image is used in the method for the effective thresholding of the retinal image. Threshold value is estimated considering green channel histogram. The threshold is used to estimate the average number of pixels occupied by OD. Applying this threshold, all bright regions within image called clusters are detected. Then two different criteria: area criterion and density criterion is applied on these clusters. In area criterion, each of the clusters in the thresholded image is labelled and total number of pixels in each cluster is calculated. The clusters having more than 125% or less than 10% of the OD area is discarded. This criterion minimizes the possibility to miss the OD from the selected candidate clusters. The density criterion is applied to clusters which have already satisfied the area criterion. According to the density criterion, if the ratio of number of pixels occupied by cluster to the number of pixels occupied by rectangle surrounding the cluster is less than 40%, the cluster is discarded. From the remaining clusters the cluster having highest density is considered to be the primary region of interest. The centroid of this cluster is determined using calculus method. A square shaped search window with side equal to twice of OD diameter (ODD) is defined around the centroid such that the centroid is center of the search window. A circular window called an oculus of radius ODD/2 is moved across the search area. Each pixel within the square window of side equal to ODD is tested for its distance (d) from the centre of the window. If the distance, d is less than or equal to the radius of the oculus, it is considered as inside pixel. The total intensity of the oculus is calculated by adding squares of intensities of all inside pixels. The centre of maximum intensity oculus is marked as a centre of OD.

An automatic OD segmentation method based on watershed transform is discussed in Kaur and Sharma (2014). The retinal images are pre-processed in the method to remove non uniform illumination before OD segmentation. Morphological closing operation is then applied to remove the blood vessels. To find the approximate position of OD three independent methods were used to obtain candidate optic disc pixels (ODP). The final ODP is selected by taking into account the three candidate pixels obtained from three different methods and their location with respect to their centroid. If the three OD candidate pixels are close to the centroid the selected ODP is the centroid. If only two candidates are close to the centroid the selected ODP is the average point in these two referred pixels. Otherwise, the selected ODP is the candidate pixel obtained with the most reliable method. Then stochastic watershed transform is used to find the exact contour of the OD.

The study of the macular region may provide a means to detect and diagnose macular abnormalities.

Macula Detection

An automated system for the localization and detection of macula in digital retinal images is discussed in Mubbashar, Usman and Akram (2011). Approximate location of macula is first localized with the help of OD center and enhanced blood vessels. Finally macula is detected by taking the distance from center of OD and thresholding, then combining it with enhanced blood vessels image to locate the darkest pixel in this region, making clusters of these pixels. The largest pixel is located as macula.

An automatic macula detection technique is discussed in Lu and Lim (2010) that makes use of the circular brightness profile of the macula: the macula is usually darker than the surrounding pixels whose intensities increase gradually with their distances from the macula center. A line operator is designed to capture the macula circular brightness profile, which evaluates the image brightness variation along multiple line segments of specific orientations that pass through each retinal image pixel. The orientation of the line segment with the minimum/ maximum variation has specific patterns that indicate the position of the macula efficiently.

The concept of bit plane decomposition and mathematical morphology is used in Kumar, Priya and paul (2013) for detection of macula. Green plane of the colour retinal image is used in the method of detection. The contrast of the green channel is further increased by adding the image to the top-hat filtered image, and then subtracting the bottom hat filtered image from the same. The resulting image is the converted into gray scale image and bit plane slicing is applied on it to decompose it into its bit planes. Bit plane 0 and bit plane 1 is then used for further processing. Morphological opening operation is used on bit plane 0 to obtain a clear dark region corresponding to the macula. A suitably processed bit plane 1 can be used to compensate for errors, if any. The outline of the obtained macula region is then dilated and the macula and fovea is localized by superimposing the outline on the original grayscale image.

A novel method for detection of macula in retinal image is described in Minar, Riha, Krupka and Tong (2014). The method uses multilevel thresholding of retinal image and ellipse detection using OpenCV (Open Computer Vision) framework. The red channel image is used in the method for the effective thresholding of the retinal image. Input retinal image is pre-processed using median blur filter before macula detection. The retinal image is then segmented in the loop, where loop is created over all threshold level. The thresholding is computed for all 256 levels, as red channel image consist of 8-bit information. The required macula region is obtained for thresholding levels from 100 to 230. Thresholded layers are then blurred again to make the macula region clearer and to detect its elliptical contour. The contour of macula is detected in all thresholding level by using functions from OpenCV framework. All ellipses detected in each level are stored in buffer for further processing. Then all detected ellipses are split into group with the same coordinates of centroid with toleration of 15 pixels. The group with the biggest amount of detection is marked as group with possible macula location.

A method to detect the macula centre using the aggregation of seeded mode tracking in retinal image is discussed in Wong et al. (2012). All the images are pre-processed in the method before macula detection to remove un-useable areas of the image. In the green channel of the colour retinal image blood vessels are first detected using a vessel detector based on the morphological top-hat transform. The resultant image is a binary mask containing an approximate segmentation of the retinal vessels. So, only the region bounded by the detected blood vessels is considered. This results in exclusion of hazy regions as well as the exterior halo. OD is then detected in the method by using region growing technique and active contour model. Location of OD is used to identify if the image belongs to a left or right eye. This information is used to define a ROI around the macula region. Seeded mode seeking approach is then used to locate the macula in the ROI by tracking the aggregation of seeds. Morphological opening operation is used to reduce the effect of vessels during tracking. Then an initial grid of n x n seeds equally distributed in the ROI at time $t = 0$ is defined. At time $t = 1$, each seed searches its r x r pixel neighbourhood, where r is the minimum distance between each seed at initialization. The seed moves to a location of local minimum in its neighbourhood. This tracking process is repeated for each seed, and termination occurs when $t > t_{end}$. At termination of the tracking process, the seeds aggregate in locations representing regions of local minima. The aggregated location having largest number of seeds is detected as macula location.

Exudates Detection

Retinal lesions like exudates can be detected by using some machine learning (Karegowda, Nasiha, & Jayaram, 2011; Ravishankar, Jain, & Mittal, 2009) and image processing methods like thresholding, edge detection, morphological operations (Sanchez, Garcia, Mayo, Lopez, & Hornero, 2009; Sharma et al. 2013). Statistical classification (Wang, Hsu, Goh, & Lee, 2000) and neural network (Gardner, keating, Williamson, & Elliot, 1996) were also attempted for exudates detection, which are catalogued into machine learning approach.

Back propagation neural network (BPN) is used in Karegowda et al. (2011) for detection of exudates. To prevent the OD from interfering with exudates detection, the OD is eliminated. Features like hue, intensity, mean intensity, standard deviation intensity and distance between OD & intensity are identified from the images by using Decision tree and GA-CFS approach. Then the feature set obtained is used as input to the BPN model to detect the exudates and non-exudates at pixel level.

An automatic exudates detection method based on mixture models is discussed in Sanchez et al. (2009). A dynamic threshold is used in the method to separate the exudates from the background. The threshold is set based on estimation of the histogram. By modelling each histogram with a different mixture model, a dynamic threshold for each image is obtained. A post processing technique, based on the edge detection, is then applied to distinguish hard exudates from the background and other artifacts. The method obtained a sensitivity of 90.2% on an independent database of small clinical set of retinal images. But this method fails to identify faint exudates in the retina.

The high gray level variation of exudates is exploited in Nayak, Bhat, Acharya, Lim and Kagathi (2008) to detect them and to determine their contour by morphological reconstruction techniques. The method obtained a sensitivity of 88.5% and specificity of 99.7%. The method is unable to detect exudates if they are similar in brightness and size to the optic disc.

In Xu and Luo (2009), a novel method is used to identify hard exudates from digital retinal images. A feature combination based on stationary wavelet transform (SWT) and gray level co-occurrence matrix (GLCM) is used to characterize hard exudates candidates. An optimized support vector machine (SVM) with Gaussian radial basis function is employed as a classifier. A sample dataset consisting of 50 hard exudates candidates is used for identifying hard exudates.

An automatic method for exudates detection based on image processing techniques that utilize colour, intensity gradients, and image textures in retinal image is discussed in Abbadi and Al-Saadi (2013). OD is also a bright region which has similar appearance to that of exudates. So, it is removed in the method before exudates detection. Then green channel colour space of retinal image is used for exudates detection. Intensity and texture information is used for exudates detection. Exudates region have higher intensity and has similar texture throughout the region. Each pixel in the image has intensity value ranging from 0 (darkest pixel), and 255 (light pixel). The retinal image is segmented using a threshold value of 110. The resultant binary image represents the candidate exudates as white pixels and all the other image details are changed to background as black colour. Then true exudates and false exudates are detected in the resultant image using texture analysis. Texture measures like average intensity, standard deviation, smoothness, third moment, uniformity and entropy are calculated. The entropy, average intensity and standard deviation of the false exudates are higher than the true exudates, and false exudates region is the least smooth and the least uniform as compared to the true exudates region. False exudates are removed by labelling it using 'unionfind' algorithm and then true exudates are segmented.

Another method for detection of exudates in retinal image using random forest classifier is discussed in Akila and Kavitha (2014). Retinal image is pre-processed by using Contrast Limited Adaptive Histogram Equalization (CLAHE) technique to improve the contrast of the image. K-means clustering and Fuzzy C-means (FCM) clustering is used in the method to detect the candidate exudate regions in the pre-processed image. From the segmented region, features like standard deviation, mean, energy, entropy and homogeneity are extracted. The features show distinct variation between normal and abnormal images. These features are used as a input to classifier. Random Forest (RF) classifier is used in the method for classification of abnormalities. The classifier obtained a sensitivity of 88.8%, specificity of 94% and accuracy of 92.94%.

Grading of Disease Stages

Progression of maculopathy is slow, very often without any symptoms in the early stages. Hence it is required to evaluate different stages of maculopathy which affects the vision to different levels. In this direction, simple and efficient computer based automatic methods for grading the severity levels of maculopathy have been proposed (Siddalingaswamy, Prabhu, & Jain, 2011; Sharma et al. 2013; Hani, & Nugroho, 2010; Jaafar, Nandi, & Nauimy, 2011; Akram, Akhtar, & Javed, 2012).

In Hani et al. (2010), the Gaussian Bayes classifier is used to determine diabetic retinopathy (DR) severity level. The colour fundus images from the database FINDeRS are analyzed by a computerized DR system to determine the areas of foveal avascular zone (FAZ). The FAZ area distribution for each DR severity class is determined and modelled with a Gaussian probability density function. A Gaussian Bayes classifier is then developed to determine DR severity based on the measured FAZ area in pixels. The method obtained sensitivity greater than 84%, specificity greater than 97% and accuracy of 95% for all DR stages.

In Siddalingaswamy et al. (2011), diabetic maculopathy is graded by the location of exudates in marked region of macula. Exudates are detected using clustering and mathematical morphological techniques. The possible exudates regions are coarse segmented by clustering technique. This technique separates the exudates region and background. After eliminating the OD from the clustered image, fine segmentation of exudates is done using morphological reconstruction. Finally the exudate regions are obtained by thresholding the difference between the original image and the reconstructed image. The method is tested on maculopathy images from a local dataset and shows a sensitivity 95.6% and specificity of 96.15%.

An automated method to detect hard exudates and grade the severity of maculopathy is discussed in Jaafar et al. (2011). The method uses top-down image segmentation and local thresholding to find the region of interest. To detect the exudates in this region, a combination of edge detection and region growing method is used. Polar coordinate system, centered at the fovea is used to evaluate the presence of exudates. The result of this is then used for grading of severity. They reported a sensitivity of 98.4% and specificity of 90.5%.

An automated system for the grading of diabetic maculopathy is discussed in Akram et al. (2012). Macula is detected as the darkest pixel region in the image. Exudates are detected by using gabor filter bank followed by adaptive thresholding. Feature set is then formulated and supplied to SVM classifier. The output of classifier is used to identify the stage of diabetic maculopathy.

Automatic detection of Diabetic Macular Edema (DME) and classification of DME severity is discussed in Vasanthi and Banu (2014). The colour retinal images are pre-processed in the method before DME detection. This includes green channel separation from RGB image, filtering by median filter to remove the presence of noise, image enhancement by row interpolation and column interpolation. Then the retinal images are standardized to a size of 576 x 720 and the morphological closing operation is performed. Since the OD shares the brightness characteristics of exudates, it is removed from the retinal image. The Hard Exudates (HE) presence in macula region is detected and the features are extracted. Gray level Co-occurence Matrix (GLCM) is then created and its parameters are evaluated for classifications which are considered as features in the method. Dataset is formed by using the features such as contrast, correlation, energy, homogeneity and area of exudates. This dataset is used as input of classifier for classification of various stages of abnormalities. Adaptive Neuro Fuzzy Inference System (ANFIS) and Extreme Learning Machine (ELM) classifier are used in the method to classify the retinal images as normal, mild, moderate and severe stages. The method obtained a sensitivity of 100%, specificity of 90% and accuracy of 96.49% for ANFIS classifier. Sensitivity, specificity and accuracy for ELM classifier is 94.28%, 100% and 96.49% respectively.

A two-stage methodology for the detection and classification of DME severity from colour retinal images is described in Deepak and Sivaswamy (2012). In a colour retinal image, a circular region of interest (ROI) is first defined around the macula region then an intermediate representation known as the motion pattern (I_{MP}) of the ROI is created. The motion pattern generated by inducing motion on the ROI results in the smearing of retinal lesions if present along the motion path. The image I_{MP} is then projected to obtain a vector response for every angle. The feature vector is formed by concatenating the obtained vector responses angular projection for different orientations. The spatial extent of exudates is enhanced in the I_{MP}. So, the feature vector for an abnormal retinal image shows several peaks in its profile due to intensities corresponding to exudates. The feature vectors for a normal retinal image have relatively uniform values resulting in a compact normal subspace. These feature vectors are used for learning the subspace corresponding to normal retinal images. Two single class classifiers: Gaussian data description (Gaussian DD) and principal component analysis data description (PCA DD) is used in the method for classification of retinal images into normal and DME category. A classification boundary is formed in the feature space around the subspace corresponding to normal retinal image. If an image feature space lies within this boundary, then it is classified as normal image otherwise it is taken as DME image. DME severity is then assessed using a rotational asymmetry metric by examining the symmetry of macular region. Macula in a normal image is relatively darker than other regions in the retinal image and is characterized by rotational symmetry. This symmetry information of macular region is used in the method for grading the severity stages of DME into moderate and severe case.

In all the above described methods, retinal images from various databases are used for the experimental evaluation. A brief description of these databases is given below:

DRIVE Database

The DRIVE database comprises 40 eye fundus colour images. The seven of these images present pathological cases. The images are pictured with a Canon CR5 non-mydriatic 3CCD camera with a 45 field-of-view (FOV). Each image was captured at 768×584 pixels, 8 bits per colour plane. The database is divided into two sets: a test set and a training set, each of them containing 20 images.

DIARETDB0 Database

This is a public database for standardising diabetic retinopathy detection from digital images.

The database comprises of 130 colour fundus images of which 20 are normal and 110 contain signs of the diabetic retinopathy. Images were captured with a 50 degree field-of-view digital fundus camera with unknown camera settings. The data correspond to practical situations, and can be used to evaluate the general performance of diagnosis methods. This data set is referred to as "calibration level 0 fundus images".

DIARETDB1 Database

This is also a public database for standardising diabetic retinopathy detection from digital images. The database contains 89 colour fundus images. Among these, 84 images are with mild non -proliferative signs of the diabetic retinopathy and 5 are considered as normal which do not contain any signs of the diabetic retinopathy. Images were captured using the same 50 degree field-of-view digital fundus camera with varying imaging settings. All the images are verified by 4 medical experts. This data set is referred to as "calibration level 1 fundus images".

MESSIDOR Database

This is a public database established to facilitate computer aided diagnosis of DR. The images are acquired by using a colour video 3CCD camera on a Topcon TRC NW6 non- mydriatic fundus camera with 45° field of view. The images were captured at 1440×960, 2240×1488 or 2304×1536 with 8 bits per colour plane. It contains total 1200 images which are divided into three sets of 400 images. Each set is further divided into 4 parts to facilitate thorough testing. Each set contains an excel file with medical findings which can be use for testing purposes.

ROLE OF COMPUTER ASSISTED METHODS IN RETINAL IMAGE ANALYSIS: DETECTION OF EXUDATES AND GRADING OF MACULOPATHY

With the advances of technology, image processing, analysis, and computer vision techniques are increasing in prominence in the fields of ophthalmology. Automatic image analysis and grading for the diagnosis of different retinal abnormalities like diabetic retinopathy, maculopathy and glaucoma benefit mass screening programs that need to examine a large number of retinal images in a short period of time. Given the diversity and complexity of eye functions, a large number of equipment, automatic computer assisted methods, and algorithms for diagnosis have been developed. The main idea of these techniques is to assist the physicians in interpreting medical images by using dedicated computer systems. Although a doctor can often identify certain diseases after a visual analysis of a retinal image, in some cases the diagnosis may be difficult due to lack of experience, fatigue, poor image quality, etc. In such situations, a computer assisted diagnosis system would be very useful (Dougherty 2011). Computer assisted diagnosis systems reduce the level of uncertainty regarding similar diseases and lighten the burden of increasing workload of the physician. This helps to improve the primary and evolutional detection of disease and allow monitoring of the health status of a patient during treatment (Ravishankar et al. 2009). Such systems are discussed in Ravishankar et al. (2009); Akram et al. (2012); Akila et al. (2014); Jaafar et al. (2011); Siddalingaswamy et al. (2011); Hani et al. 2010; Karegowda et al. 2011; Xu et al. (2009) and Vasanthi et al. (2014). The methods discussed in Karegowda et al. (2011); Xu et al. (2009) and Akila et al. (2014) use classifier for detecting the exudates. This requires a large amount of labelled training sets. These set of images are time consuming to create, difficult to obtain and computational complexity is more in these methods.

Hence simple but efficient methods are preferred for retinal image analysis. The results of such analysis may be used for classification of retinal images into healthy and diseased. The diseased images are further evaluated for identifying the stages of a disease. Two such methods of retinal image classification and grading of disease stages is available in Sharma et al. (2013, 2014). In these methods, apart from the publicly available databases, the images acquired from a local eye hospital Sri Sankaradeva Nethralaya, Guwahati are also used. It is a postgraduate teaching hospital, situated in Guwahati. A total of 74 images with large variability in terms of fundus disease and image quality are taken after consulting with the retinal expert. The image sets comprises of 30 normal and 44 diseased images. The retinal classification methods are discussed in detail in the following sections.

Method 1: Use of Image Processing Techniques for Retinal Image Analysis

An algorithm for classification of retinal images for certain medical applications such as screening is discussed in Sharma et al. (2013). Automatic retinal image classification system that is able to distinguish retinal images with and without any abnormal signs can be very helpful for the retinal experts as they can focus solely on the abnormal cases. Different image processing techniques are used in this method to detect the presence of abnormalities in the retinal images. The method consists of two stages.

In the first stage, the bright optic disc region is located. The blood vessels that emerge from the OD are nearly vertical in the vicinity of OD. Hence the vertical edge image is generated and OD is detected by directly projecting the vertical edge pixels onto the horizontal axis. The resulting 1-D projections are then searched to determine the location of the OD. There is a larger peak near the OD region because of many vertical edge pixels as shown in Figure 2.

Figure 2. OD localisation (a) Vertical edge image (b) Projection of vertical edge pixels.

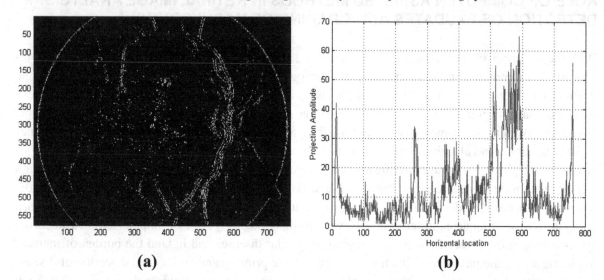

(a) **(b)**

In the second stage, bright exudates in a retinal image are detected. The colour retinal image is converted to grayscale image for further processing. Results obtained during exudates detection is shown in Figure 3.

The important steps used for exudates detection are:

1. Each image is pre-processed to improve the contrast and strengthening the texture of the image before exudates detection. This is done by applying adaptive histogram equalization to the image. This technique adjusts the local variation in the contrast by increasing or decreasing the contrast depending on the brightness. Pre-processed image is shown in Figure 3 (c).
2. Some exudates lie very close to the blood vessels. These may be missed during the process of detection. Hence, blood vessels are removed to improve exudates detection. This is done by morphological closing operation with disk shape structuring element. The image obtained after closing operation contains some candidate exudates regions as shown in Figure 3 (d).
3. The region containing exudates are higher on variance as compared to the other regions in the image. Therefore, a variance image is generated using this blood vessel removed image. This variance image emphasizes the bright region as shown in Figure 3 (e).
4. This variance image is converted to a binary image with a suitable threshold value to filter out the bright objects. The threshold value is taken from the histogram of the variance image and averaged over number of images. Then to fill the gaps within the border of the detected bright regions, morphological opening operation is used. A disk shaped structuring element is used in this operation.
5. The OD is also a bright circular region in the image. To avoid confusion with the exudates, OD is removed for accurate detection of exudates. A circular mask is used to block the OD. Image obtained after removing the OD is shown in Figure 3 (g).
6. Finally the candidate regions of exudates are obtained by removing the circular border of the retina image as shown in Figure 3 (h).

Figure 3. Exudates detection (a) Original image (b) Grayscale image (c) Pre-Processed image (d) Blood vessel removed image (e) Variance image (f) Binary image (g) OD removed image (h) Exudates

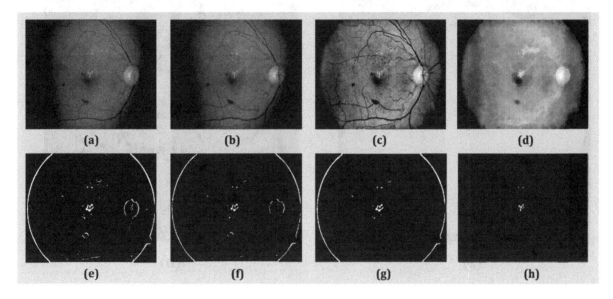

In case of normal retinal images, there are no bright exudates. So, after removing the OD no bright region remains in the image as shown in Figure 4.

Depending on the existence of exudates, retinal images are classified into normal and abnormal categories. The output image of a diseased retinal image has some white regions which indicate the presence of abnormal signs. So, the image is classified in abnormal category. In case of normal retinal image the entire resultant image appear as black with no white patches. This shows that the image is healthy. So, it is classified in normal category.

Experimental Results

The method is tested on 100 retinal images to determine its effectiveness. Among these, 49 are normal retinal images and 51 images are with some sign of abnormalities. The images are obtained from various sources including DIARETDB1 database (Kauppi et al., 2007), DRIVE database, STARE database and from a local eye hospital. The method successfully classifies all the normal images with an accuracy of 100%. From 51 abnormal images, 50 images are correctly classified with an accuracy of 98.2%. Results for specific databases are shown in Table 1. All these results are reported in Sharma et al. (2013).

Method 2: Grading of Diabetic Maculopathy Severity Level

An automated system for grading the severity level of diabetic maculopathy is discussed in Sharma et al. (2014). In this method grayscale image is used for macula detection and grading disease stages. The macula is localized based on its distance and position with respect to the OD as discussed in Siddalingaswamy et al. (2011).

Figure 4. Results of exudates detection for normal retinal image (a) Normal image (b) No exudates detected

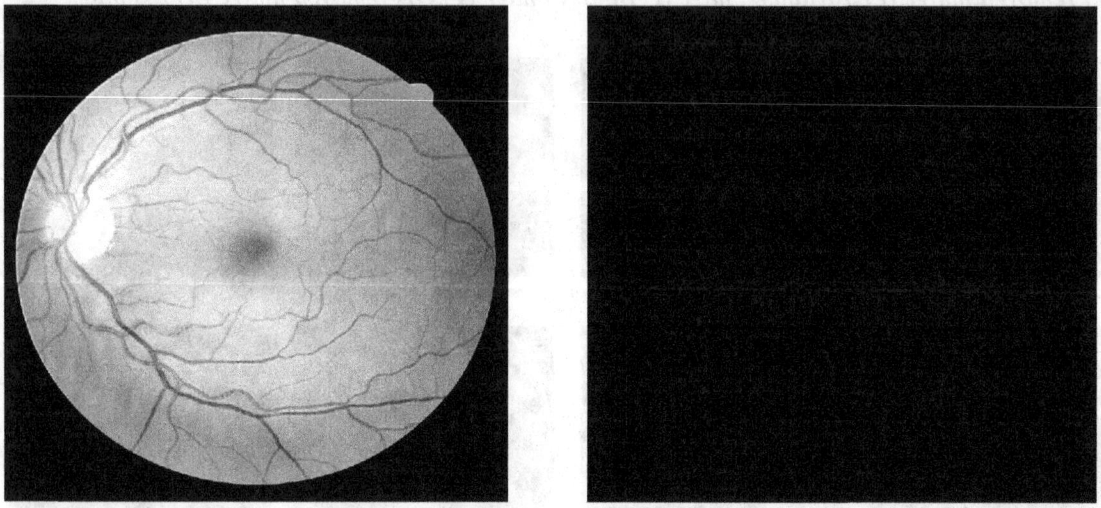

(a)   **(b)**

Macula Detection

The center of OD is detected by projecting the vertical edges pixel intensities as discussed in Method 1. Once the OD is detected, the macula is localized by finding the darkest region within the specified area in the image. Macula is situated approximately 2 disc diameter (DD) temporal to the OD in standard retinal images. Angle between the center of macula and the center of OD against the horizon is found to be in the range of -2.3 to -8.9 degrees (Siddalingaswamy et al. 2011). Using this factor, a rectangular search area is localized. The width of the search area is taken as 2 DD. A small sliding window is formed to scan the search area. For each position of the local window, the local average intensity is calculated. From various average intensity values, the lowest average intensity is calculated. Then center of the window having the lowest average intensity is taken as center of the macular region. From this center, a region of size approximately 2/3 DD along all direction is marked as shown in Figure 5. This region is considered as the macular region.

Table 1. Results of the method for different databases

Source	Normal Image	Abnormal Image	Correctly Detected	Success Rate
Hospital	15	-	15	100%
	-	21	21	
DRIVE	20	-	20	100%
STRAE	-	13	13	100%
DIARETDB1	14	-	14	98%
	-	17	16	

Figure 5. Marked location of Optic Disc, search area and macular region

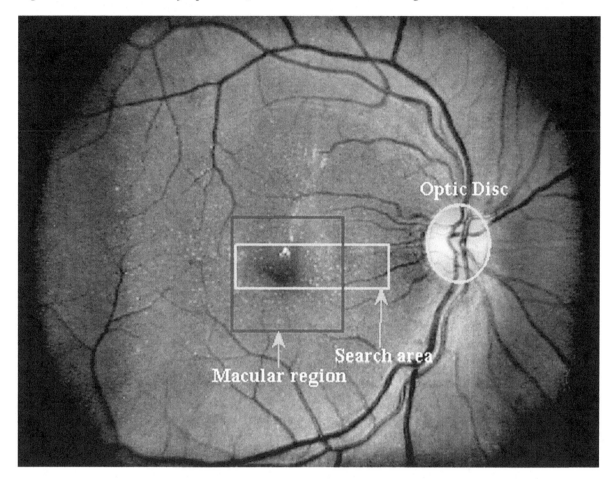

After detecting the OD and masking, the next step is to detect the exudates. Exudates detection stage is same as discussed in method 1.

Severity Level Grading of Maculopathy

Automatic grading of diabetic maculopathy is done based on international grading standard (Wilkinson et al. 2003). This method is used for grading the severity of maculopathy into severe, moderate and mild stages. After detecting macula and exudates, the macular region is divided into three concentric geometric windows x1, x2 and x3 as shown in Figure 6. The x1 is the inner most region of radii slightly greater than 1/3 of OD diameter (DD) but less than 2/3 DD. The x2 region is of radii 2/3 DD. The x3 is the outer most region of radii greater than 1 DD but less than 1.5 DD.

If exudates are present outside the x1, x2 and x3 regions of an image then it is classified as clinically non significant maculopathy. If exudates are present around the macular region then grading of maculopathy severity levels is done by estimating the number of exudates pixel in each window. The relative numbers of exudates in each window are computed. Depending on the number of exudates pixel present in different windows, the images are graded as follows:

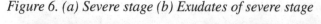

Figure 6. (a) Severe stage (b) Exudates of severe stage

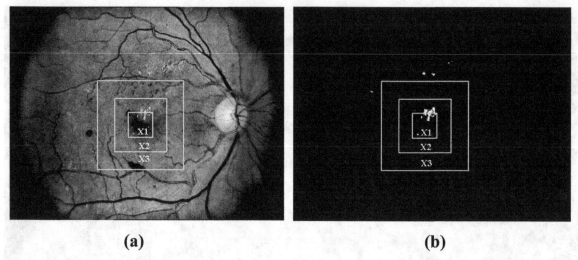

(a)   **(b)**

1. If some exudates are present in x1 region covering the center of macula, then the image is classified to be in severe stage. In this stage there is a high risk of vision loss. An example of this case is shown in Figure 6.
2. If exudates are absent in x1 region but present in x2 region, then the image is classified to be in moderate stage irrespective of its presence or absence in x3 region. Such an image is shown in Figure 7.
3. If exudates are present only in the x3 region then it is classified as mild case as shown in Figure 8.

Experimental Results

The method is evaluated on 110 retinal images. Among these, 20 are normal retinal images without any signs of maculopathy and 90 images are at different stages of maculopathy. These images are obtained from various sources including DIARETDB1 database (Kauppi et al., 2007), DIARETDB0 database (Kauppi et al., 2006), MESSIDOR database and an eye hospital. The total image set is initially classified into normal and abnormal images using the system discussed in the method 1. This system is considered as first stage of classification where all the 20 normal images are successfully classified as normal and from 88 abnormal images 90 images are correctly classified as abnormal. Then in the second stage, only the abnormal images are used for further processing.

The performance of the algorithm in grading the maculopathy images into different stages is evaluated using the four parameters, sensitivity (Se), specificity (Sp), Positive predictive value (PPV) and accuracy. They are computed on the basis of four measures: True Positive (TP), False Negative (FN), True Negative (TN), and False Positive (FP). TP represents the correctly classified stage of diabetic maculopathy by the method. FN represents the stage of diabetic maculopathy which is wrongly classified. TN represents the absence of diabetic maculopathy stage which is correctly diagnosed by the method. FP represents the absence of a particular stage of diabetic maculopathy which is diagnosed as present by the method. The Se, Sp and PPV is computed as,

Figure 7. (a) Moderate stage (b) Exudates of moderate stage

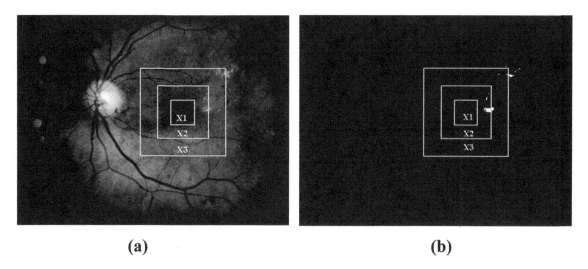

(a)   **(b)**

$$Sensitivity = \frac{TP}{\left(TP + FN \right)}$$

$$Specificity = \frac{TN}{\left(TN + FP \right)}$$

$$PPV = \frac{TP}{\left(TP + FP \right)}$$

Accuracy is computed as the ratio of truly classified images to the total number of images. The method successfully classified all the 36 images with severe stage of diabetic maculopathy as severe with a sensitivity of 100%. From 26 images with moderate stage of diabetic maculopathy, 25 were correctly classified with a sensitivity of 96.15%. From 17 images with mild stage of diabetic maculopathy, 15 were correctly classified as mild stage with a sensitivity of 88.2%. And rest 9 images were correctly classified as clinically non significant maculopathy. PPV obtained for normal category is 90.9% and for abnormal category is 100%. The method shows an overall Sensitivity of 96.2%, Specificity of 100% and accuracy of 96.5%. Results for specific databases are shown in Table 2. All these results are available in Sharma et al. (2014).

When this method is compared with the other methods described in Siddalingaswamy et al. (2011), Jaafar et al. (2011) and Vasanthi et al. (2014), it is observed that presented method gives promising results. The comparison results are shown in Table 3.

Table 2. Results of grading method for different databases

Source	Severe Stage	Moderate Stage	Mild Stage	Correctly Detected
Hospital	6	-	-	6
	-	8	-	8
	-	-	7	6
DIARETDB1	11	-	-	11
	-	4	-	3
	-	-	4	4
DIARETDB0	9	-	-	9
	-	8	-	8
	-	-	3	2
MESSIDOR	10	-	-	10
	-	6	-	6
	-	-	3	3

CONCLUSION

Retinal diseases have become one of the rapidly increasing health threats worldwide. Computer based intelligent system helps the ophthalmologists in early diagnosis of some sight threatening retinal diseases effectively. Automatic retinal image analysis system developed to detected retinal features like OD, macula, exudates can be effective in categorising retinal images in normal and abnormal categories. This can be done depending on the presence of abnormal signs in the image. Such a system will allow retinal experts to give more emphasis on diseased cases. Then further processing can be done on the abnormal images to get more information about the diseases. Computer assisted methods also allows to generate diagnosis databases that can be explored in research and specialized teaching.

Figure 8. (a) Mild stage (b) Exudates of mild stage

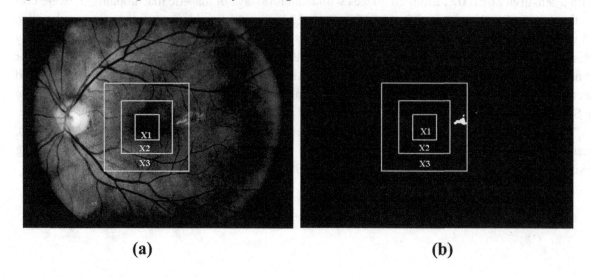

(a)   (b)

Table 3. Comparison table

Technique for Severity Grading	Sensitivity	Specificity	Accuracy
Clustering and mathematical morphological techniques (Siddalingaswamy et al., 2011)	95.6%	96.15	-
Top-down image segmentation, local thresholding and polar coordinate system (Jaafar et al., 2011)	98.4%	90.5%	-
Gray level co-occurence matrix and ELM classifier (Vasanthi et al., 2014)	94.28%	100%	96.49%
Presented Image Processing method (Sharma et al., 2014)	96.2%	100%	96.5%

FUTURE RESEARCH DIRECTIONS

Automated analysis of retinal images is an ongoing active field of research. Some of the simpler and more recent automatic methods bought to analyse retinal images is discussed in this chapter. Although the methods discussed above gives promising result, the performance of the method is affected if the image is of low contrast where macula is not visible and if the image is not macula centered. The performance of the methods can be improved by extracting the characteristic features of the image and using them in machine learning techniques.

The beginners in this field of research may find this book chapter very useful to start their research. The different chapters on computer assisted methods give an insight of its application in different fields of science, technology and biomedical engineering. In this direction, this chapter contributes to help and motivate young researchers to start with the basic knowledge of what has been done and what is the future scope to do research in this field.

REFERENCES

Abbadi, N. K. E., & Al- Saadi, E. H. (2013). Automatic detection of exudates in retinal images. *International Journal of Computer Science Issues*, *10*(2), 237–242.

Akila, T., & Kavitha, G. (2014). Detection and classification of hard exudates in human retinal fundus images using clustering and random forest methods. *International Journal of Emerging Technology and Advanced Engineering*, *4*(2), 24–29.

Akram, M. U., Akhtar, M., & Javed, M. Y. (2012). *An automated system for the grading of diabetic maculopathy in fundus images. Proceedings of Neural Information Processing (LNCS)* (Vol. 7666, pp. 36–43). Springer.

Deepak, K. S., & Sivaswamy, J. (2012). Automatic assessment of macular edema from color retinal images. *IEEE Transactions on Medical Imaging, 31*(3), 766–776. doi:10.1109/TMI.2011.2178856 PMID:22167598

Dougherty, G. (2011). *Medical image processing-Techniques and Application.* New York, NY: Springer; doi:10.1007/978-1-4419-9779-1

Gardner, G. G., Keating, D., Williamson, T. H., & Elliott, A. T. (1996). Automatic detection of diabetic retinopathy using an artificial neural network: A screening tool. *The British Journal of Ophthalmology, 80*(11), 940–944. doi:10.1136/bjo.80.11.940 PMID:8976718

Godse, D. A., & Bormane, D. S. (2013). Automated localization of optic disc in Retinal images. *International Journal of Advanced Computer Science and Applications, 4*(2), 66–71. doi:10.14569/IJACSA.2013.040210

Goldbaum, M. (1975). *STARE database.* Retrieved from http://www.parl.clemson.edu/stare/nerve/

Hani, A. F. M., Nugroho, H. A., & Nugroho, H. (2010). Gaussian bayes classifier for medical diagnosis and grading: application to diabetic retinopathy. *Proceedings of IEEE EMBS Conference on Biomedical Engineering and Sciences* (pp. 52-56). Kuala Lumpur, Malaysia. IEEE. doi:10.1109/IECBES.2010.5742198

Image Sciences Institute. (2004). *DRIVE database.* Retrieved from http://www.isi.uu.nl/Research/Databases/DRIVE

Jaafar, H. F., Nandi, A. K., & Nuaimy, W. (2011). Automated detection and grading of hard eudates from retinal fundus images. *Proceedings of 19th European Signal Processing Conference* (pp. 66-70). Barcelona. IEEE.

Karegowda, A. G., Nasiha, A., & Jayaram, M. A. (2011). Exudates detection in retinal images using back propagation neural network. *International Journal of Computers and Applications, 25*(3), 25–31. doi:10.5120/3011-4062

Kauppi, T., Kalesnykiene, V., Kamarainen, J. K., et al. (2006). *DIARETDB1 database.* Retrieved from http://www2.it.lut.fi/project/imageret/diaretdb1/

Kauppi, T., Kalesnykiene, V., Kamarainen, J. K., et al. (2006). *DIARETDB0 database.* Retrieved from http://www2.it.lut.fi/project/imageret/diaretdb0/

Kaur, A., & Sharma, R. (2014). Optic disc segmentation based on watershed transform. *International Journal of Advanced Research in Computer Science and Software Engineering, 4*(5), 681–685.

Khan, C. R., Weir, G. C., King, G. L., Jacobson, A. M., Moses, A. C., & Smith, R. J. (2005). *Joslin's diabetes mellitus.* USA: Lippincott Williams & Wilkins.

Kumar, T. A., Priya, S., & Paul, V. (2013). A novel approach to the detection of macula in human retinal imagery. *International Journal of Signal Processing Systems, 1*(1), 23–28. doi:10.12720/ijsps.1.1.23-28

Li, H., & Chutatape, O. (2004). Automated feature extraction in color retinal images by a model based approach. *IEEE Transactions on Bio-Medical Engineering, 51*(2), 246–254. doi:10.1109/TBME.2003.820400 PMID:14765697

Lu, S., & Lim, J. H. (2010). Automatic macula detection from retinal images by a line operator. *Proceedings of IEEE 17th International Conference on Image Processing* (pp. 4073-4076). Hong Kong. IEEE. doi:10.1109/ICIP.2010.5649080

Methods to evaluate segmentation and indexing techniques in the field of retinal ophthalmology. *MESSIDOR database*. Retrieved from http://messidor.crihan.fr/AccesBaseMessidor/new-index.php

Minar, J., Riha, K., Krupka, A., & Tong, H. (2014). Automatic detection of the macula in retinal fundus images using multilevel thresholding. *International Journal of Advances in Telecommunications, Electronics, Signals and Systems*, *3*(1). doi:10.11601/ijates.v3il.78

Mubbashar, M., Usman, A., & Akram, M. U. (2011). Automated system for macula detection in digital retinal images. In *Proceedings of Conference on Information and Communication Technologies* (pp. 1-5), Karachi. IEEE.

National Eye Institute. (1968). Retrieved from https://www.nei.nih.gov/health/diabetic/retinopathy

Nayak, J., Bhat, P., Acharya, R., Lim, U., & Kagathi, M. (2008). Automated identification of diabetic retinopathy stages using digital fundus images. *Journal of Medical Systems*, *32*(2), 107–115.

Osareh, A., Mirmehdi, M., Thomas, B., & Markham, R. (2002). Colour morphology and snakes for optic disc localisation. *Proceedings of 6th Medical Image Understanding and Analysis Conference* (pp. 21-24).

Padmanaban, K. & kannan, R. J. (2013). Localization of optic disc using fuzzy c means clustering. *Proceedings of International Conference on Current Trends in Engineering and Technology* (pp. 184-186), Coimbatore: IEEE. doi:10.1109/ICCTET.2013.6675941

Ravishankar, S., Jain, A., & Mittal, A. (2009). Automated feature extraction for early detection of diabetic retinopathy in fundus images. *Proceedings of IEEE Conference on Computer Vision and Pattern Recognition* (pp. 210-217). Miami, FL: IEEE. doi:10.1109/CVPR.2009.5206763

Sanchez, C., Garcia, M., Mayo, A., Lopez, M., & Hornero, R. (2009). Retinal image analysis based on mixture models to detect hard exudates. *Medical Image Analysis*, *13*(4), 650–658. doi:10.1016/j.media.2009.05.005 PMID:19539518

Sekher, S., Al-Nuaimy, W., & Nandi, A. K. (2008). Automated localisation of optic disc, and fovea in retinal fundus image. *Proceedings of 16th European Signal Processing Conference*. Lausanne, Switzerland. IEEE.

Sharma, P., Nirmala, S. R., & Sarma, K. K. (2013). Classification of retinal images using image processing techniques. *Journal of Medical Imaging and Health Informatics*, *3*(3), 341–346. doi:10.1166/jmihi.2013.1185

Sharma, P., Nirmala, S. R., & Sarma, K. K. (2014). A system for grading diabetic maculopathy severity levels. *Network Modeling Analysis in Health Informatics and Bioinformatics, Springer*, *3*(1), 49. doi:10.1007/s13721-014-0049-y

Siddalingaswamy, P. C., Prabhu, K. G., & Jain, V. (2011). Automatic detection and grading of severity level in exudative maculopathy. *Journal on Biomedical Engineering: Applications. Basis and Communications*, *23*(3), 173–179. doi:10.4015/S1016237211002608

Ter, F. & Haar. (2005). Automatic localization of the optic disc in digital color images of the human retina [M.S. thesis]. Computer Science Department, Utrecht University, Netherlands.

Thongnuch, V., & Uyyanonvara, B. (2007). Automatic optic disk detection from low contrast retinal images of ROP infant using GVF snake. *Suranaree Journal of Science and Technology, 14,* 223–226.

Vasanthi, S., & Banu, R. S. D. W. (2014). Automatic segmentation and classification of hard exudates to detect macular edema in fundus images. *Journal of Theoretical and Applied Information Technology, 66*(3), 684–690.

Wang, H., Hsu, W., Goh, K. G., & Lee, M. L. (2000). An effective approach to detect lesions in color retinal images. *Proceedings of IEEE Computer Society Conference on Computer Vision and Pattern Recognition* (pp. 181–187). Hilton Head Island, SC. IEEE

Wild, S., Roglic, G., Green, A., Sicree, R., & King, H. (2004). Global prevalence of diabetes: Estimates for the year 2000 and projections for 2030. *Journal of Diabetes Care, 27*(5), 1047–1053. doi:10.2337/diacare.27.5.1047 PMID:15111519

Wilkinson, C. P., Ferris, F. L. III, Klein, R. E., Lee, P. P., Agardh, C. D., & Davis, M. et al. (2003). Global diabetic retinopathy project group: Proposed international clinical diabetic retinopathy and diabetic macular edema disease severity scales. *Journal of Ophthalmology, 110*(9), 1677–1682. doi:10.1016/S0161-6420(03)00475-5

Wong, D. W. K., Liu, J., Tan, N. M., Yin, F., Cheng, X., Cheng, C. Y., et al. (2012). Automatic detection of the macula in retinal fundus images using seeded mode tracking approach. In *proceedings of* Engineering *in Medicine and Biology Society (EMBC)* (pp. 4950-4953). San Diego, California USA. IEEE.

Xu, L. & Luo, S. (2009). Support Vector Macidne Based Methodfor Identifying Hard Exudates In Retinal Images. *Proceedings of IEEE Youth Conference on Information, Computing and Telecommunication* (pp. 138-141). Beijing. IEEE.

Youssif, A., Ghalwash, A., & Ghoneim, A. (2008). Optic disc detection from normalized digital fundus images by means of a vessel's direction matched filter. *IEEE Transactions on Medical Imaging, 27*(1), 11–18. doi:10.1109/TMI.2007.900326 PMID:18270057

ADDITIONAL READING

Abrmoff, M. D., Garvin, M. K., & Sonka, M. (2010). Retinal imaging and image Analysis. *IEEE Reviews in Biomedical Engineering, 3,* 169–208. doi:10.1109/RBME.2010.2084567 PMID:22275207

Dougherty, G., Johnson, M. J., & Wiers, M. D. (2010). Measurement of retinal vascular tortuosity and its application to retinal pathologies. *Journal of Medical and Biological Engineering and Computing, 48*(1), 87–95. doi:10.1007/s11517-009-0559-4 PMID:20012560

Fleming, A. D., Goatman, K. A., Philip, S., Olshen, J. A., & Sharp, P. F. (2007). Automatic detection of retinal anatomy to assist diabetic retinopathy screening. *Physics in Medicine and Biology, 52*(2), 331–345. doi:10.1088/0031-9155/52/2/002 PMID:17202618

Haun, W., Wynne, H., & Mong, L. (2009). Effective detection of retinal exudates in fundus images. *Proceedings of IEEE Conference on Biomedical Engineering and Informatics*. Tianjin, China. IEEE.

Jelinek, H. F., & Cree, M. J. (2010). *Automated image detection of retinal pathology*. Boca Raton, FL: CRC press, Taylor and Francis group.

Marin, D., Aquino, A., Gegndez-Arias, M. E., & Bravo, J. M. (2011). A new supervised method for blood vessel segmentation in retinal images by using gray-level and moment invariants-based features. *IEEE Transactions on Medical Imaging*, *30*(1), 146–158. doi:10.1109/TMI.2010.2064333 PMID:20699207

Niemeijer, M., Abrmoff, M. D., & Ginneken, B. V. (2009). Fast detection of the optic disc and fovea in color fundus photographs. *Medical Image Analysis*, *13*(6), 859–870. doi:10.1016/j.media.2009.08.003 PMID:19782633

Tariq, A., Akram, M. U., & Javed, M. Y. (2013). Computer aided diagnostic system for grading of diabetic retinopathy. *Proceedings of* IEEE *Fourth International Workshop on Computational Intelligence in Medical imaging* (pp. 30-35). Singapore. IEEE.

Tariq, A., Akram, M.U., Shaukat, A. & Khan, S.A. (2013). Automated detection and grading of diabetic maculopathy in digital retinal images. *Journal of Digital imaging*, *26*(4), 803-812.

Zhanga, X., Thibaulta, G., Decencierea, E., Marcoteguia, B., & Lay, B. (2014). Exudate detection in color retinal images for mass screening of diabetic retinopathy. *Medical Image Analysis*, *18*(7), 1026–1043. doi:10.1016/j.media.2014.05.004

KEY TERMS AND DEFINITIONS

Adaptive Histogram Equalization (AHE): This is an image processing technique used to improve contrast in images. This method computes several histograms, each corresponding to a distinct section of the image, and uses them to redistribute the lightness values of the image.

Diabetic Retinopathy: A retinal pathology caused by complications of diabetes, which can eventually lead to blindness.

Exudates: Exudates are the yellow lipid deposited in the retina by leaky blood vessels.

Grayscale Image: Grayscale image is the 8-bit image in which the only colours are shades of gray. In this image all the red, green and blue components have equal intensity in RGB space. So, each pixel is represented by a single intensity value unlike RGB colour image where three intensities are required to specify each pixel.

Hemorrhages: Retinal hemorrhages are the bleeding of retentive tissue on the back wall of the eye.

Maculopathy: A retinal pathology caused by complication of diabetic retinopathy where central vision of a patient is affected.

Ophthalmology: Ophthalmology is the branch of medicine that deals with the anatomy, physiology and diseases of the eye.

Chapter 11
A Review on Vision–Based Hand Gesture Recognition and Applications

Ananya Choudhury
Gauhati University, India

Anjan Kumar Talukdar
Gauhati University, India

Kandarpa Kumar Sarma
Gauhati University, India

ABSTRACT

In the present scenario, vision based hand gesture recognition has become a highly emerging research area for the purpose of human computer interaction. Such recognition systems are deployed to serve as a replacement for the commonly used human-machine interactive devices such as keyboard, mouse, joystick etc. in real world situations. The major challenges faced by a vision based hand gesture recognition system include recognition in complex background, in dynamic background, in presence of multiple gestures in the background, under variable lighting condition, under different viewpoints etc. In the context of sign language recognition, which is a highly demanding application of hand gesture recognition system, coarticulation detection is a challenging task. The main objective of this chapter is to provide a general overview of vision based hand gesture recognition system as well as to bring into light some of the research works that have been done in this field.

INTRODUCTION

Presently, vision based hand gesture recognition has become a highly developing research field for the purpose of human computer interaction. Such recognition systems are deployed to serve as a replacement for the commonly used human-machine interactive (HCI) devices such as keyboard, mouse, joystick etc. in real world situations. Recently, gestures have become an important segment of such HCI devices. A

DOI: 10.4018/978-1-4666-8493-5.ch011

Figure 1. Types of hand gestures

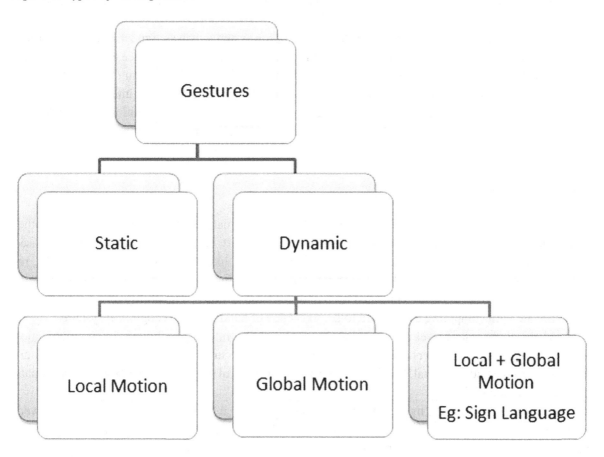

gesture may be defined as a physical movement of body parts such as hands, arms, head, face etc. to express some information or feelings (Murthy & Jadon, 2009). Gestures play an important role in our day to day communication. The ability of a computer or any processing system to understand the meaning of these gestures is referred to as gesture recognition. Among the various types of gestures, hand gestures are the most commonly used, as they are natural, easy to use and more convenient for communication. Hand gestures are basically of two types- static and dynamic (as shown in Figure 1). Static hand gestures do not involve any kind of hand movement in comparison to dynamic hand gestures, where either the entire hand moves (global motion) or only the fingers move (local motion) (Ahmeda, Alexanderb, & Anagnostopoulos, 2008).

There are mainly two approaches of hand gesture recognition: glove-based and vision-based. In glove-based method, the user needs to wear a sensor glove or a colored glove, which serves as an interface to communicate with the computer. Although, this approach gives accurate results, it affects the ease and naturalness with which the user interacts with the computer. Vision-based approach overcomes the drawback of glove based approach as it serves as a natural means of interaction. This method adopts computer vision and machine learning algorithms for recognizing the hand gestures. However, obtaining highly accurate results is a challenging task for vision based approaches (Rautaray & Agarwal, 2012).

In this chapter we have surveyed the literature on various vision-based hand gesture recognition systems and its application in different domains.

There are several applications of hand gesture recognition systems such as sign language recognition, human-robot interaction, controller less video gaming, smart TV, video surveillance etc.. Among these, sign language recognition has become an active topic of research as it provides an opportunity for the hearing impaired to communicate with the normal people without the need of an interpreter.

This chapter provides an insight into the basic process of hand gesture recognition, the detailed description of each of the sections and the related works which have been done in this field.

BACKGROUND

Gesture is a natural mode of communication which enables human beings to interact with each other from distance without the need of physical devices. The necessity of computing devices has increased tremendously in recent times. There are many physical devices like keyboards, mouses, joysticks, remote control etc. which can be used as interface for communicating with computers. However, the ease of this interaction can be greatly enhanced by the use of hand gestures. The ability of hand gestures to communicate with computing devices led to the existence of hand gesture recognition systems.

Hand gloves or sensor gloves were primitively used in 1990 as interface technique for communication between humans and computers. Although they provide very accurate recognition results, yet they are very cumbersome and unnatural. So, this led to the development of vision-based techniques for human-computer interaction (HCI).

Cameras of single lenses, multi-lens, depth perception lens, infra-red lens and kinect sensor were used as vision based HCI devices. Different lenses provide different information. The more information utilized, the higher will be the recognition rate. However, special installations may be required for these cameras and thus will be costly (Hsieh, Liou, & Lee, 2012). In comparison to these, there are other improved vision based hand gesture recognition techniques based on Principle Component Analysis (PCA), Finite State Machine (FSM), Particle Filtering, Artificial Neural Network (ANN), Dynamic Time Warping (DTW), Hidden Markov Model (HMM), Conditional Random Field (CRF) etc.

The basic block diagram of vision based hand gesture recognition system is shown in Figure 2. The image frames are firstly acquired from the input video and then processed through the subsequent stages for the system to get it as a gesture output.

The chapter is organized as follows: the first section provides a brief introduction of the chapter. The next section presents a historical background of hand gesture recognition system. The hand segmentation, hand tracking, feature extraction and classification stages of the hand gesture recognition system are respectively described in the subsequent sections. One section presents an upcoming application of hand gesture recognition system, followed by a section that describes the key issues involved in a hand gesture recognition system and finally the last section concludes the chapter.

HAND SEGMENTATION

Segmentation partitions an image into its constituent parts or objects. One of the most challenging tasks in a vision-based hand gesture recognition system is hand segmentation because hand segmentation is

Figure 2. Basic block diagram of hand gesture recognition system

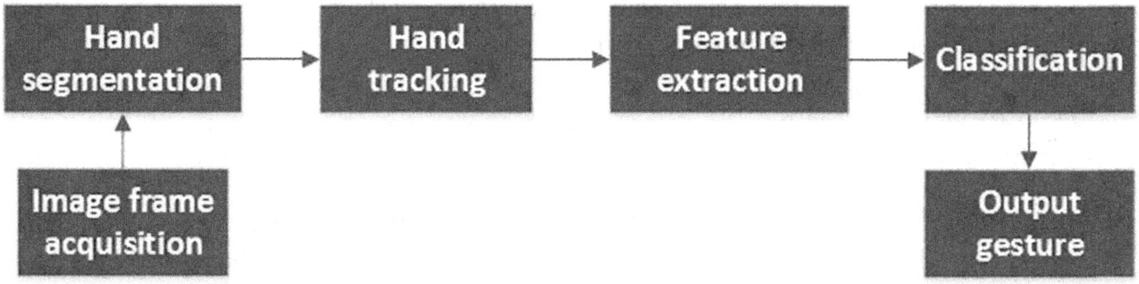

greatly affected by background conditions like complex background, dynamic background, background with multiple gestures and varying illumination. All subsequent steps greatly depend on the accuracy of segmentation. If data is lost due to improper segmentation, a proper gesture input to the system cannot be obtained which will consecutively lead to incorrect recognition. Two of the commonly used hand segmentation techniques are skin color segmentation and background subtraction.

Skin Color Segmentation

In skin color segmentation, a input image is first converted into HSV or YCbCr color space, because in HSV color space Hue and Saturation are independent of luminance and reflectance and in YCbCr color space Y alone can be used to control intensity of the image compared to RGB where color intensity has to be controlled individually. After this conversion, thresholding is done to convert it into a binary image. Disadvantage of this method is that if the background contains any object having same color as skin, noise will be very high (Phung, Bouzerdoum, & Chai, 2005).

Background Subtraction

In background subtraction method, one frame is subtracted from another to detect the regions in motion. Disadvantage of this method is that if the lighting condition changes abruptly, then there will be a change in pixel value where the light intensity changed and hence additive noise will add to the system (Lu, 2011).

This basic technique involves taking two frames as input and producing the output. The output is simply a third image produced after subtracting the second frame pixel values from the first frame pixel values. The general operation performed for this purpose is given by:

$$DIFF[i,j] = \left| I_1[i,j] - I_2[i,j] \right| \tag{1}$$

where *DIFF[i,j]* represents the difference image of two frames I_1 and I_2 respectively (Prabhakar, Vaithiyanathan, Sharma, Singh, & Singhal, 2012).

A hand gesture detection and segmentation system in complex background was presented by Zhang et al. (2008). It was based on differencing the background images of consecutive frames and it uses 3σ principle of normal distribution for updating the background. During training of the background, the algorithm first calculates the gray value of mean-variance of a Kth video frame i.e $\sigma_{K.}$ The algorithm uses $2.8\sigma_K$ as the criteria of judgement and calculates the difference (D_K) between pixel value of current image (C_K) and that of background image (B_K) using:

$$D_K = |\ C_K - B_K\ |$$

(2)

If $D_K \leq 2.8\sigma_K$, then it is considered to be illumination and shadow changes.

If $D_K \geq 2.8\sigma_K$, then it is considered to be the hand gesture that caused the change and B_K is set to $C_{K.}$

Thus the method is effective to reduce factors of illumination and gesture shadow. But the system fails for video sequences with background having multiple gesturers and changes due to adding or removing parts of background.

Contour Matching

Contours are sequences of points that represent a line/curve in an image. Every entry in the sequence encodes information about the location of the next point on the curve/line. Contour matching is most often used for recognizing and classifying image objects.

The contour model, containing pixels that are on the edge of (a part of) the object is placed on all possible positions in the search image (or another contour), computing a match value for every position. The match value is now based on the edge pixels in the contour model only. All the search image/contour pixels that correspond to an edge pixel in the contour model are added. The higher this value is, the better the resemblance between the contour model and search image/contour.

Contour matching proves to be a more preferable choice over template matching as the matching algorithm is restricted to only the edge pixels rather than the whole image as in template matching. Hence it faster, yields sharp matches and invariant under imaging transformations like scaling, translation, rotation, intensity. However, the hindrance of this method is that since a smaller number of pixels is involved in recognition, the influence of each pixel is greater, i.e. a few deviating pixels (due to noise, distortion) may hinder recognition. This has to be taken care of.

The most commonly used method for matching contour is by finding the Hu invariant moments (h_1 to h_7) which are linear combinations of the central moments (moment is a gross characteristic of a contour computed by summing over all the pixels of the contour). The Hu invariant moments are invariant to scale, rotation and reflection (except h_1). The match value is given by:

$$I(A, B) = \sum_{i=1}^{7} \left| \frac{1}{m_i^A} - \frac{1}{m_i^B} \right|$$

(3)

m_i^A and m_i^B are defined as:

$$m_i^A = sign(h_i^A) \cdot \log \left| h_i^A \right|$$

(4)

$$m_i^B = sign(h_i^B).\log\left|h_i^B\right| \tag{5}$$

where h_i^A and h_i^B are the Hu moments of contours A and B respectively (Choudhury, Talukdar, & Sarma, 2014).

Shape Matching Based Method

A hand shape estimation technique under complex background was proposed by Hamada et al. (2004) by using a shape transition network. The hand shape was estimated by selecting the best matched model from the aligned candidate models. The matching is based on the edge existence probability in the background and that of the true hand contour. In order to avoid incorrect match caused by the blurred hand image during fast hand movement, models without contour are added in the network and the models were correctly traced in the transition network. The expected value of the number of edge points (n_e) to be observed on a shape model is calculated using:

$$n_e = l_T P_T + (l - l_T)P_F \tag{6}$$

where,

l_T is the number of the model contour points caused by the correct hand contour,
P_T is the edge existence probability on correct hand boundary, and
P_F is the edge existence probability in the background.

Entropy Based technique

Entropy analysis was carried out by Lee et al. (2004) for recognizing one-handed gestures under complex background. Their proposed system incorporates frame differencing for subtracting one image frame from another, measures the entropy, separates the hand region from images and finally tracks the hand region to recognize the hand gestures. Entropy offers color information as well as motion information at the same time. To quantify the entropy of an image, Picture Information Measure (PIM) was used which is given by (Shin et al., 2006):

$$PIM = \sum_{i=0}^{L-1} h(i) - Max_j h(i) \tag{7}$$

where,

$h(i)$ means i^{th} histogram value of each image or block. *PIM* value is evaluated by subtracting the total number of pixels in each block from the histogram value of maximum frequency. If all the pixel value of block is same that is the block entropy is '0', PIM value becomes '0'. This method enables extraction of hand region even in change of lighting condition and irrespective of any user.

HAND TRACKING

Hand tracking is a high-resolution technique that is employed to know the consecutive position of the hands of the user while performing a gesture. One of the most commonly used method for hand tracking is calculation of the centroids of the segmented hand and subsequently connecting them to get the gesture trajectories. The centroid *(x,y)* of 2D binary image *I(x,y)* is given by:

$$(x,y) = \left(\frac{M_{10}}{M_{00}}, \frac{M_{01}}{M_{00}} \right) \tag{8}$$

where,

M_{00} i.e. the zeroth moment gives the number of pixels (area) of the binary image and, an image moment *Mpq* is calculated using (Sminchisescu, Kanaujia, Li, & Metaxas, 2006):

$$M_{pq} = \sum_{i=1}^{n} I(x,y)x^{p}y^{q} \tag{9}$$

where,

p is the x-order and q is the y-order. The summation is over all the pixels of the contour boundary or image (as denoted by *n* in the equation (9)).

Hand tracking is a very crucial phase for gestures involving global motion because in the subsequent process, important features are extracted from the output of hand tracking, which in turn are used for recognizing a particular dynamic gesture. So efficient hand tracking helps in getting accurate recognition results.

Color-Based Method

- A combination of motion, skin color and edge information was used to implement a real-time hand tracking method by Chen et al. (2003). At first frame differencing is done to extract the moving regions. The difference image $D_i(x,y)$ between frames *i* and *i+1* is given by:

$$D_i(x,y) = T_i\{| F_i(x,y) - F_{i+1}(x,y) |\} \tag{10}$$

where T_i is a thresholding function. It is applied over the frame difference to extract the possible moving regions in complex background.

After frame differencing, skin color detection is performed to segment out only the moving skin colored regions. Edge detection is then applied to separate the arm region from the hand region as there are fewer edges on the arm region than on the palm region. Finally, a logical 'AND' operation is used to combine all the three types of information. The output is thus given by:

$$C_i(x,y) = D_i(x,y) \wedge S_i(x,y) \wedge E_i(x,y) \tag{11}$$

where, $D_i(x,y)$, $S_i(x,y)$, $E_i(x,y)$ and $C_i(x,y)$ indicates the movement, skin color, edge and combined images respectively.

This method is robust and reliable in complex background.

- Yuang et al. (2009) proposed a color classification based hand tracking method. This method comprises of two major tasks: training and tracking. In the training phase, the user selects a region on the hand to obtain the training data in the L*a*b* color space. Based on the skin-color distribution of this selected region, the training data is classified into several color clusters using randomized list data structure.

For an input color signal x, the proposed algorithm calculates the distance

$$d_i = \sqrt{\sum_{j=1}^{?} (w_{ij} - x_j)^2} \tag{12}$$

where,

w_{ij} is the set of weight connections between the clusters and each of the input signals.

If the distance does not fall into any existing clusters, a new cluster i will be created and x is set as the weight vector of cluster i. This new cluster is then stored at the end of a randomized list data structure.

In the hand tracking phase, hand is segmented from the background in real-time using the randomized lists that have been obtained from the training procedure. The proposed method is fast since image segmentation algorithm is automatically performed on a small region surrounding the hand, as well as it is effective under different lighting conditions.

Filter-Based Method

- Kalman filter and hand blobs analysis was used for hand tracking by Binh et al. (2005). Kalman filter is used to predict location of the hand in the present frame based on its location detected in the previous frame. The advantage of using Kalman filter is that it accelerates the hand segmentation process and helps in choosing the correct skin region when multiple image regions are skin color. Thus, instead of segmenting the entire input image into multiple skin regions and then selecting the region, Kalman filter estimate is used as the starting point of search for a skin colored region in subsequent frame.

- Particle filtering and mean shift (MS) was integrated by Shan et al. (2007) for getting improved tracking results. The proposed mean shift embedded particle filter (MSEPF) improves the sampling efficiency considerably. This method has the advantage that it doesnot take any assumptions into consideration like constrained viewpoint, static background, clutter-free environments etc.

FEATURE EXTRACTION

In feature extraction, some important features are extracted from the available hand trajectory obtained after hand tracking. Feature extraction is important in terms of giving input to a classifier by means of which it can understand the meaning of a gesture. In pattern recognition and in image processing, feature extraction is a special form of dimensionality reduction (Duda, Hart, & Stork, 2009). The major features used for gesture recognition are templates, global transformations, zones and geometric features (Yang, Ahuja, & Tabb, 2002). Templates are simply the input data in their raw form. Global transformations include features which are invariant to rotation, translation, scaling etc. For e.g. Fourier descriptors which are invariant with respect to rotation of the input pattern. To extract features by zoning, the space of the hand trajectory is divided into a number of zones and the path is transformed into the sequence of zones which the path traverses. Finally, geometric features are mainly used to represent global properties of the path obtained from hand tracking. For e.g. length of the path, its orientation, velocity etc.

Researchers have proposed several distinguishing features for representation of gestures. It has been often experimentally observed that considering multiple distinguishing features (suitable according to the type of application) on a common platform enable to get better recognition rates.

- A combination of shape descriptors, histogram of oriented gradient (HOG) descriptors and scale invariant feature transform (SIFT) was used as a feature vector for recognizing two-handed signs of Indian Sign Language (ISL) by Agrawal et al. (2012). Shape descriptors used were eccentricity of ellipse, aspect ratio, compactness, extent, solidity, orientation, spreadness and roundness. HOG descriptors describe the articulated or occluded gestures by the distributions of local intensity gradients and it is also invariant to illumination change and orientation. Each cell in the image has a histogram which is constructed using the directions and the magnitudes of pixel gradients in the cell.

$$Magnitude = \sqrt{dA^2 + dB^2} \tag{13}$$

where,

dA and dB are the gradients which are computed by applying filter on image X by A and B respectively where A direction = [-1, 0, 1] and B direction = [1, 0,-1].

SIFT finds key points all over the image that are invariant to scale and orientation.

- Zaki & Shaheen (2011) fused three appearance based features viz. Principle Component Analysis (PCA), Kurtosis Position and Motion chain code (MCC) to implement a sign language recognition system. These three features were mapped to four manual components of sign language: hand shape, place of articulation, hand orientation, and movement which were then given to three separate HMM networks for classification. PCA represents a global image feature to provide a measure for hand configuration and hand orientation. Kurtosis position is used as a local feature for measuring edges and reflecting the place of articulation recognition. Kurtosis is a fourth order moment that measures edgeness (non-Gaussianity). It gives a measure of how outlier-prone a distribution is and it is defined by:

$$Kurt(x) = E(x - \mu)^4 / \sigma^4 \tag{14}$$

where,

μ is the mean of the original image x and σ is the standard deviation.
MCC represents the hand trajectory.

  - B-Spline curve was used as a feature for recognizing Indian Sign Language (ISL) Alphabets and Numerals (Geetha & Manjusha, 2012). The proposed method at first approximates the boundary extracted from the Region of Interest, to a B-Spline curve by taking the Maximum Curvature Points (MCPs) as the control points. Then the B-Spline curve is subjected to iterations for smoothening resulting in the extraction of Key Maximum Curvature Points (KMCPs), which are the key contributors of the gesture shape. A translation and scale invariant feature vector is obtained from the spatial locations of the KMCPs in the 8 Octant Regions of the 2D Space which is given for classification.
  - An algorithm for extracting 2D motion trajectories for implementation in hand gesture recognition systems was proposed by Yang et al. (2002). At first, a multiscale segmentation is performed to generate homogeneous regions in each frame. Regions between consecutive frames are then matched to obtain two-view correspondences. Affine transformations are computed from each pair of corresponding regions to define pixel matches. Pixels matches over consecutive image pairs are concatenated to obtain pixel-level motion trajectories across the image sequence.
  - A method for dynamic gesture trajectory modeling and recognition was presented in by Wang et al. (2012). Adaboost algorithm is used to detect the user's hand and a contour-based hand tracker is formed combining condensation and partitioned sampling. Each dynamic hand gesture instance is represented by a time series of the hand's location using:

$$p_t = (x_t, y_t), t = 1, 2, ... T \tag{15}$$

where,

T represents the length of gesture path and varies for different gesture instances.

Orientation of hand movement is considered as local feature and it is computed using:

$$\theta_t = \arctan\left(\frac{y_{t+1} - y_t}{x_{t+1} - x_t}\right), t = 1, 2, ..., T \tag{16}$$

Cubic B-spline curve is considered as a global feature. It is obtained by approximately fitting the trajectory points into a curve. The cubic B-Spline curve is represented using:

$$p(t) = \sum_{m=0}^{3} B_m(t) CP_m \tag{17}$$

where,

$B_m(t)$ represents the B-Spline function and CP_m indicates the control points.

However, the same gesture may vary in speed. So, to overcome this problem, all curves are scaled such that they lie within the same range. Those curves for faster moves are relatively expanded by interpolation and those of slower moves are contracted.

Moreover, the trajectories of the same gesture may vary in size and shape. So, invariant B-spline curve moments are considered as global features to represent the trajectory. Such moments are invariant to translation, rotation, and scale.

CLASSIFICATION

Classification is a statistical method that takes feature set as input and gives a class labeled output, which are the required output gestures (Theodoridis & Koutroumbas, 2006). The classifiers which are widely used in gesture recognition are:

Artificial Neural Network (ANN)

ANN is a feed-forward network consisting of an input layer, one or more hidden layers and an output layer interconnected by modifiable weights represented by links between layers. Such type of networks are used in pattern recognition where the input units represent the components of a feature vector and where signals emitted by the output units will be the values of the discriminant functions used for classification (Duda, Hart, & Stork, 2009). ANN's are preferred for representing and recognizing static gestures, however, they are not suitable for interpreting dynamic gestures because these gestures change sequentially over time and hence a single trained ANN cannot be used for recognition of these gestures. Figure 3 shows the graphical representation of an ANN.

Figure 3. Graphical representation of ANN
(Wikimedia Commons, n.d.a)

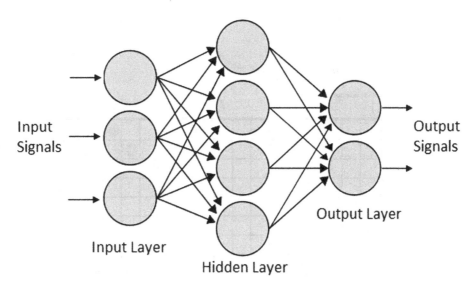

Dynamic Time Warping (DTW)

DTW approach is used for measuring similarity between two sequences which may vary in time or speed. It aims at aligning two sequences of feature vectors by warping the time axis iteratively until an optimal match between the two sequences is found (Theodoridis & Koutroumbas, 2006). The major drawback of this method of classification is that it is very time consuming since a huge number of training templates will be required to obtain a correct match for the given input pattern and the matching process has to be performed for each and every template. Moreover, recognizing non gesture patterns is a major problem in case of DTW. Figure 4 shows the DTW path for aligning two time sequences A and B. As shown in the figure, the procedure for finding the best alignment between A and B involves finding all possible routes through the grid and for each one computing the overall distance, which is defined as the sum of the distances between the individual elements on the warping path. Consequently, the final DTW distance between A and B is the minimum overall distance over all possible warping paths.

Statistical Models

Hidden Markov Model (HMM) and Conditional Random Field (CRF) are statistical models based on probabilistic approach for recognizing and labelling sequential data i.e. patterns which appear over a sequence of time (Yang, Sclaroff, & Lee, 2009).

Hidden Markov Model

HMMs are used to find out the most probable hidden states that generates a sequence of observable states. The graphical representation of HMM is shown in Figure 5. It finds a hidden state sequence which maximizes the joint probability $P(X,Y)$, where X refers to observations and Y refers to label sequences/ hidden states. It is given by:

Figure 4. DTW warping path
(GenTxWarper, n.d.a)

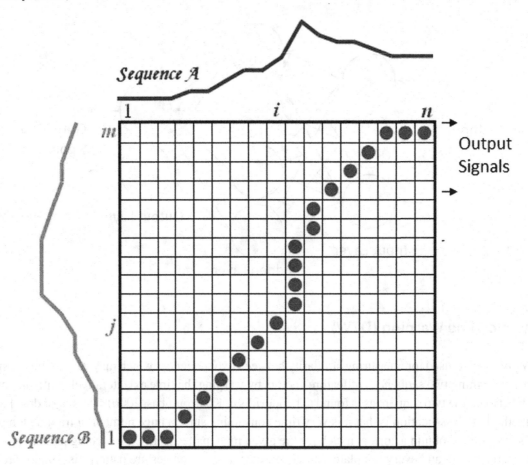

$$P(X,Y) = \prod_{t=1}^{T} P(Y_t \, / \, Y_{t-1})P(X_t \, / \, Y_t) \tag{18}$$

where,

$P(Y_t \, / \, Y_{t-1})$ is the transition distribution which represents the probability of going from one state at time *t-1* to another at time *t* and, $P(X_t \, /Y_t)$ is the observation distribution which indicates the probability that observation X_t was generated by the state Y_t (Nazerfard, Das, Cook, & L. B. Holder, 2010).

Conditional Random Field

CRFs are a framework based on conditional probability approaches for segmenting and labelling sequential data. CRFs use a single exponential distribution to model all labels of given observations. The graphical representation of HMM is shown in Figure 6. In CRFs, the probability of label sequence *Y*, given observation sequence *X*, is found using a normalized product of potential functions. Thus the conditional probability is given by (Yang, Sclaroff, & Lee, 2009):

Figure 5. Graphical representation of HMM
(Wang et al., 2006)

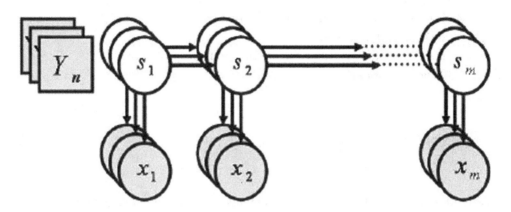

Figure 6. Graphical representation of CRF
(Wang et al., 2006)

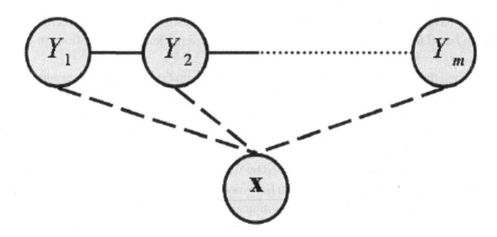

$$P_\theta\left(\frac{Y}{X}\right) = \frac{1}{Z_\theta(X)} exp\left(\sum_{i=1}^{n} F_\theta\left(Y_{i-1}, Y_i, X, i\right)\right) \tag{19}$$

In equation (19),

$$F_\theta\left(Y_{i-1}, Y_i, X, i\right) = \sum_v \lambda_v t_v\left(Y_{i-1}, Y_i, X, i\right) + \sum_m \mu_m S_m\left(Y_i, X, i\right) \tag{20}$$

where,

$t_v(Y_{i-1}, Y_i, X, i)$ is a transition feature function of observation sequence X at positions i and $i-1$. A transition feature function indicates whether a feature value is observed between two states or not.

$s_m(Y_i, X, i)$ is a state feature function of observation sequence at position *i*. A state feature function indicates whether a feature value is observed at a particular label or not.

Y_{i-1} and Y_i are labels of observation sequence *X* at position *i* and *i-1*.

n is the length of the observation sequence.

λ_v and μ_m are weights of transition and state feature functions, respectively.

$Z_\theta(X)$ is the normalization factor and is given by:

$$Z_\theta\left(X\right) = \sum_Y exp\left(\sum_{i=1}^{n} F_\theta\left(Y_{i-1}, Y_i, X, i\right)\right) \tag{21}$$

A serious limitation of HMM is its difficulty in representing multiple interacting activities due to its very strict independence assumptions (on the observations). However, in some practical scenario there might be substantial amount of dependence between observations. CRF is advantageous in comparison to HMM because CRF doesn't consider strong independent assumptions about the observations and can be trained with a fewer samples than HMM (Yang & Sarkar, 2006).

Researchers have implemented different types of classifiers for the purpose of recognition of gestures in vision based hand gesture recognition system. Some remarkable contributions in this area are reported below:

A HMM-based threshold model was proposed by Lee and Kim (1999) to recognize and spot gestures using Motion Chain Code (MCC) as a feature. The threshold model was constructed by connecting all the states of the trained gesture models in the system. A gesture is spotted only when the likelihood of the best gesture model is higher than the adaptive threshold and the boundary points are detected using Viterbi back tracking algorithm.

A model for gesture recognition was developed by Wang et al. (2006) which incorporate hidden state variables in a discriminative multi-class random field model extending previous models for spatial CRFs into the temporal domain. The hidden state conditional random field (HCRF) model can be used either as a gesture class detector, where a single class is discriminatively trained against all other gestures, or as a multi-way gesture classifier, where discriminative models for multiple gestures are simultaneously trained. The latter approach has the potential to share useful hidden state structures across the different classification tasks, allowing higher recognition rates. In their work they have implemented HCRF-based method for arm and head gesture recognition.

Binh et al. (2005) proposed a Pseudo two-dimensional hidden Markov models (P2-DHMMs) for real-time construction of hand gesture. Since hand images are two-dimensional, it is natural to believe that the 2-D HMM, an extension to the standard HMM, will be helpful and will offer a great potential for analyzing and recognizing gesture patterns. However a fully connected 2-DHMMs lead to an algorithm of exponential complexity. To avoid the problem, the connectivity of the network has been reduced by using pseudo 2-DHMMs which retains all of the useful HMMs features. The P2-DHMMs use observation vectors that are composed of two-dimensional Discrete Cosine Transform (2-D DCT) coefficients. Unlike most other schemes, the system is robust to background clutter, does not use special glove to be worn and yet runs in real time. Furthermore, the method to combine hand region and temporal characteristics in P2-DHMMs framework is new contribution of this work.

Sminchisescu et al. (2006) have advocated an approach to human motion recognition based on extensions to Conditional Random Fields (CRF) and Maximum Entropy Markov Models (MEMM). A CRF conditions on the observation without modelling it, and therefore it avoids independence assumptions and can accommodate long range interactions among observations at different instants of time. The approach is based on non-locally defined, multiple features of the observation, represented as log-linear models, to account for correlations among successive class labels. They have demonstrated the algorithm on the task of recognizing both broader classes of human motions like walking, running, jumping, conversation or dancing, and also for finely discriminating among motion styles like slow walk or wander walk. Compared to HMMs the conditional models can significantly improve recognition performance in tests that use not only features extracted from 3D reconstructed joint angles, but also in recognition experiments that use feature descriptors extracted directly from image silhouettes.

APPLICATION OF HAND GESTURE RECOGNITION: AUTOMATIC SIGN LANGUAGE RECOGNITION

Sign languages are natural languages that use different means of expression for communication in everyday life. Automatic sign language recognition has a significant impact on human society as it can provide an opportunity for the deaf to communicate with non-signing people without the need for an interpreter.

The task of automatic sign language recognition is highly challenging due to the presence of unpredictable and ambiguous non-sign hand motions that appear in between meaningful signs. In general, Coarticulation is the phenomenon that associates one sign to another during a signed utterance. It primarily describes the modification of a given sign when performed within an utterance compared to its performance isolated (Segouat & Braffort, 2010). Movement epenthesis is a special form of coarticulation, where an additional link occurs between two consecutive signs in a signed utterance.

Researchers have put forward efforts to overcome the problems of coarticulation and movement epenthesis.

Yang et al. (2009), the authors proposed a CRF based adaptive threshold model for segmenting out signs in vocabulary and non-sign patterns. A CRF is initially constructed without a label for non-sign patterns. Then, a CRF threshold model (T-CRF) is constructed by adding a label for non-sign patterns using the weights of state and transition feature functions of the original CRF. Therefore, the proposed CRF threshold model does not need non-sign patterns for training the model. A short-sign detector, a hand appearance-based sign verification method, and a sub-sign reasoning method are also incorporated to improve sign language spotting accuracy. They have used two motion-based (directional codeword between the current and previous positions of left and right hand) and four location-based features (position of left hand and right hand, vertical symmetry of the two hands and occlusion of two hands) for recognition.

Acceleration was used as a feature for detecting the co-articulated hand strokes from the rest of the meaningful hand positions by Bhuyan et al. (2005). The idea used for estimating coarticulation from a gesture model is that co-articulation is generally characterized by fast hand movement, while that during a gesture is generally smooth and slow. The main aspect of this technique is the construction of Finite State Machine (FSM) (consisting of a finite number of key frames and the corresponding key frame durations) for each and every gesture of the predefined gesture vocabulary and subsequent classification using these FSMs. State transition occurs only when the shape similarity of Key Video Object Planes

(KVOP) and duration criteria are met. The shape similarity is measured by Hausdorff distance measure. During FSM based classification if all the states of the FSM are passed successfully then a gesture is recognized. Else, co-articulation said to be detected.

Yang and Lee (2010) proposed a novel method for spotting signs and fingerspellings, which can distinguish signs, fingerspellings, and non-sign patterns. This is achieved through a hierarchical framework consisting of three steps: Firstly, candidate segments of signs and fingerspellings are discriminated with a two layer CRF where at first the conventional CRF is trained with the extracted features and then a threshold CRF (T-CRF) is built by augmenting the CRF with one additional label that can play the role of an adaptive threshold. The two-layer CRF is then built, consisting of a T-CRF and conventional CRF. Secondly, hand shapes of detected signs and fingerspellings are verified by BoostMap embeddings. Thirdly, the motion of fingerspellings are verified using CRF in order to distinguish those which have similar hand shapes and differ only in hand trajectories.

A HMM based gesture recognition system is presented by Kelly et al. (2009) which accurately classifies a given gesture sequence as one of the pre-trained gestures as well as calculates the probability that the given gesture sequence is a movement epenthesis or not. The novelty of this work is that the movement epenthesis detection is carried out by a single HMM and requires no extra data collection or training.

A technique for generation of movement epenthesis was formulated by Chuang et al. (2006) using a non-uniform rational B-spline (NURBS) based interpolation function. The NURBS function accepts an arbitrary number of control points and can construct curves according to these irregular control points. To generate movement epenthesis, the beginning cut point (where the previous sign should stop) and end cut point (where the next sign should start) are determined based on the concatenation cost, which is a linear combination of the distance, smoothness, and image distortion costs. The distance cost is defined as the normalized Euclidian distance between the palm locations at two cut points. The smoothness cost is determined by accumulating the second derivative of the curve. The image distortion cost is then estimated from the normalized Euclidian distance between the real and generated hand images.

A continuous sign language recognition system was developed by Yang and Sarkar (2006) using a two step approach. In the first step, the sentence is segmented into individual signs and then in the second step, recognition of those signs is done. In this paper, they have shown the process of sign segmentation from continuous stream. To reduce the complexity of the segmentation process, key frames are identified as those frames in the sentence that are most different from each other and different from sign frames. Each frame in a sequence is represented using a motion snapshot based representation, capturing short term movement over few frames by considering motion of salient corner points, as detected and tracked by the KLT (Kanade-Lucas-Tomasi) method.

An enhanced level building approach was addressed Yang et al. (2010) to simultaneously segment and match signs to continuous sign language sentences in the presence of movement epenthesis using dynamic time warping (DTW) based approach. The novelty of this method is that it doesnot require explicit modelling of movement epenthesis.

KEY ISSUES

There are several real-time issues that should be handled in vision-based hand gesture recognition systems. Some of these are as follows:

- **Background Conditions:** In certain practical situations, hand gesture recognition may have to be performed under different types of backgrounds like complex background, background with multiple gesturers, dynamic background and even under different illuminations. Under such situations, the systems have to be designed in such a manner that it gives effective and accurate recognition results. Such problems are most often overcome by designing efficient algorithms in the hand segmentation stage.

- **Real-Time Hand Tracking:** Robust and real-time hand tracking holds significant importance for HCI applications like sign language recognition, controlling video games, robotics etc. (Qian et al., 2014). This is because most of the applications require high real-time tracking performance with acceptable processing speed. So, tracking of free and complex hand motions in real-time and also under complex background situations can highly facilitate the interaction with computers in a more perceptive way and as such the communication becomes more natural. From the state of art survey it is seen that combining point of interest (hand location) and color likelihood often provides improved hand tracking results (Donoser and Bischof, 2008).

- **Feature Selection:** Selection of appropriate features plays a fundamental role in efficient recognition. Features should be selected in such a manner that it justifies the type of application which is to be performed. In many cases it is seen that combining multiple features for recognizing hand gestures provides better recognition rates than considering single feature.

- **Coarticulation and Movement Epenthesis (ME):** Coarticulation is a vital aspect that needs to be handled in continuous sign language recognition systems. Due to this phenomenon, the appearance of signs especially at the beginning and at the end can be significantly different under

Figure 7. Cartoon images of hand shapes representing letters of interest
(Jerde, Soechting, & Flanders, 2003)

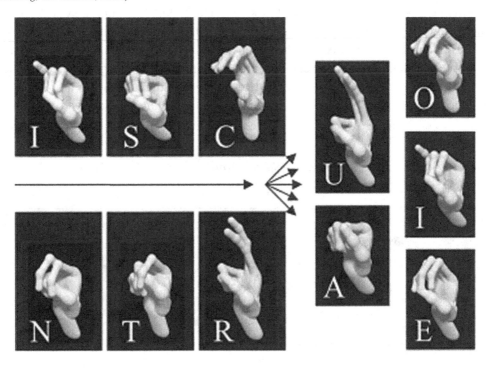

different sentence contexts, which makes the recognition of signs in sentences hard (Yang & Sarkar, 2006). Coarticulation may occur due to hand shape, hand position, sign language speed (Li, Wang, & Kong, 2013), contact type (Ormel, Crasborn, & Koochi, 2013), pinky finger extension (Keane,), thumb position (Crasborn, 2001) etc.

- **Coarticulation in American Sign Language (ASL) Finger Spelling:** Coarticulation in finger spelling is typically characterized as assimilation (where sequential hand shapes become more similar to one another) or dissimilation (where sequential hand shapes become more different). Fig. 7 shows some cartoon images of letters of interest in ASL. Here we can see that the letter C is almost similar to A, but has a significant difference with U. If we consider the spelling of the letters one by one for the words DISCUSS and DISCARD (having same preceding letters before I and different following letters after C, we will observe that there is a difference in movements from S to C for the two words. Similarly, if we consider the words DISCARD and CONFISCATE (having different preceding letters before I and same following letters after S), then also the same phenomenon happens (Jerde, Soechting, & Flanders, 2003).

- **Movement Epenthesis:** Movement Epenthesis is a special form of coarticulation, where an intermediate movement occurs between two signs as shown in Figure 8 (Yang, Sarkar, & Loeding, 2010).

Table 1 presents a summary of some of the research works which have focused on resolving the critical problems hindering vision-based hand gesture recognition.

CONCLUSION

In this chapter, various types of hand gesture recognition methods and its application in automatic sign language recognition is highlighted. Various blocks of hand gesture recognition system are discussed with related research works. As the hand gesture recognition is suffered from background conditions, a few glimpses about relevant works have been considered. A few serious problems like movement epenthesis and coarticulation which prevent from proper continuous sign language recognition are also covered. It is seen that although glove-based hand gesture recognition techniques are accurate, vision-based techniques are preferable because of the naturalness of the hand movement and ease of operation.

Figure 8. Movement Epenthesis in continuous hand gestures
(Bhuyan, Ghosh, & Bora, 2005)

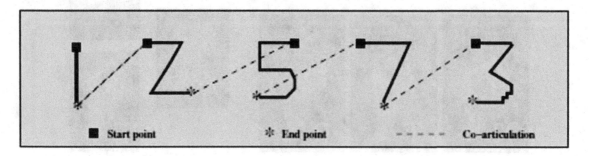

Table 1. Various research issues in vision based hand gesture recognition

Reference	Problem Identified	Method Used	Inference
Zhang et al., 2008	Complex background	Based on differencing background image between consecutive image frames using 3σ principle of normal distribution	Effective to eliminate noise due to illumination and shadow changes.
Lee et al., 2004	Complex background	(1) Frame differencing followed by entropy measurement to get color information in order to separate out the hand region (2) Chain code of the detected hand contour is taken as feature for recognition	(1) Invariant to change in lighting condition and is user-independent (2) System is able to recognize 6 types of hand postures with around 95% recognition rate
Saavedra et al., 2013	Variation in lighting condition	(1) Hand location is obtained by using STELA, which is then used to extract a training region for the hand (2) The color of the training region is used as a tool for segmenting the hand region from the background	Handles a variety of skin colors and illumination conditions
Chen et al., 2003	Real time hand tracking	(1) Hand region is extracted by combining motion, skin color and edge information (2) Fourier descriptor as spatial feature and motion analysis as temporal feature comprises of the feature vector which is fed to a HMM for recognition	(1) Robust and reliable in complex background (2) The system is tested for 20 different types of gestures and provides a recognition rate of around 90%
Binh et al., 2005	Real time hand tracking	(1) Hand location estimated by using a Kalman filter, serves as a starting point for searching a skin colored region (2) The skin color region which gives the best match to the estimated hand location is the segmented hand region.	(1) The system is fast and fairly robust to background clutter. (2) Recognition accuracy up to 98% has been achieved on a single handed database comprising of 36 American Sign Language (ASL) alphabets and digits
Agrawal et al., 2012	Feature selection	Shape descriptors, HOG and SIFT are combined to form a feature vector for recognizing two-handed signs of ISL using a multiclass Support Vector Machine (SVM)	(1) Provides a recognition rate of around 95% while testing 36 different signs performed by 4 users (2) Incorporating multiple features provides better results than considering the features individually
Zaki et al., 2011	Feature selection	(1) Feature vector comprises of three appearance based features: PCA, Kurtosis position and MCC to represent four important components of sign language viz. hand shape, place of articulation, orientation and movement (2) A three-layer HMM network is used for recognition	(1) Recognizes manual gestures of ASL. Different combinations of features were tested for recognition purpose. Amongst them, fusing all the three proposed features provided the least error rate. (2)Limitation is that the system fails to detect the hand in case of hand over face occlusion

continued on following page

Table 1. Continued

Reference	Problem Identified	Method Used	Inference
Yang et al., 2009	Coarticulation	(1) A CRF based threshold model is built for separating out signs in vocabulary and non-sign patterns (2) Two motion based features viz. MCC for left and right hand and four location based features viz. position of left hand and right hand, vertical symmetry of the two hands and occlusion of two hands are used for recognition (3) A short sign detector, hand appearance based sign verification system and a sub-sign detector are also included to enhance the sign spotting accuracy	(1) The proposed system does not require non-sign patterns for training the CRF model (2) Provides a recognition rate of 87% for spotting signs from continuous data and 93.5% for spotting signs from isolated data
Yang et al., 2006	Coarticulation	(1) To reduce the computational complexity of the sign segmentation process, the key frames are identified as those frames which are most alike from each other. This is done by finding the short term motion over frames (2) Key frames are then modelled as sign or coarticulation using a CRF	(1) The proposed CRF based model for sign segmentation proves to be more efficient than HMM based one (2) It is computationally efficient as it requires to label only the key frames instead of all the frames in the sign sentence video
Bhuyan et al., 2005	Coarticulation	(1) Acceleration is used as a feature for identifying the coarticulation phase from a continuous gesture sequence (2) A Finite State Machine (FSM) is trained for each and every gesture taking shape of gesture and duration as features	(1) Two sets of sequentially connected gestures were tested: The first set comprises of gestures which are performed one after another at a specific interval, and they can be accurately classified by using acceleration as feature. The second set comprises of gestures where the endpoint of one gesture is the start point of the next gesture, and they can be separated out using FSM based classification
Chuang et al., 2006	Movement Epenthesis (ME)	For generating ME, the beginning and end cut points (where the NURBS curve depicting ME is fitted) are determined based on concatenation cost which is a linear combination of distance, smoothness and image distortion costs	The proposed method enables to concatenate sign language video clips performed by real signers to create sign language sentences without abrupt change in palm movement, face rotation or hand shape difference
Yang et al., 2010	Movement Epenthesis (ME)	An enhanced level building algorithm is formulated to simultaneously segment and match signs to continuous sign language sentences using DTW based approach	(1)The efficiency of the proposed algorithm was tested on a dataset comprising of 39 different signs articulated in 25 different continuous sentences, providing a recognition rate of around 83% (2) Novelty of this approach is that it doesnot require explicit modelling of ME
Kelly et al., 2009	Movement Epenthesis (ME)	A HMM based threshold model is constructed for classifying a given sign sequence as one of the pre-trained signs or ME	ME detection is carried out using a single HMM and does not require extra data collection or training

REFERENCES

Agrawal, S. C., Jalal, A. S., & Bhatnagar, C. (2012). Recognition of Indian Sign Language using Feature Fusion. *Proceedings of 4th International Conference on Intelligent Human Computer Interaction.* Kharagpur. IEEE. doi:10.1109/IHCI.2012.6481841

Ahmed, S. M. H., Alexander, T. C., & Anagnostopoulo, G. C. (2008). Real-time, Static and Dynamic Hand Gesture Recognition for Human-Computer Interaction. Retrieved December 22, 2014 from http://www.machine-learning.net/amalthea-reu.org/pubs/amalthea_tr_2008_01.pdf

Bhuyan, M. K., Ghosh, D., & Bora, P. K. (2005). *Co-articulation Detection in Hand Gestures. TENCON.* Melbourne: IEEE.

Binh, N. D., Shuichia, E., & Ejima, T. (2005). Real-Time Hand Tracking and Gesture Recognition System. *Proceedings of International Conference on Graphics, Vision and Image Processing (GVIP).* Cairo.

Chen, F., Fu, C., & Huang, C. L. (2003). Hand Gesture Recognition using a Real-Time Tracking Method and Hidden Markov Models. *Image and Vision Computing, 21*(8), 745–758. doi:10.1016/S0262-8856(03)00070-2

Choudhury, A., Talukdar, A. K., & Sarma, K. K. (2014). A Conditional Random Field based Indian Sign Language Recognition System under Complex Background. *Proceedings of International Conference on Communication Systems and Network Technologies (CSNT).* Bhopal. IEEE. doi:10.1109/CSNT.2014.185

Chuang, Z. J., Wu, C. H., & Chen, W. S. (2006). Movement Epenthesis Generation Using NURBS-Based Spatial Interpolation. *IEEE Transactions on Circuits and Systems for Video Technology, 16*(11), 1313–1323. doi:10.1109/TCSVT.2006.883509

Crasborn, O. (2001). Phonetic Implementation of Phonological Categories in Sign Language of the Netherlands [Doctoral dissertation]. Leiden University Repository.

Cui, Y., & Weng, J. (1999). A Learning-Based Prediction-and-Verification Segmentation Scheme for Hand Sign Image Sequence. *Pattern Analysis and Machine Intelligence, 21*(8), 798–804. doi:10.1109/34.784311

Donoser, M., & Bischof, H. (2008). Real Time Appearance based Hand Tracking. *Proceedings of International Conference on Pattern Recognition (ICPR).* Tampa: IEEE.

Duda, R. O., Hart, P. E., & Stork, D. G. (2009). *Pattern Classification.* India: Wiley India.

Geetha, M., & Manjusha, U. C. (2012). A Vision Based Recognition of Indian Sign Language Alphabets and Numerals Using B-Spline Approximation. *International Journal on Computer Science and Engineering, 4*(3), 406–415.

DTW algorithm. (n. d.). GenTxWarper. Retrieved from http://www.psb.ugent.be/cbd/papers/gentxwarper/DTWalgorithm.htm

Hamada, Y., Shimada, N., & Shirai, Y. (2004). Hand Shape Estimation under Complex Backgrounds for Sign Language Recognition. *Proceedings of 6th International Conference on Automatic Face and Gesture Recognition*. IEEE. doi:10.1109/AFGR.2004.1301597

Hsieh, C. C., Liou, D. H., & Lee, D. (2012). A Real Time Hand Gesture Recognition System using Motion History Image. *Proceedings of International Conference on Signal Processing Systems (ICSPS)*. Dalian. IEEE.

Jerde, T. E., Soechting, J. F., & Flanders, M. (2003). Coarticulation in Fluent Fingerspelling. *The Journal of Neuroscience*, 23(6), 2383–2393. PMID:12657698

Keane, J. (n. d.). Variation in Fingerspelling Time, Pinky Extension and What it Means to be Active. *Cognition and Computation Workshops*. University of Chicago.

Kelly, D., McDonald, J., & Markham, C. (2009). Recognizing Spatiotemporal Gestures and Movement Epenthesis in Sign Language. *Proceedings of 13th International Machine Vision and Image Processing Conference*. Dublin. IEEE. doi:10.1109/IMVIP.2009.33

Lee, H. K., & Kim, J. H. (1999). An HMM-Based Threshold Model Approach for Gesture Recognition. *Pattern Analysis and Machine Intelligence*, 21(10), 961–973. doi:10.1109/34.799904

Lee, J. S., Lee, Y. J., Lee, E. H., & Hong, S. H. (2004). Hand Region Extraction and Gesture Recognition from Video Stream with Complex Background through Entropy Analysis. *Proceedings of 26th Annual International Conference of Engineering in Medicine and Biology Society*. San Francisco. IEEE.

Li, S., Wang, L., & Kong, D. (2013). *Synthesis of Sign Language Coarticulation based on Key Frames*. Multimed Tools Appl. Doi:10.1007/s11042-013-1724-1

Lu, Y. C. (2011). Background Subtraction Based Segmentation Using Object Motion Feedback. *Proceedings of 1st International Conference on Robot Vision and Signal Processing (RVSP)*. Kaohsiung. IEEE. doi:10.1109/RVSP.2011.9

Murthy, G. R. S., & Jadon, R. S. (2009). A Review of Vision Based Hand Gestures Recognition. *International Journal of Information Technology and Knowledge Management*, 2(2), 405–410.

Nazerfard, E., Das, B., Cook, D. J., & Holder, L. B. (2010). Conditional Random Fields for Activity Recognition in Smart Environments. *International Symposium on Human Informatics (SIGHIT)*. doi:10.1145/1882992.1883032

Ormel, E., Crasborn, O., & Koochi, E. (2013). Coarticulation of Hand Height in Sign Language of the Netherlands is Affected by Contact type. *Journal of Phonetics*, 41(3-4), 156–171. doi:10.1016/j.wocn.2013.01.001

Phung, S. L., Bouzerdoum, A., & Chai, D. (2005). Skin Segmentation Using Color Pixel Classification: Analysis and Comparison. *Pattern Analysis and Machine Intelligence*, 27(1), 148–151. doi:10.1109/TPAMI.2005.17 PMID:15628277

Prabhakar, N., Vaithiyanathan, V., Sharma, A. P., Singh, A., & Singhal, P. (2012). Object Tracking Using Frame Differencing and Template Matching. *Research Journal of Applied Sciences. Engineering and Technology*, *4*(24), 5497–5501.

Qian, C., Sun, X., Wei, Y., Tang, X., & Sun, J. (2014). Real Time and Robust Hand Tracking from Depth. In *Proceedings of Computer Vision and Pattern Recognition* (pp. 1106–1113). CVPR.

Rautaray, S. S., & Agrawal, A. (2015). Vision Based Hand Gesture Recognition for Human Computer Interaction: A Survey. *Artificial Intelligence Review*, *43*(1), 1–54. doi:10.1007/s10462-012-9356-9

Saavedra, J. M., Bustos, B., & Chang, V. (2013). An Accurate Hand Segmentation Approach using a Structure based Shape Localization Technique. *Proceedings of International Conference on Computer Vision Theory and Applications (VISAPP)*.

Segouat, J., & Braffort, A. (2010). Toward Modeling Sign Language Coarticulation. *Gesture in Embodied Communication and Human-Computer Interaction*, *5934*, 325–336. doi:10.1007/978-3-642-12553-9_29

Shan, C., Tan, T., & Wei, Y. (2007). Real-Time Hand Tracking using a Mean Shift Embedded Particle Filter. *Pattern Recognition*, *40*(7), 1958–1970. doi:10.1016/j.patcog.2006.12.012

Shin, J. H., Lee, J. S., Kil, S. K., Shen, D. F., Ryu, J. G., & Lee, E. H. et al. (2006). Hand Region Extraction and Gesture Recognition using Entropy Analysis. *International Journal of Computer Science and Network Security*, *6*(2A), 216–222.

Sminchisescu, C., Kanaujia, A., Li, Z., & Metaxas, D. (2006). Conditional Models for Contextual Human Motion Recognition. *Proceedings of International Conference on Computer Vision (ICCV)*. Beijing. IEEE. doi:10.1016/j.cviu.2006.07.014

Stenger, B., Mendonça, P., & Cipolla, R. (2001). Model-Based Hand Tracking using an Unscented Kalman Filter. Proceedings of British Machine Vision. UK. doi:10.5244/C.15.8

Tewari, D., & Srivastava, S. K. (2012). A Visual Recognition of Static Hand Gestures in Indian Sign Language based on Kohonen Self- Organizing Map Algorithm. *International Journal of Engineering and Advanced Technology*, *2*(2), 165–170.

Theodoridis, S., & Koutroumbas, K. (2006). *Pattern Recognition*. USA: Elsevier.

Wang, S. B., Quattoni, A., Morency, L. P., Demirdjian, D., & Darrell, T. (2006). Hidden Conditional Random Fields for Gesture Recognition. *Proceedings of Computer Society Conference on Computer Vision and Pattern Recognition (CVPR)* (Vol. 2, pp. 1521-1527). IEEE.

Wang, X., Xia, M., Cai, H., Gao, Y., & Cattani, C. (2012). Hidden-Markov-Models-Based Dynamic Hand Gesture Recognition. *Mathematical Problems in Engineering*, 2012 (2012). Article ID 986134. Retrieved from.10.1155/2012/986134

Artificial Neural Network. (2014, December 22). Retrieved Wikimedia Commons. from http://commons.wikimedia.org/wiki/Artificial_neural_network

Yang, H. D., & Lee, S. W. (2010). Robust Sign Language Recognition with Hierarchical Conditional Random Fields. *Proceedings of 20th International Conference on Pattern Recognition (ICPR)*. Istanbul. IEEE. doi:10.1109/ICPR.2010.539

Yang, H. D., Sclaroff, S., & Lee, S. W. (2009). Sign Language Spotting with a Threshold Model Based on Conditional Random Fields. *Pattern Analysis and Machine Intelligence, 31*(7), 1264–1277. doi:10.1109/TPAMI.2008.172 PMID:19443924

Yang, M. H., Ahuja, N., & Tabb, M. (2002). Extraction of 2D Motion Trajectories and its Application to Hand Gesture Recognition. *Pattern Analysis and Machine Intelligence, 24*(8), 1061–1074. doi:10.1109/TPAMI.2002.1023803

Yang, M. H., Ahuja, N., & Tabb, M. (2002). Extraction of 2D Motion Trajectories and Its Application to Hand Gesture Recognition. *Pattern Analysis and Machine Intelligence, 24*(8), 1061–1074. doi:10.1109/TPAMI.2002.1023803

Yang, R., & Sarkar, S. (2006). Detecting Coarticulation in Sign Language using Conditional Random Fields. *In Proceedings of International Conference on Pattern Recognition (ICPR)* (Vol. 2, pp. 108-112). Hong Kong. IEEE. doi:10.1109/ICPR.2006.431

Yang, R., Sarkar, S., & Loeding, B. (2010). Handling Movement Epenthesis and Hand Segmentation Ambiguities in Continuous Sign Language Recognition Using Nested Dynamic Programming. *Pattern Analysis and Machine Intelligence, 32*(3), 462–477. doi:10.1109/TPAMI.2009.26 PMID:20075472

Yuan, M., Farbiza, F., Manders, C. M., & Yin, T. K. (2009). Robust Hand Tracking using a Simple Color Classification Technique. *International Journal of Virtual Reality*, 7-12.

Zaki, M. M., & Shaheen, S. I. (2011). Sign Language Recognition Using a Combination of New Vision Based Features. *Pattern Recognition Letters, 32*(4), 572–577. doi:10.1016/j.patrec.2010.11.013

Zhang, Q., Chen, F., & Liu, X. (2008). Hand Gesture Detection and Segmentation Based on Difference Background Image with Complex Background. *Proceedings of International Conference on Embedded Software and Systems*. Sichuan. IEEE. doi:10.1109/ICESS.2008.23

KEY TERMS AND DEFINITIONS

Conditional Random Field (CRF): CRFs are a framework based on conditional probability approaches for segmenting and labelling sequential data. CRFs use a single exponential distribution to model all labels of given observations.

Dynamic Time Warping (DTW): DTW approach is used for measuring similarity between two sequences which may vary in time or speed. It aims at aligning two sequences of feature vectors by warping the time axis iteratively until an optimal match between the two sequences is found.

Gesture Recognition: A gesture may be defined as a physical movement of body parts such as hands, arms, head, face etc. to express some information or feelings and the ability of a computer or any processing system to understand the meaning of these gestures is referred to as gesture recognition.

Human-Computer Interaction (HCI): It is the study, planning, design and uses of the interfaces between human and computers.

Sign Languages: Sign languages are natural languages that use different means of expression for communication in everyday life.

Chapter 12
Acoustic Modeling of Speech Signal using Artificial Neural Network:
A Review of Techniques and Current Trends

Mousmita Sarma
Gauhati University, India

Kandarpa Kumar Sarma
Gauhati University, India

ABSTRACT

Acoustic modeling of the sound unit is a crucial component of Automatic Speech Recognition (ASR) system. This is the process of establishing statistical representations for the feature vector sequences for a particular sound unit so that a classifier for the entire sound unit used in the ASR system can be designed. Current ASR systems use Hidden Markov Model (HMM) to deal with temporal variability and Gaussian Mixture Model (GMM) for acoustic modeling. Recently machine learning paradigms have been explored for application in speech recognition domain. In this regard, Multi Layer Perception (MLP), Recurrent Neural Network (RNN) etc. are extensively used. Artificial Neural Network (ANN)s are trained by back propagating the error derivatives and therefore have the potential to learn much better models of nonlinear data. Recently, Deep Neural Network (DNN)s with many hidden layer have been up voted by the researchers and have been accepted to be suitable for speech signal modeling. In this chapter various techniques and works on the ANN based acoustic modeling are described.

INTRODUCTION

Acoustic and temporal modelings are the two major issues associated with an Automatic Speech Recognition (ASR) system. Speech is naturally dynamic in nature. The spectral and temporal variations of speech signals are due to speech production nature. Speech signal is produced by moving the articulators

DOI: 10.4018/978-1-4666-8493-5.ch012

to different position necessary for the target sound unit. Due to the variation in the articulator's motions, instead of producing a sequence of clean identical phonetic units, a sequence of trajectories or signature is obtained in the form of a speech signal. This makes it difficult to extract exact timing information as well as spectral information of the speech units from the speech signal. Therefore, modeling of speech signal needs to consider both these issues.

An ASR system uses acoustic models to extract information from the acoustic signal. In the pattern recognition based approach of speech recognition, basic recognition units are modeled acoustically based on some lexical description, which is essentially a mapping between acoustic measurement and phoneme. Such mappings are learned by a finite training set of utterances. The resulting speech units are called phone like unit (PLU) which is an acoustic description of that speech unit as present in the training set (Brown, 1987).

Thus handling temporal and spectral variability are the main challenges of ASR and currently the best known speech recognition technology prefers Hidden Markov Model (HMM), which provides solution to both these problems. Acoustic modeling is performed by discrete density models and temporal modeling is performed by state transitions (Xiong, 2009). HMM considers the speech signal as quasi- static for short durations and models these frames for recognition. It breaks the feature vector of the signal into a number of states and finds the probability of a signal to transit from one state to another (Rabiner & Juang 1993). Viterbi search, forward-backward and Baum-Welch algorithms are used for parameter estimation and optimization (Rabiner, 1989) (Juang & Rabiner, 1991). But in speech recognition HMM based acoustic modeling has a serious disadvantage. It suffers from quantization errors and poor parametric modeling. The standard Maximum Likelihood (ML) training criterion leads to poor discrimination between the acoustic models. Also the independence assumption makes it hard to exploit multiple input frames; and the first-order assumption makes it hard to model co- articulation and duration (Tebelskis, 1995)

Later after the introduction of Expectation Maximization (EM) algorithm (Rolf, 1974), GMM has been used for acoustic modeling. The probability distribution of the feature vectors associated with the HMM states can be modeled by GMM with higher accuracy. This facilitates the successful implementation of GMM-HMM systems for speech recognition as preferred by present day systems.

Despite of its outstanding performance in terms of accuracy, GMM has some disadvantages, like it requires huge amount of training data and processing speed. But the major drawback of GMM is that it requires a large number of diagonal Gaussians or a large number full covariance Gaussians to model data which lies near a non linear surface in the data space (Hinton, Deng, Yu, Dahl, Mohamed, Jaitly, Senior, Vanhoucke, Nguyen, Sainath & Kingsbury, 2012). Using large coefficients is not statistically efficient since underlying structure of speech signal is much lower dimensional.

This makes the researchers to think about some other methods for acoustic modeling. In this regard, Artificial Neural Network (ANN) appears to be an effective alternative, due to its inherent capability to learn data both linear and non-linear, show adaptive behavior, exhibit robustness to sudden variations like noise, parallel and discriminative nature of learning, retain and use it subsequently. In this respect, it closely resembles the processing nature of the human brain. Further, recent advances in very large scale integrated (VLSI) circuit technology system on chip (SoC) design of ANN have enabled implementation of bio-inspired attributes in ASR systems. ANN can model a diversity of speaking styles and background conditions with much less training data, because of the distributive representation of input. ANNs are constituted many layers of artificial neurons each of which individually can learn, retain the learning, use it subsequently and contribute to the cumulative processing capability of the network. Many neurons simultaneously process each of the stimulation received which maybe segments of a pattern and produces a response which collectively represent the total response to an input vector. This make ANN exponentially compact than GMM and enables it to generate true non-linear computing so essential for dealing with a complex phenomena like speech signal processing. ANN can also combine diverse features including both discrete and continuous. Further, ANN does not require detailed assumptions about the data distribution while estimating HMM states. Thus ANN provides potential advantage in acoustic modeling (Mohamed, Dahl & Hinton, 2012). The best ASR systems today prefer ANN as a tool to model the speech template and generate class labels to assist HMM based classifiers. Therefore, there is necessity to highlight some of the recent developments in this regard and present a review of the trend which focuses on the use of ANN as a part of an evolving ASR system.

This chapter provides a review on the state of art of ANN based acoustic modeling of speech unit used in ASR technology. Fist section of the chapter provides brief introduction of the acoustic modeling of speech signal and current approaches. In the second section statistical approaches of acoustic modeling using HMM and GMM are considered. The relative merits and demerits of these approaches are also described. The third section of the chapter covers the ANN based acoustic modeling where initially various woks sing various structure of ANN is described. Later, a few works using deep neural networks are described specifically.

ACOUSTIC MODELING OF SPEECH SIGNAL USING HMM AND GMM FOR ASR

Acoustic model is used to model the statistics of speech features for each speech unit of the language such as a phone or a word. Figure 1 shows the basic block diagram of a speech recognition system. As can be seen from Figure 1, acoustic models are required to analyze the speech feature vectors for their acoustic content. The acoustic models can be a template of the speech unit to be modeled. During recognition, an unknown word can be recognized by simply comparing it against all known templates and finding the closest match. But templates cannot model acoustic variability. Hence, acoustic models basically build using the probability distribution over the acoustic space. Probability distributions can be modeled by using both parametric and non-parametric techniques. In the parametric way, the basic assumption is the Gaussian distribution which simply finds the parameters to represent it (Rabiner & Juang, 1993).

ASR technology has shown significant improvement during the last two decades. Current best known systems are reliable in recognizing telephone quality and spontaneous speech, whereas earlier systems were only able to recognize isolated words. However, the basic acoustic modeling and feature extraction techniques have not gone through any evolution phase and the ASR system is far away from human like performance in real usage scenarios. Most of the improvements in ASR systems are basically in the domain of pre-processing, feature extraction, language modeling or model adaptation of such HMM/GMM systems. Therefore, it has been a core area of research.

The ASR problem is formulated initially as a statistical classification problem. Classes have been defined as the sequence of words W from a closed vocabulary and the parametric representation of the input speech signal defined as X. The classification problem is then stated as finding the sequence of words W which maximizes the quantity, $P(W \mid X)$, given as

Figure 1. Basic block diagram of a speech recognition system

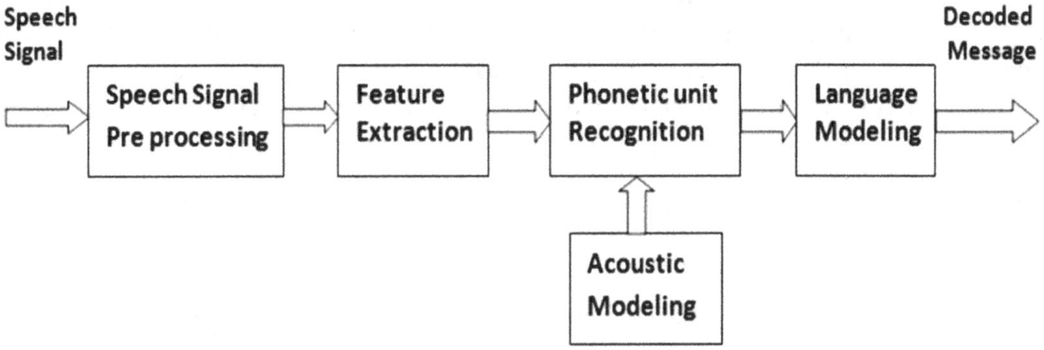

$$P\left(W \mid X\right) = \frac{P\left(X \mid W\right) P\left(W\right)}{P\left(X\right)}$$

The quantity $P\left(W\right)$ is usually referred to as the *language model* which depends on high-level constraints and linguistic knowledge about allowed word strings for that specific task. The quantity $P\left(X \mid W\right)$ is known as the *acoustic model*. It describes the statistics of sequences of parameterized acoustic observations in the feature space given the corresponding uttered words (Brown, 1987) (Salvi, 2006) (Trentin & Gori, 2001).

Earlier ASR system had used HMM for these acoustic modeling. In ASR, an HMM can be used to model a word in the task-dependent vocabulary, where each state of the hidden part represents a phoneme or phonetical unit, whereas the observable part accounts for the statistical characteristics of the corresponding acoustic events in a given feature space. Examples of event that is to be modeled are collected and used in conjunction with training algorithm like Viterbi or Baum-Welch re-estimation algorithm in order to learn proper estimates of the HMM parameters. Once training has been done, the HMM can be used for recognition. Recognition or classification means assigning each new sequence of observations to the most alike model using the maximum likelihood (ML) criteria. However, HMM suffers from some limitations. Standard continuous density HMMs, trained with Baum-Welch or Viterbi algorithms, present poor discriminative power among different models, since they are based on the ML criterion. The classical HMMs rely on strong assumptions of the statistical properties of the phenomenon at hand. For instance, the stochastic processes involved are modeled by first-order Markov chains and the parametric form of the probability density functions (PDF) that represents the emission probabilities associated with all states is heavily constraining. In addition, the number of parameters in HMMs strongly limits their suitability for hardware implementation (Hagen & Morris, 2005) (Trentin & Gori, 2001) (Frikha & Hamida, 2012).

Later HMM/GMM hybrid ASR system come, which has HMM as a model of the sequential structure of speech signals, with each HMM state using a GMM to model the acoustic characteristics of sound unit. The most common spectral representation is a set of mel frequency cepstral coefficients (MFCC)s or perceptual linear prediction (PLP) derived from a window of about 20 ms of speech overlapped by about 10 ms frame and each frame of coefficients is augmented with differences and differences of differences with nearby frames. The GMM can be viewed as a hybrid between parametric and non-parametric density models. Like a parametric model, it has structure and parameters that control the behavior of density in known ways. Like non-parametric model it has many degrees of freedom to allow arbitrary density modeling. Each state of HMMs is represented by a GMM to model the distribution of feature vectors for the given state. A GMM is a weighted sum of M component Gaussian densities and is described by

$$P(x \mid \lambda) = \sum_{i=1}^{M} w_i g(x \mid \mu_i \Sigma_i)$$

where, $p(x \mid \lambda)$ is the likelihood of a D-dimensional continuous-valued feature vector x, given the model parameters $\lambda = \{w_i, \ \mu_i, \ \Sigma_i\}$ and w_i are the mixture weight which satisfies the constraint $\sum_{i=1}^{M} w_i = 1$. The component Gaussian densities are given as

$$g(x \mid \mu_i, \Sigma_i), \ i = 1, 2, \dots M$$

where, each component density is a D-variate Gaussian function of the form,

$$g(x \mid \mu_i, \Sigma_i) = \frac{1}{\left(2\pi\right)^{D/2} \left|\Sigma_i\right|^{1/2}} \exp\left\{-\frac{1}{2}\left(x - \mu_i\right)' \Sigma_i^{-1}\left(x - \mu_i\right)\right\}$$

with mean vector μ_i and covariance matrix Σ_i (Reynolds, Quatieri & Dunn, 2000).

GMM considers a signal to contain different components that are independent of each other. These components represent the broad acoustic classes that represent certain vocal tract configurations (Reynolds & Rose, 1995). Thus it is more inclined towards modeling features concerning to words having specific characteristics. Each component is optimized using EM algorithm (Dempster, Laird & Rubin, 1977). The EM algorithm is an iterative method for calculating maximum likelihood distribution parameter estimates from incomplete data such as elements missing in feature vectors. The EM update equations are used which gives a procedure to iteratively maximize the log-likelihood of the training data given the model is linked (Rolf, 1974) (Singh, 2005). Various ways of combining these models have been proposed. One simple way is to use a 3 state HMM and implement GMM on the middle state to obtain the observation probabilities for that state (Rodriguez, Ruiz, Crespo & Garcia, 2003).

Although HMM/GMM frameworks have dominated other techniques for continuous speech recognition, they have some inherent limitations. First of all, HMM/GMM systems use short time spectral features such as MFCCs and PLPs. However, their design criteria are not consistent with the objective of increasing accuracy in ASR systems (Rahim, Bengio & Lecun, 1997). In addition, information about phones is spread out in a long temporal context (Hermansky & Sharma, 1999) (Schwarz, Matejka & Cernocky, 2004) (Schwarz, Matejka & Cernocky, 2006), while MFCCs or PLPs are only able to capture short time information even when their time derivatives are used. The second limitation of HMM/GMM is the assumption that observation frames at different times are conditionally independent given the state sequence. This means that the observations depend only on the state that generates them, not on neighboring observations. Next, HMM/GMM systems are generative models. However, the goal of ASR is pattern classification. Therefore, use of discriminative models for acoustic modeling seems to be more appropriate. In this regard, machine learning paradigms like ANN, Support Vector Machine (SVM) etc. have emerged for acoustic modeling as potential tools and HMM/GMM based approaches are challenged by the recent HMM/ANN systems. The following section provides a brief review of ANN based methods for acoustic modeling.

ANN FOR ACOUSTIC MODELING OF SPEECH SIGNAL

During 1980s, ANN technology was introduced in the domain of speech recognition (Hu & Hwang, 2002). The brain's impressive superiority at a wide range of cognitive skills like speech recognition has motivated the researchers to explore the possibilities of ANN models in the field of speech recognition in 1980s, with a hope that human neural network like models may ultimately lead to human like performance.

One of the core advantages of ANN in speech recognition is its ability to approximate non linear dynamical systems. Speech is basically a nonlinear signal produced by an inherently non linear system. Nonlinearity in speech signal is observed to be present in both phonetic and supra segmental domain. Speech sound production is described as a filtering process in which a speech sound source excites the vocal tract filter. If the source is periodic it produces voiced speech and if the source is noisy it produces unvoiced speech. The source of the periodicity for the voiced speech is in the larynx, where vibrating vocal cords interrupts the airflow from the lungs, producing pulses of air. The lungs provide the airflow and pressure source for speech and the vocal cords usually modulate the airflow to create many sound variations. Vocal fold oscillation, the turbulent sound source and the interaction phenomena are the evidence of non linearity. Because of nonlinear behavior of vocal fold oscillations, the spectral envelop of the glottal pulse changes with its pitch frequency and the spectral content changing with its amplitude. Similarly, the rapid variations of formant frequencies which are the resonance of vocal tract filter, is also an evidence of non linearity in phonetic level. On the other hand, rapid variation of speaking rate, speech energy, variation in fundamental frequency value, variation of acoustic realization of sound unit by different speaker etc. are the evidence of non linearity in supra segmental domain (Deng & Shaughnessy, 2003) (Faundez-Zanuy, 2002) (Esposito & Marinaro, 2002).

ANN which is also called a parallel distributed processing model, is a dense interconnection of simple non linear computation elements called neurons and this non linearity is distributed throughout the network (Haykin, 2003) (Kumar, 2009). The basic neuron model is shown in Figure 2. Here, neuron k is receiving input from $x_1, x_2, \ldots, x_N$ from N neurons, which are weighted by the connection weight W_{kj}, where, $j = 1, 2, \ldots N$. The output of neuron j is given as

$$y_k = f\left(u_k + b_k\right)$$

where

$$u_k = \sum_{j=1}^{N} x_j w_{kj}$$

Figure 2. Basic non linear neuron model

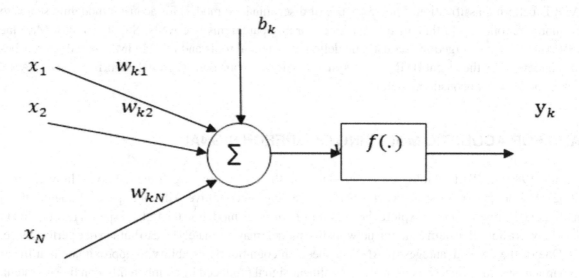

Here b_k is an internal threshold or offset and f is the nonlinear function (Haykin, 2003) (Kumar, 2009).

Such a neural network structure inherently posses non linearity in each computational element and hence a large neural network can approximate any non linearity or non linear dynamical system. They provide an efficient way of implementing non linear transform between arbitrary input and output. Thus the connectionist models, which establish nonlinear units interconnected in a large network, can be functionally used for prominent speech behavior modeling (Rabiner & Juang, 1993).

Early attempts at using ANNs for speech recognition centered on simple tasks like recognizing a few phonemes or a few words or isolated digits, with good success (Lippmann, 1990) (Evermann, Chan, Gales, Hain, Liu, Mrva, Wang, & Woodland, 2004) (Matsoukas, Gauvain, Adda, Colthurst, Kao, Kimball, Lamel, Lefevre, Ma, Makhoul, Nguyen, Prasad, Schwartz, Schwenk & Xiang, 2006), using pattern mapping by multilayer perceptron (MLP), where ANN was used for both temporal and acoustic modeling. However, limited ability of ANNs to capture temporal information from the speech signal was the major drawback. To address this issue, Time delay Neural Network (TDNN) and Recurrent Neural Network (RNN) were proposed. TDNNs are an extension of MLPs for time-sequence processing. TDNNs convert a temporal sequence input into a spatial sequence over corresponding units and can be trained by the back propagation algorithm. In contrast to TDNNs, RNN captures the dynamics of a temporal sequence by having an architecture which allows the ability to connect any pair of units such as self recurrent loops as well as backward connections. With such architecture, RNNs operate like dynamical systems and hence can be used for sequence processing. In (Waibel, Hanazawa, Hinton, Shikano & Lang, 1989), a TDNN approach to phoneme recognition is described. Using a 3 layer arrangement of simple computing units, a hierarchy is constructed that allows the formation of arbitrary nonlinear decision surfaces. The TDNN learns these decision surfaces automatically using error back propagation. Here, the time-delay arrangement enables the network to discover acoustic-phonetic features and the temporal relationships between them independent of position in time and hence not blurred by temporal shifts in the input. In (Robinson & Fallside, 1991), Robinson et al. describe speaker independent phoneme and word recognition system based on a fully recurrent error propagation network trained by propagating backwards the gradient signal in time. During recognition, a dynamic programming match is used to find the most probable string of symbols. Similarly, works described in (Robinson, 1992) (Robinson & Fallside, 1990) also proved the effectiveness of RNN for phoneme and word recognition. In (Robinson, 1992), a real-time recurrent error propagation network word recognition system implemented in DSP board is described where connectionist model employs internal feedback for context modeling and provides phone state occupancy probabilities for a simple context independent Markov model. In (Robinson, 1994), an application of recurrent nets to phone probability estimation is described in case of large vocabulary speech recognition. It describes that recurrent net is suitable for efficient exploitation of context information.

Despite of these successes, ANNs were not found to be successful in dealing with long time-sequences of speech signals. Therefore, by the beginning of the 1990s, a new research area explored the use of HMM for temporal modeling and ANN for acoustic modeling. This hybridization considers the advantages of both HMMs and ANNs improving flexibility and recognition performance (Trentin & Gori, 2001). The reason is that ANNs are found to be more able than GMMs to capture the dynamic information in extended feature windows, with frame level performance (Bourlard & Morgan, 1994) (Hochberg, Cook, Renals, Robinson & Schechtman, 1995) (Bourlard & Dupont, 1997). Feed forward ANNs offer several potential advantages over GMMs. First of all, estimation of the posterior probabilities of HMM states by feed forward ANN does not require detailed assumptions about the data distribution and they allow an easy way of combining diverse features including both discrete and continuous features. Further, ANNs have traditionally been trained purely discriminatively, whereas GMMs are typically trained as generative models. Generative training allows the data to impose many constraints on the parameters. Hence, it partially compensates for the fact that each component of a large GMM must be trained on a very small fraction of the data (Mohamed et al., 2012).

In the HMM/ANN hybrid system, an ANN is trained to output a posterior probability for each model state. During decoding, these probability mass outputs are converted to scaled likelihoods given as

$$\frac{p(x_t \mid q_k)}{p(x_t)} = \frac{p(q_k \mid x_t)}{p(q_k)}$$

Here, x_t feature vector at time step t, q_k kth state of k HMM states in model (Hagen & Morris, 2005). This scaled likelihood is used directly to replace the state likelihoods which are modeled by GMMs in HMM/GMM systems. In early attempts, ANN used was a MLP with one hidden layer of sigmoid units and an output layer with one output unit per class. It is trained with labeled data to maximize the mutual information or ''cross entropy'' between input features and target output class posteriors. When HMM/ANNs are used with sub-word units such as phonemes. Usually size of the ANN is restricted by one ANN output per phoneme and use of the scaled likelihood value from this output for all states of this phoneme. In HMM/GMM systems, the state transition probabilities used in decoding are estimated as part of the EM training procedure. But in HMM/ANN systems state transition probabilities are fixed as a common value like 0.5. However, better transition probability estimation can be achieved by using one output per hidden state (Hagen & Morris, 2005) (Morris, Payne & Borlard et al., 2002). Afterwards many different ways are described by various researchers to combine time sequence modeling power of HMM with the ANNs ability to model speech unit. Pavelka et al has replaced GMM using a MLP as an emission probability estimator in HMM based ASR (Pavelka & Kral, 2008). They

Figure 3. Long Short-Term Memory (LSTM) for Speech Recognition
Used in (Sak, Senior & Beaufays, 2014)

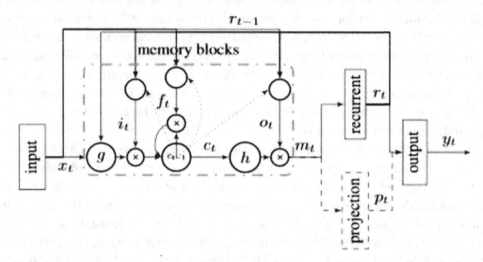

have presented a solution on how to model tri-phone phonetic units with MLP and show that it leads to better performance in comparison with GMMs in both recognition accuracy and recognition speed. Recently, Sak et al explains a RNN architecture called Long Short-Term Memory (LSTM) (Sak, Senior & Beaufays, 2014) as shown in Figure 3. It has been designed to address the vanishing and exploding gradient problems of conventional RNNs. Unlike feedforward ANNs, RNNs have cyclic connections making them powerful for modeling sequences. They have shown that LSTM based RNN architectures makes more effective use of model parameters to train acoustic models for large vocabulary speech recognition. Similarly, Lewandowski et al. explains phone sequence modeling with RNNs (Lewandowski, Droppo, Seltzer & Dong, 2014). They have introduced a hybrid architecture that combines a phonetic model with an arbitrary frame-level acoustic model.

From the last 5-10 years, HMM/ANN hybrid system research is concentrated around the use of deep belief neural network (DBNN) for acoustic modeling. In the following section, is a brief review related to DBNN for acoustic modeling.

Deep Belief Neural Network (DBNN) for Acoustic Modeling

Deep Belief Neural Networks (DBNNs) have recently proved to be very effective for a variety of machine learning problems as well as acoustic modeling as part of HMM/ANN based hybrid speech recognition systems. Initially, DBNNs were proposed for acoustic modeling in speech recognition, because they have a higher modeling capacity per parameter than GMMs. Further, they also have a fairly efficient training procedure that combines unsupervised generative learning for feature discovery with a subsequent stage of supervised learning that fine tunes the features to optimize discrimination. DBNN for acoustic modeling are efficient because the low level, local, characteristics are taken care of using the lower layers while higher-order and highly non-linear statistical structure in the input is modeled by the higher layers. This is somewhat identical with human speech recognition which appears to use many layers of feature extractors and event detectors (Hinton, Deng, Yu, Dahl, Mohamed, Jaitly, Senior, Vanhoucke, Nguyen, Sainath & Kingsbury, 2012) (Mohamed et al., 2012).

DBNNs contain many layers of non-linear hidden units and a very large output layer. When HMM considers phones on either side, each phone is modeled by a number of different tri-phone and many of the states of these tri-phone HMMs are tied together giving rise to thousands of tied states. In such situations, the large output layer of DBNN is effective to accommodate the large number of HMM states. Presently, due to the advances in machine learning algorithms and computer hardware, various efficient methods for training DBNN are explored. Using the new learning methods, several different research groups have shown that DBNNs can outperform GMMs at acoustic modeling for speech recognition on a variety of datasets.

DBNN is a graphical model with multiple layers of binary latent variables that can be learned efficiently, one layer at a time, by using an unsupervised learning procedure that maximizes a variation lower bound on the log probability of the acoustic input. Because of the way it is learned, the graphical model has the convenient property that the top-down generative weights can be used in the opposite direction for performing inference in a single bottom-up pass. This allows the learned graphical model to be treated as a feed forward multi-layer ANN which can then be fine-tuned to optimize discrimination using back-propagation. The resulting feed forward ANN is called DBNN (Mohamed et al., 2012). During training each hidden unit, j, typically uses the logistic function to map its total input from the layer below, x_j, to the scalar state, y_j that it sends to the layer above. The logistic function has the form

$$y_j = logistic\left(x_j\right) = \frac{1}{1 + e^{-x_j}}$$

and

$$x_j = b_j + \sum_i y_i w_{ij}$$

where, b_j is the bias of unit j, i is an is an index over units in the layer below and w_{ij} is a the weight on a connection to unit j from unit i in the layer below. For multiclass classification, output unit j converts its total input, x_j, into a class probability, p_j, by using the softmax non-linearity

$$p_j = \frac{\exp\left(xj\right)}{\sum_k \exp\left(x_k\right)}$$

where k is an index over all classes (Hinton et al., 2012).

DNN's can be discriminatively trained by back propagating derivatives of a cost function that measures the discrepancy between the target outputs and the actual outputs produced for each training case. When using the softmax output function, the natural cost function C is the cross-entropy between the target probabilities d and the outputs of the softmax, p,

$$C = -\sum_j d_j \log p_j$$

where the target probabilities, typically taking values of one or zero, are the supervised information provided to train the DBNN classifier. For large training sets, it is typically more efficient to compute the derivatives on a small, random "mini-batch" of training cases, rather than the whole training set, before updating the weights in proportion to the gradient. This stochastic gradient descent method can be further improved by using a "momentum" coefficient, $0 < \alpha < 1$, that smooths the gradient computed for mini-batch t, thereby damping oscillations across ravines and speeding progress down ravines:

$$\Delta w_{ij}(t) = \alpha \Delta w_{ij}(t-1) - \in \frac{\partial C}{\partial w_{ij}(t)}$$

The update rule for biases can be derived by treating them as weights on connections coming from units that always have a state of one (Hinton et al., 2012).

A few works on acoustic modeling using DBNN is described below.

1. Improved phone recognition performance on TIMIT database is reported by Mohamed et al (Mohamed et al., 2012) by replacing GMM with DBNN. In this work, networks are first pre trained to create a multilayer generative model for feature vectors lying within a window, where no discriminative information is used. After that providing discriminative information these models are tuned to predict the probability distribution over the states of monophone HMMs. The training is done by back propagation. They have used a context window of successive *n* frames of speech coefficients to set the states of the visible units of the lowest layer of the DBN To generate phone sequences, the sequence of predicted probability distributions over the possible labels for each frame is fed into a standard Viterbi decoder.

2. In (Mohamed et al.), Mohamed et al investigated two types of DBNN for acoustic modeling, the back propagation DBN (BP-DBN) and the associative memory DBN (AM-DBN) architectures. The effect of model depth and hidden layer size has been investigated. Both architectures have mechanisms to avoid over fitting. The use of a "bottleneck" in the last layer of the BP-DBN proved to help avoid over fitting while hybrid generative and discriminative training prevent over fitting in the AM-DBN. Both types of DBN consistently outperform other techniques for a wide variety of choices of the number of hidden layers and the number of units per layer on the standard TIMIT corpus and the best DBN achieves a phone error rate (PER) of 23.0% on the TIMIT core test set.

3. Dahl et al (Dahl, Yu, Deng & Acero, 2012) proposed a context-dependent (CD) model for large-vocabulary speech recognition (LVSR) using DBN. Pre-trained DBNN HMM hybrid architecture is described in this work that trains the DNN to produce a distribution over tied tri-phone states as its output. Throughout the experiments on a challenging business search dataset, they have demonstrated that CD-DNN-HMMs can significantly outperform the conventional CD GMM/HMMs, with an absolute sentence accuracy improvement of 5.8% and 9.2% (or relative error reduction of 16.0% and 23.2%) over the CD-GMM-HMMs trained using the minimum phone error rate (MPE) and maximum-likelihood (ML) criteria, respectively.

4. Siniscalchi et al. demonstrated that word recognition accuracy can be significantly enhanced by arranging DBNNs in a hierarchical structure to model long-term energy trajectories. They have evaluated the proposed system on the 5000-word Wall Street Journal task and achieved consistent and significant improvements in both phone and word recognition accuracy rates (Siniscalchi, Yu, Deng & Lee, 2013).

5. Gehring et al. proposed a modular combination of two popular applications of ANNs to large-vocabulary continuous speech recognition. First, a DBNN is trained to extract bottleneck features from frames of mel scale filter bank coefficients. In a similar way, as is usually done for GMM/HMM systems, this network is then applied as a nonlinear discriminative feature-space transformation for a hybrid setup where acoustic modeling is performed by a DBNN. This effectively results in a very large network, where the layers of the bottleneck network are fixed and applied to successive windows of feature frames in a time-delay fashion. They have shown that bottleneck features improve the recognition performance of DBN/HMM hybrids and that the modular combination enables the acoustic model to benefit from a larger temporal context. They have evaluated the architecture on Tagalog corpus containing conversational telephone speech (Gehring, Lee, Kilgour, Lane, Miao & Waibel 2013).

6. Palaz et al Estimates Phoneme Class Conditional Probabilities from Raw Speech Signal using Convolutional Neural Networks (CNN). They have investigated a novel approach on TIMIT phoneme recognition task, where the input to the ANN is raw speech signal and the output is phoneme class conditional probability estimates. The CNN architecture shows a great improvement compared to the single layer MLP architecture, confirming that convolution-based architectures are better suited for temporal signals. Moreover, it slightly outperforms the baseline, with almost no pre-processing on the data. These results suggest that deep architecture can learn efficient features (Palaz., Collobert & Doss, 2013).

7. Graves et al. describes speech recognition with deep RNNs. End-to-end training methods such as connectionist temporal classification make it possible to train RNNs for sequence labeling problems where the input-output alignment is unknown. They have investigated deep RNNs, which combine the multiple levels of representation that have proved so effective in deep networks with the flexible use of long range context that empowers RNNs. By training end-to-end with suitable regularization, they have found that deep LSTM RNNs achieve a test set error of 17.7% on the TIMIT phoneme recognition benchmark (Graves, Mohamed & Hinton, 2013)

8. Mimura et al. used DBNN for reverberant speech recognition. In this system, a deep auto encoder is used for enhancing the speech features in the front end and at the back end recognition is performed using DNN-HMM acoustic models trained on multi-condition data. They have evaluated the system on the ASR task in Chime Challenge 2014. The DNN-HMM system trained on the multi-condition training set achieved a conspicuously higher word accuracy compared to the MLLR-adapted GMM-HMM system trained on the same data. Furthermore, feature enhancement with the deep auto encoder, contributed to the improvement of recognition accuracy especially in the more adverse conditions (Mimura, Sakai & Kawahara, 2014).

9. Heigold et al reported a work on multilingual acoustic model building using distributed DBNN. They have presented an empirical comparison of mono-, cross-, and multilingual acoustic model training using deep neural networks with experimental results for cross- and multi-lingual network training of eleven Romance languages on 10k hours of data. The average relative gains over the

monolingual baselines are 4%/2% (data-scarce/data-rich languages) for cross- and 7%/2% for multi-lingual training (Heigold, Vanhoucke, Senior, Nguyen, Ranzato, Devin & Dean, 2013)

In all the above cases, it has been observed that the trend is to use ANNs in different forms and structures as part of hybrid systems being used and formulated for ASR systems. The trend is aided by more interest being generated by the success of use of ANN based architectures in ASR and the growth of VLSI technology. The ultimate ASR shall be similar to the human processing paradigm design of which shall be critically linked to advances in ANN and related technology.

CONCLUSION

In this chapter, a review on acoustic modeling of speech signal is provided. Acoustic model of speech units is an integral part of automatic speech recognition (ASR) system. The basic purpose of acoustic modeling is to model sound units based on the information extracted from the acoustic feature vectors, so that during recognition the incoming sound unit can be compared with the stored acoustic models. The non linear dynamic nature of the speech signal makes acoustic modeling a challenging task. Two basic approaches of acoustic modeling are observed in the literature. These are statistical modeling and ANN based non linear modeling approaches. HMM was initially introduced for acoustic modeling which can handle both temporal and spectral variability of speech signal. But later after the introduction of EM algorithm, GMM-HMM systems have been introduced, where GMM is used for acoustic modeling and HMM models the sequential structure of speech signals. But HMM/GMM systems are generative models, whereas the goal of ASR is pattern classification. Therefore, use of discriminative models like ANN for acoustic modeling seems to be more appropriate. Further, the inherent non linearity in each computational unit of ANN makes it more suitable for speech sound unit modeling. Thus HMM/GMM based systems have been slowly replaced by HMM/ANN systems. During the last decade MLP, RNN are being increasingly used for acoustic modeling. Currently, DBNNs due to its many layers of non-linear features and generative training have become a very competitive alternative to GMMs for relating states of a HMM to frames of coefficients derived from the acoustic input. The ultimate ASR shall be similar to the human processing paradigm design of which shall be critically linked to advances in ANN and related technology.

REFERENCES

Bourlard, H., & Dupont, S. (1997). Sub-band-based speech recognition. *Proceedings of IEEE International Conference on Acoustics, Speech, and Signal Processing*. Munich.

Bourlard, H., & Morgan, N. (1994). *Connectionist Speech Recognition – A Hybrid Approach*. Norwell, MA, USA: Kluwer Academic Publishers. doi:10.1007/978-1-4615-3210-1

Brown, P. A. (1987). The Acoustic Modeling Problem in Automatic Speech Recognition [Doctoral dissertation]. School of Computer Science at Carnegie Mellon University.

Dahl G. E., Yu D, Deng Li & Acero A. (2012). Context-Dependent Pre-Trained Deep Neural Networks for Large-Vocabulary Speech Recognition. *IEEE Transactions on Audio, Speech, and Language Processing*. 20(1), 30-42.

Dempster, A. P., Laird, N. M., & Rubin, D. B. (1977). Maximum likelihood from incomplete data via the EM algorithm. *Journal of the Royal Statistical Society. Series B. Methodological, 39*(1), 1–38.

Deng, L., & Shaughnessy, D. (2003). *Speech Processing, A Dynamic and Optimization-Oriented Approach*. New York, NY, USA: Marcel Dekker Inc.

Esposito, A., & Marinaro, M. (2002). *Some Notes on Nonlinearities of Speech. Nonlinear Speech Modeling and Applications. Advanced Lectures and Revised Selected Papers*. Germany: Springer.

Evermann, G., Chan, H. Y., Gales, M. J. F., Hain, T., Liu, X., & Mrva, D. et al. (2004). Development of the 2003 CU-HTK conversational telephone speech transcription system. *Proceedings of IEEE International Conference on Acoustics, Speech, and Signal Processing*. Montreal, Canada. doi:10.1109/ICASSP.2004.1325969

Faundez-Zanuy, M. (2002). *Nonlinear Speech Processing: Overview and Possibilities in Speech Coding. Nonlinear Speech Modeling and Applications. Advanced Lectures and Revised Selected Papers*. Germany: Springer.

Frikha, M., & Hamida, A. B. (2012). A Comparitive Survey of ANN and Hybrid HMM/ANN Architectures for Robust Speech Recognition. *American Journal of Intelligent Systems, 2*(1), 1–8. doi:10.5923/j.ajis.20120201.01

Gehring, J., Lee, W., Kilgour, K., Lane, I., Miao, Y., & Waibel, A. (2013). Modular Combination of Deep Neural Networks for Acoustic Modeling. *Proceedings of Interspeech*. Lyon, France.

Graves, A., Mohamed, A. R., & Hinton, G. (2013). Speech Recognition with Deep Recurrent Neural Networks. *Proceedings of IEEE International Conference on Acoustics, Speech and Signal Processing*. Vancouver, BC, Canada. doi:10.1109/ICASSP.2013.6638947

Hagen, A., & Morris, A. (2005). Recent advances in the multi-stream HMM/ANN hybrid approach to noise robust ASR. *Computer Speech & Language, 19*(1), 3–30. doi:10.1016/j.csl.2003.12.002

Haykin, S. (2003). *Neural Networks A Comprehensive Foundation (2nd ed)*. New Delhi, India: Pearson Education.

Heigold, G., Vanhoucke, V., Senior, A., Nguyen, P., Ranzato, M., Devin, M., & Dean, J. (2013). Multilingual Acoustic Models using Distributed Deep Neural Networks. *Proceedings of IEEE International Conference on Acoustics, Speech and Signal Processing*. Vancouver, BC, Canada. doi:10.1109/ICASSP.2013.6639348

Hermansky, H., & Sharma, S. (1999) Temporal patterns (TRAPs) in ASR of noisy speech. *In Proceedings IEEE International Conference on Acoustics, Speech, and Signal Processing* (pp. 289 -292). doi:10.1109/ICASSP.1999.758119

Hinton, G., Deng, L., Yu, D., Dahl, G., Mohamed, A. R., & Jaitly, N. et al. (2012, November). Deep neural network for acoustic modeling in speech recognition. *IEEE Signal Processing Magazine*, 82–97. doi:10.1109/MSP.2012.2205597

Hochberg, M., Cook, G., Renals, S., Robinson, A., & Schechtman, R. (1995). ABBOT hybrid connectionist-hmm large vocabulary recognition system. *Proceedings of Spoken Language Systems Technology Workshop* (pp. 170–176).

Hu, Y. H., & Hwang, J. N. (2002). *Handbook of Neural Network Signal Processing. The Electrical Engineering and Applied Signal Processing Series*. USA: CRC Press.

Juang, B. H., & Rabiner, L. R. (1991). Hidden Markov Models for Speech Recognition. *Technometrics*, *33*(3), 251–272. doi:10.1080/00401706.1991.10484833

Kumar S. (2009). *Neural Networks A Classroom Approach*. India: TATA McGRAW HILL.

Lewandowski, N. B., Droppo, J., & Seltzer, M. Yu Dong (2014). Phone Sequence modeling With Recurrent Neural Networks. *Proceedings of IEEE International Conference on Acoustics, Speech and Signal Processing*. Florence, Italy.

Lippmann, R. P. (1990). Review of Neural Networks for Speech Recognition. *Neural Computation*, *1*(1), 1–38.

Matsoukas, S., Gauvain, J. L., Adda, A., Colthurst, T., Kao, C. I., & Kimball, O. et al. (2006). Advances in transcription of broadcast news and conversational telephone speech within the combined EARS BBN/LIMSI system. *IEEE Transactions on Audio. Speech and Language Processing*, *14*(5), 1541–1556. doi:10.1109/TASL.2006.878257

Mimura, M., Sakai, S., & Kawahara, T. (2014). Reverberant Speech Recognition Combining Deep Neural Networks and Deep Autoencoders. *Proceedings of REVERB Workshop*, F.orence, Italy.

Mohamed, A. R., Dahl, G. E., & Hinton, G. (2012). Acoustic Modeling using Deep Belief Networks. *IEEE Transactions on Audio, Speech, and Language Processing*, *20*(1), 1–10. doi:10.1109/TASL.2011.2109382

Mohamed, A. R., Dahl, G. E., & Hinton, G. (2012). Acoustic Modeling using Deep Belief Networks. *IEEE Transactions on Audio, Speech, and Language Processing*, *20*(1), 1–10. doi:10.1109/TASL.2011.2109382

Mohamed, A. R., Dahl, G. E., & Hinton, G. (n. d.). *Deep Belief Networks for phone recognition*. Department of Computer Science, University of Toronto. Retrieved from http://www.cs.toronto.edu/~gdahl/papers/dbnPhoneRec.pdf

Mohamed, A. R., Hinton, G., & Penn, G. (2012). Understanding How Deep Belief Networks Perform Acoustic Modelling. *Proceedings of IEEE International Conference on Acoustics, Speech and Signal Processing* (pp. 4273 – 4276). Kyoto. doi:10.1109/ICASSP.2012.6288863

Morris, A., Payne, S., & Borlard, H. (2002). Low cost duration modelling for noise robust speech recognition. *Proceedings of IEEE International Conference on Spoken Language Processing* (pp. 1025–1028. United States.

Palaz, D., Collobert, R., & Doss, M. M. (2013) Estimating Phoneme Class Conditional Probabilities from Raw Speech Signal using Convolutional Neural Networks. Proceedings of Interspeech. Lyon, France.

Pavelka, T., & Kral, P. (2008). Neural Network Acoustic Model with Decision Tree Clustered Triphones. *In Proceedings of IEEE Workshop on Machine Learning for Signal Processing* (pp. 216 – 220). Cancun. doi:10.1109/MLSP.2008.4685482

Rabiner, L. (1989). A tutorial on Hidden Markov Models and Selected Applications in Speech Recognition. *Proceedings of the IEEE, 77*(2), 257–286. doi:10.1109/5.18626

Rabiner L., & Juang B. H. (1993). *Fundamentals of Speech Recognition.* New Delhi, India: Pearson Education.

Rabiner, L., & Juang, B. H. (1993). *Fundamentals of Speech Recognition.* New Jersey: Prentice Hall.

Rahim, M., Bengio, Y., & Lecun, Y. (1997). Discriminative feature and model design for automatic speech recognition. In Proceedings of Eurospeech (pp. 75-78).

Reynolds, D. A., Quatieri, T. F., & Dunn, R. B. (2000). Speaker Verification Using Adapted Gaussian Mixture Models. *Digital Signal Processing, 10*(1-3), 19–41. doi:10.1006/dspr.1999.0361

Reynolds, D. A., & Rose, R. C. (1995). Robust text-independent speaker identification using Gaussian mixture speaker models. *IEEE Transactions on Speech and Audio Processing, 3*(1), 72–83. doi:10.1109/89.365379

Robinson, A. (1994). An application of recurrent nets to phone probability estimation. *IEEE Transactions on Neural Networks, 5*(2), 298–305. doi:10.1109/72.279192 PMID:18267798

Robinson, T. (1992). A Real-Time Recurrent Error Propagation Network Word Recognition System. *Proceedings of the IEEE International Conference on Acoustics, Speech, and Signal Processing* (Vol. 1, pp. 617 – 620). San Francisco, CA. doi:10.1109/ICASSP.1992.225833

Robinson, T., & Fallside, F. (1990). Word recognition from the DARPA resource management database with the Cambridge recurrent error propagation network speech recognition system. Retrieved from http://assta.org/sst/SST-90/cache/SST-90-Chapter13-p14.pdf

Robinson, T., & Fallside, F. (1991). A recurrent error propagation network speech recognition system. *Computer Speech & Language, 5*(3), 259–274. doi:10.1016/0885-2308(91)90010-N

Rodriguez, E., Ruiz, B., Crespo, A. G., & Garcia, F. (2003). Speech/Speaker Recognition Using a HMM/GMM Hybrid Model. *Proceedings of the First International Conference on Audio- and Video-Based Biometric Person Authentication* (pp. 227- 234).

Rolf, S. (1974). Maximum likelihood theory for incomplete data from an exponential family. *Scandinavian Journal of Statistics, 1*(2), 49–58.

Sak, H., Senior, A., & Beaufays, F. (2014) Long Short-Term Memory Based Recurrent Neural Network Architectures For Large Vocabulary Speech Recognition. *Google.* Retrieved from http://arxiv.org/abs/1402.1128

Salvi, G. (2006). Developing acoustics models for automatic speech recognition [Master's Thesis]. Speech Music and Hearing Department at Royal Institute of Technology, Stockholm, Sweden.

Schwarz, P., & Matejka, P. & J. Cernocky J. (2006). Hierarchical structures of neural networks for phoneme recognition. *Proceedings of IEEE International Conference on Acoustics, Speech and Signal Processing*. 325-328. doi:10.1109/ICASSP.2006.1660023

Schwarz, P., Matejka, P., & Cernocky, J. (2004). Towards lower error rates in phoneme recognition. *Text, Speech and Dialogue. Lecture Notes in Computer Science*, *3206*, 465–472. doi:10.1007/978-3-540-30120-2_59

Singh, A. (2005). The EM Algorithm. Retrieved from, http://www.cs.cmu.edu/~awm/10701/assignments/EM.pdf

Siniscalchi, S. M., Yu, D., Deng, L., & Lee, C. H. (2013). Speech Recognition Using Long-Span Temporal Patterns in a Deep Network Model. *IEEE Signal Processing Letters*, *20*(3), 201–204. doi:10.1109/LSP.2013.2237901

Tebelskis, J. (1995). Speech Recognition using Neural Networks [Doctoral dissertation]. School of Computer Science at Carnegie Mellon University.

Trentin, E., & Gori, M. (2001). A survey of hybrid ANN/HMM models for automatic speech recognition. *Neurocomputing*, *37*(1-4), 91–126. doi:10.1016/S0925-2312(00)00308-8

Waibel, A., Hanazawa, T., Hinton, G., Shikano, K., & Lang, K. (1989). Phoneme recognition using time-delay neural networks. *IEEE Transactions on Acoustics, Speech, and Signal Processing*, *37*(3), 328–339. doi:10.1109/29.21701

Xiong, X. (2009). Robust Speech Features and Acoustic Models for Speech Recognition [Doctoral Dissertation]. School of Computer Engineering At Nanyang Technological University.

KEY TERMS AND DEFINITIONS

Artificial Neural Network: Artificial Neural Networks are non-parametric models inspired by biological central nervous systems. These are particularly the brain that are capable of machine learning and pattern recognition and usually presented as systems of interconnected ``neurons" that can compute values from inputs by feeding information through the network.

Automatic Speech Recognition: Automatic Speech Recognition is a technology by which a computer or a machine is made to recognize the speech of a human being.

Back Propagation: Back Propagation Algorithm is a common supervised method of training ANN where in reference to a desired output, the network learns from many inputs.

Deep Belief Neural Network: Deep Belief Neural Network is an ANN architecture with many hidden layers and a large output layer.

Expectation Maximization Algorithm: Expectation-Maximization is an iterative method for finding maximum likelihood or maximum a posteriori (MAP) estimates of parameters in statistical models, where the model depends on unobserved latent variables.

Gaussian Mixture Model: Gaussian Mixture Model is a probabilistic model for representing the presence of subpopulations within an overall population, without requiring that an observed data-set should identify the sub-population to which an individual observation belongs where mixture distribution is Gaussian.

Hidden Markov Model: Hidden Markov Model is a statistical Markov model in which the system being modeled is assumed to be a Markov process with unobserved or hidden states. It can be considered to be the simplest dynamic Bayesian network.

Mel-Frequency Cepstral Coefficients: Mel Frequency Cepstral Coefficients are coefficients that collectively make up an Mel Frequency Cepstrum which is a representation of the short-term power spectrum of a sound, based on a linear cosine transform of a log power spectrum on a nonlinear mel scale of frequency.

Multi-Layer Perceptron: Multi Layer Perceptron is a feed forward artificial neural network model that maps sets of input data onto a set of appropriate outputs.

Perceptual Linear Prediction Coding: Perceptual Linear Prediction Coding is a technique of speech analysis which uses the concepts of the critical-band spectral resolution, the equal loudness curve and the intensity-loudness power law of psychophysics of hearing to approximate the auditory spectrum by an autoregressive all pole model.

Recurrent Neural Network: Recurrent Neural Network: Recurrent Neural Network is a class of ANN where connections between units form a directed cycle which creates an internal state of the network which allows it to exhibit dynamic temporal behavior. It is an ANN with feed forward and feedback paths.

Time Delay Neural Network: Time Delay Neural Network is an ANN architecture whose primary purpose is to work on continuous data.

Section 3
Communication

This section includes three contributions which represent recent advances in communication and related areas.

Chapter 13
A New Coding Scheme for Data Security in RF based Wireless Communication

Irfan Habib
Assam Don Bosco University, India

Suman Chetia
Assam Don Bosco University, India

Atiqul Islam
Assam Don Bosco University, India

Samar Jyoti Saikia
Assam Don Bosco University, India

ABSTRACT

A radio-controlled (RC) aircraft is controlled remotely by a hand-held transmitter and a receiver within the craft. The working mechanism of such an arrangement designed using an AT89S51 microcontroller is reported in this chapter. The primary focus of the chapter is to describe the design of the interfacing of transceiver module with AT89S51 microcontroller and control the movement of the aircraft according to the instruction given remotely. The microcontroller reads the input given by the user and transmits the data to the receiver at the aircraft. The receiver module receives the transmitted signal and demodulates it and gives the data as serial sequence of bits at the output. The serial data are then given to the decoder which transforms the data from serial to parallel. This set of data is used to control motors and any related device. A special coding technique is used to secure the transmitted data.

INTRODUCTION

The Unmanned Aerial Vehicle or the wireless plane can be used in various ways. It can reach a place where other plane can't reach. It can also reach a place where the weather may be harmful for human being. It can be used in surveillance over an area, traffic control etc. But in today's world the main use of these wireless plane or unmanned aerial vehicle is as a bomber over various parts of the world without losing any human life and now a day's various countries are using this technology in their military build up.

The main components of the microcontroller based RC plane has two parts transmitter and receiver, which consists of Atmel's AT89s51 microcontroller IC, brushless DC motor, servo motors, current

DOI: 10.4018/978-1-4666-8493-5.ch013

controller, transceiver module, push buttons and the foam-wooden mechanical body of the plane. The transmitter part consists of microcontroller and the transmitter module. The encoder converts the parallel data entered by the user to serial and gives it to the transmitter module and it transmits the data. The receiver receives the exact serial data and gives it to the microcontroller. The microcontroller again converts the data to parallel form and according to the program the brushless DC motor and the servos are controlled, where the servos need a PWM signal to move the rotor to left or right and the brushless DC motor needs a continuous current to keep running. By using ASK and different bit streams the movements of the plane can be controlled. Microcontroller is used to rotate different motors according to the transmitted data.

Wireless communication has grown largely in last decade and it is constantly expanding. It can also be used for data communication to control various remote devices such as airplanes, cars etc. Data security plays a vital role in these kinds of design issues. Different coding schemes can be used to encrypt the data. In our work we have implemented a simple and unique coding scheme by generating a bit sequence to secure the data transmission along with already available coding schemes.

LITERATURE SURVEY

Some of the recent works have given stress on the design mechanical modelling and encoding and decoding methods used in wireless channels. A few related works are covered and included which have been referred while caring out the work.

1. The paper entitled hardware/software architecture designed for use as avionics for mission and payload control by E. Pastor, J Lopez and P Royo in the area of Unmanned Aerial Vehicles. Here the design tackles a number of elements critical for the operation of these systems. The architecture is a LAN-based pure distributed system, being therefore highly modular and scalable according to the requirements of the applications. A small connectivity infrastructure is required among the modules, but yet enough connectivity bandwidth could be obtained (Pastor, Lopez & Royo, 2007).

2. A work by S. Naskar, S. Das, A. K. Seth, A. Nath, which defines robot as "a machine that looks like a human being and perform various complex acts; a device that automatically performs complicated, often repetitive tasks; a mechanism guided by automatic controls." a paper on military robots .This work is an extension to it. A new feature called 'back tracking' has been introduced in the robot described in this paper. The design and the Microcontroller of this robot have been improved and a cost- benefit analysis is shown to justify the feasibility of military robots in Indian Defence (Naskar, Das, Seth & Nath, 2011).

3. The Impact of Human-Automation Collaboration in Decentralized Multiple Unmanned Vehicle a paper by M. L. Cummings, J. P. How, A. Whitten and O. Toupet in the future concept of one operator supervising multiple collaborative UxVs, the potential exists for high operator workload and negative performance consequences. As a result, significant autonomy is needed to aid the operator in this multiple UxV control task. Due to the dynamic and uncertain nature of the environment, control of collaborative and decentralized UxVs requires rapid automated replanting. However, as demonstrated in this study, human management of the automated planners is critical, as automated

planners cannot always generate accurate solutions for every combination of events. Though fast and able to handle complex computation far better than humans, computer optimization algorithms are often Bbrittle [in that they can only take into account those quantifiable variables identified as critical during the design stage (Cummings, Whitten, How & Toupet, 2011).

4. "Flight Demonstrations of Cooperative Control for UAV" by J. Howc, E. King, and Y. Kuwata a paper presented hardware demonstrations of the receding horizon task assignment and trajectory design on a new UAV test bed. This multi-vehicle test bed provides a unique platform to evaluate various distributed co-ordination and control strategies. Future work will integrate distributed collision avoidance formulations, task assignment with the formation of dynamic sub-teams, and missions with heterogeneous vehicles (How, King & Kuwata, 2004).

5. Within this study of the paper entitled "Open Source Image-Processing Tools for Low-Cost UAV-Based Landslide Investigation", a couple of public domain image processing tools for low-cost ortho-rectification and mosaic blending were used. Different open source GIS projects have also been made available, thus enabling analysis of the planar remote sensing data. Even photogrammetric processing of hundreds of UAV-based images acquired with un calibrated cameras was managed by applying open source software tools. The used algorithms can easily handle unordered image collections and have provided digital surface models of landslides without any ground control point information (Niethammer, Rothmund, Schwadere, Zeman & Joswig, 2011).

6. American Institute of Aeronautics and Astronautics describes about the Ad Hoc UAV Ground Network (AUGNet).This paper describes an implementation of a wireless mobile ad hoc network with radio nodes mounted at fixed sites, on ground vehicles, and in small (10kg) UAVs. The ad hoc networking allows any two nodes to communicate either directly or through an arbitrary number of other nodes which act as relays. We envision two scenarios for this type of network. In the first, the UAV acts as a prominent radio node that connects disconnected ground radios. In the second, the networking enables groups of UAVs to communicate with each other to extend small UAVs' operational scope and range. The network consists of mesh network radios assembled from low-cost commercial off the shelf components (Brown, Argrow, Dixon & Doshi)

7. The article "Vision-Based Multi-UAV Position Estimation" by L. Merino, J. Wiklund, F. Caballero, A. Moe, J. R. M.-De Dios, P. E. Forssen, K. Nordberg and A. Ollero, shows a vision-based method for multi-UAV motion estimation. First, a method for single-UAV motion estimation from homographies between images of the same planar scene is described. These homographies are computed from matches between features extracted from consecutive images. To reduce the influence of the drift errors in the motion estimation, the homography estimation is refined by using a mosaic that stores past information. Moreover, this article proposes the use of blob features to obtain natural landmarks in low-structured scenes. If these blobs can be matched between images from different UAVs, provided that the scene is planar, the relative displacement between the UAVs can be estimated (Merino et al., 2006).

8. "Unmanned Arial Vehicles -Revolutionary Tools in War and Peace" by Lieutenant Colonel R. P. Schwing, where it examines the future doctrinal, organizational, and operational effects of the UAV across the Department of Defence. The examination includes: (1) an overview of the background and historical development of UAVs and the concept of the "revolution in military affairs"; (2) a review of current major DoD UAV systems and operational concepts; (3) an analysis of the strategic impact of UAV systems, assessing whether the UAV can be considered a revolutionary instrument for the military services (Schwing).

9. A paper entitled "Predicting Controller Capacity in Supervisory Control of Multiple UAVs" This research extends previous work by M.L. Cummings, P.J. Mitchell attempting to predict the number of homogeneous and independent unmanned vehicles a single operator can control. They propose that any predictive model of operator capacity that includes human-in the- loop remote interaction should include various sources of wait time which include wait time due to human-computer interactions (including cognitive reorientation), queuing wait time, and wait time due to a loss of situation awareness. Using data from a simulation examining control of multiple homogeneous and independent UAVs, capacity predictions that included these sources of delay dropped by up to 67 percent, with loss of situation awareness as the primary source of wait time delays (Cummings & Mitchell, 2008).

10. The purpose of the paper entitled "The Navigation and Control technology inside the Drone micro UAV" is to present the navigation and control technologies embedded in the commercial micro UAV Drone. As it appears, a main problem is the state estimation which has required embedding numerous sensors of various types. Among these are inertial sensors and cameras. The resulting estimation architecture is a complex combination of several principles, used to determine, over distinct time-horizons, the biases and other defects of each sensor. The outcome is a sophisticated system but this complexity is not visible by the user. This stresses the role of automatic control as an enabling but hidden technology (Bristeau, Callou, Vissière & Petit, 2011).

In our work we have designed a plane that can be controlled from ground. The movements of the plane are controlled by some servo motors. The main thrust to the plane is given by the BLDC motor with a propeller. In the receiver a microcontroller is there to control the functions of different motors.

DESCRIPTION OF THE COMPONENTS

Microcontroller

The AT89s51 is a low-power, high-performance CMOS 8-bit microcomputer with 4Kbytes of flash programmable and erasable read only memory (PEROM). It is compatible with the industry-standard MCS-51 instruction set and pin configuration. Thus the interfacing and programming is same in Intel's 8051 microcontroller with an advantage of EPROM technology. That is the same hardware can be improved by changing the program. The AT89s51 provides the following standard features: 4K bytes of Flash, 128 bytes of RAM, 32 I/O lines, two 16-bit timer/counters, five vector two-level interrupt architecture, a full duplex serial port, and on-chip oscillator and clock circuitry. In addition, the AT89s51 is designed with static logic for operation down to zero frequency and supports two software selectable power saving modes. The Idle Mode stops the CPU while allowing the RAM, timer/counters, serial port and interrupt system to continue functioning. The Power-down Mode saves the RAM contents but freezes the oscillator disabling all other chip functions until the next hardware reset.

Pin Configuration

The Pin configuration of AT89s51 microcontroller is shown in Figure 1. It is same for all MSC-51 microcontrollers like Intel 8051, Intel 8052, AT89C51, AT89S51 etc. It has 40 pins. 32 pins constitute the four 8-bit ports. Apart from those, it has two pins (Vcc and GND) for power supply, two pins (XTAL1 and XTAL2) for connecting the external crystal oscillator to complete the internal clock circuit of the microcontroller. Most of the pins of 8051 microcontroller have more than one function.

Programming Model of 8051 Microcontroller

AT89s51 is similar to 8051 (MSC-51 family) as far as the programming and interfacing is concerned. The 8051 microcontroller has three types of memory as follows:

1. On-Chip Memory refers to any memory (Code, RAM, or other) that physically exist on the micro-controller itself. On-chip memory can be of several types.
2. External Code Memory is code (or program) memory that resides off-chip. This is often in the form of an external EPROM.
3. External RAM is RAM memory that resides off-chip. This is often in the form of standard static RAM or flash RAM. Code memory is the memory that holds the actual 8051 program that is to be run. This memory is limited to 64K and comes in many shapes and sizes. Code memory may be found on-chip, either burned into the microcontroller as ROM or EPROM. Code may also be stored completely off-chip in an external ROM or, more commonly, an external EPROM.

Flash RAM is also another popular method of storing a program. Various combinations of these memory types may also be used–that is to say, it is possible to have 4K of code memory on-chip and 64k of code memory off-chip in an EPROM.

On Chip RAM

The 8051 includes a certain amount of on-chip memory. On-chip memory is of two types: Internal RAM and Special Function Register (SFR) memory. The layout of the 8051's internal memory is presented in the following memory map: the 8051 has a bank of 128 bytes of Internal RAM. This Internal RAM is found on-chip on the 8051 so it is the fastest RAM available, and it is also the most flexible in terms of reading, writing, and modifying its contents. Internal RAM is volatile, so when the 8051 is reset this memory is cleared.

*   **Register Memory:** 8051 has 32 bytes of register memory which are classified into four register banks each containing eight registers R0 to R7.
*   **Bit Accessible Memory:** 8051 has 16 bytes of general purpose bit accessible memory (bit address 00H to 7FH). When the system does not require bit-access, these 16 bytes can be used as general purpose memory.
*   **General Purpose/Stack Memory:** The 80 bytes remaining of Internal RAM, from addresses 30h through 7Fh, may be used by user variables that need to be accessed frequently or at high-speed. This area is also utilized by the microcontroller as a storage area for the operating stack.

Figure 1. Pin configuration of AT89s51 microcontroller.

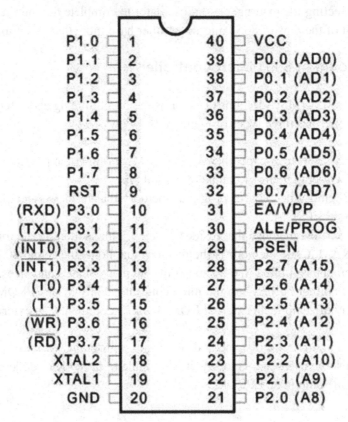

Timers

The 8051 comes equipped with two timers, both of which may be controlled, set, read and configured individually. The 8051 timers have three general functions: 1) Keeping time and/or calculating the amount of time between events, 2) Counting the events themselves, or 3) Generating baud rates for the serial port. There are six SFRs for reading and controlling timer of 8051. TCON (Timer Control, Addresses 88h, Bit-Addressable): The Timer Control SFR is used to configure and modify the way in which the 8051's two timers operate. This SFR controls whether each of the two timers is running or stopped and contains a flag to indicate that each timer has overflowed. Additionally, some non-timer related bits are located in the TCON SFR. These bits are used to configure the way in which the external interrupts are activated and also contain the external interrupt flags which are set when an external interrupt has occurred. TMOD (Timer Mode, Addresses 89h): The Timer Mode SFR is used to configure the mode of operation of each of the two timers. Using this SFR the program may configure each timer to be a 16-bit timer, an 8-bit auto-reload timer, a 13-bit timer, or two separate timers. Additionally, we may configure the timers to only count when an external pin is activated or to count "events" that are indicated on an external pin. TL0/TH0 (Timer 0 Low/High, Addresses 8Ah/8Ch): These two SFRs, taken together, represent timer 0. Their exact behaviour depends on how the timer is configured in the TMOD SFR; however, these timers always count up. What is configurable is how and when they increment in value.

TL1/TH1 (Timer 1 Low/High, Addresses 8Bh/8Dh): These two SFRs, taken together, represent timer 1. Their exact behaviour depends on how the timer is configured in the TMOD SFR; however, these timers always count up. What is configurable is how and when they increment in value.

Encoder

The encoder begins a 4-word transmission cycle upon receipt of a transmission enable (TE). This cycle will repeat itself as long as the transmission enable (TE) is held low. Once the transmission enables returns high the encoder output completes its final cycle and transmits the 4 bit data through D-OUT pin of the encoder. The encoders are a series of CMOS LSIs for remote control system applications. They are capable of encoding information which consists of N address bits and 12N data bits. Each address/ data input can be set to one of the two logic states. The programmed addresses/data are transmitted together with the header bits via an RF or an infrared transmission medium upon receipt of a trigger signal. The capability to select a TE trigger on the HT12E or a DATA trigger on the HT12A further enhances the application flexibility of the 212 series of encoders. The HT12A additionally provides a 38 kHz carrier for infrared systems. The status of each address/data pin can be individually pre-set to logic high or low. If a transmission-enable signal is applied, the encoder scans and transmits the status of the 12 bits of address/data serially in the order A0 to AD11 for the HT12E encoder and A0 to D11 for the HT12A encoder. During information transmission these bits are transmitted with a preceding synchronization bit. If the trigger signal is not applied, the chip enters the standby mode and consumes a reduced current of less than 1A for a supply voltage of 5V. Usual applications preset the address pins with individual security codes using DIP switches or PCB wiring, while the data is selected by push buttons or electronic switches. Figure 2 and Figure 3 shows the pin diagram of HT12E encoder and HT12D decoder.

Figure 2. Pin configuration of HT12E encoder.

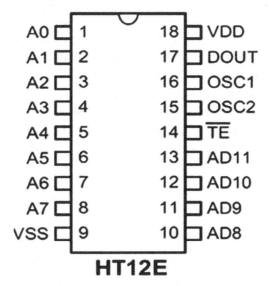

Figure 3. Pin configuration of HT12D decoder.

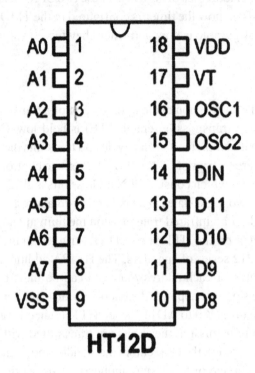

HT12D

DECODER

After reception of the signal, it interprets the first N bits of code period as addresses and the last bits as data. The decoders will then check the received address. If the received address codes all match the contents of the decoders local address, the data bits are decoded to activate the output pins and the VT pin is set high to indicate a valid transmission. This will last unless the address code is changed or no signal is received. The 212 decoders are a series of CMOS LSIs for remote control system applications. They are paired with series of encoders. For proper operation, a pair of encoder/decoder with the same number of addresses and data format should be chosen. The decoders receive serial addresses and data from a programmed 212 series of encoders that are transmitted by a carrier using an RF or an IR transmission medium. They compare the serial input data three times continuously with their local addresses. If no error or unmatched codes are found, the input data codes are decoded and then transferred to the output pins. The VT pin also goes high to indicate a valid transmission. The series of decoders are capable of decoding information that consists of N bits of address and 12N bits of data. Of this series, the HT12D is arranged to provide 8 address bits and 4 data bits, and HT12F is used to decode 12 bits of address information.

MOTORS

Servo Motors

A servo motor consists of several main parts, the motor and gearbox, a position sensor, an error amplifier and motor driver and a circuit to decode the requested position. RC servos are hobbyist remote control devices servos typically employed in radio-controlled models, where they are used to provide actuation for various mechanical systems such as the steering of a car, the control surfaces on a plane, or the rudder of a boat. Due to their affordability, reliability, and simplicity of control by microprocessors, RC servos are often used in small-scale robotics applications. RC servos are composed of an electric motor mechanically linked to a potentiometer. A standard RC receiver sends pulse-width modulation (PWM) signals to the servo. The electronics inside the servo translate the width of the pulse into a position. When the servo is commanded to rotate, the motor is powered until the potentiometer reaches the value corresponding to the commanded position. Figure 4 shows the internal block diagram of servo motor.

PWM MODULES

Many microcontrollers are equipped with PWM generators and most people initially consider using these to generate the control signals. Unfortunately they are not really suitable. The problem is that we need a relatively accurate short pulse then a long delay; and generally we only have one PWM generator share between several servos which would require switching components outside the microcontroller and complicate the hardware. The PWM generator is designed to generate an accurate pulse between 0 percent and 100 percent duty cycle, but we need something in the order of 5 percent to 10 percent duty cycle (1ms/20ms to 2ms/20ms). If a typical PWM generator is 8 bits, then we can only use a small fraction of the bits to generate the pulse width we need and so we lose a lot of accuracy.

TIMERS

A more beneficial approach can be implemented with simple timers and software interrupts. The key is realising that we can run a timer at a faster rate and do a single servo at a time, followed by the next and the next etc. Each of the outputs is driven in turn for its required time and then turned off. Once all outputs have been driven, the cycle repeats. The timer is configured so that we have plenty of accuracy over the 1 to 2 millisecond pulse time. Each servo pin is driven high in turn and the timer configured to interrupt the processor when the pulse should be finished. The interrupt routine then drives the output low. For simplicity, the output pins can be arranged on a single port and the value zero (0x00) written to the port to turn off all pins at once so that the interrupt routine does not need to know which servo output is currently active.

BRUSHLESS DC MOTOR

Brushless DC motors (BLDC motors) also known as electronically commutated motors are synchronous motors which are powered by a DC electric source via an integrated inverter, which produces an AC electric signal to drive the motor; additional sensors and electronics control the inverter output. The motor part of a brushless motor is often a permanent magnet synchronous motor, but can also be a switched reluctance motor, or induction motor. Brushless motors may be described as stepper motors; however, the term stepper motor tends to be used for motors that are designed specifically to be operated in a mode where they are frequently stopped with the rotor in a defined angular position.

MOTOR CONTROL POWER SUPPLIES

Typical brushless motors are permanent magnet synchronous AC motors, combined with sensor electronics and an AC signal generator (Inverter) driven by a DC supply. Typical brushless inverters use a switched power supply pulse width modulation to generate an AC drive signal. Various terms are used to refer to the inverters/electronic control systems

Motion Control Systems

Brushless motors are commonly used as pump, fan and spindle drives in adjustable or variable speed applications. They can develop high torque with good speed response. In addition, they can be easily automated for remote control. Due to their construction, they have good thermal characteristics and high energy efficiency. To obtain a variable speed response, brushless motors operate in an electromechanical system that includes an electronic motor controller and a rotor position feedback sensor.

Model Engineering

A microcontroller controlled BLDC motor powering a remote-controlled airplane. This external rotor motor weighs less than 200 grams, consumes approximately 11 watt and produces thrust of more than twice the weight of the plane with a proper propeller. Brushless motors are a popular motor choice for model aircraft. Their favourable power to-weight ratios and large range of available sizes, from under 5 gram to large motors rated at thousands of watts, have revolutionized the market for electric-powered model flight, displacing virtually all brushed electric motors. They have also encouraged a growth of simple, lightweight electric model aircraft, rather than the previous internal combustion engines powering larger and heavier models. The large power-to-weight ratio of modern batteries and brush less motors allows models to ascend vertically, rather than climb gradually. The low noise and lack of mess compared to small glow fuel internal combustion engines that are used is another reason for their popularity.

Transceiver Module

A transceiver is a device comprising both a transmitter and a receiver which are combined and share common circuitry or a single housing. When no circuitry is common between transmit and receive func-

Figure 4. Internal Block diagram of Servo motor.

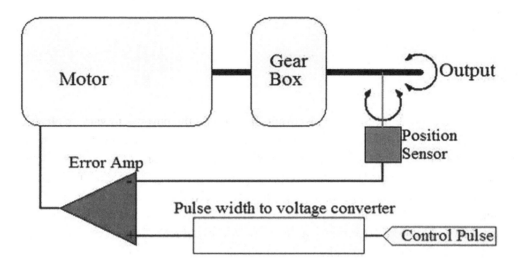

tions, the device is a transmitter-receiver. The term originated in the early 1920s. Technically, transceivers must combine a significant amount of the transmitter and receiver handling circuitry. Similar devices include transponders, transverters and repeaters.

In radio terminology, a transceiver means a unit which contains both a receiver and a transmitter. From the beginning days of radio the receiver and transmitter were separate units and remained so until around 1920. Amateur radio or "ham" radio operators can build their own equipment and it is now easier to design and build a simple unit containing both of the functions: transmitting and receiving. Almost every modern amateur radio equipment is now a transceiver but there is an active market for pure radio receivers, mainly for shortwave listening (SWL) operators.

TRANSMITTER

The transmitter consists of transmitter module of 434MHz frequency as well as the Encoder. The encoder converts the parallel data entered by the user from switch or any other thing to serial data which are different data and gives it to the transmitter module. The transmitter module takes the input data and modulates it with higher frequency signal and transmits. The modulation used here it is amplitude shift keying. The data which are sent may be used as simple data transmission or to control a remote device.

RECEIVER

The receiver consists of a receiver module of same frequency that of the transmitter and decoder. The receiver module receives the transmitted signal and demodulates it and gives the data as serial at the output. The serial data are then given to the decoder which transforms the data from serial to parallel. That data may be used in different motors to control any device. So in this case any receiver which is having the same frequency that of this receiver and having amplitude shift keying demodulation technique which is a simple envelope detector can receive the signal and will get the data which was transmitted by the receiver.

BLDC ESC

An electronic speed control or ESC is an electronic circuit with the purpose to vary an electric motor's speed, its direction and possibly also to act as a dynamic brake. ESCs are often used on electrically powered radio controlled models, with the variety most often used for brushless motors essentially providing an electronically-generated three phase electric power low voltage source of energy for the motor.

An ESC can be a stand-alone unit which plugs into the receiver's throttle control channel or incorporated into the receiver itself, as is the case in most toy-grade R/C vehicles. Some R/C manufacturers that install proprietary hobby-grade electronics in their entry-level vehicles, vessels or aircraft use onboard electronics that combine the two on a single circuit board.

THE MECHANICAL PLANE

Aerodynamic Forces

In simple terms, drag is the resistance of air molecules hitting the airplane (the backward force), thrust is the power of the airplane's engine (the forward force), lift is the upward force and weight is the downward force. So for airplanes to fly and stay airborne, the thrust must be greater than the drag and the lift must be greater than the weight (so as we can see, drag opposes thrust and lift opposes weight). This is certainly the case when an airplane takes off or climbs. However, when it is in straight and level flight the opposing forces of lift and weight are balanced. During a descent, weight exceeds lift and to slow an airplane drag has to overcome thrust. Thrust is generated by the airplane's engine (propeller or jet), weight is created by the natural force of gravity acting upon the airplane and drag comes from friction as the plane moves through air molecules. Drag is also a reaction to lift, and this lift must be generated by the airplane in flight. This is done by the wings of the airplane. The Figure 5 shows the mechanical model of the plane and the force acting on it.

Elevators

The elevators are located on the rear half of the tail plane, or horizontal stabiliser. Like the ailerons they cause a subtle change in lift when movement is applied which raises or lowers the tail surface accordingly. In addition, air hitting deflected elevators does so in the same way as it hits the rudder i.e. with an exaggerated effect that forces the airplane to pitch upwards or downwards. Moving the elevator up will cause the airplane to pitch its nose up and climb, while moving them down will cause the airplane to pitch the nose down and dive. Elevators are linked directly to each other, so work in unison unlike ailerons. The tail plane, that the elevators are part of, counteracts the natural forces that are generated about a plane's Centre of Lift, and essentially it stops the plane from just uncontrollably diving in to the ground.

Rudder

The rudder is located on the back edge of the vertical stabilizer, or fin, and is controlled by servo motor. When the pilot pushes the left switch the rudder moves to the left. The air flowing over the fin now pushes harder against the left side of the rudder, forcing the nose of the airplane to rotate to the left.

Flaps

Flaps are located on the trailing edge of each wing, usually between the fuselage and the ailerons, and extend downward (and often outward) from the wing when put into use. The purpose of the flaps is to generate more lift at slower airspeed, which enables the airplane to fly at a greatly reduced speed with a lower risk of stalling. When extended further flaps also generate more drag which slows the airplane down much faster than just reducing throttle. Although the risk of stalling is always present, generally an airplane has to be flying very slowly to stall when flaps are in use at, for example, 10 degrees deflection. Obviously though stall speeds and safe airspeeds vary from airplane to airplane. Radio control model airplanes can be simpler - for example, just have rudder and elevator control or perhaps just rudder and motor control. But the same fundamental principles always apply to all airplanes, regardless of size, shape and design.

QUANTITATIVE ANALYTICAL EXPLANATION OF THE THEORETICAL MODELLING

In digital communication there are various kinds of modulation techniques, such as Amplitude Shift Keying, where it uses a finite number of amplitudes; each assigned a with unique pattern of binary digits. Usually, each ASK encodes an equal number of bits. The ASK demodulation is the simplest form of demodulation in digital communication, which can be demodulated by an envelope detector. It consists of a rectifier and a low-pass filter. The rectifier may be in the form of a single diode, or may be more complex. In our case for communication we are using a 434 MHz transceiver module. The data will be transmitted through the transmitter and the receiver will receive the data. Then it is given to the microcontroller, where the decision is taken for what data, which motor needs, pulse for the current controller. The microcontroller gives a low signal to the timer circuit where a different pulse is generated for particular duration to control the BLDC motor.

TECHNICAL DETAILS

Transmitter and Receiver

The microcontroller based RC plane has two parts for communication the transmitter and the receiver, the transmitter shown in the Figure 6 consists of various parts and components. It consists of transmitter module as well as the encoder and switches. One point of the switch is connected to the ground and

Figure 5. Mechanical model of a plane

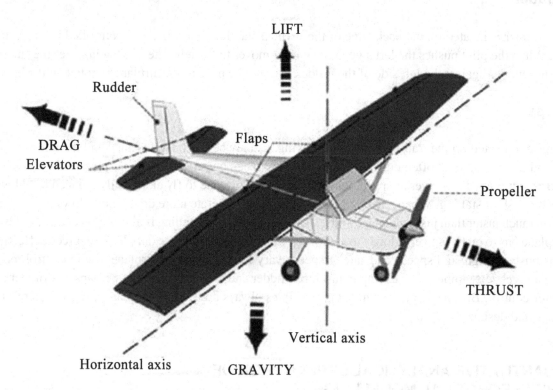

other one is to the encoder. For different switches different connections are made with the encoder. When switches are pressed, then the encoder checks the input data and address four times with the speed which is controlled by the resistor connected with the encoder.

After checking it four times, the data is send to the serial output pin of the encoder. Then the serial data is given to the RF module where this digital data is modulated with the higher frequency signal, which works as the carrier signal. In our case the carrier signal is 434 MHz. Then the signal goes to the power amplifier inside the module then to the antenna, which is an omni directional antenna.

The receiver block diagram shown in the Figure 7 receives the signal which was transmitted by the transmitter, where the antenna used is also the omni directional antenna. Upon receiving the signal it is amplified by the amplifier inside the module. Then the signal is demodulated by an envelope detector and error detection and correction is done. Then at the output of the module we find the exact serial data which was transmitted by the transmitter. The serial data is now given to the decoder where it initially checks the address of the data and then the original data. Similar to the encoder, the decoder also checks it four times. Then it decodes the data from the address and gives it to the four bit output pin of the decoder. Out of that 4 bit, 3 bit is connected to the microcontroller port P0 and the 4th bit is connected to the reset pin of the microcontroller. For controlling the servos, different pulses are generated inside the microcontroller according to the input received. Pin P1.1 and pin P1.2 are connected to the servos. The pin P1.0 is used to control the BLDC controller. This pin is connected to the pin number 2 of the 555 timer which is used as monostable multivibrator. So after receiving the signal The P1.0 pin triggers the 555 timer and the timer circuit gives a high voltage at the output for around 11 seconds. The time is controlled by the resistor used in the circuit. That means for one signal pulse it will give output for 11 seconds. Now the output of this timer is connected as the supply voltage of the second 555 timer which is used as astable multivibrator. The astable multivibrator gives output which depends upon the monostable multivibrator. The circuitry of the astable multivibrator is made as such that it gives an output pulse of 1.8 mS of 50Hz frequency. Then it is given to the not gate, because the astable multivibrator gives high voltage for longer time than the low voltage. But we need a signal that is high for 1.8 mS and the rest low. So, it can be achieved by only connecting not gate. The output signal of the not gate is then connected to the BLDC current controller or BLDC ESC. Which gives a continuous current to the BLDC motor and it runs at the full speed.

So there is a process of connecting the BLDC and the throttle input and that is as shown:

- **Entering Programming Mode:** After switching on the transmitter and giving full throttle we need to wait for 2 seconds. Then ESC emits tone like "Beep-Beep" then waiting for another 5 seconds, ESC will emit 5 beep tones. Then ESC is entered in the programming mode.
- **Select Programmable Items:** BLDC ESC emits different types of tones to communicate, when BLDC motor is connected to it. It actually uses BLDC motor to generate these tones. We will identify these tones by hearing the tones. "Beep" stands for the short tone. "Beeeep" stands for the long tone. Here One long "Beeeep" = 5 short "Beep" After entering in the programming mode as mentioned in step 1 we will hear these 8 Beep sequences with the interval of 3 seconds. After hearing the tone the throttle is disconnected.
- **Set Item Value:** Now we will hear several tones in loop. Setting the value matching to the tone by moving throttle to full position. If new setting is saved successfully then we will hear special tone "Beep Beeeep Beep Beeeep" which indicates that value is successfully set and saved. Now if we still keep the throttle sticks to top then we will be reverted back to previous step to go to other items. Moving throttle stick to full within 2 seconds will result in program mode exit.
- **Exiting the Program Mode:** There are 2 ways to exit program modes.
  - In previous step after hearing special tone "Beep Beeeep Beep Beeeep", then moving throttle to zero position within 2 seconds.
  - In second step after hearing tone Beeeep-Beeeep, then moving throttle to zero within 8 seconds.

Now during landing if the motor runs at the full speed it may damage the plane. So to control it the fourth pin of the decoder is connected to a relay. The relay controls the connection between the throttle input of the current controller and the output pulse of the not gate. If a particular switch is pressed at the receiver for that data the microcontroller is reset and the connection in the relay is disconnected. So the current controller does not receive the throttle input and the BLDC motor stops rotating. During takes off one particular data is transmitted which is received by the receiver and gives 1.8ms pulse to the controller. Then the controller gives maximum current output and the motor runs at full speed giving maximum thrust. During flight the direction and the altitude is controlled by the servos. The first 555 timer is used to control the main motor output for a particular time which is used as monostable multivibrator. The output of the monostable multivibrator is used as supply source to the astable multivibrator. When it needs to land, another control signal is send to the receiver for the motor controller. At this time the

Figure 6. Transmitter Section

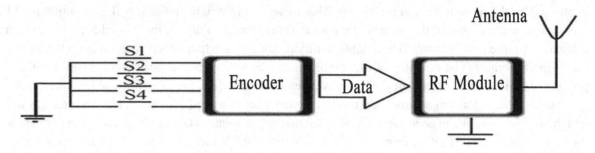

transmitter sends a data so the motor stops and the plane falls like a glider and at that time the direction and elevation can be controlled by the remote, so the plane comes down to proper landing place.

In our work we have used a particular bit sequence both at the transmitter and at the receiver. The circuit will generate one or more particular bit sequence and that bit sequence is merged with the original data. The generated bit sequence changes after every clock cycle. To generate a complex bit sequence, let say first circuit generated bit sequence is X1 and another circuit generated bit sequence is X2. Then between these two bit sequence XOR operation is done and the output is Y1 (X1 XOR X2 = Y1). Then again XOR operation is done between this output sequence Y1 and the original data bit say as D1.Then we will get a new sequence say as Y2 (Y1 XOR D1 = Y2).

This is then given to the transmitter. The transmitter sends the data to the receivers which are using same frequency as it is. That means every receiver can receive this signal which is using the frequency

Figure 7. Receiver Section

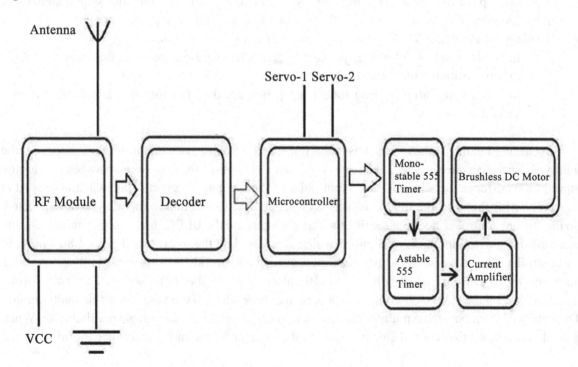

Figure 8. Block diagram of transmitter with coding scheme.

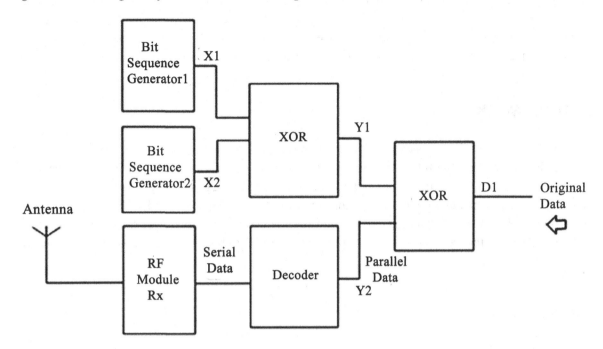

in this case 434MHz. So every receiver can extract the data Y2. But Y2 is not the original data, so to get the original data the receiver has to know the coding scheme. So at the receiver the same setup of bit generation circuit will be there which will generate the bit X1 and X2 and after XOR operation it will be Y1. So after generating the bit again XOR operation is done among the generated bit Y1 and the bit which is extracted from the received signal Y2, then we get the original data or bit (Y1 XOR Y2 = D1). The Figure 8 shows the block diagram for the coding scheme.

The final generated bit sequence can be made more complex by doing various operations among two, three or more no of bits. In this method the transmitter and the receiver setup should met two conditions one it should be switched on at the same time, so that the generation of the bit sequence starts at the same time. Because the bit sequence is changing after every clock cycle and it should generate the same bit sequence at the transmitter and the receiver at the same time, otherwise the receiver will be unable to extract the original data. Another condition is that the clock cycle speed should not be less than the transmission delay, because when the data is transmitted at the receiver after transmission delay the generated sequence should be same then only it can extract the original data

To generate the bit sequence the circuit may be made by shift registers and XOR gate. In our work we have used microcontroller to generate the bit sequence.

CONCLUSION

RC aircrafts or UAVs are likely to become more widely deployed, as there is considerable demand in both the public and private sectors to make use of these technologies. This explored the privacy concerns associated with RC aircraft technologies. These concerns may be identified and addressed by undertaking privacy impact assessments in order to ensure the appropriate collection, use, disclosure, and disposal of personal information. Various research activities show advanced capabilities in design, construction, system development, flight control and guidance, and operation of RC aircrafts. These capabilities and RC aircraft technologies have either been demonstrated in flight or through simulation.

FUTURE WORK

In future we thought of using a camera mounted on the plane so that by looking at the monitor we can fly the plane as well as it will be useful for survey from top. We will be using data encoding technique to secure the data which will be transmitted with a technique. By generating a particular code which will be changing depending upon the function we used, that will be controlled by highly synchronized pulse both at the transmitter and the receiver and we merge the data signal with the generated signal at the transmitter. At the receiver it will be able to extract the data because at the generated bit is known by the receiver.

REFERENCES

Bristeau, P. J., Callou, F., Vissière, D., & Petit, N. (2011). The Navigation and Control technology inside the AR. Drone micro UAV. *Proceedings of 18th IFAC World Congress Milano (Italy)* (pp. 1477-1484).

Brown, T. X., Argrow, B., Dixon, C., Doshi, S., Thekkekunnel, R.-G., Henkel, D. (2004). Ad Hoc UAV Ground Network. Proceedings of *AIAA 3rd "Unmanned Unlimited" Technical Conference, Workshop and Exhibit*. Chicago, Illinois.

Cummings, M. L., & Mitchell, P. J. (2008). Predicting Controller Capacity in Supervisory Control of Multiple UAVs. *IEEE Transactions on Systems, Man, and Cybernetics. Part A, Systems and Humans, 38*(2), 451–460. doi:10.1109/TSMCA.2007.914757

Cummings, M. L., Whitten, A., How, J. P., & Toupet, O. (2011). The impact of human-automation collaboration in decentralized multiple unmanned vehicle. *Naval Research STTR under the guidance of Aurora Flight Sciences,* 1-11. DOI:.10.1109/JPROC.2011.2174104

How, J., King, E., & Kuwata, Y. (2004). Flight Demonstrations of Cooperative Control for UAV teams. *Proceedings of AIAA 3rd "Unmanned Unlimited" Technical Conference, Workshop and Exhibit* (pp. 1-9).

Merino, L., Wiklund, J., Caballero, F., Moe, A., De Dios, J. R. M., & Forssen, P. E. et al. (2006). Vision-Based Multi-UAV Position Estimation. *Robotics & Automation Magazine, IEEE, 13*(3), 53–62. doi:10.1109/MRA.2006.1678139

Naskar, S., Das, S., Seth, A. K., & Nath, A. (2011). Application of Radio Frequency Controlled Intelligent Military Robot in Defense. *Proceedings of International Conference on Communication Systems and Network Technologies* (pp. 396-401). Doi:10.1109/CSNT.2011.88

Niethammer, U., Rothmund, S., Schwaderer, U., Zeman, J. & Joswig, M. (2011). Open Source Image-Processing Tools for Low-Cost UAV-Based Landslide Investigation. *International Archives of the Photogrammetry, Remote Sensing and Spatial Information Sciences,* XXXVIII-1/C22, 1-6. Retrieved from http://www.geometh.ethz.ch/uav_g/proceedings/niethammer

Pastor, E., Lopez, J., & Royo, P. (2007). UAV Payload and Mission Control Hardware/Software Architecture. *Aerospace and Electronic Systems Magazine, IEEE, 22*(6), 3–6. doi:10.1109/MAES.2007.384074

Schwing, R. P. Unmanned Arial Vehicles Revolutionary Tools in War and Peace. *United States Air Force USAWC Strategy Research Project*, 2–18.

KEY TERMS AND DEFINITIONS

Brushless DC Electric Motor (BLDC): Brushless DC electric motor are synchronous motors that are powered by a DC electric source via an integrated inverter/switching power supply, which produces an AC electric signal to drive the motor.

Decoder: Decoders are digital ICs which are used for decrypt or obtain the actual data from the received code, i.e. convert the binary input at its input to a form. It consists of n input lines and 2^n output lines. A decoder can also be used for obtaining the parallel data from the serial data received.

Encoder: Encoders are digital ICs used for generating a digital binary code for every input. An Encoder IC generally consists of an Enable pin which is usually set high to indicate the working. It consists of 2^n input lines and n output lines. In RF communication, the Encoder can also be used for converting parallel data to serial data.

Microcontroller: A microcontroller is a small computer on a single integrated circuit containing a processor core, memory, and programmable input/output peripherals.

Servomotor: A servomotor is a rotary actuator that allows for precise control of angular position, velocity and acceleration. It consists of a suitable motor coupled to a sensor for position feedback.

Transceiver: A transceiver is a device comprising both a transmitter and a receiver which are combined and share common circuitry or a single housing. When no circuitry is common between transmit and receive functions, the device is a transmitter-receiver.

Chapter 14
Exploiting Power Line for Communication Purpose:
Features and Prospects of Power Line Communication

Banty Tiru
Gauhati University, India

ABSTRACT

Power Line Communication (PLC) uses the available power line as a communication medium. The purpose of this chapter is to present the salient features, current trend and future scope of PLC with emphasis in the Indian context. Unlike other channels available, power lines are harsh media for data transfer and require efficient modeling and simulation techniques to propose and implement suitable mitigation schemes for achieving acceptable performance. Designed equipments have to adhere to strict mandates at the national and international levels to account for issues related to electromagnetic compatibility (EMC). In spite of this, PLC is expected to occupy an important place in the networking market in applications of smart grid and as a component of heterogeneous/hybrid communication system. The chapter is also backed by results from experiments carried on a typical power line in a test site with a presentation of noise, transfer characteristics, modeling and an estimate of the channel capacity.

INTRODUCTION

Power lines are readily available infrastructure that may be exploited for communication purposes. The idea started way back in the 1920's when two patents were issued to the American telephone and telegraph company (patent number 1,607,668 and 1,672,940) in the field of "Carrier Transmission over Power Circuits" involving communication over three- phase AC power wiring (Fetter, 1926). Consequently a rapidly growing field known as Power Line Communication (PLC) or Power Line Carrier Communication (PLCC) has emerged in the developed countries as well as in some developing ones.

The objective of this chapter is to review the work done on PLC based on available literature; present the salient features that are required for understanding the system and discuss some of the future prospects

DOI: 10.4018/978-1-4666-8493-5.ch014

and expectations. The chapter starts with a note on the utilities benefitted from PLC. A description of the power line grid and a generic PLC system with the mandating standards is given. The associated problems and the characteristics that make it unique and different from others channels available are discussed using results from experiments carried out in a typical indoor power line. Next, modeling, simulation and mitigation methodologies that is indispensible for successful implementation has been presented. Issues relating to electromagnetic compatibility (EMC) and controversies that limit extensive usage have been discussed in brief. The current research and future prospects which is the driving force behind all research has been presented. In the end, the available scope in the Indian context has been discussed with an estimate of the channel capacity from experimental results.

POWER LINE COMMUNICATION UTILITIES

PLC is often heralded as the "third wire" technology offering applications in attractive modes. The ubiquity nature of power lines make it a suitable candidate for delivering new energy added values and telecommunication services of various natures. With large production, and decrease in cost, PLC aims to capture the last mile and last inch applications in areas of *access*, *in-house* and *control*. Access PLC provides communications to and among houses using either the overhead or underground electrical distribution lines. In-house devices enable resource sharing, offer easy integration of equipments within the home, provide internet sharing and even telephony. Utilities of control include automatic meter reading, real- time monitoring, voltage control and load management, scheduling and forecasting through smart grids that could improve reliability and safety to electrical customers.

THE POWER LINE GRID

The power line grid is the largest network connecting urban, sub-urban and rural places with nearly 100% electrification in some countries and even in some rural areas. Depending on voltage levels, the grids can be divided into high voltage (HV), medium voltage (MV), and low voltage (LV) lines as shown in Figure 1. Electricity is generated at the generating station and transmitted at HV $\left(\geq 120kV\right)$ over overhead lines to long distances for nationwide and even international transfers. In the distribution stage, the HV is first step down to MV $\left(1 \leq V \leq 30kV\right)$ via primary transformer substations (PTS) and distributed to towns, cities and industrial complexes through buried or overhead cables. Finally the MV is stepped down to LV $\left(V \leq 1kV\right)$ through a secondary transformer substation (STS) and distributed to the end users. Electricity usually enters a customer's premise through a *house access point* (HAP) followed by an electric meter and a distribution box. The grid structures vary from country to country in terms of length of the LV line, number of homes reached by each line, voltage levels and method of injection. These pose a problem in generalizing the construction of PLC system and have been discussed in later sections.

Figure 1. Generic power line grid and power line communication system

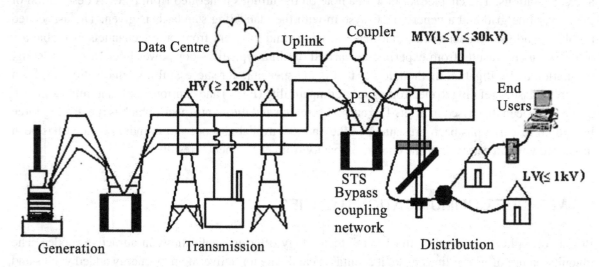

SALIENT FEATURES OF POWER LINE COMMUNICATION

Generic Power Line Communication System

Power line can be used for communication in all the three voltage levels, each having its own pros and cons. As HV has very few or no branches, the attenuation of high frequency signal is very less compared to that in their MV and LV counterparts (Lazaropoulos, 2012). However, time varying voltage arching, corona noise (Suljanovic, Mujcic, Zajc & Tasic, 2003) and difficulty in coupling prevent this to be commonly used for communication. Duckhwa and Younghun (2008), have reported successful trials of communication in HV lines. In a generic system (Figure 1), MV lines can act as the first pipelining for high speed data connection from a backbone powered by optical fiber, satellite or wireless. From here, data flows through the LV and delivered to the customer's premise through the HAP for different utilities. Transfer of signal across $MV \Leftrightarrow LV$ requires bypass coupling networks in the secondary transformers to reduce losses. Communication outside and to the HAP is called the *access* PLC. The communication within the house is called the *in-house* PLC. Repeaters may be used to exploit the full capacity this mode of communication in the global scale.

PLC Standards

At present, PLC is commercially implemented in more than 60 sites worldwide; following standards aiming efficiency of multiple users, immunity to interference and to render electromagnetically safe. Several bodies lead the complex standardization process co-operating in the international and national level. Depending on the standards, PLC can broadly be categorized into *narrowband* and *broadband*. Narrowband (NB) devices allow low data rates for control applications. For Western Europe, the NB regulations are in the CENELAC (European Committee for Electrotechnical Standardization) Standard EN 50065 ("Signaling on low voltage," 1991). The standard allows communication in the range 3 kHz to 148.5 kHz, with transmitted power depending on the specific channel and coupling method but not exceeding 500mW. The frequency band 3-95 kHz is reserved for energy providers (9 – 95 kHz known as the A band). Bands B (95-125 kHz), C (125-140 kHz) and D (140-148.5 kHz) are reserved for domestic use. In North America, the Federal Communications Commission (FCC) regulates the use of PLC in the band 9 - 530 kHz (Part 15 Subpart B, "Unintentional radiators", 2014). Part 15 of the FCC also allow communication outside this frequency in the band 535-1705 kHz. Broadband devices also known as Broadband Power Line Communication (BPL) systems use a large bandwidth (1.8-250MHz) and cater to high data rate requirements for access and in-house. BPL is governed by standards like HPA (Home Plug Power line Alliance), UPA (Universal Power line Association), OPERA (Open PLC European Research Alliance), and CEPCA (Consumer Electronics Powerline Communication Alliance) and IEEE. At present, the IEEE P1901 and ITU-T G.hn have replaced many existing standards.

PROBLEMS WITH POWER LINE CHANNELS

Though PLC seems to be a plausible solution to last-mile connectivity, the problems encountered are many. The reason for this is that power lines were not initially designed keeping communication in mind but for low frequency 50/60Hz AC signals. Some power line characteristics and associated problems are presented here.

1. **Frequency and Time Dependent Transfer Characteristics:** Experimental results and simulation. Power line channel is different from other communication channels like wireless and co-axial. To get an ideal of the characteristics an experiment is conducted in a typical indoor power line setting of a floor in the university building.
    a. **Study of Transfer Function:** In the experiment carried (layout in Figure 2a) referred to as the *test site*, high frequency signal from a signal generator is inserted to the power line at room A and the same received at various distances in rooms B,C,D and E. The distribution boxes (DB1 and DB2) distribute power to various rooms and are fed from the distribution room (DR). Both the transmitter and receiver are connected to the power line via couplers. The couplers (Figure 2b) are constituted of transformers (T) and capacitors (C1 and C2) with suitable protecting circuits (FUSE, metal oxide varistors or 'mov' and diodes) that act as high pass filters (Figure 2c) protecting the connected instruments from the power line voltage. It was seen in Figure 3 that the received signal in the different rooms decreases with frequency and the length of the transmission path and characterized by notches at which the received signal was minimal. The signal traversing through the DB (A to C, D and E) show more attenuation than that without (A to B) even though the difference in the lengths of the path is only a few meters. On traversing the communication path, the signal has to pass through pieces of wires having varying transmission parameters with taps and bridges (Tiru and Boruah, 2012) with different loaded conditions. Signal traversing from a transmitter to a receiver suffer reflections from the discontinuities and cause occurrences of notches in the transfer function making it highly frequency selective. The experiment is carried in the evening when the variation of channel conditions is minimal.
    b. **Time variance of the Transfer Function:** To study the time variance of the transfer function with load, a power line network with known topology was simulated using the two wire transmission line theory using the parameters from a real situation. As such, the inductance

Figure 2. (a) Experimental site for studying the transfer function of indoor power line (b) design of the coupler (c) frequency response of the coupler

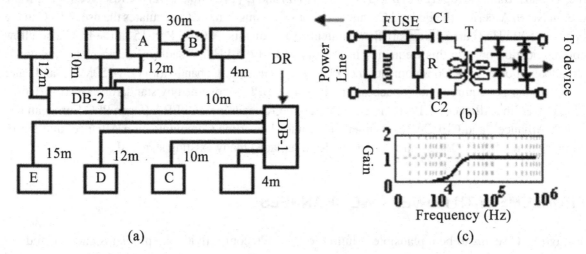

(a) (b) (c)

per unit length (L), conductance per unit length (G), capacitance per unit length (C) and the high frequency characteristics impedance $\left(Z_o \right)$ of the power line cable is taken to be 0.69μH/m, 0.018μmho/m, 38pf/m and 135 Ω respectively. The network consisted of a number of plug points between the transmitter and receiver. In the simulation, a load is shifted to various plugs keeping the position of the transmitter and receiver same. It is seen in Figure 4a that for different position of the load, the transfer function changes considerably. Similarly, Figure 4b shows the transfer function of the same system when different types of loads are selected randomly. There are situations when the transfer function is flat while on other cases there are deep that occur at unpredicted frequencies. Thus the transfer function is highly time variant which makes it unique compared to other channels.

The power line characteristics cannot be generalized and according to Chen and Chiueh (2002) can even show "contradictory results". The channel impedance is varying and leads to insufficient coupling between the transceivers and the power line.

2. **Time Varying Noise Characteristics:** Modeling the experimental results. The noise in the power line cannot be modeled as Additive White Gaussian Noise or AWGN (Tiru and Boruah, 2010) commonly used in conventional communication systems. This is because the noise is usually man made originating from equipments being plugged on to the line and the unshielded wires become easy target of electromagnetic interferences. Hooijen and Vinck (1998) segregated the noise as consisting of colored background noise, impulse noise (synchronous and asynchronous to the AC mains), switching transients and narrowband interferences due to nearby radio stations.

a. **Background Noise:** Background noise has a relatively low power spectral density (PSD), non-stationary, and caused by summation of numerous noise sources with low power. In an experiment carried at the *test site* referred earlier, it is seen that PSD of background noise in the CENELAC band follows a linearly decaying function modeled by $N\left(f \right) = mf + c\, dB/Hz$

Figure 3. Received signal in different plugs

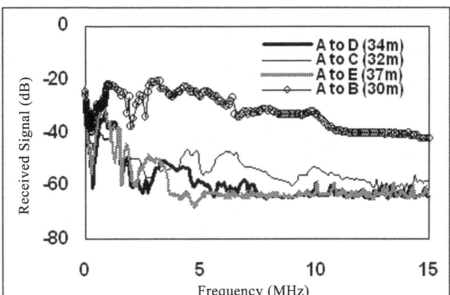

(Tiru, 2012). For high frequencies the noise is modeled by an exponentially decaying function given by $N(f) = a \ \exp^{bx} + c \ \exp^{dx} \ dB / Hz$ (Tiru and Boruah, 2010).The values of the constants in the equations are given in Table 1. The background noise varies in terms of minutes and even hours and changes between a maximum (worst case) and minimum (best case) limits. Different papers have modeled the background noise using different models (Table 1). A comparison between different models show that the best case (~-135dB/Hz) is recorded by Hooijen (1997) and the worst case (~-72 dB/Hz) by Tiru (2012) for CENELAC A band. For BPL, the best case (~-191 dB/Hz) is recorded by Biglieri (2003) and worst case (~-111dB/Hz) recorded by Liu, Gao, Bilal and Korhonen (2004) at the highest frequency of the observation (61.5MHz). Thus the noise scenario faced by PLC devices cannot be generalized and vary from place to place.

Figure 4. Transfer function of a network known a-priori for (a) varying position of the same load in the network (b) random load

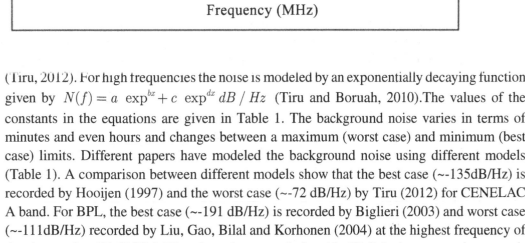

Table 1. Power line models and parameters for background noise; B=Best case, W=Worst case.

Band	Model	Constant	Ref.
CENELAC A	$N(f) = 10^{K-3.95*10^{-5}f} \left(W/Hz\right)$	K=-9.64 (B) ;-7.64(W)	Hooijen, 1997
	$V_n = 0.001f_{kHz}^2 - 0.25f_{kHz} - K(dBV)$	K=52(B) ; 40(W)	Yavuz et al., 2000.
	$N(f) = mf + c$	m,c=-0.0001,-77.73(B);-0.0002,-53.41 (W)	B.Tiru, 2012
BPL	$N(f) = 10^{a-b^c} (W/Hz)$	a,b,c=-115, 100, -0.8	Liu et al., 2004
	$S_n(f) = a + b|f|^c \ dBm/Hz$	a,b,c=-140, 38.75, -0.720 (B); -145, 53.23, -0.337 (W)	Biglieri, 2003
	$N(f) = a \ \exp^{bx} + c \ \exp^{dx} dB/Hz$	a,b,c,d=-142.9, -2.7x10^{-17}, 24.3, -1.47x10^{-13} (B) -111.9, 1.5x10^{-10}, 21.02, -2.94x10^{-7} (W)	B.Tiru et al, 2010

b. **Impulsive Noise:** Periodic asynchronous impulsive noise are usually caused by switching power supplies and have in a repetition rate between 50 kHz to 200 kHz, thus resulting in a spectrum with discrete lines. Periodic synchronous noise is caused by power supplies operating synchronously with the mains cycle. Asynchronous impulsive noise is caused by switching transients in the network. Figure 5 gives a snapshot of the different types of noise in power line captured in the *test site*. Proposals of different models for different components of power line noise are available in papers. Some of these are Middleton noise model, Markov chains, Bernoulli processes and Gaussian Mixture models. It is to be noted that the models must be easily implementable on computer simulations and must be realistic enough to portray the statistical properties.

c. **Narrowband Interferences:** The PSD of noise showed two narrowband peaks at 730 kHz and 1.03 MHz (Figure 5) which are the frequencies of the radio transmitter situated close to the *test site*.

3. **Variation of Grid Structures:** Another problem with implementation of PLC is that the topology used for power line wiring varies amongst and within countries. Power may be introduced using the balanced (USA, Europe and Japan) or unbalanced lines (Australia and UK) ("Broadband Power Line Communications", 2003). The methodology used determines a number of issues like mode of injection and the amount of radio emission expectable. The devices designed comply with the standards operable in the region and cannot be used universally in all countries.

In addition to the above cited problems, simplified models are available for other competing links like wireless and telephone networks but not for power line channels and a solid approach is still lacking (Biglieri and Torino, 2003).

Figure 5. Snapshots of different types of noise in power line and PSD

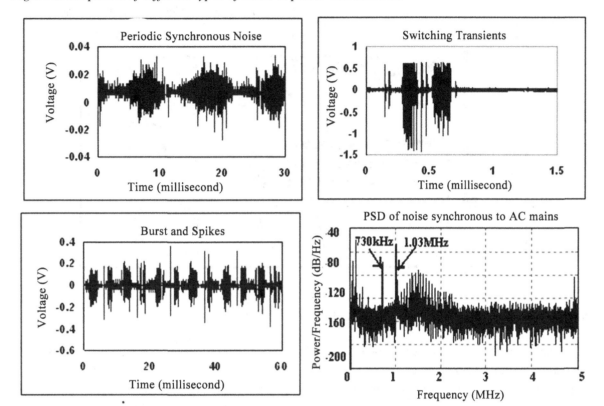

Modeling of Power Line Channels: Simulation Results

An integral part of the study of any channel for communication is the modeling and simulation of the channel conditions leading to testing and optimization of suitable transmission scheme as a preliminary requisite before implementation in actual hardware. This requires extensive study of the channel characteristics and efficient modeling. Modeling methodologies to replicate a power line channel can broadly be divided into top down and bottom up approach. In the top down approach, the model parameters are estimated after the measurement of the actual transfer function while in the later, the same is estimated theoretically. The power line environment can be analyzed in the time domain using a multi-path dependent echo model or in the frequency domain using scattering or transmission matrices. The multi-conductor transmission line theory also incorporates the return ground wire in simulation and requires the grounding practices to be elaborately known.

To find out the applicability of modeling to power line channels an experiment was conducted in which a network was simulated with all the elements known a-priori and the transfer function found out. The same system was implemented in reality and the experimental transfer function was also determined. It is seen that the simulated transfer function shows 80-90% correlation between the experimental results when complete information of the channel was known (Figure 6) with increased attenuation. However when the experimental network is connected with the power line of the other part of the building, the correlation decreases due to incomplete information of the network. The simulation methods therefore opted has to take into account the extent of reliability of the models.

Figure 6. Modeling of in-house power lines using transmission matrices: Simulated and experimental results; Experimental (1): complete information, Experimental (2): Incomplete information of the channel

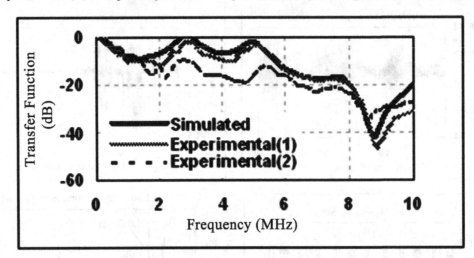

MITIGATION TECHNIQUES FOR A HARSH CHANNEL

PLC devices must incorporate sophisticated encoding and signal processing techniques to combat the cited odds. Most of the devices use spread spectrum (DSSS, CDMA) and multi-carrier modulation like Orthogonal Frequency Division Multiplexing (OFDMA) techniques to cope with frequency selective channels and offer robustness against interferences. The performance of the system is optimized by adaptively varying the transmitted power level, constellation size, code rate, symbol transmission rate etc depending on the channel conditions. At present, commercially available BPL devices give a data rate of more than 500 Mbps. The devices usually use carrier sense multiple access with collision avoidance (CSMA/CA) and carrier sense multiple access with collision detection (CSMA/CD) for channel access. Some of the available technologies and their salient features are given in Table 2

ISSUES AND CONTROVERSIES

In the past decade, a lot of controversies have developed on the future applicability of PLC. Power line cables are unshielded and acts as an antenna radiating the signal into space (Phillips, 1999). These emissions relate directly to the "common mode current" caused by electrical unbalance of the power line network. The emissions are exaggerated by faults and discontinuities in the wired network and increase with the transmitted signal power and frequency. The radiation interfere with amateur radio, maritime communications, aeronautical, defense and navigation services. The regulatory bodies like FCC, European Communications Committee (ECC) of CEPT, the Radio-communications agency in the UK, British Broadcasting Corporation (BBC), International Electro-technical Commission (IEC), International special Committee on radio interference (CISPR) and Japanese Ministry of telecommunications provide mandatory rules for limiting the emissions and operation of these devices. Moreover, standards that are "safe" in some countries may be "unsafe" in others. PLC services are under close surveillance in many countries.

Table 2. Some available PLC Technologies

Device	Technology	Band	Data Rate	Modulation	Uses
NB	X-10	120kHz	60bps	ASK	Control
	LonWorks	125-140kHz	10kbps	SS, CSMA	Home automation
	CEbus	<500kHz	10kbps	SS, CSMA/CDCR	Home automation
BPL	HomePlug AV	2-28MHz	200Mbits/s	OFDM,CSMA/CA, TDMA	In house
	HomePlug AV2	30-86MHz	>500Mbits/s	OFDMA, MIMO	In house
	HomePlug Green PHY	2-30MHz	10Mbits/s	OFDM	Smart Grid

Siding aside the EMC issues, PLC has to compete with other matured technologies wired and wireless alike in terms of efficiency, complexities and cost. The advantage over wireless is that there is no limitation caused by brick walls and requires no extra investment in lying of additional cables. However, till date, the cost of a PLC device is quite high compared to other available options. Critics disagree whether PLC will be opted more than the far matured counterpart (Tongia, 2004). Some researchers are of the opinion that though PLC does not appear to be a major disruptive technology in the competitive market, it must be considered strategically and technically for future decisions (Fink and Rho, 2008) on rural networking. The next few years are decisive for whether PLC can compete successfully in the broadband market.

CURRENT RESEARCH AND FUTURE SCOPE

Present research in PLC incorporates robust decoding, optimizing of error codes, physical layer security, noise mitigation schemes, efficient simulation, modeling, coupling and Multiple Input Multiple Output (MIMO) PLC to envisage an efficient workable system in various fields. Apart from these there are a few emerging branches which are expected to occupy an important place in the networking market in the recent future.

Development of Smart Grid

The most important application of PLC expected to rule the decades to come is the implementation and application of the Smart Grid. Smart Grid is a modernized electrical grid system that enables analog and digital communications via it to gather information about the grid condition and acts upon it in an automated fashion. It must be noted that the world's energy generation has been spaced out by the growth of energy demand. According to the analysis done by the *International Energy Outlook 2013* (*IEO2013*), the world energy consumption will grow by 56% between 2010 (524 quadrillion British thermal units) and 2040 (820 quadrillion British thermal units). India's 223GW production in 2013 is less than half of 575GW, forecasted in 2027. Balancing generation and demand at a granular level requires an efficient strategy for protection and control which can only be done by extensive use of smart grid technology.

Smart Grid have the potential to lead to sustainable development by reducing emissions from generating plants, efficient monitoring, control, deployment of dynamic pricing and demand response strategies.

Heterogeneous/Hybrid Networking

PLC can also be used with other networking options forming a part of a heterogeneous or hybrid communication system thus minimizing some of its disadvantages. A hybrid system may inject a BPL signal onto a MV power line and use a special extractor to translate the signal to wireless channel which is delivered to the end-users. Alternately, hybrid systems can also capture wireless signal and inject them directly onto the LV power line for distribution. A hybrid system is found to be very efficient for smart grid systems (Salvadori, Gehrke, Campos, Oliveira and Sausen, 2013) and home networking. The recently developed IEEE 1905.1 provides a common interface to widely deployed home networking technologies both wireless and wired supporting four media: Ethernet (IEEE 802.3), Wi-Fi (IEEE 802.11), power line(IEEE 1901) and co-axial cabling using the Multimedia over Co-Ax (MoCA) specification. An example of a heterogeneous network for home networking is shown in Figure 7. The PLC signals can also be converted to visible light for indoor wireless networking (Komnie, Haruyama and Nakagawa, 2006) using suitable devices like light emitting diodes considered by many researchers as the future lighting technology

Figure 7. IEEE 1905.1 Heterogeneous/Hybrid home networking

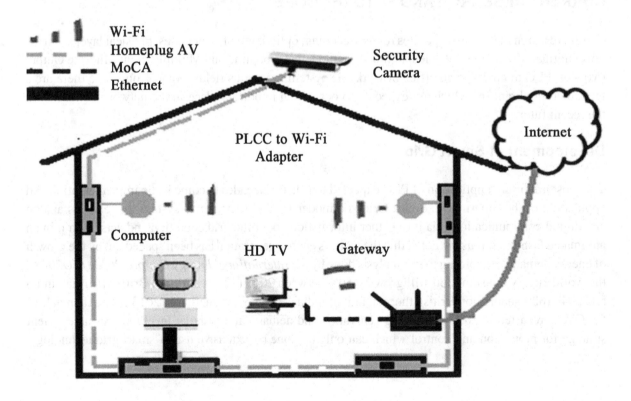

SCOPE OF PLC IN INDIA

Even after years of development, India still lags behind in areas of networking and control. Automated data acquisition and control in industries, offices and other monitoring plants are rare because of unavailability of the necessary networking infrastructure. The tele- density of rural areas is still low (40.96%, Sept, 2013) compared to that in urban (137.93%) areas ("Energy, Infrastructure and Communication", 2013). As such, India still needs a technology that can penetrate every nook and corner of the country at minimum cost. It must be noted that India has a wide coverage of the power grid that reaches well above 83% of the population with 100% penetration in many towns and villages ("Number of Towns," 2008). However, use of the same for communication is still limited to voice and SCADA between two power substations in a low frequency range (30 kHz-500 kHz). To get an idea of the channel capacity in the Indian power line network, the same was evaluated using the experimental findings of transfer function and noise in the *test site*.

Channel Capacity in a Typical Indian Power Line Network

Channel capacity estimate in the *test site* incorporates a rough estimate using Shannon's capacity theorem followed by narrower bounds given by the water filling approach. In the former, the power line channel is considered as an ideal filter $\left(\|H(f)\| = 1\right)$ with additive white noise approximation. The best and worst white noise approximation is the noise detected at the highest frequency of the allowed band for the best case noise model and the lowest frequency for the worst case noise model respectively. The estimation shows that at the maximum transmitter power of the allowed bands, a capacity of ~ 1.48-0.57, 0.47-0.29, 0.29-0.21 and 0.12-0.1 Mbps can be obtained for CENELAC-A,B,C and D respectively. The water filling approach considering the frequency selectivity of the channel and the non white nature of noise gives a tighter limits for the channel capacity to 1.358-0.812, 0.445-0.313, 0.279-0.218 and 0.119-0.097 Mbps in the respective bands. Similarly, in the bandwidth of 1-10 MHz at a transmit power of only 0.1mW, the water filling channel capacity of 52.42 Mbps and 270 kbps could be obtained for channel A to B and A to E (Figure 2a) respectively .

It is found that the channel capacity for NB transmission is enough for control applications. The capacity for BPL can be increased for larger bandwidths. Indian power grid thus offers a large scope for various networking utilities in accessible and inaccessible points thereby increasing the efficiency of the existing industries and plants. Giving serious consideration and priority to BPL would be worthwhile when backhauled by wireless communication (Krishna, Siddhartha, Kumar, Jogi, 2014) in a country where serious financial constraints exist.

CONCLUSION

In this chapter a bird's eye view of PLC is given with the results from experimental readings taken at a local site. Though the problems are many, PLC holds a promising future assuring high performance to the end users using advanced and complex technologies. Large production of the devices is expected to reduce the cost of adapters and enhance implementation of the system. Development of heterogeneous/ hybrid systems reinstates the necessity of exploitation of power line as a communication channel. Government in many countries encourages deployment of PLC to solve problems of the digital divide which is mandatory for development. However, the same is materialized only if the researchers, energy providers, telecommunication engineers and policy makers join hands together to exploit the infrastructure to the fullest. For countries where laying down of copper cables and short haul satellite is costly, PLC provides an option to be considered and can even be the driving force to provide power to the remote areas still un reached.

REFERENCES

Biglieri, E., & Torino, P. (2003). Coding and Modulation for a horrible channel. *IEEE Communications Magazine, 41*(5), 92–98. doi:10.1109/MCOM.2003.1200107

Broadband Powerline Communications Systems. (2003). *Australian Communications Authority*. Retrieved from http://acma.gov.au/webwr/radcomm/frequency_planning/spps/0311spp.pdf

Chen, Y. F., & Chiueh, T. D. (2002). Baseband Transceiver Design of a 128-Kbps Power-Line Modem for Household Applications. *IEEE Transactions on Power Delivery, 17*(2), 338–344. doi:10.1109/61.997894

Duckhwa, H., & Younghun, L. (2008). A study on the compound communication network over the high voltage power line for distribution automation system. *Proceedings of the 2nd International Conference on Information Security and Assurance* (pp. 410–414). Busan, Korea.

Energy, Infrastructure and Communication (2013). Retrieved from http://www. indiabudget.nic.in/budget2013-2014/es2012-13/echap-11.pdf

European Committee for Electrotechnical Standardization (CENELEC). EN 50065-1 (1991). Signaling on Low Voltage Electrical Installations in the Frequency Range 3 kHz to 148.5 kHz-Part 1: General Requirements, Frequency Bands and Electromagnetic Disturbances. Retrieved from http://www.bsi-global.com/en/Shop

Fetter, C. H. (1926). *Carrier transmission over power circuits, US 1607668 A*. Retrieved from http://www.google/patents/US1607668

Fink, D., & Rho, J. J. (2008). Feasible connectivity solutions of PLC for rural and remote areas. *In Proceedings of the International Symposium on Power-Line Communications and its Applications* (pp. 158-163). New Orleans, LA, USA. doi:10.1109/ISPLC.2008.4510416

Hooijen, O. G. (1997). A channel model for low voltage power line channels: measurement and simulation results. *Proceedings of the International Symposium on Power-Line Communications and its Application* (pp. 51-56). Essen, Germany.

Hooijen, O. G., & Vinck, A. J. H. (1998). On the channel Capacity of a European Style Residential Power Circuit. *Proceedings of the IEEE International Symposium on Power-Line Communications and its Applications* (pp. 31-44). Essen, Germany.

Konnie, T., Haruyama, S., & Nakagawa, M. (2006). Performance evaluation of narrowband OFDM on integrated system of power line communication and visible light wireless communication. *Proceedings of the 1st International conference on wireless pervasive computing*. Fort Worth, Texas, USA

Krishna, R., Siddhartha, R. K., Kumar, N., & Jogi, G. L. (2014). Broadband over Power Lines (BPL) for Indian Telecom Network. Retrieved from http://www.tec.gov.in/studypaper/BPL%20[Final].pdf

Lazaropoulos, A.G. (2012). Broadband Transmission Characteristics of Overhead High Voltage Power Line Communication channels. *Progress in Electromagnetics Research B,* 373-399.

Liu, E. R., Gao, Y., Bilal, O., & Korhonen, T. (2004). Broadband Characterization of Indoor Power Line Channel. *Proceedings of the International Symposium on Power-Line Communications and its Applications.* Zaragosa, Spain.

Number of towns and villages electrified in India (2008). Retrieved from http://mospi.nic.in/Mospi_New/upload/statistical_year_book_2011/SECTOR-3-INDUSTRY%20SECTOR/CH-16-ENERGY/Table%2016.14.xls

Philipps, H. (1999). Modeling of powerline communication channels. *Proceedings of the International Symposium on Power-Line Communications and its Applications* (pp. 14-21). Lancaster, UK.

Salvadori, F., Gehrke, C.S., Campos, Oliveira, A.C. M., & Sausen, P.S. (2013). Smart Grid Infrastructure Using a Hybrid Network Architecture. *IEEE Transaction on Smart Grid,* 4(3), 1630-1639.

Suljanović, N., Mujcic, A., Zajc, M., & Tasic, J. F. (2003). Corona noise characteristics in high voltage PLC channel. *Proceeding of the IEEE conference on Industrial technology* (Vol. 2, pp. 1036–1039). IEEE.

Tiru, B., & Boruah, P. K. (2010). Multipath effects and adaptive transmission of Indoor Power Line Back ground noise. *International Journal of Communication Systems,* 23, 63–76.

Tiru, B., & Boruah, P. K. (2012). Modeling Power Line Channel Using ABCD Matrices for Communication Purposes. *Lecture Notes in Information Technology,* 9, 374–379.

Tongia, R. (2004). Can Broadband over powerline carrier (PLC) complete? A techno-economic analysis. *Telecommunications Policy,* 28(7-8), 559–578. doi:10.1016/j.telpol.2004.05.004

Unintentional radiators C.F.R. Part 15 Subpart B. (2014). *Cornell Law.* Retrieved from http://www.law.cornell.edu/cfr/text/47/part-15/subpart-B

US Energy Information Administration. (2013). *International Energy outlook 2013.* Retrieved from http://www.eia.gov/forecasts/ieo/pdf/0484(2013).pdf

Yavuz, E., Kural, K., Coban, N., Ercan, B., & Safak, N. (2000). Modeling of Power Lines for digital communications. *Proceedings of the International Symposium on Power-Line Communications and its Applications.* Lancaster, UK.

KEY TERMS AND DEFINITIONS

Disruptive Technology: A technology that will capture the communication market disrupting all the other earlier technologies.

Power Line Grid: The power line grid is the largest network connecting urban, sub-urban and rural places with nearly 100% electrification in some countries and even in some rural areas.

Power-Line Communication (PLC): PLC carries data on a conductor that is also used simultaneously for AC electric power transmission or electric power distribution to consumers.

Smart Grid: Smart Grid is a modernized electrical grid system that enables analog and digital communications via it to gather information about the grid condition and acts upon it in an automated fashion.

Ubiquity: The capacity of a system to be everywhere and having omnipresent nature.

Chapter 15
Different Aspects of Interleaving Techniques in Wireless Communication

Barnali Das
Gauhati University, India

Manash Pratim Sarma
Gauhati University, India

Kandarpa Kumar Sarma
Gauhati University, India

ABSTRACT

This chapter describes the use of certain interleavers for use in a wireless communication set for better accuracy and constancy of the transmitted data. Different interleaver techniques and methods are explored, including the variation of associated system parameters. The performance derived is discussed and the most suitable design is ascertained which is essential for better reliability of a wireless communication system. Bit Error Rate (BER), computational time, mutual information and correlation are the parameters analysed, in case of four types of interleavers viz. general block interleaver, matrix interleaver, random interleaver and convolutional interleaver, considering a fading environment. The hardware implementation using a block interleaver is reported here as a part of this work that shows encouraging results and maybe considered to be a part of a communication system with appropriate modifications.

INTRODUCTION

The development of wireless communication is at such a great pace in this century that it becomes an indispensable part of day-to-day life. Wireless communication is one of the fastest growing industries nowadays. From the onset of the 20th century, technology has been uprising at a remarkable note to provide new techniques and products for wireless communications. Wireless communication services are penetrating into our lives with an explosive growth rate. Most of the handheld and portable electronics

DOI: 10.4018/978-1-4666-8493-5.ch015

we use in our day to day life such as cell phone, television, internet, etc. are all contributions of wireless communication. It has been a boon to the mankind, without which we cannot imagine a single day.

Multiple access is one of the key techniques in wireless communication system, especially, in the cellular mobile communication systems. In the recent years, the demand for bandwidth has increased fast. Since the demand for bandwidth is increasing, the information received at the destination should be as close as possible to the transmitted information from the source. It is very important that wireless channels are accurately simulated for designing and evaluating the performance of wireless communication systems. Therefore, different techniques have been proposed to meet the desired bandwidth requirement by trying to increase the spectral efficiency. But, in a wireless environment, when a signal is transmitted, it is subjected to reflection, diffraction and scattering due to the presence of obstacles like mountains, buildings, etc. in the medium. Because of this multipath behaviour, the signal received at the receiver have fluctuated amplitude, phase or multipath delay. This fluctuation of amplitude or phase in the received signal is known as signal fading. Hence, it can be said that the main cause of fading is multipath propagation. As the reliability and fidelity of transmitted data is always a matter of concern, there have been continuous efforts to achieve appreciable performance over different wireless media. Several techniques have been proposed and implemented to achieve such a goal. Interleaving is one of the simplest and convenient techniques which can be used efficiently in wireless applications. It has found its application for minimizing burst errors that creeps up in transmission. Thus, interleavers (Andrews, Heegard & Kozen, 1997) are used which provides a reliable transmission of data.

BACKGROUND

From the history of wireless communication, we see that wireless communication is that area of technology which has witnessed an explosive growth over a century. The basic question related with this technology is; how to send a message over the air medium? However, the solution to this question was given by Guglielmo Marconi in 1897, when he invented the radio through which people were able to communicate. After the invention of the radio, another question was raised; what is the best way to send a message across a noisy channel? Since then, many efforts are being taken to improve the performance over a noisy channel. These efforts has led to the birth of many new concepts in the field of wireless communication technology such as digital communication, channel estimation, channel allocation, signal processing for communications, encryption, decryption etc. In the 1940s, one of the important areas of wireless technology called *error correcting codes* was introduced, which deal with the corrupted information in a noisy channel. Before introduction of the error correcting codes, error detection codes were used to detect errors but the only way to correct the corrupted information was to repeat the transmission. The retransmission of information is not fruitful enough and sometimes it becomes unacceptable for many applications, since it does not guarantee a correct transmission (Asghar, 2010).

Claude Elwood Shannon demonstrated the theory of coding known as "coding theory" which says that the effect of errors and noise that are induced by a channel into the system can be minimized without affecting the information transfer rate, if the message bits are properly encoded. The coding theory describes the optimal design of a communication system. The main objective of the theory was to transmit maximum possible amount of information over a noisy channel, and detect and correct the errors that occurs due to noise. Shannon proved that there are good chances for information to transmit safely with the existence of a noisy channel, by properly encoding the message before transmission. The theories that were formulated were based on digital communication scheme, but none of them were able to provide specific codes which can prove that it gives the desired accuracy for a given channel. At the same time along with Shannon, two other well known mathematicians Richard Hamming and Marcel Golay were working in the same area. The error correcting codes known as Hamming codes were first constructed by Hamming and later, Marcel Golay generalized the Hamming codes and provided the codes which are able to detect and correct multiple errors in a transmission. Since then, many algebraic and mathematical techniques have been developed by the coding theory, which has enabled to bring more diversity in today's communication technology. The advent of cellular telephony in 1979 in Japan with first cellular communication network has changed the human life drastically, even though the field of radio telephony was already invented by Guglielmo Marconi back in 1897 and the first long range signal transmission was performed in 1902 over the Atlantic Ocean. The other techniques which merged with cellular telephony are the personal computer (1980's) and the WWW i.e. world wide web (1994). Due to merging of these three technologies into a single mobile device has evolved the progress in the field of communication at a growing speed. Since then customer demands have been rising. The throughput demands have gone very high and demand to incorporate multiple communication systems on to a single device has now become a basic necessity (Asghar, 2010).

Looking at the emerging trend of communication, different techniques have been formulated to achieve better transmission rate. Interleaving is one such technique which is used to combat burst of errors in combination with an error control coding. With the help of interleaving, the burst noise is spread and the noise induced bit errors can be corrected by rearranging the bits at the receiver. With the evolution of communication systems and substantial increase in bandwidth requirements, use of coding for forward error correction (FEC) has become an integral part in the modern communication systems. Dividing the FEC sub-systems in two categories i.e. channel coding/de-coding and interleaving/de-interleaving, the later appears to be more varying in permutation functions, block sizes and throughput requirements.

Therefore, it can be said that interleaver is an important part of a communication system. Since the key purpose of a wireless communication system is to transmit maximum amount of information and receive nearly equal amount of data by the receiver, interleaver helps in fulfilling this goal upto some extent.

Literature Review

Before writing this chapter, a thorough knowledge about the topic was important. So, here in this section, some previous works related to interleavers are reviewed.

In (Giannakis, Martret & Zhou, 2002), a novel multiuser-interference (MUI)-free code division multiple access (CDMA) transceiver is developed for frequency-selective multipath channels. Orthogonality among different users' spreading codes is maintained at the receiver by relying on chip-interleaving and zero padded transmissions, even after frequency-selective propagation. Deterministic multiuser separation with low-complexity code-matched filtering becomes possible without loss of maximum likelihood optimality. In addition to MUI-free reception, the proposed system guarantees channel-irrespective symbol detection and achieves high bandwidth efficiency by increasing the symbol block size. A study on the performance of turbo codes with matrix interleaving is given in (Kousa, 2003). Investigations of various issues related to the code performance are done. These include the design of the relative dimensions of the matrix interleaver, the effect of the interleaver length, the interaction between the interleaver and the number of decoding iterations, and the effect of interchanging the interleaver. Simulation results show that matrix interleavers can be very competitive to random interleavers for short frame lengths.

A novel interleaving scheme for MC-CDMA system is proposed in (Feng & Shixin, 2004). In this type of interleaving, a circular shifting register is introduced into each subcarrier branch to decrease the correlation between subcarriers. The authors in (Benedetto, Montorsi & Tarable, 2005), has dealt with the design of interleavers in a coded code-division multiple-access (CDMA) scenario, where an iterative turbo-like structure is employed at the receiver to perform multiuser detection. The choice of interleavers affects both the maximum-likelihood (ML) performance and the impact of the sub-optimality of the iterative receiver. In (Kabir, Shams & Ullah, 2012), the impact of Forward Error Correction (FEC) code namely Trellis code with interleaver, has been investigated on the performance of wavelet based MC-CDMA wireless communication system with the implementation of Alamouti antenna diversity scheme in terms of Bit Error Rate (BER). Simulation shows that the performance of the interleaved coded based proposed system outperforms than that of the uncoded system in all modulation schemes over Rayleigh fading channel. The performance of turbo codes with different types of interleaver have been studied in (Ali & Synthia, 2011). Various issues related to the code performance are investigated which include the effect of the interleaver length, the interaction between the interleaver and the number of decoding iterations, and the effect of interchanging the interleaver between input and output. In (Ngo, Niu & Ouyang, 2006), interleaver design for MIMO-OFDM based high throughput WLAN transmission has been proposed which enjoys higher spatial diversity and frequency diversity. From (Chauhan, Rai & Yadav, 2010), we come to know about a comparison of the frequency of operation and hardware requirement of two interleavers, viz. random and master random interleaver. A theoretical analysis and simulation results of a communication system for application in physical layer for wireless sensor networks has been presented in (Berber, Suh & Yuan, 2011). In order to mitigate the fading effect of the channel, the chip interleaving technique is investigated. From the theoretical derivations of closed form expressions for the bit error rate (BER), it is proved that the BER can be significantly improved using the interleaver/deinterleaver technique. A bit-interleaved time-frequency coded modulation (BITFCM) scheme for OFDM has been proposed in (Huang, Letaief & Lu, 2005) to achieve both the time diversity and frequency diversity inherent in broadband time-varying channels. For a relatively low maximum normalized Doppler frequency, a low complexity maximum-likelihood decoding approach is proposed to achieve good performance with low complexity using the BITFCM scheme. For high maximum normalized Doppler frequency, the inter-carrier interference (ICI) is very large, and an error floor gets induced. Two ICI mitigation schemes have been proposed in order to solve this problem, by taking advantage of the second-order channel statistics and the complete channel information, respectively. In (Jootar, Proakis & Zeidler, 2006), the Chernoff bound of the pair-wise error probability (PEP) and the exact PEP of convolutional codes in a time-varying Rician fading channel has been derived. With the assumptions that the channel estimator is a finite impulse response filter and the interleaving depth is finite, investigation on the estimation-diversity trade-off resulting from the effects of the Doppler spread on the system performance via the channel-estimation accuracy and the channel diversity has been done. A new channel interleaving method, called chip interleaving, for direct sequence code division multiple access (DS-CDMA) mobile radio is proposed in (Adachi & Garg, 2002). It was also found that the bit error rate (BER) performance improves with increasing spreading factor (SF) and increasing frame length. An investigation of the optimization of binary turbo code through good interleaver design is performed in the work given in (Harbi, 2012). For this purpose, different types of interleaver have been designed here and have evaluated their performance. Basically the performances of the turbo code using block interleaver, helical interleaver, random interleaver and odd-even interleaver have been evaluated. From the investigation it has been seen that for small code length, the performance of the block interleaver is superior in non-puncturing case and the performance of the odd-even interleaver is superior in puncturing case, but for large code length the performance of the random interleaver is better in both of puncturing and non-puncturing condition. In (Adachi & Liu, 2006), chip interleaving technique has been proposed for DS-CDMA to eliminate the multiple-access interference (MAI). In this work, this technique is developed to provide the single- or multicarrier CDMA with flexible low-to-high bit rate transmission by jointly using 2-dimensional (2D) OVSF spreading and chip interleaving for quasi-synchronous uplink transmissions in time- and frequency-selective fading channels. The authors in (Sanyal & Upadhyaya, 2009) presents an efficient technique to model convolutional interleaver using a hardware description language is proposed and implemented on field programmable gate array (FPGA) chip. The proposed technique reduces consumption of FPGA resources to a large extent compared to conventional implementation technique using flip flop. This implies lower power consumption and reduced delay in the interconnection network of the FPGA. A description on the performance analysis of a four arm interleaver design is presented in (Kumari & Lodhi, 2013). The four arm interleaver generates each sequence of random pattern with four independently generated patterns, due to which the memory requirement decreases in comparison with power interleavers. The permuting pattern that has to be send at receiver also decreases. Due to decrease in this complexity, maximum operating frequency increases and the hardware requirement decreases. The authors in (Badrinarayanan, Hemamalini & Mathana, 2014) have designed an architecture with minimal hardware complexity and maximum reusable interleaver that can support two standards 3GPP WCDMA and 3GPP LTE. The proposed interleaver/ deinterleaver architecture receives an input data stream of any size established by the 3GPP standard and delivers the interleaved or deinterleaved stream depending on the user requirements.

Contribution

From the literature review, it can be said that different techniques of interleaving have been employed to improve the system performance. In this chapter, four types of interleavers viz. general block interleaver, matrix interleaver, random interleaver and convolutional interleaver have been implemented and analysed; and performance evaluation was carried out for a wireless system. Bit Error Rate (BER), computational time, mutual information and correlation are the evaluation parameters that have been taken into account to estimate the system performance.

The performance evaluation undergoes in the following few steps. Firstly, BER for each interleaver is analysed considering AWGN, Rayleigh and Rician channels. Secondly, computational time for the entire process is calculated starting from generation of the data till its reception, for each of the interleavers considering all the three channels mentioned. Thirdly, mutual information between channel input and channel output is also found out. And finally, correlation property is also checked for the transmitted and received data. From the proposed approach, it is observed that the overall BER performance using block interleaver is better than other interleavers. BER obtained through AWGN and Rician is better than that obtained using Rayleigh channel. The reason behind the poor BER performance in case of Rayleigh channel might be the inability of the designed system to cope up in non-line-of-sight (NLOS) environment i.e. in presence of large number of obstacles in its path, which can further be improved. The computational time for the system using block interleaver is better in case of AWGN channel. In case of Rayleigh and Rician, matrix and random interleavers are respectively found to be better. Again computational time of convolutional interleaver is poor since it consists of a set of shift registers with a fixed delay. The mutual information between input and output of AWGN and Rician fading channel is better compared to that of Rayleigh fading channel for each interleaver. The correlation property holds good for the system using block, matrix and random interleaver. For convolutional interleaver, the correlation is a bit discouraging compared to the other interleavers.

Realization of the optimized system using a block interleaver in the FPGA platform in order to achieve a low complexity hardware architechture of an interleaver is another contribution to this work.

Organization of the Chapter

Section 1 gives a brief introduction and background about the topic and a brief overview of related works of implementations of interleavers. In Section 2, a brief explanation about the types of interleavers, a description of the fading channels and the system parameters to analyse the performance of the communication system are described. The description of the proposed approach and the system model are included in Section 3. Results are shown in Section 4. Conclusion and future work are included in Section 5.

THEORETICAL CONSIDERATION

Interleaving (Andrews, Heegard & Kozen, 1997) is a process, which is performed before transmission to disperse the data bits so that even if a part of the information is corrupted while passing through the channel, it can be recovered by rearranging the data after reception. There are different types of interleavers, which affects the performance of a system.

In a digital communication system, interleaving is used to attain time diversity without any addition of redundant bits. Due to the rapid proliferation of digital speech coders which transform analog voices into efficient digital messages that are transmitted over wireless links, interleaving has become an extremely useful technique in all second and third generation wireless systems. Speech coders attempt to represent a wide range of voices in a uniform and efficient digital format. The encoded bits i.e. the source bits which consists maximum amount of information are more important than others and must be free from errors. Many speech coders produce several important bits in succession, and it is the function of the interleaver to spread those bits in time so that even if a deep fade or noise burst occurs, these important bits will not be corrupted. Spreading of these bits over time is necessary, because it becomes possible to make use of channel coding which protects the source data from corruption by the channel. Error correcting codes are designed to protect against channel errors, while interleavers scramble the time order of source bits before they are channel encoded (Rappaport, 2002).

Role of an Interleaver

The primary role of an interleaver is to disperse the sequences of bits in a bit-stream so as to minimize the effect of burst errors introduced in transmission. An interleaver is usually used in conjunction with some type of error correcting code. The error correcting codes can correct the lost information as long as the amount of lost bits in a single codeword is within the limit defined by $d_{\min}$. The limits sometimes get violated due to existence of errors in the form of bursts. The usual sources of bursty errors are listed below (Asghar, 2010):

- Channel distortion and channel fading effects in wireless communications due to multipath propagation of the transmitted signal caused by reflection, diffraction, scattering, etc.
- Lightening and switching effects.
- Use of concatenated coding schemes, e.g. use of convolution code (Viterbi decoding) at the first stage usually generates a burst of errors when the decoding fails.

A basic interleaver is taken as a sequential device with single input and single output. A parallelism can be devised but the basic function remains the same. The interleaver takes a sequence of information bits with fixed width and generates another sequence of same width but in different order. It is then the role of a de-interleaver to retrieve back the original order. Thus the interleaver and deinterleaver strictly work in pair with each other.

An interleaver carries a specific permutation pattern π and the mapping of an input sequence $x \rightarrow x_0, x_1, x_2, \ldots\ldots, x_k$ on to an output sequence $y \rightarrow y_0, y_1, y_2, \ldots\ldots, y_k$ can be defined as:

$$y_i = x_{\pi(i)} \tag{1}$$

The reverse of this function (i.e. de-interleaving) is:

$$y_{\pi(i)} = x_i \tag{2}$$

Interleaver Types

Based on different implementation aspects, the interleavers are divided in two main categories named as block interleaver and convolutional interleaver. There are some other classifications based on their properties, which will also be discussed briefly later.

- **Block Interleaver:** A block interleaver (Figure 1(a)) accepts a sequence of bits at the input row-wise and the new sequence with the same number of bits is released at the output of the interleaver column-wise. Block interleavers (Guzman-Renteria, Michel & Sanchez-Ortiz, 2009) are very important for applications, and form the basis of most turbo code schemes. According to the 802.11n standard, the interleaving is defined using three permutations. The first permutation is performed over the block of data, which is arranged as a matrix of N_{ROW} rows and N_{COL} columns, with the rule:

$$i = N_{ROW}\left(k \bmod N_{COL}\right) + floor\left(\frac{k}{N_{COL}}\right), k = 0, 1, 2, \ldots\ldots, N_T - 1 \tag{3}$$

where N_T is the number of symbols in the block, k is the index for original data and i denotes the new position of the k symbol. The operation modulus is denoted by $\bmod$, while *floor* stands for largest integer below the argument. The second permutation is defined by:

$$j = s * floor\left(\frac{1}{s}\right) + \left(i + N_{CB} - floor\left(N_{COL} * \frac{i}{N_T}\right)\right) \bmod s, i = 0,1,2,\ldots\ldots, N_T - 1 \tag{4}$$

where j is the index for the position of the permutation, N_{CB} and s are parameters that depend on some configurations in the standard such as block size and symbol rate. The third permutation is applied to the output symbols of the second permutation and is defined by the rule:

$$r = j - \left[\left(i_{ss}2\right)\bmod 3 + 3floor\left(\frac{i_{ss}}{3}\right)\right]N_{ROT}N_{CB} \bmod N_T, j = 0,1,2,\ldots\ldots, N_T - 1 \tag{5}$$

where r is the final position of permuted signals, and N_{ROT} is a rotation parameter.

- **Convolutional Interleaver:** A convolutional interleaver (Figure 1(b)) is an interleaver which consists of a number of shift registers. The shift registers have a fixed delay each, which are positive integer multiples of a fixed integer. Every new data to the input of the interleaver is feeded to the next shift register and the previous data in that register becomes part of the interleaver output. A convolutional interleaver (Guzman-Renteria, Michel & Sanchez-Ortiz, 2009) has memory; that is, its operation depends not only on current symbols but also on previous symbols. In a typical convolutional interleaver, the delays are nonnegative multiples of a fixed integer (although a general multiplexed interleaver allows unrestricted delay values). The general way to represent the permutation of a convolutional interleaver is as follows:

$$i = \pi\left(k \bmod N\right) + \alpha\left(k \bmod N\right)N + floor\left(\frac{k}{N}\right)N \tag{6}$$

where π is a finite basic permutation of length N, k is the index for original data and i denotes the new position of the k symbol. α is the shift vector with N elements. The operation modulus is denoted by $\bmod$, while *floor* stands for largest integer below the argument.

Other Interleaver Types

Other than the two main categories i.e. block interleavers and convolutional interleavers, block interleavers can further be classified into many different classes.

1. **Matrix Interleaver:** Matrix Interleaver (Figure 2(a)) is a type of block interleaver that performs interleaving by filling the input symbols row by row in a matrix of m rows and n columns and then output of the interleaver is read column by column. The column size n is called the *depth* and the row size m is the span. Such an interleaver is completely defined by m and n and is thus referred to as (m,n) matrix interleaver. At the deinterleaver, information is written column-wise and read out row-wise (Das, M. Sarma & K. Sarma, 2014).

Figure 1. (a) Block Interleaver (b) Convolutional Interleaver

1	2	3	4	5	6	7	8
A	B	C	D	E	F	G	H
9	10	11	12	13	14	15	16
I	J	K	L	M	N	O	P
17	18	19	20	21	22	23	24
Q	R	S	T	U	V	W	X
25	26	27	28	29	30	31	32
Y	Z	a	b	c	d	e	f

INTERLEAVING

1	A	9	I	17	Q	25	Y
2	B	10	J	18	R	26	Z
3	C	11	K	19	S	27	a
4	D	12	L	20	T	28	b
5	E	13	M	21	U	29	c
6	F	14	N	22	V	30	d
7	G	15	O	23	W	31	e
8	H	16	P	24	X	32	f

(a)

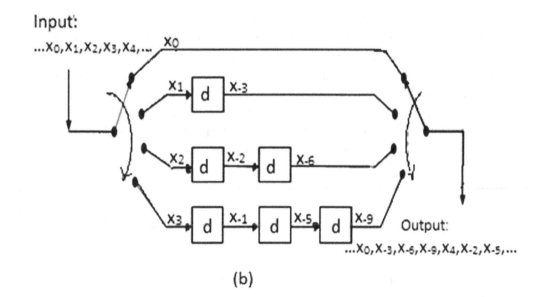

(b)

2. **Helical Interleaver:** A helical interleaver (Figure 2(b)) writes data into row–wise but reads data from its matrix diagonally instead of by column in such a way that consecutive interleaved data are never read from the same row or column. The principle design rule of helical interleavers is to start off from a pre-defined interleaver as a master interleaver, from which the family of helical interleavers are generated by reading the interleaver indices in a deterministic order (Ali & Synthia, 2011).

3. **Random Interleaver:** In random interleaver (Figure 2(c)), the base station (BS) has to use a considerable amount of memory to store the random patterns of interleaver which may cause serious concern of storage when the number of users is large. Also, during the initial link of setting-up

phase, there should be messages assigned between the BS and mobile stations (MS) to inform each other about their respective interleaver. Random interleaver scrambles the data of different users with different pattern. Patterns of scrambling the data of users are generated arbitrarily. Because of the scrambling of data, burst error of the channel is randomized at the receiver side. The user specific Random Interleaver rearranges the elements of its input vector using a random permutation. The incoming data is rearranged using a series of generated permuter indices. A permuter is essentially a device that generates pseudo-random permutation of given memory addresses. The data is arranged according to the pseudo-random order of memory addresses. If random interleaver is employed for the purpose of user separation, then lot of memory space will be required at the transmitter and receiver ends for the purpose of their storage. Also, considerable amount of bandwidth will be consumed for transmission of all these interleaver as well as computational complexity will increase at receiver ends. After randomization of the burst error which has rearranged the whole block of the data the latter can now be easily detected and corrected. Spreading is the important characteristic of random interleaver (Ali & Synthia, 2011).

4. **Odd-Even Interleaver:** An odd-even interleaver is a block interleaver in which the number of rows and columns must be odd numbers. The odd-even interleaver design is specifically for the $r = \frac{1}{2}$ turbo code. A $r = \frac{1}{2}$ turbo code is obtained by puncturing the two coded (non systematic) output sequences of a $r = \frac{1}{3}$ turbo code. However, by puncturing these two coded output sequences, it is possible that an information (systematic) bit may not have any of its coded bits (both of the associated coded bits may be punctured out). Likewise, it is also possible for an information bit to have one or both of its coded bits. Thus, if an error occurs for an unprotected information bit (without any of its coded bits), the turbo code decoder may degrade on its performance. The odd-even interleaver design overcomes this problem by allowing each information bit to have exactly one of its coded bits. As a result of this interleaver, the error correction capability of the code is uniformly distributed over all information bits (Ali & Synthia, 2011).

Channels

A communication channel is defined as a medium over which information can be transmitted or in which information can be stored. Fiber optic, coaxial cables, ionospheric propagation, free space, magnetic and optical disks are examples of communication channels. There are many factors that cause the output of a communication channel to be different from its input; among these factors are attenuation, non-linearities, multipath propagation and thermal noise. In order to study the effects of these various factors there exist some well-known channel models among which the Gaussian and slow flat independent Rayleigh fading channel and Rician fading channel with BPSK modulation will be the focus of our study.

Additive White Gaussian Noise Channel

The Additive White Gaussian Noise (AWGN) (Babu & Rao, 2011) channel is one of the most commonly used channel model and is generally used to model an environment with a very large number of additive noise sources. Most additive noise sources in modern electronics are a direct consequence of zero-mean thermal noise, which is caused by random electron motion within the resistors, wires, and other components. By the Central Limit Theorem, we can model these additive sources as a Gaussian

Figure 2. (a) Matrix Interleaver (b) Helical Interleaver (c) Random Interleaver

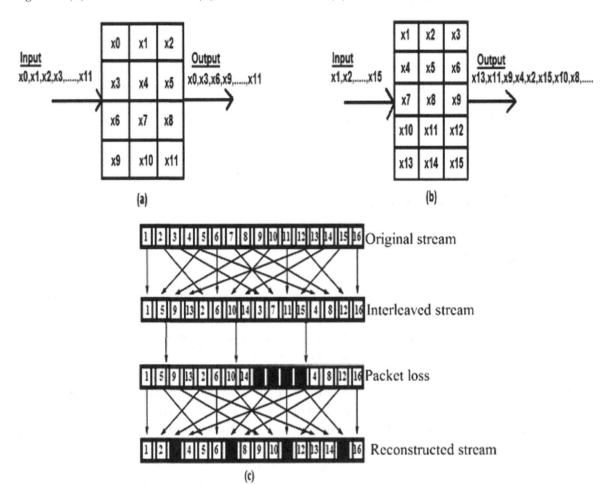

random process. This assumption becomes more accurate as the number, and variety of noise sources is increased. The statistical model for the AWGN channel with zero mean is given by its probability density function in (7) along with its variance $\left(\sigma^2\right)$ (for BPSK modulation) in (8)

$$p\left(x\right) = \frac{1}{\sqrt{2\pi\sigma^2}} \exp\left(-\frac{1}{2\sigma^2} x^2\right) \tag{7}$$

$$\sigma^2 = \frac{N_0}{2RE_b} \tag{8}$$

where, R is the coding rate

$$\left(R = \frac{\text{number of information bits}}{\text{number of transmitted bits}} \right)$$

and $\dfrac{E_b}{N_0}$ is the ratio of the bit energy to noise power spectral density. The modulated and the received signal r at any time instant t is given as follows:

$$r_t = x_t + \eta_t \tag{9}$$

where, x_t represents the information sequence and η_t is the white noise added by the channel at time t.

Multipath Fading Channels

In a cellular mobile radio environment, the surrounding objects such as houses, buildings, and trees act as reflectors of radio waves. These obstacles produce reflected and scattered waves with attenuated amplitude and a shifted phase. If a modulated signal is transmitted, multiple reflected waves of the transmitted signal will arrive at the receiving antenna from different directions with different propagation delays. These reflected waves are called multipath waves. Due to the different arrival angles and times, the multipath waves at the receiver site will have different phases. When the receiver antenna at any point in space collects them, they may combine either in a constructive or a destructive way, depending on their random phases. The sum of these multipath components forms a spatially varying standing wave field. The mobile unit moving through the multipath field will receive a signal, which can vary widely in amplitude and phase. When the mobile unit is stationary, the amplitude variations in the received signal are due to the movement of surrounding objects in the radio channel. The amplitude fluctuation of the received signal is called signal fading and it is caused by the time-variant multipath characteristics of the channel.

Causes of Fading

Fading is caused by different physical phenomenon:

Doppler Shift

When a mobile is moving at a constant velocity v along a path, v_s is the velocity of the source, f' is the observed frequency and f is the emitted frequency. All these terms will be related by the following equation:

$$f' = \left(\frac{v}{v \pm v_s} \right) f$$

From the above equation, it can be said that the detected frequency increases for objects moving towards the observer and decreases when the source moves away. This phenomenon is known as the Doppler Effect (Babu & Rao, 2011).

Reflection

When a propagating electromagnetic wave impinges on object which has generated large dimensions wave length, when compared to wavelength of the propagating wave, then reflection will occur. Actually we know that if the plane wave is incident on a perfect dielectric, part of the energy is transmitted and part of the energy is reflected back into the medium. If the medium is a perfect conductor, all the energy is reflected back. Reflections occur from the surface of the earth and from buildings and walls. In practice, not only metallic materials cause reflections, but dielectrics also cause this phenomenon (Babu & Rao, 2011).

Diffraction

The sharp irregularities (edges) of a surface between transmitter and receiver and obstructs the radio path then diffraction will occur. The bending waves around the obstacle, even when a Line of Sight does not exist between transmitter and receiver the secondary waves will be spread over the space. Diffraction looks like a reflection at high frequencies depends on the amplitude, phase and polarization of the incident wave and geometry of the object at the point of diffraction (Babu & Rao, 2011).

Scattering

The wave travels through the medium consists of smaller dimension objects compared to the wavelength and having larger volumes of obstacles per unit volume, then scattering will occur. Due to rough surfaces, small objects and irregularities in the channel scattered waves are produced. In practice, in mobile communications, electrical poles and street signs etc. induces scattering in communication (Babu & Rao, 2011).

Multipath fading channels exhibit different behaviours. The channel behaviour is mainly characterized by the time delay spread and the Doppler spread. The fading effects due to these parameters are described as follows:

1. **Flat Fading:** Flat fading implies that the signal bandwidth is small as compared to the channel bandwidth so that the received signal will have varying amplitude according to the gain fluctuations of the channel. In case of flat fading, the coherence time of the faded symbol is much smaller than the symbol period of the transmitted signal. For flat fading mobile radio channels, the phase response is linear and hence, the receiver is able to track the phase variations, and hence can compensate for it using a phase locked loop technique. This enables coherent detection of the received signal (Babu & Rao, 2011).
2. **Frequency Selective Fading:** Frequency selective fading occurs in a situation where the channel's bandwidth is smaller than the bandwidth of the transmitted signal. For frequency selective fading the coherence time is larger than the symbol period. A common rule of thumb to determine that a channel is frequency selective is that the symbol period should be at least ten times smaller than the root mean square delay spread. Frequency selective fading occurs due to the time dispersion

of the transmitted symbols within the channel, and hence, induces intersymbol interference (Babu & Rao, 2011).

3. **Slow Fading:** For a slow fading channel, the channel's impulse response exhibit slower variations than the transmitted baseband signal. In slow fading channels, the coherence time of the channel is greater than the symbol period of the transmitted signal. In frequency domain it implies that the Doppler spread of the channel is much less than the bandwidth of the baseband signal. In this situation, the channel can be understood to be static over one or several reciprocal bandwidth intervals (Babu & Rao, 2011).

4. **Fast Fading:** In a fast fading channel, the channel impulse response varies rapidly within the symbol duration. In technical terms this implies that the coherence time of the channel is smaller than the symbol period of the transmitted signal or, equivalently, the Doppler spread of the channel is greater than the bandwidth of the transmitted signal (Babu & Rao, 2011).

Rayleigh Fading Channel

The Rayleigh fading is primarily caused by multipath reception. Rayleigh fading (Kumar, Sarumathi & Sumithra, 2013) is a statistical model to account the effect of a propagation environment on a radio signal. It is a reasonable model for troposphere and ionospheres' signal propagation as well as the effect of heavily built-up urban environments on radio signals. Rayleigh fading is most applicable when there is no line of sight between the transmitter and receiver. Rayleigh fading is a type of fading, where the envelope of the carrier signal is Rayleigh distributed. Rayleigh fading is caused due to multipath effect. In case of multipath propagation, the dominant signal becomes weaker, which is a non-line-of-sight (LOS) case. The received signal is the resultant of many reflected components that are reflected from the surrounding obstacles. Rayleigh fading is a type of fast fading since it occurs very rapidly. A rapid power fluctuations at a scale of about 30 to $50dB$ can be caused due to Rayleigh fading that is comparable to one wavelength, and therefore it is referred as small-scale fading. The two-ray model is commonly used as the multipath model to illustrate Rayleigh fading. The impulse response of Rayleigh fading channel is given by:

$$h(t) = \alpha_1 e^{j\theta_1 t} \delta(t) + \alpha_2 e^{j\theta_2 t} \delta(t - \tau) \tag{10}$$

where α_1 and α_2 are independent random variables with a Rayleigh pdf, θ_1 and θ_2 are two independent random variables with uniform pdf over $[0$ to $2\pi]$ and τ is the time delay. The received signal is composed of multipath components. The different delays of these components lead to a multipath delay spread. If the time differences of these components are significant compared to one symbol period, intersymbol interference (ISI) occurs. The multipath delay spread has a spectrum with null magnitudes at frequency intervals of $1/\tau$, where τ is the time delay. Thus, this type of fading is called frequency-selective fading. When the delay spread is much less than a symbol period, the channel is said to exhibit flat fading. The statistical model for the envelope of the Rayleigh random variable is given by its probability density function in eqn. (11),

$$p(a) = \begin{cases} \dfrac{a}{\sigma^2} \exp\left(-\dfrac{a}{2\sigma^2}\right), & a \geq 0 \\ \\ \qquad 0, a < 0 \end{cases} \tag{11}$$

Rician Fading Channel

The Rician fading is similar to the Rayleigh fading, except that in Rician fading (Kumar, Sarumathi & Sumithra, 2013), a strong dominant component is present. This dominant component is a stationary (non fading) signal and is commonly known as the Line of Sight (LOS) Component. Rician fading is suitable for characterizing satellite communications or in some urban environments. Rician fading is also a type of small-scale fading. When the dominant component is stronger, the resulting phase becomes closer to the phase of the dominant component. This is similar to a delta function. Flat Rician fading channel is suitable for characterizing a real satellite link. Because of the line of sight path, the effect of Rician fading on the transmitted signal will be less than in the case of Rayleigh fading. The Rician probability density function of the received signal envelope is given by:

$$p(a) = \frac{a}{\sigma^2} \exp\left[-\frac{\left(a^2 + A^2\right)}{2\sigma^2}\right] I_0\left(\frac{aA}{\sigma^2}\right), \text{for } a \geq 0, A \geq 0 \tag{12}$$

where $I_0\left(\dfrac{aA}{\sigma^2}\right)$ is the modified Bessel function of zero order and A is the peak magnitude of the line of sight signal component. In Rician fading channel, the K-factor is one of the inputs that defines the ratio of the power of the line of sight component and the multipath components

$$\left(K = \frac{A^2}{2\sigma^2}\right).$$

The Rice distribution approximates the Rayleigh distribution with mean value A as $K \ll 1$, and reduces to it at $K = 0$. It approximates the Gaussian distribution with mean value A as $K \gg 1$, and reduces to the Gaussian as $K \rightarrow \infty$. The factor K typically shows an exponential decrease with range, and varies from 20 near the BS to zero at a large distance. The dominant component changes the phase distribution from the uniformly random distribution of Rayleigh fading to clustering around the phase of the dominant component. The stronger the dominant component, the closer is the resulting phase to the phase of the dominant component. This is similar to a delta function. Flat Rician fading channel is suitable for characterizing a real satellite link.

System Parameters

In this section, a brief description of the system parameters is given which are important to determine the performance of a wireless communication system.

1. **Bit Error Rate:** The BER (Babu & Rao, 2011; Kumar, Sarumathi & Sumithra, 2013; Ali, 2013), or quality of the digital link, is calculated from the number of bits received in error divided by the number of bits transmitted.

$$BER = \frac{\text{Bits in Error}}{\text{Total bits received}}$$

In digital transmission, the number of bit errors is the number of received bits of a data stream over a communication channel that has been altered due to noise, interference, distortion or bit synchronization errors. The BER is the number of bit errors divided by the total number of transferred bits during a particular time interval. BER is a unit less performance measure, often expressed as a percentage. IEEE 802.11 standard has ability to sense the bit error rate (BER) of its link and implemented modulation to data rate and exchange to Forward Error Correction (FEC), which is used to set the BER as low error rate for data applications. BER measurement is the number of bit error or destroys within a second during transmitting from source to destination. Noise affects the BER performance. Quantization errors also reduce BER performance, through incorrect or ambiguous reconstruction of the digital waveform. The accuracy of the analog modulation process and the effects of the filtering on signal and noise bandwidth also effect quantization errors. BER can also be defined in terms of the probability of error (POE) and represented in Eq. (13), (14) and (15).

For AWGN channel,

$$POE = \frac{1}{2}\left(1 - erfc\right)\sqrt{\frac{E_b}{N_0}} \tag{13}$$

For Rayleigh fading channel,

$$POE = \frac{1}{2}\left(1 - \sqrt{\frac{E_b/N_0}{\sqrt{\left(E_b/N_0\right)+1}}}\right) \tag{14}$$

For Rician fading channel,

$$POE = \frac{1}{2} erfc \sqrt{\frac{kE_b/N_0}{k + \left(E_b/N_0\right)}} \qquad (15)$$

where $erfc$ is the error function, E_b is the energy in one bit and N_0 is the noise power spectral density (noise power in a 1Hz bandwidth). The error function is different for the each of the various modulation methods. The POE is a proportional to E_b/N_0, which is a form of signal-to-noise ratio. The energy per bit, E_b, can be determined by dividing the carrier power by the bit rate. As an energy measure, E_b has the unit of Joules. N_0 is in power that is Joules per second, so, E_b/N_0, is a dimensionless term, or is a numerical ratio.

Here, in this work, BER is calculated for the system using block, matrix, random and convolutional interleavers separately by transmitting the signal over AWGN, Rayleigh and Rician fading channels.

2. **Computational Time:** The time required to execute a computational process is known as the computational time. It is a very important parameter since it is concerned with the time efficiency of a system. Time efficient systems are always preferred over a time consuming system which is an important consideration for real time system design. Therefore, the computational time of the entire system i.e. from generation of data till its reception using the interleavers (block, matrix, random and convolutional) has been calculated (Das, M. Sarma & K. Sarma, 2014).

3. **Mutual Information:** The measure of amount of information that a random variable X contains about another random variable Y, is known as mutual information. It reduces the uncertainty of one random variable due to the knowledge of the other. Mutual information (Guo, Shamai & Verd, 2005; Abhayapala, Perera & Pollock, 2006) can be defined as,

$$I\left(X;Y\right) = \sum_{x \in X}\sum_{y \in Y} p\left(x,y\right) \log\left[\frac{p\left(x,y\right)}{p\left(x\right)p\left(y\right)}\right] \qquad (16)$$

where $p\left(x,y\right)$ is the joint probability density function of the random variables X and Y, and $p\left(x\right)$ and $p\left(y\right)$ are the individual probability density function of X and Y respectively. For example, if X and Y are independent, then knowing X does not give any information about Y and vice versa, so their mutual information is zero. At the other extreme, if X is a deterministic function of Y and Y is a deterministic function of X then all information conveyed by X is shared with Y: knowing X determines the value of Y and vice versa. As a result, in this case the mutual information is the same as the uncertainty contained in Y (or X) alone, namely the entropy of Y (or X). Moreover, this mutual information is the same as the entropy of X and as the entropy of Y. In this work, X is taken as the channel input and Y as the channel output. We can rewrite the definition of mutual information $I(X;Y)$ as:

$$I(X;Y) = -\sum_{x \in X}\sum_{y \in Y} p(x,y) \log p(x) + \sum_{x \in X}\sum_{y \in Y} p(x,y) \log p(x|y)$$

$$I(X;Y) = -\sum_{x \in X} p(x) \log p(x) - \left(-\sum_{x \in X}\sum_{y \in Y} p(x,y) \log p(x|y)\right)$$

$$I(X;Y) = H(X) - H(X|Y) \tag{17}$$

where $H(X) = entropy$.

To understand the mutual information, we need to understand entropy. According to Shannon, entropy is a measure of uncertainty- the higher the entropy, the more uncertain one is about a random variable. Thus the mutual information $I(X;Y)$ is the reduction in the uncertainty of X due to the knowledge of Y.

The maximum number of messages that can be transmitted almost error free is a function of the mutual information between X and Y. If a communication channel is considered that transmits 0s and 1s, and transmit correctly with probability q.

$$P_{Y|X}(1,1) = P_{Y|X}(0,0) = q$$

Since binary bits 0 and 1 are used in transmitting messages, $P_X(0) = P_Y(1) = \frac{1}{2}$. The probability of making error or the probability particular message to occur is given by,

$$P_n = \left[\left(\frac{1}{2}\right)^{n/2} \frac{\left(\frac{n}{2}\right)!}{\left(\frac{qn}{2}\right)! \left(\frac{(1-q)n}{2}\right)!}\right]^2 \tag{18}$$

$\left(\frac{1}{2}\right)^{n/2}$ is the probability of a particular message occurring and rest computes all the ways to arrange symbols.

Correlation: Correlation is the degree of similarity between two or more quantities (Das, M. Sarma & K. Sarma, 2014). Correlation is a mathematical operation that uses two signals to produce a third signal. This third signal is called the cross-correlation of the two input signals. If a signal is correlated with itself, the resulting signal is instead called the autocorrelation. The cross-correlation $r_{12}(n)$ between two data sequences $x_1(n)$ and $x_2(n)$ each containing N data might therefore be written as,

$$r_{12} = \frac{1}{N} \sum_{n=0}^{N-1} x_1(n) x_2(n) \tag{19}$$

where $x_1(n)$ is assumed to be the transmitted sequence and $x_2(n)$ as the received sequence. In case of autocorrelation, $x_1(n) x_2(n)$. Therefore, the autocorrelation function can be written as,

$$r_{11} = \frac{1}{N} \sum_{n=0}^{N-1} x_1^2(n) \tag{20}$$

Field Programmable Gate Arrays

A field-programmable gate array (FPGA) is an integrated circuit created to be configured by the customer after manufacturing hence "field-programmable". The FPGA configuration is generally defined using a hardware description language (HDL), similar to that used for an application-specific integrated circuit (ASIC). FPGAs can be used to implement any logical function that an ASIC can perform. FPGAs contain programmable logic components called "logic blocks", and a hierarchy of reconfigurable interconnects that allow the blocks to be "connected together" somewhat like a one-chip programmable breadboard. Logic blocks can be configured to perform complex combinational functions, or merely simple logic like AND and NAND. In most FPGAs, the logic blocks also include memory elements, which may be simple flip-flops or more complete blocks of memory.

Verilog: The Language of Hardware

Verilog HDL is one of the two most common Hardware Description Languages (HDL) used by integrated circuit (IC) designers. The other one is VHDL. HDL allows the design to be simulated earlier in the design cycle in order to correct errors or experiment with different architectures. Designs described in HDL are technology-independent, easy to design and debug, and are usually more readable than schematics, particularly for large circuits.

Verilog can be used to describe designs at four levels of abstraction:

1. Algorithmic level (much like c code with if, case and loop statements).
2. Register transfer level (RTL uses registers connected by Boolean equations).
3. Gate level (interconnected AND, NOR etc.).
4. Switch level (the switches are MOS transistors inside gates).

PROPOSED APPROACH

This work has been divided into two phases. In the first phase, performance of the proposed model has been evaluated by considering the system parameters – Bit Error Rate, computational time, mutual information and correlation. In the second phase, a block interleaver is constructed for use in wireless channels, based on the result obtained from the first phase.

1. Simulation of a Few Interleaver Techniques for Fading Conditions

The system model of the proposed architecture is illustrated in the Figure 3(a) and flow diagram of the model is shown in Figure 3(b). The proposed model is implemented in Matlab Simulink.

Random Integer Generator

Random numbers are taken as the information source in this proposed approach. The random integer generator generates random integers uniformly distributed in the range $[0, M-1]$, where M is the M-ary number. Random numbers are useful for a variety of purposes, such as generating data encryption keys, simulating and modelling complex phenomena and for selecting random samples from larger data sets.

Integer to Bit Converter

The output from the random integer generator is fed to the input of the integer to bit converter block. The vector of integer-valued or fixed-valued sequence is mapped to a vector of bits with the help of this block. The number of bits per integer parameter value present in the integer to bit converter block defines how many bits are mapped for each integer-valued input. Number of bits per integer is equal to $\log_2(M)$. Thus we get a binary sequence of data.

Interleaver

Here in this work, as discussed earlier four types of interleavers are used (block, matrix, random and convolutional). For each of the interleavers, the system is simulated separately.

1. **Block Interleaver:** A Block Interleaver accepts a sequence of bits at the input row-wise and the new sequence with the same number of bits is released at the output of the interleaver column-wise. Block interleavers are very important for applications, and form the basis of most turbo code schemes. The flow chart for the proposed block interleaver is given in Figure 4(a).
2. **Matrix Interleaver:** The matrix interleaver interleaves the input vector by writing the elements into a matrix row-by-row and reading them out column-by-column. The product of number of rows and number of columns must match the input signal width. The flow chart for the proposed matrix interleaver is given in Figure 4(b).
3. **Random Interleaver:** Random interleaver interleaves the elements of the input vector using a random permutation. The flow chart of the proposed random interleaver is given in Figure 4(c).

Figure 3. (a) Block diagram (b) Flow diagram of the implementable model

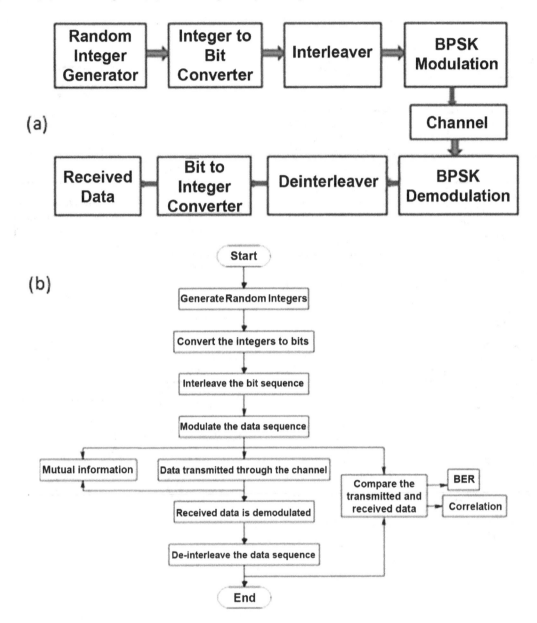

4. **Convolutional Interleaver:** The convolutional interleaver block permutes the symbols in the input signal. Internally, it uses a set of shift registers. The delay value of the ith shift register is $(i-1)$ times the register length step parameter. The number of shift registers is the value of the rows of shift registers parameter. The flow chart of the proposed convolutional interleaver is given in Figure 4(d).

Thus, applying the four types of interleaving techniques, we get the interleaved sequence of data.

Figure 4. Flow charts of (a) Block Interleaver (b) Matrix Interleaver (c) Random Interleaver (d) Convolutional Interleaver

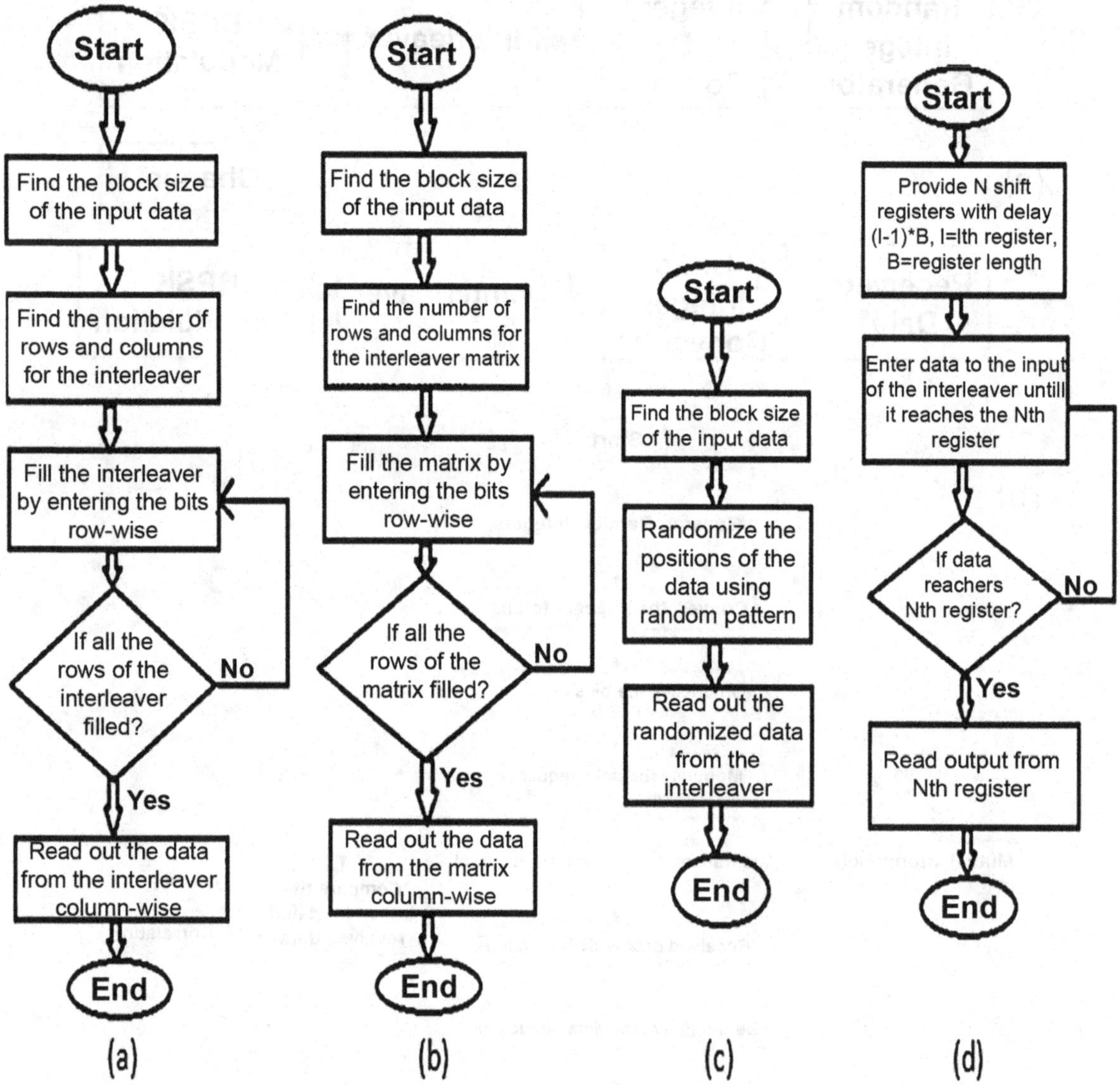

BPSK Modulator

The interleaved sequence is modulated by a Binary Phase Shift Keying (BPSK) modulator. BPSK is the simplest form of phase shift keying (PSK). In BPSK, the phase of a constant amplitude carrier signal is switched between two values according to the two possible signals m_1 and m_2 corresponding to binary 1 and 0 respectively. Normally, the two phases are separated by 180^0. If the sinusoidal carrier has an amplitude A_c and energy per bit

$$E_b = \frac{1}{2}A_c^2 T_b,$$

then the transmitted BPSK signal is,

$$s(t) = m(t)\sqrt{\frac{2E_b}{T_b}}\cos\left(2\pi f_c t + \theta_c\right) \tag{21}$$

Hence a BPSK modulated signal is achieved which would be transmitted over the wireless channel.

Channel

As mentioned earlier, three types of channels are considered in this work. The BPSK modulated signal is transmitted over the AWGN, Rayleigh and Rician fading channels where the signal gets distorted due to addition of noise. The AWGN channel takes as input the desired E_b/N_0 (here $-5:10dB$) value, the signal power (1Watts) and bit duration $\left(\log_2 M\right)$. As the signal passes through the channel, it adds noise to the signal with appropriate variance to the signal. The block, matrix, random and convolutional interleavers are employed separately and the interleaved signal is passed through the AWGN channel.

The multipath Rayleigh fading channel block implements a baseband simulation of a multipath Rayleigh fading propagation channel. The parameter of the Rayleigh fading channel block, Doppler shift is the relative motion between the transmitter and receiver. Here, we have taken the maximum Doppler shift=40 Hz. The discrete path delay vector is the propagation delay for each path, where it is taken to be $\left[0\ 2e\text{-}6\right]$ seconds. The average path gain vector is the gain of each path. The average path gain vector is $\left[0\ \text{-}3\right]$ dB. The discrete path delay vector and the path gain vector must have the same length if they are vectors. If they are scalar, the larger length of either the discrete path delay vector or the average path gain vector parameters will become the number of propagation paths at the receiver.

The multipath Rician fading channel block implements a baseband simulation of a multipath Rician fading propagation channel. Most of the parameters are the same as the multipath Rayleigh fading channel. If the K-factor parameter is a scalar, the first discrete path of the channel is a line of sight component while the remaining paths are non-line of sight components. If the K-factor parameter is a vector of the same size as discrete path delay vector, each discrete path is a line of sight path with a given K-factor. Here, we have taken $K=1$ as a scalar. The Doppler shifts of line of sight components and initial phases of line of sight components parameters must be the same size as the K-factor parameter. The maximum Doppler shift is taken as 50 Hz.

BPSK Demodulator

The output signal from the channel block is demodulated to recover the original signal with the help of a BPSK demodulator. The output of this block gives a binary sequence.

De-Interleaver

The data sequence from the demodulator is fed to the de-interleaver block so to rearrange the position of the data bits. De-interleaver performs the inverse function of an interleaver. Block de-interleaver re-order the elements of the input vector by writing the inputs to the de-interleaver column-wise and reading them out row-wise. Matrix de-interleaver deinterleaves the input vector by writing the elements into a matrix column-by-column and reading them out row-by-row. The product of number of rows and number of columns must match the input signal width. Random de-interleaver deinterleaves the elements of the input vector using a random permutation. A convolutional de-interleaver consists of N shift registers. The ith register has delay $(N - i) * B$ where B is a specified register length step. With each new input symbol, a commutator switches to a new register and the new symbol is shifted in while the oldest symbol in that register is shifted out. When the commutator reaches the Nth register, upon the next new input, it returns to the first register.

Bit to Integer Converter

The bit to integer converter maps a vector of bits to a corresponding vector of integer values. The number of bits per integer parameter defines how many bits are mapped for each output.

Received Data

From the bit to integer converter block output we get back the random integers. Thus, original data is recovered along with some errors.

2) Implementation of a Block Interleaver for Use in Wireless Channels

The communication system model that has been designed to implement in the FPGA platform is given in Figure 5(a). The flow diagram is given in Figure 5(b).

At the transmitter side, random data is taken as the source of information. The random data stream is generated with the help of T-flip flops. The random data that has been generated is then interleaved using block interleaving technique as described in the flow chart shown in Figure 5(b). A RAM has been created for the purpose of using as an interleaver, whose size differs as the length of the input codeword changes. The interleaved sequence is then modulated using BPSK modulation. The channel is modelled using the tap delay model of a finite impulse response (FIR) filter.

At the receiver, the received data is now demodulated using BPSK demodulation technique. The demodulated data is then deinterleaved which follows the inverse operation of interleaver. Thus the original data can be recovered.

RESULTS AND DISCUSSIONS

The results are shown in this section.

Figure 5. (a) Block diagram (b) Flow diagram of the FPGA implementable diagram

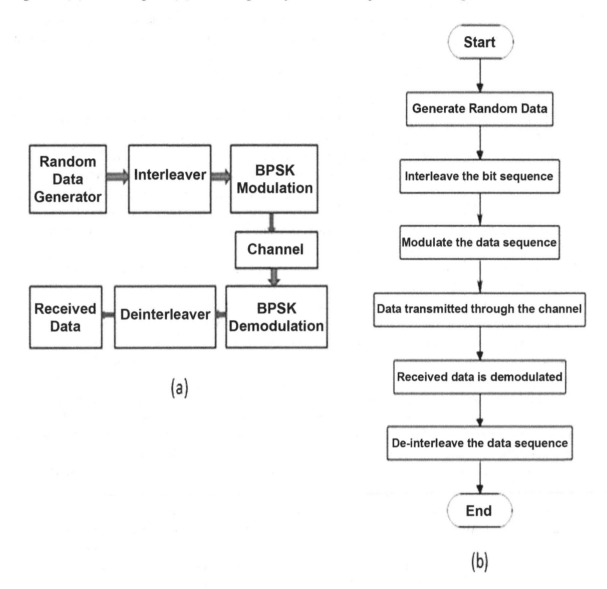

1) Simulation of a Few Interleaver Techniques for Fading Conditions

As mentioned earlier that the parameters that have been considered to evaluate the performance of the system are BER, computational time, mutual information and correlation. From the system model, it is seen that the random integers are converted into binary numbers and then interleaved. The interleaved sequence is then modulated using BPSK modulation technique. The modulated data is then transmitted over the channel. The data from the channel is then demodulated using BPSK demodulation technique. The demodulated data is then passed through a de-interleaver to recover the original bit sequence. The data which was in terms of bits is now converted into integer. Thus we get the received data.

In order to verify the proper operation of this simulation, the output data is fed into an error rate calculator block. The error rate calculator block takes the received data and the original data sequence signal as inputs and compares them. The error rate calculator will give a bit error rate for the received signal based on doing a bit to bit comparison. The curves in Figures 6(a), 6(b), 7(a) and 7(b) is generated by performing the simulation multiple times with different E_b/N_0 (-5 to 10 dB), for each type of interleavers i.e. block, matrix, random and convolutional interleaver passing through AWGN, Rayleigh and Rician fading channels. This is plotted along with the theoretical probability of error for BPSK.

From the curves obtained in Figures 6(a), 6(b), 7(a) and 7(b), we observed that the BER curves of the theoretical and simulation almost match with each other in case of all the interleavers, hence verifying the correct operation of this simulation. But we found the performance using block interleaver is better than other interleavers. BER obtained through AWGN and Rician is better than that obtained using Rayleigh channel. The BER in case of Rayleigh channel is slightly higher than other channels since it is a non-line-of-sight (NLOS) method, which consists of many obstacles in its path. The BER plot of all the interleavers for Rayleigh channel is shown in Figure 8.

Computational time which is also an important parameter to determine the performance of a wireless system, are checked using the different type of interleavers for the entire process i.e. from generation of the information at the transmitter till its reception at the receiver.

From Table 1, showing the computational time, we find that block interleaver is better in case of AWGN channel. In case of Rayleigh and Rician, matrix and random interleavers are respectively found to be better. Computational time of convolutional interleaver is poor since it consists of a set of shift registers with a fixed delay.

Mutual information gives the measure of amount of information that a random variable contains about another random variable. So, in this case, mutual information between the channel input and channel output has been determined. Higher the mutual information, higher will be the performance because if the channel output contains relatively more information about the channel input then it would be easier for the receiver to recover the original data. The mutual information curves for each of the interleavers are shown in Figures 9(a), 9(b), 10(a) and 10(b).

From the curves in Figures 9(a), 9(b), 10(a) and 10(b), we see that the mutual information between input and output of AWGN and Rician fading channel is better compared to that of Rayleigh fading channel for each interleavers. In case of Rayleigh fading channel due to its NLOS behaviour, a sizeable section of the information is corrupted due to reflections from the obstacles. As a result, the output contains less information about the channel input. The mutual information plots of all the interleavers for Rayleigh channel are shown in Figure 11.

Finally, the correlation properties between the transmitted and received bits are also checked for the system. Since from correlation, we come to know about the degree of similarity between two sequences, therefore we can say that the system performance will be better if the correlation between transmitted and received data is high.

From Figures 12(a), 12(b), 13(a) and 13(b), it is seen that the correlation property holds good for the system using block, matrix and random interleaver. For convolutional interleaver, the correlation property is not so fruitful compared to the other interleavers.

From the experimental details and results, we can summarize the work in the Tables 2, 3 and 4.

From Tables 2, 3 and 4, we see that the overall performance of block interleaver is better than the other interleavers.

Figure 6. BER plots for (a) Block Interleaver (b) Matrix Interleaver

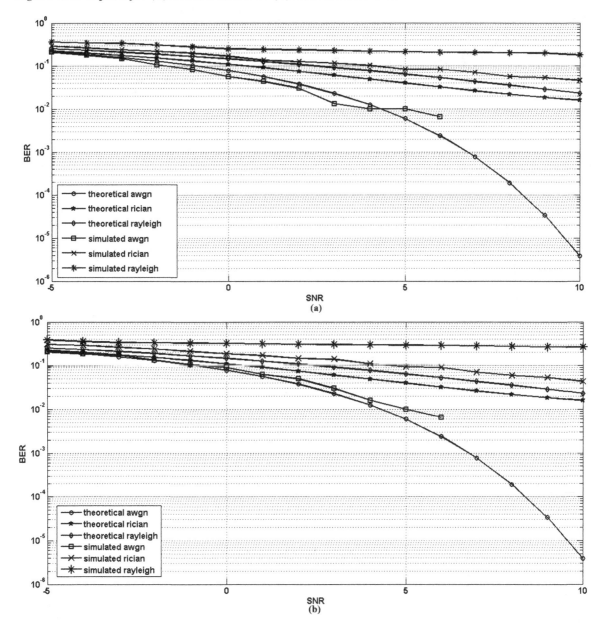

In this section, simulation of the proposed model has been verified considering some important parameters to determine the performance of the system. We have seen from the literature review that various techniques of interleaving have been proposed to improve the link performance of a wireless channel. Hence, using four types of interleaving techniques, we have tried to evaluate the performance of the system by simulating the model in terms of BER, computational time (Das, M. Sarma & K. Sarma, 2014), mutual information and correlation. From the results, we can conclude that using a block interleaver, the simulation of the model gives better results as compared with the other types. Therefore, a

Figure 7. BER plots for (a) Random Interleaver (b) Convolutional Interleaver

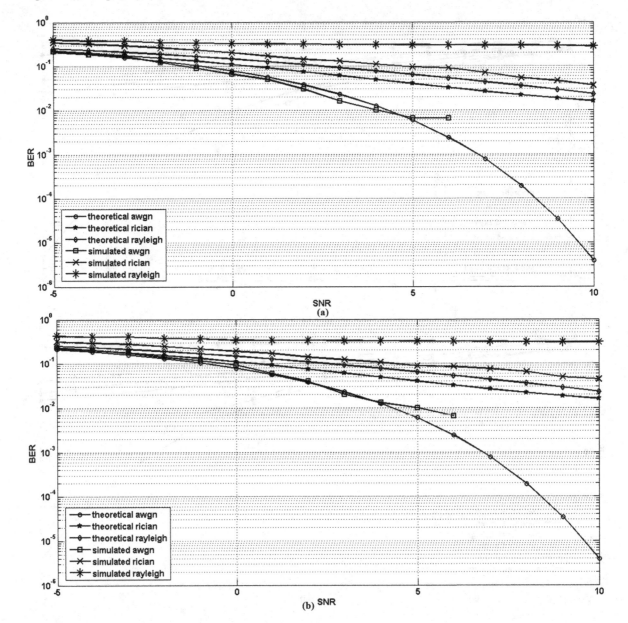

new model is proposed using a block interleaver which is explained elaborately in the next section. This new method is expected to provide improved performance.

2) Implementation of a Block Interleaver for Use in Wireless Channels

Based on the results obtained previously, in this section hardware implementation of a block interleaver has been done. In our experimentation, we have used Xilinx ISE Design Suite 13.2. To verify the proposed model, every module is implemented separately at first.

Figure 8. BER of BPSK modulated signal through Rayleigh channel for all the interleavers.

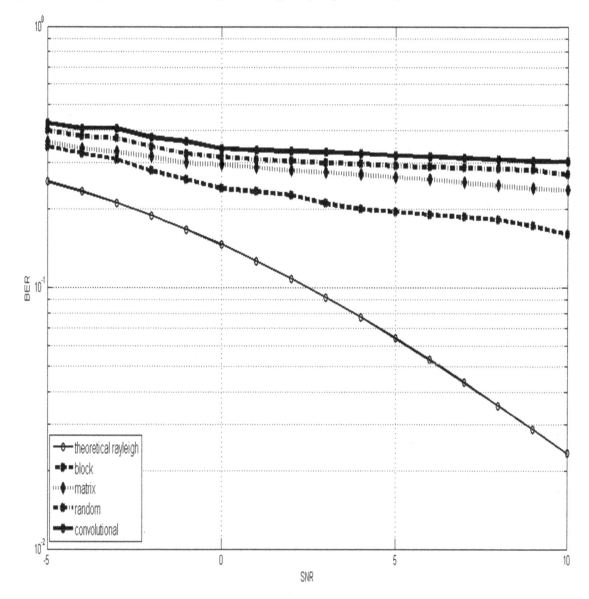

Table 1. Computational time of different Interleavers through Wireless Channels

Interleavers	AWGN	Rayleigh	Rician
General Block	10.26 s	13.09 s	13.53 s
Matrix	13.92 s	11.80 s	18.84 s
Random	12.86 s	15.47 s	13.16 s
Convolutional	16.89 s	16.02 s	21.07 s

Figure 9. Mutual Information for (a) Block Interleaver (b) Matrix Interleaver

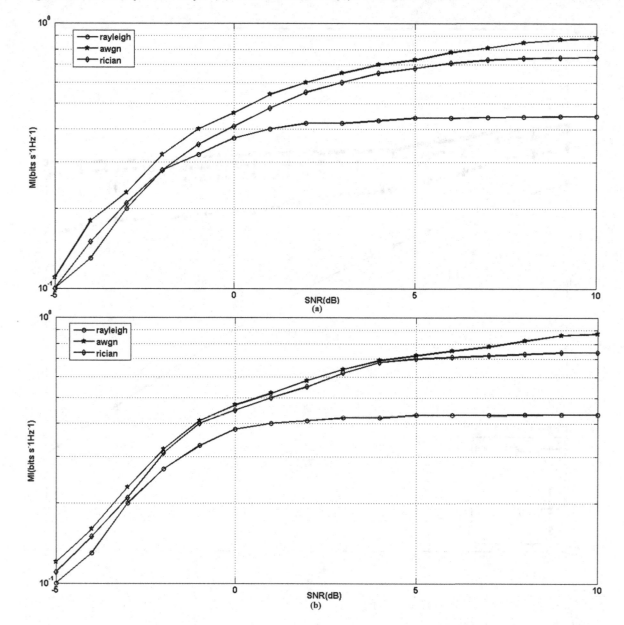

Let us now verify the transmitter and receiver. At the transmitter, we have generated 8-bit, 16- bit, 32-bit and 64-bit codeword separately, which would be fed to the input of the interleaver. The interleaver memory size is accordingly generated for different size of the codeword. Each code symbols of the codeword is applied to the respective rows of the interleaver. The codeword gets scrambled as it progresses through the interleaver. The scrambled codeword is then applied to the input of a BPSK modulator for modulation. Thus, we get a modulated codeword which is ready for transmission.

At the receiver, the data from the transmitter output is now fed to the input of the BPSK demodulator. The codeword from the output of the demodulator is applied as input to the deinterleaver. It is observed

Figure 10. Mutual Information for (a) Random Interleaver (b) Convolutional Interleaver

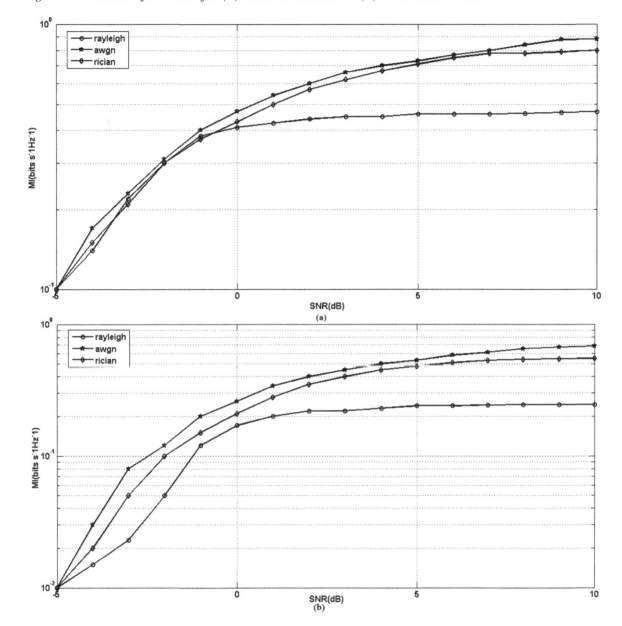

that the scrambled codeword is converted into its original form at the output of the deinterleaver in which some bits are corrupted.

For an 8-bit input codeword 11010010 transmitted, we receive the codeword 11000010 at the receiver i.e. 1-bit of the data gets corrupted.

For a 16-bit input codeword 0101100101010101 transmitted, we receive the codeword 0101100001010111 at the receiver i.e. 2-bits of the data get corrupted.

For a 32-bit input codeword 11001010101001001101001010101010 transmitted, we receive the codeword 11001010111001001001001010001010 at the receiver i.e. 3-bits of the data get corrupted.

Figure 11. Mutual Information of Rayleigh channel for all the interleavers

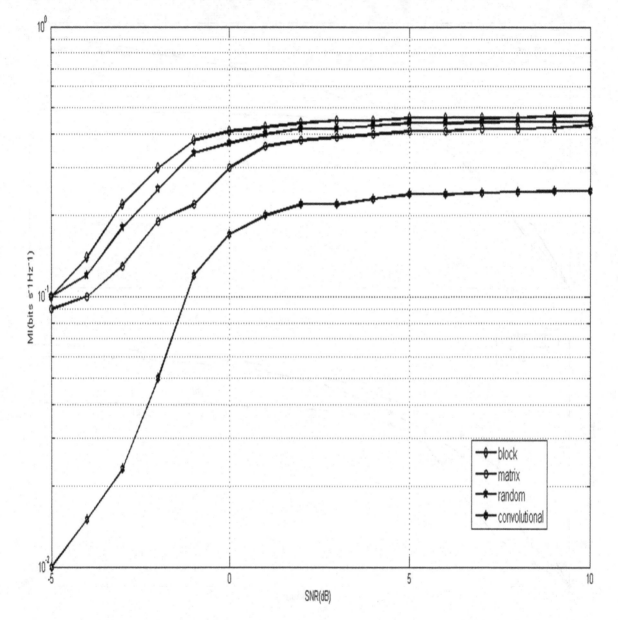

For a 64-bit input codeword 1110001110001110001110001110001110001110001110001110001110001110 0001110 transmitted, we receive the codeword 1110001110101110001110000110001010001111001 110001110001100001110 at the receiver i.e. 5-bits of the data get corrupted.

The number of bits corrupted for the different length of input codeword is tabulated in Table 5.

From Table 5, it is noticed that the percentage of error decreases as we increase the length of the input codeword. Table 6, 7, 8 and 9 gives the device utilization summary of the interleaver for different length of input codeword.

Figure 12. Correlation for (a) Block Interleaver (b) Matrix Interleaver

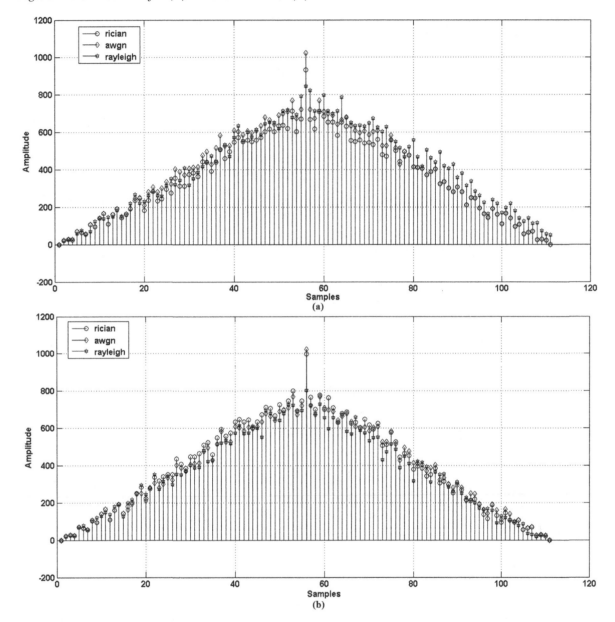

From the device utilization summary, we see that the number of slice and flip flop usage increases as the length of the input codeword increases. Therefore, the memory usage of the device also increases. The memory utilization of the interleaver for the various input codeword length are tabulated in Table 10.

The power estimation for different input codeword length which is measured using Xilinx Power Estimator (XPE) 13.2 is shown in Table 11 and 12.

From the power consumption table of the interleaver tabulated in Table 12, it is clear that interleaving with higher length of codeword consumes more power. A set of the entire work done is reported in (Das, Mastorakis, M. Sarma & K. Sarma, 2014).

Figure 13. Correlation for (a) Random Interleaver (b) Convolutional Interleaver

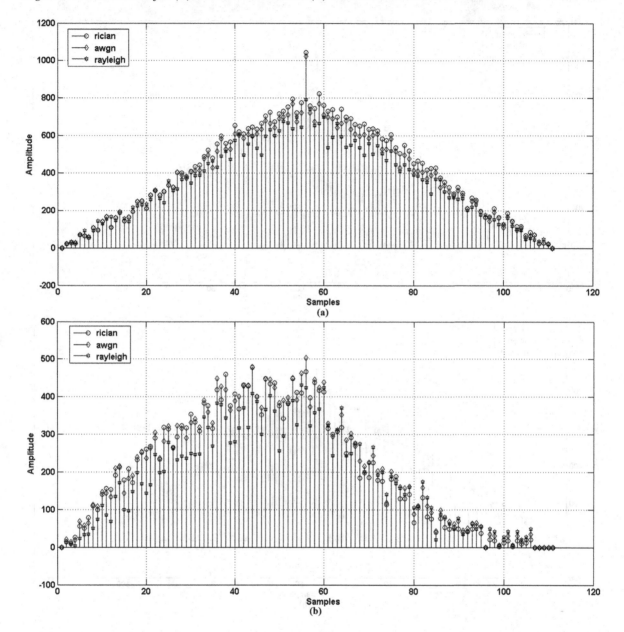

Table 2. Performance summary for AWGN channel

Interleavers	BER	Computational Time	Mutual Information	Correlation
Block	Lesser	Lower	High	Very good
Matrix	Less	High	High	Good
Random	Less	Low	High	Good
Convolutional	Less	Higher	Low	Poor

Table 3. Performance summary for Rayleigh fading channel

Interleavers	BER	Computational Time	Mutual Information	Correlation
Block	Lesser	Low	High	Average
Matrix	Less	Lower	High	Average
Random	Less	High	High	Average
Convolutional	Less	Higher	Low	Poor

Table 4. Performance summary for Rician fading channel

Interleavers	BER	Computational Time	Mutual Information	Correlation
Block	Lesser	Low	High	Good
Matrix	Less	High	High	Good
Random	Less	Lower	High	Very good
Convolutional	Less	Higher	Low	Poor

In this section, implementation of a block interleaver on FPGA platform has been shown. The main objective was to build an interleaver design with minimum possible resources and verify the transmission and reception process of the given system model. The proposed model is verified by implementing every module separately. Simulation result in the form of timing diagram using Xilinx ISE Design Suite 13.2 is presented which endorses the successful operation of the model. This technique reduces FPGA resource utilization and power consumption compared to other implementation technique.

Table 5. Performance comparison for different length of input codeword

Codeword Length	No. of Errors (in Bits)	% of Error (per Frame)
8-bit	1	12.5%
16-bit	2	12.5%
32-bit	3	9.375%
64-bit	5	7.81%

Table 6. Device utilization summary of the interleaver for 8-bit codeword

Device: XILINX xa3s50vqg100-4	Utilized	Available	Percentage Utilization
Number of Slices:	9	768	1%
Number of Slice Flip Flops:	16	1536	1%
Number of 4 input LUTs:	1	1536	0%
Number of bonded IOBs:	18	63	28%
Number of GCLKs	1	8	12%

Table 7. Device utilization summary of the interleaver for 16-bit codeword

Device: XILINX xa3s50vqg100-4	Utilized	Available	Percentage Utilization
Number of Slices:	18	768	2%
Number of Slice Flip Flops:	32	1536	2%
Number of 4 input LUTs:	1	1536	0%
Number of bonded IOBs:	34	63	53%
Number of GCLKs	1	8	12%

CONCLUSION

Since wireless channels are prone to errors, it is necessary to minimize the errors in order to get better reception of data. Interleavers are such devices which help to mitigate the burst of errors that arises in the channel. Initially, the system model of the proposed approach has been simulated using the MatLab Simulink. The system model is verified for the four types of interleavers (block, matrix, random and convolutional) considering AWGN, Rayleigh and Rician channels. The performance of the system has been estimated by taking into account some important parameters like BER, computational time, mutual information and correlation. From the analysis of the results obtained, we found the block interleaver performance to be better than the other types. Therefore, considering a block interleaver to be efficient in improving the link performance, it is designed using Verilog hardware language to implement on FPGA platform. The interleaver structure that has been designed, is implemented for different codeword length. We find that as the length of the input codeword increases, percentage of error decreases. Device utilization and power consumption is also reduced using the block interleaver.

LIMITATION

1. The computational time evaluated in presence of the interleaver from the simulation is observed to be more than that in absence of the interleaver. Though it is expected within the present framework but still it is desired to have reduction in time with more efficient algorithms.
2. The length of input codeword is limited to only 64 bits in case of hardware implementation, since it is dependent on the specifications of the FPGA on which it is designed to be implemented.

Table 8. Device utilization summary of the interleaver for 32-bit codeword

Device: XILINX xa3s50vqg100-4	Utilized	Available	Percentage Utilization
Number of Slices:	37	768	4%
Number of Slice Flip Flops:	64	1536	4%
Number of 4 input LUTs:	1	1536	0%
Number of bonded IOBs:	56	63	78%
Number of GCLKs	1	8	12%

Table 9. Device utilization summary of the interleaver for 64-bit codeword

Device: XILINX xa3s50vqg100-4	Utilized	Available	Percentage Utilization
Number of Slices:	74	768	9%
Number of Slice Flip Flops:	128	1536	8%
Number of 4 input LUTs:	1	1536	0%
Number of bonded IOBs:	63	63	100%
Number of GCLKs	1	8	12%

Table 10. Memory usage of the interleaver for different length of input codeword

-	8-Bit	16-Bit	32-Bit	64-Bit
Memory usage(kilobytes)	239892	239956	240020	241108

Table 11. On- Chip Power Summary of the interleaver

On-Chip	8-Bit(W)	16-Bit(W)	32-Bit(W)	64-Bit(W)
Clock	0.004	0.006	0.007	0.010
Logic	0.000	0.000	0.000	0.001
BRAM	0.005	0.091	0.181	0.272
PLL	0.114	0.114	0.114	0.114
Other	0.332	0.332	0.332	0.332
IO	0.766	0.766	0.766	0.766
Device Statistics	0.185	0.186	0.187	0.188

Table 12. Power consumption of the interleaver

Length of Input	Power(W)
8-bit	1.406
16-bit	1.495
32-bit	1.588
64-bit	1.683

3. The design is limited only for single user. Hence multi-user environment may lead to more complexities which needs to be solved further.
4. The design is limited only for a linear system. Non-linearity may also lead to some complexities which needs to be solved further.

FUTURE DIRECTION

1. Techniques can be devised to address the issue of time consumption to make the system more efficient for real time high data rate situations.
2. Block interleavers can be designed for multi-user environment. This will help to make use of the system in more realistic situations.
3. The issue of power consumption can be addressed with the considerations of actual power consumption factors to make the system well implementable on FPGA/ASIC platforms. This is also a very important requirement for high data rate communications.

REFERENCES

Abhayapala, T. D., Perera, R. R., & Pollock, T. S. (2005). Bounds on Mutual Information of Rayleigh Fading Channels with Gaussian Input. *In Proceedings of Communications Theory Workshop*, 6, 62 – 67.

Adachi, F., & Garg, D. (2002). Chip Interleaved Turbo Codes for DS-CDMA in a Rayleigh Fading Channel with Diversity Reception. *In Proceedings of IEEE 56th Vehicular Technology Conference Proceedings* (Vol. 3, pp. 1777-1781).

Adachi, F., & Liu, L. (2006). Chip-interleaved Multi-rate CDMA with 2-dimensional OVSF Spreading. *Proceedings of IEEE 63rd Vehicular Technology Conference* (Vol. 4, pp. 1767-1771).

Ali, I. (2013). Bit-Error-Rate (BER) Simulation Using MATLAB. *International Journal of Engineering Research and Applications*, 3(1), 706–711.

Ali, Md. S. & Synthia, M. (2011). Performance Study of Turbo Code with Interleaver Design. *International Journal of Scientific and Engineering Research*, 2(7), 1–5.

Andrews, K., Heegard, C., & Kozen, D. (1997). A Theory of Interleavers [Technical Report]. Cornell University, Ithaca, New York.

Asghar, R. (2010). *Flexible Interleaving Sub-systems for FEC in Baseband Processors* [Doctoral Thesis]. Sweden: Linkoping University Electronic Press.

Babu, A. S., & Rao, K. V. S. (2011). Evaluation of BER for AWGN, Rayleigh and Rician Fading Channels under Various Modulation Schemes. *International Journal of Computers and Applications*, 26(9), 23–28. doi:10.5120/3132-4317

Badrinarayanan, S., Hemamalini, R. R., & Mathana, J. M. (2014). VLSI Architecture of Dual Standard Interleaver for Turbo Codes. *Journal of Theoretical and Applied Information Technology*, 60(2), 408–416.

Benedetto, S., Montorsi, G., & Tarable, A. (2005). Analysis and Design of Interleavers for Iterative Multiuser Receivers in Coded CDMA Systems. *IEEE Transactions on Information Theory, 51*(5), 1650–1666. doi:10.1109/TIT.2005.846848

Berber, S., Suh, B. & Yuan, Y. (2013). Derivation of BER Expressions and Simulation of a Chip Interleaved System for WSNs Application. *Recent Advances in Telecommunications and Circuit Design*, 128-133.

Chauhan, P., Rai, A., & Yadav, N. (2010). Performance Comparison of Interleavers. *International Journal of Electronics Engineering, 2*(2), 277–278.

Das, B., Mastorakis, N., Sarma, K. K., & Sarma, M. P. (2014). Implementation of a Block Interleaver Structure for use in Wireless Channels. *Proceedings of 16th International Conference on Automatic Control, Modelling & Simulation (ACMOS'2014)* (pp. 277-281). Bulgaria.

Das, B., Sarma, K. K., & Sarma, M. P. (2014). Implementation of Certain Interleaver Designs for Application in Wireless Channels. *Proceedings of National Conference on Emerging Global Trends in Engineering and Technology (EGTET)*. Guwahati.

Feng, S., & Shixin, C. (2004). Interleaving Scheme for Multicarrier CDMA System. *Journal of Electronics (China), 21*(1), 16–22. doi:10.1007/BF02687793

Giannakis, G. B., Martret, C. L., & Zhou, S. (2002). Chip-Interleaved Block-Spread Code Division Multiple Access. *IEEE Transactions on Communications, 50*(2), 235–248. doi:10.1109/26.983320

Guo, D., Shamai, S., & Verd, S. (2005). Mutual Information and Minimum Mean-Square Error in Gaussian Channels. *IEEE Transactions on Information Theory, 51*(4), 1261–1282. doi:10.1109/TIT.2005.844072

Guzman-Renteria, M. E., Michel, R. P., & Sanchez-Ortiz, C. R. (2008). Design and Implementation of a Multi-Standard Interleaver for 802.11a, 802.11n, 802.16e and DVB Standards. *Proceedings of International Conference on Reconfigurable Computing and FPGAs* (pp. 379-384).

Harbi, Y. J. (2012). Effect of the Interleaver types on the Performance of the Parallel Concatenation Convolutional Codes. *International Journal of Electrical and Computer Sciences (IJECS-IJENS), 12*(3), 25-31.

Huang, D., Letaief, K. B., & Lu, J. (2005). Bit-Interleaved Time-Frequency Coded Modulation for OFDM Systems Over Time-Varying Channels. *IEEE Transactions on Communications, 53*(7), 1191–1199. doi:10.1109/TCOMM.2005.851561

Jootar, J., Proakis, J. G., & Zeidler, J. R. (2006). Performance of Convolutional Codes With Finite- Depth Interleaving and Noisy Channel Estimates. *IEEE Transactions on Communications, 54*(10), 1775–1786. doi:10.1109/TCOMM.2006.881363

Kabir, M. H., Shams, R. A., & Ullah, S. E. (2012). Effect of Interleaved FEC Code on Wavelet Based MC-CDMA System with Alamouti STBC in Different Modulation Schemes. *International Journal of Computer Science, Engineering and Information Technology, 2*(1), 23–33.

Kousa, M. A. (2003). Performance of turbo codes with Matrix Interleavers. *The Arabian Journal for Science and Engineering, 28*(2B), 211–220.

Kumar, P., Sarumathi, M. & Sumithra, S. M. G. (2013). Performance Evaluation of Rician Fading Channels using QPSK, DQPSK and OQPSK Modulation Schemes in Simulink Environment. *International Journal of Engineering Science Invention*, 2(5), 07-16.

Kumari, S. & Lodhi, Md. E. (2013). Four Arm Interleaver: Performance analysis. *International Journal of Scientific Research*, 2(8), 140–142.

Ngo, C., Niu, H., & Ouyang, X. (2006). Interleaver Design for MIMO-OFDM based Wireless LAN. *Proceedings of IEEE Wireless Communications and Networking Conference* (Vol. 4, pp. 1825-1829).

Rappaport, T. S. (2002). *Wireless Communication, Principle and Practice* (2nd ed.). India: Prentice Hall.

Sanyal, S. K., & Upadhyaya, B. K. (2009). VHDL Modeling of Convolutional Interleaver- Deinterleaver for Efficient FPGA Implementation. *International Journal of Scientific Research*, 2(6), 66–68.

KEY TERMS AND DEFINITIONS

Burst Error: A burst error is a string of corrupt data, such that first and last symbols are in error.

Fading: A variation in the strength of the signal.

Interleaving: This is the process of interchanging the position of the message bits before transmission.

Multipath Propagation: This is the phenomena that results in reaching the signals at the receiving antenna from more than two paths. Causes of multipath propagation include atmospheric ducting, ionospheric reflection and refraction, and reflection from water bodies and terrestrial objects such as mountains and buildings.

Signal to Noise Ratio: It is a measure that compares the level of a desired signal to the level of background noise.

Xilinx: It is an American technology company, primarily a supplier of programmable logic devices. It is known for inventing the field programmable gate array (FPGA).

Compilation of References

Artificial Neural Network. (2014, December 22). Retrieved Wikimedia Commons. from http://commons.wikimedia. org/wiki/Artificial_neural_network

Abbadi, N. K. E., & Al- Saadi, E. H. (2013). Automatic detection of exudates in retinal images. *International Journal of Computer Science Issues, 10*(2), 237–242.

Abhayapala, T. D., Perera, R. R., & Pollock, T. S. (2005). Bounds on Mutual Information of Rayleigh Fading Channels with Gaussian Input.*InProceedings of Communications Theory Workshop, 6*, 62 – 67.

Adachi, F., & Garg, D. (2002). Chip Interleaved Turbo Codes for DS-CDMA in a Rayleigh Fading Channel with Diversity Reception. *In Proceedings of IEEE 56th Vehicular Technology Conference Proceedings* (Vol. 3, pp. 1777-1781).

Adachi, F., & Liu, L. (2006). Chip-interleaved Multi rate CDMA with 2 dimensional OVSF Spreading.*Proceedings of IEEE 63rd Vehicular Technology Conference* (Vol. 4, pp. 1767-1771).

Adams, R., & Choi, A. (2012). Using Neural Networks to Predict Cardiac Arrhythmia.*Proceedings of Conference on Recent Advances in Robotics (pp. 1-6).*Florida. doi:10.1109/ICSMC.2012.6377734

Agrawal, S. C., Jalal, A. S., & Bhatnagar, C. (2012). Recognition of Indian Sign Language using Feature Fusion.*Proceedings of 4th International Conference on Intelligent Human Computer Interaction.* Kharagpur. IEEE. doi:10.1109/ IHCI.2012.6481841

Ahmad, A., Mansoor, A., Mumtaz, R., Khan, M., & Mirza, S. (2014). Image processing and classification in diabetic retinopathy: A Review. *Proceedings of the 5th European workshop on visual information Processing* (EUVIP 2014) (pp 1-6). France. IEEE

Ahmed, S. M. H., Alexander, T. C., & Anagnostopoulo, G. C. (2008). Real-time, Static and Dynamic Hand Gesture Recognition for Human-Computer Interaction. Retrieved December 22, 2014 from http://www.machine-learning.net/ amalthea-reu.org/pubs/amalthea_tr_2008_01.pdf

Ahsan, R., Ibrahimy, M., & Khalifa, O. O. (2009). EMG Signal Classification for Human Computer Interaction: A Review. *European Journal of Scientific Research, 33*, 480–501.

Akila, T., & Kavitha, G. (2014). Detection and classification of hard exudates in human retinal fundus images using clustering and random forest methods. *International Journal of Emerging Technology and Advanced Engineering, 4*(2), 24–29.

Akram, M. U., Akhtar, M., & Javed, M. Y. (2012). *An automated system for the grading of diabetic maculopathy in fundus images. Proceedings of Neural Information Processing (LNCS)* (Vol. 7666, pp. 36–43). Springer.

Alfredson, J. (2007). *Differences in situational awareness and how to manage them in development of complex systems* [Doctoral dissertation No. 1132]. Linköping, Sweden: Linköping University.

Alfredson, J., & Andersson, R. (2013). Designing for Human Factors in the Technology-Intensive Domain of Fighter Aircraft. *International Journal of Aviation Technology, Engineering and Management, 1*(2), 1–16. doi:10.4018/ijatem.2013070101

Alfredson, J., Holmberg, J., Andersson, R., & Wikforss, M. (2011). Applied cognitive ergonomics design principles for fighter aircraft. In D. Harris (Ed.), *Proceedings of the 9th International Conference on Engineering Psychology and Cognitive Ergonomics (EPCE 2011)* (pp. 473–483). Springer-Verlag. doi:10.1007/978-3-642-21741-8_50

Alfredson, J., Lundqvist, A., Molander, S., & Nordlund, P.-J. (2010). Decision support for the Gripen aircraft and beyond. *Proceedings of the 27th International Congress of the Aeronautical Sciences ICAS 2010.*

Ali, I. (2013). Bit-Error-Rate (BER) Simulation Using MATLAB. *International Journal of Engineering Research and Applications, 3*(1), 706–711.

Ali, Md. S. & Synthia, M. (2011). Performance Study of Turbo Code with Interleaver Design. *International Journal of Scientific and Engineering Research, 2*(7), 1–5.

Andolfi, F., Aquilani, F., Balsamo, S., & Inverardi, P. (2000). Deriving performance models of software architecture for message sequence charts.*Proceedings of the Workshop On the Softaware and Performance* (pp. 45-57). New York, NY: ACM. doi:10.1145/350391.350404

Andrews, K., Heegard, C., & Kozen, D. (1997). A Theory of Interleavers [Technical Report]. Cornell University, Ithaca, New York.

Anguita, D., Boni, A., & Ridella, S. (2003). A digital architecture for support vector machines: Theory, algorithm and FPGA implementation. *IEEE Transactions on Neural Networks, 14*(5), 993–1009. doi:10.1109/TNN.2003.816033 PMID:18244555

Arnaud, J. (1986). Use of unidirectional data flow in bit level systolic array chips. *Electronics Letters, 22*(10), 540–541. doi:10.1049/el:19860368

Asghar, R. (2010). *Flexible Interleaving Sub-systems for FEC in Baseband Processors* [Doctoral Thesis]. Sweden: Linkoping University Electronic Press.

ATMEGA32A-PU Atmel 8 Bit 32K AVR Microcontroller. (n. d.). *Protostack.com*. Retrieved from http://www.protostack. com/microcontrollers/atmega32a-pu-atmel-8-bit-32k-avr-microcontroller

Babu, A. S., & Rao, K. V. S. (2011). Evaluation of BER for AWGN, Rayleigh and Rician Fading Channels under Various Modulation Schemes. *International Journal of Computers and Applications, 26*(9), 23–28. doi:10.5120/3132-4317

Badrinarayanan, S., Hemamalini, R. R., & Mathana, J. M. (2014). VLSI Architecture of Dual Standard Interleaver for Turbo Codes. *Journal of Theoretical and Applied Information Technology, 60*(2), 408–416.

Bajwa, I. S., Nigar, N., & Arshad, M. J. (2010). An Autonomous Robot Framework for Path Finding and Obstacle Evasion. *International Journal of Computer Science and Telecommunications, 1*(1), 1–6.

Banuchandar, J., Kaliraj, V., Balasubramanian, P., Deepa, S., & Thamilarasi, N. (2012). Automated Unmanned Railway Level Crossing System. *International Journal of Modern Engineering Research, 2*(1), 458–463.

Barret, H. H. (2004). Foundation of Image Science (3rd ed.). Hoboken, New Jersey: John Wiley and Sons. U. K. Publications.

Benedetto, S., Montorsi, G., & Tarable, A. (2005). Analysis and Design of Interleavers for Iterative Multiuser Receivers in Coded CDMA Systems. *IEEE Transactions on Information Theory, 51*(5), 1650–1666. doi:10.1109/TIT.2005.846848

Berber, S., Suh, B. & Yuan, Y. (2013). Derivation of BER Expressions and Simulation of a Chip Interleaved System for WSNs Application. *Recent Advances in Telecommunications and Circuit Design*, 128-133.

Berggren, P., Nählinder, S., & Svensson (2014). *Assessing command and control effectiveness: Dealing with a changing world*. Farnham, England: Ashgate.

Bertalmio, M., Sapiro, G., Caselles, V., & Ballester, C. (2000). Image Inpainting.*Proceedings of the 27th Annual Conference on Computer Graphics and Interactive Techniques* (pp. 417–424), New York: ACMPress/Addison-Wesley.

Bevilacqua, V., Cambo, S., Cariello, L., & Mastronardi, G. (2005), A combined method to detect Retinal Fundus Features. *Proceedings of European Conference on Data Analysis.*

Bhuyan, M. K., Ghosh, D., & Bora, P. K. (2005). *Co-articulation Detection in Hand Gestures. TENCON.* Melbourne: IEEE.

Biasi, I., Boni, A., & Zorat, A. (2005). A reconfigurable parallel architecture for SVM classification.*Proceedings of IEEE International Joint Conference on Neural Networks* (Vol. 5, pp. 2867 – 2872)

Biglieri, E., & Torino, P. (2003). Coding and Modulation for a horrible channel. *IEEE Communications Magazine, 41*(5), 92–98. doi:10.1109/MCOM.2003.1200107

Binh, N. D., Shuichia, E., & Ejima, T. (2005). Real-Time Hand Tracking and Gesture Recognition System.*Proceedings of International Conference on Graphics, Vision and Image Processing (GVIP)*. Cairo.

Borea, R., Boquete, L., Maza, M., Lopez, E., & Lledo, A. G. (2013). EOG Technique to Guide a Wheelchair. Retrieved from https://www.researchgate.net/publication/228965183_EOG_Technique_to_guide_a_wheelchair

Bourlard, H., & Dupont, S. (1997). Sub-band-based speech recognition.*Proceedings of IEEE International Conference on Acoustics, Speech, and Signal Processing*. Munich.

Bourlard, H., & Morgan, N. (1994). *Connectionist Speech Recognition – A Hybrid Approach*. Norwell, MA, USA: Kluwer Academic Publishers. doi:10.1007/978-1-4615-3210-1

Bristeau, P. J., Callou, F., Vissière, D., & Petit, N. (2011). The Navigation and Control technology inside the AR. Drone micro UAV. *Proceedings of 18th IFAC World Congress Milano (Italy)* (pp. 1477-1484).

Broadband Powerline Communications Systems. (2003). *Australian Communications Authority*. Retrieved from http://acma.gov.au/webwr/radcomm/frequency_planning/spps/0311spp.pdf

Brown, P. A. (1987). The Acoustic Modeling Problem in Automatic Speech Recognition [Doctoral dissertation]. School of Computer Science at Carnegie Mellon University.

Brown, T. X., Argrow, B., Dixon, C., Doshi, S., Thekkekunnel, R.-G., Henkel, D. (2004). Ad Hoc UAV Ground Network. Proceedings of *AIAA 3rd "Unmanned Unlimited"Technical Conference, Workshop and Exhibit*. Chicago, Illinois.

Burges, J. C. (1998). A Tutorial on Support Vector Machines for Pattern Recognition.

Buzbee, B., Wang, W. & Wang, A. A. (n. d.). Power Saving Approaches and Trade-off for Storage Systems. Florida State University.

Cadambi, S., Durdanovic, I., Jakkula, V., Sankaradass, M., Cosatto, E., Chakradhar, S., & Graf, H. (2009). A massively parallel FPGA-based coprocessor for support vector machines.*Proceedings of 17th IEEE Symposium on Field Programmable Custom Computing Machines* (pp. 115 -122). doi: doi:10.1109/FCCM.2009.34

Canny, M., Whirter, M. J. G., & Wood, K. W. (1984). Optimized bit level systolic array for convolution. IEEE Proc. F, Commun, Radar and Signal Process, 6, 632-637.

Cardoso, J., & Blanc, C. (2001). Ordering actions in sequence diagram of UML.*Proceedings of the International conference on Information Technology Interfaces* (pp. 3-14). Croatia: IEEE.

Casner, S. M., & Schooler, J. W. (2014). Thoughts in flight: Automation use and pilots' task-related and task-unrelated thought. *Human Factors, 56*(3), 433–442. doi:10.1177/0018720813501550 PMID:24930166

Castor, M. (2009). *The use of structural equation modeling to describe the effect of operator functional state on air-to-air engagement outcomes* [Doctoral dissertation No. 1251]. Linköping, Sweden: Linköping University

Chai, S. M., Wills, D. S., & Jokerst, N. M. (1997). Systolic processing architectures using optoelectronic interconnects. *Proceedings of the Fourth International Conference on Massively Parallel Processing Using Optical Interconnections* (pp. 160-166). doi: doi:10.1109/MPPOI.1997.609179

Chaudhuri, G. S., Chatterjee, S., Katz, N., Nelson, M., & Goldman, M. (1989). Detection of blood vessels in retinal images using two dimensional matched filters. *IEEE Transactions on Medical Imaging, 8*(3), 263–269. doi:10.1109/42.34715 PMID:18230524

Chauhan, P., Rai, A., & Yadav, N. (2010). Performance Comparison of Interleavers. *International Journal of Electronics Engineering, 2*(2), 277–278.

Chavhan, Y., Dhore, M. L., & Yesaware, P. (2010). Speech Emotion Recognition Using Support Vector Machine. *International Journal of Computers and Applications, 1*(20), 6–9.

Chazal, P., Dwyer, M. O., & Reilly, R. B. (2004). Automatic Classification of Heartbeats Using ECG Morphology and Heartbeat Interval Features. *IEEE Transactions on Bio-Medical Engineering, 51*(7), 1196–1206. doi:10.1109/TBME.2004.827359 PMID:15248536

Chen, F., Fu, C., & Huang, C. L. (2003). Hand Gesture Recognition using a Real-Time Tracking Method and Hidden Markov Models. *Image and Vision Computing, 21*(8), 745–758. doi:10.1016/S0262-8856(03)00070-2

Chen, M., Hu, C., & Chang, T. (2011). The Research on Optimal Parking Space Choice Model in Parking Lots.*Proceedings of International Conference on Computer Research and Development* (Vol. 2, pp. 93-97). DOI: doi:10.1109/ICCRD.2011.5764091

Chen, Y. F., & Chiueh, T. D. (2002). Baseband Transceiver Design of a 128-Kbps Power-Line Modem for Household Applications. *IEEE Transactions on Power Delivery, 17*(2), 338–344. doi:10.1109/61.997894

Choudhury, A., Talukdar, A. K., & Sarma, K. K. (2014). A Conditional Random Field based Indian Sign Language Recognition System under Complex Background.*Proceedings of International Conference on Communication Systems and Network Technologies (CSNT)*. Bhopal. IEEE. doi:10.1109/CSNT.2014.185

Choudhury, S. R., Venkataramanan, S., Nemade, H. B., & Sahambi, J. S. (2005). Design & Development of a novel EOG Biopotential Amplifier. *IJBEM, 7*(1), 271–274.

Chuang, Z. J., Wu, C. H., & Chen, W. S. (2006). Movement Epenthesis Generation Using NURBS-Based Spatial Interpolation. *IEEE Transactions on Circuits and Systems for Video Technology, 16*(11), 1313–1323. doi:10.1109/TCSVT.2006.883509

Ciardo, G., Muppala, J., & Trivedi, K. S. (1992). Analyzing concurrent and fault-tolerant software using stochastic reward nets. *Journal of Parallel and Distributed Computing, 15*(1), 255–269. doi:10.1016/0743-7315(92)90007-A

Coleman, J. O., & Yurdakul, A. (2001). Fractions in the canonical-signed-digit number system.*Proceedings of Conference on Information Sciences and Systems, the Johns Hopkins University*.

Cooper, K., Dai, L., & Deng, Y. (2003). Modeling performance as an aspect: a UML based approach.*Proceedings of the 4th workshop on AOSD modeling with UML*. San Francisco, CA.

Cortes, C., & Vapnik, V. (1995). Support-vector networks, Machine Learning. *Journal Machine Learning, 20*(3), 273–297. doi: doi:10.1007/BF00994018

Crasborn, O. (2001). Phonetic Implementation of Phonological Categories in Sign Language of the Netherlands [Doctoral dissertation]. Leiden University Repository.

Creteil, G. C. (2010). *Macular edema- a practical approach*. Paris: Karger.

Csorba, M., Heegaard, P., & Hermann, P. (2008). Cost-Efficient deployment of collaborating components. Proceedings of the 8th IFIP WG 6.1 *International conference on Distributed applications and interoperable systems* (pp. 253-268). Oslo, Norway. Springer. doi:10.1007/978-3-540-68642-2_20

Cui, Y., & Weng, J. (1999). A Learning-Based Prediction-and-Verification Segmentation Scheme for Hand Sign Image Sequence. *Pattern Analysis and Machine Intelligence, 21*(8), 798–804. doi:10.1109/34.784311

Cummings, M. L., Whitten, A., How, J. P., & Toupet, O. (2011). The impact of human-automation collaboration in decentralized multiple unmanned vehicle. *Naval Research STTR under the guidance of Aurora Flight Sciences,* 1-11. DOI:.10.1109/JPROC.2011.2174104

Cummings, M. L., & Mitchell, P. J. (2008). Predicting Controller Capacity in Supervisory Control of Multiple UAVs. *IEEE Transactions on Systems, Man, and Cybernetics. Part A, Systems and Humans, 38*(2), 451–460. doi:10.1109/TSMCA.2007.914757

Dahl G. E., Yu D, Deng Li & Acero A. (2012). Context-Dependent Pre-Trained Deep Neural Networks for Large-Vocabulary Speech Recognition. *IEEE Transactions on Audio, Speech, and Language Processing.* 20(1), 30-42.

Das, B., Mastorakis, N., Sarma, K. K., & Sarma, M. P. (2014). Implementation of a Block Interleaver Structure for use in Wireless Channels.*Proceedings of 16th International Conference on Automatic Control, Modelling & Simulation (ACMOS'2014)* (pp. 277-281). Bulgaria.

Das, B., Sarma, K. K., & Sarma, M. P. (2014). Implementation of Certain Interleaver Designs for Application in Wireless Channels.*Proceedings of National Conference on Emerging Global Trends in Engineering and Technology (EGTET)*. Guwahati.

Davidsson, S., & Alm, H. (2014). *Context adaptable driver information – Or, what do whom need and want when?* Applied Cognitive Ergonomics.

Davies, D. (2000). Automatic Train Protection for the Railway Network in Britain.

Deepak, K. S., & Sivaswamy, J. (2012). Automatic assessment of macular edema from color retinal images. *IEEE Transactions on Medical Imaging, 31*(3), 766–776. doi:10.1109/TMI.2011.2178856 PMID:22167598

Dekker, S. W. A. (1996). Cognitive complexity in management by exception: Deriving early human factors requirements for an envisioned air traffic management world. In D. Harris (Ed.), Engineering psychology and cognitive ergonomics, Volume I: Transportation systems (pp. 201-210). Aldershot, England: Ashgate.

Dekker, S. W. A., & Woods, D. D. (1999). Extracting data from the future: Assessment and certification of envisioned systems. In S. Dekker & E. Hollnagel (Eds.), *Coping with computers in the cockpit* (pp. 131–143). Aldershot, England: Ashgate.

Dekker, S. W. A., & Woods, D. D. (2002). MABA-MABA or Abracadabra: Progress on human automation cooperation. *Cognition Technology and Work, 4*(4), 240–244. doi:10.1007/s101110200022

Dempster, A. P., Laird, N. M., & Rubin, D. B. (1977). Maximum likelihood from incomplete data via the EM algorithm. *Journal of the Royal Statistical Society. Series B. Methodological, 39*(1), 1–38.

Deng, L., & Shaughnessy, D. (2003). *Speech Processing, A Dynamic and Optimization-Oriented Approach.* New York, NY, USA: Marcel Dekker Inc.

Desai, Y. S. (2013). Natural Eye Movement & its Application for Paralyzed Patient. *International Journal of Engineering Trends and Technology, 4*(4), 679–686.

Dewangan, A. K., Gupta, M., & Patel, P. (2012). Automation of Railway Gate Control Using Microcontroller. *International Journal of Engineering Research & Technology, 1*(3), 1–8.

Diabetic Retinopathy [Image]. (2013). *Vitreous-Retina-Macula Consultants of New York.* Retrieved from http://www.vrmny.com/education-center/educational-topcs/diabetic-retinopathy.html

Diabetic Retinopathy [image]. (2014). Retinal Eye Care Associates. Retrieved from http://www.retinaleyecare.com/common/images/diabetic-retinopathy.jpg

Diabetic Retinopathy. (2012). *St. Luke's Cataract and Laser Institute.* Retrieved from http://www.stlukeseye.com/conditions/DiabeticRetinopathy.html

Diabetic retinopathy. (2013). *NHS Choices.* Retrieved from http://www.nhs.uk/conditions/diabetic-retinopathy/Pages/Introduction.aspx

Diabetic Retinopathy. (2014). American Optometric Association. Retrieved from http://www.aoa.org/patients-and-public/eye-and-vision-problems/glossary-of-eye-and-vision-conditions/diabetic-retinopathy?sso=y

Donoser, M., & Bischof, H. (2008). Real Time Appearance based Hand Tracking. *Proceedings of International Conference on Pattern Recognition (ICPR).* Tampa: IEEE.

Dougherty, G. (2011). *Medical image processing-Techniques and Application.* New York, NY: Springer; doi:10.1007/978-1-4419-9779-1

DRIVE: Digital Retinal Images for Vessel Extraction. (2004). *Image Sciences Institute.* Retrieved from http://www.isi.uu.nl/Research/Databases/DRIVE

DTW algorithm. (n. d.). GenTxWarper. Retrieved from http://www.psb.ugent.be/cbd/papers/gentxwarper/DTWalgorithm.htm

Duckhwa, H., & Younghun, L. (2008). A study on the compound communication network over the high voltage power line for distribution automation system. *Proceedings of the 2nd International Conference on Information Security and Assurance* (pp. 410–414). Busan, Korea.

Duda, R. O., Hart, P. E., & Stork, D. G. (2009). *Pattern Classification.* India: Wiley India.

Emanet, N. (2009). ECG Beat Classification by using Discrete Wavelet Transform and Random Forest Algorithm. *Proceedings of International Conference on Soft Computing with Words and Perceptions in System Analysis Decision and Control* (pp. 1-4). Istanbul. doi:10.1109/ICSCCW.2009.5379457

Enderle, J. Blanchard, & S., Bronzino, J. (2006). Introduction to Biomedical Engineering (2nd eds). Elsevier.

Endsley, M. R. (1988). Situation Awareness global assessment technique (SAGAT).*Proceedings of the IEEE National Aerospace and Electronics Conference* (pp. 789-795). New York: IEEE.

Energy, Infrastructure and Communication (2013). Retrieved from http://www. indiabudget.nic.in/budget2013-2014/es2012-13/echap-11.pdf

Engineers Garage. (n. d). Retrieved from http://www.engineersgarage.com/electronic-components/lm324n-datasheet

Eshuis, R., & Wieringa, R. (2001). A comparison of Petri net & activity diagram variants.*InProceedings of the International collaboration on Petri Net technologies for modeling communication based systems* (pp. 93-104). Berlin, Germany. Springer.

Esposito, A., & Marinaro, M. (2002). *Some Notes on Nonlinearities of Speech. Nonlinear Speech Modeling and Applications. Advanced Lectures and Revised Selected Papers.* Germany: Springer.

European Committee for Electrotechnical Standardization (CENELEC). EN 50065-1 (1991). Signaling on Low Voltage Electrical Installations in the Frequency Range 3 kHz to 148.5 kHz-Part 1: General Requirements, Frequency Bands and Electromagnetic Disturbances. Retrieved from http://www.bsi-global.com/en/Shop

Evermann, G., Chan, H. Y., Gales, M. J. F., Hain, T., Liu, X., & Mrva, D. et al. (2004). Development of the 2003 CU-HTK conversational telephone speech transcription system.*Proceedings of IEEE International Conference on Acoustics, Speech, and Signal Processing.* Montreal, Canada. doi:10.1109/ICASSP.2004.1325969

Fatourechi, M., Bashashati, A., Ward, R. K., & Birch, G. E. (2007). EMG and EOG artifacts in brain computer interface systems: A survey. *Clinical Neurophysiology, 118*(3), 480–494. doi:10.1016/j.clinph.2006.10.019 PMID:17169606

Faundez-Zanuy, M. (2002). *Nonlinear Speech Processing: Overview and Possibilities in Speech Coding. Nonlinear Speech Modeling and Applications. Advanced Lectures and Revised Selected Papers.* Germany: Springer.

Feigh, K. M., & Pritchett, A. R. (2014). Requirements for effective function allocation: A critical review. *Journal of Cognitive Engineering and Decision Making, 8*(1), 23–32. doi:10.1177/1555343413490945

Feng, S., & Shixin, C. (2004). Interleaving Scheme for Multicarrier CDMA System. *Journal of Electronics (China), 21*(1), 16–22. doi:10.1007/BF02687793

Fetter, C. H. (1926). *Carrier transmission over power circuits, US 1607668 A.* Retrieved from http://www.google/patents/US1607668

Fink, D., & Rho, J. J. (2008). Feasible connectivity solutions of PLC for rural and remote areas. *InProceedings of the International Symposium on Power-Line Communications and its Applications* (pp. 158-163). New Orleans, LA, USA. doi:10.1109/ISPLC.2008.4510416

Fitts, P. M. (1951). Human engineering for an effective air navigation and traffic control system. Ohio State University Research Foundation Report.

Flourescein angiography. (2012, September 17). *MedlinePlus.* Retrieved from http://www.nlm.nih.gov/medlineplus/ency/article/003846.htm

Fong, D., Aiello, L., Gardner, T.W., King, G.L., Blankenship, G., Cavallerano, J.D., Ferris III, F.L., & Klein, R. (2003). Retinopathy in Diabetes. *Diabetes Care,* 26(1), 226-229. Retrieved from http://care.diabetesjournals.org/content/26/1/226.full?sid=2012dd7a-64a7-4816-929d-46b3d4591a49

Fong, D., Aiello, L., Gardner, T.W., King, G.L., Blankenship, G., Cavallerano, J.D., Ferris III, F.L., & Klein, R. (2004). Retinopathy in Diabetes. *Diabetes Care*, 27(Supplement 1), s84-s87. Retrieved from http://care.diabetesjournals.org/content/27/suppl_1/s84.long

Frikha, M., & Hamida, A. B. (2012). A Comparitive Survey of ANN and Hybrid HMM/ANN Architectures for Robust Speech Recognition. *American Journal of Intelligent Systems*, 2(1), 1–8. doi:10.5923/j.ajis.20120201.01

Fundus camera picture. (2007). *Wikipedia*. Retrieved from http://en.wikipedia.org/wiki/File:Retinal_camera.jpg

Gao, Z., Lei, J., Song, Q., Yu, Y., & Ge, Y. (2006). Research on the Surface EMG Signal for Human Body Motion Recognizing Based on Arm Wrestling Robot.*Proceedings of International Conference on Information Acquisition* (pp. 1269-1273). USA

Gardenr, T. W., Abcouwer, S. F., Barber, A. J., & Jackson, G. R. (2011). An Integrated approach to diabetic retinopathy research. Arch. Ophthalmol., *129*(2), 230–235. PMID:21320973

Gardner, G. G., Keating, D., Williamson, T. H., & Elliott, A. T. (1996). Automatic detection of diabetic retinopathy using an artificial neural network: A screening tool. *The British Journal of Ophthalmology*, *80*(11), 940–944. doi:10.1136/bjo.80.11.940 PMID:8976718

Geetha, M., & Manjusha, U. C. (2012). A Vision Based Recognition of Indian Sign Language Alphabets and Numerals Using B-Spline Approximation. *International Journal on Computer Science and Engineering*, 4(3), 406–415.

Gehring, J., Lee, W., Kilgour, K., Lane, I., Miao, Y., & Waibel, A. (2013). Modular Combination of Deep Neural Networks for Acoustic Modeling.*Proceedings of Interspeech*. Lyon, France.

Genov, R., & Cauwenberghs, G. (2003). Kerneltron: Support Vector Machine in Silicon.[PubMed]. *IEEE Transactions on Neural Networks*, *14*(5), 1426–1434. doi: doi:10.1109/TNN.2003.816345

Ghosh D., Midya, B. L., Koley, C., &Purkait, P. (2005). Wavelet Aided SVM Analysis of ECG Signals for Cardiac Abnormality Detection. *Proceedings of IEEE Indicon Conference* (pp. 9-13).

Ghuneim, A.G. (2000). *Moore-Neighbor tracing*. Retrieve from http://www.imageprocessingplace.com/downloads_V3/root_downloads/tutorials/contour_tracing_Abeer_George_Ghuneim/moore.html

Giannakis, G. B., Martret, C. L., & Zhou, S. (2002). Chip-Interleaved Block-Spread Code Division Multiple Access. *IEEE Transactions on Communications*, *50*(2), 235–248. doi:10.1109/26.983320

Godse, D. A., & Bormane, D. S. (2013). Automated localization of optic disc in Retinal images. *International Journal of Advanced Computer Science and Applications*, 4(2), 66–71. doi:10.14569/IJACSA.2013.040210

Goldbaum, M. (1975). *STARE database*. Retrieved from http://www.parl.clemson.edu/stare/nerve/

Goldberg, Y., & Elhadad, M. (2008). splitSVM: Fast, space-efficient, non-heuristic, polynomial kernel computation for NLP applications.*Proceedings of the 46st Annual Meeting of the Association of Computational Linguistics*. doi: doi:10.3115/1557690.1557758

Gonzalez, R. C., & Woods, R. E. (2002). *Digital Image Processing using MATLAB. 2nd edition*. New Delhi: Prentice Hall.

Goswami, S., Mehjabin, S., Basumatary, R., Goswami, S. R., & Kashyap, P. A. (2014). Fully Automatic Crowd Control System in Metro Train.*Proceedings of National Conference on Emerging Global Trends in Engineering & Technology*. Guwahati: Assam.Don Bosco University.

Gothwal, H., Kedawat, S., & Kumar, R. (2001). Cardiac Arrhythmia Detection in an ECG beat signal using Fast Fourier Transform and Artificial Neural Network. *Journal of Biomedical Science and Engineering* (pp. 289-296).

Graves, A., Mohamed, A. R., & Hinton, G. (2013). Speech Recognition with Deep Recurrent Neural Networks.*Proceedings of IEEE International Conference on Acoustics, Speech and Signal Processing*. Vancouver, BC, Canada. doi:10.1109/ICASSP.2013.6638947

Guller, I., & Ubeyli, E. D. (2005). ECG beat classifier designed by Combined Neural Network Model. *Journal of Pattern Recognition, 38*(2), 199–208. doi:10.1016/S0031-3203(04)00276-6

Gunn, S. R. (1998). *Support Vector Machines for Classification and Regression*. University of Southampton.

Guo, D., Shamai, S., & Verd, S. (2005). Mutual Information and Minimum Mean-Square Error in Gaussian Channels. *IEEE Transactions on Information Theory, 51*(4), 1261–1282. doi:10.1109/TIT.2005.844072

Guzman-Renteria, M. E., Michel, R. P., & Sanchez-Ortiz, C. R. (2008). Design and Implementation of a Multi-Standard Interleaver for 802.11a, 802.11n, 802.16e and DVB Standards.*Proceedings of International Conference on Reconfigurable Computing and FPGAs* (pp. 379-384).

Hagen, A., & Morris, A. (2005). Recent advances in the multi-stream HMM/ANN hybrid approach to noise robust ASR. *Computer Speech & Language, 19*(1), 3–30. doi:10.1016/j.csl.2003.12.002

Hamada, Y., Shimada, N., & Shirai, Y. (2004). Hand Shape Estimation under Complex Backgrounds for Sign Language Recognition.*Proceedings of 6th International Conference on Automatic Face and Gesture Recognition*. IEEE. doi:10.1109/AFGR.2004.1301597

Handley, H. A. H. (2014). A network model for human interoperability. *Human Factors, 56*(2), 349–360. doi:10.1177/0018720813493640 PMID:24689253

Handley, H., & Smillie, R. (2008). Architecture framework human view: The NATO approach. *Systems Engineering, 11*(2), 156–164. doi:10.1002/sys.20093

Hani, A. F. M., Nugroho, H. A., & Nugroho, H. (2010). Gaussian bayes classifier for medical diagnosis and grading: application to diabetic retinopathy.*Proceedings of IEEE EMBS Conference on Biomedical Engineering and Sciences* (pp. 52-56). Kuala Lumpur, Malaysia. IEEE. doi:10.1109/IECBES.2010.5742198

Haniza, Y., Hamzah, A., & Hazlita, M. I. (2012). Exudates segmentation using inverse surface adaptive thresholding. *Journal of Measurement, Elsevier, 45*(6), 1599–1608. doi:10.1016/j.measurement.2012.02.016

Harangi, B. & Hajdu. (2013). Improving automatic exudate detection based on the fusion of the results of multiple active contours.*Proceedings of IEEE 10th International Symposium on Biomedical Imaging* (pp. 45-48). San Francisco, CA, USA. IEEE. doi:10.1109/ISBI.2013.6556408

Harbi, Y. J. (2012). Effect of the Interleaver types on the Performance of the Parallel Concatenation Convolutional Codes. *International Journal of Electrical and Computer Sciences (IJECS-IJENS), 12*(3), 25-31.

Hassenzahl, M., & Tractinsky, N. (2006). User experience – a research agenda. *Behaviour & Information Technology, 25*(2), 91–97. doi:10.1080/01449290500330331

Hatanaka, Y., Nakagawa, T., Hayashi, Y., Hara, T., & Fujita, H. (2008). Improvement of automated detection method of hemorrhages in fundus images.*Proceedings of IEEE 30th Annual International Conference on Engineering in Medicine and Biology Society* (pp.5429-5432). Vancouver, British Columbia, Canada. IEEE. doi:10.1109/IEMBS.2008.4650442

Haykin, S. (2003). *Neural Networks A Comprehensive Foundation (2nd ed)*. New Delhi, India: Pearson Education.

Heigold, G., Vanhoucke, V., Senior, A., Nguyen, P., Ranzato, M., Devin, M., & Dean, J. (2013). Multilingual Acoustic Models using Distributed Deep Neural Networks.*Proceedings of IEEE International Conference on Acoustics, Speech and Signal Processing.* Vancouver, BC, Canada. doi:10.1109/ICASSP.2013.6639348

Helander, M., & Skinnars, Ö. (2000a). Use of cognitive walkthrough for evaluation of cockpit design.*InProceedings of the 44th Annual Meeting of the Human Factors and Ergonomics Society* (pp.616-619). Santa Monica, CA: Human Factors and Ergonomics Society. doi:10.1177/154193120004400619

Helander, M., & Skinnars, Ö. (2000b). *Use of cognitive walkthrough for evaluation of cockpit design (HFA Paper No.2000-01).* Linköping, Sweden: Swedish Centre for Human Factors in Aviation.

Helldin, T. (2014). *Transparency for Future Semi-Automated Systems* [Doctoral dissertation]. Örebro, Sweden: Örebro University.

Helldin, T., Falkman, G., Alfredson, J., & Holmberg, J. (2011). The Applicability of Human-Centred Automation Guidelines in the Fighter Aircraft Domain.*Proceedings of the 29th Annual European Conference on Cognitive Ergonomics* (pp. 67-74).Universitätsdruckerei Rostock, Germany doi:10.1145/2074712.2074727

Hermansky, H., & Sharma, S. (1999) Temporal patterns (TRAPs) in ASR of noisy speech.*InProceedings IEEE International Conference on Acoustics, Speech, and Signal Processing* (pp. 289 -292). doi:10.1109/ICASSP.1999.758119

Herrmann, P. (1997). Problemnaher korrektheitssichernder entwurf von hochleistungsprotokollen. [Dissertation]. Universitat Dortmund.

Herrmann, P., & Krumm, H. (2000). A framework for modeling transfer protocols. *Computer Networks, 34*(2), 317–337. doi:10.1016/S1389-1286(00)00089-X

High-Resolution Fundus Image Database. (2007). *Department Informatik,Technische Fakultat.* Retrieved from http://www5.cs.fau.de/research/data/fundus-images/

Hinton, G., Deng, L., Yu, D., Dahl, G., Mohamed, A. R., & Jaitly, N. et al. (2012, November). Deep neural network for acoustic modeling in speech recognition. *IEEE Signal Processing Magazine,* 82–97. doi:10.1109/MSP.2012.2205597

Hiraiwa, A., Fujita, M., Kurosu, S., & Arisawa, S. (1990). Implementation of ANN on RISC processor array.*Proceedings of the International Conference on Application Specific Array Processors* (pp.677–688). doi:10.1109/ASAP.1990.145502

Hochberg, M., Cook, G., Renals, S., Robinson, A., & Schechtman, R. (1995). ABBOT hybrid connectionist-hmm large vocabulary recognition system.*Proceedings of Spoken Language Systems Technology Workshop* (pp. 170–176).

Hollnagel, E. (1999). From function allocation to function congruence. In S. Dekker & E. Hollnagel (Eds.), *Coping with computers in the cockpit* (pp. 29–53). Aldershot, England: Ashgate.

Hollnagel, E., & Woods, D. D. (1983). Cognitive systems engineering: New wine in new bottles. *International Journal of Man-Machine Studies, 18*(6), 583–600. doi:10.1016/S0020-7373(83)80034-0

Hollnagel, E., & Woods, D. D. (2005). *Joint cognitive systems: Foundations of cognitive systems engineering.* Boca Raton, FL: Taylor & Francis. doi:10.1201/9781420038194

Hooijen, O. G. (1997). A channel model for low voltage power line channels: measurement and simulation results. *Proceedings of the International Symposium on Power-Line Communications and its Application* (pp. 51-56). Essen, Germany.

Hooijen, O. G., & Vinck, A. J. H. (1998). On the channel Capacity of a European Style Residential Power Circuit. *Proceedings of the IEEE International Symposium on Power-Line Communications and its Applications* (pp. 31-44). Essen, Germany.

Hosseini, H. G., Reynolds, K. J., & Powers, D. (2001). A Multi-Stage Neural Network Classifier for ECG Events. Proceedings of IEEE Engineering in Medicine and Biology Society. Istanbul, Turkey.

How, J., King, E., & Kuwata, Y. (2004). Flight Demonstrations of Cooperative Control for UAV teams. *Proceedings of AIAA 3rd "Unmanned Unlimited" Technical Conference, Workshop and Exhibit* (pp. 1-9).

Hsieh, C. C., Liou, D. H., & Lee, D. (2012). A Real Time Hand Gesture Recognition System using Motion History Image. *Proceedings of International Conference on Signal Processing Systems (ICSPS)*. Dalian. IEEE.

Huang, D., Letaief, K. B., & Lu, J. (2005). Bit-Interleaved Time-Frequency Coded Modulation for OFDM Systems Over Time-Varying Channels. *IEEE Transactions on Communications*, *53*(7), 1191–1199. doi:10.1109/TCOMM.2005.851561

Hu, Y. H., & Hwang, J. N. (2002). *Handbook of Neural Network Signal Processing. The Electrical Engineering and Applied Signal Processing Series*. USA: CRC Press.

Iftikar, F., & Shams, A. (2012). A. Rhythm disorders - Heart Beat Classification of and Electrocardiogram Signal. *International Journal of Computers and Applications*, *39*(11), 38–44. doi:10.5120/4867-7292

Image Sciences Institute. (2004). *DRIVE database*. Retrieved from http://www.isi.uu.nl/Research/Databases/DRIVE

Jaafar, H. F., Nandi, A. K., & Nuaimy, W. (2011). Automated detection and grading of hard eudates from retinal fundus images. *Proceedings of 19th European Signal Processing Conference* (pp. 66-70). Barcelona. IEEE.

Jerde, T. E., Soechting, J. F., & Flanders, M. (2003). Coarticulation in Fluent Fingerspelling. *The Journal of Neuroscience*, *23*(6), 2383–2393. PMID:12657698

Johansson, C. (1999). Modellering av luftstridsavdömningar [Air Combat Resolution Modeling]. Linköping, Sweden: Linköping Institute of Technology.

Jootar, J., Proakis, J. G., & Zeidler, J. R. (2006). Performance of Convolutional Codes With Finite- Depth Interleaving and Noisy Channel Estimates. *IEEE Transactions on Communications*, *54*(10), 1775–1786. doi:10.1109/TCOMM.2006.881363

Juang, B. H., & Rabiner, L. R. (1991). Hidden Markov Models for Speech Recognition. *Technometrics*, *33*(3), 251–272. doi:10.1080/00401706.1991.10484833

Kabir, M. H., Shams, R. A., & Ullah, S. E. (2012). Effect of Interleaved FEC Code on Wavelet Based MC-CDMA System with Alamouti STBC in Different Modulation Schemes. *International Journal of Computer Science, Engineering and Information Technology*, *2*(1), 23–33.

Kampouraki, A., Manis, G., & Nikou, C. (2009). Heartbeat Time Series Classification with Support Vector Machines. *IEEE Transactions on Information Technology in Biomedicine*, *13*(4), 512–518. doi:10.1109/TITB.2008.2003323 PMID:19273030

Karegowda, A. G., Nasiha, A., & Jayaram, M. A. (2011). Exudates detection in retinal images using back propagation neural network. *International Journal of Computers and Applications*, *25*(3), 25–31. doi:10.5120/3011-4062

Kauppi, T., Kalesnykiene, V., Kamarainen, J. K., et al. (2006). *DIARETDB0 database*. Retrieved from http://www2.it.lut.fi/project/imageret/diaretdb0/

Kauppi, T., Kalesnykiene, V., Kamarainen, J. K., et al. (2006). *DIARETDB1 database*. http://www2.it.lut.fi/project/imageret/diaretdb1/

Kauppi, T., Kalesnykiene, V., Kamarainen, J. K., et al. (2006). *DIARETDB1 database*. Retrieved from http://www2.it.lut.fi/project/imageret/diaretdb1/

Kaur, A., & Sharma, R. (2014). Optic disc segmentation based on watershed transform. *International Journal of Advanced Research in Computer Science and Software Engineering, 4*(5), 681–685.

Keane, J. (n. d.). Variation in Fingerspelling Time, Pinky Extension and What it Means to be Active. *Cognition and Computation Workshops*. University of Chicago.

Kelly, D., McDonald, J., & Markham, C. (2009). Recognizing Spatiotemporal Gestures and Movement Epenthesis in Sign Language.*Proceedings of 13th International Machine Vision and Image Processing Conference*. Dublin. IEEE. doi:10.1109/IMVIP.2009.33

Khafri, Y. Z., & Jahanian, A. (2012). Improved Line Tracking System for Autonomous Navigation of High-Speed Vehicle. *International Journal of Robotics and Automation, 1*(3), 163–174.

Khan, F. M., Arnold, M. G., & Pottenger, W. M. (2005). Hardware-Based Support Vector Machine Classification in Logarithmic Number Systems. *Circuits and Systems, 2005. ISCAS 2005.Proceedings ofIEEE International Symposium* (Vol. 5, pp. 5154 – 5157).

Khan, R. H. (2011). Performance and performability modeling framework considering management of service components deployment [Dissertation]. Norwegian University of Science and Technology.

Khan, A., Memon, A., Jat, Y., & Khan, A. (2012). Electrooculogram Based Interactive Robotic Arm Interface for Partially Paralytic Patients. *International Journal of Information Technology and Electrical Engineering, 1*(1), 1–4.

Khan, C. R., Weir, G. C., King, G. L., Jacobson, A. M., Moses, A. C., & Smith, R. J. (2005). *Joslin's diabetes mellitus*. USA: Lippincott Williams & Wilkins.

Khandpur, R. S. (2006). *Handbook of Biomedical Instrumentation* (2nd ed.). Tata: McGraw Hill.

Khan, E. R., & Nam, L. (1991) Two-dimensional multi rate systolic array design for artificial neural networks.*Proceedings on First Great Lakes Symposium on VLSI* (pp. 186 – 193). doi:10.1109/GLSV.1991.143964

Khan, R. H., & Heegaard, P. (2010). A performance modeling framework incorporating cost efficient deployment of collaborating components. *Proceedings of the International Conference of the Software Technology and Engineering* (pp. 340-349). San Juan, PR. IEEE. doi:10.1109/ICSTE.2010.5608859

Khan, R. H., & Heegaard, P. (2010). From UML to SRN: A performance modeling framework for managing behavior of multiple collaborative session and instances. *Proceedings of the International Conference on Computer Design and Application* (pp. 72-80). Qinhuangdao, China. IEEE.

Khan, R. H., & Heegaard, P. (2011). A Performance modeling framework incorporating cost efficient deployment of multiple collaborating components.*proceedings of the International Conference Software Engineering and Computer Systems* (pp. 31-45). Pahang, Malaysia. Springer. doi:10.1007/978-3-642-22170-5_3

Kianpisheh, A., Mustaffa, N., Limtrairut, P., & Keikhosrokiani, P. (2012). Smart Parking System (SPS) Architecture Using Ultrasonic Detector. *International Journal of Software Engineering and Its Applications, 6*(3), 51–58.

Kicmerova, I. D. (2009). Methods for Detection and Classification in ECG Analysis [Ph D. Thesis]. Brno University of Technology.

Kim, S., Lee, S. & Cho, K. (2012). Design of High-Performance Unified Circuit for Linear and Non-Linear SVM Classifications. *Journal of semiconductor technology and science, 12*(2), 162-167.

Klass, K. (1991). Efficient systolic array for linear discriminant classifier. *IEEE, Delft university of Technology.* (pp. 701-704).

Klein, G., Orasanu, J., Calderwood, R., & Zsambok, C. (Eds.). (1993). *Decision making in action: Models and methods*. Norwood, NJ: Ablex.

Knuth, D. (1997). *The Art of Computer Programming* (3rd ed.). Addison Wesley.

Kohli, N., & Verma, N. K. (2011). Arrhythmia Classification Using SVM with Selected Features. *IACSIT International Journal of Engineering and Technology, 3*(8), 122–131.

Kong, F., & Tan, J. (2008). A Collaboration-based Hybrid Vehicular Sensor Network Architecture.*Proceedings of International Conference on Information and Automation ICIA 2008* (pp. 584-589). DOI: doi:10.1109/ICINFA.2008.4608067

Konnie, T., Haruyama, S., & Nakagawa, M. (2006). Performance evaluation of narrowband OFDM on integrated system of power line communication and visible light wireless communication.*Proceedings of the 1st International conference on wireless pervasive computing*. Fort Worth, Texas, USA

Kousa, M. A. (2003). Performance of turbo codes with Matrix Interleavers. *The Arabian Journal for Science and Engineering, 28*(2B), 211–220.

Kraemer, F. A., & Herrmann, P. (2006). Service specification by composition of collaborations-an example. *Proceedings of the WI-IAT workshops* (pp. 129-133). Hong Kong. doi:10.1109/WI-IATW.2006.121

Kraemer, F. A., & Herrmann, P. (2007b). Semantics of UML 2.0 Activities and Collaborations in cTLA [Avantel Technical Report 3]. Norwegian University of Science and Technology.

Kraemer, F. A., & Hermann, P. (2007a). Formalizing collaboration-oriented service specifications using temporal logic. *Proceedings of the International conference on networking and electronic commerce research conference (pp.*194-220). Italy.

Krishna, R., Siddhartha, R. K., Kumar, N., & Jogi, G. L. (2014). Broadband over Power Lines (BPL) for Indian Telecom Network. Retrieved from http://www.tec.gov.in/studypaper/BPL%20[Final].pdf

Kumar S. (2009). *Neural Networks A Classroom Approach*. India: TATA McGRAW HILL.

Kumar, P., Sarumathi, M. & Sumithra, S. M. G. (2013). Performance Evaluation of Rician Fading Channels using QPSK, DQPSK and OQPSK Modulation Schemes in Simulink Environment. *International Journal of Engineering Science Invention, 2*(5), 07-16.

Kumari, S. & Lodhi, Md. E. (2013). Four Arm Interleaver: Performance analysis. *International Journal of Scientific Research, 2*(8), 140–142.

Kumar, T. A., Priya, S., & Paul, V. (2013). A novel approach to the detection of macula in human retinal imagery. *International Journal of Signal Processing Systems, 1*(1), 23–28. doi:10.12720/ijsps.1.1.23-28

Kung, H. T. Why Systolic Architectures? *Carnegie-Mellon University*.

Kyrkou, C. (2010). Embedded hardware architecture for object detection.

Kyrkou, C., & Theocharides, T. (2009). SCoPE: Towards a systolic array for SVM object detection. *Embedded Systems Letters, IEEE, 1*(2), 46–49. doi:10.1109/LES.2009.2034709

LabVIEW help. (n. d). *General format*. Retrieved from http://www.ni.com/labview

LabVIEW. (n. d). In *Encyclopedia Wikipedia online*. Retrieved from http://en.wikipedia.org/wiki/LabVIEW

Lamport, L. (2002). *Specifying Systems*. New York: Addison-Wesley.

Lazaropoulos, A.G. (2012). Broadband Transmission Characteristics of Overhead High Voltage Power Line Communication channels. *Progress in Electromagnetics Research B, 373-399.*

Lee, H. K., & Kim, J. H. (1999). An HMM-Based Threshold Model Approach for Gesture Recognition. *Pattern Analysis and Machine Intelligence, 21*(10), 961–973. doi:10.1109/34.799904

Lee, J. S., Lee, Y. J., Lee, E. H., & Hong, S. H. (2004). Hand Region Extraction and Gesture Recognition from Video Stream with Complex Background through Entropy Analysis. *Proceedings of 26th Annual International Conference of Engineering in Medicine and Biology Society.* San Francisco. IEEE.

Lewalle, J., Farge, M., & Schneider, K. (n. d.). Wavelet Transforms (pp. 1378-1387). In C. Tropea, A. Yarin, & J. F. Foss (2007), *Springer Handbook of Experimental Fluid Mechanics, Vol. 1.*

Lewandowski, N. B., Droppo, J., & Seltzer, M. Yu Dong (2014). Phone Sequence modeling With Recurrent Neural Networks. *Proceedings of IEEE International Conference on Acoustics, Speech and Signal Processing.* Florence, Italy.

Li, T., Zhu, S., & Ogihara, M. (2006). Using discriminant analysis for multiclass classification: an experimental investigation (pp. 453-472). London: Springer, Verlag.

Li, H., & Chutatape, O. (2004). Automated feature extraction in color retinal images by a model based approach. *IEEE Transactions on Bio-Medical Engineering, 51*(2), 246–254. doi:10.1109/TBME.2003.820400 PMID:14765697

Lippmann, R. P. (1990). Review of Neural Networks for Speech Recognition. *Neural Computation, 1*(1), 1–38.

Li, S., Wang, L., & Kong, D. (2013). *Synthesis of Sign Language Coarticulation based on Key Frames.* Multimed Tools Appl. Doi: doi:10.1007/s11042-013-1724-1

Liu, E. R., Gao, Y., Bilal, O., & Korhonen, T. (2004). Broadband Characterization of Indoor Power Line Channel. *Proceedings of the International Symposium on Power-Line Communications and its Applications.* Zaragosa, Spain.

Llata, M. R., Guarnizo, G., & Calvino, M. Y. (2010). FPGA Implementation of a Support Vector Machine for Classification and Regression. Proceedings of *WCCI 2010 IEEE World Congress on Computational Intelligence* (pp. 2037-2041).

Lochan, K., Sah, P., & Sarma, K. K. (2012). Innovative Feature Set for Retinopathic Analysis of Diabetes and its Detection. *Proceeding of 2nd IEEE National Conference on Emerging Trends and Applications in Computer Science,* Shillong, India.

Loong, J. L. C., Subari, K. S., & Abdullah, M. K. (2010). A New Approach to ECG Biometric System. *World Academy of Science. Engineering and Technology, 4*(8), 644–650.

Lopez-Grao, J. P., Merseguer, J., & Campos, J. (2004). From UML activity diagrams to SPN: application to software performance engineering. *Proceedings of the 4th International conference on software and performance* (pp.25-36). New York, NY. ACM.

Lowth, M. (2014). Macular disorders. *Patient.* Retrieved from http://www.patient.co.uk/doctor/macular-disorders

Lu, S., & Lim, J. H. (2010). Automatic macula detection from retinal images by a line operator. *Proceedings of IEEE 17th International Conference on Image Processing* (pp. 4073-4076). Hong Kong. IEEE. doi:10.1109/ICIP.2010.5649080

Lu, Y. C. (2011). Background Subtraction Based Segmentation Using Object Motion Feedback. *Proceedings of 1st International Conference on Robot Vision and Signal Processing (RVSP).* Kaohsiung. IEEE. doi:10.1109/RVSP.2011.9

Lyons, J. B., & Stokes, C. K. (2012). Human-human Reliance in the context of automation. *Human Factors, 54*(1), 112–121. doi:10.1177/0018720811427034 PMID:22409106

Maculopathy and macular degeneration. (2014). *ILMO.it*. Retrieved from http://www.ilmo.it/en/solutions/surgery-at-ilmo/vision-problems-and-eye-diseases /maculopathy-and-macular-degeneration/

Madzarov, G., Gjorgjevikj, D., & Chorbev, I. (2009). A Multi-class SVM Classifier Utilizing Binary Decision Tree. *Informatica*, *33*, 233–241.

Mahdi, A. S., Al-Zuhairi. (2013). Automatic Railway Gate and Crossing Control based Sensors & Microcontroller. *International Journal of Computer Trends and Technology*, *4*(7), 2135–2140.

Majumder, P., & Medhi, J. P. (2014). Automatic exudate detection based on amalgamation of results of multiple contours. *Proceedings of International Conference on Green Materials through Science, Technology and Management*. Assam, India.

Mandal, B., Sarma, M. P., & Sarma, K. K. (2014). Design of Systolic array based Multiplierless SVM Classifier. Proceedings of *IEEE International Conference on Signal Processing and Integrated Networks* (pp. 35-39). Noida.

Manna, Z., & Pnueli, A. (1992). *The Temporal Logic of Reactive and Concurrent Systems*. Berling: Springer-Verlag. doi:10.1007/978-1-4612-0931-7

Martin, A., & Leslie, L. (1995). Conjoining Specifications. *ACM Transactions on Programming Languages and Systems*, *17*(3), 507–535. doi:10.1145/203095.201069

Matsoukas, S., Gauvain, J. L., Adda, A., Colthurst, T., Kao, C. I., & Kimball, O. et al. (2006). Advances in transcription of broadcast news and conversational telephone speech within the combined EARS BBN/LIMSI system. *IEEE Transactions on Audio. Speech and Language Processing*, *14*(5), 1541–1556. doi:10.1109/TASL.2006.878257

Mazidi, M. A., Naimi, S., & Naimi, S. (2012). *AVR Microcontroller and embedded system: Using C and Assembly Language*. USA: Pearson Custom Electronics Technology.

McKendrick, R., Shaw, T., de Visser, E., Saqer, H., Kidwell, B., & Parasuraman, R. (2014). Team performance in networked supervisory control of unmanned air vehicles: Effects of automation, working memory, and communication content. *Human Factors*, *56*(3), 463–475. doi:10.1177/0018720813496269 PMID:24930169

Medhi, J. P., Nath, M. K., & Dandapat, S. (2012). Automatic grading of macular degeneration from color fundus images. *Proceedings of World Congress on Information and Communication Technologies* (pp. 511-514). IEEE. doi:10.1109/WICT.2012.6409131

Meher, P. K. (2010). Systolic VLSI and FPGA Realization of Artificial Neural Networks. *Springer Berlin Heidelberg*, *7*, 359–380.

Merayo, M. G., Núñez, M., & Rodríguez, I. (2008). Formal testing from timed finite state machines. *Computer Networks*, *52*(2), 432–460. doi:10.1016/j.comnet.2007.10.002

Merino, M., Rivera, O., Gomez, I., Molina, A., & Dorronzoroa, E. (2010). A Method of EOG Signal Processing to Detect the Direction of Eye Movement. *Sensor Device Technologies and Applications*, 100-105. DOI: .10.1109/SENSORDEVICES.2010.25

Merino, L., Wiklund, J., Caballero, F., Moe, A., De Dios, J. R. M., & Forssen, P. E. et al. (2006). Vision-Based Multi-UAV Position Estimation. *Robotics & Automation Magazine, IEEE*, *13*(3), 53–62. doi:10.1109/MRA.2006.1678139

Methods to evaluate segmentation and indexing techniques in the field of retinal ophthalmology. *MESSIDOR database*. Retrieved from http://messidor.crihan.fr/AccesBaseMessidor/new-index.php

Milentijevic, I. Z., Milovanovic, I. Z., Milovanovic, E. I., & Stojcev, M. K. (1997). The design of optimal planar systolic arrays for matrix multiplication. *Computers & Mathematics with Applications (Oxford, England)*, *33*(6), 17–35. doi:10.1016/S0898-1221(97)00028-X

Milovanovic, I. Z., Milovanovic, E. I., Randjelovic, B. M., & Jovanovic, I. C. (2003). Matrix multiplication on bidirectional systolic arrays. *FILOMAT*, *17*(17), 135–141. doi:10.2298/FIL0317135M

Mimbela, L. E. Y., & Klein, L. A. (2000). *A summary of vehicle detection and surveillance technologies used in intelligent transportation systems. Federal Highway Administration s (FHWA) Intelligent Transportation Systems Joint Program Office, the Vehicle Detector Clearinghouse.* NMSU.

Mimura, M., Sakai, S., & Kawahara, T. (2014). Reverberant Speech Recognition Combining Deep Neural Networks and Deep Autoencoders.*Proceedings of REVERB Workshop*, F.orence, Italy.

Minar, J., Riha, K., Krupka, A., & Tong, H. (2014). Automatic detection of the macula in retinal fundus images using multilevel thresholding. *International Journal of Advances in Telecommunications, Electronics, Signals and Systems*, *3*(1). doi: doi:10.11601/ijates.v3il.78

Ming, Y. F. (2009). Identification of diabetic retinopathy stages using digital fundus images using imaging [Master's thesis]. SIM University.

Mohamed, A. R., Dahl, G. E., & Hinton, G. (n. d.). *Deep Belief Networks for phone recognition.* Department of Computer Science, University of Toronto. Retrieved from http://www.cs.toronto.edu/~gdahl/papers/dbnPhoneRec.pdf

Mohamed, A. R., Dahl, G. E., & Hinton, G. (2012). Acoustic Modeling using Deep Belief Networks. *IEEE Transactions on Audio, Speech, and Language Processing*, *20*(1), 1–10. doi:10.1109/TASL.2011.2109382

Mohamed, A. R., Hinton, G., & Penn, G. (2012). Understanding How Deep Belief Networks Perform Acoustic Modelling. *Proceedings of IEEE International Conference on Acoustics, Speech and Signal Processing* (pp. 4273 – 4276). Kyoto. doi:10.1109/ICASSP.2012.6288863

Moody, G. B., & Mark, R. G. (2001, May-June). The impact of the MIT-BIH Arrhythmia Database. *IEEE Eng in Med and Biol*, *20*(3), 45-50. Retrieved from http://www.physionet.org/physiobank/database/mitdb

Morris, A., Payne, S., & Borlard, H. (2002). Low cost duration modelling for noise robust speech recognition. *Proceedings of IEEE International Conference on Spoken Language Processing* (pp. 1025–1028. United States.

Moura, P., Borges, R., & Mota, A. (2012). Experimenting formal methods through UML. Retrieved November 19 2012, from http:// www.imamu.edu.sa/ DContent/ IT_Topics/ Experimenting Formal Methods through UML.pdf

Mubbashar, M., Usman, A., & Akram, M. U. (2011). Automated system for macula detection in digital retinal images. *Proceedings of Conference on Information and Communication Technologies* (pp. 1-5). Karachi. IEEE.

Mukhopadhyay, A. (2012). *Control a DC Motor using Arduino and l293d chip.* Retrieved from http://obliblog.wordpress.com/2012/05/30/control-motor-arduino-l293d-chip

Murthy, G. R. S., & Jadon, R. S. (2009). A Review of Vision Based Hand Gestures Recognition. *International Journal of Information Technology and Knowledge Management*, *2*(2), 405–410.

Nagamachi, M. (1989). *Kansei Engineering.* Tokyo: Kaibundo.

Nagamachi, M. (2011). *Kansei/Affective Engineering.* Boca Raton, FL: CRC Press.

Naskar, S., Das, S., Seth, A. K., & Nath, A. (2011). Application of Radio Frequency Controlled Intelligent Military Robot in Defense.*Proceedings of International Conference on Communication Systems and Network Technologies* (pp. 396-401). DOI: doi:10.1109/CSNT.2011.88

National Eye Institute. (1968). Retrieved from https://www.nei.nih.gov/health/diabetic/retinopathy

Nayak, J., Bhat, P., Acharya, R., Lim, U., & Kagathi, M. (2008). Automated identification of diabetic retinopathy stages using digital fundus images. *Journal of Medical Systems, 32*(2), 107–115.

Nazerfard, E., Das, B., Cook, D. J., & Holder, L. B. (2010). Conditional Random Fields for Activity Recognition in Smart Environments.*International Symposium on Human Informatics (SIGHIT)*. doi:10.1145/1882992.1883032

Ngo, C., Niu, H., & Ouyang, X. (2006). Interleaver Design for MIMO-OFDM based Wireless LAN.*Proceedings of IEEE Wireless Communications and Networking Conference* (Vol. 4, pp. 1825-1829).

Nguyen, H. N. (2011). *Automatic Train Control* [PDF document]. Retrieved from [REMOVED HYPERLINK FIELD] http://www.cs.swan.ac.uk/~csmarkus/.../Slides/Railway_Seminar_Talk6.pdf

Niemeijer, M., Abramoff, M. D., & Bram, V. G. (2007). Segmentation of the Optic Disc, Macula and Vascular Arch in Fundus Photographs. *IEEE Transactions on Medical Imaging, 26*(1), 116–127. doi:10.1109/TMI.2006.885336 PMID:17243590

Niethammer, U., Rothmund, S., Schwaderer, U., Zeman, J. & Joswig, M. (2011). Open Source Image-Processing Tools for Low-Cost UAV-Based Landslide Investigation. *International Archives of the Photogrammetry, Remote Sensing and Spatial Information Sciences,* XXXVIII-1/C22, 1-6. Retrieved from http://www.geometh.ethz.ch/uav_g/proceedings/ niethammer

Noor, N. M., & Ahmad, S. (2013). Analysis of Different Level of EOG Signal from Eye Movement for Wheelchair Control. *International Journal of Biomedical Engineering and Technology, 11*(2), 175–196. doi:10.1504/IJBET.2013.055043

Norman, D., Miller, J., & Henderson, A. (1995). *What you see, some of what's in the future, and how we go about doing it: HI at Apple Computer.*Proceedings of CHI* (p. 155). New York: ACM Press.

Number of towns and villages electrified in India (2008). Retrieved from http://mospi.nic.in/Mospi_New/upload/statistical_year_book_2011/SECTOR-3-INDUSTRY%20SECTOR/CH-16-ENERGY/Table%2016.14.xls

Ollero, A., & Maza, I. (2007). *Multiple hetrogenous unmanned aerial vehicles. Springer Tracts on Advanced Robotics.* NY: Springer. doi:10.1007/978-3-540-73958-6

OMG. (2009a). OMG Unified Modeling Language (OMG UML) Superstructure. Version 2.2. *Object management group.* Retrieved from http://www.omg.org/spec/UML/22/Superstructure/PDF/

OMG. (2009b). UML Profile for MARTE: Modeling and analysis of real-time embedded systems. Version 1.0. *Object management group.* Retrieved from http://www.omg.org/omgmarte/Documents/Specifications/08-06-09.pdf

Ormel, E., Crasborn, O., & Koochi, E. (2013). Coarticulation of Hand Height in Sign Language of the Netherlands is Affected by Contact type. *Journal of Phonetics, 41*(3-4), 156–171. doi:10.1016/j.wocn.2013.01.001

Osareh, A., Mirmehdi, M., Thomas, B., & Markham, R. (2002). Colour morphology and snakes for optic disc localisation.*Proceedings of 6th Medical Image Understanding and Analysis Conference* (pp. 21-24).

Osowski, S., Hoai, L. T., & Markiewicz, T. (2004). Support Vector Machine-Based Expert System for Reliable Heartbeat Recognition. *IEEE Transactions on Bio-Medical Engineering, 51*(4), 582–589. doi:10.1109/TBME.2004.824138 PMID:15072212

Padmanaban, K. & kannan, R. J. (2013). Localization of optic disc using fuzzy c means clustering. *Proceedings of International Conference on Current Trends in Engineering and Technology* (pp. 184-186), Coimbatore: IEEE. doi:10.1109/ICCTET.2013.6675941

Palaniappan, R., Gupta C. N. and Krishnan, S. M. (2008) Neural Network Classification of Premature Heartbeats. *Special Issue on Multimedia Data Processing and Classification* 3(3).

Palaz, D., Collobert, R., & Doss, M. M. (2013) Estimating Phoneme Class Conditional Probabilities from Raw Speech Signal using Convolutional Neural Networks. Proceedings of Interspeech. Lyon, France.

Parasuraman, R., Sheridan, T., & Wickens, C. (2008). Situation Awareness, Mental Workload and Trust in Automation: Viable, Empirically Supported Cognitive Engineering Constructs. *Journal of Cognitive Engineering and Decision Making, 2*(2), 140–160. doi:10.1518/155534308X284417

Parhi, K. K. (2012). VLSI digital signal processing system. New Delhi: Wiley India (P.) Ltd.

Pastor, E., Lopez, J., & Royo, P. (2007). UAV Payload and Mission Control Hardware/Software Architecture. *Aerospace and Electronic Systems Magazine, IEEE, 22*(6), 3–6. doi:10.1109/MAES.2007.384074

Patil, R. A., Gupta, G., Sahula, V., & Mandal, A. S. (2012). Power aware Hardware prototyping of multiclass SVM classifier through Reconfiguration. Proceedings of *25th International Conference on VLSI Design* (pp. 62-67). doi:10.1109/VLSID.2012.47

Pavelka, T., & Kral, P. (2008). Neural Network Acoustic Model with Decision Tree Clustered Triphones. *InProceedings of IEEE Workshop on Machine Learning for Signal Processing* (pp. 216 – 220). Cancun. doi:10.1109/MLSP.2008.4685482

Persson, M. (2014). *Future technology support of command and control: Assessing the impact of assumed future technologies on cooperative command and control* [Doctoral dissertation]. Uppsala, Sweden: Uppsala University.

Petriu, D., & Shen, H. (2002). Applying the UMl Performance Profile: Graph grammar based derivation of LQN models from UML specifications. *Proceedings of the TOOLS* (pp. 159-177). Springer-Verlag. doi:10.1007/3-540-46029-2_10

Philipps, H. (1999). Modeling of powerline communication channels. *Proceedings of the International Symposium on Power-Line Communications and its Applications* (pp. 14-21). Lancaster, UK.

Phung, S. L., Bouzerdoum, A., & Chai, D. (2005). Skin Segmentation Using Color Pixel Classification: Analysis and Comparison. *Pattern Analysis and Machine Intelligence, 27*(1), 148–151. doi:10.1109/TPAMI.2005.17 PMID:15628277

Poshtyar, A., Ghassabi, Z., & Shanbehzadeh, J. (2011) Detection of Optic Disc Center and Macula using Spatial Information of Optic Cup. In *Proceedings of 4th International Conference on Biomedical Engineering and Informatics* (pp.255-258). Shanghai: IEEE. doi:10.1109/BMEI.2011.6098351

Prabhakar, N., Vaithiyanathan, V., Sharma, A. P., Singh, A., & Singhal, P. (2012). Object Tracking Using Frame Differencing and Template Matching. *Research Journal of Applied Sciences. Engineering and Technology, 4*(24), 5497–5501.

Pradeep, S. G., Govada, A., & Swamy, K. (2013). Eye Controller Human Machine Interface. *International Journal of Advanced Research in Computer and Communication Engineering, 2*(5), 2205–2209.

Preman, J. A., & Suapura, D. M. (1991). *Neural Networks: algorithms, application and programming techniques.* Addison-Wesly.

Premi, M.S. G. (2015). Novel approach for retinal blood vessels extraction and exudates segmentation. *Journal of Chemical and pharmaceutical Research, 7*(1), 792-797.

Pritchett, A. R., Kim, S. Y., & Feigh, K. M. (2014). Modeling human-automation function allocation. *Journal of Cognititve Engineering and Decision Making*, *8*(1), 33–51. doi:10.1177/1555343413490944

Punetha, D., Kumar, N., & Mehta, V. (2013). Development and Applications of Line Following Robot Based Health Care Management System. *International Journal of Advanced Research in Computer Engineering & Technology*, *2*(8), 2446–2450.

Qian, C., Sun, X., Wei, Y., Tang, X., & Sun, J. (2014). Real Time and Robust Hand Tracking from Depth. In *Proceedings of Computer Vision and Pattern Recognition* (pp. 1106–1113). CVPR.

Quellec, G., Lamard, M., Josselin, P. M., Cazuguel, G., Cochener, B., & Roux, C. (2008). Optimal wavelet transform for the detection of microaneurysms in retinal photographs. *IEEE Transactions on Medical Imaging*, *27*(9), 1230–1241. doi:10.1109/TMI.2008.920619 PMID:18779064

Rabee, A., & Barhumi, I. (2012). ECG Signal Classification using Support Vector Machine Based on Wavelet Multiresolution Analysis. *Proceedings of 11*[th] *International Conference on Information Sciences, Signal Processing and their Applications*: Special Sessions (pp. 1319-1323).

Rabiner L., & Juang B. H. (1993). *Fundamentals of Speech Recognition*. New Delhi, India: Pearson Education.

Rabiner, L. (1989). A tutorial on Hidden Markov Models and Selected Applications in Speech Recognition. *Proceedings of the IEEE*, *77*(2), 257–286. doi:10.1109/5.18626

Rabiner, L., & Juang, B. H. (1993). *Fundamentals of Speech Recognition*. New Jersey: Prentice Hall.

Rahim, M., Bengio, Y., & Lecun, Y. (1997). Discriminative feature and model design for automatic speech recognition. In Proceedings of Eurospeech (pp. 75-78).

Rail Automation in Mass Transit Systems . (2013). Seimens. Munich: Media relations.

Rappaport, T. S. (2002). *Wireless Communication, Principle and Practice* (2nd ed.). India: Prentice Hall.

Rautaray, S. S., & Agrawal, A. (2015). Vision Based Hand Gesture Recognition for Human Computer Interaction: A Survey. *Artificial Intelligence Review*, *43*(1), 1–54. doi:10.1007/s10462-012-9356-9

Ravishankar, S., Jain, A., & Mittal, A. (2009). Automated feature extraction for early detection of diabetic retinopathy in fundus images.*Proceedings of IEEE Conference on Computer Vision and Pattern Recognition* (pp. 210-217). Miami, FL: IEEE. doi:10.1109/CVPR.2009.5206763

Reddy, D. C. (2006). *Biomedical Signal Processing- Principles and Techniques*. Tata: McGraw Hill.

Reve, S. V., & Choudhri, S. (2012). Management of car parking system using wireless sensor network. *International Journal of Emerging Technology and Advanced Engineering*, *2*(7), 262–268.

Reyna, R., Esteve, D., Houzet, D., & Albenge, M. F. (2000). Implementation of the SVM neural network generalization function for image processing.*Proceedings Fifth IEEE International Workshop on Computer Architectures for Machine Perception* (pp. 147 -151). doi:10.1109/CAMP.2000.875972

Reynolds, D. A., Quatieri, T. F., & Dunn, R. B. (2000). Speaker Verification Using Adapted Gaussian Mixture Models. *Digital Signal Processing*, *10*(1-3), 19–41. doi:10.1006/dspr.1999.0361

Reynolds, D. A., & Rose, R. C. (1995). Robust text-independent speaker identification using Gaussian mixture speaker models. *IEEE Transactions on Speech and Audio Processing*, *3*(1), 72–83. doi:10.1109/89.365379

Robinson, T. (1992). A Real-Time Recurrent Error Propagation Network Word Recognition System. *Proceedings of the IEEE International Conference on Acoustics, Speech, and Signal Processing* (Vol. 1, pp. 617 – 620). San Francisco, CA. doi:10.1109/ICASSP.1992.225833

Robinson, T., & Fallside, F. (1990). Word recognition from the DARPA resource management database with the Cambridge recurrent error propagation network speech recognition system. Retrieved from http://assta.org/sst/SST-90/cache/SST-90-Chapter13-p14.pdf

Robinson, A. (1994). An application of recurrent nets to phone probability estimation. *IEEE Transactions on Neural Networks*, 5(2), 298–305. doi:10.1109/72.279192 PMID:18267798

Robinson, T., & Fallside, F. (1991). A recurrent error propagation network speech recognition system. *Computer Speech & Language*, 5(3), 259–274. doi:10.1016/0885-2308(91)90010-N

Rodriguez, E., Ruiz, B., Crespo, A. G., & Garcia, F. (2003). Speech/Speaker Recognition Using a HMM/GMM Hybrid Model. *Proceedings of the First International Conference on Audio- and Video-Based Biometric Person Authentication* (pp. 227- 234).

Rokonuzzaman, M., Ferdous, S. M., Tuhin. R. A., Arman, S. I., Manzar, T. & Hasan, N. (2012). Design of an Autonomous Mobile Wheel Chair for Disabled Using Electrooculogram (EOG) Signals. *Mechatronics: Recent Technological and Scientific Advances*, 41-53, DOI:10.1007/978-3-642-23244-2_6

Rolf, S. (1974). Maximum likelihood theory for incomplete data from an exponential family. *Scandinavian Journal of Statistics*, 1(2), 49–58.

Román Osorio, C., Romero, J. A., Mario Peña, C., & Juárez, I. L. (2006). Intelligent Line Follower Mini-Robot System. *International Journal of Computers, Communications & Control*, 1(2), 73–83.

Saavedra, J. M., Bustos, B., & Chang, V. (2013). An Accurate Hand Segmentation Approach using a Structure based Shape Localization Technique.*Proceedings of International Conference on Computer Vision Theory and Applications (VISAPP)*.

Sagar, A. V., Balasubramanian, S., & Chandrasekaran, V. (2007). Automatic detection of anatomical structures in digital fundus retinal images. In *Proceedings of IAPR Conference on Machine Vision Applications* (pp. 483–486). Tokyo, Japan.

Sah, P., & Sarma, K. K. (2013). Detection of Blood Vessel and its application for Classifying Diabetic Retinopathy. *Journal of the Instrument Society of India*, 43, 72–74.

Sak, H., Senior, A., & Beaufays, F. (2014) Long Short-Term Memory Based Recurrent Neural Network Architectures For Large Vocabulary Speech Recognition. *Google*. Retrieved fromhttp://arxiv.org/abs/1402.1128

Salvadori, F., Gehrke, C.S., Campos, Oliveira, A.C. M., & Sausen, P.S. (2013). Smart Grid Infrastructure Using a Hybrid Network Architecture. *IEEE Transaction on Smart Grid*, 4(3), 1630-1639.

Salvi, G. (2006). Developing acoustics models for automatic speech recognition [Master's Thesis]. Speech Music and Hearing Department at Royal Institute of Technology, Stockholm, Sweden.

Sanchez, C., Garcia, M., Mayo, A., Lopez, M., & Hornero, R. (2009). Retinal image analysis based on mixture models to detect hard exudates. *Medical Image Analysis*, 13(4), 650–658. doi:10.1016/j.media.2009.05.005 PMID:19539518

Sandidzadeh, M. A., & Shamszadeh, B. (2012). Improvement of Automatic Train Operation Using Enhanced Predictive Fuzzy Control Method. INTECH Open Access Publisher.

Sanyal, S. K., & Upadhyaya, B. K. (2009). VHDL Modeling of Convolutional Interleaver- Deinterleaver for Efficient FPGA Implementation. *International Journal of Scientific Research*, 2(6), 66–68.

Sarma, P., Nirmala, S. R., & Sarma, K. K. (2013). Classification of ECG using Some Novel Features.*Proceedings of IEEE International Conference on Emerging Trends and Computer Applications* (pp. 187-191). Shillong. doi:10.1109/ICETACS.2013.6691420

Sarma, P., Nirmala, S. R., & Sarma, K. K. (2014). ECG Classification using Wavelet Subband Energy based Features. *Proceedings of IEEE International Conference on Signal Processing and Integrated Networks (pp.785-790)*. Noida. doi:10.1109/SPIN.2014.6777061

Schoelkopf, B., Sung, K., Burges, C., Girosi, F., Niyogin, P., Poggio, T., & Vapnik, V. (1996). *Comparing Support Vector Machines with Gaussian Kernels to Radial Basis Function Classifiers*. MA: Massachusetts Institute of Technology. Cambridge.

Schütte, S. (2005). *Engineering emotional values in product design – Kansei engineering in development* [Doktoral dissertation No. 951]. Linköping, Sweden: Linköping University.

Schwarz, P., & Matejka, P. & J. Cernocky J. (2006). Hierarchical structures of neural networks for phoneme recognition. *Proceedings of IEEE International Conference on Acoustics, Speech and Signal Processing*. 325-328. doi:10.1109/ICASSP.2006.1660023

Schwarz, P., Matejka, P., & Cernocky, J. (2004). Towards lower error rates in phoneme recognition. *Text, Speech and Dialogue. Lecture Notes in Computer Science, 3206*, 465–472. doi:10.1007/978-3-540-30120-2_59

Schwing, R. P. Unmanned Arial Vehicles Revolutionary Tools in War and Peace. *United States Air Force USAWC Strategy Research Project*, 2–18.

Segouat, J., & Braffort, A. (2010). Toward Modeling Sign Language Coarticulation. *Gesture in Embodied Communication and Human-Computer Interaction, 5934*, 325–336. doi:10.1007/978-3-642-12553-9_29

Sekher, S., Al-Nuaimy, W., & Nandi, A. K. (2008). Automated localisation of optic disc, and fovea in retinal fundus image.*Proceedings of 16th European Signal Processing Conference*. Lausanne, Switzerland. IEEE.

Shan, C., Tan, T., & Wei, Y. (2007). Real-Time Hand Tracking using a Mean Shift Embedded Particle Filter. *Pattern Recognition, 40*(7), 1958–1970. doi:10.1016/j.patcog.2006.12.012

Sharma, L. N. (2012). Multiscale Processing of Multichannel Electrocardiogram Signals [Ph D. Thesis]. Department of EEE, IIT Guwahati.

Sharma, P., Nirmala, S. R., & Sarma, K. K. (2013). Classification of retinal images using image processing techniques. *Journal of Medical Imaging and Health Informatics, 3*(3), 341–346. doi:10.1166/jmihi.2013.1185

Sharma, P., Nirmala, S. R., & Sarma, K. K. (2014). A system for grading diabetic maculopathy severity levels. *Network Modeling Analysis in Health Informatics and Bioinformatics, Springer, 3*(1), 49. doi:10.1007/s13721-014-0049-y

Shen, W., & Oruc, A. Y. (1990). Systolic array for multidimensional discrete transform. University of Maryland (Vol. 4, pp. 201-222).

Sheridan, T. B., & Verplank, W. (1978). Human and Computer Control of Undersea Teleoperators. Cambridge, MA: Man-Machine Systems Laboratory, Department of Mechanical Engineering, MIT.

Shin, J. H., Lee, J. S., Kil, S. K., Shen, D. F., Ryu, J. G., & Lee, E. H. et al. (2006). Hand Region Extraction and Gesture Recognition using Entropy Analysis. *International Journal of Computer Science and Network Security, 6*(2A), 216–222.

Shuhao, L., Ji, W., Wei, D., & Zhichang, Q. (2004). A framework of property-oriented testing of reactive systems. *Chinese Journal of Electronics, 32*(12A), 222–225.

Siahvashi, A., & Moaveni, B. (2010). Automatic Train Control based on the Multi-Agent Control of Cooperative Systems. TJMCS, 1(4), 247-257.

Siddalingaswamy, P. C., & Prabhu, K. G. (2010). Automatic grading of diabetic maculopathy severity levels.*Proceedings of International Conference on Systems in Medicine and Biology*. Kharagpur, India. doi:10.1109/ICSMB.2010.5735398

Siddalingaswamy, P. C., Prabhu, K. G., & Jain, V. (2011). Automatic detection and grading of severity level in exudative maculopathy. *Journal on Biomedical Engineering: Applications. Basis and Communications, 23*(3), 173–179. doi:10.4015/S1016237211002608

Siegel, A., & Sapru, H. N. (2006). B. Sun, (Ed.) Essential Neuroscience. Baltimore, Maryland: Lippincott Williams & Wilkins.

Singh, A. (2005). The EM Algorithm. Retrieved from, http://www.cs.cmu.edu/~awm/10701/assignments/EM.pdf

Singh, J., Joshi, G., & Sivaswamy, J. (2008). Appearance-based object detection in colour retinal images.*Proceedings of IEEE International Conference on Image Processing* (pp.1432-1435). IEEE. doi:10.1109/ICIP.2008.4712034

Siniscalchi, S. M., Yu, D., Deng, L., & Lee, C. H. (2013). Speech Recognition Using Long-Span Temporal Patterns in a Deep Network Model. *IEEE Signal Processing Letters, 20*(3), 201–204. doi:10.1109/LSP.2013.2237901

Sivanandam, S. N., Sumathi, S., & Deepa, S. N. (2006). *Introduction to Neural Networks using MATLAB 6.0. Computer Engineering Series*. Mc-Graw Hill.

Slåtten, V. (2007). Model checking collaborative service specifications in TLA with TLC [Dissertation]. Norwegian University of Science and Technology.

Sminchisescu, C., Kanaujia, A., Li, Z., & Metaxas, D. (2006). Conditional Models for Contextual Human Motion Recognition.*Proceedings of International Conference on Computer Vision (ICCV)*. Beijing. IEEE. doi:10.1016/j.cviu.2006.07.014

Society of Robots. (n. d). Retrieved from http://www.societyofrobots.com/electronics_negative_voltages.shtml

Sridhar, V. (2012). Automated System Design For Metro Train. *International Journal on Computer Science and Engineering, 1*(1), 30–41.

Steinhauser, N. B., Pavlas, D., & Hancock, P. A. (2009). Design principles for adaptive automation and aiding. *Ergonomics in Design, 17*(2), 6–10. doi:10.1518/106480409X435943

Stenger, B., Mendonça, P., & Cipolla, R. (2001). Model-Based Hand Tracking using an Unscented Kalman Filter. Proceedings of British Machine Vision. UK. doi:10.5244/C.15.8

Suljanović, N., Mujcic, A., Zajc, M., & Tasic, J. F. (2003). Corona noise characteristics in high voltage PLC channel. *Proceeding of the IEEE conference on Industrial technology* (Vol. 2, pp. 1036–1039). IEEE.

Svensson, E., Angelborg-Thanderz, M., & Sjöberg, L. (1993). Mission challenge, mental workload and performance in military aviation. *Aviation, Space, and Environmental Medicine, 64*(11), 985–991. PMID:8280046

Svensson, E., Angelborg-Thanderz, M., Sjöberg, L., & Olsson, S. (1997). Information complexity: Mental workload and performance in combat aircraft. *Ergonomics, 40*(3), 362–380. doi:10.1080/001401397188206 PMID:11536799

Svensson, E., & Wilson, G. F. (2002). Psychological and psychophysiological models of pilot performance for systems development and mission evaluation. *The International Journal of Aviation Psychology*, *12*(1), 95–110. doi:10.1207/S15327108IJAP1201_8

Takahashi, Y., & Yokoyama, M. (2005). New Cost-effective VLSI Implementation of Multiplierless FIR Filter using Common Subexpression Elimination (pp. 1445-1448).

Tariq, A., Akram, M. U., Shaukat, A., & Khan, S. A. (2012). A computer aided system for grading of maculopathy. *Proceedings of Cairo International Biomedical Engineering Conference*. Cairo, Egypt. IEEE. doi:10.1109/CIBEC.2012.6473318

Taylor, G. S., Reinerman-Jones, L. E., Szalma, J. L., Mouloua, M., & Hancock, P. A. (2013). What to automate: Addressing the multidimensionality of cognitive resources through systems design. *Journal of Cognitive Engineering and Decision Making*, *7*(4), 311–329. doi:10.1177/1555343413495396

Taylor, R. M. (1997). Human-Electronic Crew Teamwork: Cognitive Requirements for Compatibility and Control with Dynamic Function Allocation. In M. J. Smith, G. Salvendy, & R. J. Koubek (Eds.), *Design of Computing Systems, 21B* (pp. 247–250). Amsterdam: Elselvier.

Tebelskis, J. (1995). Speech Recognition using Neural Networks [Doctoral dissertation]. School of Computer Science at Carnegie Mellon University.

Ter, F. & Haar. (2005). Automatic localization of the optic disc in digital color images of the human retina [M.S. thesis]. Computer Science Department, Utrecht University, Netherlands.

Tewari, D., & Srivastava, S. K. (2012). A Visual Recognition of Static Hand Gestures in Indian Sign Language based on Kohonen Self-Organizing Map Algorithm. *International Journal of Engineering and Advanced Technology*, *2*(2), 165–170.

The role of autonomy in DoD systems. (2012). Defense Science Board Washington DC: Undersecretary of Defense.

Theelen, B., Putten, P., & Voeten, J. (2004). Using the SHE method for UML-based performance modeling. *Proceedings of the System specification and design languages* (pp. 143-160).

Theodoridis, S., & Koutroumbas, K. (2006). *Pattern Recognition*. USA: Elsevier.

Thongnuch, V., & Uyyanonvara, B. (2007). Automatic optic disk detection from low contrast retinal images of ROP infant using GVF snake. *Suranaree Journal of Science and Technology*, *14*, 223–226.

Tiru, B., & Boruah, P. K. (2010). Multipath effects and adaptive transmission of Indoor Power Line Back ground noise. *International Journal of Communication Systems*, *23*, 63–76.

Tiru, B., & Boruah, P. K. (2012). Modeling Power Line Channel Using ABCD Matrices for Communication Purposes. *Lecture Notes in Information Technology*, *9*, 374–379.

Tongia, R. (2004). Can Broadband over powerline carrier (PLC) complete? A techno-economic analysis. *Telecommunications Policy*, *28*(7-8), 559–578. doi:10.1016/j.telpol.2004.05.004

Trentin, E., & Gori, M. (2001). A survey of hybrid ANN/HMM models for automatic speech recognition. *Neurocomputing*, *37*(1-4), 91–126. doi:10.1016/S0925-2312(00)00308-8

Trivedi, K. S. (2001). *Probability and statistics with reliability, queuing and computer science application*. New York: Wiley-Interscience.

Ubeyli, E. D. A. (2007). ECG Beat Classification Using Multiclass Support Vector Machines with Error Correcting Output Codes. *Digital Signal Processing*, *17*(3), 675–684. doi:10.1016/j.dsp.2006.11.009

Understanding eye conditions related to diabetes. (2014). *RNIB*. Retrieved from http://www.rnib.org.uk/eye-health-eye-conditions-z-eye-conditions/understanding-eye-conditions-related-diabetes

Unintentional radiators C.F.R. Part 15 Subpart B. (2014). *Cornell Law*. Retrieved from http://www.law.cornell.edu/cfr/text/47/part-15/subpart-B

Urquahart, R. B. & Wood. (1984). Systolic matrix and vector multiplication methods for signal. *IEEE Proc. F, Commun., Radar and Signal processing,* 623-631.

US Energy Information Administration. (2013). *International Energy outlook 2013*. Retrieved from http://www.eia.gov/forecasts/ieo/pdf/0484(2013).pdf

Vallabha, D. R. Dorairaj, Namuduri, K., Thompson, H. (2004). Automated Detection and Classiffication of Vascular Abnormalities in Diabetic Retinopathy. *Proceedings of 38th Asilomar Conference on Signals, Systems and Computers.*

Vanschoenwinkel, B., & Manderick, B. (2004). *Appropriate Kernel Functions for Support Vector Machine Learning with Sequences of Symbolic Data*. Vrije Universiteit, Brussel.

Vapnik, V. (1998). *Statistical learning theory*. New York: Wiley.

Vasanthi, S., & Banu, R. S. D. W. (2014). Automatic segmentation and classification of hard exudates to detect macular edema in fundus images. *Journal of Theoretical and Applied Information Technology, 66*(3), 684–690.

Vissers, C. A., Scollo, G., Sinderen, M. V., & Brinksma, H. (1991). Specification Styles in Distributed System Design and Verification. *Theoretical Computer Science, 89*(3), 179–206. doi:10.1016/0304-3975(90)90111-T

Wadhwani, A. K., & Yadav, M. (2011). Filtration of ECG signal By Using Various Filter. *International Journal of Modern Engineering Research, 1*(2), 658–661.

Waibel, A., Hanazawa, T., Hinton, G., Shikano, K., & Lang, K. (1989). Phoneme recognition using time-delay neural networks. *IEEE Transactions on Acoustics, Speech, and Signal Processing, 37*(3), 328–339. doi:10.1109/29.21701

Walter, T., Massin, P., Erginay, A., Ordonez, R., Jeulin, C., & Klein, J. C. (2007). Automatic detection of microaneurysms in colour fundus images. *Journal of Medical Image Analysis, 11*(6), 555–566. doi:10.1016/j.media.2007.05.001 PMID:17950655

Wang, H. H., Goh, W., K.G. & Lee, M. L. (2000). An effective approach to detect lesions in color retinal images. *Proceedings of IEEE Conference on engineering in medicine and biology Society.*

Wang, H., Hsu, W., Goh, K. G., & Lee, M. L. (2000). An effective approach to detect lesions in color retinal images. *Proceedings of IEEE Conference on Computer Vision and Pattern Recognition* (pp. 1-6).

Wang, J. S., Chiang, W. C., & Ting, Y. C., Yang and Hsu, Y. L. (2011). An Effective ECG Arrythmia Classification Algorithm. *Inproceedings of Bio-Inspired Computing and Applications.International Conference on Intelligent Computing* (pp. 545-550). China,

Wang, S. B., Quattoni, A., Morency, L. P., Demirdjian, D., & Darrell, T. (2006). Hidden Conditional Random Fields for Gesture Recognition. *Proceedings of Computer Society Conference on Computer Vision and Pattern Recognition (CVPR)* (Vol. 2, pp. 1521-1527). IEEE.

Wang, X., Xia, M., Cai, H., Gao, Y., & Cattani, C. (2012). Hidden-Markov-Models-Based Dynamic Hand Gesture Recognition. *Mathematical Problems in Engineering*, 2012 (2012). Article ID 986134. Retrieved from.10.1155/2012/986134

Wang, C., & Wci, C. & Cheii. (1986). Improved systolic array for linear discriminant function classifier. *Elecfron. Lr., 22,* 85–86.

Wang, H., Hsu, W., Goh, K. G., & Lee, M. L. (2000). An effective approach to detect lesions in color retinal images. *Proceedings of IEEE Computer Society Conference on Computer Vision and Pattern Recognition* (pp. 181–187). Hilton Head Island, SC. IEEE

Wang, Y., Ning, B., Cao, F., De Schutter, B., & Van den Boom, T. J. J. (2011). A Survey on Optimal Trajectory Planning for Train Operations.*Proceedings of International Conference on Service Operations, Logistics, and Informatics (SOLI).* Beijing. IEEE. doi:10.1109/SOLI.2011.5986629

Warmer, J., & Kleppe, A. (1999). *The object constraint language: Precise modeling with UML.* Edinburgh: Addison-Wesley.

Wei, L., & Huosheng, H. (2011). Towards Multimodal Human-Machine Interface for Hands-free Control: A survey [Technical Report: CES–510]. HU. University of Essex, United Kingdom.

Welfer, D., Scharcanski, J., & Marinho, D. R. (2010). A coarse-to-fine strategy for automatically detecting exudates in color eye fundus images. *Journal of Computerized Medical Imaging and Graphics, 34*(3), 228–235. doi:10.1016/j. compmedimag.2009.10.001 PMID:19954928

What is age-related Macular Degeneration? (2013). *Geteyesmart.org.* Retrieved from http://www.geteyesmart.org/eye-smart/diseases/age-related-macular-degeneration/

What is Diabetic Retinopathy? (2013). *Geteyesmart.org.* Retrieved from http://www.geteyesmart.org/eyesmart/diseases/diabetic-retinopathy/

What is Optical Coherence Tomography? (2015). *Geteyesmart.org.*. Retrieved from http://www.geteyesmart.org/eyesmart/diseases/optical-coherence-tomography.cfm

Wild, S., Roglic, G., Green, A., Sicree, R., & King, H. (2004). Global prevalence of diabetes: Estimates for the year 2000 and projections for 2030. *Journal of Diabetes Care, 27*(5), 1047–1053. doi:10.2337/diacare.27.5.1047 PMID:15111519

Wilkinson, C. P., Ferris, F. L. III, Klein, R. E., Lee, P. P., Agardh, C. D., & Davis, M. et al. (2003). Global diabetic retinopathy project group: Proposed international clinical diabetic retinopathy and diabetic macular edema disease severity scales. *Journal of Ophthalmology, 110*(9), 1677–1682. doi:10.1016/S0161-6420(03)00475-5

Wissel, T., & Palaniappan, R. (2011). Considerations on Strategies to Improve EOG Signal Analysis. *International Journal of Artificial Life Research, 2*(3), 6–21. doi:10.4018/jalr.2011070102

Wong, D. W. K., Liu, J., Tan, N. M., Yin, F., Cheng, X., Cheng, C. Y., et al. (2012). Automatic detection of the macula in retinal fundus images using seeded mode tracking approach. In *proceedings of*Engineering in Medicine and Biology Society (EMBC) (pp. 4950-4953). San Diego, California USA. IEEE.

Woods, D. D., & Hollnagel, E. (2006). *Joint cognitive systems: Patterns in cognitive systems engineering.* Boca Raton, FL: Taylor & Francis. doi:10.1201/9781420005684

Wu, Q., & Sun, Y. (2003). A Novel Algorithm for Common Subexpression Elimination in VLSI implementation of high speed multiplierless FIR Filters. Institute of Microelectronics, Tsinghua University, 1-7.

Wu, S. L., Liao, L. D., Lu, S. W., Jiang, W. L., Chen, S. A., & Lin, C. T. (2013). Controlling a Human–Computer Interface System With a Novel Classification Method that Uses Electrooculography Signals. *IEEE Transactions on Bio-Medical Engineering, 60*(8), 2133–2141. doi:10.1109/TBME.2013.2248154 PMID:23446030

Xiong, X. (2009). Robust Speech Features and Acoustic Models for Speech Recognition [Doctoral Dissertation]. School of Computer Engineering At Nanyang Technological University.

Xu, P., & Chan, A. K. (2003). Support vector machine for multi-class signal classification with unbalanced samples. *Proceedings of the International Joint Conference on Neural Networks* (pp. 1116-1119). Portland, USA.

Xu, L. & Luo, S. (2009). Support Vector Macidne Based Methodfor Identifying Hard Exudates In Retinal Images.*Proceedings of IEEE Youth Conference on Information, Computing and Telecommunication* (pp. 138-141). Beijing. IEEE.

Yagi, T. (2010). Eye-gaze interfaces using electro-oculography.*Proceedings of International workshop on eye gaze in intelligent human machine interaction* (pp. 1-5). CA, USA.

Yang, H. D., & Lee, S. W. (2010). Robust Sign Language Recognition with Hierarchical Conditional Random Fields. *Proceedings of 20th International Conference on Pattern Recognition (ICPR)*. Istanbul. IEEE. doi:10.1109/ICPR.2010.539

Yang, H. D., Sclaroff, S., & Lee, S. W. (2009). Sign Language Spotting with a Threshold Model Based on Conditional Random Fields. *Pattern Analysis and Machine Intelligence, 31*(7), 1264–1277. doi:10.1109/TPAMI.2008.172 PMID:19443924

Yang, M. H., Ahuja, N., & Tabb, M. (2002). Extraction of 2D Motion Trajectories and its Application to Hand Gesture Recognition. *Pattern Analysis and Machine Intelligence, 24*(8), 1061–1074. doi:10.1109/TPAMI.2002.1023803

Yang, R., & Sarkar, S. (2006). Detecting Coarticulation in Sign Language using Conditional Random Fields.*InProceedings of International Conference on Pattern Recognition (ICPR)* (Vol. 2, pp. 108-112). Hong Kong. IEEE. doi:10.1109/ICPR.2006.431

Yang, R., Sarkar, S., & Loeding, B. (2010). Handling Movement Epenthesis and Hand Segmentation Ambiguities in Continuous Sign Language Recognition Using Nested Dynamic Programming. *Pattern Analysis and Machine Intelligence, 32*(3), 462–477. doi:10.1109/TPAMI.2009.26 PMID:20075472

Yathunanthan, Y., Chandrasena, L. U. R., Umakanthan, A., Vasuki, V., & Munasinghe, S. R. (2008). Controlling a Wheelchair by Use of EOG Signal.*Proceedings of 4th International Conference on Information and Automation for Sustainability(pp.*283-288), DOI: doi:10.1109/ICIAFS.2008.4783987

Yavuz, E., Kural, K., Coban, N., Ercan, B., & Safak, N. (2000). Modeling of Power Lines for digital communications. *Proceedings of the International Symposium on Power-Line Communications and its Applications*. Lancaster, UK.

Yongfeng, Y., Liu, B., Li, Z., Zhang, C., & Wu, N. (2010). The Integrated Application Based on Real-time Extended UML and Improved Formal Method in Real-time Embedded Software Testing. *Journal of networks, 5*(12), 1410-1416.

Youssif, A., Ghalwash, A., & Ghoneim, A. (2008). Optic disc detection from normalized digital fundus images by means of a vessel's direction matched filter. *IEEE Transactions on Medical Imaging, 27*(1), 11–18. doi:10.1109/TMI.2007.900326 PMID:18270057

Yu, Y., Manolios, P., & Lamport, L. (1999). Model checking TLA+ specifications. In L. Pierre, & T. Kropf, (Eds), Proceedings of CHARME '99. 10th IFIP WG 10.5 Advanced research working conference on correct hardware design and verification methods. Springer, Verlag.

Yuan, M., Farbiza, F., Manders, C. M., & Yin, T. K. (2009). Robust Hand Tracking using a Simple Color Classification Technique. *International Journal of Virtual Reality*, 7-12.

Zaki, M. M., & Shaheen, S. I. (2011). Sign Language Recognition Using a Combination of New Vision Based Features. *Pattern Recognition Letters, 32*(4), 572–577. doi:10.1016/j.patrec.2010.11.013

Zhang, Q., Chen, F., & Liu, X. (2008). Hand Gesture Detection and Segmentation Based on Difference Background Image with Complex Background.*Proceedings of International Conference on Embedded Software and Systems*. Sichuan. IEEE. doi:10.1109/ICESS.2008.23

Zhao, Q., & Zhang, L. (2005) ECG Feature Extraction and Classification Using Wavelet Transform and Support Vector Machines.*Proceedings of International Conference on Neural Networks and Brain (ICNNB)* (Vol. 2, pp. 1089-1092).

About the Contributors

Kandarpa Kumar Sarma, currently Associate Professor in Department of Electronics and Communication Technology, Gauhati University, Guwahati, Assam, India, has over seventeen years of professional experience. He has covered all areas of UG/PG level electronics courses including soft computing, mobile communication, digital signal and image processing. He obtained M.Tech degree in Signal Processing from Indian Institute of Technology Guwahati in 2005 and subsequently completed PhD programme in the area of Soft-Computational Application in Mobile Communication. He has authored six books, several book chapters, around three hundred peer reviewed research papers in international conference proceedings and journals. His areas of interest are Soft-Computation and its Applications, Mobile Communication, Antenna Design, Speech Processing, Document Image Analysis and Signal Processing Applications in High Energy Physics, Neuro-computing and Computational Models for Social-Science Applications. He has been conferred upon the IETE N. V. Gadadhar Memorial Award 2014 for his contribution towards wireless communication. He is a senior member of IEEE (USA), Fellow IETE (India), Member International Neural Network Society (INNS, USA), Life Member ISTE (India) and Life Member CSI (India). He serves as an Editor-in-Chief of the International Journal of Intelligent System Design and Computing (IJISDC, UK), guest editor of several international journals, and the reviewer of over thirty international journals and over a hundred international conferences.

Manash Pratim Sarma is presently working as an Assistant Professor in the Department of Electronics and Communication Engineering, Gauhati University, Assam, India. He earned M.Sc. in Electronics Science from Gauhati University, Assam, India in 2008. He also completed M.Tech. in Electronics Design and Technology from Tezpur University, Tezpur, Assam, India, in 2010. He has authored several peer-reviewed publications in international journals, international and national conference proceedings. He has also served as reviewer in many international conferences and journals. His areas of interests include wireless communication and VLSI design for high data rate communications.

Mousmita Sarma completed her MSc in Electronics and Communication Technology from Gauhati University, India in 2010. She also completed M.Tech in signal processing from the same institution in 2012. Currently she is working as a Research Engineer at M/s. SpeecHWareNet Pvt. (I) Ltd. and a Research Scholar at Gauhati University. She has co-authored two books and published several peer reviewed research papers for international conference proceedings and journals. Her areas of interest include Speech Processing and application of Soft-Computational tools.

***

Jens Alfredson is since 2006 and in an earlier period from 1996-2001, employed by Saab, developing and evaluating novel presentations for fighter aircraft displays. He received an MSc in Industrial Ergonomics from Luleå University of Technology in 1995. He received a Ph. D in Human-Machine Interaction from Linköping University of Technology in 2007. Since 1999, he is certificated as an Authorized European Ergonomist, Eur.Erg. (CREE). He has previously (2001-2006) worked as a researcher at the department of Man-system-interaction, Swedish Defense Research Agency.

Ruhul Amin has completed his B.Tech in Electronics and Communication Engineering from Don Bosco College of Engineering and Technology in the year 2014.

Hemashree Bordoloi currently working as an assistant professor at department of Electronics and Communication Engineering, School of Technology, Assam Don Bosco University. She earned her M.Tech in 2011 from Gauhati University. Currently, she is pursuing a PhD at Gauhati University. Her areas of interest are embedded systems, bio-electronics and soft computing tools.

Suman Chetia has completed a B Tech. at Assam Don Bosco University.

Ananya Choudhury completed her M.Tech. in Signal Processing and Communication at Gauhati University, Guwahati, Assam, India in 2014. Earlier she obtained B.E from the same university. Her areas of interests include Computer Vision, Gesture Recognition and related areas. She has authored several research papers published in proceedings of international conferences and journals.

Barnali Das received her B.E. degree in Electronics and Telecommunications from Girijananda Chowdhury Institute of Management and Technology, Guwahati, Assam, India in 2012. She received her M.Tech degree in Signal Processing and Communication from Gauhati University, Guwahati, Assam, India in 2014. Her areas of interests are error-correcting codes; performance of interleavers in wireless channels; and implementation of interleaver structure in hardware level.

Saurav Goswami has completed his B.Tech from Don Bosco College of Engineering and Technology in Guwahati.

Irfan Habib has completed B Tech from Assam Don Bosco University.

Atiqul Islam has completed B Tech from Assam Don Bosco University.

Parismita A. Kashyap is presently working as an Assistant Professor in the Dept. of Electronics & Communication Engineering in Assam Don Bosco University. She completed her B. E in Electronics & Telecommunication Engineering from Gauhati University in 2011 and her M. Tech in Electronics Design & Technology from Tezpur University in 2013. She has authored two journals and five conference papers. Her research areas include adaptive antennas and wireless communication.

Razib Hayat Khan has completed his PhD at Department of Telematics, Norwegian University of Science and Technology (NTNU), Norway. He completed his M.Sc. in Information & Communication Systems Security specialized in Security in Open Distributed System from Royal Institute of Technology (KTH), Sweden in 2008. He worked as a visiting researcher at Duke University, Durham, USA and served as research engineer, Multimedia technologies at Ericsson AB, Sweden. He also worked under VRIEND project as part of his M.Sc. thesis which was sponsored by Philips, AkzoNobel, Corus, and DSM. He received his B.Sc. degree in Computer Science and Information Technology from Islamic University of Technology (IUT), Gazipur, Bangladesh in 2004. He served as a lecturer in Stamford University, Dhaka, Bangladesh during the period November 2004 – August 2006. His research interest is mainly focused on software performance & dependability modeling, Information Systems Security. At present he is working with performance and dependability issues in Communication system.

Pushpanjalee Konwar is an assistant professor in the department of Electrical & Electronics Engineering, School of Technology, Assam Don Bosco University.

Bhaswati Mandal, completed her BE in Electronics and Communication Engineering from Girijananda Chowdhury Institute of Management and Technology in 2012 and received M Tech degree in Signal Processing and Communication from Gauhati University, Guwahati, Assam in 2014. Her area of interest are Classifier design, the Application of SVMs, Systolic arrays and the implementation of Classifier in hardware level.

Jyoti Prakash Medhi was born in Assam, India. He received his B.Tech. degree in ECE from SMIT, Sikkim, India and a M.Tech. degree in Bio-Electronics from Tezpur (central) University, Tezpur, India. He is with the Department of ECE, Gauhati University, Guwahati. He is a Ph.D degree student in the Department of Electronics and Electrical Engineering, Indian Institute of Technology Guwahati, India. His current research interests include Biomedical Image processing and Biomedical Instrumentation.

Semina Mehjabin Completed a B.Tech in Electronics & Communication.

S.R. Nirmala is currently working as assistant professor in the department of Electronics and Communication Engineering, Institute of Science and Technology, Gauhati University. She obtained her Ph. D degree from IIT Guwahati. Her working areas are Biomedical Signal and Image Processing.

Ulrika Ohlander MSc is a Principal Engineer and has worked at Saab Aeronautics since 1990. She has worked with systems engineering and the development of the cockpit in JAS 39 Gripen since 2000. She is currently an Industrial PhD-student and studies team performance and distributed decision making.

Joydeep Paul has completed his B.Tech in Electronics and Communication Engineering from Don Bosco College of Engineering & Technology in the year 2014.

Puspalata Sah received her M.Sc. and M. Tech. degrees in Electronics and communication Technology from the Gauhati University, India, in 2010 and 2012, respectively. In September 2012, she joined the Center of Plasma Physics–Institute for Plasma Research (CPP–IPR), India, as a Project Scientist where she was involved in simulation work of plasma stream velocity and transient magnetic field of a coaxial pulsed plasma accelerator using MATLAB programming. Since December 2013, she has been with the 'Thermal Plasma Processed Material Laboratory', at the same institute, developing a plasma assisted system for simulating Tokamak Divertor region.

Samar Jyoti Saikia is an assistant professor in department of Electronics and Communication Engineering of Assam Don Bosco University. He is an M Tech from Gauhati University and currently pursuing a PhD from Gauhati University.

Pratiksha Sarma is currently working as an assistant professor in the department of Applied Electronics and Instrumentation Engineering, Girijananda Chowdhury Institute of Management and Technology, Guwahati. She has obtained her M. Tech and B.E degree from Gauhati University. Her areas of interest are Biomedical Signal Processing and Embedded Systems.

Purabi Sharma received the B. E degree in Electronics and Telecommunication Engineering from Girijananda Chowdhury Institute of Management and Technology, Guwahati, India and M. Tech degree in Electronics and Communication Engineering from Gauhati University, Guwahati, India. Her area of interest is Bio-medical image processing.

Devkant Swargiary completed his B.Tech in Electronics and Communication Engineering from Don Bosco College of Engineering and Technology in the year 2014.

Anjan Kumar Talukdar is currently with the Department of Electronics and Communication Engineering, Gauhati University, Guwahati, Assam, India as Assistant Professor. He completed an M.Tech from Tezpur University, Assam, India in 2009 and is currently pursuing a PhD from IIT Guwahati, Assam, India. His areas of interest include Computer Vision, Image Understanding and related areas. He has authored several research papers published in proceedings of international conferences and journals.

Banty Tiru received her MSc degree in Physics from Gauhati University and is currently serving as an Associate Professor in the Department of Physics, Gauhati University. She did her PhD in 2011 in the area of Power Line Communication from the Department of Instrumentation and USIC, Gauhati Unversity, India. Her teaching activities have focused on electromagnetic theory, system simulation, digital signal processing and communication. Her research interests include signal processing and its application in communication and cosmic rays.

Index

A

B

C

D

E

F

Printed in the United States
By Bookmasters